CHICAGO'S ACCOMPLISHMENTS
and LEADERS

CHICAGO'S
accomplishments
-and
LEADERS

Compiled and published by
Glenn A. Bishop
in collaboration with
Paul T. Gilbert

Drawings on biographical pages by
Raymond E. Craig

BISHOP PUBLISHING COMPANY
308 West Washington Street
CHICAGO, ILLINOIS

FIRST EDITION

Printed in U. S. A., by Republic Printing Co., Chicago.

FOREWORD

Chicago, A City Predestined to Greatness

L ONG before the Stone Age man was building his mounds in Illinois, long before the Indian roamed the prairie or the French explorers came in their canoes, Chicago's destiny was written in the stars.

The groundwork of the city's greatness was laid far back in the dawn of geological time, when all the central plain from the Appalachians to the Rocky Mountains was fathoms deep beneath an ancient sea. The limestones of that prehistoric sea bottom, with their veins of zinc and lead, the sandstones and clay, the silt which mellowed into rich alluvial soil, were to become the source of untold wealth.

The carboniferous age slowly converted the primeval forests into coal. The Illinois coal deposits alone have been estimated at 45,000,000,000 tons—enough to last, at the present rate of consumption, for 750 years, by which time new sources of energy doubtless will have been found.

It was the great ice sheet, leaving other rich mineral deposits, which gouged out the Great Lakes basin, without which Chicago could not have come into being.

To the advantages of location must be added the advantages of climate. The Chicago area lies directly in the path of the cyclonic storms which sweep the country, gathering up the moisture from the Gulf of Mexico and precipitating it as rain, thus counteracting the effect of arid winds from the Southwest, irrigating the vast corn and wheat belts, and watering the northern forests. Nor could such weather conditions fail to produce a vigorous and energetic race of men and women.

Chicago, therefore, lies in the very heart of a territory blessed beyond all others in the bounty of its natural resources. From plains and farms, from mines and forests, Chicago draws the livestock, the grain, the minerals, and the timber which, converted into finished products, supply the needs of all the world.

Chicago's commanding position on the Great Lakes alone would have given her commercial domination, for while the city owes much to the railroads, if it were not for the Great Lakes, giving her a continual choice of two routes to the East, she would never have enjoyed the advantage of preferred freight rates.

Again, it is the contour of the lakes which forces east and west land traffic around far to the south, so that Chicago's location at the southern end of Lake Michigan is directly on the main route. Chicago is the terminus of 27 trunk lines, the natural transfer station, the natural gateway to the West. As a rail center, Chicago has a tremendous advantage over New York. The city is approachable on three sides. The railroads do not have to blast their way through rocks or tunnel under rivers.

But Chicago is as yet only on the threshold of her career. Just as she could not have helped growing in the past, so she cannot help growing in the future. To her pioneers and leaders who raised up a city out of a swamp, rebuilt it when it was in ashes, founded the stockyards, the universities, the banks, and the big commercial houses, built the railroads, turned a river backward, and laid the foundations for the city's material and cultural development, the present generation owes a debt of gratitude.

Most of these men have passed from the scene. Another and a larger group today directs Chicago's destinies. They have transformed the water front into a thing of beauty, have surrounded the city with forests, have reclaimed a principality from Lake Michigan, and have etched in a new and ever-changing skyline.

Chicago is to be congratulated on the type of leadership that has brought such miracles about, and that can always be counted on whenever a new civic enterprise or community effort needs support. It is to these men and women who are chiefly responsible for Chicago's later achievements that this volume is dedicated.

The even-numbered pages are devoted to a record of accomplishments, the subjects being treated by those best prepared to write of their respective fields. On most of the odd-numbered pages are presented brief biographical sketches of many leading Chicagoans. The pictorial treatment makes visualization easy.

CHICAGO'S ACCOMPLISHMENTS
Include

MUSEUM OF SCIENCE AND INDUSTRY
Dramatizing the Story of Man's Work upon the Earth............................ 13
  W. Rufus Abbott, Chairman, Board of Trustees

HULL HOUSE
Chicago's Melting Pot at Work.. 20

FURNITURE MART
The American Furniture Mart, World Headquarters for Home Furnishings 26
  V. L. Alward, President, American Furniture Mart Building Corporation

MAIL ORDER
Mail Order Houses that Serve Half the Population of America..................... 32

SUNDAY EVENING CLUB
A Religious Service that Goes Out to All the Nation............................. 40
  Arthur Andersen, Trustee

CONVENTION HEADQUARTERS
Chicago, the Preferred Convention City... 44

MUSIC
Men and Institutions which have Contributed to Chicago's Musical Prestige 50
  Arthur Bissell, President, Bissell-Weisert Piano Company

STEEL
A Quarter of a Century of Progress in Chicago's Steel Industry................. 56
  L. E. Block, Chairman, Board of Directors, Inland Steel Company

ORIENTAL INSTITUTE
Ancient Cultures Brought to Light by Oriental Institute Archaeologists 62

ATHLETICS AND RECREATIONS
Chicago as an All-Year-Round Resort.. 68
  Avery Brundage, President, American Olympic Association and
    Amateur Athletic Union of United States

PRINTING, PUBLISHING AND ADVERTISING
Chicago's Growing Leadership in Printing, Publishing and Advertising.... 76
  Ernest T. Gundlach

MEDICAL AND PHARMACEUTICAL CENTER
Chicago as a Medical Center—Chicago as a Pharmaceutical Center............. 81
  Dr. Edward H. Ochsner

REGIONAL PLAN
Looking Forward to 1950.. 88
  Daniel H. Burnham, President, Chicago Regional Planning Association

FOREIGN TRADE
Chicago and Its Far Flung International Trade.................................. 98

ZOOLOGICAL PARK
The Chicago Zoological Park and Its Ambitions Plans 102
  Edwin H. Clark, Architect

LIBRARIES
Chicago's Libraries and Their Vast Resources.................................. 108
  Carl B. Roden, Librarian, Chicago Public Library

SHEDD AQUARIUM
Chicago's Marine Wonder House... 116

WEST PARKS
The West Parks as a Socializing Influence..................................... 122

ELEVATED AND ELECTRIC LINES
Arteries of Steel that Lace the Metropolitan Area............................. 126

INLAND WATERWAYS
Chicago—The Center of Inland Waterways.. 132
  Lorenzo Dana Cornish, Chief Engineer, Division of Waterways, State of Illinois

ARMOUR INSTITUTE
The Development Plan of the Armour Institute of Technology................ 138
WHOLESALE TRADE
Chicago, the Great Wholesale Market................................ 140
    Frank S. Cunningham, President, Butler Brothers
1933 WORLD'S FAIR
A Century of Progress Exposition, Herald of a New Age.................... 146
    Paul T. Gilbert
CHURCHES
Chicago's Churches Minister to Almost Every Creed.................... 164
    Walter R. Mee, Executive Secretary, Chicago Church Federation
GASTRONOMICS
Dining "Around the World" in Chicago................................ 172
    John Drury, author of "Dining in Chicago" and "Chicago in Seven Days"
RAILROADS
Chicago as the Nation's Railroad Center............................ 184
    Samuel O. Dunn, Editor, Railway Age
SOUTH PARKS
The South Parks and Their Contributions to Chicago's Health,
Education and Entertainment.................................... 190
FIELD MUSEUM
Story of All Lands and All Ages in Chicago's Wonder House............ 198
    Stephen C. Simms, Director
ADLER PLANETARIUM
Dramatizing the Pageant of the Skies............................ 208
OPTICAL INSTRUMENTS IN SCIENCE AND INDUSTRY
Where Industry Approaches Mysticism............................ 214
    William Gaertner, President, Gaertner Scientific Corporation
CRIME DETECTION
The Scientific Crime Detection Laboratory........................ 218
    Calvin Goddard, Director, and Professor of Police Science,
        Northwestern University
BOARD OF TRADE
The Nerve Center of America's Agricultural Industry................ 222
    Peter B. Carey, Fifty-ninth President
TELEPHONE
How the Telephone has made Possible the Greater Chicago............ 232
    F. O. Hale, President, Illinois Bell Telephone Company
STOCK EXCHANGE
The Chicago Stock Exchange and Its Place in the City's Financial Life........ 238
INDUSTRY
Chicago as a National Manufacturing Center...................... 244
RADIO
Broadcasting in Chicago and Its Amazing Growth.................. 248
    Charles J. Gilchrest, Radio Editor, The Chicago Daily News
SCULPTURE
Masterpieces of the Sculptor's Art that Glorify Chicago 254
UNIVERSITY OF CHICAGO
A Review of Forty Years of Educational Achievement.............. 264
    Robert Maynard Hutchins, President
AVIATION
The Municipal Airport, Where Winged Cruisers Come and Go............ 276
    Walter Wright, Superintendent of Parks, Recreation and Aviation
SUBWAYS
Views of Proposed State Street Subway............................ 280
    R. F. Kelker, Jr., Chief Engineer, Bureau of Subways
LOYOLA UNIVERSITY
A Modern School Preserving Ancient Traditions.................... 282
    Rev. Robert M. Kelley, S. J., President

FOREST PRESERVES
    A People's Paradise of Fifty-one Square Miles of Woodland................... 288
        Charles G. Sauers, General Superintendent, Cook County Forest Preserve District
ACADEMY OF SCIENCES
    Chicago's Oldest Natural Science Institution................................ 292
        Alfred M. Bailey, Director
MEAT PACKING
    Chicago's Fundamental Industry.. 298
ART INSTITUTE
    The Art Institute of Chicago and Its Spirit of Service................... 304
        Robert B. Harshe, Director
SAFETY
    Combating the Rising Tide of Public Accidents.......... 314
        C. L. Rice, President, Chicago Safety Council
FARM MACHINERY
    American Farm Implements and Machines, 1833-1933...................... 322
        Herbert A. Kellar
BOATING
    Chicago as a Yachtsman's Paradise...................................... 330
        Malcolm D. Vail
LITERATURE
    Chicago and Its Place in Literature.................................... 336
        John Drury, Editor of "The Literary Tatler" in The Chicago Daily News
GAS
    How Natural Gas was Brought to Chicago................................ 346
MORTON ARBORETUM
    An Outdoor Laboratory for the Study of Trees, Shrubs and Vines......... 352
SCIENTIFIC CONTROL
    How Scientific Control Safeguards the Lives of Chicagoans............... 358
        Charles B. Nolte, President, Robert W. Hunt Co., Engineers
HISTORICAL SOCIETY
    Dramatizing the History of Chicago and the Old Northwest Territory........ 372
        Charles B. Pike, President
BUS TRANSPORTATION
    Seeing Chicago from the Bus Tops...................................... 380
        Garrett T. Seeley, Vice-president, Chicago Motor Coach Company
THE DANCE
    Chicago as a Center of The Dance...................................... 386
        Mark Turbyfill, author, and Dance Critic, The Chicagoan
HAWTHORNE
    A City Within a City... 392
        C. L. Rice, Vice-president, Western Electric Company
SURFACE LINES
    From Horse Car and Cable Car to Modern Street Car and Trackless Trolley 396
        Guy A. Richardson, President, Chicago Surface Lines
HUMAN WELFARE
    The Vast Machinery of Social Service in Chicago....................... 404
        Edward L. Ryerson, Jr.
ART
    Chicago—An Art Center.. 410
        *C. J. Bulliet, Art Critic, The Chicago Daily News, author of "Robert Mantell's
        Romance," "Apples and Madonnas," "The Courtezan Olympia,"
        "Firebrands of Art"*
NORTHWESTERN UNIVERSITY
    Its Ideals, Traditions, and Record of Public Service.................... 418
        Walter Dill Scott, President
PETROLEUM
    Chicago's Leadership in Oil Refining.................................. 432
        Keith Fanshier, Petroleum Editor, Chicago Journal of Commerce

CHICAGO PLAN
    Chicago Completes Great Civic Improvements..................................... 436
        James Simpson, Chairman, Chicago Plan Commission
SYMPHONY ORCHESTRA
    Traditions of Theodore Thomas Preserved in Chicago Symphony Orchestra 442
        Henry E. Voegeli, Manager
STADIUM
    The Chicago Stadium—The World's Greatest Indoor Arena..................... 448
ARCHITECTURE
    Chicago's Architecture—Is It Beautiful?.. 454
        Thomas E. Tallmadge, M.A., F.A.I.A., author of "The Story of
            Architecture in America"
FOODS
    The Chicago Mercantile Exchange and Its Vast Operations..................... 466
POLICE
    Chicago's Everyday Heroes, the Bluecoats.. 474
        John I. Howe, Detective, Chicago Police Department
UNDERGROUND TRANSPORTATION
    Chicago's Vast Underground Transportation System........................... 482
RETAIL TRADE
    Chicago, Its Bazaar Streets and Department Stores............................ 492
LUMBERING
    Treatment and Preservation of Wood Conserving America's
        Great Timber Resources.. 498
HARDWARE
    A Study in Evolution... 502
GREAT LAKES
    Where Corn-fed Boys are Transformed into Sailors............................ 510
WAREHOUSING
    Banks where Merchandise, Instead of Money, is Deposited................... 516
LINCOLN PARK
    Chicago's Most Popular Playground... 522
SUPERHIGHWAYS
    Chicago Needs Superhighways.. 532
        Hugh E. Young, Chief Engineer, Chicago Plan Commission
REAL ESTATE
    Chicago's Accomplishments, Chicago's Leaders, Chicago's Real Estate—
        A Trinity Inseparable... 540
        C. L. Perkins, Editor of the magazine, Real Estate

CHICAGO'S LEADERS
Include

Abbott, W. Rufus, 15

Adams, Robert McCormick, 17

Addams, Jane, 21

Adgate, Fred W., 23

Alward, V. L., 25

Andersen, Arthur, 33

Avery, Sewell L., 35

Bard, Francis N., 37

Barnard, Harrison B., 39

Barnes, Clifford W., 41

Barnes, William H., 43

Bartelme, Mary M., 45

Bendix, Vincent, 49

Bissel, Arthur, 51

Black, Walter Lauriston, 55

Block, L. E., 57

Bobb, Dwight S., 59

Boyd, Darrell S., 61

Breasted, James Henry, 63

Breuer, Adam A., 65

Brown, Charles A., 67

Brown, Scott, 69

Brundage, Avery, 71

Buck, Glen, 75

Buckley, Homer J., 77

Bullock, Edward J., 79

Burdick, Dr. Alfred S., 87

Burnham, Daniel H., 89

Burnham, Hubert, 91

Burton, Oliver M., 93
Butler, Paul, 95

Carnahan, Charles Calvin, 99
Carpenter, John Alden, 101
Carr, Robert F., 103
Carter, Donald M., 105
Cermak, A. J., 107
Channon, Vesta M. Westover, 111
Chapline, Jesse Grant, 113
Chritton, George A., 115
Chute, Walter H., 117
Clarke, Philip R., 121
Clow, William E., 123
Compton, Arthur Holly, 125
Compton, Frank E., 127
Condon, James G., 129
Cooke, George A., 131
Cornish, Lorenzo Dana, 133
Correll, Charles J. (Andy), 31
Crane, Jacob, 135
Crawford, Perry O., 137
Cunningham, Frank S., 141
Cunningham, James D., 139
Curtis, Kenneth, 143

Dalton, Ernest E., 145
Dawes, Charles G., 147
Dawes, Henry M., 149
Dawes, Rufus C., 151
De Leuw, Charles E., 153
Denoyer, L. Philip, 157
D'Esposito, Joshua, 159
Dilling, Albert W., 163
Dixon, George W., 167
Dougherty, Kathryn, 169
   (Mrs. John S. Tuomey)
Douglas, William C., 173
Doyle, Edward J., 175
Drake, John B., 177
Drake, Tracy C., 179
Drury, John, 181
Dunn, Samuel O., 185
Dyche, William A., 183

Eddy, George A., 189
Erickson, Hubbard H., 191
Essington, Thurlow G., 193
Ewing, Charles Hull, 195

Farr, Newton C., 197
Field, Stanley, 199
Fox, Philip, 209

Gaertner, William, 213
Gaw, George D., 215
Goddard, Calvin, 217

Gore, Edward E., 219
Gorham, Sidney S., 221
Gorman, James E., 223
Gosden, Freeman F. (Amos), 30
Greeley, Samuel A., 225
Griffenhagen, Edwin O., 227
Grimes, J. Frank, 229
Grunsfeld, Ernest A., Jr., 231

Hale, Floyd O., 233
Hamilton, Isaac Miller, 237
Hanna, Phil S., 239
Harbison, Leslie C., 241
Hartz, W. Homer, 243
Hastings, Samuel M., 245
Hawxhurst, Ralph R., 247
Hay, Bill, 249
Haynes, Hasbrouck, 253
Hedges, William S., 251
Holabird, John A., 255
Hopkins, Albert L., 257
Horner, Henry, 259
Hoskins, William, 261
Hughes, George A., 263
Hunziker, Otto F., 265
Hurley, Edward N., 267
Hutchins, Robert Maynard, 269

Icely, Lawrence B., 271

Jacobs, J. Louis, 273
Johnson, Philip G., 277
Johnston, Frank H., 275

Kelker, R. F., Jr., 281
Kelley, Rev. Robert Michael, S. J., 283
Knox, Frank, 287
Kohn, Rev. William C., 289
Kraft, James L., 291
Kropf, Oscar A., 293

Lane, Wallace R., 295
Langworthy, Benjamin Franklin, 296
Langworthy, Mary Lewis, 297
Lee, T. G., 299
Levinson, Salmon O., 303
Llewellyn, John T., 305
Loesch, Frank J., 307
Logan, Frank G., 309

MacChesney, Nathan William, 311
Maher, Philip B., 313
Mann, Rabbi Louis L., 315
Marriott, A. R., 317
Mather, Alonzo C., 321
Maxwell, Lloyd, 323
McCormick, Cyrus H., 325

McCormick, Robert R., 327
McDougall, Edward G., 331
McJunkin, William D., 333
McKinlay, John, 335
McKinsey, James O., 337
McLennan, Hugh, 339
Merriam, Charles E., 341
Miller, John S., 343
Mitchell, George F., 347
Monroe, Harriet, 345
Morton, Joy, 353
Morton, Sterling, 357
Mullaney, Bernard J., 351

Newcomet, Horace Edgar, 359
Nolte, Charles B., 361
Norton, John, 363
Norton, R. H., 365

O'Brien, John J., 367
Olsen, Leif E., 369

Paepcke, Walter P., 371
Pike, Charles B., 375
Pixley, Albert J., 377
Poppenhusen, Conrad H., 379
Putnam, Rufus W., 381

Randolph, Robert Isham, 383
Rapport, David M., 385
Rawson, Frederick H., 389
Reed, Frank C., 391
Rice, C. L., 395
Richardson, Guy A., 397
Ritchie, John A., 401
Rogers, Walter A., 403
Rossetter, George W., 405
Rummler, Eugene A., 407
Ryerson, Edward L., Jr., 409
Ryerson, Joseph T., 411

Sargent, Fred W., 413
Schulze, Paul, 415
Scott, Walter Dill, 419
Seubert, Edward G., 433
Sexton, Sherman J., 421
Sheridan, Leo J., 417
Simpson, James, 437
Smith, William Jones, 423
Solomon, Harry W., 425
Sprague, Albert A., 427
Squires, Dr. Benjamin M., 429
Stagg, Amos Alonzo, 435
Stevens, Eugene M., 431
Stewart, Rt. Rev. George Craig, 439
Stock, Frederick A., 443

Stone, Rev. John Timothy, 441
Strawn, Silas H., 447
Strotz, Sidney N., 449
Studebaker, Clement, Jr., 451
Sutherland, William J., 453
Swett, Arthur H., 455
Swift, Gustavus Franklin, 445
Symonds, Nathaniel G., 457
Szymczak, M. S., 459

Taft, Lorado, 461
Tallmadge, Thomas E., 463
Taylor, Orville J., 465
Tenny, Lloyd S., 467
Thomason, Samuel E., 469
Thompson, Rev. John, 473
Thompson, John R., Jr., 471
Thompson, Orvill W., 475
Thomson, Charles M., 477
Torrence, George Paull, 479
Tracy, Howard Van Sinderen, 481
Tracy, Sherman W., 483
Traylor, Melvin A., 485

Urbain, Jules, Jr., 487

Vail, Malcolm D., 489
Valentine, Louis L., 491
Varney, William P., 493
Voorhees, Henry B., 495

Walcott, Russell S., 497
Walgreen, Charles R., 501
Watkins, William T., 499
Watson, William U., 503
Wentworth, John, 505
Whipple, Charles J., 507
White, Harold F., 509
Wilder, John E., 511
Wilson, Kenneth L., 513
Wilson, Percy, 517
Wilson, Thomas E., 515
Wood, John Heath, 519
Woods, Henry C., 521
Woodworth, Philip B., 523
Wray, James Glendenning, 527
Wright, Clark Chittenden, 529
Wright, Frank Lloyd, 531
Wright, Warren, 525
Wrigley, William, Jr., 533

Yager, William A., 535
Young, Hugh E., 537

Zander, Henry G., 539

DRAMATIZING THE STORY OF MAN'S WORK UPON THE EARTH

How the Museum of Science and Industry Interprets Modern Progress

BY W. RUFUS ABBOTT

Chairman, Board of Trustees, Museum of Science and Industry

IN Jackson Park a temple of fine arts has been transformed into a theater upon whose stage the pageant of civilization passes in review.

Within those classic walls, the visitor may, by walking through ten miles of Exhibits, retrace the path that has taken mankind many centuries to travel. From the age of the Pyramid builders he may step into the age of electricity and mass production.

He sees the machine not as an intricate piece of mechanism, but as the result of a long process of evolution, brought about by social and economic pressure, based on the achievements of great minds of the past. He sees power in relation to human life, titanic power, released by the turning of a switch, the pressure of a button, replacing the oppressed slaves and the beasts of burden of the ancients.

Thus, in this great hall of histories is the record of man's work upon the earth condensed and dramatized.

The Museum of Science and Industry, the only institution of its kind in America, was made possible by a gift of $3,000,000 from Julius Rosen-

(*Chicago Architectural Photographing Company*)

The restored Fine Arts Building of the Columbian Exposition of 1893—now the
MUSEUM OF SCIENCE AND INDUSTRY, founded by the late Julius Rosenwald.

wald. Mr. Rosenwald had been impressed by similar museums in Europe, and was convinced that Chicago would profit immensely from an educational exhibit of this type.

A site was available in Jackson Park. The old Fine Arts building, a relic of the World's Columbian Exposition of 1893, which for many years after the Fair had housed the Field Museum, was slowly crumbling to dust. Architects, however, were loath to see it go. Although designed for temporary use, and built of perishable materials, it was the purest example of classic architecture outside Rome or Athens. In its colonnade, the glories of the Parthenon lived again.

The South Park Commissioners were persuaded to restore it. Accordingly, a bond issue of $5,000,000 was floated, and today the building, in all its original charm, stands rehabilitated in steel and stone and marble, its Ionic pillars reflected in the blue waters of the lagoon. Many exhibits have been offered without cost. In its completed form the Museum represents an investment of approximately $30,000,000.

Here countless wheels revolve, gears mesh, valves seat and unseat themselves. The visitor himself may set much of the machinery in motion. He may take a ride in an 18th century "traveling machine." He may see for himself the plight of an English mining town in the days before the steam pump. He may trace the evolution of street illumination from the link boy to the electric light. He may see how the electric car, the automobile, the telephone, the elevator, and the steel "birdcage" have contributed to the development of our cities.

The primary purpose of the Museum is the simplifying and explaining of machines. When we consider that the student of engineering must read voluminous textbooks and study complicated diagrams before he can form a mental picture of a piece of mechanism, we realize just how complete must be the details of an industrial exhibit.

This great Museum of the machine age has divided pure science and its applications in the fields of basic industry and engineering into six major divisions, as follows:

(1) The fundamental sciences of physics, chemistry, and astronomy; (2) geology, mining, and metallurgy; (3) agriculture and forestry; (4)

From alchemy to chemistry.

The glass room.

W. RUFUS ABBOTT

While W. Rufus Abbott, chairman of the board of the Illinois Bell Telephone Company, is associated in the public mind with the development of the telephone in Chicago and the middle west, he has found time thoughout his busy career to give generously of his services to many other business and civic activities. Mr. Abbott, son of William McKee and Hester (Beggs) Abbott, was born in New York, N. Y., September 18, 1869. He started his telephone work in 1889 in the offices of the Westchester Telephone Company in New York. He came to Chicago in 1893, the year of the first World's Fair. For eleven years he was superintendent of the telephone company's Suburban Division. Then he became successively general commercial superintendent, general manager, vice-president, and in 1922 president. He gave up the presidency in 1930 to become chairman of the board.

Mr. Abbott is a director of the First National Bank of Chicago, the Chicago and North Western Railway Company, and the Omnibus Corporation. He is chairman of the board of trustees of the Museum of Science and Industry, founded by the late Julius Rosenwald. He has been prominent for many years in the councils of the Chicago Association of Commerce, having been a director and chairman of the executive committee. He is a past president of the Commercial Club of Chicago, the Industrial Club of Chicago, and the Chicago Athletic Association. He was one of the founders of the Chicago Crime Commission and for five years its secretary. He was also one of the founders of the First State Industrial Wage Loan Society. He is a past vice-president for the North Central Division for the Chamber of Commerce of the United States, and a member of the Chicago Plan Commission. He was appointed (1931) by President Herbert Hoover to serve on the Advisory Committee of the National Committee on Unemployment Relief, which was headed by Walter S. Gifford. He is a member of the Chicago, Mid-Day, Glenview, and Delavan Country clubs.

Mr. Abbott married Mabel Rosalie Harland of Chicago, June 1, 1892. They have two children, Hester (Mrs. Louis E. Tilden), and William Rufus, Jr.

motive power and transportation; (5) civil engineering and public works; (6) printing and the graphic arts.

Just as the beginner in any new language must first learn its alphabet, so in the Museum the visitor begins first by learning the fundamental alphabet of all science—the unchanging principles of physics and chemistry that have served as the tools with which to build the fabric of the material world in which we live. He sees levers moving masses of matter, gravity pulling matter toward the center of the earth; he learns that the invisible air which we are breathing is composed of very definite and fixed quantities of gases; he sees matter torn apart, turned inside out and reduced to simplest terms. Here he can look in on the laboratory of Michael Faraday, and live over again the hours this greatest of experimenters spent in the tests that led up to his discovery of electrical induction.

In chemistry the visitor obtains some idea of what takes place in the research laboratories that are today an integral part of great industries. He sees, for example, how an objectionable substance such as coal-tar is, through chemical changes, fashioned into perfumes, dyes, photographic developers, patent medicines, anesthetics and lacquers, and how cellulose, the basic element of wood-pulp, is treated to become artificial silk.

In the section devoted to geology, mining and metallurgy the visitor is placed in a mine-skip and taken down into a replica of a real coal mine. He feels the dampness beneath his feet and sees veins of real coal, upon which the miners are working. Here are the old and new machines that aid the miner, stripped of their shells, with their mechanism laid bare and explained. Step by step the story of mining is unfolded and, whenever circumstances and safety permit, the visitor is permitted to operate the machines. Upon leaving the mine, a metallurgist is ready to show the visitor each step in the evolution of metal from the time it was formed by nature up to the finished product.

Agriculture is the oldest industry of man and in this division of the Museum are to be found tools of all ages—from the primitive bent stick of the ancients to the sharp, power-driven multiple disc steel implement, ma-

Shipbuilding section, Water Transportation Division.

(From Drawing by F. Enid Stoddard)

ROBERT McCORMICK ADAMS

Mr. Adams, member of the law firm of Gordon, Adams, Pierce and Edmonds, was born in Webster Groves, Missouri, June 17, 1890, son of Robert McCormick and Virginia (Claiborne) Adams. He received his A. B. (Bachelor of Arts) degree at Princeton University in 1913 and his LL.B. (Bachelor of Laws) degree at North-western University in 1916. He was admitted to the Illinois bar in 1916 and was associated in practice with Scott, Bancroft, Martin & Stephens from 1919 to 1920. He was a member of the law firm of Ross, Adams and King from 1920 until 1924, senior member of Adams and King from 1924 until 1928, and has been a member of Gordon, Adams, Pierce and Edmonds since 1928.

He enlisted in the United States Navy as a seaman in 1917, ensign, 1918 to 1919, and served as executive officer of United States mine-sweeper, Price. Mr. Adams is interested in political and civic affairs. He was secretary of the Young Men's Lowden League in 1920, Republican candidate for Cook County Commissioner (Chicago) in 1923, and Acting Ward Committeeman of the Harmony Republican groups in the 42d ward during 1923, 1924 and 1925. He was secretary of the People's ticket against coalition for Circuit and Superior Judges of Cook County in 1929, and was executive chairman of the Business Men's Republican Organization, Inc., which sponsored a com-plete list of independent civic candidates for the Board of Cook County Commissioners in the April elections of 1930. Mr. Adams is a member of the American, Illinois State, and Chicago Bar Associations, the Law Club of Chicago, Legal Club of Chicago, American Legion, Northwestern Alumni Association (director), and Phi Delta Phi Fraternity. His clubs are: University, Princeton, City (director), Onwentsia, Barring-ton Hills Country, Army and Navy (director), and Chicago Yacht. His favorite pastime is golf.

On May 3, 1924, he married Janet Lawrence of Chicago, and they have three children, Kyle, Robert McCormick, Jr., and Mervyn Winston.

chined to comply with exact measurements and curves. Here are shown and explained plant processes and structures, farm implements and tools, fencing, drainage, crops, dry farming, irrigation, economic entomology, livestock, foods, milling, packing, textiles and textile machinery, and forestry.

The section on motive power discloses to the visitor the development of the steam engine. He is shown, among other things, the earliest efforts and results obtained by Newcomen, Savery and Watt. He sees the steam engine supplying power in transportation and production and is made to realize that the steam engine, more than any other factor, was the influence that brought about what historians have called the first industrial revolution.

Evolution of the sailing ship.   Hall of timekeeping.

The story of transportation starts with the travois and sled of primitive man and proceeds step by step down to the monsters of rail and air of today. Here may be found Stephenson's "Rocket" of 1829, the historic wood-burning "Mississippi" of 1836, a model of Robert Fulton's "Clermont," an old horse car, a cable car, the first electric car to run in Chicago and a modern trolley car operatable by the visitor. Nor has air travel been neglected. Airplanes and dirigibles hang from the roof trusses. Propellers spin and model wind tunnels enable the visitor to test velocities, wind resistance and the stream-line possibilities of various shapes and structures.

The story of communication has been dramatized by taking the visitor back to the earliest forms of communication used by man. First is shown how a message had to be physically transported from one place to another and then how man learned to signal with fire, smoke, sound, and semaphores. The history of communication was changed by the introduction of electricity and in the Museum the visitor traces the evolution of the telephone, telegraph, radio and wireless and televisor. Not only are historic replicas of these instruments shown, but wherever possible they are put into actual operation so that the visitor, for example, standing in one room, may have his face squeezed through a wire and registered on a screen in another room and thus learn exactly what happens when an image is televised.

The division of civil engineering and public works illustrates such subjects as city planning, road construction, the building of canals and bridges. Here is shown in miniature a modern city, with skyscrapers piled against each other, cities within cities, each housing thousands of people. Means of conveying these people to their homes is demonstrated by the transportation engineer. To point out the evolution of the road, a single length of roadway of about fifty feet shows the primitive footpath of the savage, the Via Appia of ancient Rome, the muddy, bumpy road of the middle ages and the modern smooth hard road of concrete or macadam. A part of the modern avenue is cut away to reveal the myriad conduits, the sewer system and the subways that run beneath it. Models of all types of bridges show how they are tested to determine the stress they can stand.

In the section devoted to printing and the graphic arts in general are displayed primitive writing instruments and the means of recording thought and speech that man has used since the beginning of time. The invention of printing, models of the crude machine that ushered in the era of the printed word, movable type, typesetting machines and modern presses that print, count, cut, fold and deliver books, newspapers and magazines to wait- ing trucks are all explained and dramatized. Paper making and inking, lithography, blueprinting, photostating and many other processes also are illustrated. Here, as in all of the other divisions, the visitor is invited to operate the machines himself.

In addition to its wealth of equipment, the museum contains a lecture hall and a well-selected library of scientific works.

Hall of agricultural machinery.

CHICAGO'S MELTING POT AT WORK

Hull House, Where New American Citizens Are Made

THE triangle bounded by Polk and Halsted streets and Blue Island avenue is a meeting place of many nations. The first great wave of European immigration brought the Germans and the Irish, and the few surviving families of these pioneers now make up the aristocracy of the district.

Following them, came the Russian Jews; then the Italians and Sicilians. Finally, the Greeks, and their tenure just now is being challenged by the Mexicans.

At one corner of this triangle, at Polk and Halsted streets, in the heart of a city more cosmopolitan than any you will find in Europe, stands Hull House, a symbol of Americanism and the Promised Land. Stepping from the reek and roar of Halsted street into the calm and peace of the Hull House courtyard is like stepping into another world.

Perhaps no institution in Chicago is more widely and more favorably known than Hull House. Distinguished visitors from the old world seldom miss an opportunity of seeing it.

Drop in some night when a score or more of the clubs and classes are in session; when a play is going on in the theater, and a basket-ball game in the gymnasium; when the shops are humming and the sewing rooms are buzzing; when the boys' band is rehearsing; when boys and girls of a dozen different nations are busy with their English, their typing, their folk dancing, their debating, their singing, or their free-hand drawing, and you will see the melting pot at work, turning out young American citizens.

Hull House was established more than forty years ago—in 1889—by Jane Addams and her former schoolmate, Ellen Gates Starr, in recognition of the fact that the mere foothold of a house, easily accessible, ample in space, hospitable and tolerant in spirit, situated in the midst of the large foreign colonies which so easily isolate themselves, would be in itself a serviceable thing for the city.

Miss Addams' sympathies for the "submerged tenth" were aroused while, as a young woman, she was visiting London. As a member of a slumming party, she found herself one Saturday night in the East End, where the weekly sale of decaying vegetables and fruits was in progress.

"At the end of a dingy street, lighted only by occasional flares of gas, we saw two masses of ill-clad people clamoring around two hucksters' carts. They were bidding their farthings and ha' pennies for a vegetable hung up by the auctioneer, which he at last scornfully flung, with a gibe for its cheapness, at the successful bidder. . . . One man detached himself from the groups. He had bidden in a cabbage, and when it struck his hand, he instantly sat down on the curb, tore it with his teeth, and hastily devoured it, uncooked and unwashed as it was . . . Yet the final impression was not of ragged, tawdry clothing, nor of pinched and sallow faces, but of myriads

(Fernand de Gueldre Photo)

JANE ADDAMS

Miss Addams, settlement worker and author, was born in Cedarville, Illinois, September 6, 1860, daughter of the Hon. John H. and Sarah (Weber) Addams. She received her A. B. (Bachelor of Arts) degree from Rockford College in 1881, studied in Europe from 1883 to 1885, and at the Women's Medical College in Philadelphia, in 1888. Honorary degrees conferred on her are LL.D. (Doctor of Laws) by the University of Wisconsin, 1904, Smith College, Tufts, 1923, Northwestern and University of Chicago, 1929; and A. M. (Master of Arts) by Yale, in 1910. With Ellen Gates Starr she founded the Social Settlement of Hull House in Chicago, in 1889, and has been head resident ever since. For three years she served as inspector of streets and alleys in the neighborhood of Hull House. She was president of the National Conference of Charities and Correc-tions, in 1909; president of the Woman's International League for Peace, presiding over the conventions at the Hague in 1915, Zurich in 1919, Vienna in 1921, The Hague in 1922, Washington in 1924, Dublin in 1926, and Prague in 1929. She was active in the movements for women suffrage and took a prominent part in the formation of the progressive party in 1912.

Miss Addams has been awarded the Gold Medal of Military Merit (Greece); received the Bryn Mawr achievement award of $5,000, in 1931; and shared the Nobel peace prize with Nicholas Murray Butler, in 1931. She is the author of Democracy and Social Ethics, 1920; Newer Ideals of Peace, 1907; The Spirit of Youth and the City Streets; Twenty Years at Hull House, 1910; A New Conscience and an Ancient Evil, 1911; The Long Road of Women's Memory, 1916; Peace and Bread in Time of War, 1922; and The Second Twenty Years at Hull House, 1930. She is also a writer and lecturer on social and political reform.

of hands, empty, pathetic, nerveless and workworn . . . clutching forward for food which was already unfit to eat."

Returning to America, Miss Addams found an ideal place for her experiment in the old brick residence of one of Chicago's pioneer settlers, Charles J. Hull. The building was in ill repair, and was being used as a factory. It stood between an undertaker's shop and a saloon. It was said even to be haunted by a ghost.

Miss Addams and her co-worker rehabilitated the property and "settled" there, to live among the poor. Mothers and children came, at first by ones and twos, drawn by curiosity; then by hundreds—the men, too. Today, Hull House occupies almost an entire city block. It houses the Mary Crane Nursery, the Pre-School branch of the Illinois Institute for Juvenile Research, an Infant Welfare station, the offices of the Juvenile Protective Association and of the Immigrants' Protective League. The Visiting Nurse Association has an office there. There is a branch of the Chicago Public Library. The Boys' Club alone occupies a five-story building. Hull House has a public cafeteria and a large private dining room for the residents. The residents, numbering about sixty-five, mostly university graduates, occupy the dormitories (men's and women's) and the Hull House apartments, some of which are beautifully furnished. They give their leisure time to social work, and live together as in a cooperative club. The Hull House Labor Museum is an institution in itself. The Jane Club, a coopera-

(*Chicago Architectural Photographing Company*)
WACKER DRIVE, LOOKING EAST.

(Daguerre Studio Photo)

FRED W. ADGATE

Mr. Adgate, consulting engineer and Chicago manager of The Foundation Company of New York, son of George and Martha (Whitney) Adgate, was born in Keeseville, New York, on June 5, 1868. He is a descendant of Francis White, who settled in Plymouth, Massachusetts, about 1621. He is vice-president of Chariton Fur Corporation; a director of the Money Corporation, Glasgow Hotel Company, Gary-Wheaton Bank, and Chariton Fur Corporation, and is known throughout the country for his engineering achievements. Was engineer and superintendent for various construction projects until 1902, when he joined the newly organized Foundation Company, as an engineer. Later became superintendent, assistant Western manager, and in 1909 was made manager.

He has built numerous large bridges, power plants, mining shafts, foundations, etc. Some of the most outstanding are: Omaha Bridge for Illinois Central Railroad, East Omaha, Nebraska; Foundations, Chicago & Northwestern Station, Chicago, Illinois; Clinton Bridge for Chicago & Northwestern Railroad, Clinton, Iowa; U. S. Government Dams Nos. 12 and 19, Ohio river; McClure Dam, Upper Peninsula of Michigan; 250 K. W. Power Station below Cincinnati; 150 K. W. Power Station at Cincinnati; 100 K. W. Power Station at Pekin, Ill. He has developed a system of sinking mining shafts through quicksand which has been very successful. He was in charge of ship building and dry dock during the World War. He is a member of American Society of Civil Engineers, American Society of Mechanical Engineers, and Western Society of Engineers. Clubs: Union League; Medinah Country; Michigan North Woods; Wawohin Golf, Ishpheming, Michigan; Cincinnati Club, Cincinnati, Ohio. Next to his interest in engineering, his hobby is golf.

On June 21, 1904, Mr. Adgate married Dolly May Triplett, of St. Marys, West Virginia. They have two children, George and Dorothy.

tive club for working girls, was established in 1891, and has been self-governing ever since.

The Hull House Players, organized by the late Laura Dainty Pelham, famous soubrette of a past generation, has its own well-equipped theater, where it has presented not only some notable first performances, but many significant revivals. The theater is also constantly used by other dramatic clubs of young people and many foreign groups present plays in their own languages.

More than 6,000 people, mostly from the immediate neighborhood, visit Hull House every week. They come to attend the clubs and classes and the entertainments. English classes meeting twice a week draw their members from ten different nationalities. Classes in citizenship were established in 1906, and were helpful in securing the passage of the Illinois Adult Education Law. The most popular classes for adults are those in literature, languages, history, mathematics, drawing, and painting. The Hull House Art School holds classes both for adults and children, and the annual exhibits are a revelation.

In connection with the Labor Museum, classes in spinning and weaving are conducted, and special courses for the blind have been established. Identified with the same institution are the classes in pottery, metal work, batik, and wood carving. The products of the Hull House Kilns, an outgrowth of the pottery classes, are distributed through a wholesale dealer with show rooms in Chicago and New York. The Hull House Music School, from whose classes have been graduated many professional musicians, offers courses in piano, violin, organ, theory, and singing. Its annual Christmas concerts, accompanied by tableaux, staged by the art department, never fail to draw appreciative audiences.

The Hull House Woman's Club, one of the pioneer organizations of its kind, comes into its own with its New Year's Day reception to old settlers and its annual children's May party.

In addition to its kindergarten, Hull House supports more than sixty clubs for boys and girls, and a score of social clubs for various national groups, including ten for girls.

You will find no gangs in the neighborhood of Hull House. The Boys' Club, with its gymnasium, bowling alleys, pool and game rooms, library, band room, class and study rooms, and shops, is infinitely preferable to anything the gang or the corner pool room has to offer. The Boys' Club has its own printing plant, and publishes its official paper. It has its savings bank and its Boy Scout troop. Intramural athletic contests, which draw their galleries of more than 3,000 a month, have produced amateur boxing and wrestling champions, and champions in field events.

(*Moffet-Russell Photo*)

V. L. ALWARD

Mr. Alward, president of the American Furniture Mart Building Corporation, was born in New Brunswick, Canada, November 10, 1873, the son of Fred H. Alward and Sara (Mullin) Alward. He was educated at the New Brunswick Normal School, received the principal's certificate and began teaching at the age of eighteen years . When just twenty years of age he became principal of the Fairville Schools in Saint John, New Brunswick. Teaching, however, failed to hold his interest as a vocation. In 1897 Mr. Alward began his business career at Kenosha, Wisconsin, with the Simmons Company. He was made vice-president in 1917. Mr. Alward is credited with an appreciable share in the development of the Simmons Company's business from a volume of less than $1,000,000 annually to one of approximately $35,000,000 in his last year with the organization, 1923.

While the Furniture Mart was in course of construction, he accepted the offer of the presidency of the American Furniture Mart Building Corporation, in 1924. Mr. Alward has also served as vice-president of the Chicago Association of Commerce. He is a member of the Chicago Athletic Association, Lake Geneva Country Club, and the Lake Shore Athletic Club (serving as president 1930, 1931 and 1932). His favorite diversions are hunting and fishing.

Mr. Alward was married at Chicago, Illinois, June 5, 1905, to Winifred Nightingale, daughter of the late Dr. Augustus F. Nightingale. They have three children, Winifred-Lee, Vincent and Betsy Jane.

THE AMERICAN FURNITURE MART, WORLD HEADQUARTERS FOR HOME FURNISHINGS

Style Shows Which Attract Thousands of Buyers

BY V. L. ALWARD,
President, American Furniture Mart Building Corporation

I MAGINE a bazaar street twenty blocks long, lined on each side with furniture stores, each 100 feet in depth. Picture in these shops hundreds of thousands of dollars worth of home furnishings—period furniture, reproductions of Sheraton, Chippendale, and Hepplewhite; gay sun room and garden furniture; modernistic furniture in chaste geometric designs; dignified swivel chairs and glass-topped desks and directors' tables; "Mother Goose" furniture for the nursery. Imagine these displays behind plate glass windows fronting on five miles of corridors, and you will have a conception of the interior of the American Furniture Mart at 666 Lake Shore Drive.

The exterior of this beautiful building, the largest in the world devoted to a single industry, and the world's third largest commercial building, its seventeen stories surmounted by a 474-foot tower, is familiar to all. The interior, however, is seldom viewed by the public. Admission is by pass, and, as a rule, only members of the trade are admitted.

The Mart was built in 1924, and the tower was added three years later. In ground area 500 by 200 feet in dimensions, it occupies an entire city block in the heart of the Gold Coast, overlooking Lake Michigan. It represents an investment of more than $15,000,000, and its 2,000,000 square feet of floor space are given over to displays of furniture from the leading manufacturing houses of the United States.

Chicago is the central market place for the output of furniture makers in such strongholds of the industry as Grand Rapids, Rockford, Sheboygan, and Evansville. Furnishings shown in the Mart are made in factories of 235 cities distributed among thirty states, including Illinois, Indiana, Ohio, North Carolina, Virginia, Pennsylvania, Wisconsin, Michigan, and New York. If all this merchandise were not concentrated in Chicago, it would take a furniture buyer eight months to visit the factories represented, allowing him only one day in each city. There are approximately 700 exhibitors. The furniture exhibited at the Mart represents seventy-five per cent of all such merchandise sold at wholesale in the United States.

The Mart is open every business day of the year, but attendance reaches a peak twice yearly, in July and January, when the semi-annual furniture style shows are held. To these great fairs, which last two weeks, come buyers—more than 6,000 of them, from every important city in the country, and from Canada and Europe, to study the new designs, compare styles and values, and to lay in stocks. During the year approximately 25,000 buyers visit the Mart.

Within the Mart are samples of practically every type of period furnishings: Georgian, Early American, Early English, French Empire and French Provincial; Federal American, Contemporary, Biedermeier, Queen Anne, Directoire, each telling its story of human vanities and fluctuations of tastes and manners as dictated by monarchs, foreign trade, and other influences.

(Shigeta-Wright Photo)

The AMERICAN FURNITURE MART, located at 666 Lake Shore drive. This is the largest building in the world devoted exclusively to a single industry. Nimmons, Carr & Wright and N. Max Dunning, associate architects.

The most popular period style, authorities at the Furniture Mart agree, is Georgian. Reproductions of the masterpieces of the eighteenth century designers seem to have found general acceptance in the American home.

Contemporary furniture, although greatly subdued as compared with the "modernistic" which began to attain prominence in 1928 and 1929, is still too individual to appeal to the volume market, its sale being restricted mostly to the metropolitan centers such as Chicago, New York, and Los Angeles.

The exhibits are as complete in regard to types of furnishings as they are to styles. There are beds, chairs, tables, buffets, china cabinets, dressers, vanities, chiffoniers, radios, lamps, stoves, refrigerators, washing machines, springs, mattresses, pillows, baby carriages, bedding chests, nursery furniture, pictures, clocks, china and pottery, davenports, garden and beach umbrellas, fireplace equipment, desks, rugs and linoleums, metal furniture, sun room furniture, wrought iron products, and toys in endless variety.

On the seventeenth floor are the elaborately appointed club rooms of the Furniture Club of America, the walls of which are decorated with rich tapestries and costly paintings. The club provides for visiting merchants, manufacturers, and buyers a common meeting ground and a Chicago home complete in every respect except for sleeping quarters. The walnut-paneled Club restaurant is patronized by 250,000 furniture men during the year.

The Mart also is the headquarters of the National Retail Furniture Association and the National Association of Furniture Manufacturers, and is the home of Radio Station W C F L, Chicago.

With sales averaging more than $100,000,000 a year—and these sales do not include those of the department stores—the retail furniture business ranks fifth among Chicago's retail trades. There are about 1,200 retail furniture establishments with combined inventories of $20,000,000.

Facing east in Whiting Hall—main entrance
to the American Furniture Mart.

(*Underwood and Underwood Photo*)

World's largest light—the gigantic two billion-beam candle power LINDBERGH
BEACON atop the Palmolive Building, which guides aviators to Chicago.
Holabird & Root, architects.

AMOS

(*Maurice Seymour Photo*)

"AMOS"—FREEMAN F. GOSDEN

Mr. Gosden, well-known to millions of radio listeners as "Amos," was born in Richmond, Virginia, on May 5, 1899. He began as a traveling tobacco salesman for the American Tobacco Company. He met Charles J. Correll and associated with him in the promotion of amateur theatricals. The partners, under title of "Sam and Henry," broadcasted from radio station W G N for two years. On March 19, 1928, the characters of "Amos 'n' Andy" were created when Correll and Gosden joined the Chicago Daily News Radio Station W M A Q. So popular did they become that other radio stations began to demand their episodes. To supply this demand the two began making electrical transcriptions of their broadcast, and thirty-five other stations were supplied by the Chicago Daily News with records of these transcriptions. "Amos 'n' Andy" were the first team to make transcriptions exclusively for radio. Their audience continued to grow to such an extent that the Pepsodent Company of Chicago signed a long-term contract for their services and now they are heard in person five days a week over the National Broadcasting System.

The preparation of their episodes is a fifty-fifty proposition, but it is no over-worked "Amos" who sits down at the typewriter to write the next story; it is "Andy" who does this, while "Amos" paces back and forth trying lines and dictating. It is difficult to say which of them is responsible for any one line or situation.

On June 13, 1927, Mr. Gosden married Leta Marie Schreiber. They have two children, Freeman F., Jr., and Virginia Marie.

ANDY

(*Maurice Seymour Photo*)

"ANDY"—CHARLES J. CORRELL

Mr. Correll, also well known to the same millions of radio listeners as "Andy," was born in Peoria, Illinois, February 3, 1890. On January 27, 1927, he married Marie Janes. He began as a newsboy, learned the brick-laying trade under his father, played the piano in moving picture theaters, later developing into a producer of amateur theatricals. He spent six years on the road with Freeman F. Gosden and has since been associated with him, first representing "Henry" in the dialogues of "Sam and Henry" at Radio Station W G N. Since March 19, 1928, he has been the lordly, over-bearing "Andy" of the famous team of "Amos 'n' Andy." Mr. Correll and Mr. Gosden write every line they speak and take the parts of all the charac-ters presented in each episode. The program is usually written two or three days before it goes on the air. They have an office in one of Chicago's largest skyscrapers and spend many hours every day writing the continuity and discussing the future adventures of their famous characters.

In their broadcasting Amos and Andy demand absolute privacy. This is because they throw themselves so wholeheartedly into their characters. The world they have created around the "Fresh Air Taxicab Company, In-corpolated" and their many other enterprises is so real to them that they must guard against any outside influence that might spoil that illusion. With-out question, Amos and Andy have created and maintained the largest listening audience in the history of radio broadcasting. The musical com-position that introduces each of their episodes is "The Perfect Song."

MAIL ORDER HOUSES THAT SERVE HALF THE POPULATION OF AMERICA
An Idea That Revolutionized Merchandising Methods

CHICAGO, the birthplace of the mail order business, is the mail order center of the entire world.

Its two leading mail order houses, Montgomery Ward & Co. and Sears, Roebuck & Co., serve half the population of the United States. Their elaborate catalogues, read from cover to cover almost religiously by millions of people, have carried the name and fame of Chicago into every village and hamlet in the land, and into the far corners of the earth.

Merchandise ranging from a collar button to a completely setup house, finds its way not only into every part of the United States, but into twentyseven foreign countries. Regular customers of Montgomery Ward will be found in China, Japan, the Philippines, India, Central and South America.

These two big houses operate on a truly imperial scale. Montgomery Ward maintains branch houses in Kansas City, St. Paul, Baltimore, Portland, Oregon, Oakland, Fort Worth, Denver, and Albany. It has in operation more than 500 retail stores, including a number of large city department stores. Its customer families number 12,000,000.

Sears has ten branch houses, each an institution in itself, and has a chain of 250 retail establishments, one of the latest of which is its new State street department store in Chicago.

Buying offices are maintained by both these firms in the chief marketing centers of the world, and large staffs of buyers devote their time to traveling and collecting merchandise. Designers located in such fashion capitals as London, Paris, and New York, enable their concerns to keep abreast the everchanging trends of style.

Immense stocks are necessary to supply orders running into millions of dollars, and each firm owns outright or controls the output of many factories of many kinds.

To visit the Chicago headquarters of Montgomery Ward or Sears, Roebuck is to visit an exposition. One can wander through mile after mile of goods.

Yet, vast as this business is today, it had absurdly small beginnings. A. Montgomery Ward, the originator of the mail order idea, came to Chicago from Niles, Michigan, in 1865, with some experience as a small town merchant. After making and severing several connections, he became the traveling representative of a St. Louis firm, and was thereby given an opportunity to study at first hand the problems that confronted the farmer and the resident of the rural community.

He found them virtually at the mercy of the local merchant, whose stock was unattractive and inadequate, and whose prices were unchecked by competition. These Main Street tradesmen, blind to the opportunities for

(*Blank & Stoller, Inc. Photo*)

ARTHUR ANDERSEN

Mr. Andersen, founder and senior partner of Arthur Andersen & Co., certified public accountants, was the first alumnus to be elected to the office of president of the board of trustees of Northwestern University, from which office he recently resigned. He was born at Plano, Illinois, on May 30, 1885, and is the son of John William and Mary (Aabye) Andersen. In 1917 he was awarded the degree of Bachelor of Business Administration by Northwestern University. He also received the degree of Certified Public Accountant from the University of Illinois. Mr. Andersen's own firm was organized in Chicago in 1913 and now the firm has offices in eight principal cities in the United States and also has foreign representation. After organizing the accounting department of the School of Commerce of Northwestern University, Mr. Andersen served as professor of accounting for many years. In 1927 he was elected a trustee of the University to succeed the late Judge Elbert H. Gary. In October, 1930, he was elected president of the board.

Mr. Andersen is a director of the State Bank and Trust Company of Evanston. He is a trustee of A Century of Progress, Chicago's (1933) World's Fair and is a member of the Board of Governors of Northwestern University Foundation. He is a member of the Chicago, Chicago Athletic, University, Attic, Mid-Day, Sky Line, Commercial, Industrial, Commonwealth, Economic, University of Evanston, Glen View Golf, Bob-O-Link, Milwaukee of Milwaukee, and Broad Street of New York clubs, and Wisconsin Society of Chicago. He also is a member of American Institute of Accountants (member executive committee and council), Illinois Society of Certified Public Accountants, Society of Industrial Engineers, American Economic Association, and United States Chamber of Commerce. He is a trustee and director of the Chicago Sunday Evening Club, director of the United Charities of Chicago, and member of Chicago Red Cross Citizens' Committee for Disaster Relief. Mr. Andersen takes an active interest in civic, industrial and educational affairs.

On August 8, 1906, Mr. Andersen married Emma Arnold of Chicago. They have three children, Ethyl Bernice (Mrs. Vilas Johnson), Arthur Arnold, and Dorothy Emma.

building up good will and reputation for fair dealing, were rapidly advancing the day of the chain store and the mail order concern. Some progress had been made in the development of the Farmers' Granges, whose secretaries served as purchasing agents in a cooperative way for the members of the local chapters.

In a fourth story room of what is now 825 North Clark street, Mr. Ward started, in 1872, with one clerk, a capital of $2,400, and an idea, to build up a business which was to revolutionize merchandising methods. He proposed to make the United States Postoffice Department his salesman. Associated with him in the enterprise was his friend George H. Thorne.

Wiseacres laughed his plans to scorn. The notion that goods could be sold "sight unseen" and through the printed word alone, they pointed out, was visionary and impractical. Time was to prove how wholly wrong they were.

Montgomery Ward's first catalogue was a modest affair of eight pages, printed on a foot-power press. The firm issues today a 700-page catalogue, sumptuously illustrated in black-and-white and color, in which 40,000 items are not only accurately described, but described so attractively as to make unusually fascinating reading. Catalogue making, in fact, has come to be an art—a profession in itself, calling for the same painstaking efforts and technical skill as dictionary or encyclopedia making.

It was quite natural that in launching his enterprise, Mr. Ward should bid first for the patronage of the Grange secretaries, and he was so successful in his efforts that for many years the firm carried the slogan, "The Original Grange Supply House." But he soon discovered that if he should serve the Granges, he could just as easily serve the members direct. By dealing with his house, the out-of-town customer could save money by the elimination of the middleman.

It was not long before the Montgomery Ward catalogue became to thousands of people throughout the Middle West the very symbol of Chi-

MONTGOMERY WARD & COMPANY, CHICAGO

(*Underwood and Underwood Photo*)

SEWELL L. AVERY

Mr. Avery, president of the U. S. Gypsum Company and Montgomery Ward and Company, was born in Saginaw, Michigan, November 4, 1874, son of Waldo A. and Ellen (Lee) Avery. He graduated from the Michigan Military Academy and received his LL.B. (Bachelor of Laws) degree from the University of Michigan in 1894. In this same year he became an officer in the Alabaster Company, which merged with other gypsum companies, in 1901, to make the present U. S. Gypsum Company, of which he has been president since 1905. Mr. Avery has been president of Montgomery Ward & Company since January, 1932. He is a director of Armour & Company, Chicago, Chicago Daily News, Chicago Great Western Railroad, Northern Trust Company, State Bank & Trust Company of Evanston, U. S. Steel Corporation, Container Corporation of America, Continental Illinois National Bank & Trust Company, and the Illinois Manufacturers' Association.

Mr. Avery is a trustee of the University of Chicago, the Museum of Science and Industry, and Hull House. He is chairman of the Banking and Industrial Committee of the Seventh Federal Reserve District; and vice-president of the United Charities of Chicago and the Chicago Crime Commission. He is a member of Delta Tau Delta Fraternity. His clubs are, Casino, Chicago, City, Commercial, Mid-Day, Old Elm, Racquet, University, Attic, Chicago Riding, Chicago Yacht, Evanston Country, Glenview, Les Cheneaux, Wild Wing, and Grand Island Lodge.

He married Hortense Lenore Wisner, of Pontiac, Michigan, October 11, 1899. The children are Sewell Lee (deceased), Arla, Lenore (deceased), and Nancy.

cago. It was to most of them their only contact with the city. In countless Mississippi Valley homes the name of Montgomery Ward became a household word, and the annual catalogues, invested as they were, somehow, with the spirit of fair play and good will, were eagerly awaited and carefully treasured. To the country and village folk of the early '70's, this mail order service was almost indispensible, for the automobile was as yet undreamed of, the roads were often seas of mud in Winter, and the "general store" was fossilized. And as confidence in the firm increased, the business grew.

Success in any line invariably invites competition. Many small mail order concerns sprang up, some to survive only a few months or years. One, however, survived permanently and became a leader. This was the firm of Sears, Roebuck & Co. Its success under the able management of the late Julius Rosenwald is among the miracles of Chicago achievement.

Inauguration of the Parcels Post System in 1912, coupled with the spread of rural free delivery, imparted a new impetus to the mail order business. So great today is the volume of mail and parcel post that both Montgomery Ward and Sears Roebuck maintain in connection with their plants complete postoffices.

By means of tests conducted over many years it is possible, simply by weighing the incoming mail, to determine with a fair degree of accuracy the amount of checks and money orders received in any given delivery.

An interesting department of the big mail order houses is the laboratory in which goods of all kinds are subjected to grueling tests for strength and durability and other qualities. Here a fountain pen or a machine may be required to do a lifetime's work in a few hours.

FRANCIS N. BARD

Mr. Bard, president of the Barco Manufacturing Company of Chicago, was born in Cleveland, Ohio, on April 25, 1882, son of George M. and Helen N. (Norwood) Bard. He received his early education at military school; spent two years at the University of Chicago in an academic course; and graduated from Cornell University in 1904 with the degree of Mechanical Engineer.

He has been actively connected with the Barco Manufacturing Company since 1908; first as vice-president and then as president. The Barco Manufacturing Company is known as a railway supply company and Mr. Bard has always been very active in railway supply circles. Part of the products of his company, however, is used in every major industry in this country and in many foreign countries. He has taken out many patents, most of them applying to the products of his company. Mr. Bard is an officer and director of a number of companies. He is a member of the Union League Club, University Club, Chicago Athletic Association, Exmoor Country Club, Duquesne Club of Pittsburgh, Pennsylvania, Illinois Chamber of Commerce, and Illinois Manufacturers' Association. He is a member of the board of Railway Business Association and the National Association of Manufacturers. His favorite hobbies are big game hunting and deep-sea fishing.

He married Edith M. Decker of Chicago and Stroudsburg, Pennsylvania, April 8, 1909. They have two daughters, Dorothy and Marion.

A sketch of this kind would be incomplete without at least brief reference to the public service records of the two men whose names have been
most closely identified with the mail order business in Chicago; Mr. Ward,
quiet and retiring outside his own institution; Mr. Rosenwald, the genial
humanitarian, with an acquaintance seldom equaled among modern indus-
trialists.

Each had his distinct place in the Chicago of his day. Of Mr. Rosenwald's vast and endless charitable projects, his Negro and Jewish welfare
work, the whole world knows.

Mr. Ward's signal service to Chicago was in his guardianship of the
lake front. Designated in mockery "the watch dog of the lake front," for
many years he fought a battle single-handed against the encroachment of
public buildings in Grant Park. At the time, he was treated harshly by the
public and the press, but he lived to see the day when his efforts were
appreciated and acknowledged. It was he, and he alone, who preserved
for Chicago the beauty of Grant Park.

(Underwood and Underwood Photo)

An unusual photographic effect—cloud formations above the buildings along Michigan avenue.

HARRISON B. BARNARD

Mr. Barnard, building contractor and president of the Builders and Manu-facturers Mutual Casualty Company of Chicago, was born in Seville, Ohio, May 11, 1872, son of William Edwin and Emily (Nye) Barnard. He received his preparatory education at Wooster (Ohio) University and in 1895 re-ceived his A. B. (Bachelor of Arts) degree at the University of Chicago. He is a member of the Society of Mayflower Descendants, Society of Colo-nial Wars, Sons of the American Revolution, and the Order of Founders and Patriots of America. His ancestors were among those who came to America on the Mayflower.

Mr. Barnard has been a builder and contractor in Chicago on his own account since 1892 and has built some of the finest buildings in Chicago and other cities. He has been a trustee of the University of Chicago since 1927. His clubs are the Union League (of which he was president in 1927-1928), Architects, South Shore Country, and Beverly Country. He belongs to Delta Tau Delta Fraternity.

On June 30, 1917, Mr. Barnard married Elizabeth Tidholm, of Chicago; the children are, Harrison Blake, William Robert, Marshall Nye, Barton Wayne, and John Brewster.

A RELIGIOUS SERVICE THAT GOES OUT TO ALL THE NATION

How the Sunday Evening Club Ministers to Town and Country

BY ARTHUR ANDERSEN

Trustee, Chicago Sunday Evening Club

IT is Sunday night. In a prairie farm house in Nebraska, an elderly couple sit before the radio. It would be lonesome there without the radio. The sons and daughters have grown up and scattered. The last to go, the youngest daughter, is a stenographer in Chicago. Though far away, she is united— for tonight—with the old folks. All three are listening to the same religious service, broadcast from the Sunday Evening Club, Orchestra Hall, Chicago. Daughter is in the audience. Father and mother tune in on the radio. All three are brought together in a community of spirit. In her next letter, daughter will ask the old folks how they liked the "meeting."

In a tiny crossroads church in Alabama, a small congregation has gathered. But they have come to hear no provincial preacher expound the Gospel. They have come to hear no village choir or country organist. Over the ether waves float the strains of the great Orchestra Hall organ, with a master organist at the console. . . . The hundred trained voices of the chorus are lifted in song. Occupying the pulpit, perhaps, is Rabbi Abba Hillel Silver of Cleveland, or it may be Henry van Dyke or Hugh Black.

Multiply these scenes by a thousand . . . by ten thousand, by hundreds of thousands, and you will have a faint idea of the widespread influence exerted by Chicago's unique institution, the Sunday Evening Club.

Organized in 1907 by a group of influential business men, of which Clifford W. Barnes was the leading spirit, the Chicago Sunday Evening Club was intended as a strangers' church.

Here, in accordance with the purposes of its founders, the traveling man marooned over Sunday in Chicago, the newcomer, the art student, the young man or woman just entering business, would be sure to find a welcome.

The Sunday Evening Club was to be a place of common worship for people of all denominations. Its object was "to maintain a service of Christian inspiration and fellowship in the business center of Chicago, and to provide for the moral and religious welfare of the city."

Its success as a nonsectarian religious movement was instantaneous. While the audience at the first meeting numbered only 800, attendance rapidly increased, until today, the seating capacity of the hall, which accommodates close to 3,000, is sometimes inadequate.

Out-of-town arrivals at Chicago's hotels would find in their rooms an invitation to attend the Sunday night service. Those who availed themselves of the privilege were not disappointed. What would otherwise have been a lonesome evening had been made a profitable one.

(Maryland Studio, Pasadena, California, Photo)

CLIFFORD W. BARNES

Mr. Barnes, president and founder of the Chicago Sunday Evening Club, was born in Corry, Pennsylvania, son of Joseph and Anna (Webster) Barnes, and is a direct descendant of Daniel Webster. He received his A.B. (Bachelor of Arts) degree from Yale in 1889, his B.D. (Bachelor of Divinity) in 1892, his A.M. (Master of Arts) from the University of Chicago in 1893. The honorary degree of LL.D. (Doctor of Laws) was conferred on him by Lake Forest University in 1913 and Illinois College, 1925. Mr. Barnes came to Chicago in 1892 with President Harper and a group of Yale men, interested in the establishment of the new University in Chicago. He served in the Department of History during the first year, and at the same time entered into settlement life at Hull House, organizing the Nineteenth Ward Men's Club which administered the first defeat to "Johnny" Powers and his ring.

He was called to be president of Illinois College, and after his return to Chicago five years later, he began the organization of the Sunday Evening Club, in 1908, and other welfare agencies, which have gained national and international reputation. Mr. Barnes was president of the Legislative Voters League for fifteen years, founder of the Committee of Fifteen and president for eight years, and has been chairman of the Chicago Community Trust since its organization in 1915. He has been vice-president of the Chicago Association of Commerce in charge of civic affairs, and is a member of its executive committee and board of directors. He is chairman of the Chicago World Court Committee, vice-president of the World Alliance for International Friendship, and is active in various other national and international organizations. For war service, as Major, he received from Greece the Medal of Military Merit with silver palm, and was created Knight of the order of the Golden Cross.

Mr. Barnes married Alice Reid of Lake Forest, Illinois, May 5, 1898. They have one daughter, Lilace Reid.

As the years went on, the Sunday Evening Club became an institution. It was advertised everywhere by commercial travelers who, during their stay in Chicago had enjoyed the Club's speakers and music. On Pullman coaches, in club cars, on steamships, in hotel lobbies, when the conversation turned to Chicago, reference to the Sunday Evening Club was inevitable.

During the first fifteen years of its existence, however, its sphere of influence was local. It was adopted as their church by the hotel guests and the boarding house colonies. The radio was as yet undreamed of.

But in 1922, with the development of broadcasting, the Sunday Evening Club went on the air, one of the first religious services to be broadcast. Since then, its message has been sent out weekly to uncounted homes in cities, towns, and hamlets everywhere. Its program has become known as the "Sunday evening service of the nation." In the invisible audience are not only lonesome fathers and mothers, small-town church goers, and family groups, but sailors on the seas, lumberjacks in isolated camps, trappers, forest rangers, prospectors, many on the "Gold Coast." The program reaches countless hotel rooms. It is picked up by the speeding motorist.

But perhaps where it does the most good is in the hospitals, the asylums, the old people's homes, where it reaches the shut-ins, bringing comfort to the aged, hope to those on beds of sickness. It sheds its light even in the jails.

The Club is liberal, and has introduced from its platform leaders of every faith and creed—Roman Catholics and Jews, as well as Protestants, leaders in many professions, and renowned statesmen of other lands.

Among the famous men who have addressed the Club's Sunday night audiences were former Secretary of State Charles E. Hughes, William Howard Taft, then President, and Lyman Abbott. William Jennings Bryan was another. Marshal Joffre, Baron d'Estournelles de Constant, and Henry Wickham Steed have been Sunday Evening Club speakers.

Most of the famous American churchmen of the past twenty years have been on the Club's roster. Recent speakers include Harry Emerson Fosdick, Robert E. Speer, Bishop George Craig Stewart, Bishop William F. McDowell, Bishop Edwin H. Hughes, Robert Freeman, and Henry Howard. Among church dignitaries from abroad were the Lord Bishop of London, the Lord Bishop of Scotland, the Archbishop of York, and the Rev. Geoffrey A. Studdert-Kennedy, of London.

Mr. Barnes serves as president of the organization. Directing the club as trustees are some of Chicago's most prominent and public-spirited leaders.

The officers and the board of trustees are looking forward to the time when perpetuity of the Club's work for Chicago and the nation will be assured by adequate endowment to supplement the normal support of annual subscribers.

(Gabor Eder Photo, New York)

WILLIAM H. BARNES

Mr. Barnes, organ architect and business executive, was born in Chicago, November 10, 1892, son of Charles Osborne and Nettie Ann (Shedd) Barnes. He attended the Evanston High School and received his A. B. (Bachelor of Arts) degree at Harvard University in 1914. He was granted the honorary degree of Doctor of Music from Park College in 1931. At the age of ten he began his piano studies and two years later he added organ study, which became his chief interest in life. He studied the organ with the Dean of the New England Conservatory, Wallace Goodrich, and Clarence Dickinson of New York. By the time he was fifteen he had completed the building of an organ of usual church size in his father's home, which is today part of the large instrument in his own home in Evanston. At the age of seventeen he was organist for the Church of the Ascension, Chicago. He has gradually acquired, by study and prac- tice, a thorough knowledge of organ building, especially concentrating on acoustics and tonal effects. Mr. Barnes is considered one of the world's foremost authorities on organ construction. He has planned a large number of organs for churches, schools, and colleges throughout the United States.

Mr. Barnes was secretary and treasurer of A. R. Barnes & Company, railroad and commercial printers, from 1916 to 1922, and has been vice-president and treasurer since 1922. During the World War, he served as associate of the Committee on Classification of Personnel in the Army, Adjutant General's Office, Washington, D. C. He has been organist in various churches since 1909 and has been choirmaster and organist of the First Baptist Church, Evanston, Illinois, since 1928. He has been president of North- western University Settlement since 1928 and is a member of the committee of manage- ment, Y. M. C. A. Hotel. He was formerly state president of the National Association of Organists; and is a member of the American Guild of Organists, Pro Musica, Chicago Artists Association (ex-president) and Phi Mu Alpha Fraternity. He is author of two books entitled, The Contemporary American Organ, 1930, and The Odyssey of an Organ Enthusiast, 1932. He is also associate editor of The American Organist. His clubs are Cliff Dwellers, University, Bohemians (Chicago), University (Evanston), and Har- vard (New York).

He married Edith McMillan, of St. Paul, Minnesota, October 22, 1927.

CHICAGO, THE PREFERRED CONVENTION CITY
Where History in Presidential Nominations Has Been Written

ONE of the great crystalizing forces in America is the convention. There is hardly a trade or industry, a branch of science, or a religious movement but that is organized and holds its national or sectional conventions annually or at more frequent intervals. The social influence of all these conclaves, their influence on business ethics, on educational or scientific technique, on the direction of philanthropic enterprise or political policy, cannot be estimated. It is overwhelming.

Whenever a convention meets, several cities usually are nominated as the place of the next meeting. Despite the keener competition of the last few years, Chicago almost invariably wins. Many associations return again and again to Chicago for their meetings.

Chicago is a convention city par excellence.

In June, 1932, Chicago entertained the National Conventions of both major political parties. Even this experience was not unique, for in 1884, both the Republicans and Democrats chose Chicago as the place to nominate their respective standard-bearers, Blaine and Cleveland.

Since Abraham Lincoln was named in the old Wigwam in 1860 to lead the Republican party to victory at the polls, sixteen Presidential candidates have been nominated in Chicago.

Of these nominees, seven were sent to the White House, while two Vice-Presidents nominated in Chicago, Chester A. Arthur and Calvin Coolidge, later became President.

Here Grant, Garfield, Blaine, Harrison, Roosevelt, Taft, Hughes, Harding, and Hoover were nominated on the Republican ticket, Taft being renominated in 1912. Here George B. McClellan was nominated by the Democrats, and Grover Cleveland was twice nominated. Here William Jennings Bryan delivered his famous Cross of Gold speech that made him his party's choice in 1896. Here in 1912 convened the short-lived "Bull Moose" party which placed Roosevelt again in nomination for the Presidency.

The old brick Wigwam, where Lincoln was named, and the Stadium, where both parties convened in 1932, present contrasting pictures, both typical of the Chicago of their periods. The Stadium, today the last word in convention halls, is only one of a number of reasons why Chicago is America's preferred meeting ground.

Stroll into a hotel lobby almost any day and you will see men and women wearing badges identifying themselves as delegates to some convention.

More than 800 associations and societies hold their annual conclaves in Chicago every year, bringing to the city altogether about 1,000,000 delegates and guests.

MARY M. BARTELME

Judge Bartelme, of the Juvenile Court of Cook County, was born in Chicago, daughter of Balthasar and Jeanette (Hoff) Bartelme. She attended the Chicago public schools and received her LL. B. (Bachelor or Laws) degree from North-western University Law School in 1894. On March 3, 1913, she was appointed by Judge Pinckney, of the Juvenile Court, as his assistant and to try the cases of delinquent girls. She was public guardian of Cook County for sixteen years, having been appointed by each governor of Illinois during that period. She was elected Judge of the Circuit Court, November 6, 1923, was assigned to the Juvenile Court and was reelected in 1927 for the term of 1927 to 1933.

Judge Bartelme is a member of the American, Illinois State, and Chicago bar associations, and the League of Women Voters. Her clubs are Chicago Woman's, Woman's City, and Cordon.

These conventions are of every kind and description. Scientists, philosophers, contract bridge teachers, shoe manufacturers, canners, confectioners, educators, missionary workers, insurance men, newspaper publishers, farmers, representatives, in fact, of almost every industry and profession and endeavor meet here to discuss their various problems.

When a convention comes to Chicago, it comes to America's center. A circle with a radius of 500 miles described around Chicago would reach from Lincoln, Nebraska, to Buffalo, and from Little Rock, Arkansas, to the northern shores of Lake Superior. It would include wholly or in part, the States of Minnesota, South Dakota, Iowa, Wisconsin, Michigan, Illinois, Indiana, Missouri, Kansas, Arkansas, Mississippi, Alabama, Georgia, Tennessee, Kentucky, Ohio, Pennsylvania, New York, West Virginia, Virginia, North Carolina and the Canadian Province of Ontario.

All roads—transcontinental highways, airways, railroads, lead to Chicago, as well as several steamship routes. From almost any part of the country, with the exception of the Far West, the distance is less than five hours by air.

Here commerce, industry, education, and amusement unite to constitute a life which attracts visitors from all parts of the world. A successful

The "WIGWAM," rambling frame convention hall in which Abraham Lincoln was nominated for the presidency in Chicago in 1860, reproduced on the grounds of A Century of Progress Exposition.

convention city must have five essential things—transportation, hotels, halls and exhibit spaces, market facilities, and amusements. Chicago has them all.

Chicago can be reached by thirty-eight railroads. Sixty million people live within a night's ride of the city.

One may have the choice of a centrally located hotel in the Loop, or one on the lake front, either near the heart of the city, or out among the treetops of the parks.

At the time of the World's Fair of 1893, Chicago had only about fifty hotels. A few of these old hostelries have disappeared, among them the Grand Pacific, the Briggs House, the Stratford, the Wellington, the Victoria, and the Virginia. But replacing them, the new Sherman, the new Palmer House, the new Bismarck, the La Salle, the Blackstone, the Fort Dearborn, the new Morrison, the new Brevoort, the Atlantic, and the Stevens have added more than 10,000 rooms to the downtown area alone.

(© *Kaufman & Fabry*)

Interior of the Chicago Stadium, where thousands attended the Republican and Democratic conventions of 1932.

North of the river, the Drake, the Edgewater Beach, the Ambassador, the Sovereign, the Belmont, the Lake Shore Drive, the Pearson, the Knickerbocker, the Parkway, the Sheridan Plaza, the Surf, the Webster, and others provide approximately 20,000 rooms.

On the South Side, the Chicago Beach, the Windermeer, the Cooper-Carlton, the Shoreland, the Flamingo, the East End Park, the Hayes, and the Southmoor have some 15,000 rooms. These outlying hotels while they are patronized chiefly by permanent guests and tourists, are available also to transients, and the convention guest is always welcome.

The larger hotels have banquet halls which seat hundreds. They have accommodations also for pretentious trade shows. The Chicago Stadium seats 25,000 people, and can be used either as an auditorium or as an exposition hall. The Coliseum provides space ample enough for a cross section of any industry. Navy Pier and the Merchandise Mart are available for exposition purposes.

(*Chicago Architectural Photographing Company*)

Looking north on Michigan avenue. On the right is the Tribune Tower, Medinah Athletic Club, Allerton Hotel, and in the distance the Palmolive. Building. On the left in the foreground are the Wrigley buildings.

(Portrait by Fernand de Gueldre)

VINCENT BENDIX

Mr. Bendix, president of the Bendix Aviation Corporation and donor of the famous World's Fair Golden Pavilion of Jehol, was born in Moline, Illinois, August 12, 1881, son of John and Alma M. Bendix. His father was born in Smoland, Sweden, and his mother's birthplace was Ostergotland, Sweden. They emigrated from their native land about sixty-five years ago and settled in Moline, where Vincent Bendix attended the public schools. At the age of sixteen he obtained his first position, in New York City, as an elevator operator in a Manhattan hospital and studied to become a lawyer, but his interest was in the invention and production of mechanical devices. In 1907 he returned to Chicago and became sales manager for the Holsman Automobile Company, and the following year he produced an automobile bearing his own name. The manufacturers of these pioneer motor vehicles realized that something must be done to eliminate the hand crank starting systems to assure the future success of the horseless carriage. Mr. Bendix started to work on this problem and produced the first connecting "link" between a starting motor and the fly-wheel of the motor car's engine. It is called the Bendix Drive. More than 35,000,000 of these starter-drives have been produced.

Mr. Bendix next perfected the four-wheel braking principle and through acquisitions and affiliations he now manufactures mechanical, air, hydraulic, and vacuum brakes, brake boosters, and brake testers for automobiles and double-disc landing wheels and brakes for airplanes. Next Mr. Bendix interested himself in equipment that would keep these vehicles going, so his organization acquired the Stromberg Motor Devices Company, now the Bendix-Stromberg Carburetor Company. Subsequently other prominent automotive and aviation accessory concerns were acquired. Today Bendix Aviation Corporation is recognized as one of the foremost manufacturers of automotive and aviation equipment in the world, with fifteen plants in this country and abroad. Companies now controlled by the Bendix Aviation Corporation include: Bendix Brake Company, South Bend, Indiana; Hydraulic Brake Company, Detroit, Michigan; Bragg-Kliesrath Corporation, South Bend, Indiana; Eclipse Machine Company, Elmira, New

17900.   Continued on page 545

MEN AND INSTITUTIONS WHICH HAVE CON-TRIBUTED TO CHICAGO'S MUSICAL PRESTIGE

Cultural Assets of the Orchestra, the Civic Opera, Ravinia, the Apollo Club, and Others

BY ARTHUR BISSELL

President, Bissell-Wiesert Piano Company

THE early struggles of Chicago's pioneers to establish music as a cultural asset were carried on amidst seemingly hopeless surroundings and all possible discouragements. We who now enjoy the priceless opportunity of listening to the world's greatest music little realize what it cost in self-sacrificing effort to establish and make permanent these opportunities.

Can a more hopeless environment for musical culture than Chicago must have presented in the '40's and '50's be imagined—a squalid town, just emerging from the aspects of a frontier settlement, digging itself out of the mud as it were, a glorified swamp. Yet there were those among its inhabitants who were imbued with pioneer zeal, who foresaw the future, who planned comprehensively and laid the foundation for a musical life that now ranks with that of the world's leading capitals.

It is a significant fact that while other older and longer established communities were lying dormant as far as music was concerned, Chicago was active in the foundation of musical societies that later became the cornerstone of our present position in the musical world.

In this article little more than a brief chronological account of the musical development of Chicago is possible. From the best available records it would seem that Chicago's musical activities began about 1850. In that year Julius Dyhrenfurth established the Philharmonic Society and was its conductor, until 1856. Then Theodore Thomas first appeared in Chicago as first violinist in a concert troupe in 1854. A second visit was made in 1858. On these occasions Mr. Thomas acted as ticket taker at the door until time to appear on the platform.

In 1857 the Mendelssohn Singing Society was formed by George P. Upton under the leadership of Adolph W. Dohn. This organization later became the Apollo Musical Club of which Charles D. Hamill, later president of the Orchestral Association, was president, and whose son, Charles H. Hamill, is now president.

In 1860 a new Philharmonic Society was established under the direction of Hans Balatka, who continued as its conductor until 1869.

Theodore Thomas' third visit to Chicago in 1869 marked an important epoch in the city's musical history, for he came as the conductor of an orchestra of forty pieces. He returned in 1870, and on October 9, 1871, the first concert of his third season was announced, but never given because the great Chicago fire on that day destroyed the old Crosby Opera House in which the concert was to have been held. During the next twenty years he came to Chicago frequently with his orchestra, and during that period

BISSELL-WEISERT

(Fernand de Gueldre Photo)

ARTHUR BISSELL

Mr. Bissell, president of Bissell-Weisert Piano Company, was born in Chicago, January 1, 1870, son of George Francis and Jerusha (Woodbridge) Bissell. He received his education in the Chicago public schools, Chicago Manual Training School, Lake Forest Academy, and Lake Forest University. During his entire business career, Mr. Bissell has been associated with the musical world. For five years he was with the Weber Piano Company, and then for five years with Lyon, Potter & Company. From 1898 to 1907 he was secretary of the Clayton F. Summy Company, piano and music dealers; from 1907 to 1910 he was president of the Bissell-Cowan Piano Company; and was resident manager of the Aeolian Company of New York City from 1910 to 1913. In 1913 he organized Bissell-Weisert Piano Company, of which he was president until 1928 when this company merged with Lyon & Healy, of which he became vice-president. In June, 1931, Mr. Bissell resumed business as the Bissell-Weisert Piano Company and opened a piano salon in the Diana Court Building, 540 North Michigan avenue, where they represent the Bechstein, the most famous piano in the world, and Wm. Knabe & Co., celebrated American piano manufacturers, and the Ampico, the reproducing piano of international fame.

Mr. Bissell was formerly president of the Chicago Musical Art Society, and is chairman of the executive committee and vice-president of the International Society for Contemporary Music. He is a member of the Racquet, Arts, Cliff Dwellers (secretary), Tavern, and Onwentsia clubs, and his chief recreations are golf and music.

He married Emily Greeley Tredway, St. Louis, Missouri, December 1, 1897, and their children are Emily Greeley Tredway, and Arthur Dwight.

between 1877 and 1891 inaugurated the famous summer night concerts in the old Exposition Building, where the Art Institute now stands. In 1891 he came to Chicago to stay and gave series of concerts yearly in the Auditorium up to the season of 1904-1905.

Prior to the establishment of the Orchestra on a permanent basis, the Apollo Musical Club was organized and is still in existence in its 55th season. Its first conductor, Mr. Dohn, was succeeded in 1875 by W. L. Tomlins.

In 1882 a brilliant musical festival was given in the old Exposition Building with Thomas directing an orchestra of 174 pieces, and Tomlins conducting a chorus of 900. The soloists were Anna Louise Cary, Companini the great tenor, George Henschel and Myron Whitney. Two years later a second festival was given enlisting the services of Materna, Christine Nillsen, and Enna Juch, with Thomas conducting the orchestra of 170 instruments and Tomlins the chorus of 900 voices.

A most important and impressive occasion was the dedication, in 1889, of the Auditorium, with President Benjamin Harrison as guest of honor, and Adelina Patti as soloist. The famous Auditorium is still standing and may yet continue as a home of opera, concert, and drama.

Between 1901 and 1904 a public fund was raised to house the Chicago Symphony Orchestra in its own home in Orchestra Hall. The sum of $650,000 was subscribed by citizens, and $200,000 borrowed. The first concert was given during the season of 1904 and 1905. Thomas conducted the first two concerts on December 14 and 23, 1904, which were his last, as he died on January 4, 1905. A great memorial concert was held on January 6 and his funeral services were conducted at St. James Church on the same day. His passing marked the close of a great musical career which influenced the history of American music more than any other single factor. He was succeeded by the present director, Frederick Stock, one of the world's most gifted conductors, and the Chicago Symphony Orchestra now ranks as one of the half dozen leading ensembles of the world.

Now let us turn to the history of opera in Chicago. From the best available records it would seem that the first performance of opera was given in the "New Theatre" on Monday, July 29, 1850. The offering was La Somnambula, and the admission prices were 25 and 50 cents. The seating capacity was three hundred. This theater was burned a year later and replaced by a larger one which was dedicated in 1851, and in 1853 Lucia was presented, followed by Norma, with seats as high as $2.00. In 1858 McVickers Theater was dedicated, and a season of opera began on September 27 of that year. During the following year no less than three opera companies visited Chicago. Later Theodore Thomas conducted the American Opera Company at this theater, and the first season of German opera was presented about 1887 or 1888, with Anton Seidl wielding the baton and with Max Albory as the leading tenor. About this period a grand opera festival was presented at the old Exposition Building with Mesdames Cary,

Nevada, Scalchi and Fursch-madi as the prima donnas. This led to the building of the Auditorium of which Ferd. W. Peck was the guiding spirit, and in 1891 the first real bona fide season of opera in Chicago was inaugurated, with Eames, Lehman, Scalchi, Jean and Edouard De Reszke, Plancon, and other old time notables of the operatic world. Opera continued to be given in the Auditorium under various auspices up to 1910, when Chicago's very own Opera Company started operations and continued under many vicissitudes until the season of 1931-1932. In 1929, largely through the efforts of Samuel Insull, the New Civic Opera House on Wacker Drive, was opened and the activities of the Opera Company transferred there, where two seasons of opera were given.

Before concluding this short resume of opera in Chicago, brief mention must be made of the several seasons of opera at Ravinia Park, under the auspices of Louis Eckstein, which enlisted the services of the Chicago Symphony Orchestra and the world's leading singers from both the Metropolitan and Chicago Opera forces. Here opera was heard under ideal conditions, and the fame of Ravinia has spread throughout the musical world.

Space limitations preclude mention of the thousands of important concerts and recitals which have added to the musical prestige of Chicago.

(*Chicago Architectural Photographing Company*)

Michigan avenue, looking north from Adams street. This boulevard is considered one of the most beautiful in the world.

Mention must be made, however, of the series of Music Festivals given in Evanston each spring. Inaugurated in 1908, and still continuing, they have presented to their audiences the Chicago Symphony Orchestra and the most distinguished contemporary artists. Peter C. Lutkin, Dean of the Northwestern University School of Music, was the original sponsor of the Festivals, and for many years directed them in conjunction with Mr. Stock.

In concluding this article a brief reference to the history of the music trades should be made, for this history is indissolubly interwoven with the development of music as an art in Chicago.

One can hardly do more than list the pioneer music firms that established themselves in Chicago's early days. In 1857 W. W. Kimball came to Chicago and started business as a piano dealer. The company bearing his name later became one of the largest manufacturers of pianos in the world. In 1864 the firm of Lyon & Healy was established under the protection of the parent house of Oliver Ditson Company of Boston. Under the guidance of Patrick J. Healy this house has achieved world wide reputation as a manufacturer and retailer of musical merchandise. William Henry Bush landed in Chicago in 1854 and made a fortune in the lumber business. In 1886 he embarked in the manufacture of pianos with his son, W. L. Bush, and John Gertz under the firm name of Bush & Gertz. In 1857 the firm of Julius Bauer was established, and continued the manufacture of pianos until a few years ago. In 1868 the firm of Story & Camp was organized and became one of the leaders in the piano and organ trade of the West. From this concern later grew the firm of Esty and Camp which was for many years one of Chicago's largest retail piano houses. Mathias Schulz started a cabinet making shop in Chicago in 1869. Shortly afterward he began the manufacture of organs. In 1889, incorporated as M. Schulz Company, he continued in the manufacture of both pianos and organs, and the firm is still in business. In 1880 H. D. Cable formed a partnership with F. R. Wolfinger, organizing the Wolfinger Organ Company, later to become the Western Cottage Organ Company, then the Chicago Cottage Organ Company.

In later years such large manufacturers as the Gulbransen & Dickinson Company, The Cable Company, The Melville Clark Piano House, whose founder, Melville Clark, was responsible for many important inventions in connection with the pneumatic player piano, the Story & Clark Company, the Smith, Barnes & Strobher Company, the Cable Nelson Company, Adam Schaaf, the Steger Piano Company, Price & Teeple, Bush & Lane, the Schiller Piano Company, and the Haddorf Piano Company, all combined to make Chicago one of the leading piano manufacturing centers of the world.

Among the more prominent houses now retailing pianos are Lyon & Healy, the Cable Company, the Baldwin Company, the W. W. Kimball Company, and the Bissell-Weisert Piano Company.

(*Blank and Stoller, Inc., Photo*)

WALTER LAURISTON BLACK

Mr. Black, president of Central States Service Company and Central States Edison Company, which now control public utility subsidiaries in Wisconsin, Minnesota, Missouri, Nebraska, Kansas, Oklahoma, Indiana, and Alabama, was born in Stockton Springs, Maine, September 9, 1887, son of Alfred G. and Mary E. (Smith) Black. He was educated at the Everett, Massachusetts, High School and University of Maine. The utility subsidiaries are: Gasconade Power Company, North Kansas Power & Light Company, Beatrice Power Company, Collinsville Gas Company, Natural Gas Utilities Company, The Skiatook Service Company, Northern Wisconsin Power Company, Grand Marais Light & Power Company, Riviera Utilities Corporation, Madison Utilities Corporation, Gulf Ice & Cold Storage Company, and The Sedan Gas Company. He handles all engineering problems of construction and is in complete charge of the operations of these properties which supply variously electric, water, gas, and ice services in more than 60 cities and towns.

Mr. Black was formerly associated with the Bangor Railway and Electric Company and Boston Elevated Railway Company during the period 1908-1911; assistant superintendent of the Porto Rico Light & Power Company during 1911 and 1912; general manager of the Panama Tramways Company during construction and early operation (1913-1914) of first electric street railway on the Isthmus of Panama. During the period 1914-1925 (except two years in the United States Army during the World War) he was associated with Robert M. Feustel, consulting engineer, Fort Wayne, Indiana, in consulting engineering on public utility operation and investigations for franchises, rates, etc. Enlisted in Field Artillery, U. S. A., in 1917, but was transferred to Engineering Corps and shortly afterward commissioned and placed in command of 63d Engineers for organization, training and service overseas. During the latter part of 1925 and early 1926 Mr. Black assisted Kelker, De Leuw and Company in a special survey and report on traffic conditions in the City of Baltimore. From 1926-1928 he was associated with Day & Zimmermann, Inc., Philadelphia, Pennsylvania. He was elected to his present position in 1928. He is a member of the Midland Club, Riverside Golf Club, and Tredyffrin Country Club at Paoli, Pennsylvania. His principal hobbies are engineering and golf.

On January 17, 1925, Mr. Black married Alice L. M. Tubbs of Baltimore, Maryland. They have two daughters, Julia Lee, and Anne Lauriston.

A QUARTER OF A CENTURY OF PROGRESS IN CHICAGO'S STEEL INDUSTRY

Miles of Sandy Wastes Transformed Into Belching Furnaces

BY L. E. BLOCK

Chairman, Board of Directors, Inland Steel Company

ENTERING Chicago from the south, one passes literally through the jaws of a fiery furnace. Spectacular indeed are the lurid tongues of flame leaping from a myriad of funnels. Magic cities of steel have sprung up on the dunes at the foot of Lake Michigan. Here, in an inferno of roaring furnaces and white-hot metal, armies of men labor like Titans. On the result of their labors rests the very foundation of our civilization.

This is the Steel Age. Outstanding in its history is the record of the last quarter century. Nothing short of phenomenal has been the expansion during this period of the steel industry in the Chicago area.

True it is that the industry's progress locally has, in many respects, followed the general trend, but it is noteworthy that the rate of expansion here has far surpassed that of the country as a whole.

In 1905 the output of steel in the Chicago metropolitan district was only about 9 per cent of the total produced in the United States. In 1929,

INLAND STEEL COMPANY'S INDIANA HARBOR, INDIANA, WORKS

At the start of the present century this site was marked merely by a railroad tower house— elsewhere only sand and water. Today, with ore unloading facilities, blast furnaces, coke ovens, open hearth steel furnaces and a large number of finishing mills, it serves a great and comprehensive steel plant.

the industry's banner year, the tonnage in this area was 23 per cent of the country's total. While national steel production had been augmented 150 per cent during this period, the local increase amounted to 350 per cent.

Two factors contributed to this amazing growth—an inadequate producing capacity and the selection by this district generally as a point of distribution.

(From Drawing by John Doctoroff)

L. E. BLOCK

Mr. Block, chairman of the board of directors of the Inland Steel Company, Chicago, was born in Cincinnati, Ohio, January 13, 1869, son of Joseph and Rose (Cohn) Block. He received a public school education. A pioneer in the steel business of the Central West, Mr. Block was among the founders of Inland Steel Company and has been prominent in the management of that company for thirty-six years. Through the efforts of Mr. Block, his brothers, and other associates, the company has risen from insignificance to become the largest independent steel company in the Central West and the sixth largest producer in the United States. He has been a director of the American Iron and Steel Institute for sixteen years and is considered one of the leaders in the industry.

Mr. Block is active as a director of the Michael Reese Hospital, Chicago, and is a member of the Mid-Day, Standard, Lake Shore Country, and other clubs. His favorite sport is golf.

On June 20, 1900, he married Cora B. Bloom, of Chicago, and they have four children, Joseph, Leigh, Babette, and Eleanor.

In the early days of the twentieth century, the steel production of the Chicago territory was by no means equal to the demand for steel products, and many thousands of tons were shipped in annually from the eastern mills. It was, therefore, in accord with the oldest of our economic laws that a building program was projected which should furnish a source of supply more capable of meeting the demand. Men of vision, recognizing the needs of the district, by their energy and application gave the impetus, which now seems like a magic touch, to the transforming of miles of sandy wastes into a Tartarus of belching furnaces and whirling mills, veritable dynamos of activity.

During these years, the center of population had moved westward. Manufacturers in every field, eager for a central distributing point, and influenced in no small measure by the admirable railroad and water shipping facilities, located plants here at a far greater rate than in other parts of the country. New users of steel and western branches of eastern consumers have sprung up all about us. This increase of local demand had the obvious result of further stimulating the development of additional means of supply.

Many transformations have taken place in the methods of steel production. Power plants as well as furnaces and mills of twenty-five years ago have, to a very large degree, become obsolete. Steam driven units have been abandoned for electrical drives; furnaces and mills have been replaced by modern units designed for much greater and more economical output.

These changes, together with many refinements, involved almost incredible capital expenditures, but happily resulted in reduction of costs which has made possible an increase of more than 250 per cent in the minimum wage rate, with an advance of only 40 per cent in the average realizing price of steel.

Improved methods of manufacture, in which electricity has played an important part, have made for more stable and healthful conditions for the working man. In former days, the "man in the mills" "puddled" the iron in the furnace or fed the red-hot steel to the mills with his tongs. Today he stands at electric controls. Hugh cranes of uncanny power handle the molten metal.

Thousands of workers in the steel plants today hold stock in their respective companies which they were granted the privilege of acquiring on

ACME STEEL COMPANY ROLLING MILLS AT RIVERDALE, ILLINOIS

(*Kellogg Photo*)

DWIGHT S. BOBB

Mr. Bobb, lawyer, son of Daniel Bingham and Arminda Frost (St. John) Bobb, was born at Dakota, Illinois, July 19, 1876. His first maternal ancestor in America came with Marquis LaFayette. He entered Northwestern University, graduating in 1899 with an A. B. (Bachelor of Arts) degree. Then he entered Harvard University, obtaining his A. M. (Master of Arts) degree in 1900 and his LL.B. (Bachelor of Laws) degree in 1903. He was assistant in history at Harvard and Radcliffe College in 1900 and 1901; and from 1901 to 1902, assistant in economics at Harvard. Mr. Bobb was admitted to the bar at Boston, Mass., in 1903. From 1904 to 1909 he was lecturer on public service corporations at Northwestern University Law School. In 1909 Mr. Bobb became a member of the law firm of Adams, Bobb and Adams, now Sanders, Childs, Bobb and Westcott, with offices in Chicago and Washington, D. C., engaged chiefly in corporation, public utility, banking, and insurance law.

Mr. Bobb is a director of the Commercial Trust and Savings Bank, American Mutual Underwriting Corporation, Evanston Bond and Mortgage Company, International Bond and Share Securities Corporation, Englewood Investment Company, Inland Metal Products Corporation, King Pneumatic Tool Company, and various other corporations. He is chairman of the Committee on Character and Fitness for examination of applicants for admission to the bar. He is a member of the American, Illinois State, and Chicago Bar Associations; American Economic Association; Chicago Association of Commerce; Art Institute of Chicago; Sons of the American Revolution (president of Evanston chapter); Phi Beta Kappa and Alpha Kappa Phi fraternities and a director of the Chicago Boys' Clubs, Inc. His clubs are University, Mid-Day, Union League, Electric, Exmoor Country, Harvard, Evanston, and University of Evanston. His hobbies are golf, farming, and horseback riding.

On July 5, 1927, he married Sonia A. Erler of Odessa, Russia.

unusually favorable terms. This is a development which has given the work-ing man added interest in his firm as well as increased income, and has pro-moted harmonious relations between employers and employees.

Great strides have been made in the improvement of the quality of steel products during the last twenty-five years. In this development the metal-lurgists of the steel companies have cooperated to the fullest extent with the consumers. Specifications have been worked out to meet exacting re-quirements for various grades of steel, for heat treating, forging, deep draw-ing, and welding. Much progress also has been made in the alloying of steel with other metals to impart added strength, hardness, corrosion resistance, and other desirable qualities.

Most interesting is the question of distribution of steel products. Where did all the steel go at the start of the century? Where does it go today?

In earlier days, the principal consumers were the railroads. This chan-nel of distribution far exceeded all others. When the railroads purchased, the steel industry flourished; when they ceased to buy, the mills remained comparatively inactive. In 1905, 20 per cent of the steel produced in the United States went into rails alone, and the aggregate consumption by the railroads amounted to more than 40 per cent of the total steel production.

In recent years the automotive industry has used more steel than the railroads, while the building and construction industry has required almost as much. Among other large consumers are the oil, gas, water, and mining interests, agricultural, and machine tool interests. About five per cent of the total steel output is exported.

The pre-eminence of the automobile as the ranking customer of the mills is not difficult to understand when we reflect that this industry, which pro-duced only 22,000 cars in 1905, turned out more than 4,000,000 in 1929, a year when its production reached the peak.

While the automotive and building industries and the railroads are the leaders in steel consumption, they have been by no means the only sources of outlet. On the farm, in the home, at the office, in the factory, every-where, we find steel entering into our lives. Products formerly made of other materials, or which were non-existent at the beginning of the century, are now made of steel.

Any forecast of the steel industry's future must be to a certain extent conjecture. It is probable that the production of steel will continue to in-crease as population increases. In this connection it is interesting to note that, whereas the consumption of rolled steel products amounted to about 300 pounds per capita in 1905, this figure had risen in 1929 to more than 600 pounds per capita. Research and invention are daily finding new uses for steel products, and the per capita consumption seems destined for a steady climb.

The mid-western production still seems inadequate in periods of extreme activity. The federal waterways program, now under way, undoubtedly will stimulate activity in the Chicago district.

(Underwood and Underwood Photo)

DARRELL S. BOYD

Mr. Boyd, lawyer, is a New Yorker by birth, a Chicagoan by choice. He was born at North Tonawanda, New York, November 12, 1889, son of George A. and Anna F. (Wagstaff) Boyd. Shortly after that event the family moved to Rochester, New York, where he received his elementary and high school education. He then attended and graduated with honors from Wesleyan University. He enrolled and completed one year at Columbia University Law School, then moved to Chicago transferring to the North-western University Law School from which he graduated in 1913.

Immediately after graduation he took up the practice of his profession in Chicago with the then firm of Matz, Fisher and Boyden. He later became a member of the firm and has continued his association through its subsequent reorganizations into the firm of Fisher, Boyden, Bell, Boyd and Marshall, specializing in corporation, banking and securities law. For several years prior to its consolidation into Central Republic Bank and Trust Company, he was general counsel and a director of Central Trust Company of Illinois. He is a director of Sullivan Machinery Company, Globe American Company and Central Republic Trust Company. Mr. Boyd is a member of University, Attic, and Indian Hill Country clubs. When he finds time for recreation, he can usually be found playing a round of golf at Indian Hill.

Mr. Boyd married Emily F. Matz, of Winnetka, Illinois, June 25, 1921, and is the father of three children, Charlotte D., Denman H., and Darrell H.

ANCIENT CULTURES BROUGHT TO LIGHT BY ORIENTAL INSTITUTE ARCHAEOLOGISTS

A Unique University of Chicago Organization and Its Work

DEDICATED to "the unfolding life of man," the Oriental Institute of the University of Chicago is the largest archaeological organization in the world, a research institution devoted to tracing the course of human development from archaic savagery to social idealism. The Oriental Institute has set for itself the dual task of salvaging by scientific processes the evidence of this evolution, and of drawing from the evidence, through constructive interpretation and correlation, the epic story of the origins of modern civilization.

The existence in the city of Chicago of so significant an institution as the Oriental Institute is the result of the vision and scholarship of Dr. James Henry Breasted, its director. Forty years ago Dr. Breasted conceived the plan of organizing in comprehensive fashion the investigation of early human development, and his hopes were completely realized with the dedication, in December, 1931, of the new building of the Institute on the University quadrangles.

The Institute had its origin in 1919 in a gift by John D. Rockefeller, Jr., and its subsequent expansion has been due not only to Mr. Rockefeller's generosity but to substantial appropriations by the General Education Board and the International Education Board, and the individual gifts of Julius Rosenwald, Theodore W. Robinson, Robert P. Lamont, Henry J. Patten, and others.

Today there is no doubt that the cradle of civilization was the ancient Near East, the region folded like a horseshoe around the eastern end of the Mediterranean. Into that area the Oriental Institute has despatched thir-

Entrance of the new Oriental Institute Building at the University of Chicago. The sculpture over the door suggests the gradual transition of civilization from the east to the west. Mayers, Murray and Phillips, architects.

JAMES HENRY BREASTED

Dr. Breasted, Orientalist and historian, was born in Rockford, Illinois, August 27, 1865, son of Charles and Harriet N. (Garrison) Breasted. He received his A. B. (Bachelor of Arts) degree from North Central College, in 1888; studied at the Chicago Theological Seminary (particularly Hebrew), from 1888 to 1890; received his A. M. (Master of Arts) degree from Yale University, in 1891; received his A. M. and his Ph. D. (Doctor of Philosophy) from the University of Berlin, in 1894. Honorary degrees have been conferred on him by the Chicago Theological Seminary, B. D. (Bachelor of Divinity), in 1898; University of California, LL. D. (Doctor of Laws), in 1918; Princeton University, LL.D., 1929; and by Oxford University, D. Litt. (Doctor of Literature), in 1922. From 1894 to 1925 Dr. Breasted was, respectively, assistant in Egyptology, instructor of Egyptology and Semitic languages, assistant, associate and then professor of Egyptology and Oriental history (latter since 1905) at the University of Chicago. He has been assistant director, director, and is now chairman of the department of Oriental languages (since 1915) and director of the Oriental Institute of the University of Chicago. He was relieved of all responsibility for instruction in the University of Chicago after August, 1925, in order to take full charge of the work of the Oriental Institute in the Near East and related research projects.

Dr. Breasted collected for the University of Chicago in Egypt, during 1894 and 1895; was Thomas lecturer, Richmond (Virginia) College, in 1898; appointed (1900) on mission to the museums of Europe by commission of the Royal Academies of Germany (Berlin, Leipzig, Munich, Göttingen), to copy and arrange the Egyptian inscriptions in those museums for an Egyptian dictionary. He directed the Egyptian Expedition of the University of Chicago, 1905-1907; director of the Oriental Institute of Chicago University, since 1919; and was in charge of the archaeological survey in Mesopotamia for the Institute, in 1920. He served as Morse lecturer at the Union Theological Seminary, 1912; Earl lecturer, Pacific School of Religion and University of California, 1918; Hale Foundation lecturer, National Academy of Science, Washington, D. C., 1919; Haskell lecturer, Oberlin College, 1922; Messenger lecturer, Cornell University, 1925; and Mary Flexner lecturer, Bryn Mawr College, 1929. He is associate editor of the American Journal of Semitic Languages; was a member of the advisory council of the League of Nations Association, in 1930; is a member of the advisory board of the

Continued on page 545

teen expeditions, and is still maintaining twelve, to carry on a series of related research projects. The new Oriental Institute building is the headquarters for these expeditions which range along a 3,500-mile front from
Persia on the east through Iraq, where the ancient Assyrian and Babylonian
empires flourished, along the bend of the "Fertile Crescent," past Syria and
Anatolia, into Palestine and Egypt. Here were the great cities of the past,
such as Persepolis, Babylon, Baghdad, Nineveh, Aleppo, Megiddo, Jerusa-
lem, Memphis, and Thebes, whose names have persisted through the centuries and to which the Institute's labors are bringing the spark of reality.

The Institute has begun its story of man with his first appearance as a
thinking creature. The Prehistoric Survey, under Dr. Kenneth S. Sandford,
has made the first detailed investigation of the geological history of the
Nile Valley, and has found the oldest human artifacts yet discovered in the
Near East; flint implements produced in lower Pleistocene time, while Europe
was under a great ice sheet. The Prehistoric Survey has also established, in
tracing the history in the Faiyum Lake depressions, that the dessication
which created the Sahara Desert began in the middle of the Old Stone Age.

During the last seven years the Epigraphic and Architectural Survey of
the Institute has been copying and preserving the fast disappearing inscriptions of the Temple of Medinet Habu, built by Ramses III, of 1200 B. C.,
at ancient Thebes, which is opposite modern Luxor. These inscribed and
sculptured records are of fundamental importance because they disclose
Europe for the first time entering the arena of oriental history and reveal
something of the migratory movements which carried the Etruscans from
Asia Minor to Italy. The Epigraphic Survey is under the field direction of
Professor Harold H. Nelson, and has already issued two of a series of ten or
twelve folios which will preserve the records of the temple for all future
scholars. The temple also is in such a state of preservation as to reveal much
of the architecture of the Theban palaces, and an Institute project directed
by Professor Uvo Holscher has been concerned with this aspect. At Abydos,
similar epigraphic work is being done at the temple of Seti I, the colored
reliefs of which are among the finest works of art surviving from ancient
times. This effort is being made in association with the Egypt Exploration
Society and under the editorship of Dr. Alan H. Gardiner.

Another Institute group, with Associate Professor Prentice Duell as
field director, is engaged in the production of five folio volumes in color and
in black and white, recording the magnificent wall-reliefs of masonry tombs
at Sakkara, the cemetery of ancient Memphis. At Cairo, Dr. Gardiner and
Dr. A. DeBuck have completed the task of copying the texts, written
with pen and ink on the inner surface of the wooden coffins, which
disclose as early as the 23rd century B. C. the dawnings of the belief that
happiness beyond the grave is dependent upon the ethical qualities of man's
earthly life. A somewhat analogous project is the copying in color of the
ancient paintings on the walls of tombs in the great Theban cemetery, likewise directed by Dr. Gardiner, and executed by Mrs. Nina de Garis Davies.

(*Blank and Stoller, Inc., Photo*)

ADAM A. BREUER

Mr. Breuer, president of Breuer Electric Manufacturing Company, Inc., manufacturers of electric equipment for industry, was born in Chicago, September 11, 1883, son of Adam and Caroline (Fallscher) Breuer. He attended the public schools and business college in Chicago, and started in the sales department of the American Steel and Wire Company in 1899, where he remained for four years. The next six years he worked in the sales department of the International Harvester Company and the following two years with the Duntley Manufacturing Company, from which place he resigned to assist in organizing the Clements Manufacturing Company of Chicago, manufacturers of electric vacuum cleaners. He became vice-president and secretary of this organization. He was vice-president of the Jewel Vacuum Cleaner Company until March, 1927, when he resigned to organize the Breuer Electric Manufacturing Company, Inc., of which he is now president. This company manufactures portable electric blowers for cleaning motors and machinery, vacuum cleaners for cleaning automobiles and furnaces, heat blowers for melting grease in differentials and transmissions of automobiles, trucks, etc., and sprayers for use with insecticides and disinfectants.

Mr. Breuer is a member of the Illinois Manufacturers' Association, the Illinois Chamber of Commerce, and the Germania Club. He has always taken an active part in politics and is an advocate for good government. He is interested in all athletics. On March 16, 1918, he married Beulah Richardson, Chicago; their children are Grant William, Beulah, and Adam A., Jr.

In Western Asia, about thirty-one miles northeast of Baghdad, the Iraq expedition, directed by Dr. Henri Frankfort, is engaged in excavating the ancient Babylonian cities at Tell Asmar and Khafaji. A third division of the Iraq expedition has been uncovering the ruins of Assyrian civilization.

Two years ago (1930) Professor Edward Chiera, then in charge of the Iraq expedition and now directing the work on the Assyrian dictionary, discovered a temple of Sennacherib near Khorsabad, and excavated the palace of Sargon II, at which he found the winged bull, a colossal stone sculpture which is now in the Oriental Institute museum.

In eastern Anatolia, Dr. H. H. von der Osten has surveyed the country of the Hittites, and has carried on extensive excavations at the site of one of their cities at Alishar, uncovering twenty-three culture levels.

Early in 1931 the French government gave permission for excavations in North Syria, and the Institute's explorations have tentatively identified a site about halfway between Aleppo and Alexandretta as that of the ancient city of Calneh, founded by the Hittites, and referred to by the Hebrew prophets Amos and Isaiah as one of the powerful western enemies of Assyria.

On the western end of the "Fertile Crescent," P. L. O. Guy is in charge of an expedition that is excavating the mound of Armageddon, or Megiddo, in Palestine, commanding the most famous battlefield of the ancient world. The Institute has control of the entire site of the historic city, an area of over thirteen acres, and is now stripping off the stratified series of cities built one upon the other. Here were found, in 1927, the Stables of Solomon, and in 1930-1931 there was revealed a water system dating back to the Canaanite kings of pre-Hebrew days. Most recent of the expeditions is that in Persia, at Persepolis, capital of the great Persian emperors, Darius and Xerxes. Here the noted German specialist in Persian archaeology, Dr. Ernst E. Herzfeld, housed in Darius' palace, is now excavating the city.

The first floor of the new building of the Institute, at Fifty-eighth street and University avenue, houses one of the world's finest museums of ancient Near Eastern civilization, the exhibits affording a revelation of the rising course of mankind. In the Babylonian halls the transformation of the work of man into more highly developed forms of human organization, commercial and social relations, is illustrated by masses of business documents which date back nearly to 3,000 B. C. There are records of Babylonian astronomical observations surpassing in continuity those of modern times, and furnishing the basis for all later astronomical science.

The Egyptian exhibits show much of the complex social organization of the pyramid builders, and point further to the first glimpses of moral vision, the evidence of the transition from the age of materialism to the age of conscience and character, constituting one of the most vivid of the displays. In addition to the Egyptian and Assyro-Babylonian, there are halls devoted to the civilization of Persia and Islam, Palestine, and the Hittites, all contributing to an understanding of the process by which the Institute is creating what Dr. Breasted terms the "New Past."

CHARLES A. BROWN

Mr. Brown, patent lawyer and senior member of the firm of Brown, Jackson, Boettcher and Dienner, was born in Manchester, New York, August 25, 1858, son of Thomas A. and Emily A. Brown. He is descended from Scottish Covenanters who came to this country in 1685 and whose posterity fought in the American Revolution. He attended the University of Rochester and received his A. B. (Bachelor of Arts) degree in 1879 and his A. M. (Master of Arts) degree in 1889. In 1890 he received his LL.B. (Bachelor of Laws) degree at Lake Forest University and in 1891 his LL.M. (Master of Laws). In 1879 Mr. Brown entered the employ of the Western Electric Manufacturing Company and became manager of its successor, the Western Electric Company. He resigned in 1891 to practice patent law and is now the senior member of the patent law firm of Brown, Jackson, Boettcher and Dienner.

Mr. Brown has been president of the Hinsdale Cemetery Association since 1910. He is a member of the Patent Bar Association, American, Illinois State, and Chicago Bar Associations, and Phi Beta Kappa Fraternity, and trustee of the University of Rochester. His clubs are Union League, Law and University.

On July 27, 1892, he married Caroline Cotton of Chicago and they have seven children, Kenneth, Malcolm (died in World War), Meredith (Mrs. Ralph Fisher Skelton), Winifred (Mrs. D. G. Ghrist), Barbara (Mrs. Frederick P. Bowes), Marian (Mrs. Eliot F. Porter), and Gordon.

CHICAGO AS AN ALL-YEAR-ROUND RESORT
World's Premier Vacation City Offers Recreation and Amusement for Every Age Span, Mood and Taste

BY AVERY BRUNDAGE

President, American Olympic Association, and Amateur Athletic Union of United States

WITH its twenty-five miles of lake front, its yacht harbors and bathing beaches, its fifteen large and 193 small parks, its 130 miles of boulevards, its 200 golf courses, its amusement parks, ballrooms, and show places, and its 35,000 acres of forest preserve, Chicago is a vacation city par excellence.

To Chicagoans themselves, who prefer to spend their vacations at home, as well as to the thousands of visitors, who regard Chicago as a playground, the city offers unrivaled facilities for recreation and amusement.

(*H. Albrecht Photo*)

Lincoln Park, looking south from Field House, showing tennis courts, bird sanctuary, and Belmont Harbor.

Golfer, yachtsman, baseball fan, racing enthusiast, sun bather, theatergoer, ski jumper, motorist, equestrian, nature lover, trap shooter, fisherman, hiker—every red-blooded person, in fact, who goes in for sport and outdoor life, will find here something to his taste.

Chicago's hotels, with a capacity of more than 100,000 rooms, are unsurpassed. They offer everything in the way of luxury, and their cuisine, whether of the lunchroom, the table d'hote, or the palatial dining room, is

(Kaiden-Keystone Studios Photo)

SCOTT BROWN

Mr. Brown, lawyer, born in 1875; graduated from the University of Chicago in 1897 and from Northwestern Law School in 1899. Shortly after, he became managing director of Chautauqua Institution of which he is now a trustee. In 1905 he was elected an officer of Studebaker Bros. Mfg. Co., and, upon its organization, became secretary and general counsel of The Studebaker Corporation. In 1915 he was one of the original organizers and owners of the North American Light & Power Company and was vice-president, secretary, and director of that company and allied and subsidiary operating utility companies, including Illinois Power and Light Corporation and Illinois Traction Company. In 1926 he and the other owners of these utilities disposed of their interests and he again went back to the law.

Mr. Brown is a former president of the Illinois Chamber of Commerce and interested in various industrial enterprises. He is actively associated with various civic, educational, and charitable organizations, being a director of United Charities of Chicago and an Associate of California Institute of Technology in Pasadena, California. He is a member of the Chicago, Union League, University, Quadrangle and Glen View Clubs of Chicago; Lotos (New York) and Annandale and Midwick (California).

all the *bon vivant* could wish. Some of the outlying hotels, with their roof gardens, tennis courts, private bathing beaches, swimming pools, and open-air ballrooms, are summer resorts in themselves, resorts where outdoor recreation may be enjoyed amid all the refinements of the city. To vaca-tionists who like bath tubs, personal service, and French chefs with their holidays, these lakeside hotels make a strong appeal.

The Art Institute, with its many special exhibitions; Field Museum, the Adler Planetarium, the Shedd Aquarium, the Lincoln Park Zoo and Aquarium, the magic city of the Century of Progress Exposition grounds, the Historical Society's new museum; Hull House, where the melting pot is seen at work; the Board of Trade and its famous wheat pit; the Merchan-dise Mart and the National Broadcasting Company's super studios; Navy Pier, home of the lake breezes; the University of Chicago campus, with its mile and a quarter façade of Tudor Gothic; Northwestern University's Evanston and McKinlock campus; Buckingham Memorial Fountain, the Union Stockyards, the steel plants at Gary, the industrial town of Pullman, the Riding Club, home of Chicago's famous Black Horse Troop; the Tribune Tower, the North Shore suburbs, Fort Sheridan, and the Naval Training Academy at Great Lakes are among the "sights" no visitor can afford to miss.

(*Chicago Architectural Photographing Company*)
State street, one of the world's greatest shopping thoroughfares.

President
AMERICAN
OLYMPIC
ASSOCIATION

(Murillo Photo, St. Louis, Missouri)

AVERY BRUNDAGE

Mr. Brundage, president, Avery Brundage Company, general contractor, was born in Detroit, Michigan, September 28, 1887, the son of Charles and Amelia (Lloyd) Brundage When he was very young, his parents moved to Chicago; he attended primary school here, graduated from Chicago English High School, and entered the University of Illinois as a student in civil engineering. He completed his technical course, graduating in 1909. While at the University, he was a star track athlete. In 1915, after having spent six years as a superintendent and builder with various Chicago architects and contractors, he started in business for himself and in a short time became one of Chicago's leading contractors. Among the many buildings credited to Avery Brundage Company are the Shoreland Hotel, Ford Motor Company Chicago Plant, 3800 Sheridan Road apartment building, Canada Dry Ginger Ale Plant, Illinois Life Insurance Company and Public Life Insurance Company office buildings, James S. Kirk Soap Works, 1448 Lake Shore Drive, and 1540 Lake Shore Drive apartment buildings, Chicago Yacht Club, Garrett Biblical Institute, Sheridan-Brompton Apartments, River Forest (Illinois) Community House.

Mr. Brundage continued his participation in athletics as a member of the Chicago Athletic Association track team and was a member of the Olympic team at the Games in Stockholm in 1912. As a member of the Cherry Circle team he won the amateur all-round championship in 1914, 1916, and 1918. After giving up track athletics, his interest turned to handball and he became one of the outstanding players of the United States. Following his days as a competing athlete he became interested in the administrative side and was elected vice-president of the Amateur Athletic Union, of the United States. He has been president since November, 1928. In November, 1930, he was elected president of the American Olympic Association, the highest office in amateur athletics in the United States. Mr. Brundage is also vice-president of the International Amateur Athletic Federation and is chairman of the managing committee on sports for A Century of Progress, Chicago's (1933) World's Fair, where it is expected the major sport events of the year 1933 will be conducted. He is a member of Sigma Alpha Epsilon Fraternity, and among his club affiliations are Chicago Athletic, Illinois Athletic, Chicago Engineers, Knollwood, and Chicago Yacht.

On December 22, 1927, Mr. Brundage married Elizabeth Dunlap, of Chicago.

State street and Michigan avenue take rank among the world's greatest bazaar streets.

A trip to Chinatown (preferably at night), to Little Italy, or to the Ghetto, with its picturesque Maxwell street market, will reveal colorful Oriental or Old-World pictures.

From Navy Pier or from the other docks along the river, one may take an excursion boat to Milwaukee, Michigan City, South Haven, Grand Haven, St. Joseph, Benton Harbor, or Holland. Smaller boats ply along the lake shore to Lincoln and Jackson Parks, or take parties out on the lake for moonlight dancing.

At the Municipal Airport, Curtiss Field, or Sky Harbor, airplanes are available for sky tours of Chicago and its environs, and a dirigible is now making trips over the city and the Exposition grounds.

Chicago is the home of two major league baseball clubs. During the summer, the pennant-winning Cubs may be seen in action at Wrigley field, or the White Sox at Cominsky Park on the South Side.

Those who like to invest in the speed of horses will find four splendid racetracks in the Chicago area; Washington Park, where the American Derby, one of the classics of the turf, with its $50,000 purse, is run annually; Hawthorne, Lincoln Fields, at Crete, and Arlington Park, a few miles north-west of the city, where some of the most famous thoroughbreds in America run during the season.

Soldier Field, its classic stadium seating more than 100,000 people, is the scene of many spectacles, athletic contests, and pageants, among them the British-American Track Meet, and the Post-Olympic Games. Here the great Eucharistic Congress was held in 1926. Here the Army-Navy football game was played in the fall of the same year; here Notre Dame's warriors have battled the best Conference teams. Here Gene Tunney wrested from Jack Dempsey the world's heavyweight championship. At Soldier Field are held the annual Chicagoland Music Festivals and the spectacular Army Show.

The best football in America is on view at Dyche Stadium in Evanston, the home of Northwestern's "Wildcats," and at Stagg Field, named in honor of the "Grand Old Man," coach of the University of Chicago's Maroons for forty years.

An August attraction that lures many visitors, including Chicagoans, is the Cook County Fair, at the Fair Grounds at North avenue and River road. The Aurora Fair is another popular fall attraction.

The International Livestock Show and Horse Show at Dexter Pavilion, with its marvelous displays of fat hogs, sheep, and cattle, and its dashing ex-hibitions of horsemanship, attracts thousands of spectators and fanciers.

A season of old-fashioned revivalism, with chicken dinners thrown in for good measure, is offered by the annual Methodist campmeeting at Desplaines.

For winter sports, Chicago offers ice hockey and skating at the Stadium, and ski jumping at Cary, Illinois.

For all-year-round amusements, such as opera, the theater, and dancing, Chicago is exceptionally well equipped. Some of the most gorgeous voices in the world are heard on the stage of the Chicago Civic Opera House and at the "Opera House in the Woods" at Ravinia. Orchestra Hall is the home of the famous Chicago Symphony Orchestra, whose concerts, under the baton of Frederick Stock, provide Chicago with the best in music. At Orchestra Hall and the Auditorium during the fall and winter season, as well as at the Goodman Theater and other smaller halls, concerts are given every Sunday by world-famous singers and virtuosos. Next to Broadway, Chicago's Rialto is the brightest in America. The public ballrooms are palatial; some of them as luxurious as the Petit Trianon at Versailles. Dinner dancing to the music of orchestras of nation-wide fame at the hotel cafés or night clubs is another popular diversion.

(*Chicago Architectural Photographing Company*)

Olympia Fields Country Club. Nimmons, Carr & Wright, architects.

During the summer, the amusement parks, with their miles of scenic and "thrill" rides, their dance halls and outdoor vaudeville, their whirligigs and chutes and sideshows attract merrymakers by the thousand.

Of recent years Chicago has become water conscious. On a sultry day, its fifteen public bathing beaches, its sixty street-end beaches, and its children's wading pools are thronged with swimmers, splashers, and sun worshipers.

The recreational facilities of Lincoln Park alone are amazing. Here the fly-caster can test his skill, the trap shooter can bang away at clay pigeons, the archer can send his shafts speeding toward the target. In the lagoon, oarsmen, singly or in crews, train for the regatta in their racing shells. Children race their model yachts. Rowboats can be rented by the hour. There is a pony track for boys and girls, and there are bridle paths for more expert equestrians. There are diamonds for baseball; courts for croquet and tennis. One of the city's sportiest golf courses recently has been opened near the Waveland avenue entrance of the park. Diversey Beach offers an opportunity to enjoy the swimming. One could easily, and without being bored, spend an entire two weeks', or even a longer, vacation in the park, exploring its miles of inviting paths, visiting the Academy of Science, the Historical Society's Museum, the zoo, the bird house, the conservatory, the aquarium; rowing, playing golf or tennis.

Belmont Harbor shelters a fleet of motor boats and white-winged yachts, which on a fair day may be seen dancing far out on the sparkling waters of Chicago's inland sea. There are other yacht harbors in Jackson Park and Grant Park, and off Wilmette.

Jackson Park invites the visitor to enjoy beach parties at the bathing beach or picnics on its rustic Wooded Isle, where the squirrels are so tame that they will climb on your shoulder and eat out of your hand. There is boating, and—in season—fishing in the lagoon. Golfers will find a nine and an eighteen hole course. Tennis players are accommodated on 100 clay and grass courts. The children's playground is equipped with everything the little folk could desire. Garfield, Humboldt, and Douglas Parks also offer many recreational facilities.

While yachting has always been a popular sport in Chicago, and the many regattas have developed fine seamanship among its followers, outboard motorboat racing has of late attained a considerable vogue, the Burnham Park lagoon, off the Century of Progress Exposition grounds being a favorite course for the short-distance events. Longer races are held over a course from Milwaukee to Chicago.

Including private clubs, public fee courses, and public courses in the parks and forest preserves, Chicago has more than 200 golf grounds. Those owned by the public are to be found in Lincoln, Jackson, Garfield, Columbus, and Marquette Parks, and in five of the forest preserve tracts—the Turnbull Woods tract, Glencoe; Harms Woods, Edgebrook, Palos, and Burnham.

Chicago's miles of well-paved boulevards constitute a motorist's paradise. A drive of less than an hour will carry one out to the picturesque Dunelands, to the forest preserves girding the city, or along the beautiful North Shore, past the Northwestern University campus, the Marshall studio, the Baha'i temple, No Man's Land, a Coney Island in miniature; through the sequestered suburbs of Kennilworth, Winnetka, Glencoe, and Highland Park, through deep ravines and glens, past golf courses and country clubs and private estates, to Fort Sheridan, Great Lakes, and Lake Forest.

In the forest preserves, golf courses, swimming holes, baseball diamonds, picnic grounds, and camping sites will be found amid sylvan surroundings, along winding paths, and winding waterways.

(J. D. Toloff Photo, Evanston, Ill.)

GLEN BUCK

Mr. Buck, president of The Glen Buck Company, advertising agency, was born in Cedar Springs, Michigan, November 4, 1876, son of Judge Curtis Buck and Elizabeth (McRae) Buck. He attended public and high schools and later was a student at Lawrence University and at Northwestern University from 1893 to 1897. He received the honorary degree of D. B. A. (Doctor of Business Administration) from Lawrence University in 1929. In 1906 he married Anne E. Flaherty, of Chicago, and they have one daughter, Peggy (Mrs. Albert Rixon Hansen). Mr. Buck became the owner and editor of the Park River (N. D.) News in 1898, and Gogebic Daily Journal, Ironwood, Michigan, in 1900; was with the Chicago Record, 1901; was advertising manager for Olds Motor Works during 1902; and was with Butler Brothers, Chicago, from 1903 to 1909. He established the present advertising firm of The Glen Buck Company in 1909 and is now its president. He has handled some of the largest advertising campaigns in America, particularly for the Ford, Lincoln, Packard, and Stutz automobiles, the Mimeograph, Sheaffer pens, Phoenix hosiery. He wrote the first electric refrigeration and air-craft advertising appearing in national publications, and was one of the first regular advertising managers employed in the automobile field. During the World War he was employed by the United States Government as a writer of propaganda and general publicity.

Mr. Buck is a trustee of the Evanston Public Library and a life member of the Audubon Society and American Game Protective Association. His clubs are Cliff Dwellers, Union League (Chicago), Evanston, and Glenview Golf. His recreations are ornithology and book-collecting. He lectures on business subjects and is the author of "Trademark Power" (1916), "This American Ascendency" (1927), "The Cost of Confusion" (1929), also many other books.

CHICAGO'S GROWING LEADERSHIP IN PRINTING, PUBLISHING AND ADVERTISING

A One-third Billion Dollar Industry that Ranks First in Chicago in Number of Employees

BY ERNEST T. GUNDLACH

A T the beginning of the present century, Chicago ranked a modest third or fourth in the field of printing, publishing, and advertising. Chicago's daily newspapers were published in editions of ten or twelve, sometimes eight pages; when a sixteen-page issue ran off the press, it was a red letter day.

New York was, of course, America's printing and publishing center. The greatest dailies, the largest number of magazines, the big printing establishments, and, with two exceptions, the leading advertising agencies, were concentrated in that city. Philadelphia ranked second; it was the home of several of the best daily newspapers in America; of the Ladies' Home Journal, then already the leader in its field, and of the N. W. Ayer Agency, at that time by far the largest advertising agency in America, and still today, in 1932, one of the three outstanding leaders. Boston was then a conspicuous factor in the publication of school books and in various types of printing.

All three of these cities have grown greatly in publishing, printing, and advertising, during the past thirty years.

(*Chicago Architectural Photographing Company*)

Chicago's new POSTOFFICE—world's largest postal building contains every convenience and detail for the handling of mail that it is possible for human ingenuity to provide.
Graham, Anderson, Probst & White, architects.

(*Underwood and Underwood Photo, New York*)

HOMER J. BUCKLEY

Mr. Buckley, president, Buckley, Dement & Company, was born in Rock Island County, Illinois, March 16, 1879, son of John A. and Mary (Sullivan) Buckley. He attended St. Ignatius College and Bryant & Stratton Business College, Chicago. He began as a messenger at Marshall Field & Company in 1891, working there until 1905 as cash boy, shipping clerk and finally as manager of circular advertising and the follow-up system, under H. Gordon Selfridge. In 1905 he organized Buckley, Dement & Company, of which he is now president. This organization, one of the largest direct mail houses in the country, does business for advertisers in all parts of the United States and Canada. It employs 400 people and occupies its own six-story building.

Mr. Buckley is a pioneer in organized advertising, being one of the charter members of the Advertising Club of Chicago and a member of the organization committee for the first convention of the Associated Advertising Clubs of the World. He is the founder of the Direct Mail Advertising Association, of which organization he is now an honorary vice-president; is president of the National Council of Business Mail Users; and former chairman of the Advertising Council of Chicago. He is chairman of the committee on public information and trustee of A Century of Progress, Chicago's (1933) World's Fair. He is a director of the Illinois Manufacturers' Association and a director of the Fidelity Investment Association (Wheeling, West Virginia). Mr. Buckley is on the staff of the following schools: Cleveland Advertising School, New York Advertising School, Y. M. C. A. School of Commerce, Northwestern University, University of Chicago, and Notre Dame University. He is a member of the Chicago Association of Commerce (executive committee) and belongs to the following clubs: Union League, Irish Fellowship, Chicago Athletic Association, and Butterfield Country (director). He is the author of Science of Marketing by Mail, 1924.

Mr. Buckley married Lucile Kathleen Wallace of New York City, September 23, 1908. They have one daughter, Marihelyn.

But it was shortly after the beginning of the century that Chicago put on seven-league boots.

In that time, the printing business made the greatest strides of any Chicago industry. From an annual volume of $40,000,000 to $50,000,000, the total value of products had expanded by 1929 to nearly one-third billion dollars. This refers exclusively to printing, publishing, and advertising without allied industries. Think of it! Nearly 333 million dollars in one year within the limits of the Chicago area. Accurate figures since the last census are not as yet available. There has been, of course, a large reduction in volume, though not in the same ratio as in various other industries. In number of employees in Chicago, printing and publishing still ranks first.

Today Chicago has the largest printing plants in the country; it has the greatest linotype plants, the most completely equipped binderies, the largest composing rooms, and the largest plants for map printing.

In the last few years, one by one, magazines edited in New York have come here for their printing work. Many a periodical, bearing a New York address, comes to you from a Chicago printing plant. Catalogs and booklets of the great mail order houses, having an annual circulation of more than 120,000,000 a year, together with innumerable special circulars, are products of Chicago presses.

There are more presses for color printing here than in any other city in the United States. Unique edition bookwork has been growing extensively. And in general, there is a larger number of highly specialized printing plants in this city than in any other in the world.

Furthermore, Chicago stands at, or near, the top in the manufacture of printing presses and of other printing machinery. Newspapers from New England to California and in Europe use Chicago-made presses.

In the field of publishing, Chicago is one of the leading cities, though not the leader. Two of Chicago's dailies have been known for a generation as being among America's most consistent successes, The Chicago Tribune and the Chicago Daily News. The Chicago American is said to rank near the top in the long list of Hearst papers as a profit-maker. The Herald & Examiner and the Tribune have Sunday circulations of about a million each. The Illustrated Times came up within one and one-half years to over 160,000 circulation. There is also the Chicago Journal of Commerce, which is read by business executives not only in Chicago but throughout the country. In addition, there are about forty foreign language newspapers.

Several good monthlies are published and printed in Chicago; also many of the leading trade journals, both monthlies and weeklies. There are more than two hundred of these technical publications. The Agricultural Publishers' Association, embracing the farm papers from coast to coast, maintains its headquarters in Chicago. Some of the largest book publishing organizations in the country are located here.

EDWARD J. BULLOCK

Mr. Bullock, vice-president and director of the Standard Oil Company (Indiana) since 1922, was born in Cleveland, Ohio, September 16, 1873, and is the son of John and Elizabeth (Davis) Bullock. He attended the public schools of Milwaukee, Wisconsin, and started earning his living in the Milwaukee office of the Standard Oil Company (Indiana). In 1904 he was transferred to the Chicago office of the company, where a few years later he was promoted to the position of manager of all sales for the Chicago Division. Today, in addition to other duties, he supervises all purchases, which run into millions of dollars annually.

Mr. Bullock has held office of president of the Oak Park Club. He is a member of the Union League, Oak Park, Oak Park Country, River Forest Country, and River Forest Tennis clubs, Ohio Society of Chicago, and of many fraternal organizations and civic enterprises. He is interested in golf and all other outdoor sports.

On July 12, 1904, he married Cora Ardelia Wells, of Portage, Wisconsin, (deceased), and is the father of four children, John, Miriam, Elizabeth, and Grace.

In the field of advertising, Chicago ranks second to New York. It is significant that the majority of the associations working for the good of advertising were originated in this city. The Agate Club of Chicago is said to be the first advertising club in the world. It was organized in 1893. A few years later, the National Advertising Association was formed here. Out of this grew the Associated Advertising Clubs of the world. Their first convention was held in this city.

The American Association of Advertising Agencies had its germ in Chicago. The plan was initiated by the late Stanley Clague in 1912. The Association has developed into a strong organization advocating higher ethics in publicity.

The Audit Bureau of Circulation was founded in Chicago in 1914; and it was again Mr. Clague who originated the idea. This Audit Bureau has been of inestimable value to the advertising business. In fact, it has revolutionized our attitude toward "space buying." The Bureau has established faith in circulation statements and in exact values, also to a large degree, as to equality of rates to all advertisers.

The Financial Advertisers' Association maintains its central office in Chicago. There are various other organizations and affiliated associations with headquarters in this Central Western City.

There are about 160 partly and fully recognized general agencies in Chicago and their total volume ranks second among the cities of this country. The leading eastern agencies all maintain branches in Chicago, some of them with large forces.

The general offices and the main plant of the greatest outdoor advertising concern in the world are located in Chicago. The making of outdoor and window displays in various processes has become a large industry. There are a great number of oil paint, lithograph, offset, and rotogravure plants here. Street car advertising in Chicago represents a monthly circulation of approximately 125,000,000 car riders.

The manufacturers of advertising specialties in Chicago are said to have an annual output in excess of $30,000,000. The Advertising Specialty Association maintains its headquarters in this city. Some of the largest direct mail organizations are also located here. Outstanding among them is Buckley, Dement & Company, the foremost direct advertising organization in the world.

It is not the writer's desire to pile Olympus on Parnassus, but the impression of hugeness grows when we delve into statistics on the electric sign business, on specialty manufacture for point-of-sale material, and on the volume of a variety of industries otherwise allied to publishing, printing, and advertising.

CHICAGO AS A MEDICAL CENTER
How the Health of the People is Safeguarded
BY DR. EDWARD H. OCHSNER

MANY factors are involved in the consistent growth and development of a great city like Chicago. Natural advantages of location, and adequate transportation facilities are not enough to insure a city's permanence. Sanitary provisions and medical supervision in the interests of public health are essential if any large community is to endure. For these, the medical profession is in large measure responsible.

Chicago has been fortunate from the start in having capable, far-sighted, public-spirited physicians who have taken pride in their city and have done everything possible to safeguard the health of its inhabitants.

As was so often the case in frontier settlements, a doctor was one of the first white men to locate in the straggling little community that grew into Chicago. He was Dr. William C. Smith, and he arrived in 1803 as the first post surgeon at Fort Dearborn. He remained five years, looking after the health of the garrison and attending to such private practice as offered. He was succeeded by Dr. John Cooper, who in turn was succeeded by Dr. Isaac Van Voorhees in 1811.

Dr. Van Voorhees, who was among the victims of the Fort Dearborn massacre the following year, is described by one of his contemporaries as "a young man of unusual breadth of vision and loftiness of ideals." That he had a prophetic vision is indicated by a letter which he wrote to a friend a few months after his arrival here.

(*Chicago Architectural Photographing Company*)
SPIRES OF BUSINESS

"In my solitary walks," he wrote, "I contemplate what a great, powerful republic will arise in this new world. Here, I say, will be the seat of millions yet unborn, the asylum of oppressed thousands yet to come."

In the Indian massacre of August 15, 1812, the entire white population was wiped out, the few survivors being scattered, and only three families, the Ouilmettes, the Du Pins, and the Beaubiens, were found living in the neighborhood when Capt. Hezekiah Bradley, U. S. A., arrived in 1816 with two companies of infantry to build a new fort on the ruins of the old.

The tomahawk and the scalping knife, however, were not the only perils the early settlers had to face. Located on marshy ground so slightly elevated above the lake level as to provide practically no drainage, the community for many years suffered from epidemics of malaria, small-pox, cholera, diphtheria, enteritis, and typhoid fever.

The settlement was without a physician for some time, but in 1820, Dr. Alexander Wolcott was appointed Indian agent here, and combined the practice of medicine with his official duties.

On several occasions, cholera threatened to destroy the entire settlement. Severe visitations of this scourge occurred in 1832 and 1833. In 1837, shortly after the first municipal election, a board of health was organized, consisting of Dr. J. W. Eldredge, D. Cox, and A. N. Fullerton. Dr. Daniel Brainard was appointed health officer. One of the first duties of this board was to deal with the cholera situation.

In 1849, after a brief respite, the dread disease, brought to Chicago by a traveler from New Orleans, broke out in an unusually virulent form, and in that year, out of a population of 23,000, six hundred and seventy-eight cholera victims were buried. It was four years before the disease was again temporarily stamped out. It recurred, however, in 1856, and again in 1866, when it caused 990 deaths. The board of health, which had been disbanded, was reorganized, and a successful campaign was waged against the plague. Drainage of the swampy areas not only banished cholera, but greatly reduced the death rate from malaria, a disease virtually unknown in the Chicago region today. Smallpox, which had taken heavy tolls, especially in 1848 and 1859, was gradually brought under control by vaccination.

But as the city grew in population, typhoid fever and enteritis became more and more prevalent, constituting a serious menace not only to the health, well-being, and lives of its citizens, but to the growth and development of the city itself. The wastes of the city, street washings, building sewage, refuse from the slaughter houses, distilleries, and rendering plants, were turned into the lake, causing the contamination of the source of drinking water. By 1870, the range of impurity extended a mile out from the shore, half way to the crib, and it was evident that remedial measures were imperative.

The Illinois and Michigan Canal was deepened so as to draw the water from the lake, but the pumps which kept the water flowing were inadequate,

(Chicago Architectural Photographing Company)
A BRILLIANT PAGEANT OF LIGHT

especially in times of flood, when the accumulated sewage would be backed up, and the situation would become intolerable.

In 1891, Chicago, with a population of approximately 1,000,000, lost 1,997 persons by death from typhoid fever, while some 15,000 were incapacitated for months because of this disease. Enteritis wrought almost as much havoc, the majority of its victims being children.

During the late '80's, the medical profession came to the conclusion that typhoid and enteritis were largely water-borne diseases, caused by pollution of drinking water with sewage. Another serious attempt to overcome these scourges took the direction of extending the water tunnels farther out into the lake. One tunnel, completed in 1894, extended out five miles from shore. This greatly reduced the number of typhoid cases, but the medical profession soon realized that even this precautionary measure would not suffice so long as the city continued to grow and to pour its ever increasing volume of waste into Lake Michigan.

As the result of agitation started by the medical men, the Sanitary District was created in 1890, the trustees of which were commissioned to build a new canal, and to make the Chicago River flow backwards. This monumental undertaking—comparable to the construction of the Suez Canal—was begun in 1892 and completed in 1900 at a cost of approximately $70,000,000. Some 15 miles of the canal were cut through solid rock. With the opening of the canal, the death rate in Chicago fell off significantly; typhoid and enteritis became almost negligible.

The longer intake tunnels, together with the Drainage Canal, soon gave Chicago the reputation of being one of the healthiest cities of its class in the world. While the death rate from typhoid in 1891 was 173.8 per 100,000 population, it dropped so rapidly after these sanitary improvements had been installed, that in 1901 it was only 29.1 per 100,000. It remained at about this figure, varying somewhat from year to year, and no further improvement occurred until it was discovered that certain foods, such as milk and green vegetables, sometimes were contaminated, and that the lake was still being polluted by sewage poured into it from the suburbs to the north and south of Chicago.

Chlorination at the intakes was now instituted. This, with regular inspection and control of the milk supply, further cut down deaths from enteritis and typhoid until in 1931, the low of 0.4 per 100,000 from the latter disease was attained.

Chlorination of the drinking water is, however, only a makeshift, and already the Drainage Canal, despite its extensions, is becoming inadequate to carry off all the sewage. The problem now before the medical profession, and the authorities, local, state, and national, is how best and most economically to treat sewage not only in Chicago, but in every other center of population, and how to keep our inland waters unpolluted.

In the field of medical education, as well as in the field of preventive and curative medicine, Chicago's physicians have added to the prestige of the city.

Chicago today has three great medical centers; one on the West Side, in the vicinity of the Cook County Hospital; one on the South Side, on the University of Chicago campus; one on the North Side, on the McKinlock campus of Northwestern University.

To the vision of Dr. Daniel Brainard Chicago is indebted for its oldest and most famous medical school. Largely through his efforts, Rush Medical College obtained its charter in 1837. The school was opened in 1843 in rented quarters, but a year later moved into its own building, a one-story brick and stone structure at Dearborn and Indiana streets (Dearborn street and Grand avenue) representing an investment of $3,500.

Dr. Brainard not only was an outstanding teacher of anatomy and surgery, but he had the personality which attracted to him other men of high standing. Thus he was able to secure for his faculty such representative men as Dr. James V. Z. Blaney, Dr. N. S. Davis, Dr. Austin Flint, Dr. M. L. Knapp, and Dr. John McLean. Dr. Blaney occupied the chair of chemistry and materia medica; Dr. Knapp taught obstetrics; Dr. McLean, theory and practice. Dr. Davis was the organizer of the American Medical Society. Dr. Flint was the originator of the Principle of Ethics of the American Medical Association.

It was at Rush Medical College that "laughing gas" was first administered, in 1847, and that chloroform was first used in Chicago as an anesthetic in a surgical operation.

Efficient medical teaching and medical service to the public required, in addition to capable practitioners, adequate hospitals. Here again, public-spirited and far-sighted laymen have cooperated with the members of the medical profession.

In 1848, a charter for an "Illinois General Hospital" was taken out by a group of Rush Medical College professors, and in 1850, a hospital of twelve beds was opened at Rush and North Water streets, the only institution of its kind in a city that was far from being a health resort. A year later, it was turned over to the Sisters of Mercy, and during the Civil War, Mercy Hospital, as it was then known, was the only public hospital in Chicago. It was located at that time in Wabash avenue near Van Buren street, but in 1866 moved to its present site at 26th street and Prairie avenue.

The County Hospital, a model of its kind, and the largest in the world, is an outgrowth of a small hospital established by Dr. McVicker, when he was commissioner of health, in 1853. In 1866, during the cholera epidemic of that year, it came under its present management.

This hospital has grown steadily and served thousands of poor. Its clinics, presided over by talented and brilliant specialists, have attracted students and physicians from all parts of the world. Many of the foremost medical men of the United States have received their early training at this institution.

Later years have seen the establishment of many private and semi-private hospitals, more than 100 in number—Passavant, Wesley Memorial, the Lying-In, the McCormick Children's hospital, St. Luke's are among those that come first to mind. All these hospitals are magnificently equipped, and have been giving excellent service to thousands of patients annually.

Chicago has been indeed fortunate in having had and still having so many outstanding general practitioners, specialists, research workers, and medical teachers. The John B. Murphy Memorial is a monument only to one physician who has contributed to the betterment of Chicago.

Chicago has been fortunate in having had and still having splendid medical schools and hospitals. It has every reason to be proud and grateful to these men and these institutions for the services they have rendered to the community. Without such institutions and without these medical men or others of the same professional accomplishments and civic pride, Chicago could never have risen to the enviable position which she holds today. The past and present bespeak an even more glorious future.

CHICAGO AS A PHARMACEUTICAL CENTER

Since the World War, Chicago has come forward rapidly as a manufacturing center for medical chemicals and fine pharmaceutical products, used and prescribed by the medical profession.

During the years 1914 to 1918, when the import supply of medicinal chemicals was cut off, the Abbott Laboratories, of Chicago, was requested by the Government to enter this field. A research staff was organized at that time under the direction of Dr. Alfred S. Burdick, and a number of medicinal chemicals, never before manufactured in this country, were made available to the medical profession and to hospitals. Such products included the Dakin antiseptics, Chlorazene and Dichloramine-T, Barbital, Acriflavine, Procaine and Cinchophen.

In 1922, the Dermatological Research Laboratories, Philadelphia, the first to manufacture arsenical preparations in this country, was purchased by the Abbott Laboratories. Later the Jno. T. Milliken Company, of St. Louis, and the Swan-Myers Company, of Indianapolis, were also acquired.

ABBOTT LABORATORIES, NORTH CHICAGO, ILLINOIS

This company now owns twenty-four acres of manufacturing property in North Chicago, where its main plant is located. All wholesale and retail druggists in the United States now sell the Abbott pharmaceutical products and their distribution is world-wide.

The superior rail and water shipping facilities of Chicago have led other pharmaceutical companies to maintain their plants in the Chicago area. Notable among these are G. D. Searle & Co., Chicago Pharmacal Company, Wilson Laboratories, Bauer & Black, and Petrolagar. All leading pharmaceutical manufacturers in the United States find it necessary to maintain branches and stocks in Chicago.

The medical schools of the University of Chicago, the University of Illinois, and Northwestern University, with their affiliated hospitals, research laboratories, and clinics, have done much to put Chicago into the forefront of medical and pharmaceutical activity.

(Moffett-Russell Photo)

DR. ALFRED S. BURDICK

Dr. Burdick, president of Abbott Laboratories, manufacturers of pharmaceutical and biological specialties of the Abbott, Swan-Myers, and Dermatological Research Laboratories, was born in DeRuyter, New York, February 15, 1867, son of Rev. Stephen and Susan (Maxson) Burdick. He received his A. B. (Bachelor of Arts) degree at Alfred University in 1886 and his M. D. (Doctor of Medicine) degree at Rush Medical College, Chicago, in 1891. He started a general practice of medicine at Dunlap, Illinois, later practicing at Tampa, Florida, and Hinsdale, Illinois, and was associate professor in the practice of medicine at Illinois Medical College from 1899 to 1904.

Dr. Burdick became vice-president and assistant general manager of Abbott Laboratories in 1916 and in 1921 became president and general manager, which position he now holds. The Abbott Laboratories, with executive offices and main plant at North Chicago, Illinois, also controls the Dermatological Research Laboratories at Philadelphia and Abbott Laboratories, Limited, of Montreal, Canada. Dr. Burdick was a member of the Selective Service Board number 59 in Chicago from 1917 to 1919. He was a member of the board of governors, 1922 to 1929, and vice-president, 1923 to 1924, of the Synthetic Organic Chemical Manufacturers' Association; was president of the American Drug Manufacturers' Association from 1923 to 1925. He has been a Lieutenant Colonel in the Medical Reserve Corps, United States Army, since 1923. He wrote Standard Medical Manual in 1904, The Remedy in 1915, and Common Emergencies in 1915. He was editor of Medical Standard from 1899 to 1904 and American Journal of Clinical Medicine from January, 1904 to 1931. He is a member of the American, Illinois State, and Chicago medical societies, and American Medical Editors' Association. His clubs are City, Chemists of Chicago, and Chemists of New York.

On July 9, 1891, Dr. Burdick married Ella Grace Brown of West Hallock, Illinois.

LOOKING FORWARD TO 1950
How the Regional Planning Association is Anticipating the Future
BY DANIEL H. BURNHAM
President, Chicago Regional Planning Association

THE automobile, the railway, and the telephone, bringing the delights of country life to city workers, have made possible Chicago's wonderful suburban development. Towns and villages once isolated are today a part of Greater Chicago. Air transportation, still in its infancy, may spread the city out still farther.

Chicago grew too fast during the 19th century. Like most American cities, she grew like Topsy. The most serious problem confronting the city in those days was that of drainage, and because of the inadequacy of drainage facilities, Chicago was swept by repeated epidemics of cholera, typhoid, and small-pox. Again, nobody could look ahead and forsee the skyscraper and the automobile. Had it been possible in the days before steel and concrete construction and the internal combustion engine to forecast the future, and to plan for future needs, Chicago's downtown streets would have been much wider. A comprehensive thoroughfare system, such as is materializing today, could have been laid out years in advance.

Chicago keeps on growing, and will continue to grow. She has a future that gives one a thrill to contemplate. But far-seeing men are looking forward to that future and anticipating the needs of the community in the

(*Trowbridge Photo*)
A home in Lake Forest, Illinois.
Russell Walcott, architect.

(*Trowbridge Photo*)
A home in Lake Forest, Illinois.
Walcott and Work, architects.

(Loubell Studios Photo)

DANIEL H. BURNHAM

Mr. Burnham, vice-president and secretary of A Century of Progress Exposition, Chicago's (1933) World's Fair and president of the Chicago Regional Planning Association, was born in Chicago, February 22, 1886, son of Daniel H., to whose genius not only Chicago, but American architecture owes it renaissance, and Margaret S. (Sherman) Burnham. He received his education in the Evanston grammar and high schools, and in the Middlesex School, Concord, Massachusetts. After completing a special course in architecture at Lawrence Scientific School, Harvard University, he became a partner in his father's firm, D. H. Burnham and Company, in Chicago. On the death of his father, in 1912, Mr. Burnham became a partner in the firm of Graham, Burnham and Company, but in 1917, he reestablished the original firm, the name of which was changed later to Burnham Brothers, Inc.

In such structures as the Bankers' Building, the Carbide and Carbon Building, and the Burnham Building, Mr. Burnham has given Chicago some excellent examples of Twentieth Century architecture, while his departures in the Century of Progress buildings have been even more daring. It is significant that the son of the chief architect of the World's Columbian Exposition, Chicago's first World's Fair, should be largely responsible for the architecture and design of the World's Fair of 1933. The Chicago Plan, the conception of the senior Burnham, which has resulted in such improvements as Wacker Drive, North Michigan avenue, and the reclamation of the Lake front, have gone forward in recent years under the Chicago Plan Commission of which Mr. Burnham is a member. He is a member of the American Institute of Architects, the Illinois Society of Architects, the Western Society of Engineers, the Chicago Commercial, Union League, University, Cliff Dwellers, and Commonwealth clubs.

Mr. Burnham was married, June 21, 1913, to Helen Otis of Chicago. They have two children, Daniel H. III, and Spencer Ottis.

years to come. Thus, it is possible to plan improvements that will mean a
vast saving of money; to carry out a zoning program that will conserve real
estate values and at the same time provide for industrial development; to set
aside grounds for recreational uses and for rights of way before land prices
have gone skyrocketing, and above all, to provide for arterial highways radiating from the Loop. The object of planning such improvements far in advance is to avoid, so far as possible, the mistakes of the past—costly mistakes,
such as granting to the Illinois Central railroad the right of way along
Chicago's lake front, which fortunately, though at a tremendous cost, has
been reclaimed by the extension of the shore line.

(*Trowbridge Photo*)

A home in Winnetka, Illinois.   Russell Walcott, architect.

Place the point of a giant compass at State and Madison streets and de-
scribe a circle with a 50-mile radius. You will have a fan-like land area
reaching out into the adjacent states of Indiana and Wisconsin, and embracing not only all of Cook county, but fifteen counties, three in Indiana, three
in Wisconsin, and nine in Illinois.

This is the metropolitan area, and it is filling up with residents at the rate
of more than a million every decade. It is evident that the soundness of this
population growth and the success of the industries within the Chicago area
are dependent on the proper physical provisions for this increase, and that
such provisions must look far into the future.

If the present population trends hold constant, this area, in which 280
cities and villages are located, will have by 1950 between 7,500,000 and

(*Underwood and Underwood Photo, New York*)

HUBERT BURNHAM

Mr. Burnham, architect, son of Daniel Hudson Burnham and Margaret (Sherman) Burnham, was born in Chicago, September 7, 1882. He is a graduate of the Chicago Manual Training School and the Phillips Academy, Andover, Massachusetts. He attended the United States Naval Academy, graduating in 1905, and graduated from the École des Beaux Arts, Paris, France, in 1912. Upon his return to America in 1910 he became a member of the firm of D. H. Burnham and Company (founded by his father), of Chicago. In 1912 the firm name was changed to Graham, Burnham and Company and so remained until 1917 when it was re-established as D. H. Burnham and Company to be changed in 1928 to Burnham Brothers, Inc. Mr. Burnham served as a lieutenant in the United States Navy during the World War and did aviation construction work in France for fourteen months. The Burnham organization has planned and been architects for some of Chicago's most beautiful buildings, including the Carbide and Carbon Building, Bankers Building, Engineering Building, Burnham Building, as well as many other buildings throughout the country.

Mr. Burnham is a Fellow of the American Institute of Architects, a member of the Illinois Society of Architects, Society of Beaux Arts Architects, and Chicago Architectural Club. His clubs are University, Cliff Dwellers, Chicago, Glenview, and Indian Hill. He is a member of the Architectural Commission of Chicago's 1933 World's Fair.

On June 24, 1908, he married Vivian Cameron, of Washington, D. C.

A bank in Evanston, Illinois.
Childs & Smith, architects.

A school in Evanston, Illinois.
Childs & Smith, architects.

8,000,000 inhabitants, more than twice as many as shown by the 1920 census figures.

Chicago, it is estimated, will have a population of 4,500,000 and Cook county, of 5,300,000. For this tremendous population, and in exact relation to it, many facilities must be provided, such as streets and highways, parks, forest preserves, sewers, sewage treatment plants, water works, electric power, gas, and telephone systems.

Working quietly in the Chicago area is a rapidly growing force of regional planners set in motion and supported by public officials and business men in every part of the region. This force is fast bringing together and coordinating the many local plans for future development, both public and private; and out of them it is forming a number of comprehensive programs for orderly and systematic growth.

This body is known as the Chicago Regional Planning Association. Cooperating with it are local authorities, public utilities executives, and others whose interests are bound up in the future development of Greater Chicago. These men are contributing their time and thought not only to the shaping of sound policies and definite plans, but also to carrying them out by actual construction.

The problem of sanitation, water supply, and drainage in the Chicago area is one which will affect the future population to a greater degree than any other factor. Roads can be built, districts can be zoned, parks can be laid out; but unless adequate provision is made for supplying the residents of this region with clean, pure water, and adequate means for the treatment and disposal of sewage, the capacity of the land in this congested segment will be definitely limited.

Already there are towns and villages close to the metropolis whose water supplies are inadequate, although they are within a few miles of the inexhaustible supply provided by Lake Michigan. Engineers, representatives of industries, members of city and village councils have in hand the task of building the works that will secure satisfactory water for the areas to be populated during the coming decades.

Under the direction of a regional committee on highways, which includes federal, state, county, and municipal officials, a comprehensive map

(*Moffett-Russell Photo*)

OLIVER M. BURTON

Mr. Burton, president and treasurer of the Burton-Dixie Corporation, manufacturers of box springs, mattresses, pillows, automobile seat cushions and allied lines, is the son of John and Elizabeth Lucy (Long) Burton, and was born in Geneva, Illinois, on March 18, 1877. He received his education in the Chicago public schools and business colleges. He began his active business career with his father in 1895; became secretary and treasurer of the Oliver M. Burton Company in 1899 and has been president and treasurer since 1905. The name of the company is now the Burton-Dixie Corporation.

He is a member of the Chicago Association of Commerce, Illinois Manufacturers' Association, Chicago Association of Credit Men, and his clubs are Chicago Athletic, Racquet, Indian Hill in Chicago, and the Detroit Athletic, of which he is a non-resident member.

Mr. Burton married Ann J. Tatham, of Chicago, on October 20, 1909.

was prepared showing the paved highways and those expected to be paved by every state and county in the region. The next step was to plan for the connection of existing and proposed paved routes at state and county lines where breaks occurred. The third step was to bring city and village officials into touch with state and county executives so that the former might co-ordinate their street plans to dovetail with the county and state programs.

During the few years in which the Regional Planning Association has been active, the highway systems of Illinois, Indiana, and Wisconsin have been so coordinated as to develop a system of more than 3,000 miles of paved road with few hiatuses between one county and another or at the lines dividing the states. Much of the existing mileage has been widened from eighteen and twenty foot lanes to multiple traffic lanes of forty feet or more.

Street and highway plans have been made for the future which already are materializing in a comprehensive system of boulevards, parkways, and forestways. More than 150 miles of boulevard rights of way 200 feet in width have been ceded by private property owners in accordance with this plan. In Cook county the Forest Preserve Commissioners have been ac-quiring broad belts of land as connecting links between isolated forest pre-serves so that the tracts may be extended into a unified system. In these new belts will be laid trails, bridle paths, and eventually driveways. On the other broad rights of way, pavement is to be laid as needed. Trees will be planted along the boulevards wherever possible. As the communities grow, the arteries of traffic will have been provided for at far less expense and in more favorable locations than would have been the case if they had to be widened or opened after the area had been built up.

Carefully watching the development of the region, the zoning authorities of the municipalities, as well as the county authorities, have been planning sufficient industrial areas for the future, properly located so as to preserve adequate and attractive residential districts. Chicago and its environs are essentially industrial, and plenty of industrial sites must be set aside in order that the region may maintain its supremacy in this respect.

Essential in zoning is the maintenance of some areas for strictly single family use, others for apartment buildings, and still others for retail business, all being tributary to the industrial areas. A correct balance of such zones is the objective of the committee of experts which makes up the zoning de-partment of the association.

The Airways Committee is made up of practical flyers who are familiar with the needs of aviation in the region. These men have located approxi-mately 200 landing field sites in the fifteen counties. It is obvious that there will hardly be a call for that many airports in this territory for many years to come, but the sites have been "spotted" so that the best of them may be acquired at minimum expense for future development. Engineers have pre-pared detailed maps of each of these potential landing fields so as to expedite the development of private airports. Large, well-equipped airports along all

(*Loubell Studios, Photo*)

PAUL BUTLER

Mr. Butler, vice-president of the J. W. Butler Paper Company and of Butler Paper Corporations, Chicago, was born in Chicago, June 23, 1892, son of Frank O. and Fannie (Bremaker) Butler. He was in the class of 1916 at the University of Illinois. Mr. Butler is also president of the Butler Paper Company (Denver); Southwestern Paper Company (Fort Worth); Pacific Coast Paper Company (San Francisco); and Southwestern Paper Company (Houston). He is a director of the Missouri-Interstate Paper Company (Kansas City); Butler Paper Company (Detroit); Southwestern Paper Company (Dallas); Standard Paper Company (Milwaukee); Sierra Paper Company (Los Angeles); and Butler Brothers Development Company, Butler Company, and Central Waxed Paper Company, all of Chicago. He is chairman of the board of directors of McClellan Paper Company, Minneapolis.

Mr. Butler served as a lieutenant in the air service of the United States Army during the World War and as civilian aide to the Secretary of War from 1928 to 1932. He is Commander of Chicago Black Horse Troop Reserve, Headquarters Troop, 160th Cavalry. He is a member of the Art Institute of Chicago, Field Museum, Chicago Historical Society, Society of Colonial Wars, and Phi Delta Theta Fraternity. He is a director of American Sentinels and American Citizenship Foundation. His clubs are Union League, Mid-Day, Army and Navy (vice-president and acting president, 1924-1926), Racquet, Chicago Yacht, Chicago Riding, Oak Brook Polo (president, 1924-1930), York Golf (president, 1926-1932), Hinsdale (Illinois) Golf, India House (New York), Everglades (Palm Beach), and San Mateo-Burlingame Polo (California). He is an expert horseman and a well-known polo player.

In 1924 Mr. Butler married Marjorie Stresenreuter of Chicago. They have three children, Paul, Jr., Frank O. II, and Marjorie.

the airways radiating from Chicago have already been completed and private aviation clubs have been and will be established.

An interesting division of the plans for the Chicago region is that devoted to the acquisition of city and village park land and playgrounds; of township and county parks and forest preserves, and of state parks and wild life sanctuaries. Already there are more than 50,000 acres of parks, playgrounds and forest preserves under public ownership in the region. The goal for 1950 is 140,000 acres. Instead of 40,000 acres of state and county parks, there must be 65,000 acres; and to supply the needs of the community for active recreation the municipalities of the region should have 75,000 acres of parks and playgrounds, instead of the present 12,000 acres.

Two Wisconsin counties, three in Illinois and one in Indiana, have acquired their first county parks, while the State of Indiana has acquired and developed the 2,400-acre Dunes State Park.

Cook county, which leads all counties in the United States in the possession of forest preserve lands, now owns and maintains 33,000 acres of woodland, extending in a sweeping belt around the city, and visited by thousands of Chicagoans. Certain open areas are maintained as playgrounds, athletic fields, golf courses, and picnic grounds, while the reforestation of the boundaries of these open areas is going on at the rate of 400,000 trees per year.

While the population is spreading outward from Chicago into the suburban districts, the residents are profiting by the experience of those in the more congested areas, and are acquiring their recreation acreages before the cost of land becomes prohibitive. With the plans already on foot, and the even more ambitious plans for tomorrow, one would not be over-optimistic in predicting that Greater Chicago will in time be the best laid-out metropolitan area in the world.

(Hornby & Freiberg Photo)

A modern manufacturing plant in Niles Center, Illinois. Olsen and Urbain, architects.

(*Hornby & Freiberg Photo*)

A modern factory in Bellwood, Illinois. Olsen and Urbain, architects.

(*Trowbridge Photo*)

A home in River Forest, Illinois. Olsen and Urbain, architects.

CHICAGO AND ITS FAR FLUNG INTERNATIONAL TRADE

Waterway Projects Which Will Bring the Fleets of All Nations to the City's Door

FOR many years Chicago has dreamed of a waterfront lined with ships flying the flags of the great mercantile nations of the world. Nor is the day far distant when this dream shall be realized and Chicago will take her place among the nation's seaports.

Most well-informed Chicagoans are fully cognizant of the city's position as the commercial center of the United States. They need not be reminded that Chicago supplies one-eighth of the material needs of the nation; that the total retail, wholesale, and manufacturing volume of the Chicago Metropolitan District is in excess of thirteen billion dollars annually; that the total retail trade of Chicago amounts to two and one-half billion dollars a year, which in per capita volume is fifty per cent greater than the national average.

There are many, however, who do not realize the tremendous importance of foreign trade in these imposing figures. They would be incredulous if told that one Chicago firm alone exports $75,000,0000 worth of its goods in a single year; that a widely known Chicago building material house exports eighteen per cent of its output through foreign representatives permanently established in every country of recognized commercial standing.

A Chicago confectionery manufacturer imports $20,000,000 worth of raw material in a year—nuts, flavoring extracts, chocolate, and other ingredients, from many lands. The annual imports of one Chicago department store represent the purchase of $10,000,000 worth of general merchandise.

These are the leaders. Hundreds of smaller companies, many engaged exclusively in international trade, swelled the combined total of the export and import volume of foreign trade of the Chicago district to over nine hundred million dollars for the last year for which figures are available.

The introduction of steam power on the Great Lakes early brought Chicago into prominence as a port. As far back as 1860, goods were arriving from the Orient. Only a few customs officers were needed in those days, but the increasing demand for imported luxuries has made the United States Custom House a busy place. A staff of several hundred is required for the customs service today, and millions of dollars in duty are paid to the United States Treasury from the Port of Chicago.

Chicago is one of the few ports of entry in America for antique furniture. From France come the latest creations of the milliner, the coutourier, and the perfumer. Rare laces, hand-embroidered handkerchiefs, Italian damasks, kid and suede gloves, tapestries, organdie, and georgette are among the many importations from Europe. Oriental rugs from Persia, China, and other lands of the Far East, also find ready acceptance in the Chicago market.

(Moffett-Russell Photo)

CHARLES CALVIN CARNAHAN

Mr. Carnahan, lawyer, was born at Cochran's Mills, Pennsylvania, April 3, 1868, son of William H. and Maria L. (McKee) Carnahan. He attended the public schools of Armstrong County, Pennsylvania, Hillsdale College in Michigan, and the Chicago College of Law. In 1891 Mr. Carnahan came to Chicago, was admitted to the Illinois bar in 1892, and has since been engaged in general practice with the firm of Carnahan & Slusser, with offices in the Westminster Building, Chicago. Mr. Carnahan is identified with a number of corporations. He has always taken an active interest in politics. In 1900, he was Republican nominee for Congress, 5th Illinois District, and in 1930, Republican nominee for the Superior Court Bench.

Mr. Carnahan is a member of the American, Illinois State, and Chicago bar associations, and the Chicago Law Institute. He is a founder member of A Century of Progress, Chicago's (1933) World's Fair, a member of its board of trustees and chairman of its legal committee. The law firm of Carnahan & Slusser, of which Mr. Carnahan is senior partner, are general attorneys for the Fair. He is a Mason (32°), Oriental Consistory. He is a member of Phi Delta Theta Fraternity, Civil Legion (life member), Chicago Athletic Association, Union League Club, Westmoreland Country Club, and Men's Club of Wilmette (ex-president). Mr. Carnahan takes his recreation on the golf links but prefers an occasional hunting or fishing trip.

On June 15, 1894, he married Katherine A. Hawkes of Chicago, and they have one daughter, Madeleine R. (Mrs. Donald F. Simmons).

In these days of drastic economic readjustments much is being said of the extent to which international commerce has suffered. In many respects commerce has suffered, but it is refreshing to note that in spite of interna-tional tariff wars, quota systems, exchange restrictions, and other adverse influences, substantial *increases* were made in the exportation and importa-tion of many important articles of commerce during the depression-ridden years of 1931 and 1932.

While fully recognizing the gravity of the current international business recession, experienced exporters and importers of Chicago look to the future with confidence. Material readjustments are inevitable. Markets that were formerly ours will be lost. On the other hand, new and potentially great foreign fields will be opened. Competition will continue, on an ascending scale, to be intelligent and keen. But the possibilities of realizing lucrative profits will continue to exist for those companies that are alert and aggres-sive. Already are appearing unmistakable signs of a desire to cease hostilities in the trade wars that have been raging. Trade barriers will come down, and international commerce will resume its even flow.

Chicago, business heart of the greatest industrial nation in the world, and already a most important center of international trade activities, will receive a tremendous impetus upon the completion of the Lakes-to-the-Gulf Waterway.

This undertaking is expected to be consummated during 1933, thereby making available an all-water barge route from Chicago to the Gulf of Mexico. The availability of this more economical mode of transportation will prove a great boon to Chicago's foreign trade, particularly with Latin America.

(*Moffett-Russell Photo*)

JOHN ALDEN CARPENTER

Mr. Carpenter, composer and business man, was born in Park Ridge, Illinois, February 28, 1876, son of George B. and Elizabeth Curtis (Greene) Carpenter. He received his A. B. (Bachelor of Arts) degree at Harvard University in 1897 and his honorary A. M. (Master of Arts) degree in 1922. He studied music under Bernard Ziehn and Sir Edward Elgar. Mr. Carpenter entered the business of George B. Carpenter and Company, mill, railway, and vessel supplies, in 1897 and has been vice-president since 1909. Although Mr. Carpenter has spent his entire career in the business founded by his grandfather, he has, at the same time, become one of America's leading composers.

A few of his most famous compositions are, When Little Boys Sing, 1904, with Mrs. Carpenter (Rue Winterbotham); Improving Songs for Anxious Children, 1907, with wife; Sonata (for violin and piano), 1912; Gitanjali (song offerings), 1913; Adventures in a Perambulator (suite for orchestra), 1914; Concertino (for orchestra and piano), 1915; Symphony, performed first at Norfolk Festival, June, 1917; The Birthday of the Infanta, a ballet-pantomime produced by Chicago Opera Company, season of 1919-1920; Skyscrapers (ballet), produced by Metropolitan Opera Company, New York, 1926, and by State Opera, Munich, Germany, 1928; also numerous published songs. In 1932 Mr. Carpenter composed his most noteworthy work, A Song of Faith, at the invitation of the Washington Bi-Centennial Commission. He is a trustee of A Century of Progress, Chicago's (1933) World's Fair, a member of the music committee of the Chicago Exposition, and has served as director and president of the Illinois Children's Home and Aid Society. He is a member of the University, and Saddle and Cycle clubs. He was decorated by the Legion of Honor, France, in 1921.

Mr. Carpenter married Rue Winterbotham, of Chicago, November 20, 1900 (died 1931).

THE CHICAGO ZOOLOGICAL PARK AND ITS AMBITIOUS PLANS

Where the Fauna of All Lands May Be Studied in Their Natural Environment

BY EDWIN H. CLARK
Archtect, Chicago Zoological Park.

ZOOLOGICAL gardens are no longer mere show places or heterogeneous collections of animals. They are great outdoor laboratories where the student of natural history may make his observations at first hand. To the public school children, the zoo is an adjunct to the classroom, teaching invaluable lessons in geography. To the artist, it is a studio where living models are provided.

Out in the forest preserve region in Brookfield, near Riverside, within easy access of the city, the world's largest zoological gardens are assuming form. Unfortunately, the plans have been delayed somewhat by the tax muddle in Cook County, but as soon as the requisite funds are available, the building program will go forward.

BEAR DENS

The Chicago Zoological Park will have accommodations for more than 5,000 animals and birds. It will conform to the very latest style in zoos in that it will be "barless."

The specimens will be exhibited, so far as possible, in the open, and amid natural surroundings, where they can lead safe, healthful, normal lives and obey the Biblical injunction to bring forth their kind. They will be separated from the public only by moats.

Visitors to the famous Hagenbeck zoo in Hamburg have been startled on finding themselves for the first time face to face with a group of lions or tigers or a herd of rhinos. It is as if they had suddenly encountered these beasts in their native wilds. A similar experience is in store for visitors to the Chicago Zoo.

Since 1927 the work of landscaping and construction has been in progress, and is already about half completed. Exclusive of the land, which was

(Moffet-Russell Photo)

ROBERT F. CARR

Mr. Carr, president of the Dearborn Chemical Company, was born at Argenta, Illinois, November 21, 1871, son of Dr. Robert F. and Emily A. (Smick) Carr. He was educated in the public schools of Argenta, the Academy at the University of Illinois, and in 1893 he received his Bachelor of Science degree from the four-year chemical course at the University of Illinois; received honorary degree of LL.D. (Doctor of Laws) in 1929. He has been connected with the Dearborn Chemical Company since 1894, serving in the positions of secretary, vice-president, and in 1907 Mr. Carr was made president of the company. He was a director of the Standard Trust and Savings Bank from its organization in 1910 to 1924, when he resigned to become a director of the Continental and Commercial National Bank, now the Continental Illinois National Bank and Trust Company, on which board he still serves. He is also a director of Wilson & Company. He served the last six months of 1918 as Major on the General Staff, Purchase, Storage and Traffic Division, under General Goethals, engaged in the work of revising and standardizing specifications for general army commodities.

Mr. Carr was a member of the board of trustees of the University of Illinois for a term of six years beginning in 1915; president of the board in 1919 and 1920. He is the donor of a fellowship in chemistry at the University. In 1931 he was appointed a member of the Board of Education of Chicago. He has been president of the Home for Destitute Crippled Children since 1921. He is a life member of the Chicago Historical Society, the Art Institute, and the Field Museum. He is a member of Kappa Sigma Fraternity and life trustee of the Kappa Sigma Endowment Fund. He is a member of the American Chemical and other scientific societies. Mr. Carr's club affiliations are the University (president, 1924-1925), Chicago, Industrial (president, 1920-1921), Commercial, Casino, Old Elm, Shoreacres, Onwentsia, Exmoor (president, 1915, 1916), Chicago Riding (Chicago), Congressional Country (Washington), Midwick Country (Pasadena), and Vermejo (New Mexico).

Mr. Carr was married in 1906 to Louise Smiley (deceased), of Chicago. There are three children, Louise, Florence, and Robert F., Jr.

donated to the people of Chicago and Cook County by the late Mrs. Edith Rockefeller McCormick, and additional acreage acquired by the Forest Preserve District of Cook County, the Zoo will cost in the neighborhood of $4,220,000. Its operation calls for an annual budget of $300,000, and a permanent staff of more than 100 superintendents, animal keepers, vetenarians, guards, and gardeners will be required.

There will be 19 exhibition halls, 4 lions' dens, 9 elephant grottos, 9 bears' dens, and pits for the Siberian tigers, designed so that these animals may remain in the open all winter. Six buildings will house the 2,400 birds and reptiles, grouped in the following order: perching birds, running birds, tropical aquatic birds, upland birds (pheasants and quail), cranes and peacocks, parrots and macaws. There will be four flight cages for condors, eagles, and falcons. The islands of the lagoon will be populated by water fowl of all kinds, including rose-hued flamingoes from the Mississippi bayous and the Nile. Over to the west end of the gardens the visitor will find an 80-acre forest sanctuary for native birds. There will be five antelope paddocks, huge outdoor tanks for seals and sea lions, and enclosures for tortoises and alligators. Artificial crags for the mountain goats will be built up to a height of 150 feet.

The lion house, 256 feet in length, is a palace of steel, marble, and tile, and contains fifteen cages all of which lead by underground passages to outdoor dens. The house for small mammals is gaily decorated in Pompeian reds and yellows, and is equipped with a ventilating plant which can furnish a complete change of air every eight minutes. Among other important buildings are the $300,000 primate house for monkeys, and the pachyderm house for elephants, tapirs, rhinos, and hippos, on which $500,-000 has been spent. The architectural scheme follows the Italian farm style.

The buildings, numbering about sixty in all, together with the open-air enclosures, are arranged on either side of two main passageways or malls, one beginning at a rise at the east end of the park, where the refectory will stand, and extending 2,000 feet to the west, where it is terminated by the sea mammal plaza which overlooks an eleven-acre lake. The other runs from the main entrance in 34th street to the 31st street entrance, intersecting the first mall at a distance of 800 feet from the east boundary. Both avenues are flanked with Norway maple. An almost incredible amount of work has been done in landscaping, the laying out of esplanades, the creation of artificial lakes and lagoons, and the planting of thousands of trees and shrubs.

The bears, lions, tigers and other large cats, the wolves, hyenas, pachyderms, buffalo, zebras, antelope, deer, elk and hoofed animals in general, as well as the monkeys, will be exhibited in the open against scenic backgrounds typical of their native haunts. The Zoo will have its own abattoir, kitchens, and hospital.

Especially interesting to the student of zoology will be the collection of invertebrates, housed in a building of its own. Here will be seen colonies

(*Moffett-Russell Photo*)

DONALD M. CARTER

Mr. Carter, American patent lawyer, was born September 12, 1868, at Collinsville, Illinois, the son of Henry T. and Marium (Smith) Carter. The branch of the family of which he is a member was established in America by John Carter, an Englishman, who settled in Virginia in 1649. Graduating from the local high school, Mr. Carter attended Iowa State College, receiving his degree, Bachelor of Mechanical and Electrical Engineering, in 1891. Instead of entering the engineering profession, however, he went west, and remained there long enough to realize his youthful ambition of becoming a cowboy.

In 1893 he came to Chicago and while working in the law office of Francis W. Parker attended the night classes of the Chicago College of Law, taking a post-graduate course at Lake Forest University, which conferred upon him three years later the degree of LL.D. (Doctor of Laws). Specializing in patent law, he became junior partner of the firm of Parker and Carter, of which firm he is now senior partner. Among the more important suits in which he figured was that against the City of Chicago for infringement on patents for bascule bridges involving the Michigan avenue and other spans. Another was against the Chicago Tribune and the Westinghouse Electric and Manufacturing Company for alleged patent infringements on devices for feeding paper to presses. Both suits, which were won by Mr. Carter, attracted wide-spread attention.

In addition to his law practice Mr. Carter has many other interests. With President William Rainey Harper of the University of Chicago, Shailer Mathews, and Francis W. Parker, he established the publication The World of Today. As one of the early members of the Rotary Club, he is credited with the introduction of the service idea of that organization. He is especially interested in the study of government, philosophy, and history. He has also spent much time in boys and citizenship work. Mr. Carter is a member of the Chicago Patent Law Association (president 1929-1930), the Chicago Bar Association, the Union League, South Shore Country, and City clubs.

of bees and ants, clouds of moths and butterflies, and such other specimens as spiders, molluscs, sea anemonies, octopi, and crabs.

Negotiations have been under way for some time with animal dealers for supplies of mammals, reptiles, birds, and amphibians, to be forwarded as soon as the Zoo is ready to receive them. As for rare animals, it is expected that there will be at least one specimen each of the mountain gorilla, the okapi, Grant's eland, and that anomaly of nature, the duck-billed platibus of Australia.

In order that a visit to the Zoo may be more than an outing, but have educational value as well, lectures on natural history, recorded on phonograph discs, will be broadcast at frequent intervals in the main exhibition halls by means of amplifiers. For Edward Bean, superintendent of the Zoo, believes that such an institution can be made an important part of the public school system of the city and county.

"We can show the marvels and the beauties and the goodness and the badness of the animal kingdom in a supremely vivid way," he says. "People love action in a zoo, and they will get plenty of action here. But in this Zoo we intend to go deeper than that. We propose to give a vast survey of the wonders of creation from the bridge-building ant to the chimpanzee, the most intelligent of all animals below man. And if the visitor doesn't go away from here in a more reverent mood than when he came, it will be because he hasn't the intelligence of a chimpanzee."

The entire enterprise is in the hands of the Chicago Zoological Society, of which John T. McCutcheon, famous cartoonist and big game hunter, is president.

A. J. CERMAK

Mr. Cermak, one of our first citizens and World's Fair Mayor of Chicago, son of Anton and Catherine (Frank) Cermak, was born in a two-room cottage in a mining village about fifty miles from Prague, Bohemia, on May 9, 1873. Now he rules the political destinies of the second largest city in the United States. When Mr. Cermak was elected mayor of Chicago on April 7, 1931, every newspaper in the entire world announced the fact; the first time anyone from the Middle West received so great an honor.

He was one year old when he passed the Statue of Liberty and was brought to Chicago. After a brief stay at Canal and 15th streets, the family went to the mining country at Braidwood, Illinois, where they established a permanent home. His first job, at the age of eleven, paid him $2.00 a week; later he worked in the mines at Braidwood as a mule driver and earned $1.10 a day. At the age of sixteen, he arrived in Chicago and became a brakeman on the Elgin, Joliet and Eastern Railroad; then became a tow boy for the street car company, and every day rode an old white horse down Blue Island avenue. He attended business college at night and later studied law. When he was nineteen, he started in the teaming business with one team; in time this grew to forty. One of the first contracts he obtained in this business he still holds, that of hauling waste wood from the International Harvester Company. Although his brother carries on this business for him, the contract is still in his name.

In 1908 he organized the real estate firm of Cermak and Serhant, in which he is a partner; is a director of the Lawndale National Bank; president of the Lawndale Building and Loan Association since 1907; director of the 26th Street Business Men's Association; and was a member of the 43d, 44th, 45th, and 46th General Assemblies of Illinois. He served as a member of the City Council of Chicago, 1909 to 1912 and 1919 to 1922; chief bailiff of the Municipal Court, 1913-1918; and was president of the Cook County Board from 1922 until April, 1931, when he resigned to become Mayor of Chicago. He is chairman of the Cook County Democratic Central Committee, member of the nominating committee of same, national committeeman from Illinois, and president of the Bohemian Charitable Association. His clubs are Medinah Athletic Club, Steuben Club, Lake Shore Athletic, and Midwest Athletic. He is an ardent sportsman, so the time he has for recreation he spends with his family and friends at his home on Channel Lake.

Mr. Cermak married Mary Horejs (deceased), of Chicago, December 15, 1894, and he is the father of three daughters, Lillian (Mrs. Richey V. Graham), Ella (wife of Frank J. Jirka, M. D.), and Helen (Mrs. Floyd M. Kenlay).

CHICAGO'S LIBRARIES AND THEIR VAST RESOURCES

Storehouses of Knowledge Made Available to All

BY CARL B. RODEN
Librarian, Chicago Public Library

PRESERVED as a memorial collection in the Chicago Public Library, and kept carefully under lock and key, is a little group of books, which alone out of the Library's 1,733,000 volumes is not available to the general reader.

The collection includes such treasures as Sir Theodore Martin's Life of the Prince Consort, with the royal autograph of Queen Victoria on the flyleaf; Lord Macaulay's complete works autographed by Sir Charles and Lady Trevelyan, the latter the sister of the great essayist and historian; the works of Thomas Hughes, John Bright, Richard Monckton Milnes, and John Ruskin.

These books are all that remain of the 8,000 volumes presented to Chicago as the nucleus of a free public library by Great Britain's leading authors, publishing houses, and universities shortly after the great fire of 1871 as an expression of sympathy from the British people.

At the time of the fire, the Chicago Library Association, an outgrowth of the Young Men's Association, had on its shelves in the old Metropolitan Block at Randolph and La Salle streets, a collection of 30,000 books. These, together with the libraries of the Chicago Historical Society and the Chicago Academy of Sciences, were destroyed by the flames. John Robson, an Englishman, who had been in charge of the Association's library, returned to England authorized by Mayor Joseph Medill to make an appeal for books to replace those that had been lost. He interested in his quest Thomas Hughes, author of Tom Brown's School Days, and within a few months the British gifts began arriving in Chicago.

Among those who responded to the appeal were Queen Victoria, the Duke of Argyle, the British Museum, the Universities of Oxford and Cambridge, Thomas Carlyle, Gladstone, Herbert Spencer, Alfred Tennyson, Lord Churchill, Lord Macaulay, John Ruskin, Disraeli, Robert Browning, the Rossettis, Charles Kingsley, Darwin, Huxley, John Stuart Mill, Jean Ingelow, Mrs. Oliphant, Walter Besant, Lewis Carroll, James Bryce, and Francis Turner Palgrave. Supplementing the British gifts were 1,200 volumes of German literature assembled and presented to the Library by Chicagoans of Teutonic birth.

Such was the foundation—by no means modest in those days—of the Public Library's now immense collection. And from an institution housed in an abandoned water tank, the Library has grown until even the impressive building on Michigan avenue—opened in 1897 and designed to serve a population of 3,000,000—is no longer adequate. The Chicago Public

(*Shigeta-Wright Photo*)

Diana Court, the extraordinary atrium of the Michigan Square building. The beautiful statue of Diana by Carl Milles, the celebrated Swedish sculptor, glows in a resplendent setting of modern architecture. Holabird & Root, architects.

Library system today includes 44 branch libraries, 13 sub-branches, and branches in 400 public and private schools.

This far-flung system, however, by no means compasses Chicago's library resources. The Newberry Library and the John Crerar Library are institutions in themselves. Mention is made elsewhere in this book of the specialized collections of the Art Institute, the Chicago Historical Society, the Chicago Academy of Sciences, the Adler Planetarium, Field Museum, the Shedd Aquarium, and the various universities and colleges.

Information on almost everything under the sun is at one's fingertips, or the fingertips of a trained reference room attendant, in Chicago's great storehouses of knowledge. As an example of the resources of the city's libraries, there is the gas appliance salesman, who, after selling a gas range to an Italian opera singer for use in the latter's villa at Nalim, Italy, turned to the reference books in his company's own library to find out what kind of gas was supplied in that particular little town, so that he could adjust the valves of the range accordingly.

(*Chicago Architectural Photographing Company*)
Chicago Public Library, located from Randolph street to Washington street at Michigan avenue

Chicago's libraries are more than repositories of books. They are laboratories for research work of every kind. They are public school and university extensions. The Chicago Public Library lends approximately 16,000,000 books a year to 700,000 readers. More than 300,000 readers make use of its reference room annually. The Library circulates thousands of lantern slides and hundreds of books for the blind. Its work with children has come to be of great importance. Classes for instruction in the use of a library are conducted in thirty branches. Organized reading clubs have been

French
Books

American
Books

AMERICAN
LIBRARY

UNIVERSITY of
STRASBOURG
F R A N C E

VESTA M. WESTOVER CHANNON

Mrs. Channon founded the French Library of the Alliance Francaise of Chicago, in 1903, and for years was chairman of the committee. The collection then included nine thousand volumes of classical and modern French literature. She also founded the American Library, in honor of Pasteur, at the University of Strasbourg, France, in 1923, and is president of the executive board. This collection is housed in three sections (literary and historical, general, and medical) at the University.

Mrs. Channon was born at Oconomowoc, Wisconsin, and as a child was brought to Chicago by her parents, George Frederic (lawyer) and Elizabeth Q. (Miller, of New York) Westover. She graduated from high school and Grant Collegiate Seminary of Chicago. She married Harry Channon of Chicago in London, England; and has one son, Henry III, a writer, who was born 1897, in Chicago, and served in the American Red Cross with the American Expeditionary Forces during 1917 and 1918 (second lieutenant, 1918). Mrs. Channon divorced her husband in 1932. During the World War she was a member of the Allied Relief Committee of the Council of National Defense, and attended the convention of Allied Women on War Work in Paris in 1918. She is a life-member of the New Orient Society of America and is interested in Egypt; she was a guest at Tanis, 1930, for the French excavations.

She is a Daughter of the American Revolution (director of the Chicago chapter, 1924-1925), and a member of the Colonial Daughters of the XVII Century (New York) and the American Society of the French Legion of Honor. She is a member of the Neighborhood Church of Pasadena, California. She was decorated as Chevalier de la Légion d'Honneur, and Officier de l'Instruction Publique, France. Her clubs are Woman's Athletic, Woman's, College, Arts, et cetera (Chicago), Women's Athletic Club (Los Angeles), and American Women's (London, Paris).

established. Story hours, attracting the interest of many child welfare leaders, are conducted in all but four of the branches, in twelve city parks, and
in the Marks Nathan Orphan Home, the Jahn School for Crippled Children,
and the Children's Memorial Hospital. Thousands of questions asked by
children or by more mature students in connection with their school or
university work are answered by the reference room attendants, who are
supposed to be human encyclopedias. Those who find it inconvenient to go
to the library can find out what they want to know by telephone. Many
inquiries are answered by mail.

It is significant to reflect that Chicago's first attempts to establish a public
library date back to 1834, when the city had a population of only 3,500. A
group known as the Chicago Lyceum was formed, and a collection of 300
books was assembled. Out of this, in 1841, grew the Young Men's Association, whose object it was "to establish and maintain a reading room, to pro-
cure literary and scientific lecturers, and to promote the intellectual improvement of the members." Walter Loomis Newberry, founder of the magnificent library which bears his name, was the Association's first president. Its
first library and reading room occupied the second floor of John Johnson's
Building—over the barber shop. Better quarters were found later in the
Saloon Building, and finally in the Metropolitan Block. Appearing on its
lecture programs were such celebrities as Emerson, Holmes, Lowell, Sumner,
Beecher, and Rufus Choate. A lecture in 1861 on Slavery, by Wendel Phillips, almost caused a riot. The Chicago fire put an end to the Association's
activities, but not to its influence. In January, 1872, a public meeting was
called at Plymouth Church to consider the establishment of a free library.
Among the sponsors of the movement were Marshall Field, Levi Z. Leiter,
N. K. Fairbank, and Cyrus H. McCormick. Mayor Medill called the meeting to order, and Thomas Hoyne was made chairman. Legislation was
passed a few months later providing for a library tax, and Hoyne was elected
first president of the Library Board.

Curious indeed was the Library's first home—the water tank in the rear
of the old Rookery at La Salle and Adams streets. The tank was fitted up
with shelves, and the gift books from London were installed. The Library
was dedicated on New Year's Day, 1873, President Hoyne and Mayor
Medill being the principal speakers. The audience was made up of the city's
social and political leaders.

William Frederick Poole, compiler of the famous Poole's Index, who
had been librarian of the Boston Atheneum and more recently of the Cincinnati Public Library, was Chicago's first Public Librarian. The first
book—Tom Brown's School Days—was issued to Mr. Hoyne. An early
purchase of the Library Board, and one that went far toward filling the
empty spaces on the shelves, was the Tauchnitz edition of British and
foreign authors in 785 volumes. Mr. Poole, during his fourteen years as
librarian, built up a library whose resources and completeness were equalled
by few similar institutions in America.

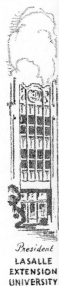

President
LASALLE
EXTENSION
UNIVERSITY

BUILDING
OPPORTUNITY
THROUGH
ADULT
BUSINESS
TRAINING

(Continental Photo)

JESSE GRANT CHAPLINE

Mr. Chapline, president and founder of La Salle Extension University, was born in Waverly, Missouri, January 13, 1870, son of William Purnell and Sallie Ann Chapline. He was educated in the public schools and at St. Louis College, St. Louis, Missouri. He was manager of John Wanamaker Century Club, Philadelphia; was vice-president of Making of America Company, publishers; and was president of the Associated Publishing Company, Chicago. Mr. Chapline has been a pioneer in adult business training. He founded La Salle Extension University in 1908—when there were few books on commercial subjects and practically no training courses on business. He evolved and perfected the idea of making available to business men, through home study courses, the best experiences of commerce and industry, and enlisted the aid of outstanding business leaders in building such experience-training. He was also instrumental in developing the modern problem method—the most effective means of business training known to educational science. Under his leadership, La Salle has grown until it has resources of $7,000,000, a total staff of 1,100, and an enrollment of over 800,000 adults in sixty-five different countries.

Mr. Chapline is president of Marye Safety Nut Corporation; director, Commercial Research Corporation; vice-president, National Home Study Council; and member, Associated Advertising Clubs, Association of National Advertisers, International Chamber of Commerce, Art Institute of Chicago, et cetera. He is a member of the South Shore Country (member, board of governors), Union League, Press, Lake Shore Athletic, and Midlothian Country clubs.

On May 12, 1909, he married Anne J. Johnson, of Chicago. He has two daughters, Marjorie Anne and Dorothy Jane.

The $2,000,000 Public Library Building, occupying what was once known as Dearborn Park, was, at the time of its dedication, the most impressive public edifice in Chicago, and is still an ornament to the city. The story of the succeeding years has been one of constant growth and increasing service.

Today the Public Library shares with two mighty compeers the domain of service to the people of Chicago, which for the first two decades of its life it occupied alone. In many departments its collections maintain an almost unchallenged supremacy. But the coming of the Newberry Library and, a few years later, of the John Crerar Library, presented opportunities for special developments, which were recognized at the beginning and have been realized with wisdom and skill. Thus Chicago has been provided with a group of institutions of research, each the complement of the others, that together are scarcely surpassed for literary wealth and completeness in America.

Walter Loomis Newberry, it will be remembered, was one of the group of ambitious young men active in the library movement of the early '40's. Remembering in the days of his prosperity the ideals of his youth, he made ample testamentary provision for the foundation and maintenance of a great free library on the North Side. His death occurred at sea in 1868, but it was not until nearly twenty years later that his trustees were enabled to proceed with the execution of his will. Their first act was to call to their aid the able librarian, Mr. Poole, under whom the Public Library had grown so rapidly.

John Crerar, merchant and capitalist, died in 1889, and in his will directed that a major part of his estate be set aside for the establishment of another free library.

The amount realized from the Newberry estate was in excess of $2,600,000, and from the Crerar estate, $2,500,000, both of which funds have been materially increased through careful administration. The trustees of these two foundations agreed after many conferences on a division of the field of service, a unique arrangement which has resulted in the symmetrical upbuilding of two great reference libraries, whose commanding position in their respective provinces is acknowledged throughout the world of letters.

The trustees of the John Crerar Library selected as its special field the natural, physical, and social sciences and their applications, while the Newberry Library, on the other hand, resolved to lay special emphasis on literature, history, philosophy, and the fine arts. The latter institution has not, however, lost sight of the duty imposed by the will of its founder of providing a general reference collection for the studious reader. Furthermore, it has built up a museum filled with priceless rarities in manuscripts and early printed books. Its collections of Americana, church history, and genealogy are outstanding.

GEORGE A. CHRITTON

Mr. Chritton, member of the law firm of Dyrenforth, Lee, Chritton and Wiles, was born in Fountain County, Indiana, June 4, 1870, the son of John W. and Sarah Ann (Brown) Chritton. He attended the district schools of Fountain County, Indiana, and Sedgwick County, Kansas; Wichita (Kansas) Business College; and the State Normal School at Emporia, Kansas. He received his LL. B. (Bachelor of Laws) degree from Kent College of Law, Chicago, (now Chicago-Kent College of Law) in 1896. He took a post-graduate course at Chicago College of Law (Lake Forest University) in 1897. He was in the law department of the Metropolitan Elevated Railroad Company from 1894 to 1904, and since 1905 has been a member of the law firm of Dyrenforth, Lee, Chritton and Wiles, special-izing in patent, trade-mark, copyright, corporation, real estate, and commercial law. He is a member of the faculty of John Marshall Law School and secretary of the Fair-Chritton Lumber Company, Chritton, Mississippi.

Mr. Chritton is a member of the American Bar Association, Illinois State Bar Asso-ciation (board of governors), Chicago Bar Association (chairman of the legal education committee for several years), Chicago Patent Law Association (president 1930), and Chicago Law Institute. He was president of the Oak Park School Board from 1910 to 1918 and was president of the Chicago Baptist Social Union. He is president of Chicago Foundlings Home and the Baptist Old People's Home; vice-president, Chicago Baptist Executive Council. His clubs are Union League, Oak Park, Oak Park Country, and River Forest Country (president 1927-1929). His recreations are motoring, golf, and book collecting.

He married Laura Fair, of Chicago, February 24, 1897. Their children are Ernest Fairfax and George Alvah, Jr.

CHICAGO'S MARINE WONDER HOUSE
THE JOHN G. SHEDD AQUARIUM

Where Fishes of All Sizes, Shapes, and Hues Delight the Visitor

CHICAGO, in addition to such show places as the Field Museum, the Rosenwald Industrial Museum, the Adler Planetarium, and the Art Institute, has two public aquariums, one at Lincoln Park, the other set amid ideal surroundings on a point of land jutting out into Lake Michigan at the east end of the Roosevelt road extension.

The latter, the John G. Shedd aquarium, is the largest and most completely equipped institution of its kind in the world, and one of the very few in America. New York, Boston, Philadelphia, San Francisco, and Detroit have aquariums, but nothing to compare with Chicago's magnificent marble home for fish.

JOHN G. SHEDD AQUARIUM   Graham, Anderson, Probst & White, architects.

The aquarium was presented to the city by the late John G. Shedd, president of Marshall Field & Company for many years, who gave $3,000,000 with which to build, stock, and maintain this wonder house.

It is controlled by the Shedd Aquarium Society, whose trustees are prominent business men, and whose president is Melvin A. Traylor, head of the First National Bank of Chicago. The upkeep is provided for by a small tax levied by the South Park Board. The director, Walter H. Chute, was formerly in charge of the Boston aquarium.

In deciding to present such an institution to Chicago, Mr. Shedd was undoubtedly motivated by the knowledge that the Government fisheries exhibits at the World's Fair of 1893 and at the St. Louis, Buffalo, and Omaha expositions, attracted more visitors than any other exhibit, and that one aquarium held, so far as known, the worlds record attendance, having at the time an average daily attendance of 5,000 over a period of twelve years.

(Bloom Photo)

WALTER H. CHUTE

Mr. Chute, director of the John G. Shedd Aquarium, was born April 12, 1891, in Boston, Massachusetts, and was educated in the Boston high schools. He first became interested in fish while convalescing from a serious illness. He found an old fish bowl in a closet of his home, and from this beginning his interest grew until he had a whole room devoted to small aquariums.

Mr. Chute was one of the organizers of the Boston Aquarium Society in 1916, and was secretary of that organization from that time until he left Boston, in 1925. He was director of the Boston Aquarium when he left to become associate director, and later director, of the Shedd Aquarium. Mr. Chute is directly responsible for many of the unique and splendid innovations incorporated in the Shedd Aquarium. In company with a representative of the architects, he visited all the aquariums in the world, in order to take advantage of the lessons learned and the experience gained by them. He worked constantly with the architects during the planning and construction, and the building is not only different from any other aquarium, but new and revolutionary methods are being devised and practiced at this institution.

On April 6, 1913, Mr. Chute married Rosetta Murphy in Boston, Massachusetts.

This record was broken as soon as the Shedd aquarium opened. By the end of October, 1931, its attendance had reached a total of 6,223,323, representing a daily average of 12,300 visitors over the entire seventeen months it had been open to the public. Of this total attendance, 5,985,188 were admitted free, while 248,135 paid the nominal admission fee charged on "pay days."

Thus it would seem that most people are at heart followers of Isaac Walton, while to others, the study and observation of the finny tribes holds a certain fascination and adventure.

Many new ideas were incorporated in the construction and equipment of the building. The exterior is of Georgia marble, in the Grecian Ionic style of architecture, and it is octagonal in shape. It consists of a main floor, a basement, a basement-mezzanine and a central tower which rises to a height of 100 feet. Only the ground floor is open to the public, however, the exhibits being so arranged that they all may be seen without climbing any stairs or retracing steps.

The aquarium proper is 300 feet in diameter, covering 74,614 square feet on the main floor, exclusive of the terrace, which is 30 feet in width. A spacious marble foyer hall opens into an octagonal rotunda, in the center of which is a 40 foot pool, arranged as a semi-tropical swamp. A beautiful piece of rockwork in the center is covered with a profusion of plants, where snakes, frogs and turtles make their home.

Radiating from the rotunda are six main exhibition halls, each 30 feet wide and 90 feet long. The interior and exterior decorations, from the great bronze doors at the front entrance to the tiles that garnish the wainscoting, take their artistic motif from forms of aquatic life in endless variety, such as fish, turtles, lobsters and reptiles. There is a wealth of interesting aquatic and nautical detail in the specially designed appointments, both decorative and utilitarian. An example is the beautiful grill work around the entrance, which is a lacy formation involving sea horses, snails, lobsters, starfish, sea-anemome, turtles, coral, shells of many kinds, rope with weights, and repetitions of Neptune's trident.

There are specially designed rooms for many purposes. There is a lecture hall with fire-proof projection room, photographer's dark-room and laboratory, hatchery, hospital, feed rooms, refrigerating rooms, work shops, and many laboratories for various purposes. On one side of the foyer hall are the executive offices and lecture hall and on the other side is a "balanced" aquarium room.

Of special interest is this "balanced" aquarium room. It is decorated in colorful Japanese style to represent an open air courtyard, lighted by eight large lanterns, each on a bamboo post. It is octagonal in shape with a central kiosk in which fancy goldfish are exhibited. An innovation in this room is the use of the new "violet ray" glass in all the skylights to insure a proper growth of marine plant and animal life, and a more faithful rendition of color. The fancy goldfish exhibited here are fine specimens, many of them prize winners costing as much as $75 apiece. The main wall of the room contains 65 smaller aquariums, planted with aquatic plant life, and in which tiny tropical fishes flash like jewels.

Octagonal hall with forty-foot semi-tropical pool, where snakes, frogs, and turtles make their home.

Portion of "balanced" aquarium room, where goldfish and tiny tropical fishes are exhibited.

Some of these fish are very tiny, measuring not more than one-half inch when completely grown. Many of them are beautifully colored, with an irridescent sheen of silver or gold, or combinations of brilliant blues, flashing reds and splendid yellows that defy description. Here may be seen the re-nowned "walking fish" of Africa, which is known in its native habitat to walk over dry land, and on occasion even to climb trees. Also from Africa is the electric catfish, capable of giving an electric shock. There is a queer armored catfish, from South America. Another odd specimen is the hatchet fish, so called because of its extremely deep thin body which resembles the head of a hatchet.

For the larger fishes exhibited in the six main galleries there are 132 permanent exhibition tanks, 95 reserve tanks and a number of portable tanks, varying in capacity from 375 gallons to 13,500 gallons. The total capacity of all the permanent tanks in the building is about 500,000 gallons. Water is supplied from four reservoirs in the basement, the total capacity of which is 2,000,000 gallons, half of which is fresh water drawn directly from Lake Michigan. The other half is salt water, which was brought 1,600 miles from the ocean at Key West, Florida, in 160 tank car-loads. The salt water probably will last for twenty years.

The water is moved through five entirely distinct and separate systems of antimonial lead piping, which material has been found to best resist the in-roads of salt water. These systems circulate heated and refrigerated salt water, and heated, natural and refrigerated fresh water. Thus the water for northern fishes is refrigerated while specimens from the tropics live in water heated by coils to the temperature to which they are accustomed.

The aquarium exhibits not only the common fishes of American fresh and salt waters, but also many rare and unusual varieties from different parts of the world. There are now in the building over 8,000 fishes, representing

345 species. Fish range in size from one-half inch in length to 585 pounds in weight.

In order to make possible this extensive collection, the aquarium owns and operates a special Pullman railroad car, the Nautilus, which is, in effect, a traveling aquarium. It is equipped with tanks and receptacles for the living fishes, and complete handling apparatus to accommodate all sizes. This car makes it possible to transport at the same time all of the five classes of fish; the cold salt water, warm salt water, natural, cold and warm fresh water fishes.

Interesting fresh water exhibits include the electric eels from South America, the large ugly salamanders from Japan, and the 585 pound sea-cow, or manatee, from Florida. Salt water fishes from Florida include the spade fishes, striped like convicts' suits, squirrel fishes as delicately pink as cameos, with very large brown eyes and spines as sharp as needles. There are the sand-colored sawfish, with his dangerous double-edged toothed saw that he carries before him; the large sharks, which an attendant has tamed so that they will eat out of his hand, and some baby dog sharks, born in the Aquarium June 8, 1930. The blue angel-fish is one of the most beautiful specimens in the Aquarium, and one of the most difficult to acquire and transport to the aquarium alive.

Crabs are present in several different varieties. There is the stone and the hermit, the green and the blue crab. The beautifully colored and patterned queen triggerfish, a fantasy in blue and gold from the tropical coral reefs, gets its name from the trigger-like arrangement of the spines in the dorsal fin. And, of course, there is that very interesting little fish, the sea horse, the only fish that has movable vertebrae so that he can bend his head and tail. It reminds one very much of the chess figure called Knight.

Space does not allow mention of the many other interesting fishes to be found in this beautiful aquarium, where there is presented to the public the opportunity of viewing and studying the most comprehensive collection of live aquatic animals ever exhibited.

The Shedd Aquarium is open every day from 10:00 to 5:00. Admission is 25c to adults except on Thursdays, Saturdays and Sundays. Children are admitted free at all times.

(Underwood and Underwood Photo, New York)

PHILIP R. CLARKE

Mr. Clarke, president of the City National Bank and Trust Company, was born in Hinsdale, June 10, 1889, the son of Robert W. and Mary Evelyn (Foster) Clarke. He graduated from the Hinsdale High School in 1906 and attended Beloit College (1906-1907). He began his business career with Farson, Son Co., bankers. In 1912, at the age of twenty-two, he organized his own investment firm, Clarke and Company, which he headed until 1919, when he became president of the Federal Securities Corporation. During the years that followed he was a director of many investment and public utilities corporations, and in 1930 was elected president of the Central Trust Company, later the Central Republic Bank and Trust Company. His success in directing the Liberty Loan campaign led to his selection in 1930 by Governor Emmerson as leader of a civic move-ment to raise $5,000,000 for unemployment relief, and the even more impressive sum of $74,000,000 to keep the City Government in operation.

Mr. Clarke has many interests in addition to banking. He is an enthusiastic deep-sea fisherman, speed boat pilot and yachtsman. His avocations include tennis, golf, baseball, amateur dramatics, and bridge. He has served as president of the Hinsdale Board of Education. He is a member of the Union League, Attic, Chicago, Industrial, Commercial, Chicago Golf, Hinsdale, and Spring Lake Country clubs; the Old Elm Golf Club; and a member of the Recess Club of New York.

He was married September 17, 1910, to Louise Hildebrand. There are three children, Philip Ream, Norman Foster, and David Griffing.

THE WEST PARKS AS A SOCIALIZING INFLUENCE
What Their Organized Programs of Sports, Work, and Play Mean to Their Respective Neighborhoods

C HICAGO's West Park System is made up of four large and fifteen small parks and 42 miles of boulevards. The large parks, Humboldt, Douglas, Garfield, and Columbus, have a combined area of more than 700 acres and the remaining 100 acres of the System are distributed among the smaller recreation centers, most of which are located in the city's most congested districts.

The socializing influence of these fifteen small parks is hard to estimate, but it is not so intangible as it might appear. With the opening of each one of them, juvenile delinquency in the immediate neighborhood has fallen off fifty per cent.

These playgrounds, or social centers, with their gardens, outdoor and indoor gymnasiums, branch libraries, and well equipped field houses, are a part of Chicago's melting pot.

Their programs of organized sports, work, and play are participated in by young people of more than thirty nationalities—Chinese, Assyrians, Greeks, Italians, Mexicans, Poles, Bohemians are just a few—and while preserving the best of Old-World institutions, are blending them with those of the New World. Out of this medley of all nations is issuing a new race, strong, vigorous, and clean-cut, a race of young Americans.

During the course of a year more than 11,000,000 people visit the West Parks, and this number does not include the millions of casual visitors. The swimming pools of the small parks have been enjoyed by as many as 45,000 boys and girls in a single day. The showers of Eckhart Park in the heart of the Polish district are used by 130,000 people a year. On the 152 tennis courts of the West Parks a quarter of a million players annually seek exercise. The golf courses are used by 174,000 people in a single season. Organized ball games in the parks draw from 20,000 to 25,000 actual players every year. Some 30,000 boys and girls are registered in the various athletic organizations. There are annually 642,000 visitors to the Garfield Park conservatory. Attendance at the fifteen small parks runs up to 1,000,000 a year.

It has been said that the West Parks offer everything from a free bath to free education in botany, music, and handicraft. Among their many activities are dramatics, dancing, and model yacht and airplane designing. Marble tournaments, kite-flying tournaments, harmonica-playing tournaments, and model yacht races are all included in the program. Ideals of good sportsmanship have replaced rowdyism.

Thus it is that the small parks have leavened entire neighborhoods and have wielded an incalculable social influence in their respective communities. Not the least of their social service is the circulation by the branch libraries of thousands of books to young and adult readers alike.

WILLIAM E. CLOW

Mr. Clow, president, James B. Clow & Sons, manufacturers of cast-iron pipe, plumbing goods, steam, water, and gas specialties, gas steam radiators, and fabricated marble, was born in Industry, Pennsylvania, September 23, 1860, son of James B. and Matilda (Ross) Clow. He was educated in the public schools of Pittsburgh, Pennsylvania, and began his business career with his father in Pittsburgh in 1876. In 1878 he started in business in Chicago forming a partnership with his father under the name of James B. Clow & Son. On October 23, 1894, the firm was incorporated as James B. Clow & Sons, and he became vice-president. After his father's death in 1907, he was made president. This company is the second largest manufacturer of cast-iron pipe in the United States and has general offices, a factory, and warehouses in Chicago, foundries in Birmingham, Alabama, and Newcomerstown and Coshocton, Ohio, as well as warehouses and branch offices in principal cities.

Mr. Clow is a member of Chicago, Union League, Commercial, Shoreacres, Saddle and Cycle, and Onwentsia clubs. His recreations are hunting, fishing, and golf.

He married Margaret A. Sarver, in Pittsburgh, June 1, 1882. Their children are, William E., Jr., Kent S., and Martha M. (Mrs. Donald B. Douglas).

(*Chicago Architectural Photographing Company*)
Administration Building, Garfield Park.

Eckhart Park, opened in 1908, was Chicago's first public playground. The second was Stanton Park, which replaced an entire block of dilapidated shacks and tenements in the Ghetto, establishing a social center in one of the most densely populated districts of the city.

While the small parks specialize in social service, the four large parks specialize in beauty. Their charming landscaped and waterscaped vistas have had a decided influence on many of the industrial houses in the neighborhood, which have improved their grounds with trees and shrubbery, fountains and lawns. Columbus Park, the newest of the chain, was originally woodland, and many of the patriarchal trees have been preserved. There are said to be more than 100 varieties of trees in the West Parks, the American elm predominating. Their sixty-seven acres of lagoons are used for boating in the Summer and for skating in the Winter. They are stocked with sunfish, bass, pickerel, and trout, and fishing is permitted during a limited season in the Fall.

The Garfield Park conservatory, the largest public-owned conservatory in the United States, houses a collection of exotic plants which includes 3,500 species and varieties, and is valued at $1,250,000. There is also an orchid collection of 432 varieties, valued at $50,000. The conservatory, however, is more than a show house. It is an educational institution, offering an organized course of lectures in horticulture and botany. The rose and peony gardens of Humboldt Park are famous for their beauty.

In addition to such sports as baseball, golf, and tennis, some of the West Parks have installed bowling greens. The West Side Bowling Green Association, with headquarters at Columbus Park, is one of the several clubs in the city devoted to the encouragement of this old English game.

Nobel Prize Winner in PHYSICS

(Moffett-Russell Photo)

ARTHUR HOLLY COMPTON

Dr. Compton, holder of the Charles H. Swift Distinguished Service Professorship of Physics at the University of Chicago, was born in Wooster, Ohio, September 10, 1892, son of Elias and Otelia Catherine (Augspurger) Compton. He received his B. S. (Bachelor of Science) degree from the College of Wooster, in 1913; his M. A. (Master of Arts) from Princeton, in 1914; and his Ph. D. (Doctor of Philosophy), in 1916. He studied at Cambridge University, England, during 1919-1920. The honorary degree of Sc. D. (Doctor of Science) has been conferred on him by the College of Wooster, 1927, Ohio State University, 1929, and Yale, 1929; that of LL. D. (Doctor of Laws) was conferred on him by Washington University, in 1928, and University of California, 1930.

He was a Porter-Ogden Jacobus fellow at Princeton University, 1915-1916; an instructor in physics at the University of Minnesota, 1916-1917; research physicist with Westinghouse Lamp Company, East Pittsburgh, Pennsylvania, 1917-1919; national research fellow in physics, Cavendish Laboratory, Cambridge University, 1919-1920; professor of physics and head of department at Washington University, 1920-1923; professor of physics at the University of Chicago, since 1923; John Simon Guggenheim fellow, 1926-1927; special lecturer at Punjab University, Lahore, India, 1926-1927. During the war he served as a civilian associated with the United States Signal Corps, developing airplane instruments, 1917-1918. He is a fellow of the American Physical Society (council, 1926-1930), the American Optical Society, and the American Association for the Advancement of Science (vice-president Section B, 1927). He is a member of the American Philosophical Society, National Academy of Sciences (1927), National Research Council (chairman of committee on X-rays and radioactivity, 1922-1925), Solvay International Congress of Physics (1927), Volta International Science Congress, Rome (1927, 1931), Alpha Tau Omega, Sigma Xi, Phi Beta Kappa, and Gamma Alpha; foreign member of Reale Accademia dei Lincei, Rome, 1925, Prussian Academy of Sciences, Berlin, 1932. He was associate editor of the Physical Review, from 1922 to 1926. He belongs to the Quadrangle and Union League clubs. He is the

Continued on page 545

ARTERIES OF STEEL THAT LACE THE METROPOLITAN AREA
How Rapid Overhead Transit Has Made Possible Chicago's Expansion

J UST as the national network of transportation has aided Chicago's development by bringing the world to its door, so have the local transit facilities advanced the growth of the city from within. By increasing the ease of travel between business centers and outlying residential areas, the local transportation lines have enabled the city to extend its borders into sections that otherwise would have been inaccessible.

To the elevated railways, established several decades ago as separate organizations and now operated as a single unified system by the Chicago Rapid Transit Company, must go a large share of credit for enabling the city to attain its present dimensions. During the early years the street car—advancing successively from horse to cable and finally to trolley operation—sufficed as a means of local transit. As the city's population grew in density, however, it was necessary to travel longer distances to find suitable sites for homes. This called for a speedier means of local transportation.

It was in 1892 that the first elevated railroad was established in the city, the Chicago and South Side Rapid Transit Company starting operation on June 6 of that year between Congress and Thirty-ninth streets. The need for faster transportation at that time is seen in the fact that the city had already passed the million mark in population and embraced an area of 169 square miles. Travel even within the city had become a matter of miles.

Some four on a Chicagoland golf course.

(Moffett-Russell Photo)

FRANK E. COMPTON

Mr. Compton was born in Wisconsin Rapids, Wisconsin, August 7, 1874, and is the son of Harry Henry and Frances (Shepard) Compton. Mr. Compton is president of F. E. Compton & Company, publishers; director, National Association of Book Publishers; director of the Chicago Daily Times; president of Subscription Book Publishers' Association (1921-22); president, National Theta Delta Chi Fraternity (1911-13); president, Skokie Country Club (1919-20); University of Wisconsin, Class of 1898; and is a pioneer in the educational publishing field. A noted proponent of making all knowledge interesting and inspiring for growing children, he has created the educational or "school" type of encyclopedia, built expressly to supplement school work. Starting in Chicago 38 years ago with an ambition and an idea, through his efforts Compton's Pictured Encyclopedia has become the student's work of reference in the home, the school, and the library, and the largest selling encyclopedia in the world. Branch offices are located in the principal cities of the United States; in London, England; and Milan, Italy.

Mr. Compton was married to Annie Wilson Howe (niece of the late President Woodrow Wilson) July 21, 1917. The children are Frank F., Edna, and Josephine Wilson.

When the World's Columbian Exposition opened in 1893, the original elevated line had been extended south to the site of the Fair in Jackson Park. Steam "dummy" engines furnished the motive power at that time. It was during the Fair that a revolutionary feature in operation of elevated trains was successfully introduced. The Intra-mural Railway circling the Fair grounds operated trains under electric power for the first time in history.

The success of the Intra-mural Railway led the Metropolitan West Side Elevated Railway Company, which followed the Lake street line as the third elevated system in Chicago, to cancel orders for steam "dummy" engines and start service in 1895 as the first electrically-operated commercial elevated railroad in the world. The other lines soon changed to electric operation, extensions were made, and the Union Loop was opened in 1897. The Northwestern elevated lines started operation between the Loop and Wilson avenue in 1900, making four elevated railroads using the Loop, but operating separately and charging separate fares.

Joint operation of all the lines as the Chicago Elevated Railways came about in 1911. Two years later through-routing of trains and universal transfer privileges were inaugurated for the greater convenience of the public.

Since the elevated system came under the present management, it has been extended and developed until today it comprises 230 miles of single track, 60 per cent of which is on elevated steel structure. A total of 5,511 trains are operated daily, service being maintained 24 hours a day under all weather conditions. Equipment includes 1,862 passenger coaches, which are operated in train units of from two to eight cars. There are 237 stations on the Rapid Transit Lines, as the unified system is known today.

In addition to serving all sections of the city on 12 branches extending fanlike from the Loop, the Rapid Transit Lines furnish fast and frequent service to many suburban communities. These include Evanston, Wilmette and Niles Center to the north, and Oak Park, Forest Park, Cicero, Berwyn, Maywood, Bellwood and Westchester to the west. Service over the entire system converges in the Loop. The importance of the Rapid Transit Lines as a transportation medium for downtown workers is seen in the fact that 190 trains of 1,040 cars enter the Loop within sixty minutes during the morning rush period, while 224 trains pass the intersection at Lake and Wells streets during the maximum rush hour.

The life and activities of Chicago are not confined to its corporate limits, however. There has developed a large metropolitan area, all sections of which are bound by ties of commerce and industry to the city proper. The area embraced in greater Chicago is no longer measured in miles, but rather in the amount of time it takes to travel from one point to another. The metropolitan area is generally considered today as including any community that can be reached within one hour after leaving the Loop.

(Chambers Photo)

JAMES G. CONDON

Mr. Condon, member of the law firm of Ryan, Condon and Livingston, was born in Bloomington, Illinois, November 28, 1871, son of William and Brigid (McNamara) Condon. He graduated from St. Viateur's College, Kankakee, Illinois, in 1892 and received his LL.B. (Bachelor of Laws) degree at Illinois Wesleyan University, Bloomington, Illinois, in 1894. He was admitted to the Illinois bar in 1894 and practiced at Bloomington until 1895, when he came to Chicago. He was a member of the law firm of Ryan and Condon from 1908 until 1914 when the name was changed to Ryan, Condon and Livingston, which it remains. Mr. Condon spends most of his time in connection with corporation work.

He is a member of the American, Illinois State, and Chicago Bar Associations (board of managers of the latter, 1924-27), and Lawyers Association of New York. His clubs are Iroquois (president, 1910-11), Chicago Athletic Association, Mid-Day, Chicago Riding, Knollwood, Edgewater Golf, and he is also actively interested in, as well as a member of, Post and Paddock at Arlington Park. Outside of work, his principal interests are golf, horseback riding, and motoring.

Mr. Condon married Lucy Dalton, of Bloomington, June 30, 1895, and they have two daughters, Marian (Mrs. Paul Gerhardt), and Jane (Mrs. William Truman Brophy III).

An important factor in extending the borders of metropolitan Chicago is embraced in the three electrically-operated interurban railroads serving the territory to the north, west and east. With the Rapid Transit Lines serving as the backbone of local high-speed transportation, these interurban lines extend their ribbons of steel to points beyond, making them easily accessible to the commuter. Corporate limits of city or county are no longer a bar to the Loop worker seeking a home in the suburbs.

To the north the Chicago North Shore and Milwaukee Railroad (North Shore Line) operates high-speed trains at frequent intervals along the lake shore, and through the beautiful Skokie Valley as far as Milwaukee. All-steel limiteds carrying parlor-buffet cars cover the distance between the hearts of Chicago and Milwaukee in less than two hours, stopping at Waukegan, Kenosha, and Racine. Frequent express service is afforded Loop commuters from suburban communities as far north as Waukegan on the Shore Line Route, and west to Libertyville and Mundelein over the Skokie Valley Route. Trains operate directly to and from the Loop over the tracks of the Rapid Transit Lines, with 63rd and Dorchester on the south side as the terminal for limiteds carrying parlor-buffet cars.

Operating to and from the Loop passenger station at Wells street and Jackson boulevard, trains of the Chicago Aurora and Elgin Railroad (Sunset Lines) serve western suburbs and cities throughout the scenic Fox River Valley. Fast and frequent service is afforded commuters from Aurora, Elgin, St. Charles, Geneva, Batavia and intermediate points in this region. Use of the Rapid Transit Lines tracks between the Loop and western city limits speeds up this service, while stops at eight stations on the west side and in adjoining suburbs add to the convenience of the Sunset Lines.

Skirting the southern shore of Lake Michigan, and passing through the famous Dunes region and the "Workshop of America" in northern Indiana, the Chicago South Shore and South Bend Railroad (South Shore Line) connects the Loop with Hammond, East Chicago, Gary, Michigan City and South Bend. Direct access to the downtown Chicago business district is gained over the tracks of the Illinois Central Railroad, with the terminus at Randolph street station, only two blocks east of the Randolph-Wabash station of the Rapid Transit Lines. Parlor cars are carried on South Shore Line limiteds at convenient hours.

With this network of Rapid Transit Lines and high-speed interurban railroads stretching through the city and its metropolitan area, Chicago is afforded the transportation facilities essential for continued expansion and development. It is upon these rapid transit arteries that the people of metropolitan Chicago must rely for quick and convenient travel, as traffic congestion reaches the saturation point with the steady increase in population.

(Underwood and Underwood Photo)

GEORGE A. COOKE

Judge Cooke, member of the law firm of Cooke, Sullivan and Ricks, was born at New Athens, Ohio, July 3, 1869, and is a son of Thomas and Vanceline (Downing) Cooke. He attended Knox College, where he was awarded his A.B. (Bachelor of Arts) and LL.D. (Doctor of Laws) degrees in 1892 and 1922. After passing the Illinois bar examination, he practiced law at Aledo, Illinois, and from 1896 to 1900 was a partner of Judge Guy C. Scott.

Judge Cooke served as a member of the Illinois House of Representatives from 1902 to 1906. In 1909 he was elected judge of the Supreme Court to fill the unexpired term of Judge Guy C. Scott and was re-elected in 1912. He also served as chief justice from June, 1913, to June, 1914. In 1918 he resigned and has been a member of the firm of Cooke, Sullivan and Ricks since January 1, 1919. He is a member of the American and Illinois State Bar Associations and Beta Theta Pi Fraternity. His clubs are: University, Tavern, of Chicago; and Oak View Country, Aledo, Illinois.

On October 20, 1896, he married Sarah Blee, of Aledo, Illinois, and their children are Margerie (Mrs. Robert P. McBride), Martha (Mrs. Claude E. Canning), George Blee and Thomas Blee.

CHICAGO — THE CENTER OF INLAND WATERWAYS

BY LORENZO DANA CORNISH

Chief Engineer, Division of Waterways, State of Illinois

T HE site of Chicago from prehistoric time has been the dividing point of the two greatest inland waterway systems in the world. During the glacier period the waters of Lake Michigan poured through this area and carved out the valley of the DesPlaines and Illinois rivers on their way to the southern seas. The forces of nature raised the land, and the waters of Lake Michigan found their way to the sea through the Great Lakes and the St. Lawrence River.

The intrepid explorer, Père Marquette, in his travels to find a water outlet to the south in 1673, found such an outlet in the present city limits of Chicago. He located a short portage between the Chicago and the Des-Plaines rivers, which in times of high water was navigable for canoes. He then envisioned a commerce-laden river route from the Great Lakes to the much sought Indies.

This divide between the waters was definitely responsible for the location of the settlement which eventually developed into Chicago. The settlers of Chicago and the State foresaw that the future development of this area could only come through the construction of a commercially navigable channel to connect Lake Michigan with the Illinois River so that the lumber and manufactured products of the Eastern States could be distributed southward and the grain from the prairies of Illinois transported to the East. The construction of the Erie Canal gave an eastern outlet to Europe through New York.

Chicagoans were the leaders in promoting a waterway to the Missis-

(*Chicago Aerial Survey Company*)

(Nieto Photo)

LORENZO DANA CORNISH

Major Cornish, Chief Engineer of the Division of Waterways, State of Illinois, was born in Lee Centre, Oneida County, New York, March 30, 1877, son of James Bennett and Frances Emeline (Ward) Cornish. He received his education in Syracuse, New York, and obtained his C. E. (Civil Engineer) degree at Syracuse University in 1902. During his engineering career of over thirty years, Major Cornish has been principally engaged in the design and construction of waterway transportation facilities and power development. From 1902 to 1906 he was Junior United States civil engineer and superintendent of construction at Pittsburgh; engineer assistant to the International Consulting Board for the Panama Canal during 1906; designing engineer for the Isthmian Canal Commission, 1907 to 1913; principal assistant engineer for the American Red Cross Board of Engineers in China during 1914; and principal United States engineer in the United States Engineering Department, Cincinnati, Ohio, from 1915 to 1917. Since 1919 he has used the experience he gained when canalizing the Ohio River and building the Panama Canal to bring to fulfillment Marquette's vision—the connection of Lake Michigan with the Mississippi River by a modern navigable waterway, the Illinois Waterways.

A veteran of the Spanish American War and the World War, Major Cornish has the unique record of the most rapid construction of track on the Western Front of any officer in France who received citation from the Commander-in-Chief—2.69 miles of track laid by 135 men under traffic in five hours, and one cubic yard of excavation per man per hour were among the records of Company C, 15th Engineers. As a member of the American Society of Civil Engineers, the Western Society of Engineers, the Mississippi Valley Association, and the National Rivers and Harbors Congress, Major Cornish has been a frequent contributor of articles to their publications. He is a member of the Medinah Athletic Club.

On January 23, 1901, he married Mary Elizabeth Brodhead of Syracuse (died 1911); one son, Lorenzo Eugene Brodhead. He married Jeanette Welsh of Cincinnati, Ohio, May 18, 1916.

sippi and their efforts were successful with the completion of the Illinois and Michigan Canal in 1848. From the opening of the canal Chicago grew at an enormous rate, soon became the greatest lumber center in the world, and quickly followed as the greatest grain center of the United States. The development of railroads by 1880 supplanted this waterway as a commercial carrier of freight.

Chicagoans never lost sight of the eventful need of a modern commercial waterway to the South and two hundred and fifty years after its conception by Père Marquette the Chicago area had contributed, at a cost of a hundred millions of dollars, the most important link of this inland water chain—a sanitary and ship canal designed and built as a bulwark against sewage contamination of Lake Michigan, the course of its water supply, together with a navigation channel through the Continental Divide, without which the Lakes-to-the-Gulf Waterway would yet be at the Père Marquette stage of contemplation. This waterway was opened in 1900 and though sufficient waters from Lake Michigan to float modern water carriers were diverted into the Mississippi, navigation could not exist owing to the rapids of the DesPlaines and Illinois rivers between Lockport and Utica.

Chicagoans were again the leaders in a state-wide movement to complete what is since known as the Illinois Waterway, and in 1908, by an amendment to the State Constitution, provided funds for its construction. Not until 1917 could legislative authority and governmental approval be secured for the construction of the waterway. Actual work was commenced in 1919 and in spite of unavoidable delay was rapidly nearing completion in 1929 when it became evident that the $20,000,000 bond issue was insufficient for the task. Chicagoans were again among the leaders in cooperating with the Government of the State in an appeal to the Federal Government for aid to complete the waterway. Federal aid was finally secured to an amount of $7,500,000 and in 1930 Federal engineers took over the completion of the channel and navigation structures of the waterway and the State continued its work by the reconstruction of all highway bridges over the waterway.

In October, 1932, the Federal engineers had completed the essential parts of the waterway and operated all five of the locks and passed boats from the Illinois River at LaSalle up through three of the locks to a bridge on the DesPlaines River near Channahon. All essential bridges will be constructed early in 1933 and with the opening of navigation after the closed winter season modern commercial navigation will be an actual fact between Chicago and all southern points.

The sight of foreign ships is a common occurrence in Chicago, which has long been a seaport in a small way. When the St. Lawrence Waterway is completed, large ocean freighters can come to Chicago and Chicago will have reached its destiny as the center of transportation between the two latest inland waterway systems in the world—the Great Lakes-St. Lawrence

(Underwood and Underwood Photo)

JACOB CRANE

Mr. Crane, a consulting plan engineer of international reputation, with projects in all parts of this country, in China and in Russia, was born in Benzonia, Michigan, September 14, 1892, and is the son of Jacob L. and Sarah T. (Maley) Crane. He was active in the campaign for Chicago's Zoning Ordinance, was a leader in the formation of the Chicago Regional Plan, and directed the survey of State Planning for Illinois under the auspices of the Illinois Chamber of Commerce. He is a consultant on planning and development for many of Chicago's suburbs and designer of such suburbs as Woodmar and Westchester.

He says: "I'm a rank visionary. Most of what I desire for this town and this district cannot be had short of fifty or a hundred years of gradually rebuilding the desolate shambles which constitute two-thirds of our built-up city and suburban area. I am not alone; five other persons, out of the four million, feel as I do. Chicago's present program is meager compared to what I would propose for the long-term job. But this latter wouldn't cost so much because it would be largely a matter of guiding and controlling the natural process of reconstruction, which is going on anyway. Meanwhile, we plan, and we do what can be done, and we dream of the magnificent future."

He is a member of the American Society of Civil Engineers, American City Planning Institute, British Town Planning Institute, American Society of Landscape Architects. He is a Tau Beta Pi. His clubs are Cliff Dwellers, Columbia Yacht, and Chicago Yacht. He wrote a chapter in "Living Architecture," also many articles for magazines.

Mr. Crane married Ruth F. Fifield, 1910 (died February, 1928), and is the father of three children, Sally C., Jacob III, and James Fifield.

Waterway on the north, with thousands of miles of shore line and industrial cities, connected with the Mississippi River system, which reaches to Minneapolis and St. Paul on the Upper Mississippi, the fertile valleys and mines of the Missouri River, the industrial centers of the Ohio River up to Pittsburgh, all of which are tributary to the Gulf Seaboard at New Orleans.

In 1933 the eyes of the world will be centered on Chicago and its Century of Progress, and Chicagoans and visitors will go aboard a boat at the Municipal Pier, travel through the Chicago River to the Chicago Drainage Canal, 160 feet wide, 24 feet deep, about forty miles to Lockport, where the boat will enter locks 600 feet long, 110 feet wide, and with the gates closed behind them the water will be lowered 41 feet. The boat will then travel into the DesPlaines River through Joliet to the locks at Brandon Road, where it will again be dropped 31 feet, then proceed down the river to the Dresden Island Lock just below where the Kankakee joins the DesPlaines to form the Illinois River. The boat will be lowered 16 feet and then proceed through a thirty-six-mile stretch of the river to Marseilles; thence two miles through a canal to the Marseilles Lock, again to drop 21 feet into the pool below; thence thirteen miles to the lock at the historic site of Starved Rock, where it will be lowered 17 feet into the Illinois River and will have passed through the Continental Divide at Chicago and over the steep portion of the river, which to the present time had formed a barrier to all navigation except canoes and flat bottom boats.

The Hall of Science of A Century of Progress. This huge structure, 700 by 400 feet, is shaped like a U, and encloses on three sides a court capable of accommodating 80,000 persons. At one corner rises a 176-foot tower equipped with a carillon. The building faces a beautiful lagoon, an island, and Lake Michigan beyond. At night it has the appearance of a brilliantly illuminated metal and glass creation, rising from colored terraces. Paul Cret, architect. McLennan Construction Company, builders.

(Fernand de Gueldre Photo)

PERRY O. CRAWFORD

Mr. Crawford, engineer and public utility operator, was born November 11, 1885, in Malvern, Carroll County, Ohio, son of James F. and Mary L. (Cox) Crawford. After spending a year at Ohio State University, he entered Stanford University, where he took the course in electrical engineering, and was graduated with the class of 1908. He began his career as construction engineer for the North California Power Company, but in 1912 he went to Afghanistan as assistant engineer on the Jabl-us-Siraj hydro-electric project at Kabul, one of the wildest and most remote outposts of civilization. Returning three years later to the United States, he reentered Stanford as a post-graduate student.

In 1916 he became associated with The California Oregon Power Company as engineer, later rising to the position of vice-president and general manager. In 1929 he resigned to become president of the Federal Public Service Corporation of Chicago, a company whose subsidiaries supply electric power, gas, water, telephone service, and ice to communities in nineteen states. Mr. Crawford is a member of the American Institute of Electrical Engineers, the American Society of Civil Engineers, the American Society of Mechanical Engineers, the Adventurers' Club of Chicago, and the Chicago Stanford Club, of which he was elected president for 1933.

He was married in London, England, February 18, 1914, to Irma J. Zschokke, and their children are Dora M., Perry O., Jr., and Kenneth Z.

THE DEVELOPMENT PLAN OF THE ARMOUR INSTITUTE OF TECHNOLOGY

Enlisting the Cooperation of Industry in Educational Problems

THE Armour Institute of Technology Development Plan was formulated in the spring of 1931 after several months of careful study, directed by the Board of Trustees and a Development Committee. This study included a thorough investigation of the methods and practices of engineering education as it is carried on in America today, and an analysis of the educational "needs" of the great industries of the Chicago industrial area which absorbs more than seventy-five per cent of the graduates of Armour Institute of Technology.

The Development Plan is based upon one broad principle, namely, that there are three groups who must always be vitally interested in engineering education; the college itself, its alumni, and industry and the engineering professions; and that all of these groups may profit if permanent channels of expression are established whereby the voice of each may become effective in shaping the policies and methods which are employed in the college.

In the past, it has been largely true that educational institutions do not look to outside sources for assistance in the solution of any problems of curriculum and teaching method, on the assumption that the educator is a specialist whose business it is to find the solution to such problems.

The new attitude at Armour Institute of Technology rejects this thought. It embraces the idea that the educator alone can never arrive at a satisfactory solution to problems in which industry is as definitely involved as it is in engineering education. The educator takes the position of the producer in a business enterprise, and he looks to consumer demand—in this case, industry and the engineering professions—to assist him by pointing out ways in which his product, the graduate engineer, might be improved.

This new principle is the most important change embodied in the Armour Plan. It is interesting to note that already consumer demand has expressed itself, that the curricula at Armour Institute are being made less specialized in answer to industry's plea for an engineer with a broader, more fundamental education.

There is every indication that industry is more than willing to continue to assume some of the responsibility for engineering education, and that both industry and the college, and, inevitably, the graduates of the college, will benefit thereby.

REPUBLIC

JAMES D. CUNNINGHAM

Mr. Cunningham, president of Republic Flow Meters Company and Autogas Corporation, was born in Chicago, Illinois, May 5, 1887, and is a son of William H. and
Josephine (Dalton) Cunningham. He attended the Chicago schools, graduating from
the Hyde Park High School in 1905. He began as a clerk with the Armour Glue
Works; later was a member of the firm of Clyde Machine Works Company; and in
1911 founded and became president of the Steam Appliance Company, now the Republic Flow Meters Company, manufacturers of industrial instruments with a factory
in Chicago and branch offices in principal cities. He is also a director of the Dominion
Flow Meters Company of Toronto, Canada, and the Electro-Flo Meter Company of
London, England.

Mr. Cunningham is also president of the Autogas Corporation, manufacturers of
Republic Conversion Gas Burners for heating homes, etc., with gas. He is a director
of the Illinois Manufacturers Mutual Casualty Association, vice-president and member of
American Society of Mechanical Engineers, and member of Western Society of Engineers.
He was president of the Illinois Manufacturers' Association during 1928 and 1929. He
is interested in engineering problems and education, and is chairman of the board of trustees, as well as chairman of the development committee, of the Armour Institute of Technology. The Armour Institute development program is based on a survey of engineering
educational requirements of the local industrial area and calls for progressive changes and
enlargements. It includes the establishment of not only an advanced engineering college
but a technical and industrial research institute. He is a member of The Chicago Club
and the Chicago Engineers Club.

CHICAGO, THE GREAT WHOLESALE MARKET

Complete Stocks, Attractive Prices, Quick Delivery With Low Transportation Costs—No Wonder Buyers Favor Chicago!

BY FRANK S. CUNNINGHAM
President, Butler Brothers

ARE you contemplating going into the retail business? Come to Chicago! In at least one Chicago wholesale establishment you can see model stores completely stocked. You can see the fixtures which experience recommends as most satisfactory. You can see the store arrangement which has proved most profitable from a selling standpoint. You will discover that retailing is no longer a hit-or-miss business, but a science which has been reduced to accurate details.

Are you in doubt as to the best location for your store? Experts will advise you, basing their suggestions on a mass of records from which inescapable facts have been drawn.

BUTLER BROTHERS CHICAGO BUILDINGS

Are you rather vague in your ideas of the proper merchandise to stock? The modern Chicago wholesaler has the information at his fingertips— what items, what colors, what sizes, what prices constitute the kind of stock which can be relied upon to turn at a profit! He will gladly furnish you with a system of stock control which prevents your running out of wanted items, and he will show you how costly such "outs" may be.

You raise your eyebrows in surprise? What has all this to do with selling at wholesale, you ask? Just this—the modern Chicago wholesaler knows that his success depends upon his customers' success. He knows there are many things about retailing which the average retailer doesn't know—facts which, if observed and accepted, would make a vast difference in the average retailer's annual business, and annual profits.

(Underwood and Underwood Photo)

FRANK S. CUNNINGHAM

Mr. Cunningham, president of Butler Brothers, was born in Bourbon, Indiana, April 16, 1866, son of Oliver W. and Bethia Ann (Simpson) Cunningham. He received his education at the high school of Goshen, Indiana. He started with Butler Brothers, wholesale general merchandise, of Chicago, in 1886, and has been president since 1918. Mr. Cunningham is one of Chicago's civic leaders and is trustee of the Northwestern University and Evanston Hospital and president of the Cradle Society of Evanston since its inception in 1923. His clubs are the Chicago, University, Union League, Commercial, and Glenview.

On September 14, 1893, Mr. Cunningham married Lucy E. Baty, of Chicago, and they had one son, Oliver Baty (captain, United States Army, killed in action during World War).

So he has made it his business to ascertain those facts and place them at the disposal of his customers. Because he reasons, correctly, that the merchant who learns modern retailing through a wholesaler—whose red figures turn to black with that wholesaler's help—will turn to that wholesaler for the major part of his purchases, other things being equal.

This is a comparatively new idea in wholesaling. But then, Chicago is a comparatively new city, and new ideas thrive here! That may be one of the big reasons for Chicago's recent growth as a wholesale center—its ever-increasing popularity with buyers, department heads, merchandise managers, and store owners, throughout the vast and fertile territory which rightfully regards Chicago as its trading center.

Chicago's night-time brilliance. In the extreme right foreground is the illuminated spire of the Chicago Temple Building.

According to the latest Federal census, there are some 9,312 wholesale houses in metropolitan Chicago, doing an annual business somewhere in the neighborhood of five billions of dollars. It is no exaggeration to say that whatever any merchant wants can be bought to advantage in Chicago —quickly, economically, satisfactorily.

Among the leaders in Chicago's development as a wholesale market must be numbered Marshall Field & Co., Carson, Pirie Scott & Co., Hibbard, Spencer, Bartlett & Co., and Butler Brothers. Each of these establishments has attained the proportions of an exposition, with stocks of gargantuan dimensions—vast displays so arranged that they are in themselves a liberal education to any merchant.

Supplementing these outstanding leaders in the dry goods and general merchandise field are thousands of smaller firms and specialty houses with-

(Moffett-Russell Photo)

KENNETH CURTIS

Mr. Curtis, president and chairman of the board of Curtis Lighting, Inc., and president of Curtis Lighting Securities Company, Curtis Lighting of New York, Inc., and Curtis Lighting of Canada, Ltd., was born in Marinette, Wisconsin, March 1, 1894, son of Augustus Darwin and Marette (Hotchkin) Curtis. He received his education at Hyde Park High School, of Chicago; Cascadilla School, Ithaca, New York; University of Wisconsin, where he received his B. A. (Bachelor of Arts) degree in 1919; and North-western University, where he received his M. B. A. (Master of Business Administration) in 1923. He also took post-graduate work in geology at the University of Chicago.

Curtis Lighting, Inc., of which Mr. Curtis is president and chairman of the board, is the largest organization of its kind in the world. It is devoted to the design, manu-facture, and installation of engineered lighting equipment which provides the correct amount of illumination for proper architectural and lighting effect. This company, with representatives in all the world's principal cities, and factories in the United States, Canada, and Europe, is developing novel lighting ideas, many of which will first be seen at A Century of Progress, Chicago's (1933) World's Fair. The company will also have an exhibit of its own at the Fair. Mr. Curtis was commissioned First Lieutenant of Infan-try at Camp Custer, Michigan, and served with the American Expeditionary Forces on the Meuse-Argonne front in France. He is a director of The Electric Association, Chicago, and The Chicago Architects Club. He is a member of the Illuminating Engineering Society. He is a Sigma Phi and a member of many clubs and fraternal organizations. His recreations are hunting, fishing, and horseback riding.

Mrs. Kenneth Curtis is the former Mary Clair Eastman, of Evanston. The children are Clair and Kenneth Augustus.

out which no market would be complete. There is ample opportunity for the out-of-town buyer to shop, to compare values, and to make his purchase wherever his judgment indicates he will receive the greatest satisfaction.

Scores of thousands of retailers are served by Chicago's wholesale houses, and the number is growing each year.

In ready-to-wear clothing, for example, records show a sales increase of 233 per cent since 1914. Buyers seeking this class of merchandise find a highly diversified market confined in a small area, which makes for desirable economy of time and effort. They can leave home in the evening, complete their buying in one day, and be back home ready for business the following morning—a program hard to duplicate in any other market.

Infants' and children's wear, accessories, and furniture—millinery—men's clothing—gift merchandise—leather goods—furs—Chicago's reputation in all of these lines is second to that of no other market in the country.

Hardware merchants find unparalleled values in Chicago's wholesale houses. The great volume of hardware business clearing through Chicago gives tremendous unit purchasing power to the wholesalers who handle this business—brings prices farther down—attracts more retailers!

Toys! The world's largest wholesaler of toys is located in Chicago! The annual Chicago Toy Fair attracts manufacturers, jobbers, and buyers from the larger stores all over the Middle West.

And so on, through the whole long category of merchandise classifications—whatever any merchant wants can be found in Chicago's wholesale houses, easily, quickly, at the right price, and for immediate delivery.

A CENTURY OF PROGRESS VIEWS

Night view showing base of tower of the Hall of Science, the walls of which are illuminated by gaseous tubes.

Concealed neon illumination makes the south view of the Hall of Science a captivating scene at night.

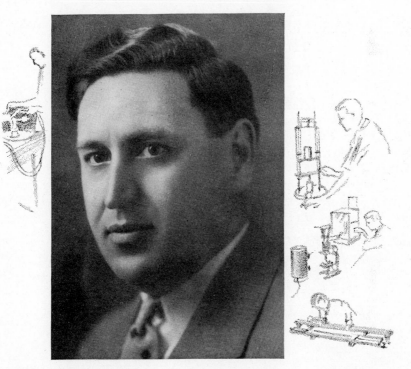

ERNEST E. DALTON

Mr. Dalton, president of Coe Laboratories, Inc., was born in Brantford, Ontario, on November 16, 1889. His parents were Dennis Dalton and Katherine (McKinnon) Dalton. Mr. Dalton attended school there but moved to Buffalo, New York, in 1901, where he finished school. At the age of fourteen he entered the employ of a dental supply house, this step being the beginning of an outstanding career in the dental industry which has never been interrupted. He was married to Cora Jeffe of Buffalo in 1910 and has one daughter, Colette. He moved to Chicago in the latter part of 1910 where he has made his home since. Mr. Dalton heads one of the unique institutions in Chicago—the Coe Laboratories, Inc.

While the Coe Laboratories, Inc., is essentially a manufacturer of materials for dentists, by far the largest part of its activities is devoted to research and educational work with the dental profession. Its museum and scientific research laboratory and educational rooms are the Mecca of dentists and technicians from all over the world. Mr. Dalton organized the Coe Laboratories, Inc., in 1924, and, under his guidance and direction, it was an immediate success. It has grown and expanded until today it is regarded as one of the leading dental institutions in the country. Coe Laboratories, Inc., through its association of 140 Certified Laboratories, is able to give the results of its research findings to dentists in every corner of the world. Mr. Dalton is a national figure in the dental industry, not only because of the products and technics his organization has given to dentistry, but also because of his genuinely friendly personality and his adherence to his high principled ideals.

A CENTURY OF PROGRESS EXPOSITION, HERALD OF A NEW AGE

Interpreting Creatively the Spirit of Today

BY PAUL T. GILBERT

ON a strip of land reclaimed from Lake Michigan, extending from Twelfth street to 39th street, a distance of nearly three and a half miles, and on Northerly Island (also man-made), separated from the shore by a narrow lagoon, an Aladdin city has sprung up.

It is a city unlike anything ever seen on earth before; the kind of a city one might expect to see on visiting Mars. It is a futuristic city, foreshadowing nobody knows exactly what. It vibrates with youth. It reflects the spirit of Today—and perhaps more daringly, the spirit of Tomorrow.

Administration building—headquarters of A Century of Progress—Chicago's 1933 World's Fair. This structure is a striking example of the application of modern architectural principles to new methods of building.

A stranger viewing it for the first time will be struck by the oddity, the wierdness, the bizarreness of its architecture. New materials have gone into its construction. New engineering principles have been experimented with, in its construction. Even the architects and engineers themselves are a bit amazed, a bit breathless, over what they've done. The roof of the Agricultural Building is made of cornstalks, and perhaps no one would be surprised if told that it was made of pumpkin pie. Anything is possible in this extraordinary city. The "breathing" dome of the Travel and Transport Building—the largest dome in the world—is suspended like a lampshade by cables from the skeleton-like steel uprights which surround it.

Here are architectural conceptions that seem upside down and topsy-turvy. Structures with their skeletons on the outside, like insects. Uncompromising horizontals and perpendiculars. Box-like rectangularity. Triangular towers. Surfaces that require tricky illumination rather than plastic art for decoration. Simplicity and usability rather than elegance. No "exposition art," no gingerbread about Chicago's second World's Fair City. No suggestion of the glory that was Greece. Nothing you have ever seen before. It is a city that epitomizes the age of steel, chromium, aluminum,

(Eugene L. Ray, Evanston, Photo)

CHARLES G. DAWES

General Dawes, lawyer, banker, author, composer, and public official, was born in Marietta, Ohio, August 27, 1865, son of General Rufus R. and Mary Beman (Gates) Dawes. He attended Marietta College and received his A. B. (Bachelor of Arts) degree in 1884, his A. M. (Master of Arts), in 1887. Working as an engineer on a small Ohio railroad, he earned sufficient money to put himself through the Cincinnati Law School, from which he graduated with an LL. B. (Bachelor of Laws) degree in 1886. He taught himself music, first mastering the flute and then the piano, and his composition, "Melody in A Minor," has been played by distinguished artists throughout the world. He was admitted to the bar in 1886; practiced in Lincoln, Nebraska, 1887 to 1894; moved to Evanston, Illinois, in 1894.

Mr. Dawes was the executive of the McKinley movement in Illinois that resulted in McKinley instructions at the Springfield Convention in 1896; member of the executive committee of the Republican National Committee in the campaign of 1896; comptroller of the currency from 1897 to 1901. He organized the Central Trust Company of Illinois in 1902 and was president until 1921; chairman of the board, 1921 to 1925; honorary chairman of the board in 1930-1931, and when reorganized in 1931 as the Central Republic Bank & Trust Company was honorary chairman of that board. He is now chairman of the board of directors of the City National Bank & Trust Company organized October 6, 1932.

He was commissioned major of engineers of the National Army, June, 1917; lieutenant colonel in July, 1917; colonel in January, 1918; and brigadier-general in October, 1918. He arrived in France as lieutenant colonel of the railway engineers; was appointed to administrative staff of commander in chief of the American Expeditionary Forces, September, 1917; served as chairman of the general purchasing board and as general purchasing agent of the American Expeditionary Forces; later, was a member of the Military Board of Allied Supply, the Liquidation Commission of the A. E. F., and the Liquidation Board of the War Department; resigned from the Army in 1919, returning to the United States August, 1919. General Dawes was awarded the Distinguished

Continued on page 546

electricity. It is the forerunner of amazing changes that will come about in America within the next twenty-five years—a pre-view of the future.

During the administration of the late Mayor William E. Dever, Chicagoans became conscious of the fact that the Prairie Metropolis was growing up, that it was approaching its one hundredth birthday.

Something should be done on a grand scale, they thought, to commemorate such an important event. One outstanding event in the history of the nation, the four hundredth anniversary of the landing of Columbus, was celebrated by the World's Columbian Exposition. Chicago's first World's Fair was a magnificent gesture. During its transitory existence it made Chicago the Queen City of the world. No exposition held since that time has been able to compare with it either in its ineffable, dream-like beauty or in the splendor of its exhibits. It ushered in a renaissance of classic architecture. For Chicago it marked the beginning of a new and a more gracious era.

Now, in 1926, Chicago seemed to be standing on the verge of another period of expansion. It was soaring cloudward, its restless skyline changing almost overnight. Wacker drive was nearing completion. The Michigan avenue bridge had provided a new gateway to the Loop.

Out of the deliberations of a group of leaders grew the conception of a second World's Fair, an exposition that would repeat the triumph of 1893 and dramatize the progress, material and spiritual, of Chicago during the century of civic life that was drawing to a close.

This progress has been almost unbelievable. In 1833, when Chicago was incorporated as a town, its population was about 150. There were 28 voters. The settlement consisted of a group of cabins clustered around a "tomahawk" fortress. The mournful howl of the prairie wolf could be heard at night. Indians loafed around Fort Dearborn or the Kinzie cabin. A log foot bridge spanned the river; vehicles were taken across on the ferry. The streets were hardly more than cowpaths. It is recalled that a stage coach, mired in Clark street between Madison and Randolph, was abandoned. A woman crossing a muddy street lost both her shoes.

By a happy coincidence the birth of Chicago as a corporate town coincided with the beginning of a century of undreamed of progress. The railroad, the harvester, the steamship, the telegraph, the telephone, the sewing machine, the typewriter, the phonograph, the electric light, the bicycle, the automobile, the motion picture, the airplane, the radio were among the products of that cycle.

An Exposition that would present in dynamic form the changes in industry and in everyday life wrought by the discoveries and inventions of these hundred years would, in the opinion of its sponsors, be justified on the occasion of Chicago's centennial celebration.

An ideal site for such a Fair was available right in Chicago's front yard. In fact, the nucleus of a Fair was already provided. Near by stood the magnificent Field Museum, one of the world's wonder houses. The new

(*Kellogg Studio Photo*)

HENRY M. DAWES

Mr. Dawes is president of the Pure Oil Company, one of the large completely integrated companies in the oil industry. He was born in Marietta, Ohio, April 22, 1877, son of Rufus R. and Mary Beman (Gates) Dawes, and graduated from Marietta College there. In 1907 Mr. Dawes came to Chicago to become associated with his brothers, Charles G., Rufus C. and Beman G. Dawes, in the public utility business. He was president of the Southwestern Gas & Electric Company and vice-president of Dawes Brothers, Inc.

Mr. Dawes was appointed Comptroller of the Currency and a member of the Federal Reserve Board by the late President Harding on May 1, 1923, resigning in December, 1924. He is chairman of the board of the Central Illinois Securities Corporation, director of the City National Bank and Trust Company of Chicago, Chicago Great Western Railroad, American Petroleum Institute, Dawes Brothers, Inc., Union Gas and Electric Company, Metropolitan Gas and Electric Company, Personal Loan and Savings Bank (Chicago), and Drovers Trust and Savings Bank of Chicago.

He is a member of the Delta Upsilon Fraternity. His clubs are the University, Chicago Club, Cosmos (Washington, D. C.), Glenview Golf (Chicago), Evanston Country, and Seaview Golf (N. J.).

On April 5, 1905, he married Helen Curtis of Marietta. Their children are Curtis and Mary G.

$6,000,000 Stadium—not yet known as Soldier Field—had just been completed and dedicated. The Art Institute with its priceless collections, was another asset. Plans for the Adler Planetarium and the Shedd Aquarium were well under way. And to the south, in Jackson Park, the old Fine Arts Building of glorious memories was being remodeled and restored for the Museum of Science and Industry founded by Julius Rosenwald.

A Century of Progress—Chicago's 1933 World's Fair—was organized as an Illinois corporation, not for profit, under the trusteeship of eighty of Chicago's most influential citizens, and work was begun with characteristic energy on the vast project.

With the Columbian Exposition as a model, and with the permanent buildings in Grant Park of a classic design, it might have been expected that the architects of A Century of Progress Exposition would have followed the conventional lines.

On the contrary, they did just the opposite, and in a way which made Chicago gasp. The Columbian Exposition of forty years before, reviewing as it did the past, was housed appropriately in buildings of the golden age of architecture. A Century of Progress Exposition, it was determined, must be more than a historic pageant. It must depart from tradition and express creatively the spirit of the new age. It must tear away the veil that shrouds the future.

Never before has a World's Fair been planned with such an extraordinary viewpoint as this. Its very opening was to be in keeping with its

(*Courtesy, Curtis Lighting, Inc.*)

Director's room in the Administration building—a remarkable room, wonderfully effective
with lighting.

PRESIDENT
A Century of Progress
CHICAGO'S
· 1933 ·
WORLDS FAIR

RUFUS C. DAWES

Mr. Dawes, president of A Century of Progress Exposition, Chicago's (1933) World's Fair, was born in Marietta, Ohio, July 30, 1867, the son of General Rufus R. and Mary (Gates) Dawes. It was one of his ancestors who accompanied Paul Revere on his famous ride. Mr. Dawes was graduated with the degree of Bachelor of Arts from Marietta College in the class of 1886, and received his Master's degree in 1889. In 1931 he was awarded the honorary degree of Doctor of Laws by Northwestern University.

His business life has been spent largely in organizing and managing public utility companies. He is president of Dawes Brothers, Inc., and of the Metropolitan Gas and Electric Company, and was formerly president of the Union Gas and Electric Company, the Central Indiana Gas Company, the New York and Richmond County Gas Company, the Seattle Lighting Company, and many other organizations. In public life Mr. Dawes has a distinguished record of service. He was a member of the Illinois State Pension Laws Commission in 1918 and 1919; a delegate to the State Constitutional Convention of 1920; adviser to the American experts who prepared the Dawes Plan of reparations settlement; and assistant to Owen D. Young, first agent of general reparations. Since 1927 Mr. Dawes has devoted most of his time and energy to the World's Fair, and it is under his administration that the Aladdin City on the Lake front has sprung up, a miracle of beauty, and the forerunner of a new age. He has served also as president of the Board of Education of his home city, Evanston. Mr. Dawes is a member of the Chicago, Commercial, University, Glenview Country, and Evanston Country clubs.

He was married June 3, 1893, to Helen B. Palmer of Washington Court House, Ohio.

theme. In 1893, the public looked on with amazement as the Columbian Exposition was started in motion by President Cleveland, pressing an electric button in the White House nearly a thousand miles away—a wonder in those days when electricity was only beginning to come into its own. A beam of light from the star Arcturus, launched into space forty years before, to be caught by a silenium cell, was to start the machinery of A Century of Progress Exposition in motion. A comparison between the two methods is in itself significant of how far civilization marched in the four decades necessary for that ray of light to reach the world.

At the beginning of that era, the completion of which the Exposition celebrates, man was groping blindly for those laws which would enable him to mold the forces of nature to his use and comfort. Today his mastery over those forces are evident in new means of transportation, of communication, of manufacturing processes, new methods of fighting disease, and new products that make our lives more comfortable and safe. Today the laboring man can enjoy luxuries that were, a century ago, beyond the conception of even kings.

Air view showing on the left a replica of Fort Dearborn, one of Chicago's most thrilling historical monuments. Near here, in 1812, the brave inhabitants of the Fort were massacred by Indians. On the right is the Lincoln group which includes replicas of the historical buildings, as well as relics, associated with the martyred President.

The object of A Century of Progress Exposition is to tell in a vivid way the story of the discoveries and inventions, their application, and the transformation they have wrought all around us.

Man himself has set the stage for this great spectacle. Every foot of the enchanted garden on which the Aladdin City stands was until very recently deep below the surface of Lake Michigan. The site is easily accessible. Suburban railways near the entrance can handle 50,000 persons an hour, motor buses, 20,000 an hour, while elevated and surface lines running within a few blocks of the grounds can carry 1,000,000 passengers

CHARLES E. DE LEUW

Mr. De Leuw, consulting engineer and president of Charles De Leuw and Company, was born in Jacksonville, Illinois, July 3, 1891, and is the son of Oscar Anthony and Bessie Mary (Tribbey) De Leuw. He received his B. S. (Bachelor of Science) degree in 1912 and his C. E. (Civil Engineer) degree in 1916 at the University of Illinois. From 1908 to 1916 he was engaged on municipal, railroad, and reclamation engineering projects, and later, as a member of the engineering firm of Kelker, De Leuw and Company, in various civil engineering and transportation projects in New York, Chicago, Los Angeles, Baltimore, St. Louis, and other cities. In 1930 the firm name was changed to Charles De Leuw and Company, consulting engineers. Since August 1, 1930, Mr. De Leuw has been assistant chief engineer of the Bureau of Subways for the City of Chicago.

He served on the Mexican Border in the First Illinois Cavalry in 1916 and as 1st Lieutenant and Captain of the 4th United States Engineers from May, 1917, to January, 1919. He actively participated in three major engagements in France during the World War and was awarded the Distinguished Service Cross and the Belgian Ordre de la Couronne. He is a member of the American Society of Civil Engineers, American Society of Military Engineers, and other technical societies.

a day. Within the grounds, trucks of the semi-trailer type, and a fleet of motor coaches offer the visitor the choice of a high-speed arterial route or more leisurely sight-seeing tours.

GENERAL MOTORS BUILDING AT A CENTURY OF PROGRESS

Here, for the first time, illumination takes the place of paint and bas-relief. The lighting engineers have worked to produce marvelous effects. First of all, one must understand that most buildings of the 1933 World's Fair are windowless. They have no natural light, but are illuminated day and night by electricity. The great halls, rotundas, and galleries are embellished with luminous panels of colored fabric, glass, and reflecting metal, in keeping with the modern architecture of these buildings. Many of the larger rooms are illuminated from sources entirely concealed. Certain rooms are flooded with light coming from "pin-hole" openings in the walls and ceilings. Neon illumination has been widely used, but not in the manner associated with the ordinary use of neon in shop window signs. No exposed tubes are employed; they are concealed behind grills and metallic planes so as to afford the rich glow of this type of lighting without the sharp effects generally associated with it. In some cases, several overlapping silhouettes or grills are used to heighten the illusion of texture and depth.

Thus, in the large, high-ceilinged, six-sided Communications Hall of the Electrical Science Group, hundreds of small metallic jewels have been attached to the lower side of the radiating ceiling beams. Concealed behind a panel at the hub of this design is a battery of slowly rotating light projectors. The light beams strike these jewels, those near the hub picking up the light first, so that there is a constantly expanding or radiating action from the hub to the circumference. This design is continued down the walls to the floor. At the entrance to the hall is a colored light pattern, emblazoned on the floor, apparently in rainbow-tinted tile, but actually by projection from the ceiling above.

Floodlighting of the exteriors, as commonly conceived, is conspicuous by its absence. Practically all exterior illumination is in color, the colors being chosen to enrich the pigments used to embellish the buildings in the daytime. Another novelty is the shimmering effects on the walls, such as is produced by the reflection of the sun's rays on rippling water. Water is actually used for these effects, and by its agitation, patterns of various forms

Electricity's wizardry is unfolded in this sickle-shaped group of buildings called the Electrical Group at A Century of Progress. Embellished with hanging gardens, steel cypress trees, electric cascades and fountains, gilded pylons and paved terraces, this structure—1,200 feet long by 300 feet wide—presents the last word in modern architectural phantasy.
Raymond Hood, architect.

are produced which, to say the least, are as mysterious as they are bewildering.

To amaze and delight the Exposition visitor and to give him a glimpse into the future, the engineers have contrived spectacular Aurora Borealis and fog effects made possible by cascades of chemical vapor released from airplanes at an altitude of 1,000 feet, and illuminated in color as they fall, by army-type searchlights similar to those installed at Niagara Falls.

As a crowning diadem of light, the Hall of Science tower has been studded with "electric jewels," converging in a solid mass at the apex. Actually, these jewels are small projectors, each throwing a high candlepower beam either north, south, east, or west. At a distance of a thousand feet or more, these jewels merge in a blaze of color which is effective for several miles.

A simple but spectacular and entirely new device is employed on the towers and pylons of the General Exhibits Building, which, coated with bright, corrugated metal, permit a play of light from hidden sources near the ground, so as to create hundreds of bright horizontal color lines, one color alternating with another, and running from top to bottom.

The sensational flaming arc ladder; a flaming Niagara, cascading down the walls of the Electrical Building's great court; electric fountains in rainbow hues, and mysterious serpentine lights creeping along the flower beds and among the shrubs are among some of the other unique lighting effects which express the spirit of the Fair.

Appropriately enough, the first completed unit of the Exposition was the replica of old Fort Dearborn, which stands in Leif Ericson drive at 26th street, almost on the site of the massacre of 1812 in which almost the entire garrison of the original fortress perished.

Time is turned back a century when one steps through the massive log gate into the stockaded enclosure. Double rows of log palisades, five and ten feet in height are so arranged that the block houses command not only the space without the four walls, but also that between the palisades. An enemy scaling the outer barrier would only find himself in a *cul de sac* which could be swept at every point by rifle or cannon.

At the northeast and southwest corners of the inclosure stand block-houses, their topmost points of vantage reached by ladders. From slits like those let into the walls, soldiers once leveled their guns. To the left of the entrance gate are the soldiers' barracks, and at right angles and on opposite sides of the parade ground are the officers' quarters, two stories high with shingled roofs. On the east side, just south of the building which housed the supplies, are the commanding officer's quarters. Between the supply building and the northeast blockhouse is the powder magazine. In the center of the grounds the American flag flies from a lofty mast.

Materials for the original fort were easily obtained. But for the repro-duction much study and effort were required. Norway pines were brought from Wisconsin to furnish logs for the stockades. Stone that had laid in the open for many years until it was thoroughly weathered, was used for the fireplaces. Hammered iron hinges were especially blacksmithed for the doors and gate. Sheets of glass as full of flaws as possible were chosen to give semblance to the crude little window panes of a century ago. The fort

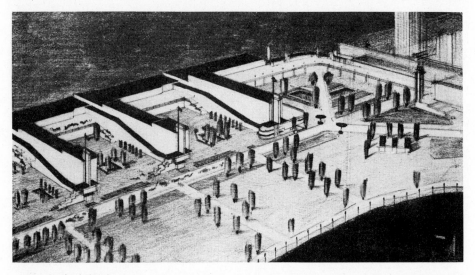

The General Exhibits group, designed by Harvey Wiley Corbett. Facing the lagoon formed by Northerly Island and Lake Michigan, this group comprises a series of pavilions each housing exhibits of a separate branch of industry.

L. PHILIP DENOYER

Mr. Denoyer, president Denoyer-Geppert Company, publishers of visual instruction aids, was born in Milwaukee, Wisconsin, December 12, 1875, and is the son of William and Lucy (Venema) Denoyer. He graduated from the State Teachers College at Oshkosh, Wisconsin, in 1899, received his A. B. (Bachelor of Arts) degree at Lawrence College in Appleton, Wisconsin, in 1901, and was a graduate student of the University of Chicago, 1908-1909. He was a teacher at the high school in Rock Island, Illinois, 1904-1906, was principal of high schools at Washburn, Wisconsin, until 1907, and at Urbana, Illinois, until 1908, and was professor of geography and geology at the State Teachers College in LaCrosse, Wisconsin, 1909-1913. On June 11, 1903, he married Flora Havighurst (died February 24, 1929), of Mt. Pleasant, Iowa, and there is one daughter, Muriel M. On March 8, 1930, he married Xenia M. Bilhorn of Chicago.

Mr. Denoyer has been president and managing editor of the Denoyer-Geppert Company of Chicago, well-known publishers of maps, charts, globes, atlases, and anatomical models for schools, colleges, hospitals, homes, etc., since 1916. He is the author of Outline of Commercial Geography (1912), Teacher's Manual for Globes (1929), and co-editor of several other teacher's manuals. He is the inventor of a new type of blackboard outline maps known as Lecturer's Charts, and has made many improvements in map rail, globe mountings, etc. The maps he has assisted in editing comprise history maps from the dawn of civilization to the present, including such subjects as changes in the distribution of population, immigration, slavery, elections, suffrage, and geography maps depicting political divisions, topography, rainfall, population density, and related subjects.

For about fifteen years, Mr. Denoyer has conducted adult Bible classes in various churches, mostly with groups of men. He has been president of the Rogers Park Sunday Evening Club, Exhibitors' Association of the National Education Association, Lawrence Alumni Club of Chicago, and the Public Welfare League of LaCrosse, Wisconsin. He is a life member of the Chicago Geographic Society and of the Art Institute of Chicago, a member of the American Geographical Society of New York City, and a charter member of the Illinois Academy of Sciences. His principal recreations are motoring, travel and golf—a member of Mission Hills Country Club.

is furnished with antiques and objects of historical interest, many of which have been loaned by the Chicago Historical Society.

Another reminder of the past, set amid twentieth century surroundings, is the Lincoln group, which includes replicas of the log cabin in which the martyred President was born; Lincoln's boyhood home in Indiana; the Lincoln-Berry general store and the Rutledge Tavern in New Salem, Ill., and the Chicago Wigwam in which Lincoln was nominated for the presidency.

The "Sky Ride," one of the spectacular features of Chicago's 1933 World's Fair—A Century of Progress Exposition. Two steel towers, 600 feet high and 2,000 feet apart connected by cables at the 200-foot level, carry rocket cars which shoot through the air at high speed.

Two buildings of outstanding interest are the Mayan Temple, a reproduction of the famous nunnery at Uxmal, one of the finest examples of pre-European culture in America, and the Golden Pavilion of Jehol, a reproduction of China's finest Lama temple. The material for the latter building—28,000 pieces of wood—was brought to Chicago for Vincent Bendix by the Swedish explorer, Sven Hedin. The Pavilion is colored in red lacquer and gold and crowned with a double-decked roof covered with copper shingles finished in pure leaf gold. Inside is a priceless collection of Chinese and Buddhist treasures.

The centerpiece of the Exposition's exhibit scheme is the impressive Hall of Science on the edge of the lagoon. A spacious interior courtyard, picturesque terraces, ramps, pylons, and a lofty tower from which the

(*Kellogg Photo*)

JOSHUA D'ESPOSITO

Mr. D'Esposito, consulting engineer, was born in Sorrento, Italy, August 18, 1878, the son of Antonio and Luisa Marie (di Pontecorvo) D'Esposito. He was educated at the Royal Nautical Institute of his native city, and came to the United States in 1898, working as a machine shop apprentice. In 1904 he entered the service of the Pennsylvania Railroad as a draughtsman. He became an American citizen in 1907, and by 1913, when he came to Chicago to initiate the Union Station project, had advanced to the position of assistant to the chief engineer.

His work on the Union Station was interrupted during the war, when he was summoned to Washington as assistant manager of the Emergency Fleet Corporation of the U. S. Shipping Board. In 1919, however, he returned to Chicago and resumed the project, which was completed in 1925. As consulting engineer for the Chicago Daily News Building, he was the instigator of air rights exploitation in this city, the Daily News building being Chicago's first commercial structure to be erected over a railroad right of way. He did the engineering work also on the spectacular Sky Ride, the principal amusement enterprise of A Century of Progress Exposition, consisting of two 620-foot steel towers, one on Northerly Island, the other on the mainland, between which "rocket" cars are operated over cables. Mr. D'Esposito has completed the plans for the proposed Consolidated Station, concentrating the freight and passenger terminals of the railroads now using the Grand Central, the La Salle street, and the Polk street stations. More recently he proposed the electrification of 50,000 miles of trunk lines in the United States, to be financed by a $3,000,000,000 Federal bond issue, as a means of furnishing employment to thousands of men and leading the country out of the depression. He is a member of the American Society of Civil Engineers, the American Railway Engineering Association, the Western Society of Engineers, the Union League, Engineers, and Illinois Golf clubs.

Mr. D'Esposito was married August 18, 1908, to Katherine Von Olnhausen of Pittsburgh. There are three children, Louise, Joshua, and Julian.

The Lincoln group, which includes replicas of his birthplace, the Indiana cabin of his boyhood, the Lincoln-Berry general store, the Rutledge Tavern in New Salem, Illinois, and the Chicago Wigwam, where the Republican Convention of 1860 nominated Abraham Lincoln for the presidency of the United States.

mellow notes of a carillon sound the passing hours, make this building an enchanting place for visitors.

An ornate bridge leads across the lagoon to the Electrical Group, which extends nearly a quarter of a mile along Northerly Island and comprises the Radio, Communications, and Electrical buildings. Hanging gardens, steel trees, and unique lighting and landscaping effects add to the interest of this strikingly modern group.

The Travel and Transport Building, windowless, and nearly a block and a half long, is so lofty and spacious that a cross section of an ocean liner may be installed under its roof. Locomotives and multiple-motored trans-

Corner of the replica of the Golden Pavilion of Jehol—finest existing example of Chinese Lama architecture—at A Century of Progress. The entire pavilion is a marvel of Chinese ingenuity, made of more than 20,000 parts cunningly joined together by dovetail joints and dowels and without the use of a single nail. The replica was built by Chinese craftsmen under the direction of Dr. Sven Hedin, eminent Swedish explorer, and is an exact reproduction of the famous Golden Pavilion which was built in 1767 at Jehol, the summer home of the Manchu emperors. Dr. Hedin was commissioned by Vincent Bendix to bring this elaborately beautiful structure to Chicago as a World's Fair exhibit.

THE "FUNNIES" IN THE MIDWAY, THE AMUSEMENT AREA OF A CENTURY
OF PROGRESS

THE HEAD OF "BOZO," ONE OF THE FEATURES OF THE MIDWAY

port planes seem dwarfed by its vast proportions. The dome of the Capitol at Washington is 135 feet in diameter; that of St. Peter's at Rome, 137 feet. The dome of the Travel and Transport building, hung by "sky hooks" at the height of a twelve-story structure, has a clear interior diameter of 206 feet. From the tops of twelve steel towers built in a circle, cables run like threads of some giant spider web, supporting the roof.

The Hall of States, partly enclosing a spacious courtyard and sunken garden, faces the Federal Building with its 75-foot dome and three triangular towers, each 150 feet in height, and representing respectively the administrative, legislative, and executive branches of the Government.

THE HALL OF STATES AND THE FEDERAL BUILDING

(*Moffett-Russell Photo*)

ALBERT W. DILLING

Mr. Dilling, consulting engineer and special counsel, was born in Salt Lake City, Utah, January 17, 1892, and is the son of William Ferdinand and Kristine (Huseby) Dilling. After graduating from the Crane Technical High School in 1909, he completed a special three-year course in civil engineering at Armour Institute of Technology, and he received his LL.B. (Bachelor of Laws) degree at the Kent College of Law in 1917. He was admitted to the Illinois bar in the same year, after which he took special work at the University of Chicago.

Mr. Dilling was associated with the engineering department of the Chicago, Milwaukee and St. Paul Railroad (now Chicago, Milwaukee, St. Paul and Pacific Railroad) from 1912 to 1917 and was field engineer for the Universal Portland Cement Company from 1917 to 1920; engineering assistant to commissioner of public works, City of Chicago, from February to December in 1920, in charge for City of $110,000,000 Union Station development; also acting engineer of bridges, City of Chicago. He was appointed chief engineer of the Sanitary District of Chicago in December, 1920, and served for two years, during which time he was in charge of projects costing over $100,000,000, including design and construction of new works. He has been in private practice in engineering and in special counsel work since 1922. He was also supervising engineer for the West Park Commission of Chicago during 1927 and 1928. He is a member of the American Association of Port Authorities, American Society of Civil Engineers, Western Society of Engineers, American, Illinois State and Chicago Bar associations, and Delta Chi Fraternity. He is a member of the Chicago Athletic Association, and his recreations are travel, gardening, and motoring.

On August 12, 1918, he married Elizabeth Eloise Kirkpatrick, of Chicago. They have two children, Kirkpatrick and Elizabeth Jane.

CHICAGO'S CHURCHES MINISTER TO ALMOST EVERY CREED

Places of Worship Number 1800

BY WALTER R. MEE

Executive Secretary, Chicago Church Federation

METROPOLITAN Chicago, as shown by a recent survey made by the Chicago Church Federation, is 90 per cent church-going. This high percentage is not surpassed by any city of half a million or more population in the United States.

Numerically, the Roman Catholic and combined Protestant groups are about equal in strength, with the individual Catholic churches excelling in size and membership, while the Protestant churches are the largest in number. The Jews also form important religious groups, orthodox and liberal. Approximately 1800 churches, synagogues, and temples are to be found in the Chicago area.

In addition to church buildings, hundreds of other buildings are maintained by the various denominations for service. Protestant churches maintain a magnificent system of hospitals, orphanages, old people's homes, colleges, and universities. The Roman Catholics have similar institutions, in addition to their many convents and parochial schools. Property values of these holdings are doubtless in excess of a quarter of a billion dollars.

In the establishment of churches in Chicago there is glory enough for all. No one denomination can claim all the priorities, though each of the "First" churches has a priority claim in some particulars.

The year of the town's incorporation, 1833, saw the beginnings of the Roman Catholic, Presbyterian, and Baptist churches in Chicago. The Methodist Episcopal and Protestant Episcopal churches were established here soon afterwards. Ten years later came the Second Baptist, the Second Presbyterian, the Canal Street Methodist Episcopal, and the Trinity Protestant Episcopal churches, the second churches of their respective denominations.

In 1843, which might be described as a year of a "church boom," the First Evangelical church and the First German United Evangelical Lutheran church, St. Paul's, also were organized. The former was located at Polk street and what was then Third avenue; the latter at Ohio and La Salle streets.

For the first religious service held in Chicago territory, we shall have to go back about 260 years, to the winter of 1674, when Father Jacques Marquette, a Jesuit missionary priest set up a crude wooden cross outside the crude cabin that formed his shelter, and taught the Indians the significance of Christianity's symbol.

Two years later, Father Claude Allouez, another Jesuit, established himself at a small mission at the mouth of the "River of Wild Onion," but remained only a short time. In 1699, a more successful mission, the Guardian

FIRST PRESBYTERIAN CHURCH, WILMETTE, ILLINOIS.
Childs & Smith, architects.

Angel, was maintained on the north branch of the river by Fathers Francois Pinet and Julien Binneteau. Then there is a gap of many years.

In the modern period, a Baptist minister, the Rev. Mr. McCoy, visiting the village, preached the first sermon to the settlers in 1825. There were three ministers of the Methodist Episcopal church working in Chicago before the arrival as a resident of a minister of any other denomination. The Rev. Jesse Walker came in 1828; the Rev. Stephen R. Beggs was regularly appointed pastor in Chicago in 1831, and the Rev. William See, a local minister who plied his trade while leading Methodist class meetings, was a resident here during the same period.

"Father" Walker, as he was called, had a log cabin at Wolf Point, where he lived and preached and organized a union Sunday school.

Philo Carpenter, a layman, assisted by John Wright and his son, had established a Sunday school, and for months had tried to organize a church, when, in 1833, the Rev. Jeremiah Porter came to Fort Dearborn as an army chaplain. The settlement, including the garrison, numbered at that time about 400, and on June 26, 1833, the First Presbyterian church came into being with a membership of 26, and was the first church incorporated by the state. Services were held in the carpenter shop of the fort, and the first sermon was preached from the text: "Herein is my Father glorified that ye bear fruit."

Congregationalists may well claim a share in this church because its pastor, Mr. Porter, was a missionary of the Congregational faith.

It remained for the Baptists to erect the first frame building used in Chicago as a church. It was a two-story building with a school on one floor and a "meeting house" on the other. Dr. J. T. Temple, a physician, was the builder. The first Baptist pastor, the Rev. Allen B. Freeman, arrived in Chicago, August 16, 1833, and his church, the First Baptist, was formally organized on October 19 of the same year.

Father J. M. St. Cyr, Chicago's first Roman Catholic priest, celebrated his first mass, May 5, 1833, in a log cabin in Lake street near Market. The Rev. J. W. Hallam, first pastor of St. James Episcopal church, preached his first sermon on October 19, 1834. The First Unitarian church was established June 29, 1836. After worshiping for some time in the fort, the Presbyterians built a church at Clark and Lake streets—in the middle of a swamp.

But it would require much space to trace the beginnings of all the denominations which are now strong and growing. Chicago today has some masterpieces of church architecture which compare favorably even with the old-world cathedrals. Outstanding among these are the Gothic chapel on the University of Chicago campus; the Chicago Temple at Clark and Washington streets; and the Fourth Presbyterian church at Delaware place and North Michigan avenue, built at the cost of $750,000. The Oriental school of architecture is represented in the unique Baha'i Temple in Wilmette, as yet uncompleted, where a sort of universal creed, based on the teachings of a Persian philosopher, is expounded. The churches of Christ, Scientist, also have impressive buildings.

Erection by the First Methodist Episcopal congregation of the Temple, Chicago's "skyscraper church," was heralded around the world as one of the most significant events in the religious life of America. This valuable site has been occupied by the congregation since 1838 when the original $600 "First church" building was brought on a scow across the North branch of the Chicago river and placed there. The Temple, together with the ground, is valued at $6,500,000. The steeple, built of translucent material, and illuminated at night, is one of the landmarks of downtown Chicago, and a striking feature of the city's fantastic skyline. One foot higher than the Washington monument, it soars to a height of 556 feet, and the golden cross at its apex was, at the time it was placed there, the highest point in Chicago. The Temple houses the offices of the Chicago Church Federation, and the headquarters of several denominations, notably the Methodists, the Presbyterians, and the Disciples of Christ, are located there.

Two recent events in Chicago's ecclesiastical history stand out as of world importance. The first of these was the elevation of His Eminence, George Cardinal Mundelein of the Chicago Roman Catholic archdiocese. Cardinal Mundelein in his audi-

(*Courtesy, Curtis Lighting, Inc.*)
Illuminated front of the First Methodist Episcopal Church, Oak Park, Illinois. Tallmadge & Watson, architects.

(*Underwood and Underwood Photo*)

GEORGE W. DIXON

Mr. Dixon, president of Arthur Dixon Transfer Company, is one of the outstanding business and civic leaders of Chicago. He was born in Chicago, September 16, 1866, and is the son of Arthur and Annie (Carson) Dixon. He is a member of more than twenty clubs and serves on thirty boards of trustees and directorates. Several years ago he conceived the idea of a churchly edifice to include a place of worship within a large building. This was done and the spire of the Chicago Temple, located at the southeast corner of Washington and Clark Streets, may be seen for miles. He is president, Board of Trustees, First Methodist Church and he has been superintendent of the Sunday School for more than thirty-seven years.

Mr. Dixon is a member of the Lincoln Park Board and Chicago Plan Commission; a director of the Personal Loan and Savings Bank, Butler Brothers, Grand Trunk Western Railway System, Baltimore and Ohio, and Chicago and Connecting Railroad. He was a member of the Illinois Senate, First District, 1902-1907; served on Staff of Governor Yates, rank of colonel; trustee, Northwestern University, American University, and Illinois Wesleyan.

He is president of Wesley Memorial Hospital, Chicago Home Missionary Society, Central Howard Association, and has been president of "Chicago Youth Week Federation" for many years. He is a trustee of the Chicago Historical Society; trustee, Chicago Zoölogical Society; trustee of Chicago's (1933) World's Fair and is chairman of Committee on Progress Through Religion. Member of Phi Kappa Psi Fraternity. Among his clubs are: Hamilton (president, 1909), Union League (vice-president, 1928), Executives, Saddle and Cycle, Casino, Optimist, Rotary, Chicago Athletic, Chicago Yacht, University, Glenview, and Chicago. His chief interests are in civic and church affairs.

Mr. Dixon married Marion E. Martin, of Chicago, March 2, 1903 (died January 4, 1926). Their children are Marion (Mrs. Stanley Zaring), and George W., Jr.

ence with Pope Pius XI and in all his public utterances has attributed his high honor not to his own personal achievements so much as to the benevolence and achievements of the Roman Catholics of Chicago. It was largely through Cardinal Mundelein's efforts that the magnificent seminary, with its library of rare Latin books, and its prim "meeting house," more reminiscent of New England than of Rome, was built at the village of Mundelein.

Another event, and one which will long be remembered, was the Eucharistic Congress of 1926. Deep indeed was the impression made by the thousands who attended the great pageant at Soldier Field by gorgeous vestments worn by the princes of the church; the inspiring music of the massed choirs and the children's choruses; the lovely candle-light service, and the sublimity and ardent religious feeling of it all. The pilgrimage to Mundelein for the final services and the procession of the Eucharist was perhaps the most significant religious demonstration since the Crusades.

Chicago has two world-famed religious organizations which have added greatly to the prestige of the city—The Sunday Evening Club, and Central Church. The former, organized by Clifford W. Barnes, who is still its president and active leader, meets weekly from October to June in Orchestra Hall. It is essentially a strangers' church, conducted for the benefit of transients. Many of America's distinguished preachers, and not a few from other countries, have occupied its platform. Its services are broadcast by radio, and its name has been carried by travelers into far corners of the earth.

Orchestra Hall also is the home of Central Church, where every Sunday morning the Rev. Frederick F. Shannon addresses a congregation founded by David Swing, and ministered to in succession by Newell Dwight Hillis and Frank W. Gunsaulus.

Notable among Chicago's religious institutions are Lincoln Center, the community house on the South side presided over for so long by the patriarchal Jenkin Lloyd Jones; Moody Institute, on the north side, the Bible school established in 1889 by the evangelist, Dwight L. Moody; Garrett Biblical Institute, Chicago Theological Seminary, Western Theological Seminary, and the Presbyterian Theological Seminary.

Chicago is to be congratulated on its truly heroic efforts to maintain churches in the downtown business district. It can no longer be said that churches have chosen the easier way of following the better residential districts while they have neglected the hotel and boarding house population and the thousands of young men and women who have come to the city to study or to enter business.

While many of the older and more substantial members of these congregations have removed to the suburbs, the churches themselves have refused to surrender. Among the churches that are giving excellent and devoted service in the transient neighborhoods are the Second Presbyterian, at 20th street and South Michigan avenue; Immanuel Baptist, at 23d street and South Michigan avenue; St. James Protestant Episcopal, at Cass and Huron streets; New England Congregational, at Delaware place and North Dear-

(Du Bois Studio Photo)

KATHRYN DOUGHERTY (MRS. JOHN S. TUOMEY)

Kathryn Dougherty, president and publisher of Photoplay Magazine and Opportunity Magazine, and one of the best known women executives in the publishing business, was born in Boone, Iowa, daughter of William Edward and Elizabeth (Cunningham) Dougherty. She received her education at the Academy of Our Lady, Chicago, Illinois. Starting in the business world in a clerical capacity, she advanced to the head of the bookkeeping department of Sharp and Smith, surgical instruments, Chicago. This position she left to enter the publishing field. Here she quickly found opportunities for the development and application of her marked abilities. Within a relatively brief period she assumed the administration of three executive offices, secretary, treasurer and business manager. On August, 19, 1932, Miss Dougherty was appointed to succeed the late James R. Quirk as president and publisher of Photoplay Magazine and Opportunity Magazine.

Miss Dougherty has a brilliant record in business organization, accounting, and finance. Perhaps no other woman in America has ever risen to a position of quite similar importance in the publishing business. Yet, in spite of her business duties, her little daughter, Joan, receives her full share of her mother's companionship. Miss Dougherty is also active in society and in church and social service.

On October 25, 1922, she married John Sylvester Tuomey, of Blue Island, Illinois. They have one daughter, Joan Kathryn.

born avenue; Grace Methodist Episcopal, at Locust and North La Salle streets, and the three Roman Catholic churches, one on each side of the city, old St. Mary's, at Ninth street and South Wabash avenue; St. Patrick's, at Desplaines and Adams streets, and Holy Name Cathedral, at North State and East Superior streets.

CHICAGO THEOLOGICAL SEMINARY
Herbert Hugh Riddle, architect.   Harrison B. Barnard, builder.

The Chicago Church Federation which represents nineteen denominations and 850 churches, is one of the achievements in church unity and in the administration of the many interests which the churches have in common but would be unable to carry out if working as separate isolated units. The federation functions through departments and commissions and touches every phase of the city's life, civic, institutional, charitable, and social.

No one can adequately estimate what the churches are doing for Chicago unless account is taken of the various agencies which derive their life and support from them. Of these we simply name a few: The United Charities, hospitals; the religious, educational and social help to reformatory and penal institutions such as the Juvenile Court, the Bridewell, the homes at St. Charles and Geneva; the Salvation Army and the Volunteers of America, the Y. M. C. A. and Y. W. C. A., summer camps, boy scouts and girl scouts, special benefactions at Christmas and Thanksgiving; work for foreigners, Chinese, Japanese, Mexicans and others; the Daily Vacation Bible schools, open air evangelism, and the far-reaching work of the great universities, Chicago and Northwestern, both founded by churches and largely maintained by them and having in connection with them theological seminaries for the training of ministers.

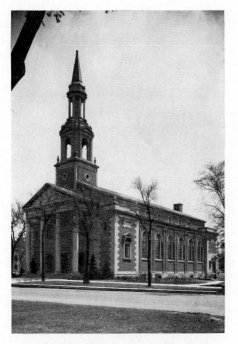

The First Congregational Church,
Evanston, Illinois.
Tallmadge & Watson, architects.

The Grace Lutheran Church of River Forest,
Illinois.
Tallmadge & Watson, architects.

(*Chicago Architectural Photographing Company*)
GARRETT BIBLICAL INSTITUTE
Holabird & Roche, architects.   Avery Brundage Company, general contractor.

DINING "AROUND THE WORLD" IN CHICAGO
Restaurants Where the Dishes of All Nations Are on the Menu
BY JOHN DRURY

Author of "Dining in Chicago" and "Chicago in Seven Days"

A RE you one of those fortunate persons who regard eating as a fine art? Do you get the same esthetic thrill out of a savory dish of *bouilla-baisse a la Marseilles* that you do out of Beethoven's "Moonlight Sonata" or a Whistler nocturne? If so, then Chicago, despite the havoc wrought by prohibition, still has gustatory delights in store for you.

It has been maintained by some that dining, under the restrictions of the noble experiment, has become a lost art. There are chefs who look back with regret on certain game dishes, the preparation of which called for a prolonged bath in wine. Bon vivants will tell you that a French or an Italian table d'hote is impossible without the grape.

To be sure, the older generation doubtless fared better than we do today. The Grand Pacific—now a memory—was famous for its cookery, and John B. Drake's game dinners, with their bewildering courses of quail, partridge, pheasants, reed birds, buffalo steak, bear steak, and venison, have passed into history.

Kinsley's is gone, and Abson's chop house. Rector's, Voegelsang's, the Edelweiss, Stillson's, Mangler's, the Hofbrau, and Old Quincy No. 9 did not survive the prohibition era, and the Tip Top Inn with its picturesque Dicken's room and "Nursery," and its sunny negro waiters, was the last to go.

But despite the casualties, Chicago is anything but a desert from the epicure's point of view. Its elegant hotel dining rooms, its historic res-taurants, and its obscure little cafés and coffee houses of the foreign quar-ters provide dishes as skillfully cooked, as appetizing, and as varied as can be found in any city of the United States—New York, San Francisco, and New Orleans included.

Certain globe-trotters perhaps will be inclined to challenge this state-ment, maintaining that it is impossible to dine anywhere but in Paris. But what kind of folk are they? Usually the kind who tell you superciliously that "they order such things better in Europe," and have never taken the trouble to investigate the gastronomical resources of their home town. They have never ventured out around the corner in search of interesting restaurants and cafés.

Yes, you can dine in Chicago! Even Brillat-Savarin, that prince of epicures, would not be disappointed. He would find everything here to satisfy his sensitive palate and to gratify his curiosity for exotic viands. Nor would he have to go more than three miles in any direction from the Loop to discover the culinary creations of practically every nation in the world— and well cooked, too.

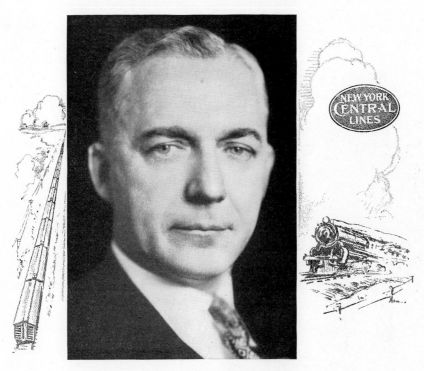

(Blank & Stoller, Inc., Photo)

WILLIAM C. DOUGLAS

Mr. Douglas, assistant general freight traffic manager, New York Central Lines, was born in Chicago, February 2, 1880, son of Thomas and Jane (Tolmie) Douglas. He attended the Chicago public schools. On October 1, 1895, as a boy of fifteen, Mr. Douglas started with the New York Central Lines in Chicago. He has been in continuous service with this organization since that date, advancing step by step in freight traffic departments at Chicago, Detroit, and Grand Rapids, becoming assistant general freight traffic manager, with headquarters in Chicago, on July 1, 1932. The New York Central Lines System includes not only the New York Central Railroad, but the Michigan Central, Big Four, Pittsburgh and Lake Erie, and the Boston and Albany Railroad. In addition there are several affiliated lines.

Mr. Douglas is a member of the following clubs: Union League, Chicago Golf, Mid-Day, Traffic, and Rotary.

He was married in 1919 to Martha Holtz and has one son, William C., Jr.

Chefs, maitres d'hotel, and head waiters who have received their early training in the establishments of his beloved Paris, or elsewhere on the continent, would be his to command. Every dish known to the French and German schools of cookery, which, as everyone knows, are the world's leading schools, would be ready for his approval.

One of the latest of the super-skyscrapers is the LA SALLE-WACKER building. A. N. Rebori and Holabird & Root, associate architects.

Go two miles south of the Loop, for example. Here, almost within shadow of the great white skyscrapers of the machine age, stands a little oriental coffee house, a bit of the Near East, where sultry-eyed Arabs eat *arische mahshi* or sit about and smoke those bubbling Turkish water-pipes. *Arische mahshi,* in case you don't know, consists of grape leaves stuffed with bits of lamb, and rice. Or go to 22nd street and Wentworth avenue, the heart of Chinatown. Here, numerous dining places, decorated in teakwood, mother-of-pearl, red lacquer, and gay with fat lanterns, cluster about the pagodas of the Chinese "city hall" and offer all the exotic viands of the Far East—chicken bird's nest soup, fried shrimps with soy sauce, *chow mien subgum,* kumquats, lichee nuts, almond cakes, and the like.

Go still farther south, to a charming restaurant in the Japanese quarter around historic Lake Park avenue, near 37th street. Dainty Nipponese maids will serve you a typical *sukiyaki* meal—a most appetizing dinner of thin slices of fried beef, fresh vegetables and various Japanese sauces. What's more, it is cooked right at your table, Japanese style. And you won't mind the fact that the Japanese quarter is located in the great south side *black belt,* for the negroes also have restaurants where Southern dishes may be had — fried chicken, beaten biscuits, barbecue sandwiches, Southern hash and red beans and rice. East of the black belt, in the white

EDWARD J. DOYLE

Mr. Doyle, president and director of the Commonwealth Edison Company, was born in Chicago on August 28, 1879. He entered the employ of the old Chicago Edison Company as office boy on March 1, 1896, at the age of 16. After entering business Mr. Doyle continued his education and was elected assistant secretary and assistant treasurer of Commonwealth Edison Company in 1913. In 1914 he was elected secretary and treasurer and in 1924 he became vice-president in charge of finances, securities and claims. On February 25, 1930, he was elected president and director of Commonwealth Edison Company.

Mr. Doyle is a director and officer of numerous companies. He holds memberships in various clubs, including the Chicago Club, Chicago Athletic Association, the Electric Club, and Evanston Golf Club.

He married Bertha Katherine Streff, of Chicago, June 27, 1910, and they have three children, Edward J., Jr., Rosemary K., and Elizabeth Jane.

section along Lake Park avenue, stands a small French restaurant serving the best oysters and soft shell crabs in town.

Most of Chicago's foreign restaurants, however, are located across the river on the near west side, adjoining the tenement areas of South Halsted street. Although placed in dingy environments, they are clean and sanitary, and the waiters are always courteous to strangers. Delicious lamb chops are the *spécialité de la maison* of a quaint Greek café a half block north of Hull House, on Halsted street. Having an old-world atmosphere unlike any other restaurant in town, the café is noted for its little summer garden in the rear.

A block southward is a Mexican restaurant, the rendezvous of consuls and consular attaches of Latin-American countries, of Mexican caricature artists, Hull House residents, and newspapermen. All the native specialties are on the menu: *sopa de arroz, gallina con molle poblado, frijoles refritos, tortillas,* and *chocolate y pan.* For the dishes of sunny Italy you have only to walk two blocks farther south, to the intersection of Halsted and Taylor streets, which is the cross-roads of the west side's "Little Italy." Italian opera singers and politicians are seen almost every night in the many spaghetti restaurants of the quarter. These places all serve an excellent cuisine— *antipasto, ravioli, spaghetti, Napolitano,* roast chicken, veal *al Marsala,* and such items.

Up and down Roosevelt road, the great highway

(*Kaufman & Fabry Co. Photo*)
THE DRAKE TOWER AND THE DRAKE HOTEL
Benjamin H. Marshall, architect.

(*Lewis-Smith Photo*)

JOHN B. DRAKE

Mr. Drake, general manager of the Drake Hotel, was born in Chicago, May 19, 1872, son of John B. and Josephine C. (Corey) Drake. He received his education at the Harvard School, Chicago, St. John's Military Academy, Ossining, New York, and Phillips Academy, Andover, Massachusetts. Upon leaving school, he traveled around the world, his grand tour being rather a ripening process and giving him a first-hand acquaintance with the best of the old-world hotels. Naturally he began his career as an employee of the Grand Pacific, which was owned by his illustrious father, John B. Drake I, where he remained two years. After leaving the Grand Pacific, he was associated for some time with the Illinois Trust and Savings Bank. For several years he was associated with his brother, Tracy, in the managment of the family estate. He combined also with his brother in the building of the Blackstone Hotel and the famous theater of the same name, and ten years later that more ambitious enterprise, the building of the Drake Hotel, which has served to perpetuate the memory of their father. To tourists the world over, both hotels are synonymous with Chicago, the Blackstone perhaps being a bit more intimate and on the order of the European guest house; the Drake being a rival of the leading metropolitan hotels of the world and a rendezvous of Chicago's smart set.

Mr. Drake is a director of the Presbyterian Hopital, member of the Art Institute of Chicago (life), Field Museum of Natural History (life), and Chicago Historical Society. He is a member of Onwentsia and the Chicago Riding clubs. He has quite a reputation as a duck hunter and as president of the Grand Island Club on the Illinois River, he usually gets his limit when shooting the feathered game.

On June 3, 1897, he married Jessie K., daughter of Samuel McClellan, in Middletown, Ohio. Their children are John B. III, William McClellan, Elizabeth, and Katherine.

of the Jewish quarter, you will find the famous kosher restaurants of the city, several of them being frequented by such famed theatrical stars as George Jessel, Eddie Cantor, and Al Jolson. Others cater to Jewish intellectuals and writers. Roumanian dining places are located along 14th street, in the district known as "the Valley," while Lithuanian restaurants serve their native dishes in the vicinity of 18th and South Halsted streets. For true Bohemian dishes, you must go to a place on West 26th street, in "Little Pilsen." Plum dumpling, with cottage cheese; roast duck, with sauerkraut; Prague salami, with raw onions; liver sausage; and the toothsome Bohemian pastries, such as *kolacky* and *buchty smaken,* are all featured on the menu.

Northwest of the Loop, along that busy highway, Milwaukee avenue, stand the restaurants of the Polish and Russian quarters. *Borscht, kasha* and *goluptse* and other Muscovite dishes are served in a workers' cooperative restaurant, operated by the communists. The foods are highly appetizing if a bit heavy; the atmosphere comes up to expectations, and you needn't be afraid that anyone will toss a bomb. Around the corner from this bit of Russia, you will find a Polish dining room. The Poles are very fond of mushrooms, and employ them as a garniture for many, if not most, of their main dishes. In this restaurant you may obtain the favorite Polish dish, *Ztrazki po Nelsonsku*—in other words, beef filet à la Nelson. It is served with sour cream gravy, mushrooms, and potatoes *en casserole.* Delicious pastries, prepared by expert chefs from Krakow, provide you with a wide choice for dessert.

Any survey of Chicago's worthwhile restaurants will convince you that the oldest and most outstanding are of German atmosphere. This is only natural, as the Germans were among the city's pioneers, and still make up one of the largest racial groups in Chicago. Their restaurants, redolent of the grand old days, are located in many parts of the Loop, and also on the near north side. One of the most famous dining parlors in the country is an unpretentious German place in Wells street, between Madison and Washington, its scoured floor, its mahogany bar, its tables and woodwork mellowed by time. Here, every Saturday at noon, Chicago's famous authors and poets regale themselves with generous helpings of *Wiener schnitzel* or *Koenigsberger klops,* seated at a big round table. Celebrities visiting Chicago during the World's Fair of 1893 came here to sample the rare wines, and practically every man of note in the world of letters who has visited the city within the last forty years has been entertained here.

Tucked away in a little side street just south of the Loop is a famous English grill, where, in a typically British atmosphere, one may enjoy his Southdown mutton chops, his juicy steaks or roasts.

Swedish restaurants, with their *smorgasbords,* abound on the North Side in the vicinity of Belmont avenue and Clark street. One must be careful, however, not to fill up on the delicacies laid out on the central table—the salt and smoked fish, the anchovies, and the sardines in oil— for these are only skirmishers; there is much more coming.

TRACY C. DRAKE

Mr. Drake was born in Chicago, September 12, 1864, son of John B. and Josephine C. (Corey) Drake. At the age of thirteen he entered the Vermont Episcopal Institute at Burlington, Vermont, receiving his preparatory education there. The two years spent at this school were followed by a three-year period at Trinity Military Institute, Tivoli, New York, and a four-year collegiate course at Rensselaer Polytechnic Institute, Troy, New York, from which college he received his degree of Bachelor of Science.

Heir to memorable family tradition, established by his father, John B. Drake (the first), it remained for Tracy Drake and his brother, John B., to perpetuate an esteemed name by building the famous Blackstone Hotel, the Drake Hotel (one of North Michigan avenue's architectural gems), the Blackstone theater, and, in association with Benjamin H. Marshall, the Drake Tower, a thirty-story structure adjoining the Drake Hotel on Lake Shore Drive, this being a residential structure, connected with, and served by, the Drake. Drake University of Des Moines, Iowa, at the fiftieth commencement and the semi-centennial celebration of the founding of the University, on June 8, 1931, conferred upon Mr. Drake the honorary degree of Doctor of Laws. He is an enthusiastic sportsman and seldom misses his yearly trip to the Canadian Rockies, with his son, Francis, where he hunts grizzlies, mountain sheep, white goats, deer, and moose. He is a member of the Interfraternity Club, Chicago Athletic Association, Lake Geneva Country Club, and Delta Kappa Epsilon Club of New York.

On January 12, 1893, he married Annie Daughaday, of St. Louis. Their children are Carlos Corey and Francis Augustus.

(*Howe & Arthur Photo*)
THE TWO BLACKSTONES
The Blackstone Theatre in the foreground,
the Blackstone Hotel in the background.
Benjamin H. Marshall, architect.

JOHN DRURY

John Drury, newspaper man, poet, author of "Chicago In Seven Days," "Dining In Chicago" and of the official Century of Progress guidebook to the city, was born in Chicago on August 9, 1898, the son of Michael and Mary (Sullivan) Drury. He graduated from St. Andrew's Roman Catholic School, where he was known as a talented artist. While still young his father, a street car conductor, died. At the age of fourteen he became interested in literature and has been writing ever since. After attending Nicholas Senn High School for two years, he was forced to leave in order to help support his mother and two sisters. He worked in drug stores, factories, bookshops, and department stores and continued his education at Lane Technical Night School.

While working in the book section of Marshall Field & Company he wrote book reviews for the Chicago Daily News and the Chicago Evening Post. During the World War he served on "home guard" duty with the 11th Regiment, Illinois National Guard, under the late Brigadier-General James E. Stuart. Later he became an active member of the poetry renaissance of the 20's, his verse appearing in the numerous poetry magazines of the period. This was later collected in a volume called "Arclight Dusks." After knocking about the world as newspaper man and sailor—Mexico, Brazil, Argentina, Canada, London, New York and Los Angeles—he settled down in his home town, feeling that romance can be found at one's door. His guidebooks to Chicago followed. He worked on the City News Bureau and then joined the staff of the Chicago Daily News. He is a member of the Midland Authors and at one time was librarian of the Press Club of Chicago.

He is married to Marion Neville, daughter of the late James Tilford Neville, veteran circuit court judge of Missouri.

For odd, colorful, and sometimes outlandish eating places, as well as for many of a foreign atmosphere, one must explore the north side "Latin Quarter" in the shadow of "Tower Town." Some of these, of course, are cheap and sordid pseudo-Bohemian gathering places, but the majority of them are worth a visit, especially those occupying the imposing old Gold Coast mansions.

This district also has a Filipino restaurant, as well as a gay dining place specializing in peppery Creole cookery and presided over by one of the Alciatores of New Orleans.

Notables, society people and the *beau monde* in general patronize the dining rooms of the city's world-famous hotels along Michigan boulevard. The foods served here are the best obtainable, and they are prepared by chefs who are past masters of Continental cookery. Numerous restaurants on the "Boul Mich" also attract discriminating diners. Outside of Chicago, along the exclusive north shore, there are many charming tea rooms and other dining places.

But for good, old-fashioned, plain American dishes, of the sort that Carl Sandburg, the Chicago poet, and thousands of other Chicagoans with him, enjoy most, you are directed to "Toothpick Row," that gay plaisance of lunchrooms in Clark street, just south of Madison, in the heart of the Loop. To the student of Americana, these places are interesting because they serve the dishes of an emerging school of American cookery—ham and eggs, Boston baked beans, strawberry shortcake, waffles, watermelon, corned beef and cabbage, baked Idaho potatoes, New England boiled dinner, Denver sandwich, minced pie, Lake Superior whitefish, and a host of others.

Such, briefly, is a survey of the gastronomic possibilities of Chicago. If you have not yet discovered the fine art of dining; if eating to you is just a physical function, then you are missing one of the most pleasurable experiences of living. Study the different kinds of foods and, above all, experiment with foreign dishes. In other words, acquire an epicure's interest in dining. If you do this then you will find one more hobby to increase the joys of living.

Remember, it was Dr. Samuel Johnson, that famous wit of the Cheshire Cheese and stout-hearted devotee of epicureanism, who said: "Some people have a foolish way of not minding, or of pretending not to mind, what they eat. For my part I mind my belly very studiously and very carefully for I look upon it that he who does not mind his belly will hardly mind anything else."

(*Eugene L. Ray, Evanston, Photo*)

WILLIAM A. DYCHE

Mr. Dyche, business manager of Northwestern University, was born in Monroe, Butler County, Ohio, May 25, 1861, son of David R., M. D., and Mary S. (Boyd) Dyche. He attended Northwestern University and received his A. B. (Bachelor of Arts) degree in 1882, his A. M. (Master of Arts), in 1888. He graduated from the Chicago College of Pharmacy in 1886. Mr. Dyche has been a trustee of the University since 1894. He served as mayor of Evanston from 1895 to 1899; was in the drug business in Chicago in 1899; has been business manager of Northwestern since 1903.

Mr. Dyche is characterized by President Walter Dill Scott of the University as being the preserver of the institution just as Dr. John Evans was the founder. The McKinlock Memorial Campus in Chicago was his dream and to a great degree his accomplishment. The development of the fraternity, sorority, and dormitory system is the result of his efforts. Plans for the stadium were formed in his mind. He has been president of the State Bank of Evanston since 1909 and vice-president and chairman of the board of the State Bank and Trust Company since 1919. He is an associate member of the Chicago Real Estate Board. He is a member of Phi Beta Kappa Honorary Fraternity. His clubs are Union League and University (Chicago); University, Glen View, Evanston, and Evanston Country clubs (Evanston). Dyche Stadium was named in his honor by Northwestern University in 1926.

On February 11, 1897, Mr. Dyche married May Louise Bennett, of Evanston, Illinois (died 1923). His children are David Bennett, Ruth Caroline, and George Frederick.

CHICAGO AS THE NATION'S RAILROAD CENTER

Steel Highways Which Radiate From the World's Greatest Rail Center to All Parts of the United States and Canada

BY SAMUEL O. DUNN

Editor, Railway Age, Chairman, Simmons-Boardman Publishing Co.

TRAVELERS rushing through the concourse of the Chicago & North Western terminal station, or waiting for the arrival or departure of trains, often pause for a moment to pay tribute to the "Pioneer," the tiny, but stanch wood-burning locomotive, mounted on a section of "strap" rails.

The Pioneer, which arrived in Chicago on the Steamship Buffalo in October, 1848, and was the first locomotive to pull a train of cars out of the city, links the present with the past, and carries one back to the very beginnings of railroading in the Middle West.

In 1836 a charter was granted to the Galena & Chicago Union Railroad, which was to become the great-great grandfather of the North Western. Galena, situated in the rich lead mining district of Illinois, was at that time a city of considerable importance—of much more importance than Chicago.

A railroad in the '30's was a dubious venture, and so doubtful were the directors of the Galena line regarding its success that they were given an option under the charter of constructing a turnpike instead, from which they could collect toll.

The panic of 1837 caused a setback to both plans, and for several years nothing was done. But in 1846, William B. Ogden, mayor of Chicago, was elected president of the railroad company, and immediately began to revive the project. The line was surveyed the following year, but the undertaking met with opposition. Local merchants had the idea that the railroad would divert trade from the city, and accordingly the city council refused to grant it a right of way within the corporate limits of Chicago. The company was allowed merely to lay temporary rails from the foot of Dearborn street at the river to the terminal at Halsted and Kinzie streets for the transfer of the rolling stock when it should arrive by boat. The "permanent" rails, which in 1848 extended only as far as the Desplaines River, were of wood on the surface of which were laid "straps" of iron three-quarters of an inch thick. Two locomotives, including the Pioneer, and six second-hand freight cars had been acquired, and with this equipment, the Galena & Chicago Union Railroad announced its official opening on November 20, 1848.

A party of about one hundred invited guests—newspaper men, executives of the road, and "distinguished citizens" embarked in gaily decorated cars on the first train trip out of Chicago. Arriving at Desplaines, they saw a farmer, city-bound, who was having difficulties trying to cart a wagonload of wheat over the rough road. Rather in the spirit of fun the wheat

(*Walinger Photo*)

SAMUEL O. DUNN

Mr. Dunn, editor of Railway Age and chairman of the board of Simmons-Boardman Publishing Company, was born in Bloomfield, Iowa, March 8, 1877, and is the son of Samuel W. and Sarah J. (Hedrick) Dunn. After graduating from the Pratt (Kansas) high school in 1894, having previously learned the printer's trade, he pursued a newspaper career. In 1895 he was editor of the Quitman, Missouri, Record; from 1896 to 1900, he was associate editor of the Maryville, Missouri, Tribune; then followed four years on the Kansas City Journal as reporter and editorial writer. In 1904 he came to Chicago and for three years was railroad editor and editorial writer of the Chicago Tribune. In 1907 he became associate and managing editor of Railway Age and since 1911 has been editor of Railway Age Gazette and its successor Railway Age, which is probably the most widely quoted trade magazine in the world, its editorials and articles being reprinted in hundreds of newspapers and magazines. In 1911 he was admitted to the Illinois bar. Since October, 1931, he has been chairman of the board of the Simmons-Boardman Publishing Company, publishers of Railway Age, Marine Engineering, Railway Mechanical Engineer, Railway Engineering and Maintenance, Railway Signaling, Railway Electrical Engineer, and the Boiler Maker, and also president of the American Builder Publishing Corporation, which publishes American Builder and Building Age.

Mr. Dunn is an author and lecturer on transportation subjects, having written the following books: American Transportation Question, 1912; Government Ownership of Railways, 1913; Regulation of Railways, 1918; and numerous articles in national magazines. In 1921 Tufts College conferred upon him the honorary degree of Master of Arts. He is a member of the Union League Club (second vice-president, 1932), Chicago, Traffic, Knollwood Country, Exmoor Country, and Western Railway. His principal recreation is golf.

On March 29, 1899, he married Carrie E., daughter of Mrs. Fayette Smith of Maryville, Missouri, and their children are Fayette Smith, Elizabeth, and Samuel O., Jr.

CHICAGO AND NORTH WESTERN
PASSENGER TERMINAL

CENTRAL STATION

was transferred to the train, and thus the first rail shipment of grain into Chicago took place.

Within a week, thirty carloads of wheat were awaiting shipment at Desplaines, and the farmers of the surrounding territory were quick to take advantage of the new transportation facilities. During its first year of operation, the road's gross earnings were $23,763. Gross earnings for the second year rose to $104,359. Railroading was on its way towards success.

Meanwhile, the road was allowed to enter the city. The first depot, at Canal and Kinzie streets, erected in 1849, was a straggling, onestory frame shack, to which were added later a second story and a cupola. From this cupola, the president of the railroad, with a spyglass, could watch the arrival of the trains, and announce them when they became visible at Austin, for it was not until 1855 that a telegraph line was strung along the right of way.

GRAND CENTRAL STATION

LA SALLE STREET STATION

The second passenger station, a pretentious three-story brick building at Kinzie and Wells streets, was destroyed by the great fire of 1871, and for nine years a wooden shed served the needs of the traveling public. In 1880, the big, red brick terminal station surmounted by the square clock tower, still remembered by many Chicagoans, was erected, but on completion of the new $25,000,000 terminal station at Canal and Madison streets in 1911, the "Wells street depot" was abandoned, finally to be torn down to make way for the palatial Merchandise Mart.

The Illinois Central had its origin in the wild dreams of the State Legislature in the early '30's. These dreams had as their objectives a state-owned railroad system consisting of two trunk lines, one running north and south, dividing the state in equal parts; the other intersecting it midway at right angles. To satisfy the demands of local politicians, construction was begun simultaneously at many points, and Illinois seemed to be entering upon a railroad age. But alas for the dreams! The bubble burst, and the scheme, impractical from the start, was finally abandoned by the State. In 1851, however, the Illinois Central was chartered under private auspices, and the following year, the first trains were in operation between the 12th street terminal and Calumet (now Kensington) station. This right of way permitted the Michigan Central to run its first trains into Chicago in 1852.

Recent electrification of the Illinois Central's suburban lines at a cost running up into millions of dollars has provided Chicago with the swiftest and most efficient suburban service in the world, eliminating the smoke nuisance, and making it possible to run noiseless, smokeless trains between Chicago and the South Shore suburbs at a speed of sixty miles an hour. Plans are under way for the construction of a splendid new Roosevelt road

(*Chicago Architectural Photographing Company*)
UNION STATION
Graham, Anderson, Probst & White, architects. Joshua D'Esposito, consulting engineer.

terminal station, harmonizing in architecture with Field Museum and other permanent structures in Grant Park. Monopoly of the lake front has been surrendered to the city, and a vast area of artificially made land, nearly four miles in extent, beautifully landscaped and boulevarded, now reaches out beyond the tracks.

The railroads, largely, have made Chicago the city it is today, and Chicago, the world's greatest transportation center, is the terminus of almost every railroad entering her gates. For hundreds of thousands of travelers Chicago is the journey's end, or the beginning of another journey.

In all, twenty-two trunk lines, seven belt and switching lines, eight industrial railroads, and four electric lines terminate in Chicago. These forty-odd railroad companies operate 133,427 miles of line, representing more than half the total railroad mileage of the United States.

It is estimated that under normal business conditions between 1,500 and 2,000 passenger trains arrive in or depart from Chicago daily—a train a minute, with a daily passenger traffic in excess of 375,000. The suburban branches alone carry between 150,000 and 200,000 passengers in and out of Chicago every working day.

More than ten per cent of all the freight handled in the United States is loaded and unloaded in the Chicago area, and more than 4,000 industries are served by private tracks.

Chicago's $50,000,000 Union Passenger Terminal Station, a monument of steel and stone, is one of the most magnificent stations of its kind in America, and a fitting gateway to Chicago.

A new development in passenger traffic is the combination air and rail service, by means of which one can travel comfortably by train at night, and transfer to an airplane for a day's journey through the clouds.

Chicago's past development and present growth are due almost entirely to its railroads. The future prosperity of Chicago likewise depends on them.

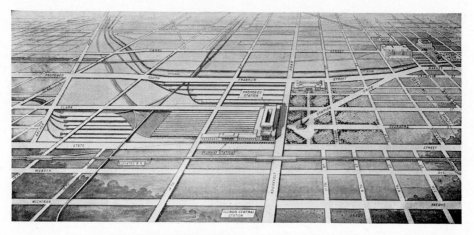

THE PROPOSED SOUTH CENTRAL STATION
Joshua D'Esposito, consulting engineer.

GEORGE A. EDDY

Mr. Eddy, president of The Goss Printing Press Company, patentees and manufacturers of newspaper and magazine printing presses, was born in Chicago, May 24, 1874, son of George Day and Mary Adeline (Charbonneau) Eddy. He attended the grammar and high schools of this city, later taking the business and technical course of Chicago Athenaeum. At the start of his business career, Mr. Eddy was an apprentice machinist with The Goss Printing Press Company for four years and has been with this organization for more than forty years, successively as machinist, chief engineer, secretary, sales manager, vice-president, and now president and general manager. The press manufactured in Chicago by the Goss Printing Press Company is used extensively for the printing of newspapers and magazines.

Mr. Eddy is also president of the R. M. Eddy Foundry Company and vice-president of The Bryant Company, both of Chicago. He is a director of the City National Bank and Trust Company of Chicago. He is a member of the Chicago Athletic Association, Evanston Golf Club, the Country Club of Evanston, Westmoreland Country Club, and the Shawnee Country Club. His favorite recreations are golf and bowling.

He married Ella Benson, June 20, 1906, and their children are Lorraine Adeline and George Albert, Jr.

THE SOUTH PARKS AND THEIR CONTRIBUTIONS TO CHICAGO'S HEALTH, EDUCATION AND ENTERTAINMENT
Where Outdoor and Indoor Activities of All Kinds Are Encouraged

CHICAGO may be said to be bounded on all sides by parks. The South Park System, when completed, will extend continuously from the Chicago River to the Indiana boundary line. The new bascule bridge, spanning the river at its mouth, with its stately north and south approaches, connecting the South Park and Lincoln Park Systems, will in time give the city a 25-mile strip of parkway reaching from the Calumet district to Devon avenue. The West Park System, whose three units, Humboldt, Garfield, and Douglas Parks, are linked together with splendid boulevards, also are connected with the two park systems on the east.

The South Park chain is made up of five large and eighteen small parks, containing in all, 3,500 acres. Within the jurisdiction of this system are 92 miles of boulevard. The new Outer Drive through Burnham Park, most of it built over what was once fifteen feet of water, is one of the longest uninterrupted driveways in America. It runs for eight miles without an intersection to 57th street, carrying the motorist out to Hyde Park in half the time required by other routes.

PART OF NAVY PIER

(Blank & Stoller, Inc. Photo)

HUBBARD H. ERICKSON

Mr. Erickson, proprietor of the Motor Boat Mart, Navy Pier, was born in Chicago, February 27, 1885, son of Daniel and Mathilda Erickson. He was educated at the Alcott Grammar and North Division High schools, the English High School, and Manual Training School of Chicago. Mr. Erickson began as an employee of George B. Carpenter and Company, ship chandlery, in 1905, and was advanced through various positions until he became general manager in 1916. He left this company in 1917 to manufacture marine accessories under the firm name of Hubbard H. Erickson & Company. He is the originator and proprietor of the Motor Boat Mart, Navy Pier, which includes the largest exhibit of motor boats and accessories in the world.

He is a member of the Chicago Association of Commerce, Chicago Association of Credit Men, and the National Association of Engine and Boat Manufacturers. His clubs are Rotary, Lake Shore Athletic, Chicago Yacht, Columbia Yacht, and Itasca Country. His favorite recreation is boating.

On November 28, 1915, Mr. Erickson married Edna Marie Laibach, of Chicago. Their children are Dorothy May and Hubbard H.

Under the very shadows of Michigan avenue's skyscrapers are 200 acres of baseball diamonds, tennis courts, and archery ranges in Grant Park alone. There is not another area of its size in all the world that provides as much free education and entertainment as Grant Park. Here are located the Art Institute, the United States Naval Reserve Armory, Field Museum of Natural History, the Shedd Aquarium, the Adler Planetarium, the Buckingham Memorial Fountain, and Soldier Field.

The great $6,000,000 Stadium—Soldier Field—its classic columns built of reenforced concrete, much of it pre-cast in the form of cut stone, has been built, as was the Parthenon, or the Coliseum of Rome, to endure through the ages. Perpetuating the memory of Chicago's sons who made the supreme sacrifice in the World War, it symbolizes in its classic architecture, in its beauty and its strength, the youth and courage and the will to win—the spirit of the city's young manhood of 1917.

The signing of the Armistice, followed by the war exhibits, the homecomings, the parades and military reviews of the first post-war months brought home to Chicagoans the need not only of erecting a suitable memorial to the hero dead, but of providing a place for the presentation of great spectacles, pageants, and festivals; for athletic events and for the national gatherings which the city attracted annually. This memorial is a U-shaped structure 300 feet wide and 1,000 feet in length, and the site covers approximately 38 acres. The colonnade, which is the distinctive feature of the edifice, rises 110 feet above the field. At either side of the open north end it terminates in monumental plazas on which are provided pedestals for heroic sculptured figures. The south end is crowned with a

SOLDIER FIELD, on the lake front, where many interesting events take place, including Army shows, music festivals, athletic games, and operas.

(Kaiden-Keystone Studios Photo)

THURLOW G. ESSINGTON

Mr. Essington was born in Streator, Illinois, May 19, 1886, son of John and Mary (Gault) Essington. As a boy in Streator he grew up with the idea that he would be a lawyer. In 1903, after his graduation from the Streator Township High School, he attended the University of Illinois and received his A. B. (Bachelor of Arts) degree in 1906. He graduated, cum laude, from the University of Chicago Law School in 1908. Immediately he went back to the "home town" to start practicing law. Later he formed the partnership of Essington and Heflin, which later became Jones, Essington and Heflin. At the age of twenty-nine he was elected City Attorney of Streator. He served successively as City Attorney for two years (1915-1917), as Mayor of Streator for two years (1917-1919), and as a member of the Illinois Senate for eight years (1919-1927) with an outstanding record. In 1923 came the climax of his brilliant political career when he was selected as a candidate for the Republican nomination for Governor of the State, the youngest man ever to run in Illinois for that office. In 1926 he came to Chicago, and, with George B. McKibbin, formed the partnership of Essington and McKibbin.

Mr. Essington is a member of the American Bar Association, the Illinois State Bar Association (chairman of the Committee on Legislation), the Chicago Bar Association (member of the Committee on Amendment of the Law), the La Salle County Bar Association, the Chicago Law Club, Delta Kappa Epsilon, Phi Delta Phi, and Phi Beta Kappa. He is also a member of the University Club of Chicago, The Electric Club, Union League Club (first vice-president, 1931), Economic Club, and the Flossmoor Country Club, and of the Masonic lodges and B. P. O. Elks. While living in Streator he was a member of the Presbyterian Church. He is now a member of the vestry of St. Paul's Episcopal Church in Chicago. In his spare time Mr. Essington plays golf, and likes to hunt, fish and ride horseback. He is an enthusiastic philatelist (stamp collector), and a collector of Indian relics. In addition, he has many civic interests.

On February 26, 1913, Mr. Essington married Davie Hendricks, of Madisonville, Kentucky. They have one daughter, Elizabeth.

Greek temple. Permanent seats in the east and west stands accommodate 75,000 people, while temporary seats increase the capacity to 150,000. Soldier Field has been the scene of such spectacular events as the Eucharistic Congress, the Dempsey-Tunney fight, football games, the United States Army tournaments, the post-Olympic athletic carnival, and the Chicago-land music festivals.

Burnham Park, the site of the Century of Progress Exposition, is only a part of a $100,000,000 lake front extension, made possible after many years of litigation. Grant Park had been built up of cinders and refuse from the great Chicago fire, but Burnham Park, like the new Lincoln Park extension, encroaches on the dominion of Lake Michigan, and establishes a new shore line. It is a tract of 1,774 acres, of which 503 acres represent enclosed water area. The lagoon thus formed gives Chicago its first straightaway course for outboard motorboat racing, furnishing the city with an ideal stage for water carnivals. The six-mile strip of reclaimed land, of which Burnham Park is a part, will shortly take on the aspects of Deauville and the Lido. Three new bathing beaches are to be located along the shore.

Jackson Park, a 553-acre playground, offers facilities for almost every kind of outdoor sport. Originally laid out by Frederick Law Olmstead of Boston, it had been only slightly improved at the time it was offered as a site for the World's Columbian Exposition in 1893. Today it is described as "the most beautiful piece of landscape development in the world."

Here, in 1902, was opened the first municipal golf course in America. The first public baseball diamonds and tennis courts were those of Jackson Park. Golfers now have access to one nine-hole and one eighteen-hole

GENERAL VIEW OF THE MICHIGAN BOULEVARD GARDEN APARTMENTS
Chicago housing project, erected for negroes by the Julius Rosenwald Fund.
Ernest A. Grunsfeld, Jr., architect.

(*Eugene Hutchinson Photo*)

CHARLES HULL EWING

Mr. Ewing, in the real estate and investment business, was born at Randolph, Cattaraugus County, New York, July 11, 1868, son of Robert Finley and Aurelia (Culver) Ewing, of early Colonial ancestry. In the paternal line were Samuel Finley, his great uncle, a president of the College of New Jersey (Princeton University) and Samuel Finley B. Morse, inventor of the electric telegraph. Mr. Ewing obtained his academic education at Oberlin College and later, at Yale University, where he graduated with an A. B. degree in 1893. During another year he studied at the Northwestern University Law School, after which he spent two years at Moorhead, Mississippi, as manager of the Moorhead Stave Company. For thirty years he was chief assistant to Miss Helen Culver in the management of her business interests, and, as such, also manager of the Helen Culver Fund of the University of Chicago from 1896 to 1909.

Since 1903, Mr. Ewing has been engaged in the real estate and investment business, controlling valuable property holdings in Illinois and Florida, and being interested in several substantial developments in the latter state. He was one of the organizers and for twenty years, from 1906 to 1926, was secretary and treasurer of the Southern Gypsum Company, Inc., of North Holston, Virginia, and is now a director of The Beaver Products Company of Virginia, Inc., its successor, a subsidiary of Certainteed Products Corporation. Mr. Ewing is also a director of the First National Bank of Lake Forest, Illinois, and of the First National Company, of Bradenton, Florida. He has been a trustee of Hull House Association since 1920, and is a life member of the Geographic Society of Chicago, which he served as president for three terms (1924-1926, 1928-1929), and during his administration established the society's endowment fund. He is also a life member of the Art Institute of Chicago, the Field Museum of Natural History, and the Press Club of Chicago; a member of Phi Beta Kappa, Phi Delta Phi, and the Elihu Club of Yale; and an honorary member of the Imperial and Royal Geographic Society of Persia. He is a member of the Chicago Real Estate Board, the National Association of Real Estate Boards, and the Chicago Historical Society. He is a member of the Yale Club of Chicago, the University Club, the City Club, the Cliff Dwellers, and the Oberlin Men's Club of Chicago, of which he is the founder; also the Onwentsia and Knollwood Clubs of Lake Forest, Illinois. He is also a member of the Sarasota Country, Beach and Sarasota Yacht clubs, in Florida. His favorite recreations are horseback riding, tennis, golf.

Mr. Ewing was married on October 8, 1906, to Mary, daughter of Dr. Thomas H. Everts of Minneapolis, and they have two daughters, Katherine Everts and Helen Culver.

course, while scores of baseball and tennis games are in progress simultaneously every Saturday and Sunday during the Summer. The site of the German Building of World's Fair days is occupied by two lawn bowling courts. The Jackson Park bathing pavilion overlooks 2,000 feet of sandy beach. A snug yacht harbor accommodates the fleet of the Jackson Park Yacht Club. The basin in the Midway, the World's Fair street of all nations, is flooded during the Winter for skating, hockey, and curling, and is bordered by an equestrian path.

Jackson Park has recently motorized its lagoons. The old row-boats have been replaced by electric launches, with a radio in each.

While the "White City" lives today only in memory, a few relics of its glory still remain. On the Wooded Island may be seen the Japanese buildings, rather pathetic and weatherbeaten after forty years of exposure, and greatly in need of repair. The Santa Maria, a replica of the Columbus flagship, rides at anchor in the harbor, her companions, the Nina and the Pinta, having fallen into decay. Daniel French's golden statue, "The Republic," marks the site of the Administration Building. Most important, however, is the old Fine Arts Building, one of the most beautiful specimens of Ionic architecture in the modern world, now restored in permanent steel, stone and brick as the home of the Industrial Museum.

Of commanding historic interest is the old Cahokia Courthouse transplanted on the Wooded Island from the village of Cahokia in St. Clair County, Illinois, where it was built in 1716, and over which the flags of France, Great Britain, and the United States have flown. The Parks' most beautiful piece of statuary is Lorado Taft's Fountain of Time.

Washington Park, with its sweeping meadows, is another popular playground. In addition to baseball diamonds and tennis courts, roquet courts, and archery butts, the Park has a cricket field and a green for lawn bowling. Here the original Lawn Bowling Club, which has revived the fifteenth century English game of bowls, has its headquarters. The model yacht basin at 51st street is the scene of weekly Summer regattas in which these small craft compete. The lagoon is available for such sports as fly-casting, fishing, skating, and curling, according to the season. The floral displays of the Washington Park conservatory and rose garden are admired and enjoyed by thousands. The new 124th Field Artillery armory is one of the show places of the city.

Among the more important small parks are Marquette Park of 322 acres, with its baseball grounds, tennis courts, golf course, skating pond, and finely equipped field house, and Calumet Park of 174 acres, with its popular bathing beach.

The eighteen small parks which complete the South Park System are highly organized educational and social centers. The field houses, with their indoor and outdoor gymnasiums, their dance halls, work shops, and assembly rooms, provide entertainment and recreation for 14,000,000 boys and girls and their parents annually.

(Blank and Stoller, Inc., Photo)

NEWTON C. FARR

Mr. Farr, realtor and civic leader, was born in Chicago, December 25, 1887, son of Marvin A. and Charlotte (Camp) Farr. He attended Harvard School of Chicago, later graduating from the Lawrenceville School of New Jersey in 1905. In 1909 he graduated from Cornell University, receiving his degree in Civil Engineering, and from that year until 1912 was an engineer with the Raymond Concrete Pile Company. In 1912 he entered the real estate business with his father, the late Marvin A. Farr, and now operates under the name of Farr and Company, specializing in the construction and financing of business buildings and appraisals. When the United States entered the war Mr. Farr enlisted in the Signal Corps, United States Army, in 1917. He was commissioned a second lieutenant in March, 1918.

Mr. Farr is treasurer of Hughes Oil Company; president and treasurer of Onekema Canning Company; chairman of Debenture Bondholders Committee of American Bond and Mortgage Company; president of the Chicago Real Estate Board, 1930, (vice-president, 1922-1925, general chairman Appraisal Committee, 1929); chairman of Real Estate Division, Chicago Association of Commerce, 1929; president of the Better Business Bureau, 1931; director of Investors Protective Bureau; and a member of Mayor Cermak's Advisory Commission. He is chairman of the Board of Managers of Hyde Park Y. M. C. A.; treasurer and trustee, Kenwood Church; trustee, Kenwood Plymouth Church Endowment Fund; trustee, Chicago Sunday Evening Club; member, Chicago Red Cross Citizens' Committee for Disaster Relief; trustee, Faulkner School; director, Manistee County Agricultural Society; member Executive Committee, Illinois Humane Society; member, Board of Governors, Delta Phi fraternity; member of the University Club and director of its Banjo Club for more than fifteen years. He is a member of the Interfraternity Club, The Tavern Club, the Sunset Ridge Country Club (vice-president in 1929), the Chicago Motor Club, Realty Club of Chicago, Cornell Club of New York, the American Legion, Indian Hill Country Club, Chicago Historical Society, the Art Institute of Chicago, the Field Museum, Civic Music Association, and the Isaac Walton League. He was president of the Cornell Club of Chicago in 1922; vice-president Cornell Alumni Corporation, 1927; member Cornell Society of Engineers, and Cornell University Athletic Association. His principal hobbies are music and golf.

STORY OF ALL LANDS AND ALL AGES IN CHICAGO'S WONDER HOUSE

Educational Opportunities Offered by Field Museum of Natural History

BY STEPHEN C. SIMMS
Director, Field Museum of Natural History

CHICAGO possesses, in Field Museum of Natural History, one of the four or five leading scientific museums of the world. Treasures and knowledge gleaned from the most distant parts of the world, covering both modern times and long past ages, are brought to the city by this institution.

Through the doors of the Museum it is possible to step from the heart of the city into the atmosphere of the jungles of Africa, the wilds of the Americas, the mysterious countries of the Orient and the South Seas, or the forbidding lands of perpetual ice and snow. It is possible also to step backwards in time to the ancient civilizations of Greece and Rome, to mystic Egypt of old, and yet further even into prehistoric ages, hundreds of millions of years ago, when strange forms of life, now long extinct, existed on the earth, and man was yet unknown.

Housed in a beautiful marble temple designed from a classic Greek model, Field Museum stands in Grant Park at Roosevelt Road and Lake Michigan. It is one of the outstanding architectural gems of Chicago. The building alone is valued at more than $7,000,000; with the collections it contains the Museum represents a value exceeding $50,000,000.

As an educational institution, Field Museum has reached a high pinnacle. It may be called a "people's college" of the sciences. All classes of people

(Henry Fuermann & Sons Photo)

FIELD MUSEUM OF NATURAL HISTORY
Graham, Anderson, Probst & White, architects.

President
FIELD MUSEUM
of
NATURAL
HISTORY

STANLEY FIELD

Mr. Field, president of Field Museum of Natural History, Chicago, was born of American parents in Manchester, England, May 13, 1875, son of Joseph Nash and Katherine (Blackwell) Field. He was educated in Repton School, England, and came to the United States in 1893. Since 1906 he has been identified with Marshall Field & Company and is now a director.

Since the first part of 1932 he has been chairman of the executive committee of the Continental Illinois National Bank and Trust Company of Chicago. He is also a director of the Merchandise Bank & Trust Company, Illinois Central Railroad, The Peoples Gas Light and Coke Company, Commonwealth Edison Company, Public Service Company of Northern Illinois, and The Mutual Life Insurance Company of New York. During 1917 and 1918 he was in charge of all purchases for the American Red Cross in France. His clubs are Racquet (New York); Chicago (president), Racquet, Chicago Yacht, Saddle and Cycle, Onwentsia, and Old Elm Golf.

Mr. Field married Sara Carroll Brown of Baltimore, April 17, 1900. Their children are Katherine Blackwell, Daphne, and Joseph Nash.

are reached by its influence. The serious student of science and the academic scholar are aided in their researches by the Museum. The institution contains a wealth of exhibits and information of an economic character, study of which is valuable to business men and industrial leaders in a practical way, frequently suggesting to them ideas for use in their commercial activities. It is a mine of inspiration and suggestion for workers in the fine arts, and also the lesser arts of craftsmanship. The novelist, the illustrator, the scenario writer, the painter, all can find objects which will aid them in establishing "local color" in their various works. The sculptor derives new conceptions from the collections of stone, bronze and wood sculptures and carvings representing the cultures of other peoples and ages. Textile makers, fashion designers, pottery makers, jewelers, goldsmiths, printers—these are but a few of the many classes of artisans whom the Museum provides with suggestive material of value to them in their arts or trades.

(*Courtesy, Field Museum of Natural History*)
STANLEY FIELD HALL
The great central exhibition hall of Field Museum of Natural History.

To the average man, woman or child, regardless of any practical value to be derived from a tour of the Museum, the institution gives a broadening cultural influence which, like many courses in universities, like good books, good music and great art, while it may have no apparent immediate practical value, makes better informed and more tolerant citizens and workers.

The Museum was founded in 1893 by the late Marshall Field. It is open every day of the year. Admission is free on Thursdays, Saturdays and Sundays; on other days adults are charged twenty-five cents. Children are always admitted free, as also are students and teachers of any accredited school or other educational institution.

The exhibits in Field Museum of Natural History have been gathered by collectors who are specialists in their respective departments of the natural sciences, and who have been dispatched to many parts of the world for the purpose of accumulating exhibition and study material. The exhibits are grouped into four departments—anthropology, botany, geology and zoology. The collections in each department are arranged systematically under their respective divisions, descriptive labels being attached for the information of visitors.

Representative collections of outstanding exhibits from each of the four departments are to be found in Stanley Field Hall, the great central exhibition hall which occupies the nave of the building. These are intended to give a glimpse of the activities of the institution in general. The visitor enters the building via this hall, and thus is introduced to the systematic collections. The hall itself is architecturally magnificent and stately, and contains, besides its collections, four fine statues, designed by Henry Hering,

(© *Field Museum of Natural History*)

Life-size restoration of a Neanderthal family and cave in which these Western Europeans of about 50,000 years ago lived. This group, the work of the sculptor, Frederick A. Blaschke, is in the Department of Geology, Field Museum of Natural History.

symbolizing "Natural Science," "Dissemination of Knowledge," "Research," and "Record." The hall is dedicated to Stanley Field, the present President of the Museum.

To the left of this hall the visitor finds the anthropological collections, and to the right the zoological exhibits. Further exhibits of these departments are also found on the ground floor beneath, and certain anthropological material in the second floor galleries overlooking Stanley Field Hall. The exhibits of the departments of botany and geology occupy series of connected halls on the second floor.

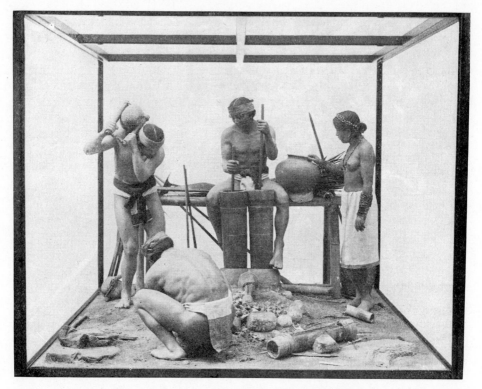

(*Courtesy, Field Museum of Natural History*)

Life-size group representing Philippine iron workers and their forge—Department of Anthropology, Field Museum of Natural History.

Few sciences are of such absorbing interest as anthropology. To trace the evolution of man from the dim past, when he was scarcely more than a highly developed animal, is tremendously fascinating. The various races have not advanced uniformly in culture, but even the most backward challenge our admiration by the skill with which they have met and solved the problems presented by their environment. Primitive peoples stand out as mile posts on the road which we ourselves have traveled.

The exhibits in the department of anthropology are designed to show the achievements in arts and industries, as well as the social and religious life, of the world exclusive of modern Europe and America, in both historic and prehistoric times. Here there are to be seen life-size groups representing Eskimos, American Indians of various tribes, Philippine natives, and other such peoples, surrounded by the weapons, implements, utensils, art products and other objects representative of their lives. Backgrounds precisely representing the environment in which they live are part of many of the exhibits. The ancient cultures of Peru, Mexico, and other parts of the American continents, and of the South Pacific islands, are all represented by collections of artifacts. Etruscan, Greek and Roman antiquities of great variety and interest are exhibited; and there is a vast Egyptian archaeological collection, including a number of mummies. There are halls devoted to ethnological collections from Africa, Polynesia, Micronesia, Melanesia, the Philippines, India, Korea, and other far places. Madagascar is represented by a remarkable collection unrivalled in any other museum of this country.

The department contains a highly important collection of treasures from the Orient. The Blackstone expedition of 1908-10, with Dr. Berthold Laufer, who is now Curator of Anthropology, as leader, penetrated far into Tibet and returned laden with collections of gorgeous dresses, grotesque masks used in religious dances "to cast out demons," and curious objects far too numerous to mention here. There are extensive exhibits of ancient Chinese jade, bronze, cast iron, mortuary pottery, clay figures, porcelain, wood carving, and unique ancient sculpture. In the Japanese collection the examples shown of sword guards, swords, tapestry, and women's costumes are particularly notable. This brief account is intended merely to indicate the value and interest of the anthropological exhibits. When it is stated that the number of objects in this department alone is more than 200,000, the extent and scope of the various collections will be readily imagined.

In the department of botany every effort is made to give a comprehensive idea of the entire plant kingdom, its large range of plant forms, and its relation to human life. Field Museum was the first general natural history museum to give to botany space comparable to that devoted to other sciences. The department maintains a vast herbarium, chiefly of purely scientific interest, and economic reference collections of considerable extent, in addition to the exhibited collections.

In exhibited botanical material, emphasis is laid on the economic uses of plant materials. These are of interest particularly to the student of economics and the business man, as well as the student of botany and the casual visitor. In the department's Hall of Plant Life is a display of characteristic plant forms from the lowest to the highest. Microscopic plants, such as bacteria and the minute algae, are represented as they are seen with the aid of a microscope. Larger plants can sometimes be preserved for a long time by drying or otherwise, but usually give a poor idea of their appearance in the living state. For this reason, they are shown at the Museum in the form of reproductions which are exact replicas of the living plants. These are produced in the Museum in special laboratories maintained through the generosity of President Stanley Field. The original material secured in all parts of the world is used variously as models and component parts of these life-like reproductions. The reproductions are supplemented in many cases with models illustrating on an enlarged scale various significant details of structure, and characteristic dry plant material, such as fruits, seeds, gums and fibers.

Two halls are devoted almost entirely to plant economics, one of them especially to food plants, the other to plant materials used in industry. Two halls contain collections of woods, one North American, the other foreign types. Sections and trunks of trees, photographs of them in the living state, closeups and reproductions of the foliage, maps showing distribution, samples of finished lumber, and labels containing essential information about their growth and uses accompany them.

(Courtesy, Field Museum of Natural History)
The Giant Panda—one of the world's rarest animals. The specimens in the group at Field Museum were obtained by Colonel Theodore Roosevelt and Kermit Roosevelt while leading the William V. Kelley-Roosevelts Expedition to Eastern Asia.

Exhibits in the department of geology classify into two groups, one illustrating the scientific, the other the economic and industrial relations of the mineral products of the earth. The scientific series begins with an extensive collection showing the various mineral species. About 700 species are illustrated by 20,000 specimens. Supplemental to this is a large collection of crystals, presented to the Museum by William J. Chalmers. There is also a very large meteorite collection containing representatives of nearly 700 falls, being in this respect the most complete collection in the world. Rock structures and the effects of natural forces, such as glaciation, erosion, folding, acting on the materials of which the earth is composed, are shown in the section devoted to physical geology. There is also a model of the moon, 19 feet in diameter, which so far as is known is the largest and most elaborate representation of the moon's surface ever made.

In the section of paleontology, or historical geology, the development of life on the earth from the age of the simplest invertebrates to that of the highest forms is illustrated in historic sequence. The largest known land animals, the dinosaurs, are represented by a huge mounted partial skeleton, 12 feet high and 30 feet long. Remains of other huge dinosaurs, including a skull of the great horned dinosaur, are also shown. Complete or partial skeletons of the extinct mammoths, mastodons, cave bears, ground sloths, saber-toothed tigers, and other animals contemporary with early man, as well as skeletons and other specimens of still more remote periods going back hundreds of millions of years, have been assembled. Recently a series of twenty-eight mural paintings showing how these prehistoric creatures are believed to have appeared in life, has been installed in the hall. They were painted by Charles R. Knight, recognized generally as one of the world's leading artists in his specialty—the depiction of paleontological subjects. The paintings are a gift to the Museum from Ernest R. Graham. Also presented by Mr. Graham are three life-size groups, one a restoration of a Neanderthal man, his family and their cave; the other of the mesohippus, a species of small three-toed horse which grew to about the size of a collie dog and lived in North America some thirty million years ago; and a restoration of Titanotheres, huge rhinoceros-like animals of prehistoric times on this continent. These are the work of sculptor Frederick A. Blaschke. There is also a restoration of a forest of the Coal Age, some 250,000,000 years ago.

The economic geological collections include among other things specimens of various ores arranged by countries, states, and mining districts, with models of mines, and metal treatment plants of various types; specimens of alkalies, salts, and various similar substances; a collection of petroleum and oil sands and a model of an oil well; a collection of coals and coal derivatives, and collections of clays, soils and other mineral substances which are important economically.

One of the most complete collections of gems and jewels in existence is included in the department of geology. It contains nearly every variety of gems, and of precious and semi-precious stones in finely cut examples, and also as crystals. cleavages and rolled grains. Many of the specimens are of historic interest and world-wide reputation, such as the diamond on which the bust of William II of Holland was engraved by DeVrees of Amsterdam, the work requiring five years.

The exhibits in the department of zoology consist of three main divisions: a classified series where each important animal can be found in its proper place; special exhibits of the animals of various countries illustrating their habits and natural surroundings; and preparations of animals or parts of animals to illustrate facts, ideas, and theories about them in their relation to each other and to man.

Recently groups of rare animals obtained by the James Simpson-Roosevelts Asiatic expedition, and the William V. Kelley-Roosevelts expedition to Eastern Asia, both led by Colonel Theodore Roosevelt and Kermit Roosevelt, have been placed on exhibition, in addition to groups obtained through the efforts of many other important expeditions which have been carried on in the past few years.

Mammals are arranged in two series, one being systematic to show one specimen of each of the principal species; the other in habitat groups to show the home life, so to speak, of especially interesting or important species. In Carl E. Akeley Memorial Hall are found the principal masterpieces of taxidermy on African mammals of the noted taxidermist, sculptor and explorer, after whom the hall is named.

North American, South American, African, Asiatic, and Australian mammals are all represented in the Museum collections. Nearly all the known species of American birds, and the principal species of foreign birds, are on exhibition. In addition to the general bird collections there is a series of beautiful habitat groups of various birds with painted backgrounds representing their natural environment. The department also has on exhibition noteworthy collections of fishes, reptiles, amphibians, and skeletons of vertebrates.

The Museum has a large general library, and four departmental libraries, containing more than 92,000 scientific books and pamphlets.

Study and reference collections, supplementing the exhibits, are made available to students and research workers upon application to the Director.

Extension of the Museum's work directly to the school children of Chicago is carried on by two special units of the Museum organization. One of these is the Department of the N. W. Harris Public School Extension, which circulates traveling exhibits in the schools. More than 1,100 such cases are in use, and two are sent to each school every two weeks. The James Nelson and Anna Louise Raymond Foundation for Public School and Children's Lectures provides free motion pictures, stereopticon slides, guide-lecture tours of the Museum, extension lectures for talks in the schools, and other forms of instructive entertainment for young people. The activities of these two branches of the Museum reach practically every school child in the city.

Guide-lecturers are available for parties of adults, as well as children, upon application to the Director. No charge is made for this service. Regular public lecture-tours of the exhibits are conducted daily, except Saturdays and Sundays, at 11:00 a. m. and 3:00 p. m., and schedules of the subjects to be covered are published every month. Series of free public lectures, illustrated with motion pictures or stereopticon slides, with eminent explorers and scientists as speakers, are given in the James Simpson Theater of the Museum each Spring and Fall.

The Museum operates its own large publishing plant, which puts out many important scientific works based chiefly on the discoveries made by the Museum's many expeditions throughout the world, and the work of its scientific staff. In addition, series of leaflets and other instructive works written in popular style are produced by Field Museum Press.

(*Chicago Architectural Photographing Company*)

This view was taken from the Congress Street entrance to Grant Park.

DRAMATIZING THE PAGEANT OF THE SKIES
The Adler Planetarium and Astronomical Museum
A Man-made Universe on a Man-made Isle

WITHIN the compass of a few hundred yards in Grant Park, one may explore the wonders of the earth, the marvels of the deep, and the mystery of the starry heavens.

The Adler Planetarium and Astronomical Museum is one of a splendid trinity of buildings devoted to such universal study. It is a fit companion to the Field Museum and the Shedd Aquarium. Its special province is the study of the heavens.

In a man-made universe, the vast dome of the heavens has been reduced to the proportions of an inverted bowl sixty-eight feet in diameter, a miniature cosmos, within which Sun, Moon, planets, and stars revolve in imitation of the stately procession overhead.

On this horizon-blue stage, unobstructed by clouds, the celestial bodies appear as actors in a majestic pageant, each enacting the role ordained when they were sent spinning into space.

The planets, Sun and Moon, and 9,000 stars make up the cast, marshaled by the operator of the Zeiss projector. From the powerful lenses of

The Adler Planetarium and Astronomical Museum, the only institution of its kind in the Western Hemisphere. Ernest A. Grunsfeld, Jr., architect.

(Eugene L. Ray, Evanston, Photo)

PHILIP FOX

Dr. Fox, director of the Adler Planetarium and Astronomical Museum of Chicago, was born in Manhattan, Kansas, March 7, 1878, the son of Simeon M. and Esther (Butler) Fox. He received his B.S. (Bachelor of Science) degree at the Kansas State College in 1897, his M.S. (Master of Science) in 1901, a B.S. degree at Dartmouth College in 1902, and attended the University of Berlin in 1905 and 1906. Dr. Fox was a Commandant and teacher of mathematics at St. John's Military School, Salina, Kansas, from 1899 to 1901; Carnegie research assistant at Yerkes Observatory, University of Chicago from 1903 to 1905; instructor in astro-physics at the University of Chicago from 1907 to 1909; professor of astronomy and director at Dearborn Observatory, Northwestern University from 1909 to 1929; and has been director of the Adler Planetarium and Astronomical Museum in Grant Park, Chicago, since its opening in 1929.

He served as second lieutenant in the 20th Kansas Infantry, United States Volunteers, in the Philippine Islands in the Spanish-American War; as major in the infantry from May 1, 1917, to September 23, 1919; while in France he was assistant chief of staff of the 7th Division, and is now a colonel in the Reserve Corps, commanding the 341st Infantry. Dr. Fox is an Officier de l'ordre du Sauveur (Greece); a Fellow of the American Academy of Arts and Sciences, the Royal Astronomical Society, and the American Association for the Advancement of Science. He is a member of the American Astronomical Society, Société Astronomique de la France, Astronomische Gesellschaft, Alpha Delta Phi, Phi Beta Kappa, Phi Kappa Phi, and Sigma Xi. He is the author of Annals of the Dearborn Observatory (volumes I and II), also several scientific brochures, and contributions to astronomical journals, principally on double stars, stellar parallax, and solar physics. In 1930 he received the honorary degree of Doctor of Laws from Drake University and that of Doctor of Science from Kansas State College, in 1931.

Dr. Fox married Ethel L. Snow, of Chicago, August 28, 1905. Their children are **Stephen, Bertrand, Gertrude, and Robert Temple.**

this projector they are thrown upon the screen and directed in their march across the sky.

In this unique theater, where astronomy is dramatized, the illusion is so compelling that one loses all sense of enclosure and the limited space seems as broad as the sky itself.

It is possible to speed up the movements of the heavenly bodies so that a day, or even the 25,800-year-long celestial cycle, measured by the precession of the equinoxes, can be reproduced within the space of a few minutes. Centuries are shortened into seconds as the electric motors drive the mechanism which controls the artificial heavens. Nor is any of the majesty of the celestial movements lost by this acceleration; on the contrary, the speeding up aids greatly in an understanding of them.

(© *Kaufman & Fabry*)
THE STARLIT DOME IN THE DARKENED PLANETARIUM CHAMBER

By operation of the instrument, different aspects of the skies as viewed from various points on the Earth's surface may be presented. Thus, from his seat in the domed theater, the spectator may be transported, as if by a magic carpet, to the North or the South pole, or to the equator. Constellations, such as the Southern Cross, not seen in northern latitudes, ascend above the horizon; or the pole star can be seen increasing in altitude as one travels northward.

Moreover, such is the wizardry of the projecting apparatus, the heavens can be shown as they appeared at any time in the past or as they will appear hundreds or thousands of years in the future. One can see them as Hipparchus, discoverer of precession of the equinoxes, saw them; as they appeared to the Chaldean astronomers, to the Pyramid builders, to Homer, or to the ancient shepherds who watched their flocks by night looking to the stars for guidance. Or one can project himself into the far-distant future, and gaze up at the stars as they will be revealed when Vega will have replaced Polaris as the cynosure.

Chicago owes its Planetarium—the only one in America—to the generosity of Max Adler, who by making possible this institution, sought to awaken popular interest in the science of astronomy and the knowledge of the heavens. That he has more than realized his hopes is evidenced by the eager crowds that visit the Planetarium summer and winter—scientists, students, school children, tourists, laymen and philosophers. Attendance records are comparable with the Planetarium's two sister institutions, the Field Museum and the Shedd Aquarium.

The Planetarium occupies a commanding site at the northern end of Northerly Island. The building was dedicated and opened to the public on May 12, 1930. Its architect is Ernest A. Grunsfeld, Jr., of Chicago, awarded the 1930 Gold Medal of the Chicago chapter of the American Institute of Architects for the design of this building.

The edifice, dodecagonal, or twelve-sided in shape, is 160 feet in diameter at the foundation, and is built of Minnesota rainbow granite. On each of its twelve exterior corners are bronze placques with the signs of the Zodiac in bas-relief, the work of Alfonso Iannelli. Centrally located within the structure is a circular hall surmounted by a copper dome rising eighty-five feet above the terrace on which the building stands. Within this hall is the Planetarium proper, in which rows of seats, concentric with the circular wall, are provided for spectators. On the interior dome is stretched the linen screen which serves as the vault of heaven.

The projection apparatus is a grotesque instrument, with ungainly steel stilts and knobs studded with lenses which resemble the highly magnified eyes of a fly. The lenses project the stars as brilliant points on the concave surface above. Manufactured at the plant of Carl Zeiss, Jena, Germany, it looks, rather as if it had been made on the planet Mars, being quite unlike anything on land or sea, except perhaps, a long-legged, double-headed insect. The instrument contains 122 separate projectors, of which thirty-two are for the stars; eighteen for the nebulae, star clusters, and the dog star, Sirius; thirty-two for the constellation names; eighteen for the members of the solar system; and nineteen for various reference points and circles.

The Planetarium is open to visitors daily, and lectures are given at frequent intervals. Each lecture is like a personally-conducted tour through the heavens, during the course of which the traveler, penetrating far beyond the solar system, meets such stars as Canopus, Vega, Arcturus, Betelgeuse, Castor, and Pollux; traces such constellations as Orion, Cassiopeia, Scorpio, Draco, Taurus, and the two Bears; and returns, sprinkled, as it were, with star-dust from the Pleiades, and the furthermost nebulae and galaxies—universes millions of light years beyond our own.

The halls surrounding the central chamber house the astronomical museum. Here are displayed historical instruments and documents relating to the science; working models of famous telescopes and observatories; horological and nautical instruments, both modern and ancient; machines for grinding lenses; and machines uncannily accurate for making computations. Spectroscopes may be seen in operation illustrating the various types of spectra. To the amateur, as well as the student, the collection of transparencies showing recent achievements in astronomical photography are perhaps the most interesting of the exhibits.

America has long stood on the frontier of astronomical research, and in these studies, Chicago has for more than half a century played a leading role. It was just as the country was emerging from the throes of the Civil War that the Chicago Astronomical Society was formed and brought to the city the largest refracting telescope then in existence, the eighteen and one-half inch lens of the Dearborn Observatory. The University of Chicago, to escape the smoke and dust and the glare of city lights, has located its great Yerkes Observatory at Williams Bay, Wisconsin. What the Adler Planetarium has done, however, is to dramatize and popularize astronomy; to stage a pageant of the heavens.

The doorway to the Adler Planetarium and Astronomical Museum where Time becomes the slave of Science.

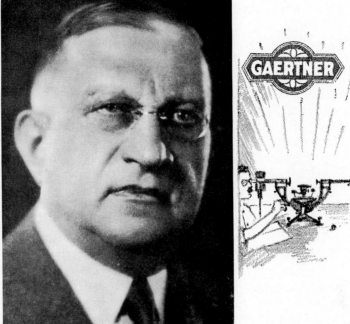

WILLIAM GAERTNER

Mr. Gaertner, president of the Gaertner Scientific Corp., makers of precision instruments for scientific purposes, was born in Merseburg, Germany, October 24, 1864, son of Karl and Luise (Pippel) Gaertner. He was educated at the public school and the School for Instrument Makers, Berlin, Germany. After starting his business career, at the age of sixteen, as an apprentice in an instrument shop at Halle, Germany, he was later employed by W. Apel, a manufacturer of chemical and physical apparatus, at Goettingen, Germany, and by F. E. Breithaupt and Son, makers of surveying and geodetic instruments at Cassel. He also worked at his craft in London and Vienna, and came to the United States in 1889 where he became instrument maker for the United States Coast and Geodetic Survey at Washington, D. C. As government employees must be American citizens, a special ruling was made in his case by the United States Treasury Department waiving the provision of the naturalization law requiring five years residence before naturalization. Mr. Gaertner became a citizen of the United States after eleven months residence in this country in recognition of his scientific achievements.

In 1893 he started work with the Smithsonian Institution, where he assisted Prof. Samuel P. Langley in his aeronautical experiments. In 1896 Mr. Gaertner opened a small shop in Chicago for the manufacture of surveying instruments. This business grew, until in 1924 William Gaertner and Company was incorporated as the Gaertner Scientific Corp., of which he is president and treasurer. He manufactured the "interferometer" for the late Prof. Albert A. Michelson, and in 1910 he made a photographic zenith telescope for determining latitude variations for the observatory of the International Geodetic Association. Mr. Gaertner has made greater progress than anyone else toward the solution of the problem of making accurate precision screws for scientific purposes, a problem which has baffled instrument makers for many years. He was awarded the Howard N. Potts gold medal "for notable achievements as a designer and maker of scientific instruments," by the Franklin Institute in 1924.

He is a member of the American Astronomical Society, the Chicago Association of Commerce, and the Press Club. He is now active in developing new instruments and improving old designs for the U. S. Air Corps. On June 14, 1917, he married Belva Eleanora Boosinger of Litchfield, Illinois.

WHERE INDUSTRY APPROACHES MYSTICISM
The Application of Optical Instruments
BY WILLIAM GAERTNER

President, Gaertner Scientific Corporation

THAT telescopes will reveal the vast depths of space and microscopes the tiniest of bacteria, is known to everyone, but the extensive use and function of optical instruments in the making and testing of objects that enter into our everyday lives is known usually only to those having some important part in their fabrication. Even when one observes these instru-ments in common use, as when the surveyor is seen looking through his level, their function is not readily understood, for the telescope on the engi-neer's level is more closely related to the sight on a rifle than it is to the sailor's spyglass. Indeed it performs both functions, for it not only permits seeing clearly the marks on the distant stadia rod but permits bringing the telescope barrel in accurate alignment with them. This combination of functions can as well be embodied in a microscope for viewing and at the same time setting on very fine markings. If a microscope with spider threads in its focal plane is mounted so as to move on a very straight guide by means of a fine and accurate screw, we have what is called a comparator.

The comparator finds applications in such diverse ways as studying and measuring the setting expansion of Portland cement, determining the "creep" of metals when heated in a furnace, gauging the hardness of steel by the width of Brinell impressions, studying the effect of heat treatment on the arrangement of the very atoms in a sample of metal by measuring the distance of the spots produced on a photographic plate when radio-graphed by X-rays, determining the chemical composition of a sample of unknown material by measurement of the photograph obtained by burning less than a millionth of an ounce of it in front of a spectrograph.

There are some problems in industry where even the microscope, meas-uring as it does to about a fifty-thousandth of an inch, is too coarse an instrument and one has to resort to an instrument whose great power was first shown by Michelson—the interferometer. The surfaces of gauge blocks to adhere and measure properly, must be flat to dimensions which cannot be seen with a microscope. They are tested for flatness, parallelism and length by observing the interference of light waves seen when a piece of quartz, polished flat to a millionth of an inch, is pressed in contact with them. The preparation of such master flats is a procedure requiring the highest skill.

The interference method has been applied to the study of the thermal expansion of ceramic materials which must be very small to avoid their cracking. Dental fillings likewise must, on setting and subsequently, main-tain their dimensions to an extremely high degree of accuracy, for the measurement of which the interference method is also preferred.

Even the interferometer, measuring to millionths of an inch, does not represent the ultimate in fine measurements. It has been found that an

(*Moffett-Russell Photo*)

GEORGE D. GAW

Col. Gaw, president of Gaw-O'Hara Envelope Company, and of the United States Paper Corporation, director of the Du-Plex Envelope Company, and Chicago's official host, was born in Owensboro, Kentucky, January 15, 1889, son of Mattison and Louise M. Gaw. After attending a parochial school in Owensboro and Owensboro College, he received his M. A. (Master of Arts) degree at St. Mary's College, St. Mary, Kentucky. He spent several years on the vaudeville stage and for two seasons was leading man in the musical comedy called "Little Johnny Jones." Constant travel gave Col. Gaw a chance to see nearly all of the cities in America, so when he decided to leave the stage and enter the business world, he deliberately chose Chicago. Col. Gaw, with Tom O'Hara, started their envelope business with only $500. Now, the Gaw-O'Hara Envelope Company, located at the intersection of Sacramento and Franklin Boulevards, is the largest direct-to-consumer envelope concern in the world—hence the slogan "P. D. Q., Price, Delivery, Quality."

Col. Gaw realizes that Chicago has been very kind to him and his co-workers and is now trying to repay this debt in every way possible. He now fills a new "payless post" which Mayor Cermak created for him, that of Chicago's "Commissioner of Hospitality." The purpose of this new position is to help sell Chicago's virtues to the outside world, as well as to some of our own citizens, and Col. Gaw meets many of the noted visitors and escorts them about the city in the white guest car. People throughout the world have erroneously heard so much about the vices in connection with Chicago that Col. Gaw believes that now they should be interested in learning the truth about its virtues; that through this procedure many thousands must change their minds about Chicago.

Col. Gaw is a member of the Illinois Athletic Club, Chicago Press, Lincoln Park Traps, Chicago Yacht Club, and the Evanston Golf Club. He enjoys motor-boating, golfing, hunting, and just meeting people.

On May 10, 1912, he married Ellen Katherine Hopkins of Rockport, Indiana, and they have one daughter, Betty Allen.

apparently homogeneous block of metal such as a steel shaft, in reality consists of a mass of interwoven microscopic crystals. These individual crystals have a regular structure, and the way the atoms are arranged in the crystal depends among other things on the heat treatment to which it has been subjected, and is closely connected with such characteristics as hardness, homogeneity and tensile strength. The atomic distances and their arrangement is revealed by the way in which the material reflects X-rays through the X-ray spectrometer. These reflected X-rays may be photographed and measured on a comparator (as mentioned above) or they may be allowed to fall in an ionization chamber and the conductivity produced measured by an electrometer.

It is coming to be realized that such minute quantities as .001 per cent, present as impurities in alloys, may have a decided influence on their physical properties. For such small percentages the usual chemical methods of analysis are not well adapted. But here optical science comes to the assistance of the chemist. For when such material is burned in an arc or spark, the elements give out their characteristic radiations with a brilliance which is in a general way proportional to the amount of the element present. Many of these radiations are in the ultra-violet, to which glass lenses and prisms are opaque. Fortunately, however, crystal quartz allows them to pass as readily as glass passes visible light. And the photographic plate is sensitive to them, even more sensitive than to visible light. A spectrograph with lenses and prisms of quartz therefore is the ideal instrument for recording these radiations. With the help of a comparator the identity of the elements producing the various radiations is readily determined, and by a study of the amount of blackening they produce on the photographic plate, the amount of each present is ascertained. This amount of blackening is estimated by some workers visually, by comparison with standards photographed on the same plate. It is, however, much facilitated by the use of an auxiliary instrument—the microphotometer. This is especially designed to measure the amount of blackening on the small area covered by each spectrum line.

Space does not permit giving more than a mere hint of the many applications of optics in industry. The field is constantly widening and is virtually unlimited.

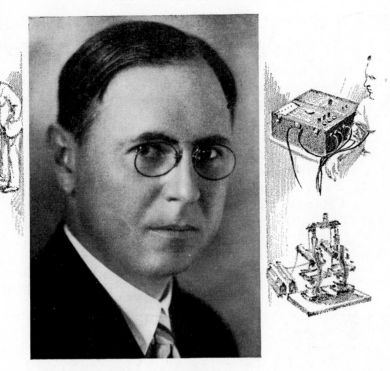

CALVIN GODDARD

Colonel Goddard, professor of police science (Law Faculty) and managing director of the Scientific Crime Detection Laboratory at Northwestern University, was born in Baltimore, Maryland, October 30, 1891, son of Capt. Henry P. and Eliza Whitman (Acheson) Goddard. He received his A.B. (Bachelor of Arts) degree in 1911, *cum laude*, and his M. D. (Doctor of Medicine), 1915, from Johns Hopkins. He was an honor graduate of the Army Medical School at Washington, in 1917. In that year he was commissioned first lieutenant of the Medical Corps; was promoted through grades to major, March 28, and is now lieutenant colonel in the Ordnance Reserve. He was assistant director (business administration) of Johns Hopkins Hospital, 1921-1924; administrative director of the Cornell Clinic, 1924-1925; associate director and director of the Bureau of Forensic Ballistics, New York, 1925-1926; director of Major Calvin Goddard and Associates, New York, 1926-1929. Colonel Goddard is technical adviser (arms and ammunition) for the Pennsylvania State Police.

He is a member of the Institute of Criminal Law and Criminology, Society of American Military Engineers, Association of Military Surgeons, Army Ordinance Association, American Society of International Law, New York Medico-Legal Society, Chicago Academy of Criminology, International Association for Identification (director), New York Country (Washington); Indian Landing Boat Club, Annapolis, (Maryland); Phi Kappa Psi (New York); Army and Navy Adventures (Chicago). Colonel Goddard is a contributor of articles on firearms identification and general ordinance subjects.

He married Eliza Cunningham Harrison, of New Kent County, Virginia, August 3, 1915. Their children are Eliza Cunningham and Mary Woodbridge.

THE SCIENTIFIC CRIME DETECTION LABORATORY
Chicago's Answer to Mass Machine Gun Murder

BY CALVIN GODDARD,
Director, Scientific Crime Detection Laboratory, Northwestern University

A SUSPECTED murderer was about to be set free. He had, apparently, an air-tight alibi. No evidence directly connecting him with the crime of which he was accused could be produced. Then science stepped in. Parts of his clothing were subjected to microscopic scrutiny. The powerful lens revealed minute bits of algae—seaweed—adhering to his clothing, a species of algae found only in the neighborhood where the crime was committed. The alibi was shot to pieces, and on the strength of this evidence, produced almost as if by magic, the man was convicted.

The ratiocination process of detectives of the Sherlock Holmes type, fascinating as they may be in fiction, have yielded to the still more fascinating methods of science.

Many phases of modern crime detection work have become highly specialized sciences in themselves. There is the science of firearm identification, built up on a study of weapons, projectiles, and exploded cartridges. Given a mere slug of lead, the expert is enabled to determine exactly the make of gun it was discharged from, and in many cases, actually to identify the weapon employed.

The modern criminal may congratulate himself upon his cleverness, and indeed, he is far more clever than the criminal of other days. But science manages to keep a jump or two ahead of him, and scientific crime detection, while still in its early stages of development, already to the uninitiated savors of wizardry and necromancy. What criminal, for instance, can persist in his denials in the face of the "Lie-detector" which is positively uncanny in its operations?

The Scientific Crime Detection Laboratory, a department of the Law School of Northwestern University, was established in the Fall of 1929, through the munificence of Burt A. Massee, who had served as foreman of the coroner's jury convened to investigate the so-called "Valentine Day Massacre" of that year.

The first institution of its kind in the United States, it is patterned partly after the scientific police labo-

Students examining laboratory specimens— cast of human hand, and fatal bullets under microscope.

President
AMERICAN
INSTITUTE
of
ACCOUNTANTS
1923-24
•
The CHICAGO
ASSOCIATION
of COMMERCE
1922
•
CHICAGO
CRIME
COMMISSION
1926-27
•

(Moffett-Russell Photo)

EDWARD E. GORE

Mr. Gore, certified public accountant and senior member of Edward Gore and Company was born in Carlinville, Illinois, December 4, 1866, son of David and Cinderella Davis (Keller) Gore. He was educated at Blackburn College, Carlinville, Jacksonville (Illinois) Business College, and the University of Illinois. He studied law from 1888 to 1893 and was elected justice of the peace at Carlinville in 1889, serving for four years. He was appointed Chief of the Building and Loan Department, State Auditor's Office, July 1, 1893. He was appointed Chief of the Banking Department of the same office, January 1, 1895, and served in both capacities until January, 1897.

Mr. Gore has engaged in public accounting practice in Chicago since January 11, 1897, practicing alone until 1904, when he became a member of the accounting firm of Barrow, Wade, Guthrie & Company. In 1922 he helped to organize the firm of Smart, Gore & Company with which he continued until 1927, when he became the senior member of Edward Gore and Company, the firm of which he is now the head. Mr. Gore has been active in the accounting field and was president of the Illinois Society of Certified Public Accountants in 1907 and has been a member of the council of the American Institute of Accountants since its organization in 1916. He was president of the American Institute of Accountants in 1923 and was re-elected in 1924. He has been active in the Chicago Association of Commerce and was a member of the auditing committee in 1906, member of the ways and means committee in 1909, 1910, and 1911, chairman of the ways and means committee in 1912, vice-president in 1913 and 1914, chairman of the executive committee in 1915 and member of the executive committee since 1912. He was president of the Association in 1922. Mr. Gore has also been active in the Chicago Crime Commission and has been a director and member of the executive committee since 1919, president in 1926 and was reelected in 1927. He belongs to the Sons of the American Revolution and to the Union League Club of Chicago. His favorite recreation is fishing.

Mr. Gore married Amanda Jeannette, daughter of William F. Burgdorff, of Carlinville, Illinois, October 6, 1892. Their children are, Florelle Jeanette (Mrs. Frank W. Hawley), Mary Amanda (Mrs. E. B. Wilcox), Virginia Cinderella, and Budd.

ratories maintained in all the larger cities of Europe, and partly after the best foreign medico-legal institutes, its services being available to law-enforcing agencies and reputable individuals throughout the United States and Canada.

Staffed with a corps of highly trained persons, it stands ready to examine and report upon any bit of physical evidence which may figure in a crime, its investigations including studies of blood, bombs, bones, bullets, code messages, counterfeits, dust, finger and foot-prints, fingernail scrapings, fire-arms, food, hair, handwriting, inks, poisons, stains, tireprints, textiles type-writing, and scores of other subjects. Its small permanent staff has available the advice of a considerably larger group of consultants, all pre-eminent in their several fields, located throughout the United States.

Aside from actual case studies, the laboratory offers short courses in the application of scientific methods to criminal investigation. At the begin-ning of 1930, it commenced the publication of "The American Journal of Police Science," a bi-monthly periodical, which fused in 1932 with the "Journal of Criminal Law and Criminology." The accomplishments of its psychology department, presided over by Leonarde Keeler, who has brought the "Lie-detector" to its present state of perfection, have elicited the praise of jurists throughout America. And finally, no less a body than the Wicker-sham Commission on Law Enforcement and Observance, in referring to the Laboratory in its report dated June 26, 1931, states that: "Scientific to the last degree, it is establishing a precedent for which there is no equal in this country at the present time."

Night view with the Merchandise Mart and the La Salle-Wacker building predominating.

SIDNEY S. GORHAM

Mr. Gorham, lawyer, was born in Rutland County, Vermont, November 6, 1874, son of Frank E. and Mary J. (Smith) Gorham. He attended the common schools there, and received his LL.B. (Bachelor of Laws) degree at Chicago College of Law (now Chicago-Kent College of Law) in 1894. He began as an office boy in the law firm of Luther Laflin Mills and George C. Ingham (Mills and Ingham) in 1890. After the death of Mr. Ingham he continued in the employ of Mr. Mills until 1904, when he was admitted to partnership with Mr. Mills and his son, Matthew Mills. Two years later, with Mr. Henry W. Wales, he organized the partnership of Gorham and Wales. In 1912 Mr. Amos C. Miller became a partner and the firm name was changed to Miller, Gorham and Wales. Mr. Gorham is the author of the first state-wide motor vehicle law of Illinois, which was passed in 1907 and became a law January 1, 1908. He represented the Chicago Motor Club in the gas tax litigation in 1927 and 1928 and this act was held unconstitutional by the Supreme Court. In 1928 he was appointed special assistant corporation counsel for the City of Chicago and assigned to advise the Citizens Traction Settlement Committee. In June, 1930, he was appointed special assistant corporation counsel for the City of Chicago to advise the Committee on Gas, Oil and Electric Light in negotiations for a contract ordinance with the Illinois Bell Telephone Company.

He is a member of the Chicago Bar Association and was treasurer during 1925 and 1926, second vice-president during 1926 and 1927, first vice-president during 1927 and 1928, and president from 1928 to 1929. He is a member of the Illinois State Bar Association, American Bar Association, and the Law Club of the City of Chicago. He is chairman of the committee on traffic control of A Century of Progress—Chicago's (1933) World's Fair. He is a director of the Terminal National Bank of Chicago, trustee and member of the Mid-Day Club, past vice-president of Chicago Athletic Association, member and director Chicago Motor Club and American Automobile Association, and member of the Glenview Club, La Grange Country Club, Illinois Seniors Golf Association, and Forty Club. His favorite recreations are golf and horseback riding. He is actively interested in civic affairs.

On July 15, 1896, he married Myrtle G. Willett of Chicago, and their children are Lucy M. (deceased), Sidney S., Jr., and Willett N.

THE NERVE CENTER OF AMERICA'S AGRICULTURAL INDUSTRY

Far-Flung Influence of the Chicago Board of Trade

BY PETER B. CAREY

Fifty-ninth President, Chicago Board of Trade

BROODING silently over the deep canyon of La Salle street, Ceres, goddess of the golden grain, symbolizing the spirit of agriculture, sheds her benediction over one of the world's business marts.

A country goddess transplanted to the heart of a great city, she stands silhouetted against the sky on her lofty pedestal atop the Chicago Board of Trade tower.

Even to the most heedless passer-by in the street below she brings a picture of millions of acres of waving wheat fields, an empire of grain, reaching out toward the sunset.

She is the guardian of America's bread basket. Sublimely aloof, detached from the turmoil of the city streets, she seems indifferent to the conflict going on below.

On the floor of the exchange, in the famous wheat pit, the battle is renewed daily. To the average spectator, the pit is Bedlam; the frantic gesticulations and the incessant roar of the traders are meaningless.

The roar is nothing less than the heart-throb of America's agricultural industry. The exchange is the clearing house of the world's grain markets. Here some 400 million bushels of grain flow from producer to consumer annually.

Beneath the massive trading floor are the terminals of 2,700 miles of wire, tapping all parts of the country, the fibers of a vast nervous system, connecting with other nerve centers in the far corners of the earth.

Quotations from the Chicago market are broadcast by radio six times daily by the Board of Trade. Farmers even in the most isolated communities are thus kept constantly informed of the market, and can act accordingly. Other radio stations, including one of the most powerful in Europe, relay to the world the price of grain which traders pay at Chicago. The widest newspaper and ticker publicity is given the commodity prices registered in this common trading place.

The story of the Chicago Board of Trade begins nearly a century ago, when Chicago itself was little more than a pioneer community, a crossroads market.

In March, 1848, a group of Chicago merchants, eager to provide an adequate market for the farmers who were bringing their crops to the city by wagon and selling them in a hit-or-miss fashion, held a preliminary meeting in the office of W. L. Whiting. The second meeting, at which the Board of Trade was formally organized, was held in dingy rooms over Gage and Haines' flour store. Thomas Dyer was elected the first president.

JAMES E. GORMAN

Mr. Gorman, president of the Chicago, Rock Island and Pacific Railway Company, occupies a position of unusual distinction among those who have contributed to Chicago's growth and achievements. Born on the West Side, December 3, 1863, and having entered railway service as a boy of thirteen, his entire business life has been spent in Chicago. Not without some experience in commercial life, more than fifty years have been devoted to the railway transportation industry, and his progress, step by step, in the freight traffic departments of the Burlington, North Western, Illinois Central, Santa Fe and Rock Island eminently fitted him for the important part he has played in both business and civic affairs.

Coming from the Santa Fe to the Rock Island as vice-president in charge of freight traffic, he was a few years later elected president, in 1917. Serving as federal manager during the War period, he resumed the presidency in 1920. His remarkably wide personal acquaintance among business men of the Middle West and his broad circle of devoted friends have been subjects of frequent comment. Despite the burdens incident to his busy life, which include the responsibilities of a bank directorship and membership on the Board of Trustees of A Century of Progress—Chicago's (1933) World's Fair, he has given liberally of his time to all important civic enterprises, and has given ready ear to those who have been aided by his wise and friendly counsels.

Daily telegraphic market reports were arranged for in 1849, and in the following year, the board was granted a charter which gave official sanction to its acts.

(Hedrich-Blessing Photo)
View of La Salle street showing the Board of Trade building, with Ceres, goddess of grains, silhouetted against the sky.   Holabird & Root, architects.

(*Moffett-Russell Photo*)

SAMUEL A. GREELEY

Mr. Greeley, member of Pearse, Greeley and Hansen, hydraulic and sanitary engineers, was born in Chicago, Illinois, August 20, 1882, son of Frederick and Florence More-house (Arnold) Greeley. He belongs to the third generation of engineers within the family. His grandfather, Samuel S. Greeley, came to Chicago in 1848 and in 1852 was city engineer of Chicago. His father, Frederick Greeley, was a well-known surveyor in Chicago, Mr. Greeley received his A. B. (Bachelor of Arts) degree at Harvard University in 1903; B. S. (Bachelor of Science) degree in sanitary engineering at Massachusetts Institute of Technology in 1906. He was assistant engineer with the firm of Hering and Fuller, New York, from 1904 to 1909; visited England and the Continental cities in 1908, 1911, and 1928; was resident engineer in charge of construction and superintendent in charge of operation at the Milwaukee Refuse Disposal Plant, 1909 to 1911; made an investigation and report on water supply and sewage treatment for Caracas, Venezuela, during 1911; was engineer with the Sanitary District of Chicago, 1912 to 1915; supervising engineer at Camp Custer, Michigan, 1917 and 1918, and sanitary engineer United States Shipping Board, operations on Pacific Coast, Northeast Coast, and Great Lakes.

Pearse, Greeley and Hansen have done work for New York City; New Bedford, Massachusetts; Toledo, Ohio; Dallas, Texas; Louisville, Kentucky; Walla Walla, Washington; Los Angeles County, California; The Twin Cities; Highland Park, Illinois; and in general throughout the country. Mr. Greeley is a member of the American Society of Civil Engineers, American Water Works Association, American Public Health Association, New England Water Works Association, Illinois Society of Engineers, and Western Society of Engineers. His clubs are University, Engineers, City, Indian Hill Country, and Commonwealth.

On October 4, 1913, he married Dorothy Coffin of Winnetka, Illinois, and their children are Samuel Sewell, Frederick, Lois, and Dorothy.

From the very first, it set about establishing standards of quality for foodstuffs. Inspectors were appointed to see that these standards were lived up to.

With a common meeting ground where buyer and seller might congregate to make their trades, and a central market place for commodities available, growers began to receive a fairer return for their efforts in the fields.

In those days, as today, the Board of Trade never made a single trade. It has simply remained an association which provides every trade facility for the use of its members.

These facilities increased simultaneously with the organization of the commodity exchange. In 1848, the first shipments by railroad were made to Chicago, and the first telegraph messages received. Prices of farm products throughout the Middle West began to stabilize for the first time, prices being based on what such products were worth in the important trading center, Chicago.

Today, the Board of Trade ranks first among the world's commodity exchanges. It occupies a monumental building, a landmark for miles around, soaring approximately 600 feet above street level. Its charter membership of 82 has grown to one of 1,500. Memberships are held by merchants, exporters, bankers, millers, elevator owners, cooperative farm groups, brokers, insurance companies, and others. Through its operations, 30,000 persons are directly given employment, while 100,000, directly or indirectly, are provided with work. Supplementing the Board's own rigid code of ethics—a model of modern business practice—is the Grain Futures Act, by virtue of which this and other exchanges are placed under the supervision of the United States Department of Agriculture. All transactions come under the constant scrutiny of government experts, with whom the officers of the exchange work in close cooperation.

In a world market of this kind, speed in handling orders is a vital factor. Member houses of this exchange have added to their systems of privately-leased wires until they throw a network over North America and complete their connections only when they penetrate to Europe, Asia, Africa, Australia, South and Central America.

So rapidly do these houses serve their customers that trades in the future contract markets frequently are dispatched from another city, received and executed in Chicago, and confirmed at the point of origin within thirty seconds. The "round trip" on orders from Europe is made well within a three-minute period.

Growth of the Chicago Board of Trade is due to one outstanding fact. It markets the farmer's grain at a lower cost than obtains in the marketing of any other staple foodstuff. The futures markets of the Board of Trade have received wide public attention. These are broad enough to absorb the largest hedging—buying and selling against previous purchases or sales to offset possible loss—by the actual owner of the grain, and enabling him to

EDWIN O. GRIFFENHAGEN

Mr. Griffenhagen, management engineer and senior partner of Griffenhagen and Associates, consultants in management, was born in Chicago, January 14, 1886, son of Oscar Fred and Anna Maria (Kleinhans) Griffenhagen. He received his B. S. (Bachelor of Science) degree in Civil Engineering at the Armour Institute of Technology in 1906; C. E. (Civil Engineer) in 1909. Starting as a mining engineer in Alaska in 1906, he was office engineer in the engineering department of the Chicago, Milwaukee and St. Paul Railway from 1907 to 1909. During 1909 he was architectural engineer for the City of Chicago and was selected to organize the technical work of the City of Chicago Efficiency Division during 1910. From 1911 to 1919 he was head of the industrial engineering department of Arthur Young & Company, Chicago and New York, reorganizing numerous corporations, utilities, and banks, and many states and cities. With his colleagues he took over the business of this department in 1920 and since has practiced as Griffenhagen & Associates, consultants in management to corporations and specialists in public administration and finance, with offices in Chicago, New York, Hartford, Washington, D. C., Los Angeles, and Toronto. Mr. Griffenhagen reorganized the Canadian Government departments during 1918 to 1921 and in 1920 was chief counselor to United States Congressional Commission on Reclassification of Salaries. He has conducted reorganizations of numerous states and cities as well as many large corporations; was directing engineer for Chicago River Bridge Survey. In 1932 he was selected to direct the preparation of a plan of reorganization of the government of the Chicago metropolitan area for the General Assembly of Illinois. He is secretary, treasurer, and managing director of Kindersley Farms Company.

Mr. Griffenhagen is president of the Institute of Management; charter member of the Association of Consulting Management Engineers; member, International Management Institute, American Society of Civil Engineers, Western Society of Engineers, Society of Industrial Engineers, and numerous other technical associations in the fields of business, political science, and engineering. He is a member of the Chicago Association of Commerce, Illinois Manufacturers' Association, United States Chamber of Commerce, Art Institute of Chicago, and Tau Beta Pi Fraternity. His clubs are University, City, Chicago Athletic Association, Collegiate, Delavan Country, Lake Shore Athletic, Rotary, Edgewater Golf, all of Chicago, and Engineers' (New York).

On January 7, 1909, Mr. Griffenhagen married Christine A. Gloeckler (Smith, 1908) of Chicago, and they have two children, Ruth Christine (Smith, 1930) and Elinor Jane.

shift the risk of price fluctuations to the futures market. Millers, exporters, and processors are thus safeguarded against losses brought about by sudden price changes in a highly speculative medium. As a result, they can operate on a narrower margin of profit.

Futures markets are maintained now on the exchange for wheat, corn, oats, rye, barley, provisions, cotton, and stocks and bonds, the cotton and securities markets having been added within recent years. In establishing the cotton market, the Board entered into a contract with the Department of Agriculture providing for delivery at Houston and Galveston of this commodity. The volume of business has increased steadily, and many innovations have been introduced which have been adopted by the older exchanges.

The securities market, made possible by the Board's private wire system, opened up a vast field for investment in sparsely settled communities unreached by ticker service.

The importance of the Board's futures markets in grain should not overshadow the importance of its cash grain markets. Since 1855, when records of grain shipments were first compiled, a market has been provided for more than 15,500,000,000 bushels of grain shipped from country points to Chicago.

Shipments of grain from Chicago in the same period are in excess of ten billion bushels, firmly fixing this city's prestige as a clearing house of the world's grain trade.

Unequalled shipping facilities, including water as well as Chicago's matchless railroad transportation, have aided fair and open marketing of farm products and in building up such a colossal market.

One department alone of the Board of Trade, that of the weighmaster, has devoted its activities for years to improving the traffic in grain so that fairer returns may be cashed in by the growers. An untiring effort has been made to reduce the extent of grain wastage through inadequate shipping equipment, and the Board of Trade has campaigned ceaselessly to the end that accurate weighing facilities be available at practically every point of shipment.

Such a program reaches the goal that it merits. And today it can be said safely that farmers in general are appreciative of the low cost and effi-

(*Henry Fuermann & Sons Photo*)
Lobby of Board of Trade building, showing modern lighting.

J. FRANK GRIMES

Mr. Grimes, president and founder of I. G. A. (Independent Grocers' Alliance of America) and I. D. A. (Independent Druggists' Alliance of America), was born in Chicago, December 17, 1881, son of Joseph Lawrence and Mary Ann (Mapes) Grimes. Educated in the public grammar and high schools of Chicago, he started in his business career in the employ of wholesale grocers in Chicago and Sioux City, Iowa. While in Sioux City he conducted a system of departmental analysis showing just where the profits in the wholesale grocery business were coming from and the territories that were showing the best results. This system was successful and was adopted quite extensively by wholesale grocers. Later Mr. Grimes became sales manager of the Baker-Vawter Company where he remained for a year and a half after which he became a partner in William W. Thompson and Company, certified public accountants, specializing in the grocery field. For over fifteen years he directed the operations of this company and devised a special cost accounting system that enabled wholesale grocers to conduct their business in an up-to-date manner. By 1926 the Thompson Company had as clients some 260 of the country's largest and most important wholesale grocers.

Mr. Grimes, realizing that stores operated by organizations with large buying powers were taking a good deal of business from his clients, made extensive investigations and surveys which showed that most of the difficulty was occasioned by a lack of organized cooperation between wholesale grocers and their retail customers. He and his associates then organized the first I. G. A. unit of seventy-five independent retail grocers around William T. Reynolds & Company, Inc., of Poughkeepsie, New York, during the summer of 1926. The Alliance immediately began an amazing growth which spread into other states until there are now, with branches, over one hundred old-established and important wholesale houses affiliated with the I. G. A., and there are from one to 250 I. G. A. stores in each of 3,500 towns and cities in forty-two States, making this the largest organization of independent grocers in the world. The I. D. A. (Independent Druggists' Alliance of America) was organized for the same purpose—to help the independent store-owner. Mr. Grimes is a firm believer in independent opportunity and individual ownership of retail organizations; he is a strong advocate of agricultural cooperative movements. In addition to the above organizations, Mr. Grimes is president

Continued on page 546

ciency of marketing their surplus crops through a house holding membership on this exchange.

There are more than one hundred such houses today with connections
with country shippers, whose sole source of income is the commission earned
on grain consigned to them to sell at Chicago.

These men, and their fathers and grandfathers before them, have built
up their trade and good will under highly competitive conditions which, in
the final analysis, insure intelligent handling and the highest prices obtainable for the country shipper.

These are the men who were heaviest hit, economically, by the government's policy in creating a Farm Board, and subsequent attempt to set up a
monopoly in the handling of grain, a scheme that failed but which almost
destroyed established markets by the indiscreet use of taxpayers' money.

The Dairy Building of A Century of Progress in which exhibits dramatize, in sculpture,
painting and with projection equipment, the contribution of dairy products to the development of mankind.

(*Koehne Photo*)

ERNEST A. GRUNSFELD, JR.

Mr. Grunsfeld, architect, was born on August 25, 1897, in Albuquerque, New Mexico. As a boy he went to New York and was raised and educated there. Prepared at Phillips Exeter Academy, he graduated from the Massachusetts Institute of Technology with a degree of Bachelor of Science in architecture in 1917, and was awarded the Medal of the American Institute of Architects, the Gold Medal of the French Society of Architects, and the Roche Prize. After graduating, he studied, and received a certificate in, naval architecture, and following this was stationed at the Charlestown Navy Yard at Boston. He was recommended to become Naval Constructor in the United States Navy but resigned to practice architecture. After two years in the office of Robert D. Kohn of New York and with Clarence S. Stein, he studied in Europe for three years, at the American Academy in Rome and in Paris. After his return to New York in 1922, he worked as chief designer for the Brooklyn Public Library and later for Andrew Thomas on housing projects, after which he became an assistant of Mr. Stein in the office of Kohn, Butler and Stein. Mr. Stein and he were consultants on the Fort Sheridan Gardens project, a housing development near Chicago containing 700 homes, and due to this commission, he located in Chicago in 1924. From 1924 to 1928 he practiced in Chicago with Mr. Eugene H. Klaber and since then, for himself. He is a member of the Illinois Housing Commission.

Some of Mr. Grunsfeld's work in Chicago includes: the Adler Planetarium, which was awarded the Gold Medal of the American Institute of Architects for the year 1931; the Jewish People's Institute, a large community center; the 21-story Whitehall Hotel on Delaware place; branch library building for the City of Chicago; the Michigan Boulevard Garden Apartments, a housing project erected for negroes by the Julius Rosenwald Fund, which contains about 2,000 rooms, covering an entire city block, with a garden of over two acres in the center of the building. It is the largest housing project in the United States contained within one building. Other work by Mr. Grunsfeld includes residences and other buildings in Chicago, Detroit, Rock Island, Savannah, Philadelphia, Columbus, Cincinnati, New York, and other cities.

In 1926 he married Mary-Jane Loeb, and they have two children, Esther and Ernest A. III.

HOW THE TELEPHONE HAS MADE POSSIBLE THE GREATER CHICAGO

City, Suburbs, and Surrounding Territory Knit Into a Social and Commercial Unit

BY F. O. HALE
President, Illinois Bell Telephone Company

CHICAGO has been called the telephone capital of the world. While not the headquarters of the telephone industry, Chicago factories have produced more telephone equipment than is produced in any other city of the world, and during the greater part of the telephone era, Chicago's tele-phone system has developed more rapidly than that of any other metro-politan center of America or Europe.

Spread out over an area of hundreds of square miles, with suburbs dot-ting the prairie within a radius of fifty miles from the Loop, Chicago could never have attained its spectacular growth had not the telephone system grown with the city and anticipated future needs.

Thirty years ago a telephone in a private home was regarded as a luxury. Today it is almost indispensable. Thirty years ago business marched to a relatively slow tempo. Today an intricate network of wires reaching into almost every home, and to almost every desk, counter, and workshop, has knit Chicago and the surrounding territory into a single social and com-mercial unit. One can call New York without hanging up the receiver. The Chicago business man, from his office in the Loop, can talk to London, Paris, and Berlin.

Manually operated switchboard in one of Chicago's large telephone central offices.

FLOYD O. HALE

Mr. Hale, president of the Illinois Bell Telephone Company, was born in West Windsor, Vermont, April 13, 1882, and is the son of Frank S. and Mary J. (Hale) Hale. He is a graduate of Dartmouth College. His entire business life has been spent in the telephone organization. Beginning with a clerical position in Pittsburgh, successive promotions took him to New York, St. Louis and finally to Chicago, where, in 1921, he became chief engineer of the Illinois Bell Telephone Company. He was elected vice-president in 1922 and president in 1930.

Mr. Hale has been called on to give the benefit of his business judgment to a number of other important Chicago enterprises. He is a director of the Harris Trust and Savings Bank, the Terminal National Bank, and the Madison-Kedzie Trust and Savings Bank. He was a vice-president of the Union League Club, chairman of the finance committee for 1930-1931, and is now a director of the club. He is a member of the Industrial Club, Chicago Commonwealth Club, Chicago Club, Chicago Association of Commerce, Western Society of Engineers, University Club, Electric Club, Chicago Golf Club and the LaGrange Country Club.

In 1905 Mr. Hale married Gail Giddings Perkins of Windsor, Vermont (died 1921); the children are Elizabeth Perkins (Mrs. John H. Beardsley), and Robert Locke.

Telephone service in Chicago began in 1878, only a year after Alexander Graham Bell in his little workshop in Boston had invented his device for carrying sound vibrations, and had taken out his first patents. A crude central office, connecting a few instruments of primitive type, was opened in a building at La Salle and Madison streets.

Bernard E. Sunny, for many years president and chairman of the board of the present operating company, and still one of its directors and guiding spirits, became superintendent of the Chicago exchange in 1879.

In 1881 the Chicago Telephone Company was incorporated. The enlarged scope of its operations dictated, in 1920, a change of name, and the organization became known, more appropriately, as the Illinois Bell Telephone Company. Present directors include, in addition to Mr. Sunny, W. R. Abbott, William Butterworth, C. P. Cooper, David A. Crawford, W. S. Gifford, F. O. Hale, Charles Piez, Theodore W. Robinson, Fred W. Sargent, and A. H. Mellinger.

While a Boston workshop was the cradle of the telephone industry, it remained for a Chicago manufacturing concern to begin the manufacture of equipment on a large scale. Production was started in a modest plant in Kinzie street by the Western Electric Manufacturing Company, now the Western Electric Company. Business expanded so rapidly as the demand for telephones and telephone lines increased that the Western Electric is now the largest industrial organization in Chicago, with immense plants at Hawthorne, other large factories in the East, and distributing warehouses in thirty-two cities.

Meanwhile the telephone itself, has grown until there are now in the United States 19,000,000 instruments in service, and calls are registered at the rate of 65,000,000 a day.

Starting with a few lengths of wire stretched across the tops of buildings, the Chicago telephone system now operates more than 5,000,000 miles of copper wire, most of it in cables underneath the streets. Long distance telephone cables, "stepped up" at frequent intervals, extend to New York, Boston, and other cities of the eastern seaboard and as far westward as St. Louis and Omaha. By means of cable and open wire the Chicago telephone user has access to 70,000 or more cities, towns and villages in every part of this country, all telephones in Cuba

Telephone cable splicer at work beneath a Chicago street.

and most of those in Canada and Mexico, while over the recently perfected transoceanic radio telephone systems, he may reach practically all other telephone users in the civilized world. Chicago makes calls to Europe and occasional calls to South America, Australia, and Africa.

It is not alone in mere extent that the telephone in Chicago has grown. Its usefulness has been multiplied manyfold. Chicagoans have always been generous users of telephone service and quick to appreciate the comfort and convenience which the telephone affords. There are now in service more than 1,000,000 telephones in the city and suburbs and from these telephones more than 5,000,000 calls are made every day in the year. The trend toward better quality has been evident throughout the whole period of existence of

the telephone in Chicago, not only in the basic handling of calls by the company but in response to the customer's desire to obtain the most satisfactory and convenient arrangements on his premises. Large business houses use private branch exchanges, which, in size and capacity, are equal to or greater than the entire facilities of many a smaller town. The Chicago home which once found a single telephone sufficient now uses two to a half dozen, and some larger homes are equipped with complete systems

"Selector frame," one of the important pieces of dial telephone switching apparatus.

giving both out-going and intercommunicating service.

The adoption of the dial method of operation in the downtown business section and some of the congested residential areas has also improved service and aided the company in meeting the problem of the vast increase in the size of force which would have been necessary under the manual system, and has made possible continued improvements which would have been difficult, if not impossible, as the human element became a larger and larger factor. The growth of the telephone has been so rapid, however, both in Chicago and its suburbs, and the remainder of the territory operated by the Illinois Bell Telephone Company, that the introduction of the dial method in Chicago and in several other population centers of the state has been accomplished without a reduction in the number of operators required in the service of the company as a whole.

For a few years after the opening of the original central office on La Salle street one switchboard took care of the telephone needs of Chicago, but soon the popularity of the service made it necessary for the company to provide additional exchanges with full equipment. This process has gone on until every part of the city is now served by a total of 107 operating units, all connected by trunk cables with each other and with the very extensive long distance switching equipment located in the company's headquarters building at 212 West Washington street. This toll operating center includes all the latest type of equipment necessary to care for the thousands of suburban and intercity calls which are made by Chicago users every day. Calls to nearby exchanges are made in the same manner as local calls and on most of the calls to any part of the country the connection is set up and the call completed while the user holds the receiver. This speedy service has been made possible by improvements in methods and the addition of ample facilities between important cities.

The company's entire plant and equipment are valued at $285,000,000. Land and buildings alone in Chicago represent an investment of more than $20,000,000. Chicago employees number about 19,000. Adding to this an estimated 10,000 operators employed by subscribers on their private switchboards, and the large number of employees of the Western Electric Company, brings the total to more than 50,000 persons regularly employed in Chicago in supplying telephone service to the city and to the nation.

While it would be hazardous to predict the exact forms which improvements in the art of communication will take in the future, it is certain that improvements will be made and the trend toward higher quality will continue. In addition to the efforts of the Illinois Bell organization, the company has at its disposal the entire facilities of the Bell System of which it is a part, and particularly the facilities of the Bell Telephone Laboratories whose staff of nearly 6,000 is working continuously for improvement. The achievements of this staff in recent years have been so outstanding as to leave no doubt of continued success in the future. Some of the progress will, no doubt, be reflected in better service, some in better apparatus, and some in economies which will tend to offset part of the increasing cost involved in developing a complex and rapidly expanding communication network.

Chicago is destined to continue its rapid progress. The energy and experience of its business men and leaders in all lines assure it a future of growing importance in national affairs. The telephone will continue to play an important part in this development. Growth in the number of telephones and in telephone usage is expected to be steady. Extension of plant and equipment which will mean the investment of many millions of dollars will continue to be planned far enough in advance to meet the requirements of the Chicago community as they arise.

(*From Drawing by John Doctoroff*)

ISAAC MILLER HAMILTON

Mr. Hamilton, president of the Federal Life Insurance Company, of Chicago, was born in Ash Grove, Illinois, September 6, 1864, son of Ephraim S. and Celia B. (Miller) Hamilton. Educated at Grand Prairie Seminary, Onarga, Illinois, and by private tutors, he began his business life in general merchandising and live stock, and later entered banking. He was admitted to the Illinois bar in 1888, engaged in the general practice of law, and was a member of the Illinois State Senate from 1896 to 1900. He has been president of the Illinois League of Republican Clubs, and president of the National Republican League.

Mr. Hamilton has been president and a director of the Federal Life Insurance Company since he organized it in 1900. This company provides life, accident, and health insurance. He is president of The Illinois Canning Company, at Hoopeston, and a director of the Lake Shore Trust and Savings Bank. Mr. Hamilton has been very active and prominent in various life and accident and health organizations. He was one of the organizers and president of the American Life Convention whose membership includes about 250 legal reserve life insurance companies located in practically all States of the Union and the Dominion of Canada. He was one of the organizers and chairman of the Association of Life Agency Officers which established the Life Insurance Sales Research Bureau. He served for two terms as president of the Health & Accident Underwriters Conference. He is a member of the Illinois Athletic, Chicago Yacht, Hamilton, Union League, South Shore Country, Chicago Athletic, Exmoor Country, Bob O' Link Golf, and Casualty and Surety clubs; also Rotary Club No. 1, Chicago.

On June 11, 1907, he married Amanda S. Ernst of Chicago now deceased. There is one daughter, Miriam Celia, who graduated from Vassar College with honorable mention in 1930 and is now a senior in the Law School of the University of Chicago. She is and for some years has been a member of the board of directors of the Federal Life Insurance Company.

THE CHICAGO STOCK EXCHANGE AND ITS PLACE IN THE CITY'S FINANCIAL LIFE

Its Growth from a Local to a National Institution

AMONG the important markets of Chicago is its securities market, and in the rapid growth of the Chicago Stock Exchange is reflected the growth of the city as a financial center. The influence of this Exchange is felt today throughout the entire country. It is of direct benefit to every commercial and industrial enterprise in the Middle West.

For nearly three quarters of a century there has been some kind of a public market for securities in Chicago. The first stock exchange, organized in 1865, aided materially during the Civil War in maintaining the prices of government issues.

It was not until 1882, however, that the present Exchange was established, opening on May 15 of that year with 134 stocks and bonds listed for trading. In its early days the Exchange encountered many vicissitudes, and in 1887 its business dropped to such a low ebb that the Western Union actually removed its instruments from the Exchange floor. The market was, at best, a small and inactive one, and a day's trading was considered good when 50,000 shares changed hands. Today transactions run as high as half a million shares.

(*From etching by Ralph Fletcher Seymour*)
TRADING FLOOR OF THE CHICAGO STOCK EXCHANGE

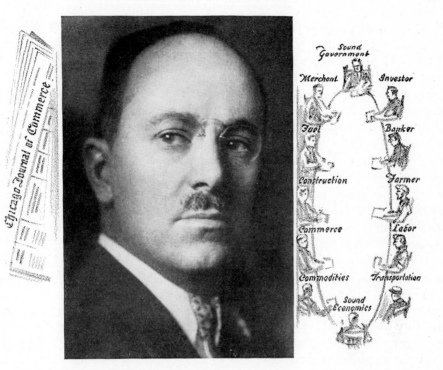

PHIL S. HANNA

Mr. Hanna, editor of The Chicago Journal of Commerce, a native of Aurora, Illinois, and a graduate of the University of Illinois, is a writer on business and political subjects. He was born March 9, 1887, son of James Carswell and Idella Medora Hanna. His father was for many years a merchant in Aurora. Shortly after becoming editor of The Chicago Journal of Commerce in October, 1931, Mr. Hanna inaugurated a vigorous attack on governmental waste and governmental competition in private business, which gained national attention and had largely to do with arousing the voters of the country to the high cost of government. His daily column, "Round Table of Business," is widely read.

The Chicago Journal of Commerce was started in October, 1920, and is unlike any other daily newspaper published. It is best described as "the business man's daily newspaper." It eliminates crime and sensation but covers in a concise manner business, financial and trade events. It contains daily more than 29,000 quotations. There are thirty-two experts in the Editorial Department, each devoting his entire time to a particular trade field. The Chicago Journal of Commerce oil and gasoline prices are the authority for a very large proportion of the petroleum industry. Its slogan is *"All the news a busy man has time to read."* He is a member of the Detroit Athletic Club, Chicago Athletic Association, Phi Kappa Psi.

Mr. Hanna married Marion Bartlett of Detroit in 1913. There are four children— Elizabeth, Barbara, Nancy and Philip, Jr.

During the fifty years of its existence The Chicago Stock Exchange has grown from a local to a national institution. It has at present 443 member-ships. These members have 619 offices in 207 cities in the United States and Canada. The members' private wires leading from Chicago total more miles than similar private wires leading from any other financial center in the world. This network of wires is supplemented by a quotation ticker service extending from coast to coast.

The nation's press associations carry the daily table of sales of The Chicago Stock Exchange transactions to the leading cities of America. The securities laws of most of the States of the Union provide that dealers in securities may buy or sell stocks listed on the Exchange without further qualifications. This widespread recognition is an indication not only of national interest in the Chicago securities market, but of confidence in the integrity of that market.

The Chicago Stock Exchange is a market place where stocks and bonds are bought, sold and delivered. It is under the direct control of its members. A significant feature of the Exchange is that only individuals or partnerships may be members, thus protecting the investor by requiring the unlimited liability of all members and their partners. No officer, director or employee of a corporation dealing with the public in securities may be a member of The Chicago Stock Exchange. The organization has maintained this high standard to safeguard the investors who deal through its members.

Naturally the question arises as to what is the future ahead of The Chicago Stock Exchange. The history of every great financial center has been that it first develops as an industrial and commercial center. As long as it is a borrowing community, requiring more capital than it possesses for the development and operation of its business enterprises, it is not of great importance as a financial market. However, in the development of every major financial market, from Genoa on down through Amsterdam, Berlin, London, Boston and New York, history shows that as soon as these communities became lending communities—as soon as they reached the point where they had more money as communities than they needed for the development and operation of their business enterprises—they started on the road to financial independence and financial leadership. Eventually these financial markets became of equal importance to the other markets of these cities.

Chicago has been slow in developing its financial independence because of the great variety of undeveloped resources of the Middle West. As the business of the Middle West increased, new fields were opened and for years funds had to be borrowed from the outside to take advantage of the opportunities that lay ahead. Approximately two decades ago Chicago, as a great economic center, passed from the borrowing to the lending stage. That is the economic reason for the expansion of The Chicago Stock Ex-change in the last few years and why it has been so outstanding.

LESLIE C. HARBISON

Mr. Harbison, president of Household Finance Corporation, was born in Batavia, Iowa, December 14, 1878, son of Samuel Morrison and Cordelia (Quig) Harbison. He received his education in the public schools of Philadelphia and Bethlehem, Pennsylvania. His first position was that of an outside representative of Frank J. Mackey, Philadelphia, in 1897. Later he was transferred to their Cleveland (Ohio) office, where he remained from 1900 to 1905; was manager of the Washington (D. C.) office from 1905 to 1908; and was in the middle-western branch offices in Chicago from 1908 to 1917. In 1918 the organization upon which Household Finance Corporation was subsequently built came into being and in 1925 it assumed its present corporate form. In that year Mr. Harbison was appointed president, and under his leadership Household Finance Corporation has become the largest organization of its kind in America, with 148 branch offices in ninety-one cities of twelve states. This organization makes loans in amounts up to three hundred dollars to families unable to obtain bank credit. Loans may be repaid any time within a year and eight months, charges being made only for the actual length of time money is used. This organization sponsors a household money management program to teach families how to spend wisely.

Mr. Harbison is a member of the Illinois Society of the Sons of the American Revolution. His clubs are Chicago Athletic Association, Medinah Athletic, Bob o'Link, and Westmoreland Country. His favorite recreations are golf, hunting, and fishing.

He married Maude E. Bower, of Boston, Massachusetts, December 31, 1900. Their children are Gladys Irene (Mrs. John H. Lawson), David Samuel, Leslie Craig, Dorothy Maude, and Elizabeth Helene.

If Chicago is to enjoy the same experience as other great trade centers, it eventually will have a stock exchange corresponding to the other markets of the city. When one realizes that this is the great grain market of the world, the great live stock market of the world, the great food distributing center of the world, the great railroad center of the world—(one could list scores of fields in which Chicago leads)—the people of the Middle West may look forward to expecting great things of The Chicago Stock Exchange as a market place for securities.

With fifty years' background of experience, with billions of dollars in securities already listed on the Exchange, with a single day's volume of business reaching $100,000,000, with the Exchange developing from a local to an international institution, it is fair to look forward to the time when The Chicago Stock Exchange will correspond in greatness to the other great markets in the city.

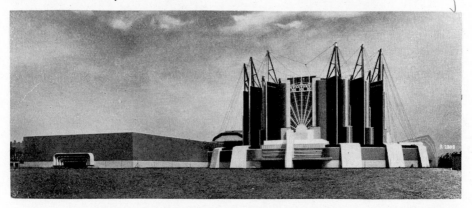

(*Chicago Architectural Photographing Company*)
THE TRAVEL AND TRANSPORT BUILDING of A Century of Progress, showing the "cable-suspended" dome which represents the first important application of the "suspension bridge" principle of support to architecture.
Edward Bennett, John Holabird, and Hubert Burnham, associated architects.

(*Moffet-Russell Photo*)

W. HOMER HARTZ

Mr. Hartz, president of Morden Frog and Crossing Works, was born in Tarrytown, New York, December 11, 1887, son of Irving Thomas and Lillian Ione (Terhune) Hartz. He graduated from the Chicago Manual Training School in 1903 and received his B.S. (Bachelor of Science) degree at Purdue University in 1907. He was with the engineer-ing corps of the Chicago Southern and Pennsylvania railways before graduating from college and was with the Baltimore and Ohio Railroad from 1907 to 1908. He worked for the Oliver Iron Mining Company in 1908, Chicago, Milwaukee & St. Paul Railroad Company in 1909, and the S. B. Chapin & Company 1909 to 1911.

In 1911 Mr. Hartz became connected with the Morden Frog and Crossing Works as a draftsman and has continued in the same company respectively as chief clerk, sec-retary, treasurer, assistant manager of sales until 1927, vice-president from 1927 to 1930, and president since 1930. This company manufactures frogs, crossings, switches, switch stands, guard rail clamps, tie bars, rail braces, et cetera, for steam, electric and industrial railroads. The company celebrated their fiftieth year of existence in 1932, having been organized in 1882. Mr. Hartz is a member of the Western Society of Engineers, Indiana Society of Chicago, and Delta Upsilon Fraternity. His clubs are Chicago Athletic Asso-ciation, Engineers, and Exmoor Country, and his favorite recreation is golf.

He married Bertha Blanchard Mead of Chicago, April 25, 1917. Their children are William Homer, Jr., and Betty Mead.

CHICAGO AS A NATIONAL MANUFACTURING CENTER

An Industrial Area That Is Producing More Than Five Billion Dollars Worth of Goods a Year

PRIOR to 1834, meat packing and tanning, both conducted on a back yard scale, were Chicago's only industries. The town's first foundry was established in 1835, and the first flour mill was erected a year later.

By 1857, there were in Chicago manufacturers of flour, soap, glue, starch, wine, beer, packed beef, and tanned leather, with a combined capital of $1,639,000, and 639 employes on the pay roll.

No women's or men's clothing, no furs, no cosmetics or perfumes, no printing materials, no bakery products, no confectionery or ice cream. Many articles for everyday use were manufactured in the home.

Meat packing today still leads Chicago's industries, and its story is told elsewhere in this book. Today, the Chicago Metropolitan Area is

ENGINEERING BUILDING
Burnham Brothers, Inc., architects.

CARBIDE AND CARBON BUILDING
Burnham Brothers, Inc., architects.

(Moffett-Russell Photo)

SAMUEL M. HASTINGS

Mr. Hastings, chairman of the finance committee of the Dayton Scale Company, was born in Rimersburg, Pennsylvania, August 14, 1860, the son of Eli and Rachel Whitehall (Kerr) Hastings. He was educated in the Gardner, Illinois, public schools. He began as a clerk in a dry goods store in Braidwood, Illinois. In 1879 he established a store of his own, which he conducted until 1884. He was also in the dry goods business in Streator, Illinois, from 1884 to 1889. Mr. Hastings came to Chicago in 1889, and with several associates, organized the Moneyweight Scale Company. After extensive travel in Europe, he returned to Chicago in 1903 to become president of the Dayton Scale Company, holding this office until 1928, when he was made chairman of the finance committee.

Mr. Hastings is a director of the International Business Machines Corporation, the Addressograph International Corporation, and the Metal Door and Trim Company of La Porte, Indiana. He is chairman of the board of the Highland Park State Bank, and was Mayor of Highland Park from 1915 to 1928. A member of the Illinois Manufac-turers' Association, he served that body as treasurer, from 1912 to 1915, as president from 1915 to 1917 and again during 1932. He is a founder member of A Century of Progress Exposition. In 1916, when it seemed inevitable that the United States would be drawn into the World War, Mr. Hastings urged on President Wilson the appointment of a commission of from twelve to twenty representative Americans to visit the European capitals and commercial centers with a view to bringing about peace. When the United States declared war against the Central Powers, he called together the members of the Illinois Manufacturers' Association, who pledged themselves and their plants to the service of the nation. Mr. Hastings advocated also a permanent commercial and industrial union of the allied nations to be based on a two hundred billion dollar bond issue by the United States, Great Britain, Italy, and Japan. Mr. Hastings is a member of the Sons of the American Revolution, the Mid-Day, Old Elm, and Exmoor Country clubs, the Chicago Athletic Association, and a life member of the Press Club.

He was married September 16, 1881, to Janette Rankin of Braidwood, Illinois, who died in November, 1922. He was married again to Miss Nettie Ann Moore of Chicago in 1925. He has an adopted son, Rolland Thomas Rankin Hastings.

the fastest growing steel center in the world. Those who regard Chicago as too utilitarian might do well to investigate the printing and publishing business of the city which in book and job work alone has an annual production in excess of $150,000,000, while that of the newspaper and periodical branch of the business is almost as great. Articles are manufactured today in Chicago that were undreamed of at the beginning of the present century.

Chicago is producing goods whose value in the course of a year amounts to approximately $4,000,000,000, while the value of the products turned out annually in Greater Chicago—an area which includes such industrial beehives as Waukegan, Gary, Indiana Harbor, Hammond, Chicago Heights, Joliet, Aurora, and Elgin—is $5,588,331,242, according to the last census returns, in 1930.

Illinois ranks third among the States in the value of its manufactured goods, but in industrial importance Chicago stands second among American cities.

Much of Illinois' industrial activity is centered in and around Chicago, where 11,774 manufacturing establishments are located. These establishments employ in normal times more than 550,000 wage earners who draw annually nearly $870,000,000 in wages. Salaried officers and "white collar" employees number approximately 113,000 with a combined annual salary of $317,000,000. The cost of materials, containers, fuel, and electrical energy used in the Chicago Area mounts up to more than $3,000,000,000 a year in normal times.

Since the total value of the finished products was $5,588,331,242, the value "added by manufacture" was in excess of $2,500,000,000—two and a half billion dollars of created wealth. This value, however, does not represent actual profit, as deductions must be made for such items as rent, interest on investment, depreciation, taxes, insurance, and advertising.

The Chicago factories alone employ normally more than 400,000 wage earners and approximately 86,000 salaried executives and other employees. These establishments pay out annually something like $870,000,000 in salaries and wages.

Conditions have been favorable for manufacturing in Illinois for many years. The Illinois State Legislature has refrained from passing bills which in other States have been so damaging to industry, and if this policy is continued, and the manufacturers are not overtaxed or harassed in other ways, there is abundant reason to believe that Illinois and Chicago plants will continue to advance in production until ultimately they will lead those of all other States in the value of their output.

(*Moffett-Russell Photo*)

RALPH R. HAWXHURST

Mr. Hawxhurst, member of the law firm of White and Hawxhurst, was born in Chicago, January 24, 1887, son of Arthur and Marie (Reynaud) Hawx-hurst. He received his preparatory education at Lewis Institute and his A. B. (Bachelor of Arts) degree at Northwestern University in 1905; LL.B. (Bachelor of Laws) in 1909. He was admitted to the Illinois bar in 1909 and has since practiced in Chicago. He is associate professor of law at Northwestern University Law School and associate editor of the Illinois Law Review. Mr. Hawxhurst is very much interested in civic affairs. For four years he was trustee of Kenilworth, Illinois, and for the past seven years has been mayor of that suburb, his present term expiring in April, 1933. During the World War he was a member of the Draft Board and a Four Minute Man. He is general counsel for many corporations and is Chicago counsel for several large surety companies and is director of many.

Mr. Hawxhurst is a member of the American, Illinois State, and Chicago Bar Associations, Beta Theta Pi, Delta Chi, Sigma Rho, Delta Theta. His clubs are Union League, City, The Law Club, Kenilworth, Bob O'Link Golf, Exmoor Country, and Illinois Whist. For recreation he enjoys tennis and golf.

He married Jeannette Leggett, of Chicago, August 23, 1910, and they have four children, Stephen, Jacqueline, Suzanne, and Ralph R., Jr.

BROADCASTING IN CHICAGO AND ITS AMAZING GROWTH

Radio Comes Into Its Own

BY CHARLES J. GILCHREST
Radio Editor, The Chicago Daily News

IT was the eve of Armistice Day, 1921. Confusion reigned backstage of the Auditorium Theater—the usual hectic scene of last-minute preparation, for tomorrow the Chicago Grand Opera Company would open its season. In the wings, a stage carpenter was hammering a weakened set. Nearby, a marimba sounded its musical note. And radio—wireless, as it was called then—was born in Chicago.

Those hammer blows and that marimba note were the first sounds to go out on the ether waves from the prairie metropolis. The following night, wireless made its official debut with the broadcasting of the opera performance. Few in the audience noticed the microphone suspended from the ceiling, and those who did failed to comprehend its significance; nor would they have known what to call it, for the word had just been coined.

Wireless came to Chicago unheralded and unsung. That first broadcast was heard by an invisible audience numbering only a few hundred amateurs and engineers who had been following the preliminary tests. They "listened in" on erratic little crystal sets with headphones glued to their ears. Some of it they got, and some of it they missed, for radio was still in its experimental stage.

It was George Foster who persuaded the Westinghouse Electric and Manufacturing Company to bring wireless to Chicago. Westinghouse was the builder and owner of the pioneer station KDKA, established in Pittsburgh in 1920. The Chicago station was given the call letters KYW, which it still uses.

At the suggestion of Mr. Foster, the microphone—it was not yet known as a "Mike"—had been installed in the opera house. An executive of the Commonwealth Edison Company, he had become enthused with the new thing, called by some a toy.

The opera management gave its consent with some misgivings. Wireless? How amusing! But it could do no harm to humor him.

Mary Garden spoke into the microphone that night, and her voice, picked up by the little crystal sets, was heard by a handful of radio fans, who also heard more or less distinctly Edith Mason in "Madame Butterfly."

Newspaper editors had been asked to listen in, and receiving equipment had been furnished for their use. When the performance was over, wireless enthusiasts rushed to the local rooms. "What did you think of it?" they asked. "Of what?" returned the editors. "Of the broadcast—the wirelessing of the opera." "Oh. that! We forgot all about it. Didn't hear it." First-page stories describing the experiment appeared, however, the following morning.

BILL HAY

Mr. Hay, chief announcer and sales director of Radio Station W M A Q of Chicago, is a genuine Scotchman and was born in Dumfries, Scotland, on April 18, 1887, the son of William Gibiral and Jessie Keiller (Menzies) Hay. He attended school in this ancient town, where Robert Burns lies buried, and worked his way through college, studying music in addition as he went along. Later he obtained employment in London, England, with Thomas Cook and Son, well-known travel agency, and finally, having decided he would do some traveling himself, he came to the United States in 1909, becoming a naturalized citizen in 1916. April 21, 1915, he married Elizabeth Webster of Chicago.

It was at Hastings, Nebraska, that he got his start in radio work. Later he returned to Chicago, where his voice and Scottish bur-r-r became familiar to a larger public through Station W G N. Not long afterward he trans-ferred his allegiance to W M A Q and became chief of its announcing staff and sales director, being in charge of the sale of time and programs to sponsors. Mr. Hay announces most of the leading programs over W M A Q, but he is probably best known as the announcer for "Amos 'n Andy" and "The Goldbergs," two of the most outstanding and popular programs broadcast over a coast-to-coast network every night except Saturday and Sunday. He is the only radio announcer used exclusively by one advertiser on a chain broadcast. His "Auld Sandy" program, heard every Sunday night over WMAQ, is a pop-ular feature with hundreds of thousands of listeners. He was decorated as a Cavaliere of the Order of the Crown of Italy. He is a member of Midland and Medinah Athletic clubs and Mission Hills Country Club. His favorite recreations are golf and squash racquets.

The end of the opera season was in sight. Broadcasting had started, and was becoming popular. How could it be continued? Then the radio studio was conceived. On the eighteenth floor of the Edison Building a single room was fitted up. Its walls were hung with burlap. A plain carpet deadened the floor. Here the first studio broadcast took place on January 23, 1922.

The program was given by Richard Czerwonky, violinist, and Frances Ingram, contralto, with Sally Menkes at the piano. KYW launched a daily

When wireless was very young this was its home, the studio on the sixteenth floor of the Edison Building, installed just a month after studio broadcasting had become a fact in Chicago. Note the embryo microphone, which, on occasion when records were to be played could be pushed up against the horn of the phonograph. Compare with picture below.

(Wesley Bowman Photo)

Studio A of the National Broadcasting Company in the Merchandise Mart—the world's largest broadcasting studio in the world's largest building. The piano is a nine-foot concert grand, the largest model made. The steps of the two-level stage are visible in the background.

(*Covington Studio Photo*)

WILLIAM S. HEDGES

Mr. Hedges, manager of Radio Station W M A Q, Chicago, was born in Elmwood, Illinois, June 21, 1895, son of LeRoy Clarke (M. D.) and Ida Erie (Ellis) Hedges. He graduated from the Colorado Springs (Colorado) High School in 1913 and was a student at the University of Chicago from 1914 to 1917. He joined the editorial staff of the Chicago Daily News in 1915, while still a student at the University and established the radio department in 1922. On April 1, 1930, when The Daily News founded the subsidiary corporation, W M A Q, Inc., to operate its station, one of the first radio stations in Chicago, Mr. Hedges was elected president of the new corporation. Now that the station is affiliated with the National Broadcasting Company, Inc., Mr. Hedges remains the manager of this radio station. He was also secretary of Press Wireless, Inc., from 1929 to 1931 and has been in control of experimental work conducted by W9XAP, the television station established by The Daily News, August 1, 1930.

In 1918 he graduated from the School of Military Aeronautics, Austin, Texas, and the Artillery School of Fire, Fort Sill, Oklahoma. He became a 2nd lieutenant in the Air Service, U. S. A., at Post Field, Oklahoma, and was attached to 311th Air Corps, Officers' Reserve Corps, from 1919 to 1924. He is a member of the International Committee on Wireless Telegraphy, and president of the National Association of Broadcasters from 1928 to 1930 (chairman legislative committee during 1927), chairman executive committee, 1930-1931, and a member of the executive committee, 1931-1932. He is a member of the American Legion, La Societe des 40 Hommes et 8 Chevaux, and Sigma Nu Fraternity. He belongs to the National Sojourners, Medinah Athletic, Shawnee Country, and Wilmette Golf Clubs, and is a 32 degree Mason and Shriner. He edited "Credit Craft and The Modern Office" from 1925 to 1931 and contributed to "Radio and Its Future," "Education on the Air," in 1930 and "Careers in Advertising" in 1932. His principal interests, outside of radio and his family, are golf, reading and travel.

On April 21, 1920, he married Margaret Elizabeth Hasenbalg of Chicago. Their children are Helen Saxby and Margaret Ann.

studio broadcast from 8 to 9 o'clock in the evening, the artists volunteering their services. The sponsored program and the salaried radio star were undreamed of. But radio had been weaned away from opera, and had moved into its own studio.

As the broadcasting idea grew in popularity, other stations sprang up, and the industry developed its own terminology. The radio announcer became an important person, even as he is today. At the same time, the crystal set, with its headphones was emerging into an elaborate multidialed affair which only an engineer—probably two engineers—could operate successfully. But the fact remained that wireless' noises were getting on the air with a fair degree of certainty and were being picked up by the ever increasing multitudes.

The chain idea came into being January 4, 1923, when telephone lines connected WEAF in New York and WNAC in Boston—and another milestone was passed. The infant had learned to walk, to get from one station to another. Of course, he didn't walk very well yet. He couldn't go very far, sometimes he'd fall down, and fans would hear nothing at all. He staggered at times, stumbled. But nevertheless he was walking in his own queer, ambling, infantile fashion.

As time progressed he walked better, farther, and with greater and greater assurance. In fact he walked all the way from New York to Chicago in April, 1927. It was then that Frank Mullen opened an office here for the National Broadcasting Company, the first network office in Chicago. He had a staff of three people. Today Vice-president Niles Trammell heads a staff of 800 NBC workers in Chicago.

And the boy grew older. Now he lives not in the dinky little room of the Edison building but in such sumptuous suites as Studio A of the National Broadcasting company's quarters in the Merchandise Mart. He can point proudly to his home, pick out Studio A and say "It's the largest broadcasting studio in the world." It floats on springs, being a room within a room in the special two-story penthouse NBC occupies on the top of the world's largest building.

Think of that little original studio—then of Studio A. "A" is large enough to accomodate 500 visitors and at the same time full size orchestras and casts of radio actors such as WMAQ and WENR use for some of their more elaborate sponsored shows. It's two-level stage is much larger than is ordinarily found in theaters. It is attractively dressed up in two-shade green walls with moveable panels instead of the old burlap drapes for accoustic purposes. Special sunlight lamps illuminate it. The stage is backed by a huge bronze grill. At the other end is a projection booth, as yet unused, but there, ready and waiting for television when the child acquires its sight.

HASBROUCK HAYNES

Mr. Haynes, chairman and president of the Haynes Corporation, inventor of the Manit System and the Salit Plan, was born in Detroit, Michigan, August 21, 1888, son of David Oliphant and Helen Dunham (Williams) Haynes. He received his M.E. (Mechanical Engineer) degree at Stevens Institute of Technology, Castle Point, New Jersey, in 1910. Upon graduation Mr. Haynes became a member of the engineering staff of Gunn, Richards & Company, production engineers and accountants, New York, and was assigned to work with Studebaker Corporation, South Bend, Indiana, and Detroit, Michigan, during its reorganization and transition from the manufacture of horse-drawn vehicles to automobiles. He was later appointed assistant general manager of Studebaker Corporation of Canada, Ltd., at Walkerville, Ontario, and subsequently became special representative of Packard Motor Car Company, organizing and promoting distribution.

Mr. Haynes became president of the Haynes Corporation in 1917 and chairman of the board in 1928. He is also chairman and president of The Eastern Haynes Corporation of New York. These companies, which are engaged in management engineering and specializing in the measurement and stimulation of human effort, have served many nationally known corporations such as Armour and Company, Quaker Oats Company, Anaconda Copper Company, Continental Can Company, Loose-Wiles Biscuit Company, and Kraft Cheese Company.

In 1922 Mr. Haynes originated the Haynes Manit (man-minute) System, which is a scientific and intensive plan for increasing labor efficiency. In 1932 Mr. Haynes developed the Haynes Salit Plan for accelerating sales and profits by the scientific application of payment to all salesmen on an incentive basis according to the gross profits which each one sells. This includes payment of bonuses to sales supervisors.

Mr. Haynes believes that much of the inertia of a depression is due to the fact that business men have been unwilling to progress by discarding outworn and unsound ideas, methods, and practices. Mr. Haynes belongs to the American Society of Mechanical Engineers, Society of Industrial Engineers, Illinois Manufacturers' Association, Chicago Association of Commerce, and Beta Theta Phi fraternity. His clubs are University, Engineers, and Country Club of Evanston. His recreations are golf and horseback riding.

On October 11, 1923, he married Elizabeth Craig of Chicago. His children are Louise Covington and Milton Covington.

MASTERPIECES OF THE SCULPTOR'S ART THAT GLORIFY CHICAGO

Charming Statues and Impressive Memorials Along the Boulevards and in the Parks

MUCH of the beauty of such Old-World cities as Paris, Vienna, Dresden, and Brussels rests to a great extent upon their public monuments and statues, and it is through such specimens of municipal art that their fame has become world-wide.

Of such, too, was the grandeur that was Greece, the glory that was Rome. Chicago, while still one of the world's youngest cities, is beginning to assume a definite character and European atmosphere by reason of the many beautiful works of statuary that have been installed along the boulevards and in the parks within recent years.

One of the most exquisite of these is Lorado Taft's "Fountain of Time," in Washington Park. In this symbolic poem, classic art reaches a high level. The speeding motorist might well pause here to reflect on the message Father Time imparts as the ages of mankind, fading away into the mists of antiquity pass before him in review. It is they who pass; he, Time, alone, remains.

Equally beautiful is the Ferguson Fountain of the Great Lakes, also the work of Lorado Taft, erected by the B. F. Ferguson Monument Fund, completed in 1913, and located at the south terrace of the Art Institute. Here, the five Great Lakes, symbolized by graceful maidens, are seen pouring crystal waters into a central basin.

In the McKinlock court of the Art Institute is the Fountain of Tritons by Carl Milles, brought from the sculptor's gardens in Sweden to Chicago by a group of public-spirited citizens in commemoration of the out-

(Henry Fuermann & Sons Photo)

333 Building, at Michigan avenue and Wacker drive.
Holabird & Root, architects.

(Kellogg Photo)

JOHN A. HOLABIRD

Mr. Holabird, senior partner in the firm of Holabird and Root, architects, was born in Evanston, May 4, 1886, the son of William and Maria (Augur) Holabird. He received his preparatory education at the Hill School, Pottstown, Pennsylvania. Graduating in 1903, he was given an appointment to the United States Military Academy at West Point, and was commissioned as a Second Lieutenant in 1907. He spent the next two years at the Engineers' School at Washington Barracks, and in 1913, enrolled in the Ecole des Beaux Arts, Paris. After an extensive preparation in architecture and engineering, he began his practice in Chicago on his return from Paris in 1913. From 1914 to 1917 he was a Captain of the Illinois National Guard, and in August, 1918, he left for overseas service as Major in the Field Artillery. Later he received the commission of Lieutenant Colonel. He was decorated with the Distinguished Service Medal, and was mustered out in March, 1919.

The firm of Holabird and Root has designed the classic Stadium at Soldier Field, the Stevens Hotel, the Palmer House, Chicago's first "skyscraper church," the Methodist Temple Building, the Palmolive Building, Board of Trade Building, 333 Building, Daily News Building and many others. As a member of the architectural commission of A Century of Progress Exposition, Chicago's (1933) World's Fair, Mr. Holabird is in a good measure responsible for many of the new and revolutionary ideas in design and engineering which have been given expression in the buildings of this miracle city.

Mr. Holabird is a trustee of the Art Institute, a member of the American Institute of Architects, and of the University, Union League, Industrial, Chicago, Saddle and Cycle, and Glenview Golf clubs.

Mr. Holabird was married May 12, 1917, to Dorothy Hackett of Chicago. He has two sons, John Augur and Christopher.

standing service rendered to the United States by the Swedish-American inventor, John Erisson.

The memory of Theodore Thomas, father of the Chicago Symphony Orchestra, is perpetuated by a magnificent statue, "The Spirit of Music," executed by Albin Polasek, and erected in Grant Park, opposite Orchestra Hall, between Adams street and Jackson boulevard.

The memorial tablet reads: "Scarcely any man in any land has done so much for the musical education of the people as did Theodore Thomas in this country. The nobility of his ideals with the magnitude of his achievement will assure him everlasting glory."

Nor have our national heroes been forgotten. The Saint Gaudens' Lincoln, an impressive bronze amid equally impressive settings at the south end of Lincoln Park has been the inspiration of thousands of young Americans. At the entrance to the Art Institute stands the heroic bronze George Washington by Jean Antoine Houdon.

The spirited equestrian statue of John E. Logan, by Saint Gaudens, was erected by the State of Illinois in Grant Park near Park row, and completed in 1897. It is at the foot of this monument that every important parade has been reviewed for the last thirty-five years. This statue also marks the tomb of the famous Civil War general.

The Alexander Hamilton monument by Bela Pratt at Washington street and the Illinois Central parapet has the following inscription on its tablet: "Liberty may be endangered by abuses of liberty as well as by abuses of power."

One of the finest equestrians to be found anywhere is that of Phil Sheridan in Lincoln Park near Belmont avenue. It depicts the general on his famous ride, and action is expressed in every line.

Not so well known as the Lincoln mentioned above, but quite as interesting is the other Saint Gaudens statue of the Emancipator, a seated figure, located east of the Illinois Central right of way near Van Buren street, in Grant Park.

Other national heroes are commemorated by the McKinley statue, the work of Charles J. Mulligan, in McKinley Park; the Kosciusko equestrian statue by Alexander Choclzinski, in Humboldt Park; the Stephen A. Douglas monument on the South Side, and the von Humboldt statue, by Felix Garling, unveiled in Humboldt Park in 1892.

The memory of two tragic events in Chicago history is preserved in the Haymarket memorial, now removed from its original site in Haymarket Square to Union Park, and dedicated to the memory of the policemen who fell in the famous West Side riot; and the Fort Dearborn Massacre memorial, which stood for many years at the foot of 26th street, but which now occupies a site in the main hall of the Chicago Historical Society's new building.

More peaceful events are commemorated by the Statue of the Republic in Jackson Park and the Illinois Centennial Monument in Logan Square.

ALBERT L. HOPKINS

Mr. Hopkins, lawyer and income tax specialist, was born in Hickory, Mississippi, April 27, 1886, son of Oliver and Helen V. (Tucker) Hopkins. He attended Millsaps College, Jackson, Mississippi, from 1900 to 1901, the University of Mississippi during 1901 and 1902. He received his A. B. (Bachelor of Arts) degree at the University of Chicago in 1905, J. D. (Doctor of Jurisprudence) in 1908, and LL.B. (Bachelor of Laws) at Harvard in 1909. Mr. Hopkins was admitted to the Illinois bar in 1908 and was appointed Assistant United States attorney, Northern District of Illinois, in 1913, which he remained until 1917, when he was made assistant counsel, United States Interstate Commerce Commission at Washington, where he served until 1919. In 1919 he was appointed special attorney for the Internal Revenue Bureau and he served in this capacity until 1920.

Later Mr. Hopkins organized the law firm of Hopkins, Starr and Hopkins, and in 1931 formed the law firm of Hopkins, Sutter, Halls and De Wolfe. He is a member of the University, Union League, Law, Quadrangle, and Flossmoor Country clubs.

On April 19, 1922, he married Florence Odil, and they have three children, Nancy Odil, Florence Catherine, and Albert L. Jr.

The former is a reminder of the World's Columbian Exposition, and stands on the site of the old Administration Building. The latter signalizes the one-hundredth anniversary of Illinois' statehood.

The early days of exploration and the American Indian are recalled by such statues as the Peace Signal, a mounted Indian in Lincoln Park; the Indians on horseback—specimens of modernistic sculptor—at the Congress street approach to Grant Park, and the cross erected at South Robey street and the river on the site of the landing of Marquette and Joliet.

A children's poet and a children's story teller still live in the charming memorial to Eugene Field and the statue of Hans Christian Anderson, both in Lincoln Park. In the former, the delicate figure of a fairy brooding like a guardian angel over the sleeping children, is most exquisite.

The Fountain of Time in Washington Park, facing the Midway. This work, by Lorado Taft, shows the human procession passing in review before the great immovable figure of Time. The idea was suggested to the sculptor by these lines from a poem,
"Time goes, you say? Ah, no
Alas, time stays; we go."

Among other Lincoln Park sculptures is the conventional Linné statue, dedicated to the memory of the famous naturalist; and the heroic, but somewhat grotesque, statue representing the spirit of Goethe.

An especially pleasing bit of statuary is the Rosenberg fountain surmounted by the bronze figure of Hebe. This work was accepted by the City of Chicago in October, 1893, and is standing in Grant Park at Michigan avenue and Park row.

A bit of ancient Greece is to be found in the graceful peristyle, seen to the best advantage by moonlight, in Grant Park at Michigan avenue and Randolph street. The semicircular row of classic columns encloses a small, but beautiful fountain.

(From Drawing by John Doctoroff)

HENRY HORNER

Judge Horner, elected Governor of Illinois on the Democratic Ticket, November 8, 1932, was born in Chicago November 30, 1878, the son of Solomon and Dilah (Horner) Horner. He was educated in the Chicago public schools, the Chicago Manual Training School, the University of Michigan, and the University of Chicago. He received his degree of Bachelor of Laws from the Kent (now Chicago-Kent) College of Law in 1898, and was admitted to the Illinois Bar in 1899. Lincoln Memorial University has conferred upon him the honorary degree of Doctor of Laws.

When Mayor Harrison called the Charter Convention of 1911 for the purpose of adopting a new city charter, Judge Horner, then engaged in private practice, was selected as Chairman of the Committee on Plans and Procedure. In 1914 he was elected Judge of the Probate Court, and was four times reelected to this office by increasing majorities. He has served also in the County Court, dealing with problems involving election machinery, tax legislation, and state institutions. Despite his arduous duties on the Bench, Judge Horner has found time for many charitable enterprises and for the study of civic affairs. He has been the arbitrator in scores of labor disputes in Cook County, and in 1929, as a member of the Illinois Society for Mental Hygiene, was active in the improvement of conditions in the State Hospital for the Mentally Defective.

A recognized authority on Lincoln, he has gathered together a priceless collection of manuscripts and documents pertaining to the Great Emancipator. He is a member of the American, Illinois, and Chicago Bar Associations, of the Chicago Geographical Society, the Art Institute, the Chicago Historical Society, the Lincoln Centennial Association, Lincoln Memorial Commission, Lincoln Highway Commission, and the Chicago Association of Commerce. He has served as a trustee of many charitable homes and asylums, and a member of the Chicago Council of Boy Scouts. His club affiliations are many, including memberships in the Law, City, Chicago Literary, Mid-Day, Standard, Iroquois, Covenant, Collegiate, Illinois Athletic, Wayfarers, Caxton, and Lake Shore Country clubs.

The story of Chicago's early days is told in the virile reliefs on the approach to the Michigan avenue bridge, only a short distance from the site of Fort Dearborn, marked by a tablet over the entrance of the London Guarantee Accident Building across the way. One of these depicts the Fort Dearborn massacre; another, entitled "The Discoverers," shows the arrival of Marquette and Joliet; a third, "The Pioneers," has for its subject the arrival of John Kinzie and his family, while the fourth, "The Regeneration," symbolizes Chicago's recovery from the great fire.

(Kaufman & Fabry Co. Photo)

In the BUCKINGHAM MEMORIAL FOUNTAIN, the gift of Miss Kate Buckingham, Chicago has not merely the largest, but the most beautiful fountain in America. Its pool is 300 feet wide, the center column of water rises 110 feet, and when illuminated in color, it is a never-to-be-forgotten spectacle. Marcel Loyau of Paris, sculptor of the sea horses. Bennett, Parsons & Frost and Jacques H. Lambert, associated architects.

At Diversey parkway and Lake View avenue, facing Lincoln Park, stands the impressive circular colonnade of the Elks' Memorial, somewhat resembling Grant's Tomb in New York, and dedicated to the memory of 70,000 Elks who served in the World War.

The modernistic school of sculpture is represented in such statues as the colossal Ceres by John Storrs, looking down upon La Salle street from the apex of the Board of Trade tower, and the monumental bust of Leif Ericsson, by Oscar J. W. Hansen. The head, cast in bronze, measures six

WILLIAM HOSKINS

Mr. Hoskins, president of Mariner and Hoskins, Inc., consulting research and analytical chemists, was born in Covington, Kentucky, July 15, 1862, son of John and Mary Ann (Hoskins) Hoskins. He graduated from the Chicago High School in 1879, followed by chemical and other instruction. In 1880 Mr. Hoskins joined Prof. G. A. Mariner in his analytical chemical laboratory, became partner in the firm of Mariner and Hoskins, Inc., in 1885, and was sole proprietor from 1890 until 1930, when the firm was incorporated as Mariner and Hoskins, Inc., and he became president.

Mr. Hoskins' discoveries number more than one hundred and range from a special chalk for billiard cues to the high resistance wire used in electric heating appliances, which made electric heat possible. He perfected safety paper, which is now used extensively in making checks and prevents alterations. One of the world's outstanding chemists, Mr. Hoskins has made thousands of experiments that have been of benefit to industry. Through chemical research, he has separated the commodities having merit from those that were frauds. He was an associate member of the Naval Consulting Board in 1917 and was a member of the sub-committee in charge of the Chicago office. He was a member of the advisory committee of the United States Bureau of Mines, and a fellow in the American Association for the Advancement of Science. He is a member of the Chicago Academy of Sciences, Western Society of Engineers, Franklin Institute (Philadelphia), American Academy of Political and Social Science, American Institute of Mining and Metallurgical Engineers, American Electrochemical Society, and Illinois Academy of Sciences. His clubs are Engineers and City (Chicago).

On December 8, 1885, Mr. Hoskins married Ada May Mariner of Chicago (deceased). The children are Minna, Edna (Mrs. Fred Scheele), William, Florence (Mrs. Harvey Melcher).

feet from the neck to the tip of the crown. The statue and base stand thirty-two feet in height alongside two 100-foot pylons on the lake front near the Century of Progress Exposition grounds. The project, costing $250,000, was financed by the Scandinavians of the United States.

Two exquisite bits of privately owned statuary that deserve mention here are the boys and dolphins group in the lobby of the Stevens hotel, and the Diana fountain in the Diana Court building, 540 North Michigan avenue.

Grace of line combined with the majesty of falling waters reaches perfection in the Buckingham Memorial Fountain. This fountain, standing in the center of a formal garden, its main pool of reinforced concrete faced with pink Georgian marble, 300 feet in diameter, is the gift to Chicago of Miss Kate Buckingham in memory of her brother, Clarence Buckingham, patron of art, and friend of the Art Institute.

The fountain is like a great jewel, a sparkling diadem set in the midst of Grant Park. Here, architecture and engineering have joined hands to produce a masterpiece. Patterned after the Latona fountain in the gardens of Versailles, the Buckingham Fountain is designed on a more epic scale than its model. The central jet rises to a height of 110 feet. The central effect is circular in form and 103 feet in diameter, rising in three cascades to a central bowl twenty-five feet above the pool level. The central jets are surrounded by jets at lower levels in the surrounding bowls, and these by jets from eight surrounding fountain groups from which the water is thrown in a trajectory more nearly horizontal. Shells, sea horses, and dolphins augment the beauty of this monumental work.

For day displays, a volume of 1,600 gallons a minute is provided, and for special occasions, 5,500 gallons. The sheets of water, falling in successive cascades, are illuminated at night by means of concealed projectors and incandescent lights, and by the manipulation of switches and dimmers, symphonies in color may be played. The effect produced is that of molten metal or liquid fire emerging from the jets. The pumping station itself is an engineering work of some importance.

(*Koehne Photo*)

GEORGE A. HUGHES

Mr. Hughes, president of the Edison General Electric Appliance Company, was born in Monticello, Jones County, Iowa, April 14, 1871, son of Alexander and Mary E. (Higginbotham) Hughes. He attended high school at Bismarck, North Dakota, and from 1887 to 1889 was a student at the University of Minnesota. From 1894 to 1895 he was the city editor of the Bismarck Daily Tribune and from 1896 to 1898 a reporter for the St. Paul Dispatch. For many years Mr. Hughes was manager of the Hughes Electric Company, operating electric power plants in Eveleth, Minnesota, Fargo, Bismarck and Dickinson, North Dakota, and Glendive, Montana. During this period he invented the electric range and formed the Hughes Electric Heating Company to manufacture it. Later this company, with the Hotpoint Company of California, consolidated with the heating device department of the General Electric Company, forming, in 1918, the Edison Electric Appliance Company (now the Edison General Electric Appliance Company of Chicago), manufacturers of electrical appliances for homes and industries. Mr. Hughes is a director of the Electric Vacuum Cleaner Company of Cleveland, Ohio. He served in the North Dakota National Guard and was state librarian of North Dakota for two years.

Mr. Hughes is president of Chicago Boys' Clubs, Inc., with five clubs in Chicago to aid under-privileged boys, and chairman of the Boys' Clubs Foundation. He is a member of the American Institute of Electrical Engineers, and his clubs are the Union League, Illinois Athletic, Electric, and Riverside Golf of Chicago, and the New York (New York). He is the author of various published addresses, including "Public Utility Problems from a Manufacturer's Standpoint," "Present Day Problems," "Government in Business," and "Politics in Business."

On June 24, 1890, he married Meta S. Scharkoff, of Chicago, and they have one daughter, Mary (Mrs. Grant Call).

THE UNIVERSITY OF CHICAGO
A Review of Forty Years of Educational Achievement

BY ROBERT MAYNARD HUTCHINS
President, The University of Chicago

IN June, 1932, the University of Chicago marked the completion of its fortieth year of service. The four decades since 1892 have seen the University develop into one of the great educational institutions of the world.

Conceived not as just another university, but as a community of scholars working for the advancement of knowledge, it has been a leader in research and a pioneer in education, productive of contributions to the progress of the world on a scale that is unparalleled.

In the plans for the organization of the University there was much of the boldly progressive spirit of the Chicago which was intent on achieving its destiny as one of the outstanding cities of the world. There had existed, from 1857 to 1886, the "old" University of Chicago, which had been concerned primarily with instruction. Those who worked for the establishment of the present university saw the necessity of a center of learning that should be part of Chicago and the Middle West. From the first they received the cooperation and support of the citizens of Chicago. The initial gift of $600,000 made by the founder, John D. Rockefeller, was contingent upon the pledging of a further $400,000 by the people of Chicago. Before the University had taken form, that initial gift of Mr. Rockefeller's had been increased by pledges of an additional two millions, and within ninety days the people of Chicago had pledged another million dollars. Mr. Rockefeller's final gift, made in 1910, brought the total of his benefactions to the University to $35,000,000, but even this large sum has been exceeded by the gifts of others, the contributions of Chicagoans comprising a large share of this additional support.

The University received its charter in 1890, and opened on October 1, 1892. Its organizer and first president, Dr. William Rainey Harper, introduced many ideas new to education, and from the first the University was imbued with the experimental attitude. The faculty of 120 included no less than nine college and university presidents, enthusiastically enlisted in Dr. Harper's "new and different" university. The entire faculty had been selected for its eminence or promise in research; the proof of its ability is to be found in the forty-year record of accomplishment. There was a student body of 594, alert and eager to participate in the opportunities of this new institution. Few of the buildings were ready for use, but the University already had a site of 24 acres and provisions for ten buildings.

When the University opened its fortieth year, it had assets in excess of $108,000,000, of which $60,000,000 were endowment. It had a campus of 110 acres, with eighty-five buildings devoted to educational purposes. The Midway front of the University extends for almost a mile, with the

(H. A. Atwell Photo)

OTTO F. HUNZIKER

Professor Hunziker, manager of manufacturing and director of research laboratories, Blue Valley Creamery Company, is considered one of the world's foremost dairy scientists. Born in Zurich, Switzerland, December 25, 1873, the son of Carl Otto and Louise (Pupikofer) Hunziker, he came to America in 1893 and became a naturalized citizen in 1904. He graduated from Bryant and Stratton Business College, Providence, Rhode Island, in 1896 and held various positions until 1898 when he entered Cornell University, obtaining his B. S. A. (Bachelor of Agricultural Science) degree in 1900 and his M. S. A. (Master of Agricultural Science) in 1901. He was instructor in dairy bacteriology, Cornell University, 1901-1902; milk expert for Scranton Condensed Milk Company, 1902-1905; professor of dairying and chief of the dairy department at Purdue University and Indiana Experiment Station from 1905 until 1916 when he took his present position with Blue Valley Creamery Company. At that time this company was operating twelve creameries; they are now operating twenty-three creameries and five milk plants.

Professor Hunziker was a delegate from the United States Department of Agriculture to the International Dairy Congresses in Stockholm, 1911; London, 1928; and Copenhagen, 1931. He was chairman of the program committee, Industry and Economics, for the World's Dairy Congress, in Washington, 1923. He has been a member of the Cook County Board of Health, and La Grange Board of Health (president, 1926-1927). He is a member of American Dairy Science Association (president, 1911-1913), Purdue Research Foundation, National Dairy Council, National Dairy Association, and Dairymen's Country Club. He is a member of the American Society of Agricultural Engineers, and Sigma Xi, Gamma Alpha, and Alpha Zeta fraternities. He was awarded the Distinguished Service gold medal by the Swiss Dairy Federation, Berne, Switzerland, in 1928. He is author of Condensed Milk and Milk Powder, 1914, 1918, 1920, 1926; and The Butter Industry, 1920, 1927. He was awarded a diploma for scientific publications by the International Exposition, in Milan, Italy, 1925. In 1927 he was invited to Australia and New Zealand for investigations and recommendations as to the dairy

Continued on page 546

towers of the Chicago Lying-In Hospital at the west balanced on the east
by those of the International House of Chicago. Dominating the Midway
front, which has been called "the world's most beautiful academic avenue,"
is the great University Chapel. South of the Midway are the new residence
halls for men. Within the past seven years the University's building program has cost in excess of $30,000,000.

The faculty today numbers approximately 900, and the student body,
during an academic year, about 14,500, with an average quarterly registration of 5,400. As originally chartered, the University was controlled by the
Baptist church, but this denominational control has been voluntarily re-
linquished. There are men and women of 30 denominations in the teaching
and student bodies, and the University has more Roman Catholic students

THE UNIVERSITY OF CHICAGO CHAPEL, one of the finest examples of Tudor
Gothic in the Western world. Bertram G. Goodhue, architect.

than Baptist. Of the 30 members of the Board of Trustees, three-fifths now
must be members of a Christian church, and 10 of this group must be Baptists. The original requirement that the president should be a member of
the Baptist church also has been removed.

President Harper and his associates conceived of the University as an
institution dedicated to the service of the Middle West, with particularly
close relations with the city of which it was a part. That relationship has

(Du Bois Studio Photo)

EDWARD N. HURLEY

Mr. Hurley, business and civic leader, was born in Galesburg, Illinois, July 31, 1864, the son of Jeremiah and Ellen (Nash) Hurley. He received his Doctor of Laws degree from the University of Notre Dame; his Doctor of Civil Law degree from Knox College, Galesburg. He started his career in 1888 as a traveling salesman for the United States Metallic Packing Company of Philadelphia, of which concern he later became manager. Mr. Hurley originated and developed the pneumatic tool industry in the United States and Europe. In 1896 he organized and headed the Standard Pneumatic Tool Company, but in 1902 sold out his interests to engage in farming and stock raising at Wheaton. Six years later he became president of the Hurley Machine Company, manufacturers of home labor-saving devices, and is now chairman of the board. In 1913 he was appointed by the United States Government as special commissioner to report on the banking and credits of the Argentine Republic, Brazil, Chile, and Peru. He was vice-chairman and later chairman of the Federal Trade Commission, resigning in 1917 to undertake his wartime duties for which General Pershing later awarded him the Distinguished Service Medal. He was chairman of the United States Shipping Board and president of the Emergency Fleet Corporation during the World War—he "built the bridge to France." Mr. Hurley served also as a member of the War Council and the American Red Cross. He was a member of the World War Funding Commission of 1924 and of President Hoover's Advisory Shipping Committee.

He is a director of the Chicago Great Western Railroad, the Pierce-Arrow Motor Car Company, the Studebaker Corporation, the Illinois Power and Light Corporation, the Illinois Traction Company, the North American Light and Power Company, Wilson and Company, the Chicago and Connecting Railways and the Collateral Trust, the Calumet and South Chicago Railroad, the Southern Street Railway Company, and the Hammond, Whiting and East Chicago Railroad. He is federal receiver for the Chicago City Railway Company, and co-receiver for Middle West Utilities Company. Mr. Hurley is alo a director of the National Foreign Trade Council; past president of the American Manufacturers' Export Association; and a member of the Illinois Manufacturers' Association, the Inter-

Continued on page 547

been realized, and the University consistently has been a vital part of the Western Empire. In the number of students from the Chicago area it has educated the University has had an important influence on the community, for 10,000 of its 28,000 degree holders live in the Chicago area. The University has been the leading institution of the country in the science of education, and its production of teachers has been one of its most important efforts. University improvements in educational techniques have been significant contributions to Chicago and to the rest of the United States. Of the 150,000 students who have matriculated at the University, some 30,000 have received degrees. There are 10,000 graduates of the University in the Chicago region.

The basic research of the University in many of its phases has been constantly in touch with reality; the experts of its faculty likewise have been in touch with the realities of the problems that have faced Chicago and the nation. The service of these experts has been constantly available, whether the problem were one of governmental consolidation, taxation, or city planning. The Social Science Research Committee has made of Chicago a vast laboratory and has, through study of more than a hundred individual problems, pointed the way toward improving the life of the community. The School of Commerce has been intimately concerned with the fundamental problems that affect especially the economic welfare of the Middle West. The University Clinics, a new development in medical teaching and research, constitutes one of the great centers of the world. Its research inures to the benefit of all humanity, but Chicago benefits most immediately and directly from the facilities the clinics provide.

Conscious as the University has been of its obligations to its region, that particular interest has not acted to limit the reach of its endeavors. The

President
UNIVERSITY
of CHICAGO

ROBERT MAYNARD HUTCHINS

Dr. Hutchins, president of the University of Chicago, was born in Brooklyn, New York, January 17, 1899, the son of William James and Anna Laura (Murch) Hutchins. He attended Oberlin College from 1915 to 1917; received his A. B. (Bachelor of Arts) from Yale University in 1921, honorary A. M. (Master of Arts) in 1922, and LL. B. (Bachelor of Laws) in 1925. The honorary degree of LL.D. (Doctor of Laws) was conferred on him by West Virginia University, Lafayette College, and Oberlin College in 1929, and by Williams College and Berea College in 1930.

Dr. Hutchins did ambulance service in the United States Army, 1917 to 1919, with the Italian Army in 1918 and 1919. He was decorated with the Groce di Guera (Italian). He was master in English and History at Lake Placid (New York) School, 1921-1923; secretary at Yale University, 1923-1927, lecturer in the Yale Law School, 1925-1927, professor of law, 1927, acting dean, 1927-1928, dean, 1928-1929; president of the University of Chicago since 1929. He is an honorary member of the Chicago Bar Association and the Tavern and Law clubs. He is a member of the Connecticut Bar Association. He is a member of Phi Beta Kappa, Phi Delta Phi, Alpha Delta Phi, Delta Sigma Rho, Torch, Order of the Coif, and Wolf's Head fraternities. His club affiliations are Graduate, Elizabethan, Yale (New York); University, Union League, Chicago, Quadrangle, Cliff Dwellers, Commercial (Chicago).

Dr. Hutchins married Maude Phelps McVeigh, of Bay Shore, Long Island, New York, September 10, 1921. They have one daughter, Frances Ratcliffe.

range of its interests as an institution dedicated to investigation has known no limits, and the University today is acknowledged to be one of the world's greatest research institutions. Five Americans have won the Nobel prize in science; four of them have been University of Chicago faculty members. Three of these four are the only American winners of the prize in physics: Albert A. Michelson, Robert A. Milliken, and Arthur H. Compton. These and other investigators won for Ryerson Physical Laboratory the designation of "the most famous physical laboratory in America." Dr. Alexis Carrell was awarded the Nobel prize in medicine for work done on surgery of the blood vessels while a member of the Chicago faculty. The spirit of investigation which has characterized the University has produced the planetesimal hypothesis of the origin of the earth; the discovery of a new anesthetic; it has brought about the founding of the modern school of sociology;

(Hedrich-Blessing Photo)
UNIVERSITY OF CHICAGO FIELD HOUSE
Holabird & Root, architects.

it has developed and implanted new educational techniques through the schools of the country. The University of Chicago has in the Oriental Institute the greatest archaeological organization in the world, with thirteen expeditions engaged in the Near East. The most complete collection of material for the study of Chaucer is to be found in the University, which has, in photostatic form, all the known manuscripts of his Canterbury Tales. These are but isolated examples of the results of the University's experimental attitude.

The prestige of the University of Chicago has been attested by independent investigations conducted to assemble the most expert and informed opinion of educational leaders as to the comparative standings of the leading universities. The results justify the international reputation of the University of Chicago as a notable educational and research center. The famous

(*Chambers Photo*)

LAWRENCE B. ICELY

Mr. Icely, president of Wilson-Western Sporting Goods Company, was born in Leaf River, Illinois, November 2, 1884, and is the son of Elias and Emma (Harrison) Icely. During his entire business career Mr. Icely has been associated with the sporting goods industry. He began his career as assistant manager of the Chicago division of Wright & Ditson Company in 1905 where he remained until 1909. 1909 to 1915 he was manager of the Pacific Coast division of the same company. Later he was made Western sales manager. In 1917 he was made general sales manager and vice-president at New York.

Mr. Icely's executive ability and genius for organization caused the Wilson-Western Sporting Goods Company to offer him the presidency of that company in 1918. This position he accepted and still holds. His development of the company has been one of the outstanding achievements of the industry. Mr. Icely has been a forceful factor in the organization of the industry through various manufacturing associations and the institution of the Chamber of Commerce of athletic goods manufacturers, Golf Ball Manufacturers Association, Golf Club Manufacturers Association, and Golf Bag Manufacturers Association. He is a member of the Chicago Athletic Association, Lake Shore Athletic Club, Illinois Golf Club, Rotary Club of Chicago, and the Olympic Club of San Francisco. He is naturally interested in sports both as a business man and sportsman.

On August 3, 1907, he married Kathryn Flynn of Chicago and they have one daughter, Kay Doris.

Miami report, which ranked twenty departments in the universities of America, placed eight Chicago departments as first in the entire country: ranked four more departments as second best; placed five in third position, two in fourth, and one, the lowest of the twenty, as fifth best. The Vischer study of 601 American scientists, ranked as most meritorius by their fellow scientists, placed Chicago first in two departments; tied for first in two others, second in four others, and third in another, the best record made by any of the leading American scientific schools. Further, this report showed that Chicago has a notable record in the undergraduate training of starred scientists. Still another study, made by Robert L. Kelly, executive secretary of the Association of American Colleges, determined that Chicago was the leading source of teachers of distinction.

The educational reorganization which became effective in October, 1931, is the most recent evidence of the University's leadership. It departs completely from the traditional methods of American colleges in organiza-tion and in spirit, and its development is being watched as the most distinc-tive and promising experiment in higher education today. The University is

Ryerson physical laboratory, with Kent and Jones chemistry laboratories in the background.

J. LOUIS JACOBS

Mr. Jacobs, consulting management engineer and Cook County Assessor, was born in Kiev, Ukraine, December 24, 1885, son of Isaac and Pearl (Tower) Jacobs. He came to the United States in 1891, becoming a naturalized citizen in 1908. After graduating in 1907 from the Sheffield Scientific School of Yale University, he took post-graduate work at Yale in economics, mathematics, and law. During 1908 he was engaged in financial and real estate reporting and in municipal engineering, and in 1909 he investigated railroad construction in the Middle West. From 1910 to 1915 he supervised technical investigations of finance, organization, personnel classification and administration for the City of Chicago. Since 1915 as a director of J. L. Jacobs & Company, management engineers and consultants to governments and industries, he has furnished professional services and given counsel to governmental, utility, industrial, and civic organizations on management, financial, statistical, and personnel problems. During the World War he was staff advisor on industrial relations and administrative methods for the Emergency Fleet Corporation, United States Shipping Board. He was also a consultant on labor classification and standardization for the United States War Labor Policies Board.

In the professional services and as consultant, he has made investigations and given counsel on employment administration, wages and classification, and management problems to the following governmental agencies: the cities of Chicago, Cincinnati, Milwaukee, Minneapolis, Oakland, California, and Philadelphia; the Sanitary District of Chicago; the Chicago Board of Education; the states of New Jersey, West Virginia, and Nebraska; the United States Railroad Labor Board; the counties of Milwaukee, Wisconsin, Cook, Illinois, and Hamilton, Ohio; Dominion of Canada employees; Federal Public Works. He was formerly a lecturer in economics and business organization at Northwestern University School of Commerce. Mr. Jacobs is a member of the American Statistical Association, American Academy of Political and Social Sciences, American Society of Civil Engineers, Society of Industrial Engineers, Western Society of Engineers, National Municipal League, et cetera. His clubs are City and Harvard-Yale-Princeton.

He married Susanne Myrtle Barker, of Chicago, March 17, 1915. Their children are, Esther Louise and Thomas Louis.

organized now into the professional schools, The College, and four Divisions: the Social Sciences, the Humanities, the Physical Sciences, and the Biological Sciences. The purpose of the College is to provide a general education; the four Divisions provide for advanced study. Through this reorganization the University has achieved the unification of related fields of knowledge, and so eliminated the isolation that prevailed under departmental organization. There are no required classes nor required courses; a student progresses by demonstrating in comprehensive examinations that he has acquired that proficiency and mastery which the University regards as essential to education. Neither are there time limits; a student advances as rapidly as his abilities permit. To achieve such a revolutionary program, the University reformed not only its organization and redefined its educational aims, but reshaped its entire curriculum, developing new courses of a radically different type. The University was not alone in its recognition of dissatisfaction with the established theories and methods of higher education, but it was the first to effect a thorough going revision designed to eliminate that dissatisfaction.

BOTANY POND

(Blank & Stoller, Inc., Photo)

FRANK H. JOHNSTON

Mr. Johnston, president of Acme Card System Company, was born in Manchester, Iowa, June 7, 1879, son of Charles H. Johnston. Educated in the public schools, he has devoted his entire business experiences toward bringing system and efficiency to modern business. In the year 1900, he was employed in Chicago by a mechanical business equipment company and shortly thereafter went into the sales division and became well acquainted with the principal retail establishments in the larger cities throughout the United States.

In 1914, Mr. Johnston founded the Acme Card System Company, which, under his leadership, is distributing its product all over the world. Many improvements in modern record keeping methods are due to his vision in analyzing the requirements of present day business. Although the active head of a growing business, Mr. Johnston has had time for outside activities. His occasional pronouncements on the trend of business are given publicity by leading economists and editors. His recreations are golf and horses.

On December 25, 1902, he married Maud Miller.

THE MUNICIPAL AIRPORT, WHERE WINGED CRUISERS COME AND GO

Chicago As the Hub of the Transcontinental Air Lines

BY WALTER WRIGHT

Superintendent of Parks, Recreation and Aviation

UNCHALLENGED as a railroad center, Chicago has within the last few years, and with the development of commercial aviation, which she has done much to encourage, become the hub of the transcontinental air lines which have spread their amazing network over the United States.

Air-conscious Chicagoans today regard St. Louis, Minneapolis, Detroit, and Cleveland, if not as suburbs, at least as near neighbors, within a few hours' hop of their doors. It is nothing at all out of the ordinary to have lunch in Chicago and dinner in New York.

Air lines radiate from Chicago in all directions. Powerful beacons guide the mail and passenger planes to the city, and the Lindbergh beacon scouring with its silver beam a circle with a 500-mile radius, nightly beckons the winged cruisers to the Nation's air capital.

To those who have not as yet realized how rapidly and how completely the new form of transportation has captured the public imagination, a visit to the new air terminal passenger station at the Municipal Airport will be

(*United Air Lines Photo*)

PHILIP G. JOHNSON

Mr. Johnson is president of United Air Lines which maintains general headquarters at Chicago for its Transcontinental, Middle West, Intermountain and Pacific Coast Lines, which fly more than one million miles per month, mostly with multi-engined passenger mail-express planes. The subsidiary companies of which Mr. Johnson is also president are National Air Transport (Chicago-New York and Chicago-Dallas), Boeing Air Transport (Chicago-San Francisco), Varney Air Lines (Salt Lake City-Seattle) and Pacific Air Transport (Seattle-San Diego). The various companies of United Air Lines on December 1, 1932, completed 50,000,000 miles of flying (nearly half of which was flown at night), making United Air Lines the largest air transport system in the world in point of mileage flown.

Mr. Johnson, who is one of the younger type of corporation executives, became interested in the aeronautical industry on graduating from the University of Washington at Seattle and became a draftsman for Boeing Airplane Company, now one of the largest builders of military and commercial airplanes in the United States. Mr. Johnson rose through various capacities to the presidency of the Airplane Company and later became president of the Air Transport units as well. When these companies became subsidiaries of United Aircraft and Transport Corporation, Mr. Johnson was elected a vice-president of that large aeronautical corporation and also took over the active direction of all the corporation's transport activities. United Air Lines is now serving forty-one cities in eighteen states, operating a fleet of more than 100 planes which carry, in addition to a larger volume of passenger business, more than all of the nation's air mail Mr. Johnson is also a vice-president of the Aeronautical Chamber of Commerce of America. He was born November 5, 1894, in Seattle, Washington.

Mr. and Mrs. Johnson, who, prior to her marriage was Miss Catherine Foley, have two children, Philip G., Jr., and Esther.

a revelation. At no other station in the world do more regularly scheduled mail and passenger planes arrive than at this, and from no other station do as many planes depart on scheduled flights.

The white, monolithic concrete depot, with its modernistic lines and comfortable appointments, the busy ticket office, the click of telegraph instruments, the attendant redcaps, the announcement of departures by the loud speaker, and even the illuminated weather maps, all give one an impression of progress and make him realize that he is living on the threshold of a new age, an age of modern transportation.

(*Kaufmann & Fabry Co. Photo*)
ADMINISTRATION BUILDING, MUNICIPAL AIRPORT
Paul Gerhardt, architect.

While waiting for his plane to take off, the passenger may hear the drone of motors overhead, while out of the clouds drops a carrier from New York or San Francisco. The door is opened, and the new arrivals step down, receive their hand baggage, and pass through the gates, while a compartment in one of the wings is let down, and the mail is transferred to a truck. The landings are made so quietly and with so little bustle and confusion that it seems impossible that the planes could have come from such distances and without adventure.

The immense hangars at the Airport not only house the resident planes, but also the shops where the planes are daily inspected and kept in perfect trim. Here too will be observed the radio and control tower, through which the field can talk to flying pilots; and the radio beacon which guides ships safely into port no matter what the weather. Everywhere is evident the combined official watchfulness of city, state, and federal government, which assures the air-traveling public of the highest degree of safety and comfort, combined with speed.

Chicago's Municipal Airport is today the busiest airport in the world.

It has outstripped even such older and world-famous ports as Croyden, Le Bourget, and Templehof, serving respectively London, Paris, and Berlin. It has outstripped them in the number of daily scheduled flights as well as in the number of passengers and amount of air mail carried. Thus Chicago has reached in the air that supremacy it holds in railroad transportation.

The Airport is under the jurisdiction of the Bureau of Parks, Recreation, and Aviation, of which Col. A. A. Sprague, Commissioner of Public Works, is the director. It occupies an area of approximately one square mile, from 55th to 63d streets, and from Cicero avenue to Central avenue. It is situated nearer the heart of the city it serves than any other airport of its class, and lies entirely within the city limits. It is readily accessible by four main traffic arteries, and by two surface lines. By bus or taxicab, it is about a half hour's ride from the Loop. The field is splendidly illuminated for night flying, with beacons, flood lights, boundary and hazard lights. Its four oiled cinder runways, in total length more than two miles, offer a perfect landing surface for planes of any size under any load. The new concrete taxi runway, a mile and a quarter long on two sides of the field, makes both clean and rapid the arrival and departure of the many ships in and from the loading zone.

The immense volume of activity at this airport can be appreciated when it is known that there are twelve lines operating forty different routes on daily schedule. Eighty planes a day leave or arrive at this port on regular schedule, and an average of twenty more independent planes arrive and depart each day. The combined total mileage of scheduled flights arriving and leaving Chicago totals over 44,000 miles daily.

Speed has made the great success of air travel—speed with safety and comfort. When one can travel from Chicago to Cleveland in approximately three hours, spend practically a day there for business and return home in the evening, at a cost which is approximately the railroad fare plus lower berth, the future can readily be seen.

With the constant use and further development of radio in connection with flying, the safety of the passenger will be assured as in no other mode of travel.

With this swift progress Chicago is keeping step. Scattered about the Chicago area in Cook county and two adjacent counties are a score of commercial and privately owned airports, including a municipal seaplane base and a military combination airport and seaplane base. Plans are under way for the establishment of a landing field on an island off the lake front within five minutes' ride of the Loop. This field, beautifully landscaped to conform to the adjacent park area, would accommodate land planes, amphibians, and sea planes. Planes arriving at and departing from this field would use the present Municipal Airport as a base, where every facility is at hand for housing, inspection, and repairs.

With this prospect in view, Chicago will have ample justification for her claim to being the transportation center of America.

SUBWAYS
Views of Proposed State Street Subway

Model showing development of a three-level street—a trend of modern design in subway construction.

State street, a triple-decked shopping mart. Cut-away drawing disclosing how the famous thoroughfare will be transformed. Above is the present street level and below that, the concourse extending across the entire width of the street. The trains will be operated in the third level.

(*Moffett-Russell Photo*)

R. F. KELKER, JR.

Major Kelker, noted consulting engineer, was born in Harrisburg, Pennsylvania, August 5, 1875, son of Luther Reily and Agnes Keyes (Pearsol) Kelker. He received his B. S. (Bachelor of Science) degree at Pennsylvania State College in 1896, and his degree in electrical engineering in 1897. He was engineer with steam and electric railways at Buffalo, Cleveland, and New York City from 1897 to 1907; with the Board of Supervising Engineers of Chicago in charge of reconstruction of railway tracks from 1907 to 1914; engineer of construction, Local Transportation Committee of Chicago, since 1914. He was a member of the firm of Kelker, De Leuw and Company, engineers, from 1919 to 1929; member of the Advisory Subway Engineering Commission and chief engineer, Bureau of Subways, City of Chicago since 1930.

He served as captain, 311th Engineers, 80th Division, U. S. A., camp adjutant, Camp Grant, Illinois, and on major staff duty in France during the World War. He is a member of the American Society of Civil Engineers, Western Society of Engineers, Illinois Society of Engineers, American Electric Railway Association, Chicago Association of Commerce, Pennsylvania Society, Sons of the Revolution. His clubs are Mid-Day, City, Westmoreland Country, University, and the Missouri Athletic, St. Louis. He is author of various reports on traffic and transportation for New York, Chicago, Los Angeles, Baltimore, St. Louis, and many other cities.

In May, 1911, he married Georgia Moore, of Rochester, New York.

LOYOLA UNIVERSITY, A MODERN SCHOOL PRESERVING ANCIENT TRADITIONS

Professional Schools Which Meet the Requirements of the New Era

BY THE REV. ROBERT M. KELLEY, S. J., President

L OYOLA UNIVERSITY, conducted by the Jesuits, is the development of St. Ignatius College which was founded on Chicago's great West Side in 1869. A new charter was obtained in 1909 in the name of Loyola University of Chicago.

From a struggling institution of thirty-seven college students and five faculty members, in 1870, it has grown into an urban university with eight divisions, six thousand students, and four hundred and eighty faculty members. More than a thousand high school students are affiliated with the institution in Loyola Academy and St. Ignatius High School.

The administrative offices and the College of Arts and Sciences are located in Rogers Park on a twenty-two-acre campus fronting on Lake Michigan. The Graduate School, the Schools of Law, Commerce and Social

(*Chicago Aerial Survey Co. Photo*)

Lake Shore campus, Loyola University, showing College of Arts and Sciences, Loyola Academy, Elizabeth M. Cudahy library, gymnasium, and athletic field.

President LOYOLA UNIVERSITY

(Laveccha Studio Photo)

REV. ROBERT MICHAEL KELLEY, S.J.

Father Kelley, president of Loyola University, was born in Manson, Iowa, July 24, 1877, son of Michael Bede and Nora M. (Foley) Kelley. He attended St. Mary's (Kansas) College from 1894 to 1897, received honorary degree of LL.D. (Doctor of Laws) in 1924; joined the Society of Jesus (Jesuits) in 1897; received his A.B. (Bachelor of Arts) degree from St. Louis University in 1903, A.M. (Master of Arts), in 1904. He studied theology at St. Louis University, 1908 to 1912. Father Kelley taught in the preparatory division of the University of Detroit, 1904-1908, and in the same division of Creighton University, Omaha, Nebraska, 1913-1914. He was ordained a priest of the Roman Catholic Church in 1911. He held the position of dean of the College of Liberal Arts at Creighton University from 1914 to 1920, regent of the Institute of Law in 1919-1920.

From 1920 to 1926 Father Kelley was president of Regis College at Denver, Colorado, and in 1926-1927 he was assistant to the provincial of the Missouri Province of the Society of Jesus. He has been president of Loyola University, the second largest Catholic school of higher education in the United States, since September 8, 1927.

Father Kelley is a member of the Union League Club.

Work are in the Downtown College Building at Franklin and Washington streets. In this building is also housed a College of Arts and Sciences. The Schools of Medicine and Dentistry are on the West Side adjacent to the Cook County Hospital.

As a Jesuit school, Loyola is a very definite kind of school, with a character, purpose and procedure fixed for it by the Institute of the Society of Jesus, and by some three hundred and fifty years of educational experience. A Jesuit school aims at giving a distinctive sort of education, based upon an experience which goes much farther back than the history of the Jesuits themselves. The Jesuits did not invent that sort of education; they inherited it.

When the Jesuits came into the field of school-education, they found three types of education in existence. The first type grew up in Greece, in its best period. Its aim was *development* of the individual. It has been called "cultural" education; but no one word will express it. The second type of education was Roman. It aimed at equipping the individual for a social task, or a small group of social tasks. It may be called "vocational education." The third type was developed more particularly in the late Middle Ages and the succeeding centuries. It aimed at equipping the few specially gifted individuals for the distinctive work of discovering, if they might, new facts and truths. It may be called education for *research*.

The Jesuits singled out for their particular work the first type of education, that which has been vaguely called the "cultural." They devoted by far the greater number of their members to training boys and youths in a Catholic, liberal education, which aimed at helping immature minds and characters to become mature.

Within the past thirty years a change has taken place in Jesuit schools. Modern impatience to achieve wealth has brought increased demand for the second type of school, the vocational. The Jesuits have been influenced by that demand, and have developed almost every sort of professional school. Loyola University, for instance, has five such schools; of medicine, law, dentistry, commerce and finance, and social work.

Despite the fact that today the professional schools far outstrip the basic college of liberal arts and sciences in number of students, the Jesuits have not surrendered their traditional aim. They are still primarily devoted to the balanced development of boys and youths into men who are cultured through training in the sciences, the humanities, and the Catholic religion. Their vocational schools are to a certain extent, concessions to immediate demands of the times.

The story of the founding and growth of Loyola University is closely connected with the history of Chicago. The seed for the religious and educational development of Chicago was planted by that intrepid Jesuit missionary-explorer, Father Jacques Marquette, S. J., who, in 1674 was the first white man to reside on the site of Chicago. After a week's sojourn at the mouth of the Chicago River, Father Marquette and his French and In-

(*Chicago Architectural Photographing Company*)
ELIZABETH M. CUDAHY MEMORIAL LIBRARY AT LOYOLA UNIVERSITY
Rebori & Wentworth, architects.

dian companions proceeded up the river to the point where Damen avenue now intersects the stream. Here they spent the Winter of 1674-1675, portaging into the DesPlaines River and down the Illinois to Kaskaskia as soon as the river was navigable.

The next link in the bond between Chicago and Loyola University was supplied by Father Arnold Damen, S. J., father of the great Holy Family parish and builder of Chicago's West Side. Father Damen became a permanent resident of Chicago on May 4, 1857. He erected a temporary church on the south side of Eleventh street between May street and Blue Island avenue and held first services there on July 12 of the same year. Simultaneously with the building of the church, Father Damen provided a school for the children of the parish by adding wings on each side of the church for use as classrooms.

When Father Damen first organized the parish, almost all that portion of the city was still unsettled prairie. The locality was speedily settled by a population drawn thither largely by Father Damen and his church. By 1870, 5,000 children were being educated in the five parochial schools of the parish and St. Ignatius College. In 1900 there was attached to Holy Family parish a congregation of more than 25,000 persons.

Father Damen was appointed Vice-Rector, or the first President, of St. Ignatius College when it opened its doors on September 5, 1870, to admit thirty-seven students. The first board of trustees was composed of the Revs. J. S. Verdin, S. J., J. DeBlieck, S. J., M. Oakley, S. J., and J. G. Venneman, S. J. All these men had had the usual course of studies prescribed to a member of the Society of Jesus, which was up to the standards of a master's degree, although it was not customary at the time to take out a degree.

St. Ignatius College awarded its first degree, master of arts, to Philip J. Reilly on June 25, 1873. Registration passed the 300 mark during the presidency of the Rev. Joseph G. Zealand, S. J., 1884-1887, and reached 496 students during the regime of the Rev. Thomas S. Fitzgerald, S. J., 1891-1894.

When a new charter was obtained in 1909, the Rev. Alexander J. Burrowes, S. J., became the first President of the newly named Loyola University of Chicago. A School of Law was established in the downtown district in the same year. The School of Sociology, now known as the School of Social Work, and extension classes in liberal arts courses were organized in the Downtown College Building during the presidency of the Rev. John L. Mathery, S. J., 1912 to 1915.

The School of Medicine was made an integral part of the University by the Rev. John B. Furay, S. J., who occupied the President's chair from 1915 to 1921. Under the guidance of the Rev. William H. Agnew, S. J., who was president from 1921 to 1927, the College of Arts and Sciences was moved to the Lake Shore Campus; a Home Study division was established; the School of Commerce was opened; and the Chicago College of Dental Surgery became Loyola's Dental School.

Since 1927 the various divisions of the University have been strengthened and consolidated. The erection of the Elizabeth M. Cudahy Memorial Library, a $330,000 gift with an additional endowment of $100,000, given by Edward A. Cudahy as a memorial to his wife, and an athletic field and stadium are the important physical improvements of the Lake Shore Campus of the University.

FRANK KNOX

Col. Knox, president and publisher of The Chicago Daily News, has been identified with the newspaper business since his cub reporter days on the Grand Rapids Herald in 1898. He was born in Boston January 1, 1874, the son of William Edwin and Sarah Collins (Barnard) Knox, and received his Bachelor of Arts degree from Alma College, Alma, Michigan. His newspaper career was interrupted by the Spanish-American war, in which he served under Theodore Roosevelt in Troop D of the First Volunteer Cavalry, the famous Rough Riders. Returning to Grand Rapids, he advanced to the position of city editor, and later, of circulation manager of the Herald, and in 1901 became publisher of the Sault Ste. Marie News. In 1912 he went to Manchester, New Hampshire, as publisher of the Manchester Leader, which newspaper a year later was merged with the Manchester Union. Col. Knox is still publisher of the Leader-Union. As publisher of the Boston American and the Boston Advertiser, in 1926, he became regional manager for the Hearst newspapers first in New England, then in Northern New York, Pennsylvania, and Washington, D. C., and from 1927 to 1931, was general manager of all the Hearst newspapers.

While in Grand Rapids he was a major on the staff of the Governor of Michigan, and in 1913 had a similar commission on the staff of the Governor of Massachusetts. Col. Knox enlisted in the World War as a private in the First New Hampshire Infantry, but was sent to an officers' training camp, where he was commissioned a cavalry Captain. Before he could be assigned to a troop, he was commissioned major in the Field Artillery, and saw service overseas with the 78th Division, being mustered out as a lieutenant-colonel. He is now a lieutenant-colonel in the 365th Field Artillery, organized reserve. He was appointed a member of the Board of Indian Commissioners in 1911 by President Taft. As chairman of the Michigan Republican State Central Committee in 1912, he worked for the nomination of Theodore Roosevelt, and was manager of Theodore Roosevelt's pre-convention headquarters in Chicago. At the "Bull Moose" convention of that year, he was chairman of the Credentials Committee. In 1920 he returned to the regular Republican fold, and at the National Convention in Chicago, was floor manager for Gen. Leonard Wood. Col. Knox came to Chicago as publisher of The Daily News in 1931, and in 1932, as chairman of the National Campaign to Combat

Continued on page 547

A PEOPLE'S PARADISE OF FIFTY-ONE SQUARE MILES OF WOODLAND

The Lure of the Forest Preserves That Gird Chicago

BY CHARLES G. SAUERS
General Superintendent, Cook County Forest Preserve District

WITHIN half an hour of State street is a realm of golden sunsets, of towering trees and dappled meadows, of lily ponds and winding streams, a sanctuary of birds, squirrels, and rabbits. Here the city is forgotten in the peace of forest glades and mossy banks and shady dells.

Surrounding Chicago on all sides except the east, which is skirted by Lake Michigan, are the Forest Preserves, the playground of 4,000,000 people. This belt of 35,000 acres or fifty-one square miles of woodland is the greatest recreational domain in the immediate proximity of any American city. The Forest Preserve district is visited by 15,000,000 nature lovers yearly.

With the completion of Forest Way, linking the various tracts by strips of land of a minimum width wherever possible of 660 feet, the motorist can drive for seventy-five miles through a continuous arcade of trees, and never see a single sign board. There are nooks and corners that can be explored only on foot, by following winding paths and trails.

With its seven golf courses, its six bathing places, its facilities for boating, camping, picnicking, hiking, horseback riding, motoring, fishing, baseball, skating, it offers ideal opportunities for winter and summer sports.

The Forest Preserve District has its own fire patrol and police force. It employs a staff of 400 foresters, caretakers, life guards, matrons, etc.

Starting in 1915 with the purchase of a 40-acre tract in Deer Grove, Palatine Township, and a 100-acre tract in Palos, the district has expanded until it has a belt of woodland about four miles wide around the city.

It contains nearly 3,000,000 trees, 50,000,000 saplings and seedlings, 25,000,000 shrubs and bushes. Reforestation of denuded tracts has been going on to such an extent that 1,000,000 trees have been planted there within the last two years.

President
CONCORDIA
TEACHERS
COLLEGE

BIBLE

(H. A. Ebert Photo)

REV. WILLIAM C. KOHN

Dr. Kohn, president of Concordia Teachers College and one of the outstanding Lutheran clergyman of the Middle West, was born in Chicago, June 2, 1865, the son of John and Dorothy (Reckett) Kohn. He attended St. James school, and was advised by its principal, his future father-in-law, to enter the ministry. Accordingly he enrolled at Concordia College, Fort Wayne, Indiana, where he studied for six years. Completing his theological studies at Concordia Seminary, St. Louis, he returned to Chicago as assistant pastor of St. James Church, of which he later became pastor. For more than twenty years he was engaged in missionary work on the South Side of Chicago. Starting in 1889 with a con-gregation of ten families, he built up a powerful church, St. Andrews, with a member-ship of more than 3,000. During this time he served his synod as a visiting officer, and in 1908 became president of the Illinois district of the Evangelical Lutheran Synod of Mis-souri, Ohio, and other States. From 1906 to 1909, during his pastorate at St. Andrews, he served as chairman of the Mission Board and of the Church Extension Board of the Northern Illinois District. Educated in architecture and in business administration, as well as in theology, Dr. Kohn directed the building activities of Concordia Teachers College, which was opened in 1913. Concordia Teachers College boasts a group of classic buildings set in beautifully landscaped grounds occupying forty acres in River Forest where young men of Lutheran faith are trained to teach in the parochial schools. Twice he refused the presidency of the institution, but finally accepted it, reluctantly turning over to others his work on the South Side. He occupies the chairs of theology, pedagogy, and Bible History, teaching both in German and in English.

Dr. Kohn was married April 26, 1888, to Sophia Bartling of Chicago. Their oldest son, William, is a missionary in Canada. Other children are Elsa (the wife of the Rev. P. Roehrs), Herbert, Gerard, Gertrude (Mrs. L. Kellerman), Luther, and Paula (Mrs. W. Schriefer.)

Further development of this vast property with its unrivaled scenic beauty and recreational possibilities has been provided for by a bond issue of $2,500,000 passed in 1930. The work will conform to a general plan drafted by an advisory committee headed by Gen. Abel Davis and acting in cooperation with the Forest Preserve District Board of which Emmett Whealan is president.

The plan calls for large allotments of space to natural forest and its maintenance and reforestation as a means for passive recreation; also for smaller allotments to grounds for active play.

To this end, 26,250 acres, or seventy-five per cent of the whole, is to be reserved in its natural state as wooded area. Picnic grounds, parking spaces, playgrounds, baseball diamonds, and field houses will occupy 4,000 acres, or fourteen per cent of the total. Existing water areas, including rivers and lakes, take up approximately 800 acres, greatly enhancing the beauty of the silvan landscape. An additional 950 acres of marsh and low-land are being cleared and converted into lagoons, available for boating and fishing.

Golf courses 1,400 acres in extent, and the Zoological Park at Riverside account for the remaining space.

Forest Way will consist of two one-way master drives, each forty feet wide, flanked by trees separated by a forested strip. Bridle paths, pedestrian trails, paved walks, and concrete roads have been provided for as well as rustic bridges spanning the many woodland streams.

The trees most in evidence are hard and soft maple, oak, walnut, linden, and elm. Many of the oaks and elms are patriarchal, and had attained a ripe age even when the Indians roamed the territory.

The buildings throughout the Forest Preserve are of a uniform design, inclining to the rustic, with huge timbers and blocks of stone predominating. The same design prevails from the pretentious headquarters and administration building down to the humblest "red hot" stand. It is characteristic of the architecture of the various lodges, pavilions, bath houses, and shelters. The lodges, with their open fireplaces, offer hospitality to all who seek the peace and quiet of these woodlands. Three modernly-equipped swimming pools, Cermak, Emmett Whealan, and Green Lake are equipped with modern machinery to purify the water and keep it in drinking water clarity. They are also equipped with commodious locker rooms and showers. More than 750,000 persons last summer dipped into their clear cool waters and played in the sand beaches that surround them. Children may be left safely with the nurses and matrons in attendance. On peak days these pools can accommodate as many as 5,000 bathers each.

It will be interesting to the fisherman to know that the waters of the Forest Preserve are kept well-stocked with fingerlings from the city and state hatcheries. Fishing, however, is permitted only in certain designated bodies of water. At all others fishing is strictly prohibited.

JAMES L. KRAFT

Mr. Kraft, president of the Kraft-Phenix Cheese Corporation, Chicago, was born in Ontario, Canada. He came to Chicago in 1903, from a clerkship in a Buffalo, New York, grocery store. With a capital of 100 pounds of cheese, a horse and cheese wagon, sixty dollars, and an idea for pasteurizing and packing cheese, Mr. Kraft built the largest cheese business in the world in less than tweny-five years. It was his idea for pasteurizing and packaging cheese which is accredited with revolutionizing cheese-making in this country. Today the business of which Mr. Kraft is president has branches in every section of the United States, in almost every state, and in many foreign countries, including Canada, England, Australia, Spain, and Germany.

Mr. Kraft has been a leader in activities of the Baptist denomination since his arrival in Chicago. He is treasurer of the International Council of Religious Education and has been superintendent of the North Shore Baptist Sunday School for twenty-three years. He was formerly vice-president of the Northern Baptist Convention, and has held executive positions in many of the working organizations of the Baptist denomination. Mr. Kraft is well known to archaeologists, collectors, and historians for his collections and studies of prehistoric stone. The Lincoln Park totem pole, one of the three standing outside museums in the United States, was a gift to the school children of Chicago from Mr. Kraft. His collections of fossil fish, American Indian relics, and uncut jade are among the finest private collections in the world. On the 150th anniversary of the founding of Sunday Schools, Mr. Kraft presented the city of Toronto with a duplicate of the London Statue of Robert Raikes, founder of Sunday Schools. Mr. Kraft is a member of the Illinois Athletic, the Lake Shore Athletic, the Mid-Day, and the Hamilton clubs, and the Congressional Country Club of Washington, D. C.

He married Pauline Elizabeth Platt, of Chicago, June 2, 1909. They have one daughter, Edith Lucile.

CHICAGO'S OLDEST NATURAL SCIENCE INSTITUTION

The Academy of Sciences and Its Seventy-Five Year Record of Service

BY ALFRED M. BAILEY
Director, Chicago Academy of Sciences

FOUNDED in 1857, the Chicago Academy of Sciences is the oldest natural science organization in the city, one of the few links between the Chicago of today and the Chicago of the days before the great fire. It has its home in Lincoln Park, near the Center street entrance, in the fine old building presented by Matthew Laflin, pioneer real estate operator, to the people of Chicago. Since 1904, the building has been a landmark of the North Side.

The Academy was founded by a group of scientists and nature lovers who believed in the value of such an institution. Charter members included James V. S. Blaney, Dr. Nathan S. Davis, Sr., James W. Freer, C. A. Helmuth, Hosmer A. Johnson, Dr. Edmund Andrews, Henry Parker, J. Y. Scammon, Franklin Scammon, Richard K. Swift, Joseph D. Webster, Eliphalet W. Blatchford, and Henry W. Zimmerman.

MATTHEW LAFLIN MEMORIAL, HOME OF THE CHICAGO ACADEMY OF SCIENCES

Robert Kennicott, the distinguished naturalist, was appointed its first director. Unfortunately, he was not permitted to serve long in this capacity, for in 1866 he lost his life while exploring a lonely section of Alaska.

It is interesting to note that the children and grandchildren of the founders, as well as the direct descendants of Matthew Laflin, also had scientific interests. Among the officers of the Academy today are Dr. Nathan S. Davis III, Dr. Edmund Andrews, and Lloyd Allan Laflin.

The Academy is open to the public every day in the year except Christ-

(Walinger Photo)

OSCAR A. KROPF

Mr. Kropf was born in Vienna, Austria, March 10, 1872. His parents, Ferdinand Michael and Eleonor Johanna Kropf, were German, and the family came to the United States in 1877. Mr. Kropf graduated from the Washburn Academy at Topeka, Kansas, in 1891. He received his B.A. (Bachelor of Arts) degree at Washburn College in 1895 and was valedictorian of his class; M.A. (Master of Arts) in 1897, and LL.D. (Doctor of Laws) in 1925. During 1897 and 1898 he was superintendent of the public schools of Hays City, Kansas. In 1901 he received his LL.B. (Bachelor of Laws) degree at Northwestern University Law School and was admitted to the Bar. He has practiced law since then continuously in Chicago and has taken an active part in civic affairs.

Mr. Kropf is chairman of the board of the Howard Avenue Trust and Savings Bank of Chicago, director of the Citizens Association and chairman of its committee for A Century of Progress. He organized the German Club of Chicago and was its first president. He also was president of the Rogers Park Sunday Evening Club. He is a 33rd degree Mason, Past Potentate of Medinah Temple A. A. O. N. M. S., and served four terms as Grand Orator of the Grand Lodge A. F. & A. M. of Illinois. He is a member of the American, Illinois State and Chicago bar associations, and of Phi Alpha Delta Fraternity. He served as chairman of the Committee on Admission of the Chicago Bar Association. His clubs are Union League (former chairman, public affairs committee), Ridgemoor Country, Law, and German of Chicago (president, 1914-1915).

On October 21, 1908, Mr. Kropf married Edith Alfreda Anderson of Chicago. Their children are Richard Thomas, who graduated from the Massachusetts Institute of Technology in 1931, and Eleanor Arletta, who is attending Northwestern University.

mas, and admission is free at all times. Its museum of natural history is one of the most complete, of a local area, in the country, and the great habitat groups with photographic backgrounds are more than eighty feet in length, the faunal and floral life which once occurred in the Chicago area, being shown in the foreground. Among the large mammals shown are the black bear, mountain lion, prairie and timber wolves, Canada lynx, and Virginia deer. Birds, insects, plants, and fossils are included in the many exhibits. Thousands of students use the collections as a basis for study; about 300,000 people visit the Academy annually.

In addition to the exhibits for the public, a free lecture program is given Sunday afternoons during the fall and winter months, with illustrated talks by some of America's foremost naturalists.

(*Chicago Academy of Sciences Photo*)
BLACK BEAR AND YOUNG

The publications of the Academy have been important contributions to science. The first record of the ornithology of Alaska, after the American occupation, was published by the Academy in 1868, and in the years that have passed have appeared many other worthwhile works on the animal and plant life and the geology of North America. Pepoon's splendid work on the plant life of the Chicago locality, under the title "The Flora of the Chicago Region," is the most recent publication, but the Academy issues quarterly a sixteen-page bulletin recording its activities.

A great part of the work upon the scientific collections is carried on by the Honorary Curators of the different departments and their aids.

Unlike most museums, the Academy does not receive tax money for its support. Its income is derived from endowments and the dues of its membership. Its affairs are administered by a board of scientific governors of which Dr. Henry C. Cowles is chairman, and a board of trustees of which Lewis C. Walker is chairman. Serving on both boards are some of Chicago's most prominent citizens.

(*Moffet-Russell Photo*)

WALLACE R. LANE

Mr. Lane, senior member of the law firm of Parkinson and Lane of Chicago, was born in Whateley, Massachusetts, August 12, 1876, son of John William and Mary (Haynes) Lane. He received his preparatory education at Hopkins Academy, Hadley, Mass., and Williston Academy, Easthampton, Mass. He was a student at Brown University, Providence, R. I., from 1895 to 1897, and received his LL.B. (Bachelor of Laws) degree at Yale Law School in 1900. He was admitted to the Connecticut bar in 1900 and first practiced at Fitchburg, Mass.; then moved to Des Moines, Iowa, where he practiced from 1901 to 1910 as a member of the law firm of Orwig and Lane; during this period he was a professor of law at Highland Park College, lecturer at Drake University, Des Moines, and the University of Nebraska at Lincoln, on patent, trade mark, and unfair competition law. In 1910, Mr. Lane moved to Chicago and became associated with Robert H. Parkinson under the firm name of Parkinson and Lane, specializing in patent, corporation, trade mark and unfair competition law. He is recognized as one of America's foremost patent counsels. His firm represents a large number of leading corporations, municipalities, and several states. Mr. Lane is a director of several corporations. He is a member of the Scarlet Fever Committee, Inc., administering the "Dick Patent" on scarlet fever antitoxin for the benefit of the public, and in recognition of his services the Lane Fellowship was established in 1930. He was appointed by President Coolidge in 1925 as a delegate representing the United States to the International Convention for Protection of Industrial Property at The Hague, which resulted in the treaty ratified by the United States Senate on December 16, 1930. He was vice-chairman of the Lawyers' National Committee during 1925 and 1926 to increase salaries of Federal Judges.

Mr. Lane is a trustee of Brown University and in 1927 received from this University the honorary degree of Master of Arts; is a trustee of Williston Academy and Hopkins Academy; was made an honorary member of the Cum Laude Society of Williston Academy, 1930, and Phi Beta Kappa (Brown), 1932. He is a member of the American Bar Association (chairman, patent section, 1919-20), American Patent Law Association (president, 1922-23), Chicago Patent Law Association (president, 1924), Chicago,

Continued on page 547

(Moffett-Russell Photo)

BENJAMIN FRANKLIN LANGWORTHY

Mr. Langworthy, senior member of the law firm of Langworthy, Stevens, McKeag and McCornack, was born in Jersey City, New Jersey, October 9, 1871, son of George Irish and Anne Lockhart (Karr) Langworthy. He is a descendant of Colonial ancestors, among them James Babcock, who settled at Portsmouth, Rhode Island, in 1642, and Col. Joseph Babcock, who was born at Westfield, Rhode Island, in 1754. He received his B. S. (Bachelor of Science) degree at Alfred University in 1892 and later studied law at the Northwestern University Law School. In 1897 he married Mary A. Lewis of Plainfield, New Jersey. Their children are Frances Lewis (Mrs. Donald Bain Murray) and Marigold Lockhart (Mrs. Dwight Taylor).

Mr. Langworthy was admitted to the Illinois bar in 1895, and has since been engaged in the practice of municipal, real property, and corporation law. For many years he was professor of real property law at John Marshall Law School and was village attorney of River Forest, Illinois, from 1909 to 1915. He is a member of the American, Illinois State, and Chicago bar associations. He was president of the Chicago Alumni Association of Alfred University in 1925. He is a member of the Sons of the American Revolution and was president of the Patriotic League of Phil Sheridan Post No. 615, G. A. R., of Oak Park, Illinois. His clubs are Union League, City, and Rolling Green Golf.

(Fernand de Gueldre Photo)

MARY LEWIS LANGWORTHY

Mrs. Langworthy, clubwoman and civic leader, a descendant of Abraham Lewis of the Revolutionary War period, was born in Alfred, New York, March 31, 1872, daughter of Abram Herbert and Augusta Melissa (Johnson) Lewis. She attended the Alfred public schools, Plainfield (New Jersey) Young Ladies' Seminary, and took special studies at Alfred University, receiving a teacher's certificate from Delsarte School of Expression, New York, in 1894.

On October 25, 1897, she married Benjamin Franklin Langworthy, of Chicago. Their children are Frances Lewis (Mrs. Donald Bain Murray), and Marigold Lockhart (Mrs. Dwight Taylor).

Mrs. Langworthy is a well-known writer and director of patriotic and educational pageants, among them River Forest Independence Day, for several years, and is director of the drama class of the River Forest Women's Club. For two terms she served as trustee of the Village of Winnetka and is vice-president of the National Congress of Parents and Teachers, director of the Illinois League of Women Voters, vice-president of the Cook County School of Nursing, secretary of the Juvenile Protective Association, and member of the Daughters of the American Revolution (George Rogers Clark Chapter).

Mrs. Langworthy is a director of the Woman's City Club, president during 1924 and 1925, and is a member of Chicago Woman's Club, Woman's Athletic Club, and Winnetka Woman's Club. Her favorite recreations are swimming, walking, motoring, and the theater.

MEAT PACKING — CHICAGO'S FUNDAMENTAL INDUSTRY
The Union Stock Yards, Where Range and City Merge

O F recent years the Union Stock Yards as a mecca for tourists has had considerable competition. But almost up to the beginning of the present century the Stock Yards stood unchallenged as Chicago's big show. Not to see the Yards was to miss seeing Chicago, and this square mile of industry was included in the itinerary of every visitor to the city. It was visited by princes and maharajas. It is still one of the starred attractions of Chicago's Baedecker.

Meat packing is, and has been for three-quarters of a century, Chicago's fundamental industry. The city, by its strategic location alone, was destined to become the world's most important packing center. Here the railroads converging from the Western plains, branched off, leading to the populous eastern cities. But if the railroads contributed to Chicago's rise as a world meat market, the packing business in itself is largely responsible for the city's railroad supremacy.

Even as long ago as 1882, more than 175,000 carloads of livestock were received at the Union Stock Yards yearly. Today the annual receipts reach 250,000 carloads, and of these, approximately one-third are reshipped to other destinations. To visualize a single day's receipts, you have only to think of a continuous freight train seven miles in length.

A SMALL PART OF THE "YARDS"

(*Moffett-Russell Photo*)

T. G. LEE

Mr. Lee, president of Armour & Company, was born on a farm near Carrollton, Ohio, February 13, 1878, the son of Erasmus W. and Nancy Isabel (Crabb) Lee, and was educated in the public schools. At the age of fifteen he came to Chicago and obtained a job in a commission house, but having raised his own pet stock at home, he had his eye on Packingtown, and, despite his youthful appearance, he managed to persuade the head of Armour's beef department to employ him as a stenographer. His first opportunity came when the department manager's stenographer resigned and Mr. Lee applied for the job. The manager had his misgivings, but tested the boy out and found that he would qualify.

Mr. Lee proceeded to grow up with the business. He became secretary to the manager of the beef department and later was placed in charge of this department, where he remained until his appointment as sales manager of the Philadelphia territory. In 1920 he became sales manager of the New York territory with supervision over the company's Eastern interests. In 1926 he was summoned from New York, elected to a vice-presidency, and placed in charge of all branch house sales as well as the operations of the beef and small stock (veal and lamb) divisions of the business. Such was his status in January, 1931, when he was elected to the directorate, and to the presidency, "because of his thirty-five years' experience in all divisions of the business and his success in discharging the various responsibilities put on him." Mr. Lee is a member of the Union League and Exmoor Country clubs.

He was married, November 8, 1902, to Harriette Jones of Charlottesville, Virginia. There are two children, Jane (Mrs. William E. Graham) and Martha.

It was in the early '60's that Chicago's pioneer packers began wresting the supremacy from other packing centers. In the early days each railroad maintained yards for livestock near its terminal, and these yards, together with the slaughter houses, were scattered widely over the city. Hogs, sheep, and steers were driven through the streets. In 1865 John Sherman and a group of his associates purchased a square mile of land several miles south-west of what was then the city limits. They arranged for rail connections, and opened Chicago's Union Stock Yards. Other yards were abandoned and concentrated there.

A year later, three quarters of a million head of cattle, sheep, and hogs found their way to the Chicago killing pens. Thirty years later there were fifteen times as many. Every year since 1895 has seen more than 10,000,000 head slaughtered and dressed—sometimes many more, as when, during the World War, the number rose to 15,000,000.

Tapping the entire prairie empire, Chicago draws its livestock from 6,000,000 farms distributed among twenty-seven States; from ranches and farms extending across the plains to the Rocky Mountains, and southwest

to the Rio Grande. Most of the cattle and hogs come from Illinois, Iowa, Indiana, Missouri and Nebraska.

The meat dressed and processed in Chicago every year is sufficient to feed the twenty-five largest cities in the United States or the entire popula-tions of France, Belgium, Holland, Denmark, Norway, and Sweden com-bined. The packers located in Chicago could furnish, in the course of a year, a two month's supply of meat for the entire United States. In other words, they produce about one-sixth of the meats consumed by the nation. The daily output is 9,000,000 pounds; the annual output is 2,500,000,000.

For stock sold in Chicago the farmers and ranchers receive more than $400,000,000 a year, and in one year, 1918, they received $900,000,000 for their steaks and chops on the hoof. What's more, they are paid in cash, and a Stock Yards receipt is equivalent to money in the pocket. The Chicago packers have an annual pay roll in the city alone of $35,000,000, distributed among 25,000 employees. Thus vast amounts of currency are kept in circulation, adding greatly to the nation's prosperity and buying power.

Profits from the sale of meats are narrow, averaging in normal times only about 2½ cents for each dollar invested, or a fraction of a cent a pound. This close figuring has been made possible largely through the utilization of by-products, formerly regarded as waste and representing fortunes thrown away.

For Chicago's pre-eminence in packing is not one of size alone. The packing firms have taken the initiative in the development of new products and of new uses for old products. Methods of packing, curing, smoking, refrigerating, distributing, and merchandising have undergone revolutionary changes within recent years.

In no other industry has science worked such wonderful transformations than in the packing industry, and it can be said truthfully that not a hair nor a hoof or an animal goes to waste. Practically every part of an animal which winds up its career in the Union Stock Yards, is turned to some commercial use. The principal by-products include hides and leather, hair

LOADING A REFRIGERATOR CAR WITH BEEF

and wool, bones and horn, fertilizer, glue, casings, oils and fats, strings for musical instruments, and glue. Science has found a use for them too in many drugs, including insulin, thus making important contributions to human welfare.

Because of the inclusion of by-products in the value of the meat animal when purchased, the packer can and does pay a higher price to the farmer. On the other hand, he can sell the meat for much less than he could if there were no by-products to make up the difference. In this way, both producer and consumer benefit.

One of the interesting sights at the packing plants is that of the government inspectors at work. Nothing escapes their eagle eye. The slightest taint is immediately spotted, and an entire carcass may be rejected. The government stamp on a slab of meat is a guarantee of purity. It is interesting also to see the bearded Jewish rabbis in the killing pens slaughtering the animals for the kosher trade.

The Institute of American Meat Packers, with headquarters in Chicago, is the trade, research, and educational division of the industry. The Institute is carrying on an extensive program of scientific and practical research, employee training, and waste elimination. It is in the laboratories of the Institute that many new uses for by-products have been developed.

In furtherance of the industry's educational program, an institute of meat packing has been established at the University of Chicago, conducted jointly by the University and the Institute of American Meat Packers. Education and research activities are carried on also by the larger individual companies.

(From Drawing by John Doctoroff)

SALMON O. LEVINSON

Mr. Levinson, senior member of the law firm of Levinson, Becker, Gilbert, Peebles & Swiren, and founder of the American Committee for the Outlawry of War, was born in Noblesville, Indiana, December 29, 1865, the son of Newman D. and Minnie (Newman) Levinson. He received his Bachelor of Arts degree from Yale University in 1888, his Bachelor of Laws degree from Lake Forest University in 1891, and was awarded the degree of Doctor of Laws by Grinnell College in 1929 and by DePauw University in 1930. Admitted to the Illinois Bar in 1891, he has practiced in Chicago since that time, specializing in the reorganization of industrials and railroads. He reorganized the Westinghouse companies and the personal business affairs of George Westinghouse in 1908; the St. Louis & San Francisco Railroad Company in 1915.

It is, however, as the instigator of the Outlawry of War movement that he has received world-wide recognition. Having had two sons in the service during the World War, the subject of the legal status of war was one which touched him closely. In 1918 he set forth his views in an article published in the New Republic. His idea—one that had never before been expressed—was to dethrone Mars from his legal pedestal, or to deprive war of its legal status rather than to try to mitigate the horrors of war. He founded and financed the American Committee for the Outlawry of War, enlisting in the campaign such workers as Raymond Robins, John Haynes Holmes, Judge Florence Allen, Dr. C. C. Morrison, and John Dewey. In 1927 Mr. Levinson went to Europe, established an office in London, and interviewed publicists, journalists, statesmen, and diplomats in England and France. The ideas thus promulgated were the foundation of the Kellogg-Briand peace pact, signed in Paris, August 27, 1928. In recognition of his services to humanity Mr. Levinson was awarded the Rosenberger medal by the University of Chicago, being one of only three to receive this honor. The other recipients are Dr. James Henry Breasted, Orientalist, and Dr. F. G. Banting, discoverer of insulin.

Continued on page 547

THE ART INSTITUTE OF CHICAGO AND ITS SPIRIT OF SERVICE

What the World's Most Democratic Art Museum Offers to the Student, to the Master and to the Public

BY ROBERT B. HARSHE
Director

THE lordly stone lions guarding the entrance to the Art Institute in Grant Park at the end of Adams Street might well be emblazoned on Chicago's coat of arms. They symbolize the cultural aspirations of the city.

Down the ages, the need of art has been as elemental as the urge for food, shelter and clothing. What we know of prehistoric man is compassed by the record of his art. Art alone endures as the measure of the slow march of mankind out of savagery.

The pomp of kings and the spiritual power of priests have in turn been served by the handmaiden of art. Their palaces and temples were the world's first art museums. Castles and cathedrals, however, were primarily storehouses. It is not strange, then, that the idea of the museum as a storehouse, to which only the scholar or the esthete hold the key, should persist today.

Proud of its title, "the world's most democratic art museum," the Art Institute of Chicago has from the first used its influence to break down these antiquated traditions.

Open to the public free of charge on Wednesdays, Saturdays, Sundays, and holidays, and with a nominal admission fee of 25 cents on other days, it is visited yearly by more than 1,000,000 art lovers. Thousands of children, viewing the great masterpieces by occidental or oriental artists, in its many halls and galleries have received an inspiration that has enriched their lives. Its Art School, the largest and most influential in the United States, is establishing new standards for American art. Many of America's foremost painters, etchers, sculptors and designers have received their training there.

As early as 1866, Chicago, which up to that time had been concerned mainly with growing, began to feel the need of something definitely cultural. In that year the Chicago Academy of Design was founded. It survived the great Chicago fire of 1871, and shortly afterwards, was reorganized as the Chicago Academy of Fine Arts. Its purpose, as defined by charter, was "the founding and maintenance of a school of art and design, the formation and exhibition of collections of objects of art, and the cultivation and extension of the arts of design by any appropriate means." In 1882, the Academy became known by its present name, the Art Institute of Chicago.

In 1882, after the Institute had outgrown two buildings, one in Van Buren Street, the other on Michigan Avenue near Van Buren Street, a site for a permanent building was obtained in Grant Park, and the imposing Italian Renaissance structure which now houses its priceless treasures was

(Koehne Photo)

JOHN T. LLEWELLYN

Mr. Llewellyn, president of the Chicago Malleable Castings Company, Allied Steel Castings Company, and the Virginia Hotel Building Corporation, was born in Briton Ferry, South Wales, July 7, 1863, son of Henry and Elizabeth (Gower) Llewellyn. Immigrated to America from his birthplace, with parents, to Chicago during his first year, and six years later moved with family to Milwaukee, Wisconsin, where he entered grammar and Bay View High schools. At the age of sixteen, entered employ of the Milwaukee Works of the North Chicago Rolling Mill Company (now Illinois Steel Company) advancing to assistant general sales agent. When the Milwaukee offices were removed to Chicago in 1895, Mr. Llewellyn accepted the position as president of the Belle City Malleable Iron Company, Racine, Wisconsin, where he remained for four years, returning to Chicago in 1899 to organize the Chicago Malleable Castings Company of which he is now president.

Trustee, Chicago Orphan Asylum; member, Executive Committee, Railway Business Association, American Iron & Steel Institute, Malleable Iron Research Institute, Chicago Athletic Association, and the South Shore Country, Midlothian Country, and Flossmoor Country clubs, the Wisconsin Society of Chicago, and others.

On June 23, 1886, married Mary Agnes, daughter of James Sheriffs of Milwaukee. They have one son, James Sheriffs Llewellyn, now deceased.

(Courtesy, The Art Institute of Chicago)
THE ART INSTITUTE OF CHICAGO
Shepley, Rutan & Coolidge, architects.

erected. Building and grounds are valued at $20,000,000. The collections could not be purchased for $40,000,000.

Although no object in the Museum has been bought by taxpayer's money, and tax receipts pay only a fraction of its upkeep, its wonderful collections, formed entirely from the gifts of individuals, and its building, paid for by private subscriptions, belong in their entirety to the people of Chicago.

It is perhaps due to this feeling of ownership that the average Chicagoan has for this institution a pride verging on affection. However poor he may be in worldly goods, these are his treasures, exhibited for his esthetic pleasure and education. Pride in the Art Institute and appreciation of its services are reflected in the size of its membership, which is larger than that of any other museum in the world. Annual and sustaining members, numbering some 15,000, contribute each year to its support, and life members, on the payment of $100, enjoy with their families the advantages of its lectures and its theater during the subscriber's lifetime.

The list of benefactors who have made gifts valued at $50,000 or more, memorialized by bronze tablets in the entrance hall, is virtually a complete roster of the men and women who have notably furthered the educational progress of Chicago.

The Institute's large attendance is due not only to its central location, but to the variety and quality of its special exhibitions which greatly outnumber the exhibitions shown in other museums. Many of these exhibitions consist wholly or in part of the work of Chicago artists who are eligible for annual prizes of $13,300.

The departmental organization of the Institute has developed specialized public interests which have resulted in the formation of various contributory

(*Underwood and Underwood Photo*)

FRANK J. LOESCH

Mr. Loesch, veteran lawyer and senior member of the law firm of Loesch, Scofield, Loesch and Burke of Chicago, was born in Buffalo, New York, April 9, 1852, and is the son of Frank and Mary (Fisher) Loesch. He enrolled in 1871 at the Old Union College of Law, Chicago, graduated in June, 1874, and was admitted to the practice of law. Mr. Loesch has been counsel for the Pennsylvania Railroad System in Illinois since 1886; general counsel, Chicago Union Station Company since 1913; special assistant state's attorney in prosecution of election frauds, 1908 and 1909; member of the Board of Education, 1898 to 1902; president of the Chicago Crime Commission, 1928 to 1932. He was appointed by President Hoover in May, 1929, as one of the eleven members of the National Commission on Law Observance and Enforcement. Some of his most notable work was following the April, 1928, primary, when he was named chief special assistant attorney general, thus becoming, at the age of seventy-six, the head of the column marching against election frauds and crimes.

Mr. Loesch is a member of the American, Illinois State, and Chicago bar associations, serving as president of the latter from 1905 to 1907. He is a trustee and vice-president of the Chicago Historical Society; honorary member of the Union League Club (president, 1916-1917), and member of the University, Law (president, 1922-1923), Saddle and Cycle, Chicago Literary (president, 1928-1929), City, and Casino clubs of Chicago, and the Cooperstown, New York, Country Club.

On October 2, 1873, he married Lydia T. Richards of Chicago (deceased); the children are Angeline L. (wife of Dr. Robert E. Graves), Winifred L. (wife of Frederick Z. Marx), Richards L., and Joseph B. He married May Browning Bausher, of Chicago and Cooperstown, New York, February 7, 1925.

societies, such as the Antiquarians, the Friends of American Art, the Orientals, the Print and Drawing Club, the Needlework and Textile Guild, the Subscribers to the Goodman Theatre.

The Institute maintains no less than three libraries, a Print Reference Library in the Department of Prints and Drawings; the Burnham Library of Architecture, founded by the late Daniel H. Burnham, and the Ryerson Library of books on the fine arts, the foundation of the late Martin A. Ryerson. These libraries serve more than 100,000 readers annually.

(Courtesy, The Art Institute of Chicago)
VIEWS OF BLACKSTONE HALL, ART INSTITUTE

The Department of Museum Instruction with a staff of five lecturers offers courses in the history and appreciation of art. Lectures given in the Institute to members, students and the children, reach annual audiences numbering approximately 100,000. Lectures given before clubs, organizations and high schools by the Extension Lecturer, Dudley Crafts Watson, each year reach over 40,000 listeners. The Scammon Lectures founded by Mrs. Maria Sheldon Scammon are given annually and are frequently published in book form. The James Nelson Raymond Lecture Fund for Children, founded by Mrs. Anna Louise Raymond has quickened the interest of over 300,000 children in the knowledge and significance of art.

The Children's Museum endowed by Mr. and Mrs. Charles Worcester provides exhibitions of especial interest to boys and girls. Talks are given Saturday mornings by its curator to children of members. Plays for children and for members of the Art Institute are presented by the students in the

(*Paul Stone-Raymor, Ltd., Photo*)

FRANK G. LOGAN

Two careers in a single lifetime is the unusual achievement of Frank G. Logan, honorary vice-president of the Art Institute of Chicago. By pursuing his vocation as founder of the well-known firm of Logan and Bryan, he rounded out one career by the time he reached his fiftieth year. Since his retirement in 1901, Mr. Logan has made his second and most active career in his avocations—the furtherance of art, education and science.

To the advancement of art, Mr. Logan has given generously of his time, energy and resources. In 1916 he established and endowed the Mr. and Mrs. Frank G. Logan Medal and Prize Fund, out of the income of which annual awards are made to all branches of art displayed in the Institute. He is a trustee of the Municipal Art League, and of the Municipal Monument Fund founded by the late B. F. Ferguson, which erects statues and monuments to beautify Chicago's public places; a trustee appointed by the City of Chicago for the purchase of art for the Municipal Collection out of the annual funds appropriated by the City Council; a trustee of the Grand Central Galleries of New York, of the Chicago Galleries Association and of numerous other art societies and associations. His own love of the beautiful is represented in his private collection, one of the finest in Chicago. It consists of Barbizon paintings, modern Dutch, Flemish masters (one of which is a self-portrait by Rembrandt painted in 1631), English portraits, and works by American artists. A trustee of Beloit College since 1892, he founded and endowed the Logan Museum of Archaeology and Anthropology, which is renowned. The Museum is decorated with twelve mural paintings by John Norton representing the twelve epochs of man's life and houses collections from more than two hundred locations covering the world, among which is one of the greatest Paliolithic (Old Stone Age) exhibits in this country, including the world-famed Aurignacian necklace of some 30,000 to 50,000 years ago. The American collection from nearly every state in the Union, among others, embraces the largest aggregation of American stone axes and a representative assemblage of rare Wisconsin coppers.

In addition to these gifts, Mr. and Mrs. Logan founded and endowed a chair of anthropology and financed five archaeological expeditions to Europe and Africa seeking

Continued on page 548

Dramatic School of the Kenneth Sawyer Goodman Memorial Theatre founded by Mr. and Mrs. William Owen Goodman.

Educational work for children is concentrated in the Saturday classes of the Art School where 500 exceptionally talented young people begin early in life to choose some form of art expression as a vocation.

The Art School of the Institute offers courses in fine and applied arts to about 5,000 students. From the General Education Board and the Association of Arts and Industry it has recently received $360,000 to found a school of Industrial Art to develop designers to serve the industries of the Middle West.

The Museum acquires and exhibits examples from the art of the world, chosen not for their historical or academic importance, but for high esthetic quality alone. These exhibits are not limited to painting and sculpture; they include prints, textiles, furniture, ceramics, from America, Europe, and the Orient. The collections are beginning to assume a coherent and sequential scheme, the most serious gaps being found in Classical and Egyptian, Medieval and Renaissance art. In American, Spanish, Primitive German and French, Impressionistic and modern French painting; in Chinese pottery and bronzes it leads all other American art museums. It is strong also in Gothic and Persian art, in Japanese Prints, in Continental glass, and in certain phases of modern prints.

The Art Institute contains the official Fine Arts Department of the Century of Progress Exhibition which will show in definite sequence the Art of the world from Gothic times to the present. It is throughout an exhibition of masterpieces such as has never been seen in the United States.

GOTHIC ROOM, LUCY MAUD
BUCKINGHAM MEMORIAL

(Courtesy, The Art Institute of Chicago)
STAIRWAY, ART INSTITUTE

(Arthur Ermates Photo)

NATHAN WILLIAM MacCHESNEY

Mr. MacChesney, senior member of the law firm of MacChesney, Whiteford & Wells, was born in Chicago, June 2, 1878, son of Alfred Brunson MacChesney (M. D.) and Henrietta (Milsom) MacChesney (M.D.) The MacChesney family came originally from Normandy in France, Scotland, and the north of Ireland, settling in America in 1689. Mr. MacChesney obtained his A. B. (Bachelor of Arts) degree at the College of the Pacific in 1898, which college conferred on him an honorary LL. D. (Doctor of Laws) in 1926. Meantime he pursued special work at Stanford University. He was a student instructor in the University of Arizona, 1898-1899, and from 1899 to 1900 he attended Northwestern University Law School, which conferred on him the LL. M. (Master of Laws) degree in 1922. He graduated from the Law Department of the University of Michigan in 1902 with the degree of LL. B. (Bachelor of Laws). His general practice has involved largely corporation, banking, probate, and real estate law, the National Association of Real Estate Boards, for which he is general counsel, being one of his clients. Mr. MacChesney was Special Assistant Attorney General of the United States in 1911 and 1912, and has been Special Assistant Attorney General for Iilinois.

General MacChesney served in the National Guard of California and of Arizona. During the war with Spain he was with the first United States Volunteer Cavalry, later known as the "Rough Riders." During the Mexican border trouble he was on duty with the Illinois National Guard. General MacChesney was commissioned in the United States Army, June, 1917, serving with the 33rd and 86th divisions, with the Secretary of War, and as Judge Advocate attached to the staff of General Pershing. He was recommended for the Distinguished Service Medal, awarded a citation by General Pershing, and has been awarded the Order of the Purple Heart by the War Department. He was commissioned Brigadier-General in the National Guard, thanked by the Illinois State Council of Defense and presented with a Commemorative Sabre, He was also thanked by England, France, Belgium, and Italy for his war services and has had conferred upon him by the King of Siam the rank of Commander in the Order

Continued on page 548

(*Hedrich-Blessing Photo*)

1301 ASTOR STREET—Modernism has invaded the smaller building, and its clean lines
and surfaces seem to have detracted nothing from the homelike qualities of this residential apartment building. Philip B. Maher, architect.

(*Loubell Studios, Photo*)

PHILIP B. MAHER

Mr. Maher, architect, was born in Kenilworth, Illinois, October 21, 1894, son of George W. (architect) and Elizabeth (Brooks) Maher. He studied architecture under his father and at the University of Michigan and started with the firm of George W. Maher, architect, of Chicago in 1914; was a member of the firm of George W. Maher & Son from 1921 to 1924. He established the present firm of Philip B. Maher, architect, in 1924.

He has designed some of Chicago's most distinguished buildings, his practice covering many classes, such as office buildings, fine shops, clubs, cooperative apartments and residences. He is best known for the many projects he has designed along North Michigan avenue when this district started its rapid development following the opening of the Michigan Boulevard Bridge. Among them were the Woman's Athletic Club, The Farwell Office Building, The Blackstone Shop, Jacques' Shop and the Decorative Arts Building. He also designed and aided in organizing the cooperative apartment buildings at 1301 and 1260 Astor Street, which are unique in that all apartments in the buildings are of totally different design and layout and are developed as so many individual homes. In addition to the above, he designed the City Hall for the City of Gary, Indiana. In many of his late buildings of a modern style he has carried out the interior decoration and furnishing complete, designing all furniture so as to carry out the individual style of the buildings. Mr. Maher served as an ensign in the U. S. Navy two and one-half years during and after the World War and was stationed at Great Lakes, Illinois, where he was engaged in the construction development of the station; later he was at Naval Headquarters, London, and after the Armistice, with the Commission to Negotiate Peace at Paris. He is a member of the American Institute of Architects. His clubs are Arts, Tavern, Saddle and Cycle, and Onwentsia.

On December 22, 1921, Mr. Maher married Madeleine Michelson of Chicago and they have two children, Philip Brooks, Jr., and Hilary.

COMBATING THE RISING TIDE OF PUBLIC ACCIDENTS

The Chicago Safety Council and Its Important Tasks

BY C. L. RICE
President of the Chicago Safety Council

THE Chicago Safety Council is a monument to the broadmindedness and vision of Chicago's industrial leaders. Organized in 1926 as a co-operative effort to reduce industrial accidents, it has become today an aggressive champion in the fight to stem the mounting toll of deaths from public accidents within its sphere of influence.

Until within recent years, the problem of industrial safety had received little attention. Accidents in factories and workshops were regarded as inevitable. The safety engineer had not begun his studies.

A survey of the situation, however, revealed the fact that in most instances life and limb could have been saved had ordinary precautions been taken.

Two things were necessary if the situation was to be relieved. The workmen themselves must be educated and shown how to avoid the most common

(*Chicago Architectural Photographing Company*)
Wacker Drive, looking west. The river that flows backward. Steel bascule bridges span this stream once arched by wooden structures.

(*From Drawing by John Doctoroff*)

RABBI LOUIS L. MANN

Dr. Mann, Rabbi of Chicago Sinai Congregation, was born January 25, 1890, in Louisville, Kentucky, the son of David and Frieda (Weiss) Mann. Graduating in 1907 from the Male High School in Louisville, he studied at Johns Hopkins University, and later at the University of Cincinnati, where he received his Bachelor's degree in 1910, and his Master's degree in 1912. Further studies at the Hebrew Union College led to the degrees of Bachelor of Hebrew Literature and Rabbi. Yale University conferred upon him the Doctor of Laws degree in 1920. Dr. Mann was Rabbi of Mishkan Israel Congregation in New Haven from 1914 to 1923, and on the death of Dr. Emil G. Hirsch in 1923, was called to Chicago to fill the Sinai Temple pulpit. He was lecturer on Comparative Ethics at Yale University, and is now professorial lecturer in the Department of Oriental Languages and Literature, University of Chicago. In 1931 he lectured on "The Evolution of the Soul" for the W. F. Ayres Foundation. As a preacher Dr. Mann prefers to deal with the problems of the day, believing that "nothing human is foreign to religion."

His civic and philanthropic interests are many. He is an acting National Director of the B'nai B'rith Hillel Foundation, a member of the Executive Committee of the Eugenics Commission of the United States, a member of the executive board of the American Committee for the Outlawry of War, vice-president of the Big Brothers and Big Sisters Movement of America, chairman of the board of the Religious Education Association of America, and a member of the board of trustees of the (Carnegie) Church Peace Union. Dr. Mann was appointed by President Hoover as a member of the White House Conference on Child Health and Protection, and by Governor Emmerson as a member of the Commission on Unemployment and of the State Planning Commission. He is Chancellor of the Jewish Chautauqua Society of America, editor of the department of ethics of the New Standard Jewish Encyclopedia, associate editor of "Unity," and contributing editor of the Dictionary of American Biography. As a member of the National Advisory Council of the American Birth Control League, Dr. Mann has been an outstanding advocate of the movement. For scholarly attainments he was decorated in 1931 by France as an Officer of the Academy. He is a member of Rotary International, the Covenant, Standard, and City clubs, and the American Oriental Society.

Dr. Mann was married June 17, 1915, to Ruth Cohen, daughter of former Senator Alfred M. Cohen, of Cincinnati. Their children are Mary Louise and Arthur Horace.

risks. The employers must be persuaded that it was to their own interests to install safety devices and to cut down the accident toll which represented such an economic waste. Employers, for the most part, were willing to co-operate with the Chicago Safety Council, and the initial expense of safe-guarding their plants was soon offset by the saving of money paid in work-men's compensation. Only a small minority remained obdurate. Among the workmen themselves, the spirit of rivalry produced good results. Groups vied with each other in accident prevention, and discovered that it paid. The traditional carelessness of the factory employee was thus gradually overcome.

With its industrial program well organized and making headway, the Council directed its attention to more general fields. A larger responsibility, it was seen, confronted it in the home and highway situation. Realizing that much of the experience gained in dealing with industrial accidents could be applied to an attack on accidents in the homes and on the streets of the com-munity, the Chicago Safety Council has swung into line with municipal officers and other agencies in this even greater fight.

The frequency and number of home accidents, minor and major, present an appalling picture. Burns, scalds, cuts, asphyxiations, explosions, electro-cutions, poisonings cause thousands of deaths and injuries yearly. And it is not an easy matter to educate the housewife.

Approximately 1,000 deaths are caused annually in Cook county by automobiles alone, and with the population, as well as registrations steadily increasing, and with roads as yet inadequate for twentieth-century traffic, it is with the greatest difficulty that the accident toll is held down even to reasonable limits. The automobile dawned swiftly on a horse-and-buggy world, and road building has not kept pace with the new transportation.

As yet, the Council is a modern David confronting a formidable Goliath. Education of the public is the sling with which it is striving to drop the giant, and to this task the Chicago Safety Council is devoting unremitting efforts.

A survey of highway accidents shows that most of them are preventable. Courtesy, consideration of others, and control of speed on the part of the motorists; safety education in the homes and schools, and watchfulness on the part of pedestrians will do much to improve the automobile accident situation. Engineers more and more are building safety into cars and roads. Vast sums of money are spent every year to safeguard grade crossings. But the personal equation still remains, and a high-powered automobile with an incompetent or careless driver at the wheel is still a thing of danger.

By means of interfleet drivers' contests—an idea borrowed from the industrial accident campaign—the Chicago Safety Council has educated legions of truck operators. As a group today they are responsible for fewer accidents in proportion to the number of vehicles involved than are the drivers of the private cars. In dealing with the latter, the Council has had recourse to free safety tests, including brake and ignition inspections, to-gether with publicity and remedial legislation.

(Blank and Stoller, Inc., Photo)

A. R. MARRIOTT

Mr. Marriott was born on a farm in DuPage county, Illinois, May 26, 1860, son of William and Kittie (Gresham) Marriott, and spent his entire business life with the Chicago Title and Trust Company and its predecessors. He became president of this pioneer Chicago organization on November 14, 1929, and was recognized as one of the outstanding authorities on Chicago real estate titles. He attended the public schools at Wheaton, Illinois, and the Chicago College of Law. He began as office boy in the abstract office of Haddock, Coxe and Company. Sixteen years later he was appointed superintendent of Haddock, Valette and Rickcords, and two years later was elected vice-president. This company later became the Security Title and Trust Company, and in 1901 was reorganized as the Chicago Title and Trust Company, of which Mr. Marriott was vice-president from 1901 until November, 1929, when he became president. He remained in that office until his death on May 20, 1931. He is survived by his wife, Mrs. Mabel R. Marriott, and seven children, Ida Elizabeth (Mrs. Robert A. McClevey), Arthur Cooper, Robert William, Thomas Benton, Rogerson, Elizabeth Jane, and David Francis.

Mr. Marriott was president of the DuPage Title Company of Wheaton and the Allman-Gary Title Company of Gary, Indiana. For twenty-five years he had been a member of the executive committee of the Illinois Abstractors' Association. He belonged to the Chicago and Cook County Real Estate boards, and the Chicago and Illinois State bar associations. He was a member of the Union League, the Oak Park, and the Big Foot Country clubs. Mr. Marriott was actively interested in the growth of Chicago.

(*Chicago Architectural Photographing Company*)

MICHIGAN AVENUE AT NIGHT

It is unfortunate that Illinois has no driver's license law such as obtains in many other States. Such a law, in the belief of the Chicago Safety Council, by eliminating the unfit and the chronically careless driver, would result in the saving of hundreds of lives yearly, not only in Chicago and Cook County, but throughout the State. A competency law, requiring drivers' tests before the issuing of a license would inconvenience and rule out a negligible minority—eliminate the "lunatic fringe" responsible for the great majority of accidents. It would benefit the others.

The Chicago Safety Council has actively sponsored a driver's license law, and though defeated in its first attempts to have it written in the statute books, is pledged to continue the battle with even firmer resolution than before.

While the Council is active in the field of public and home accidents, it has not neglected its original program of industrial safety. Realizing that eternal vigilance is the price of safety, it carries on an extensive program of industrial accident prevention. The Council conducts monthly meetings in various sections of the city and thousands of foremen, supervisors and workers fill the large auditoriums available to hear leaders in the industrial safety field discuss their common problems.

Except for a small executive staff, all activities of the Council are carried on by volunteer committees and workers. Several hundred interested individuals—the recognized leaders in the industries they represent—are engaged in this program.

Its present leaders feel that the work of the Council has but begun—that it is to play an increasingly important role in the community and that through its efforts Chicago's industry, Chicago's homes, and Chicago's streets can be the safest in the world.

(*Chicago Architectural Photographing Company*)

ELKS' WAR MEMORIAL AT LINCOLN PARK

MATHER TOWER,
a twentieth century senti-
nel standing on the site of
old Fort Dearborn.

Herbert Hugh Riddle,
architect.

(Eugene L. Ray Photo)

ALONZO C. MATHER

Mr. Mather, founder and executive head of the Mather Humane Stock Transportation Company of Chicago, commonly known as the Mather Stock Car Company, is descended from a long line of noteworthy and distinguished ancestors of English origin. Outside of his personal worth and accomplishments, there is much of interest attached to his genealogy which betokens lines of sterling worth and prominent identification with American history for many generations. Although a native of the Empire State, Mr. Mather has been a resident of Chicago for more than half a century. He obtained his early education in the Fairfield (New York) Preparatory School, of which his grand-father, Captain Moses Mather, a soldier in the War of 1812, was one of the founders, and of which his father, Dr. William Mather, was president for more than a quarter of a century. Mr. Mather first secured employment at Utica, New York, later went to Quincy, Illinois, where he remained until 1875, when he came to Chicago and started the wholesale mercantile business under the firm name of Alonzo C. Mather and Company. In 1881 Mr. Mather's humane impulses led him to investigate the trans-portation of live stock over long distances by railroads, and he devised a live stock car in which animals are shipped in comfort, fed and watered without unloading, so that there is no loss from killed or injured animals, no suffering, and no loss to owners from shrinkage due to hunger and thirst. In recognition of this achievement, in 1883 the American Humane Society awarded him an elaborate gold medal. Later he designed a refrigerator in which fresh meats are shipped and kept in perfect condition over a long journey. Thousands of Mather cars are being used by railroads in United States and Canada.

Mr. Mather had for many years been interested in and had worked out a plan to build a bridge across the Niagara River from Buffalo to Fort Erie, Ontario, including the construction of an international harbor at Fort Erie and the harnessing of water rushing between the abutments for electric power. He planned to erect the bridge as a memorial to the inventors of United States and Canada who were the first to use modern methods and steel construction in the nineteenth century. At this time a bill

Continued on page 548

AMERICAN FARM IMPLEMENTS AND MACHINES
1833-1933
BY HERBERT A. KELLAR

In 1833, the year Chicago was incorporated as a city, almost ninety percent of the population of the United States were forced to toil in the fields in order to provide bread for themselves and the remainder of the population. One hundred years later, less than fifty percent of the people not only raised enough food to feed themselves and the residue of the population but piled up a surplus for export. The invention, manufacture, introduction and use of improved agricultural machinery has been a potent factor in bringing about these changed conditions.

In 1833, the farmer plowed his fields with a cast iron plow; levelled them off with a wooden drag harrow with wood or iron points; sowed his wheat broadcast by hand; planted his corn with a hoe; cultivated with a single or double shovel plow; reaped his grain with a sickle, scythe or cradle; and finally threshed it with a flail or tramped it out with animals, later removing the chaff with the aid of the wind.

Succeeding decades witnessed many changes in the methods of preparing the soil, planting of seeds, cultivating, reaping and threshing. Consistently throughout the period improved implements and machines have displaced laborious hand labor.

The steel plow succeeded the cast iron plow before the Civil War, and a decade later its construction was still further improved by the introduction of soft center steel. The sulky or riding plow, as contrasted with the walking plow, did not become practical until about 1870, after which date it rapidly came into wide use. The basic idea of the gang plow (the use of more than one plow at the same time) was not easily applied where plows were drawn by animals and early led to experiments in traction by steam engine. The English idea of using a stationary engine with a steel cable to draw several plows across a field did not prove popular in this country and after 1865 a steam traction engine was gradually developed which was capable of drawing as many as eighteen plows at one time. Between 1880 and 1915 gang plowing with the aid of such engines became quite common on large farms. The modern internal-combustion tractor, both wheeled and crawler types, came into its own during the World War, quickly displacing steam traction in plowing and in the last few years machines have steadily superseded animal power on the farms.

Harrows, since 1833, have generally followed three types, the spike tooth, disc and spring tooth. The principle changes in the spike tooth harrow aside from the shape of the frame and method of attachment have been first—to give the teeth a backward slant and then to make them adjustable. The construction has also gradually altered from wood and iron to an iron frame and steel teeth. Disc harrows with a gang arrangement

(Blank and Stoller, Inc., Photo)

LLOYD MAXWELL

Mr. Maxwell, first vice-president of Roche, Williams and Cunnyngham, Inc., advertising agency, was born in Hicksville, Ohio, August 3, 1879, son of Isaac M. and Celesita A. (Crary) Maxwell. After graduating from high school he attended the University of Chicago, and entered the advertising field after a successful career in the automotive industry. His first advertising connection was with the Associated Sunday Magazine as Eastern manager. Subsequently, he was vice-president and partner in Erwin, Wasey & Company, president of Maxwell-McLaughlin Company, and then associated himself with Williams & Cunnyngham (now Roche, Williams and Cunnyngham, Inc.), of which he is, at the present time, first vice-president, being responsible for the advertising of many national accounts.

Mr. Maxwell is past president of the Midlothian Country Club, the Minocqua Heights (Wisconsin) Golf and Country Club, the Iowa State Golf Association, the Marshalltown (Iowa) Country Club, and the Western Advertising Golfers Association. He is a trustee of the Bendix Foundation, and also a member of the Bob O'Link Country, Union League, Chicago Athletic, Executives, Players Club of New York, Chicago Press Club, and the Society of Automotive Engineers. Fraternally, he has been a national figure in the Elks for more than twenty years, serving now as Grand Trustee. His friends are his "hobby"; golf, his favorite pastime.

On December 30, 1919, he married Mary Agnes O'Neil, of New York, and there is one daughter, Marian.

CYRUS HALL McCORMICK

were put on the market as early as the fifties but it was not until after 1870 that they were widely used. An interesting variation of these machines has consisted in placing disc furrow openers on seeders. The spring tooth harrow, although invented in the late sixties did not become popular until a device to make them adjustable was perfected in 1877. In recent years the displacement of the horse by the tractor has enabled the farmer to greatly extend the number of harrows which he can operate at one time.

Although numerous patents on seeders and grain drills were taken out in the thirties and forties, it was not until after 1850 that they began to be practical and not until 1861 that they came into general use. The chief improvements of American inventors have been in the feed and adjusting devices. An early type was the broadcast seeder. As in the case of harrows, three distinct types gradually developed; cylinder drills, slide drills and force feed drills, each of these offering a different method of depositing the seed. One of the most widely used form of the seeder was the shoe drill, so adjusted as to adapt itself to obstructions in the ground. This first came into general use about 1870. In addition to combinations of drills with harrows, which have already been mentioned, fertilizer distributors and grass-seeding attachments have frequently been added to American grain drills. Here again the tractor with its greater pulling power has increased the acreage which grain drills can cover in one operation.

Numerous attempts were made without success to develop a practical corn planter after 1833 but it was not until 1853 that a successful device appeared. Space does not permit taking up the intricate and involved subsequent development of corn planters. Suffice it to say that the modern corn planter, among other features, accurately controls the amount of seed to the hill, depth of planting, spacing arrangement of hills and rows, and adjustment to ground obstructions. One of the noticeable developments of agricultural machines has been the tendency to produce special devices for special purposes. Such an implement is the Lister, a combined plow and corn planter adaptable to dry regions because it plants the corn at the bottom of the furrow. The two row corn planter was a standard machine

CYRUS H. McCORMICK

Cyrus H. McCormick, chairman of the board of directors of the International Harvester Company, was born in Washington, May 16, 1859, son of Cyrus Hall and Nettie (Fowler) McCormick. He began his career in 1879, leaving Princeton University in that year to enter his father's business. In 1884 he succeeded his father as president of the McCormick Harvesting Machine Company, where he quickly evidenced his ability in the hand-ling of extensive and varied activities under the stress of vigorous competition. When the International Harvester Company of today finally emerged, he became its first presi-dent (1902-1919). In this capacity he guided and developed a world-wide enterprise with constant concern for the welfare of its employees and the farming public which it serves. Because of his understanding of economic conditions in foreign countries he was appointed a member of the Special Diplomatic Mission of the United States to Russia in 1917 in which connection he rendered valuable service to his country.

Mr. McCormick is a patron of music, painting and landscape gardening of the "natural school." He has contributed liberally to the Presbyterian Theological Seminary, Princeton University, The Elizabeth McCormick Memorial Foundation for Child Welfare, the Young Men's Christian Association, and other institutions.

He married Harriet Bradley Hammond, of Chicago, Illinois, March 5, 1889 (died January 17, 1921). The children are Cyrus, Elizabeth (deceased), and Gordon. He married Alice M. Hoit, of Chicago, April 22, 1927.

in the days of the horse. The tractor has made it possible to increase the number of rows planted simultaneously.

The single and double shovel plows used for cultivation in 1833 were succeeded in the fifties by the straddle row sulky corn cultivator. Various improvements were made in this machine such as regulating the depth in the soil in which it operated, adjustment to obstructions, and throwing the soil at will to or from the plants. In addition various types have been developed for special use, such as disc spring tooth and spading cultivators. As in the case of other farm implements, the tractor has increased the capacity of the cultivator at each operation.

The mechanical grain reaper although invented in 1831 did not begin to supplant the cradle until the late forties and the fifties. A self rake device was added in the sixties and before the end of the decade the hand binding harvester foreshadowed the era of automatic binding. The wire binder of the seventies, succeeded by the twine binder after 1880, brought an end to the reign of the hand binding machines. The twine binder in which one man drove a reaper, which cut, bound and discharged the grain in bundles all in one continuous operation, exercised a virtual monopoly over grain harvesting operations until after the World War. Complementary minor machines of some importance developed parallel to the grain reaper, were the horse drawn header, the push binder, and the dropper, the latter containing a reaping attachment added to a mower. The development of the tractor immediately proceeding the World War led to a further improvement upon the binder. The so called tractor binder, in which a gasoline or kerosene tractor was substituted for horses increased both the speed and capacity of the machine. The same period saw the evolution of the latest development in harvesting implements, the "Harvester-Thresher." This machine known as the "Combine," also drawn by a tractor, reaps and threshes the grain in one operation.

Attempts to devise a corn binder proceeded simultaineously with the evolution of the grain binder but did not meet with success until the early nineties. Two types proved successful at that time and are still manufactured, one binding the grain while standing upright and the other while lying horizontally. A recent development in corn binding has been the introduction of a machine which cuts and binds two rows at the same time.

The mower, used for cutting grass, first became practical in the fifties through attachments added to reapers. It did not become effective as a separate machine until the sixties. By the seventies the two wheeled front cut type became the standard and beyond improvement in general construction and the recent substitution of the tractor for horses, it has undergone little change with the years.

When a man with a scythe could only cut about an acre of grass in a day, the hand rake proved adequate to gather the hay. The introduction of the mowing machine necessitated the development of machines to handle the grass after it was cut. The first practical implement for this purpose

ROBERT R. McCORMICK

Col. McCormick, editor and publisher of the Chicago Tribune, was born in Chicago, July 30, 1880, the son of Robert Sanderson and Katharine Van Etta (Medill) McCormick. His father was American Ambassador to Vienna and St. Petersburg; his grandfather, Joseph Medill, was the greatest of the early builders of the Tribune. Col. McCormick was graduated from Yale University in 1903 and studied law at Northwestern University. In 1907 he was admitted to the Illinois Bar and became a member of the firm of Shephard, McCormick and Thomason, now known as Kirkland, Fleming, Green and Martin. He entered politics in 1904 when he was elected alderman from the old 21st ward. His interest in public affairs led to his appointment as a member of the Chicago Charter Convention in 1907. He served also as a member of the Chicago Plan Commission. During his term as alderman Col. McCormick was elected president of the Sanitary District Board, and it was under his administration that the canal, with its locks and works, was completed. In 1910 he was called on to assume the presidency of the Tribune Company.

In the military phase of his career, Col. McCormick has held several important posts. During the trouble with Mexico he served on the border as Major of the 1st Illinois Cavalry. On America's entry into the World War he was attached to General Pershing's staff, but desiring more active participation in the fighting, he joined the 5th Field Artillery. Later he became Colonel of the 61st Regiment. While in the front lines he was cited by his Brigade Commander for prompt action in battle, and was later decorated with the Distinguished Service Medal. Before returning to civil life he served as Commandant at Fort Sheridan. He is a member of the Racquet and Tennis Club of New York, and of the Chicago, Saddle and Cycle and Onwentsia clubs.

Col. McCormick was married March 10, 1915, to Amie Irwin Adams.

was the horse drawn revolving hay rake of the fifties and sixties. Gradually this type was superseded by the spring tooth hay rake. Hand and self dumping attachments aided the efficiency of these implements and this was further increased by the introduction of the side delivery rake which placed the hay in a continuous windrow suitable for loading. The desirability of stirring up the hay so that it would cure better after it had been trampled by the horses attached to a mowing machine, led to the invention of the hay tedder. Other interesting developments following the Civil War were the hay loader designed to gather the hay from the windrow; the several types of hay forks and carriers used to stack the hay in barns or in the field; and the hay press for baling hay.

The first important American development in the thresher took place in the thirties when the old ground hog or open cylinder type was combined with a fanning mill. The machine operated by horse power and was portable. Though roughly effective it was not until the vibrator principle was introduced in the fifties that all the good grain could be separated from the straw and chaff. Horse powers were used with threshers until after the Civil War. The portable steam engine then monopolized the field until the recent development of the gasoline engine and the tractor. Attempts to devise a machine to reap and thresh at the same time were made as early as the thirties and unwieldy horse-drawn contrivances were actually

Entrance to Agricultural Group of A Century of Progress, Chicago's 1933 World's Fair. Here the entire story of the evolution of agriculture from the past age of cradle and flail to the present age of tractor and combine is shown in dramatic form.

developed. These operated fairly well under special conditions. Real success with this type of machine has been attained with the introduction of the modern "Harvester-Thresher" or "Combine."

Other agricultural machines which have been highly developed in the last hundred years are corn shellers, straw and feed cutters, grinding mills and potatoe diggers. Although used to some extent before the Civil War it was not until after that time that they were improved and came into general use. More recent machines are corn huskers and shredders, potato planters, cotton planters, fertilizer distributors, stalk cutters, manure spreaders, and cream separators and milkers.

Cyrus Hall McCormick, who invented the first practical reaper in 1831, was not only a great inventor but also the founder of the agricultural machine industry. The establishment of his factory in Chicago in 1847 marked the beginning of a great industry in America. Chicago as the home of the various McCormick companies and the harvester company later built up by William Deering, both of which merged in 1902 with other leading firms to form the International Harvester Company, has long played a leading part in the manufacture of agricultural machines.

Agricultural manufacturers in the past hundred years have contributed much to the modern industry and commerce. Mass production, standardization of parts, the written guarantee, the free trial, a fixed price, a system of agents and dealers, storage warehouses in strategic locations, liberal credit, time payments, the testimonial, the field trial, and other procedure now common to the world were early practiced by these men, foremost of whom was McCormick of Chicago.

The American genius for the machine has found full scope in agriculture. If we could for the moment possess the recollections of our agrarian ancestors what glories of accomplishment could we recall: McCormick's reaper, Wood's mower, Deere's and Oliver's steel plows, Brown's corn planter, Pitt's and Case's threshers, Bickford and Huffman's and the Empire grain drills, Adams' and Galt's corn shellers, Appleby's twine binding device, and the corn binder! And then today we have the tractor and the combine.

The hundred years between 1833 and 1933 have witnessed many changes in agricultural theory and practice. The laborious hand operations of olden days, except in a few backward regions, have faded from memory. Today the civilized world is machine conscious. McCormick with his first crude reaper opened up a new vista for agriculture and civilization. Inspired by his vision men have solved the problem of production. In the next hundred years may we find the solution to the pressing problems of world marketing and distribution.

CHICAGO AS A YACHTSMAN'S PARADISE
Lake Michigan, the Scene of Many Regattas and Outboard Events
BY MALCOLM D. VAIL

CHICAGO'S yachting season opens unofficially on the first balmy day of Spring. The frost is hardly out of the ground when from the storerooms of the shipyards along the north branch of the river the yachts are taken out, or stripped of their tarpaulins, and lined up on the runways. Skippers in reefers, sweaters, and duck trousers fondly overhaul their pets. Paint-pots and brushes are produced. Hatches are thrown open. Hulls are painted, decks holystoned, and rigging put in shape. A few weeks later, the boats will be riding at anchor in the various yacht harbors along the shore of Lake Michigan, ready for the first regatta of the season.

A recent survey made for the Lake Michigan Yachting Association reveals the fact that there are more than 600 sail and power yachts in and about Chicago, representing a total valuation of $7,500,000. This census does not include the hundreds of smaller boats which make Lake Michigan their playground during the summer.

The development of Star class boats has been nothing less than sensational. Five fleets, made up of eighty boats of this class in 1921 increased during the next decade to more than fifty fleets with some 800 boats. This increase in itself is sufficient evidence of the interest that is being taken in yachting.

Hardly a week goes by from May to October without some kind of a regatta in which the schooners, yawls, and sloops, the P. Q. and R. boats, the Eagles, Stars, and Pups compete. Many of Chicago's speedy seaworthy boats have been entered in the Great Lakes Championship Series for their classes.

Along its twenty-five miles of Lake front Chicago has several snug yacht harbors, of which Belmont Harbor, where the Chicago Yacht Club has its floating home, is the showiest. Other anchorages are off the South Shore Country Club, the Jackson Park Yacht Club, Grant Park, where the Columbia and Chicago Yacht clubs have their headquarters; Navy Pier, and Wilmette, home of the enterprising Sheridan Shore Club, which is housed in the sumptuous Marshall Studio. The Saddle and Cycle Club, which is not exclusively a yacht club, is planning a spacious north side harbor. The Lincoln Park lagoon shelters a large argosy of motor boats. Both the Columbia and the Chicago Yacht Clubs have announced ambitious building plans for the downtown lake front, and space is mostly all gone in the new Montrose Harbor.

Founded in 1875, the Chicago Yacht Club has been for many years a leader in the development of the sport it sponsors. It opens the season with the Memorial Day races, and which in addition to its weekly racing has in its major events the Virginia Trophy race for Q boats, the Mackinac race over a course of 331 miles, cruises to St. Joseph and to Black Lake,

(*Koehne Photo*)

EDWARD G. McDOUGALL

Mr. McDougall, president of Libby, McNeill and Libby, was born in Fargo, Michigan, April 6, 1875, son of John D. and Christy Ann (Monroe) McDougall. A few years after his graduation from high school the Spanish-American War broke out and he enlisted in the army, being commissioned a Lieutenant. Mustered out in 1901, he entered the service of Libby, McNeill and Libby and has since been engaged in the interesting and eminently useful business of making the finest foods from many regions conveniently available to every household. First employed as a clerk, Mr. McDougall progressed steadily and by 1914 held the position of general sales manager. A short time later he was made vice-president of the company and was elevated to his present office in 1922. When Mr. McDougall first joined the Libby organization he found it a relatively small concern with only one plant producing a few canned meat products. Today Libby, McNeill and Libby is one of the largest canning companies in the world, controlling thousands of acres of orchards and farms and operating more than sixty manufacturing units extending from Hawaii to Delaware.

Among the company's "100 Famous Foods" are California fruits and vegetables, Hawaiian pineapple, pickles and condiments, canned meats, Alaska salmon, and evaporated milk. These products have been advertised extensively for many years and are distributed by an international sales organization with 250 branch offices and agencies in the principal cities of the world. Always active in movements beneficial to the industry as a whole, Mr. McDougall has served as a director of the National Canners Association and as an officer of numerous other business organizations. In Chicago he is a member of the Union League, South Shore Country, and Beverly Country clubs. His favorite recreations are horseback riding and golf.

Mr. McDougall was married, June 28, 1904, to Alice L. Fillmore of Chicago. There are three children, Clarice Louise, Chesley Edward, and Lorna Lee.

Michigan, and to Milwaukee, the Sir Thomas Lipton race for R boats, the Sir John Nutting race for Eagle Class, the open race for the Sheldon Clark Trophies, and the Gehrmann trophy for the Pups.

The Columbia Yacht Club stages the annual Michigan City classic, held early in June, from the Van Buren street gap in Grant Park to the Michigan City basin. The Jackson Park and Sheridan Shore clubs have attractive summer programs of week-end regattas and cruises.

While some of the events, such as the Mackinac and Michigan City races call for seamanship of the highest quality, yachting as a sport is attracting more and more women, and all the Chicago clubs have developed women skippers some of whom can give the men plenty of competition.

(*Chicago Architectural Photographing Company*)

Eastern yachtsmen visiting Chicago are invariably amazed at the facilities for their favorite sport offered by Lake Michigan. In the downtown harbor will be found motor yachts of all kinds, from the tiny speed boat to such floating palaces as the Kenkora, the Mizpah, or the Freedom. The Kenkora is a 190-foot auxiliary cruiser belonging to Kenneth G. Smith. The Freedom, Sterling Morton's 90-foot schooner, is one of the largest racing craft on the Great Lakes and was built in a Chicago shipyard last year. Another speedy yacht is Philip K. Wrigley's 88-foot Wasp.

Not only is Chicago gaining prestige as a yachting center, but as the center of a rapidly growing ship-building industry. Chicago-built boats are seen today in the harbors of Detroit, Cleveland, Milwaukee, New York, Boston, and several on the Florida coast, where they are competing successfully with Eastern-built craft.

(Loubell Studios Photo)

WILLIAM D. McJUNKIN

Mr. McJunkin, civic leader and advertising man, was born in Franklin, Pennsylvania, February 2, 1870, son of Jehu David and Margaret (Campbell) McJunkin. He was educated in public schools of Butler, Pennsylvania, under private tutors, and at Western University of Pennsylvania, now Pittsburgh University. Mr. McJunkin served three large State street department stores as advertising manager and then, twenty-seven years ago, formed the McJunkin Advertising Company, of which he is president.

Throughout his career he has been deeply interested in civic movements for Chicago's progress, despite the demands on his time as a leader in the advertising field and as president of many other corporations in which he is financially interested. He is a member of the Board of Education of Chicago, vice-chairman of the committee on public information of A Century of Progress, Chicago's (1933) World's Fair, a director in the Travelers' Aid Society and of the Chicago Tuberculosis Institute, and actively interested in other charitable institutions. Mr. McJunkin helped to organize the Chicago Advertising Council. He is vice-president of the National Outdoor Advertising Bureau. He is a member of the Electric Club, the Builders Club, the Chicago Athletic Association, the Elks, the Medievalists, the Irish Fellowship Club, and the Edgewater Golf Club. Golf is his favorite sport.

He married Nell Frances Barker, of Columbus, Ohio, May 30, 1894, and they have a son, William Jonathan, and a daughter, Mrs. F. W. Harvey, Jr.

Many of Chicago's yachtsmen served with distinction in the World War. Not a few qualified as officers at the Naval Training School at Great Lakes and at the emergency school conducted at Navy Pier.

Lack of an adequate course off the lake front has retarded the development of outboard motorboat racing, although the annual Milwaukee-to-Chicago race has for several years attracted the more reckless followers of this pastime. But with the completion of the lagoon east of the Century of Progress Exposition grounds, outboarding has come into its own.

There are probably about 10,000 outboard motor boats in and about Chicago, but only a small proportion of these, of course, are built for racing.

Early in 1932, the first of a series of speed trials for these craft was held on the new outboard track. This tournament was followed by others, and toward the close of the season it was announced that outboard racing would supply one of the thrills at the big Exposition.

With the further development of harbors as provided for by the "Chicago Plan"; with the completion of the palatial yacht club homes in Chicago's front yard, and increased interest shown in yacht and outboard racing, the future outlook for the sport is most encouraging.

(Underwood and Underwood Photo)

Night view of the Merchandise Mart, this, the world's largest building, is one of Chicago's first buildings to be erected on air rights.
Graham, Anderson, Probst & White, architects.

(Moffett-Russell Photo)

JOHN McKINLAY

Mr. McKinlay, president of Marshall Field and Company, was born in Greenock, Scotland, August 31, 1874, son of James D. and Mary (Wilson) McKinlay. The family emigrated to America in 1884 and settled in Chicago. He left school after completing the eighth grade and on August 29, 1888, entered the employ of Marshall Field & Company as a cash boy at $2 a week. It is reported he used his first week's pay to buy a pair of long trousers. During the first years of his employment he attended various night schools. He took a three-year law course at the Chicago College of Law and was admitted to the bar of Illinois in 1900. Mr. McKinlay was promoted steadily in the retail organization of Marshall Field & Company until he became manager of retail offices. Early in 1911 he was transferred to the wholesale offices of the company. In January, 1916, he was elected treasurer; in November, 1917, he was elected second vice-president; first vice-president in January, 1923; and president, February 14, 1930. Mr. McKinlay and Mr. Simpson, former president and chairman of the board of directors, were born within fifty miles of one another in Scotland but did not know one another until they both were employed by Marshall Field & Company.

Mr. McKinlay is a director of the Harris Trust and Savings Bank, N. W. Harris and Company, and the First State Pawners Society of Chicago. He is also the director of the Washington and James Smith Home. He is a member of the Chicago, Union League, Mid-Day, Commercial, Beverly Country, and South Shore Country clubs.

In November of 1900 Mr. McKinlay married Helen Eddington of Jackson, Michigan. They have two children, John and Dorothy (Mrs. John A. Middleton).

CHICAGO AND ITS PLACE IN LITERATURE
Authors Who Have Added to the Prestige of the City

BY JOHN DRURY
Editor of "The Literary Tatler" in the Chicago Daily News

MENTION of Chicago as a literary center recalls to the average mind Eugene Field, Finley Peter Dunne, George Ade, and perhaps Opie Read. Rex Beach, it will be remembered, began his literary career while he was a law student in Chicago. Such later writers as Carl Sandburg and Sherwood Anderson will be added to the list by way of afterthought. Even the native Chicagoan, who prides himself in the achievements of his city, has only an inadequate idea of the importance of Chicago in American literature.

It is an amazing fact that Chicago has produced more writers, especially those who have molded the new indigenous American literature of today, than any other city in the country.

These writers are not merely popular novelists, of which Chicago has its share, but are creators of genuine significance. Their influence is felt throughout the nation.

True, not all of them have drawn on the Chicago scene for inspiration, but the prairie metropolis has been their common meeting ground, providing them with the stimulation which comes from contact with others as brilliant as themselves.

Writers who have interpreted Chicago life alone have contributed almost half a hundred books, mostly novels, which express the struggles and conflicts, the sordid materialism, the melodramatic climaxes, or it may be the lyrical dreams, of this still youthful, energetic city. The majority of these books are of more or less permanent value to our native literature. Not a few have helped establish what has come to be known as the new American language as distinguished from the Queen's English. In short, portraying life in what H. L. Mencken said was "the most thoroughly American of American cities," these works may indeed be taken as cross-sections of life in the United States.

Chicago's position as a producer of significant literature came prominently before the public in 1920 when Mencken wrote an essay on the town in which he called it "the literary capital of America." He told about the vital writers of the city's first Golden Age of letters, which occurred in the '90's—Theodore Dreiser, Henry B. Fuller, George Ade and Frank Norris. All four wrote about Chicago as they saw it—Dreiser in "Sister Carrie"; Fuller in "The Cliff Dwellers"; Ade in "Fables In Slang"; and Norris in "The Pit." There were other important writers of this period who also wrote about the city—Hamlin Garland in "Rose of Dutcher's Coolly"; Finley Peter Dunne in "Mr. Dooley"; Robert Herrick in "The Common Lot"; Upton Sinclair in "The Jungle"; and Frank Harris in "The Bomb." Opie Read in "The Jucklins" pictured mid-western life.

(*Blank and Stoller, Inc., Photo*)

JAMES O. McKINSEY

Mr. McKinsey, senior partner of James O. McKinsey and Company, accountants and engineers, was born in Gamma, Missouri, June 4, 1889, son of James Madison and Mary Elizabeth (Logan) McKinney. He graduated from the State Teachers College in Warrensburg, Missouri, in 1912; received his LL.B. (Bachelor of Laws) degree from the University of Arkansas in 1913, and his Ph.B. (Bachelor of Philosophy) degree in 1916, and his A.M. (Master of Arts) degree in 1919 at the University of Chicago. From 1912 to 1916 he was a high school teacher in St. Louis, Missouri, and since 1917 has been a member of the faculty of the University of Chicago, being professor of business administration since 1926. He lectured on accounting at Columbia University from 1920 to 1921. In 1919 he became a certified public accountant in Illinois, and from that year has been engaged in professional work. Since 1925 he has been senior partner of James O. McKinsey and Company. This company which maintains offices in Chicago and New York, specializes in financial and management surveys. Mr. McKinsey spends much of his time in serving in an advisory capacity to presidents of organizations.

Mr. McKinsey is a director of Phoenix Hosiery Company, United States Radio and Television Corporation, Selected Shares Corporation, and other well-known corporations. He served as private, later as lieutenant, in the Ordnance Department, United States Army, from 1917 to 1919. He is a member of the American Institute of Accountants, American Management Association, National Association of Cost Accountants, Illinois Society of Certified Public Accountants, and Delta Sigma Pi, Phi Kappa Sigma, and Delta Theta Phi fraternities. His clubs are Attic, Union League, Quadrangle, South Shore Country, and Olympia Fields Country in Chicago, and The Rookery in New York. He is author of the following: Bookkeeping and Accounting, 1920; Budgetary Control, 1922; Managerial Accounting, 1924; Business Administration, 1925; and Accounting Principles, 1929; also several pamphlets published by American Management Association and other organizations.

On June 12, 1920, Mr. McKinsey married Alice Louise Anderson of Sioux City, Iowa, and they have two children, Robert and Richard, who are twins.

The city's second Golden Age began in 1912 and ended, if end it did, when the United States entered the World War in 1917. It produced a very influential crop of writers—Sherwood Anderson, Carl Sandburg, Edgar Lee Masters, Ben Hecht, Maxwell Bodenheim, Vachel Lindsay, Floyd Dell, Ring Lardner, Francis Hackett and Lew Sarett. It also produced two magazines which have left their impress on American literature— Harriet Monroe's **Poetry** and Margaret Anderson's **The Little Review.** The combination of two such productive periods in the city's history caused Mencken to write:

> **"In Chicago there is the mysterious something that makes for individuality, personality, charm; in Chicago a spirit broods upon the face of the waters. Find a writer who is indubitably an American in every pulse-beat, an American who has something new and peculiarly American to say and who says it in an unmistakably American way, and nine times out of ten you will find that he has some sort of connection with the gargantuan abattoir by Lake Michigan—that he was bred there, or got his start there or passed through there in the days when he was young and tender."**

In 1926, however, Mencken changed his mind. He looked out of his Baltimore study and saw no new significant figures rising on the Chicago horizon. Samuel Putnam, a local literary critic who had a leaning for all the latest European "isms," agreed with him. The result was an article in *The American Mercury* called "Chicago: An Obituary," by Samuel Putnam. Mr. Putnam, after reviewing its past achievements, pronounced the town dead; said it was "esthetically and creatively, a cactus desert." He then flew to his beloved Paris.

But the town continued to turn out writers of first-rate caliber. Ernest Hemingway was a Chicago product and some of his short stories, particularly "The Killers," reflect the city's life. John Dos Passos was born here and his novel, "Eveline Hutchins," published in **Pagany** magazine, is a Windy City story. Edna Ferber, a former Chicagoan, used local material in her novel, "So Big." Elizabeth Madox Roberts, Janet Lewis, Glenway Wescott, Yvor Winters, and Marjorie Latimer, all now doing significant novels and short stories, were stimulated by contact with each other in Chicago. Younger writers came along and pictured the city around them— Meyer Levin in "Frankie and Johnnie"; James T. Farrell in "Young Lonigan"; McKinley Kantor in "Diversey"; Lester Cohen in "The Great Bear"; Robert D. Andrews in "Windfall"; Ruth Russell in "Lake Front"; and John Gunther in "The Red Pavilion."

As for poetry, Chicago has been the nation's Parnassus for many years. Miss Monroe's **Poetry** magazine, as much as the influence of Whitman, was responsible for a poetry revival in 1914 which extended throughout the Anglo-American world. The work of outstanding figures in this revival is represented in "The New Poetry," an anthology compiled by Miss Monroe and Alice Corbin Henderson, and it includes such poets of Chicago as Carl

(Moffett-Russell Photo)

HUGH McLENNAN

Mr. McLennan, president of McLennan Construction Company, was born in Chicago, and is the son of John A. and Olive A. (Cowan) McLennan. He obtained his education at the Chicago Manual Training School and the Armour Institute of Technology. He received his LL.B (Bachelor of Laws) degree at Lake Forest University in 1899 and has been in the building construction business in Chicago since 1905. He is president of the McLennan Construction Company, Lake Shore Drive Hotel Company, Chicago Produce District Trust, 227 and 237 East Delaware Place Building Corporation, and vice-president of the 219 Lake Shore Drive Building Corporation.

McLennan Construction Company has built some of Chicago's noted buildings, including the Trustees System Building, South Water Market, A Century of Progress, Chicago's (1933) World's Fair General Exhibits Building, the Allerton Club, and many others. Mr. McLennan is a member of Phi Kappa Sigma Fraternity, and his clubs are Chicago Athletic Association, Builders, Bob o' Link Golf.

On May 28, 1921, he married Mrs. Durant Howard of Chicago, who had one son by a previous marriage, Durant Howard.

Sandburg, Edgar Lee Masters, Maxwell Bodenheim, Mary Aldis, Alice Corbin, Florence Kiper Frank, Hamlin Garland, Harriet Monroe, Helen Hoyt, Agnes Lee, Vachel Lindsay, Frances Shaw, Eunice Tietjens, and Edith Wyatt. A few years back Charles G. Blanden brought out his "Chicago Anthology," but the work represented was of no great moment.

Just how much the city itself inspired local versifiers was revealed recently when a leading poet of the city, Mark Turbyfill, printed a symposium of sixteen Chicago poets in **The Chicagoan.** Replying to a questionnaire, the majority said they were stimulated, either emotionally or intellectually, by the Chicago scene, although unable to determine whether the town caused them to write "in a manner essentially characteristic of it." Among those who replied were Sandburg, Miss Monroe, Jessica North, Mrs. Tietjens, Sterling North, Jean Toomer, George Dillon, Samuel Putnam, and Pearl Andelson. All critics agree, however, that Sandburg, especially in his "Chicago Poems," remains the true poetic voice of the city. But the town has many other poets of merit—Mitchell Dawson, Lew Sarett, Glenn Ward Dresbach, Polly Chase Boyden, Rev. Irwin St. John Tucker, Bertha Ten Eyck James, Marion Strobel, Dorothy Aldis, Douglas Malloch, and Vincent Starrett. In the past there have been Sherwood Anderson, Keith Preston, Mildred Plew Merryman, Louise Ayers Garnett, Julia Cooley Altrocchi, Wilbur D. Nesbit, Emanuel Carnevali, John V. A. Weaver, William Vaughn Moody, Eugene Field, Ben King, John Vance Cheney, Bert Leston Taylor, Franklin P. Adams, and Horace Spencer Fiske.

Further evidence of Chicago's continued position as a literary center is seen in the fact that **The Midland** magazine is published here. It is rated by Mencken and Edward J. O'Brien, of "Best Short Stories" fame, as one of the few outstanding literary magazines of America. Each month its editor, John T. Frederick, brings forth some new and talented young writer, either from Chicago or other parts of the mid-west. There is also **The Chicagoan,** a sort of local **Vanity Fair,** which has a number of worthwhile contributors.

Chicago has turned out writers who have paved the way toward what there is of an American language. Ade began it in 1902 with his Chicago books, "In Babel" and "Fables In Slang." Ring Lardner, a local reporter, followed suit with his "You Know Me, Al," as did John V. A. Weaver, with his "In American." The Big Shots of the city's second Golden Age—Sandburg, Masters, Anderson, Hecht—all made use of the American language, and so did J. P. McEvoy in "The Potters" and Farrell in "Young Lonigan." And there were the dialect writers—Dunne, making use of the Irish-American, and Frank Pixley and Kurt M. Stein, both using the German-American idiom. Today, the University of Chicago has officially taken cognizance of the American language, having brought over Sir William Craigie, the maker of the Oxford dictionary, to compile the first dictionary of our native tongue. The University has already put out an American translation of the Bible.

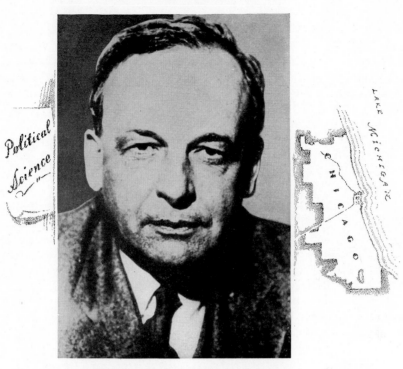

CHARLES E. MERRIAM

Professor Merriam, chairman of Chicago University's department of political science, was born in Hopkinton, Iowa, November 15, 1874, son of Charles Edward and Margaret Campbell (Kirkwood) Merriam. He received his A. B. (Bachelor of Arts) degree at Lenox College, in 1893, also from the State University of Iowa, in 1895; his A. M. (Master of Arts) from Columbia, in 1897. During 1899-1900 he studied in Berlin and Paris; received his Ph. D. (Doctor of Philosophy) from Columbia, in 1900. Professor Merriam occupies a unique position among scholars of government. He is probably the foremost advocate of the use of the scientific method in the study of political problems. He served as a Chicago alderman for six years (1909-1911 and 1913-1917, from the seventh ward), also serving as chairman of the Commission on City Expenditures; and in 1911 was the Republican nominee for Mayor of Chicago. His connection with the University of Chicago began in 1900, after he had won the Ph. D. degree at Columbia. Since then he has played a major role in organizing the University's work in the field of government upon a research basis. He served as president of the National Research Council from 1924 to 1927, and was made president of the American Political Science Association in 1924. At present (1932) he is serving as one of the five members of President Hoover's commission for the study of social trends in the United States.

Notable among the eight books published by Dr. Merriam is "the American Party System." Among the publications which he has edited is a series of eight recent volumes on the training of citizens in various modern nations. Within the past three years six semi-public groups, including the Association of City Managers, the Civil Service Assembly and the National Municipal League, have moved their headquarters to the vicinity of the University campus, where they cooperate with Professor Merriam's department. Mr. Merriam was one of the first men in academic circles to recognize the growing importance of police science and to incorporate police work into the curriculum. He has maintained considerable influence in local politics and consistently supported honest candidates and policies. He has argued especially for the unification of the Chicago metropolitan area, the centralization of planning and responsibility, and local home rule. He is a member of the Social Science Research Council (president 1924-1927) and of the American Political Science Association (president 1924-1925).

Professor Merriam married Hilda Doyle, of Constableville, New York, August 3, 1901. Their children are Charles James, John Francis, Elizabeth, and Robert Edward.

An interesting development among local writers since Putnam's "obituary" has been the growing enthusiasm for Americana, both contemporary and historical. Outstanding in this field has been Sandburg, the poet, with his monumental biography of Lincoln; his book of songs, "The American Songbag"; and his fanciful "Rootabaga Stories." Second in interest has been Lloyd Lewis' "Myths After Lincoln," and, more recently, his "Sherman: Fighting Prophet." Prof. William E. Dodd's "Lincoln or Lee" also deals with the Civil War period. Other writers in the Americana field have been Estelline Bennett, with "Old Deadwood Days"; Walter Noble Burns with "The Saga of Billy the Kid"; Franklin Meine with "Tall Tales of the Southwest"; Earl H. Reed with "Duneland Sketches"; Prof. Charles E. Merriam with "Chicago"; Harry Beardsley with "Joseph Smith: Founder of Mormonism"; and Harlan Ware and James Prindle with their "Rag Opera." Sarett, the poet and woodsman, and Mrs. Flora Warren Seymour, founder of the Bookfellows, write about the American Indian. American art is dealt with by C. J. Bulliet in his "Apples and Madonnas" and by J. Z. Jacobson in his "Thirty-five Saints and Emil Armin."

The city's newspaper life has of late been a fruitful source of inspiration to many local writers. It all seemed to begin with Hecht's "1001 Afternoons in Chicago," a volume of short stories gleaned by a wandering reporter. Other books on the same theme followed in rapid succession—Henry Justin Smith's "Deadlines"; Meyer Levin's "Reporter"; Hecht's "Erik Dorn"; and the Chicago newspaper dramas, Hecht and MacArthur's "The Front Page"; Maurine Watkins' "Chicago"; and Bart Cormack's "The Racket." Somewhat earlier than any of these books, however, is "The Briary Bush," by Floyd Dell, which detailed the career of a young reporter in the town.

Other meritorious novels which portray Chicago life include Margaret Ayer Barnes' "Years of Grace" (which won a Pulitzer prize); Janet Fairbank's "The Smiths"; Marion Strobel's "Saturday Afternoon"; Mary Synon's "The Good Red Bricks"; Woodward Boyd's "The Love Legend"; Clifford Raymond's "Our Very Best People"; Newton Fuessle's "The Flail"; Henry Kitchell Webster's "An American Family"; Howard Vincent O'Brien's "New Men for Old"; Edwin H. Lewis' "Those About Trench"; Donald Richberg's "A Man of Purpose"; Willa Cather's "The Song of the Lark"; Susan Glaspell's "The Glory of the Conquered"; Robert Morss Lovett's "A Winged Victory"; Clarence Darrow's "An Eye for An Eye"; and Isaac K. Friedman's "Poor People."

(*Blank & Stoller, Inc. Photo*)

JOHN S. MILLER

Mr. Miller, lawyer and member of the firm of Taylor, Miller, Busch and Boyden, was born in Chicago, November 8, 1888, son of John Stocker and Ann (Gross) Miller. His father was a pioneer lawyer of Chicago. He graduated from the Harvard School here, obtained his B.A. (Bachelor of Arts) degree at Harvard College in 1911 and his LL.B. (Bachelor of Laws) degree in 1914. He was admitted to the bar in 1914 and started the practice of law. He became a member of the firm of Miller, Starr, Brown, Packard & Peckham in 1915, and in 1917 formed, with Orville J. Taylor, the firm of Taylor & Miller, which has evolved into the present firm of Taylor, Miller, Busch and Boyden. Mr. Miller attended the first Citizens' Military Training Camp at Plattsburg, New York, in 1915 and went to the Mexican border with the First Illinois Field Artillery in 1916. When the United States entered the World War, he was commissioned a second lieutenant, then a major, assigned to the Eighty-Sixth Division, 161st Artillery Brigade, 333rd Field Artillery, and served throughout the war, receiving his honorable discharge in January, 1919.

Mr. Miller is president, treasurer, and director of Site of the Fort Dearborn Building Corporation; director and general counsel of Personal Loan & Savings Bank; and a member of the American, Illinois State, and Chicago Bar Associations and the Association of the Bar of the City of New York. His clubs are the Law, Legal, Wayfarers, Chicago, Attic, Cliff Dwellers, and Commercial.

On June 29, 1911, he married Judith Drew Barker of Boston, Massachusetts; children, Judith D., Portia A., and John S. April 9, 1932, he married Catherine Beacom of Pierre, South Dakota.

(Chicago Architectural Photographing Company)
The Colonnade which stretches full length of the 20 North Wacker Drive Building, giving
an old-world appearance to this busy Chicago street.
Graham, Anderson, Probst & White, architects.

HARRIET MONROE

Miss Monroe, poet, founder, and for twenty years editor, of "Poetry: a Magazine of Verse," was born in Chicago, the daughter of Henry S. and Martha (Mitchell) Monroe. She was graduated from the Visitation Academy, Georgetown, D. C., and received her Doctor of Letters degree from Baylor University, Waco, Texas. As a young poet, in 1891, Miss Monroe was selected to compose the dedicatory ode for the World's Columbian Exposition, and on October 21, 1892, the 400th anniversary of the discovery of America, she read her "Columbian Ode" before a vast assembly, and was crowned with laurel. In 1912 she established "Poetry," a magazine which was endowed by a large group of art patrons.

From the very start, the magazine became the forum of contemporary poets, publishing the first and early works of poets now world famous. It was in this magazine that Carl Sandburg's "Chicago Poems" first appeared, and Joyce Kilmer's "Trees," and Vachel Lindsay's "General William Booth Enters Into Heaven." As the "fairy godmother" of the younger poets, Miss Monroe encouraged such writers as James Joyce, Sherwood Anderson, Lew Sarett, T. S. Eliot, and Ernest Hemingway, to mention only a few of her protégés. Among the foreign writers who have contributed to her publication were Rabindranath Tagore, John Drinkwater, Rupert Brooke, and Padriac Colum. "Poetry," which goes out monthly to subscribers not only in America, but in England, France, Italy, Turkey, China, South Africa, Australia, Haiti, Brazil, and the Philippines, is largely responsible for the modern school of verse and for the free verse movement.

Miss Monroe is the author of several collections of verse, including Valeria and Other Poems, 1892; The Passing Show, modern plays in verse, 1903; You and I, 1914; and The Difference and Other Poems, 1924. Her twentieth century anthology, "The New Poetry," is generally considered the best modern collection. It was published in 1917 and revised in 1923 and 1932.

HOW NATURAL GAS WAS BROUGHT TO CHICAGO
The Story of a One Thousand-Mile Pipeline and a Unique Engineering Project

A T 4 o'clock on the afternoon of October 16, 1931, two men standing at the outskirts of the city, eyes on the watches they held, dropped their arms. Two crews of men under them began spinning the control wheels of two giant valves—and natural gas from Texas rushed into Chicago's 3,738-mile system of gas distribution mains.

That evening, housewives noticed that the gas flame under the family dinner was a deep, rich blue in color. Many of them paid no attention to it, but most of them knew that natural gas from great deposits thousands of feet beneath the Texas Panhandle, a thousand miles away from Chicago, was helping to cook the evening meal.

Thus ended the story of the construction of the world's largest and longest natural gas pipeline, an engineering feat unique in the annals of private industry. Projects of the United States Government have been larger in size—the Panama Canal, costing over $400,000,000, was several times larger than the pipeline, with its cost of $75,000,000—but no undertaking has better exemplified the courage and vision of private interests.

Perhaps we should say that the story of the pipeline began when the Chicago housewife used it to boil a pot of potatoes. For a generation or more in the future the story of this project will go on unfolding itself—

Nearing the end of the trail. Behind this pipe-laying crew is nearly a thousand miles of steel pipe, linking the gas fields of Texas with the great metropolitan center of greater Chicago. The line blazed a new trail, straight across farm lands, through miles of swamps and under a hundred-odd rivers, in its drive from Texas to Chicago.

(Moffett-Russell Photo)

GEORGE F. MITCHELL

Mr. Mitchell, president of The People's Gas Light and Coke Company, was born in Chicago, March 20, 1888. He graduated from the George Dewey Grammar School in 1902, and, at the age of fourteen years, started working for the American Steel Foundries. To continue his education he later entered the Armour Scientific Academy, subsequently taking a course in business and stenography, maintaining himself meanwhile by evening employment. In 1909 he obtained a situation as stenographer with the Commonwealth Edison Company, rose from that position to become assistant to the president's secretary, and a little later became secretary to the president. During the World War he served as Assistant Secretary of the State Council of Defense of Illinois.

In January, 1919, Mr. Mitchell joined The People's Gas Light and Coke Company, a corporation that has given continuous gas service in Chicago for the last eighty-three years, and which is one of the largest singly operated gas companies in the world. In March, 1919, he was appointed assistant to the president of that company; in June, 1921, was made treasurer; and, in May, 1924, was elected vice-president in charge of finance. He was elected a member of the board of directors in December, 1927, and was made president in February, 1930. He belongs to the Chicago, Attic, Union League, South Shore Country, and Olympia Fields Country clubs. His hobbies are golf, bridge, and hard work.

the story of a cleaner city, of a busier city, with new industries attracted by the prospect of an economical and easily usable clean fuel, of a happier city, with many household burdens taken from the shoulders of its men and women.

Whatever benefits the pipeline is now bringing to Chicago, and whatever may be the future advantages it will offer to our citizens and their children, are matters for history to record. We are interested now in the story of how this 1,000-mile pipeline was planned and completed.

The greatest gas field in the world had been discovered in Texas. Searching for oil, prospectors had drilled nearly a mile into the earth beneath the Texas Panhandle, and they had uncovered, not oil, but gas—immense domes of it, larger than any before encountered, and at unusually great rock pressure, indicating an enormous reserve.

In the proper place, these gas reserves could be of great benefit to humanity. Industries and homes could use them to solve their fuel and heating problems.

A thousand miles away, in Chicago, was the greatest fuel market in the Middle West. But between Texas and Chicago were many rivers, including the Missouri and the Mississippi, ranges of hills, miles of swampy lowlands, other miles of rocky ground—obstacle after obstacle in the path of the pipeline.

The present market for fuel in Chicago would not justify the cost of the pipeline. A market would have to be developed by aggressive sales effort, to take care of the supply of gas after it was brought from Texas.

All of these factors were carefully considered. And early in 1930, the first shovelful of earth was dug from the hard surface of the Texas Panhandle. Before the pipeline reached Chicago, 75,000,000 cubic feet of earth had been dug out—and replaced.

Survey after survey had been made of the country between the gas fields and the goal of the pipeline. Soil conditions, drainage conditions, the courses of rivers and streams, had been determined from geological survey books.

Agents for the company had interviewed every owner of property along the right of way, negotiating over 12,000 leases to clear the way for the pipeline.

Statisticians and financiers had worked for months, considering every possible phase of the project, collecting data in support of convictions and other data which showed that certain accepted beliefs were not supported by fact, writing the complete story of the project—financial, engineering, legal, and other aspects of it—for the information of the interests who would advance the money for the pipeline's construction. All of this before the first shovelful of earth was removed.

Once started, the work went ahead with great speed on several fronts. Ditch-digging machines covered several miles in a single working day . Ten thousand freight cars brought 209,000 tons of steel pipe from mills in the

Sinews of service. Constant labor in maintaining and improving the
company's facilities for distributon of gas keeps the service to Chicago
users as nearly perfect as possible.

Middle West to the scene of operations. Crews of welders joined the
lengths of pipe together, making a total of 80,000 welds. Other crews
coupled the pipe together with flexible couplings, to provide for expansion
and contraction under different temperature conditions.

Barges were floated across the Mississippi river, carrying pipe-laying
crews who lowered the pipe to the river bed, after dredges had made a
place for it in the shifting sands.

Other crews worked waist-deep in mud and water, digging by hand a
ditch for the pipe through the treacherous swamp-lands along the river
bottoms. Other crews of men used dynamite to clear obstructions.

Month after month the work went on, pushed to completion in the
midst of widespread industrial stagnation, when fears for the future were
rampant, when private capital generally was being withdrawn from circulation.

Seventy-five million dollars went to the owners of the gas-producing
land—a half-million acres of it—to the owners of property crossed by the
pipeline, to the steel mills that fabricated the pipe, to the manufacturers of

pipe-laying equipment, and to the thousands of men who worked on the project.

After the pipe had been laid, ten compressor stations, located every 100 miles along the line, were installed to keep the gas moving on its trip to Chicago. The total horsepower of these stations—100,000—is a figure hard for us to conceive.

Finally, after nearly 18 months of record-breaking labor, after a scar 1,000 miles long had been made on the face of the earth, two men stood at the outskirts of Chicago and gave the signal which completed the final step in the long journey.

And the pipeline began doing what it was built to do. The gas fields of Texas had been brought within the city limits of Chicago.

PEOPLES GAS BUILDING

(Moffett-Russell Photo)

BERNARD J. MULLANEY

Mr. Mullaney, vice-president of The Peoples Gas Light and Coke Company in charge of public and industrial relations, was born on a farm near Woodhull, New York, son of John and Catherine (Leonard) Mullaney. He was educated in the country district and village schools of Steuben County, New York. His early life was spent on a farm, in a grocery store, and as a school teacher. Later he worked on newspapers in St. Paul, Minneapolis, and Chicago as a reporter, copy reader, city editor, traveling correspondent, and political editor. After fifteen years in such work he took advertising positions with such Chicago firms as Schlesinger and Mayer, H. G. Selfridge & Company, Carson, Pirie and Scott, and Armour and Company. Later he served for four years in public office as secretary to the mayor and as Commissioner of Public Works of the City of Chicago. During the World War he served the State Council of Defense of Illinois as director of publicity.

Mr. Mullaney is active in the work of the American Gas Association: member of its board of directors since 1924; vice-president, 1927-1929; president, 1929-1930. In the Chicago Association of Commerce he is chairman of the general publicity committee and member of the executive committee and the senior council. He is an active member of the Chicago Historical Society, Geographical Society of Chicago, and Art Institute of Chicago (life member). His clubs are Chicago Athletic, The Tavern, Edgewater Golf, and Economics, of Chicago.

On December 11, 1895, Mr. Mullaney married Jane King of Chicago (died April 9, 1927). On September 5, 1932, he was married, in France, to Mrs. Georgia Blackman Pratt of Paris.

AN OUTDOOR LABORATORY FOR THE STUDY OF TREES, SHRUBS AND VINES

The Morton Arboretum and Its Unique Work

O N the Joliet road, one mile north of Lisle, Du Page county, Illinois, on a fork of the Du Page river, is located a 400-acre paradise of trees and birds and flowers. It is known to every nature lover in Chicago, and can be reached by a 25-mile drive from the city, west on Roosevelt road, or southwest on Ogden avenue, to Joliet road. Train service is provided by the Burlington from the Union station to the little town of Lisle, the second station west of Downers Grove.

The Morton Arboretum, established in 1921 through the public-spirited and far-sighted efforts of Joy Morton, is visited by thousands of tourists annually, especially in the spring, when the arboretum is an epiphany of blossoms. Every season of the year, however, in this leafy Arcadia, has its individual charm, and every passing mood of nature is revealed from the first green shimmer of the willows to the blazing banners of October, and the exquisite winter landscapes in their delicate pastel shades.

Many visitors express surprise on learning that the arboretum is neither a nursery nor a private park. The nature and purposes of the establishment are unique. It is a vast outdoor laboratory or museum for the study of such woody plants as are capable of surviving the northern climate, and is de-

Early one spring a pair of wild Canadian Geese made their appearance in the Arboretum and fortunately decided to remain.

MORTON
BUILDING

(Moffett-Russell Photo)

JOY MORTON

Mr. Morton, chairman of the board of Morton Salt Company and founder of the Morton Arboretum at Lisle, Illinois, was born in Detroit, Michigan, September 27, 1855, son of J. Sterling and Caroline (Joy) Morton. His father, J. Sterling Morton, was for many years a national figure and was a descendant of Richard Morton who is of record at Plymouth, Massachusetts, as early as 1625. J. Sterling Morton was a Nebraska pioneer and served as territorial governor. He was appointed by President Cleveland to serve as Secretary of Agriculture in 1893. His home was in Nebraska City and he gave it the name of "Arbor Lodge." Governor Morton died in 1902. In 1923 Joy Morton donated the old homestead to the State of Nebraska and it is now a state park commemorating his father who instituted "Arbor Day." J. Sterling Morton married Caroline Joy, of Detroit, a descendant of Thomas Joy, who built the first town house in Boston in 1650.

Joy Morton spent his boyhood at Nebraska City, Nebraska, and attended Talbot Hall there. He moved to Chicago in 1879 and since 1885 has been senior member of Joy Morton and Company and is also chairman of the board of Morton Salt Company, which is the largest organization in America manufacturing and distributing salt and has numerous sales offices and plants in Illinois, Michigan, Kansas, Utah, California, Texas and many other States. Mr. Morton is president of Standard Office Building Corporation, Morton Building Corporation, and Louisiana Furs, Inc., and is interested in many other organizations. He is a director of the Alton Railroad Company and of the Equitable Life Assurance Society of the United States (New York). He founded the Morton Arboretum at Lisle, Illinois, a unique experimental laboratory for the cultivation and propogation of trees, shrubs, vines and grasses. He is a member of the Chicago Historical Society, Art Institute of Chicago, Field Museum of Natural History, Chicago Zoölogical Society, Chicago Plan Commission, and American Forestry Association, Washington, D. C. His clubs are Commercial, Chicago, and Caxton, of Chicago, and Lawyers' of New York.

September 23, 1880, he married Carrie Lake (died 1915), daughter of Judge George B. Lake of Omaha. He married Margaret Gray, of Chicago, January 16, 1917. There are two children of his first marriage, Jean (Mrs. Joseph M. Cudahy); and Sterling, who married Preston Owsley, November 2, 1910, and has a daughter, Suzette Preston, now a junior at Vassar College.

signed to increase the knowledge of trees and shrubs and bring about an improvement in their growth and culture. To test the hardy timber trees of the world which might be used for reforestation purposes is another major aim. Here, trees from all parts of the temperate zone are assembled and tested for their hardiness and their economic and ornamental value.

The specimens not only are classified botanically, but grouped in land-scape paintings and arranged geographically, according to their native habitat.

For sheer beauty, the Morton Arboretum has few equals even among the most pretentious private estates of the country. Winding paths, car-peted in the Spring with fallen blossoms, or in the Fall with pine needles and fallen leaves, entice the visitor from the main driveways. They tunnel through thick foliage or skirt still waters, whose glassy surfaces, ruffled only by the wings of birds, reflect the overhanging willows. Such byways as Joy path, Willow path, or Spruce Hill path, lead to enchanting vistas, often with a sparkling bit of lake or river in the distance.

Looking eastward across Lake Marmo, a body of water frequented by birds of many kinds.

Lake Marmo is fed by the waters of this lux-uriantly bordered brook.

As the pageant of nature is unfolded, each season brings its own delights. Lovely indeed is hawthorn time, with its massed blossoms. In May, the wild plum trees, the wild crabs, and the Japanese cherry trees are clothed in bridal veils of pink and white. Lilac time is a miracle of mauves and lavenders, and October transforms the arboretum into a field of the cloth of gold. And in winter, with purple shadows cast upon the snow, and the tracery of branch and twig outlined against a chartreuse sky, a subtle spell broods over the preserve. At all times of the year it is a sanctuary of wild life, and throughout the summer, its arcades resound with the madrigals of birds.

To the forestry student, the park superintendent, the landscape architect, or the owner of a small estate, the arboretum is of inestimable service, furnishing as it does, occasional bulletins based on current research. In these bulletins, failures as well as successes in the cultivation of exported trees and shrubs are chronicled, and suggestions are made for the introduction of new and little-known varieties. Lists of shrubs for seasonal planting are sent out, together with notes as to the kind of soil and the climatic conditions most favorable for the propagation of certain recommended species. Thus, one bulletin describes the "red bud" or "the tree with the beautiful rose-pink blossoms," known also as the Judas tree, due to its resemblance to an eastern red bud which tradition has branded as the tree to which Judas Iscariot hanged himself.

To see the Arboretum in Hawthorn time is to see it in one of its most pleasing moods. These large thorn trees bordering Joy Path are particularly handsome specimens.

Another bulletin will deal with the Japanese cherry trees, such as the Haigan sakura, or Spring cherry; the Fuji cherry from the region around Mt. Fujiyama; or the Yoshino cherry, grown successfully in Potomac Park, Washington, D. C., and in the Morton Arboretum, but supposed to be unreliable north of New York City.

Many plants whose hardiness has been considered doubtful have been introduced north of the 40th latitude as a result of the experiments made in this outdoor laboratory. Conspicuous among these are the trees and shrubs of the Balkan group, including the Austrian pine, the Omorika spruce, the Balkan maple, the Russian olive, and the European beech. Various native species of pine and spruce have been thoroughly tested with reforestation in view.

Roadside planting—the improvement of the American landscape by bordering the paved highways with trees—is another enterprise sponsored by the arboretum. A special study has been made of the horse chestnut, an excellent tree for street planting or for parks, or where dense shade is required.

Other varieties, such as the fringe tree or "old man's beard" and the silver bell or "snow drop tree," introduced from the south, have made themselves at home in the Chicago area.

Of lilacs, the arboretum has many rare and beautiful varieties, including the pinkish mauve Mme. Antoine Buchner, the Lucie Baltet, the Adelaide Dunbar, the Edmund Baissier, the President Lincoln, the Princess Clementine, and others.

Set amid flowering shrubs and vase-like elms, stands "Thornhill," the Morton residence, in an ample wing of which is housed the arboretum library.

Mr. Morton comes by his love of trees naturally. In 1854, his father, J. Sterling Morton, came from Detroit to Nebraska, bringing his young bride, Caroline Joy Morton. They selected as a site for their new home one of the highest points of land near Nebraska City. Both were nature lovers, and it was not long before flowers, shrubs, and vines adorned their estate. Orchard trees as well as shade trees and evergreens were set out, and Arbor Lodge, as they named their home, became a beauty spot. The elder Morton's interest in trees began to gain wide recognition as early as 1872, when as president of the State Board of Agriculture, he persuaded Gov. Furnas to issue the first Arbor Day proclamation. Later, in 1885, the state legislature made Arbor Day a legal holiday in Nebraska, and set aside April 22, Mr. Morton's birthday, as a day for tree planting. Since that time, the Arbor Day idea has spread to almost every State in the Union.

As a further token of his interest in nature, he deeded to Nebraska City in 1888 a 23-acre tract of natural timber to be used as a State park.

At the death of Mr. Morton in 1902, Arbor Lodge and its fine colonial mansion passed into the hands of his son, Joy Morton, who made it his summer home for many years. In 1923, however, he deeded the property to the State of Nebraska for use as a State park. The old family mansion is used as a historical museum.

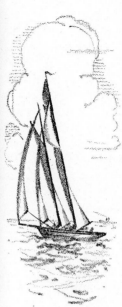

(*Underwood and Underwood Photo*)

STERLING MORTON

Mr. Morton was born in Chicago, Illinois, August 25, 1885, son of Joy and Carrie (Lake) Morton. He was educated in the Chicago Public Schools; Chateau de Lancy, Geneva, Switzerland; Princeton-Yale School, Chicago; Lawrenceville School, Lawrenceville, New Jersey; and Princeton University, from which he graduated in 1906, with the degree of Litt. B. (Bachelor of Letters). He was editor of the college literary magazine. Upon leaving college, he engaged in business with the Morton Salt Company of Chicago until 1917, being at that time in charge of manufacturing and sales of the Western Division, headquarters at Kansas City. He was elected president of Morkrum Company in 1917, which became Morkrum-Kleinschmidt Corporation in 1925 and Teletype Corporation in 1929. During his term as president, this company, which developed and manufactured printing telegraph apparatus, including such well-known devices as the Teletype and the high speed stock ticker, became one of the larger electrical manufacturing concerns of Chicago, employing 2,500 persons. In September, 1930, the Teletype Corporation became a part of the American Telephone & Telegraph Company (Bell System). Mr. Morton retired as president but remains as director.

He is president and director of International Inventions Corporation, vice-president and director of Morton Building Corporation, secretary and director of Morton Salt Company, director of Teletype Corporation, director of Elgin National Watch Company, and a member of the board of trustees of Armour Institute of Technology. He has served in various civic organizations and has been a director of the Illinois Manufacturers' Association since 1929. Being physically incapacitated for active service, he was a member of local and district draft boards and an officer in the First Regiment Illinois Reserve Militia during the World War. Mr. Morton is a member of the Chicago, Chicago Yatcht, Industrial, Saddle and Cycle, Harvard-Yale-Princeton, and Tavern clubs of Chicago; and, of the Princeton and New York Yacht clubs of New York. His principal recreations are horseback riding and sailing. He owns one of the largest schooners built in recent years on fresh water.

He married Preston Owsley, of Chicago, November 2, 1910. Their children are Suzette P., Carolyn (died 1921), and Millicent (died 1929).

HOW SCIENTIFIC CONTROL SAFEGUARDS THE LIVES OF CHICAGOANS

The Inspection and Testing Engineer and His Important Work

BY CHARLES B. NOLTE
President, Robert W. Hunt Co., Engineers

To the average layman the term "Scientific control" imparts only a vague meaning. Fortunately, the American Indian offers us an excellent illustration.

Forty miles from Hazleton, British Columbia, there is a unique suspension bridge, a span of about 140 feet, built by the Skeena River Indians over the Bulkley river. The cables are made of wire stolen from the Canadian Government Yukon Telegraph line. When the bridge was completed, the chief of the tribe was reluctant to risk his pack ponies, which were

worth $8 each. Squaws were plentiful, however. So he tested the bridge by sending a group of sixteen squaws across it.

Such a method of determining the safety of a bridge would seem barbarous to a more enlightened engineer, but it at least shows a realization on the part of the chief of the necessity for some assurance that the bridge would stand the strain; that life and property could be entrusted to it without unreasonable risk. He used the method which to him seemed best and most logical.

A unique suspension bridge about 140 foot span built by the Skeena River Indians over Bulkley River forty miles from Hazleton, British Columbia. The cables were made of wire stolen from the Canadian Government Yukon Telegraph Line. Before risking his pack ponies, which were worth eight dollars each, the Chief tested the bridge by sending sixteen Indian squaws across it.

Today, man builds more daring structures than the simple suspension bridge of the Skeena River Indians. He builds them not only with much greater efficiency, but also with the sure knowledge that they will bear the loads intended for them. No squaws are required to risk their lives to assure safety to the rest; the modern engineer employs other methods to protect his fellow men. To tell of these methods, and their place in the upbuilding of Chicago, is the purpose of this brief account.

We have heard, many times, of the wonders of science; how through it the practice of medicine grew from the chantings of a witch doctor to the almost certain curing or prevention of practically all human ills; how it enables us to survey the heavens, weigh the stars, and tell exactly of what each is composed; how it has devised ways to transmit the human voice

(Foto-Ad Photo)

HORACE EDGAR NEWCOMET

Mr. Newcomet, vice-president of the Pennsylvania Railroad, with headquarters in Chicago, started his railroad career here on February 18, 1896. Mr. Newcomet was born in Philadelphia, on April 27, 1874, son of Henry W. and Elizabeth K. (Stell) Newcomet. He attended the University of Pennsylvania and studied at the University of Chicago. Mr. Newcomet left Chicago in 1898, going to Cleveland. He steadily advanced in the operating department until September 16, 1926, when he returned to Chicago as general manager of the Pennsylvania. He was promoted to vice-president on June 16, 1929. His office is in the General Office of the Pennsylvania Railroad in the Chicago Union Station, from which he directs the activities of that company in the states of Illinois, Indiana, Michigan, Ohio, Kentucky, and Missouri.

The Pennsylvania is one of the few railroads which reaches the center of Chicago entirely over its own rails. It carries more passengers and handles more freight than any other railroad in the United States. In addition to his duties as vice-president of the Pennsylvania, Mr. Newcomet is an officer or a director of a number of other transportation companies. Mr. Newcomet is a member of the Union League Club, Chicago Club, Traffic Club and Electric Club of Chicago, the Union Club of Cleveland and the Queen City Club of Cincinnati.

He was married in 1899 to Louise Worthington, and is the father of three children, Walborn W., Edith Louise (Mrs. J. Beach Clow), and Marian Florence.

thousands of miles through space; how it has given us automobiles, engines, electric lights, and all the host of other conveniences which constitute our modern civilization.

But there is one service that science performs of which most have never heard or know very little. It is that part of science which, taking for its province all materials, gives to the engineer the assurance that his "building blocks" will not fail.

Some, having read this far, will wonder, "How can this interest me? I am not an engineer, and it is for them that this is written." But those who reason thus will be wrong. We all depend on modern materials for our safety. To realize this, consider steel and cement only, and enumerate the uses you make of structures and other objects made of these materials. The skyscrapers in which you work or shop, the railroad tracks, wheels, locomotives, upon which you rely as you travel to and from the city, and the concrete streets and boulevards providing safe paths for speeding cars, are but a few of the essentials used daily by the residents of a great city. Suppose, now, the materials of which these were made should fail; a rail could split—wrecking a train; a foundation crumple — causing a building to collapse. When materials are considered in this light they take on a greater importance even to those entirely unfamiliar with the science of engineering. Buried deep among the basic reasons for "Chicago's Accomplishments," but of vital concern to all, at least as far as her material structures are concerned, is this service

General view in chemical and metallurgical laboratory.

Tensile strength test of steel. 300,000-pound capacity Universal testing machine.

Preparing and crushing concrete control cylinders in an automatic 400,000-pound Watson-Stillman machine.

science renders in the upbuilding and safeguarding of the city.

The methods used to make sure materials are sound, and therefore safe to use, can easily be explained. We may sum them all up in three words—inspection, testing and analysis—all of which have been placed on a strictly

(Moffett-Russell Photo)

CHARLES B. NOLTE

Mr. Nolte, president and general manager of Robert W. Hunt Company, Consulting, Testing, and Inspecting Engineers, was born in Mattoon, Illinois, December 28, 1885, and is the son of Richard Beach and Anna Turner (Miller) Nolte. He graduated from the Mattoon, Illinois, High School in 1904, the Mattoon School of Commerce in 1905, and received his B. S. (Bachelor of Science) degree in Mechanical Engineering at the University of Illinois in 1909. That same year he entered the employ of Robert W. Hunt Company as a mechanical engineer; in 1912 he was made a division manager of this organization; in 1919 he was made manager and in 1923 became vice-president and general manager. In July, 1930, he was appointed president and general manager. The Robert W. Hunt Company is the largest analytical inspecting and testing engineering organization in the world, with offices and chemical, metallurgical, concrete and physical testing laboratories in Chicago, New York, Pittsburgh, St. Louis, Kansas City, Dallas, Birmingham, New Orleans, San Francisco, Los Angeles, Seattle, Portland, Montreal, Toronto, Vancouver, London, England, Brussels and Liege, Belgium, and Essen, Germany. Mr. Nolte is a member of the American Society of Civil Engineers, American Society of Mechanical Engineers, American Society for Testing Materials, American Railway Engineering Association, Western Society of Engineers, and Pacific Railway Club. He is also a member of the Union League Club, University Club of Chicago, Chicago Engineers' Club, and South Shore Country Club. Outside of his interest in scientific control which is explained more in detail in the article which Mr. Nolte furnished for this book, his principal interest is in his family, and his chief recreations are golf, hunting and fishing.

On November 8, 1911, he married Maude Alice Bacon, of Champaign, Illinois. Their children are Margaret Alice and Richard Bacon.

scientific basis. For reliable results, however, it is necessary that this inspection, testing and analysis be undertaken only by a specialist who makes this work a lifelong study. Such a specialist is the Inspection and Testing Engineer. Having the proper equipment, and armed with the technical knowledge of materials gained through experience and research, he daily cooperates with civil engineers, purchasing agents, and others who buy and use materials. The materials which come under his scientific control are too numerous to even list here, but because the basic methods of handling each are the same, we will discuss only those materials which are most widely used—cement, concrete and steel.

The lines of study science follows in developing the potentialities of materials, and of course this includes cement, take into account several considerations. The first of these is the uses for which the material is intended; secondly, defining those properties which specially fit it for these uses; thirdly, devising suitable tests to determine the extent to which these properties are present; and finally, applying such tests.

The principal use and purpose of cement is to make concrete. Those properties which cement must possess in order to make satisfactory concrete may be defined somewhat as follows: (1) it must act as a glue—binding the sand and stone into a solid mass, (2) it must stand weathering (alternate heat and cold, dryness and moisture), and (3) it must harden and remain hard. There are other qualities which may be desirable for cement, but for all practical purposes these three will suffice.

In order to measure these properties, scientists have developed specific tests for each. A sample of the cement to be used is taken and subjected to the following tests.

Perhaps the most important of all these tests is the tensile-strength test, for this measures the binding power of the cement. A small quantity of the sample is mixed with three times as much sand and a measured quantity of water. The whole mass is thoroughly mixed and then placed in molds where it hardens, within twenty-four hours, into miniature blocks of "experimental" concrete (sand, but no stone, being used). These blocks (usually six are made from one sample) are called briquettes, and are shaped somewhat like dumb-bells—the area of the smallest section (corresponding to the handle of the dumb-bell) being exactly one square inch. Now, the older cement becomes, the harder it gets. It is the general practice, therefore, to wait seven days to test half of the briquettes, and twenty-eight days to test the remaining half. The test itself consists of putting the briquettes, one by one, into a machine, equipped with a pair of jaws. These jaws grasp the two knob-like ends of the briquette and pull in opposite directions until it breaks—registering automatically in pounds the pull necessary to do this. In such a way is the "sticking capacity" of the cement determined.

The second test measures the soundness of the cement and, indirectly, its ability to withstand weathering. This is made by mixing a sample of cement with water and shaping it into what looks like a mud pie. These

(Fernand de Gueldre Photo)

JOHN NORTON

Mr. Norton, painter, was born in Lockport, Illinois, March 7, 1876, the son of John Lyman and Ada (Gooding) Norton. He attended Harvard, 1895 to 1897, and the Art Institute of Chicago, 1900 to 1902, from which he received the degree of Master of Fine Arts in 1927.

Mr. Norton has specialized in mural decorations. The principal buildings that he has decorated are the Sioux City (Iowa) Court House; Tavern Club, Daily News Building, Loyola University Library, Board of Trade Building, Chicago Motor Club (all Chicago); Beloit (Wisconsin) College Museum of Ethnology; Court House at Birmingham, Alabama; and many others. He is a representative at the Art Institute of Chicago. He was awarded a gold medal by the American Institute of Architects.

Mr. Norton served with the first United States Volunteer Cavalry of the Spanish-American War. He is a member of the Cliff Dwellers, Tavern (president), Wayfarers clubs (Chicago); and the Lake Zurich (Illinois) Golf Club.

On September 2, 1903, Mr. Norton married Margaret Francis. Their children are Margaret Francis (Mrs. Henry Garrett), John Francis, and Nancy.

"pies"—or pats, as they are called—are first put into a moist-air cabinet and left twenty-four hours. They are next put into a boiler and steamed—much like a plum pudding is cooked. After twenty-four hours of this steaming, the pats are removed and examined for cracks. Sound cement will not be affected by such treatment, whereas poor cement will.

The third and final significant test is to determine fineness. This is important because the speed with which the cement develops a high early strength is largely governed by the fineness to which its particles have been ground. This test is extraordinary in one respect and quite ordinary in another. It consists simply of placing a weighed quantity of cement (about a heaping tablespoonful) in a sieve and shaking until no more will pass

Cement laboratory—Tinius Olson Briquette Testing machines to which have been added the new type A. S. T. M. clips and disposal chutes. To the right "Hunt" mould cleaning machine.

through the mesh. The remarkable part of this test is the mesh of the sieve. Its copper wires are woven so closely that there are forty thousand openings to the square inch, and even water will be retained. Yet, in spite of the minute openings, more than three out of four of the cement particles must be small enough to pass through.

In addition to these tests, there are others of a more special nature, as well as a specific system of chemical analysis; but for everyday use these three are all that are required.

Cement is just as inseparably connected with concrete as flour is with bread. The Inspection and Testing Engineer, therefore, has not finished his job if the scientific control which he exercises stops with cement. Logically, it should and does extend to the mixing of cement with sand, stone, and water to make concrete.

(*Blank and Stoller, Inc., Photo*)

R. H. NORTON

Mr. Norton, president of the Acme Steel Company, makers of hot and cold rolled strip steel, cooperage hoop, steel strapping, and other steel reenforcements for shipping, was born in Chicago, December 27, 1875, and is the son of Oliver W. and Lucy Coit (Fanning) Norton. He attended the Chicago Manual Training School, and the University of Chicago. Starting with the Acme Steel Company in 1904, he was placed in entire charge of production in 1912, made vice-president in 1914, and has been president since 1923. Mr. Norton has taken an active part in the development of the company from assets of $100,000 to assets of over $11,000,000, practically all of which growth was brought about from profits, without the addition of outside capital.

Mr. Norton has lived in Kenwood for more than forty years and was for many years president of the Kenwood Improvement Association; vice-chairman, board of trustees of the Chautauqua Institution; trustee, Chicago Orchestral Association; and secretary, Chicago Chamber Music Society, governing member of the Art Institute of Chicago, and also a member of the Alpha Delta Phi Fraternity. Club affiliations are the Union League, University, South Shore Country, City Club, and Loyal Legion of the United States, of which he is past vice-commander of Illinois Commandery. Collecting fine violins and oil paintings are his hobbies. He is now the owner of four noted violins —two Stradivaris and two Guarneris—also about forty paintings by foremost American and European artists.

On May 9, 1908, Mr. Norton married Sallie Elizabeth Calhoun of Chicago. Their children are Beatrice, Patricia, Calhoun, and Christopher.

Ten years ago those who used concrete were in the same position as a baker who had no definite recipe for making bread. The making of concrete was largely a hit or miss procedure. Within the last few years, however, advances in the science of concrete designing have been sufficient to allow the engineer to control the quality of this material with the same precision and satisfactory results as has been the case in the manufacture of steel. The advances made in concrete control are shown graphically in the recent erection of twenty-story buildings—or higher—a feat that a decade ago would have been considered impossible or insane.

The Inspection and Testing Engineer not only assures the proper quality of cement, but he makes elaborate tests on the sand, stone, and water that is destined to become a part of the concrete. He goes even further: he supplies, through calculations based upon years of experience and research, the correct design (proportions of sand, stone, water and cement) to insure concrete of the desired strength. In doing this, he is in the same position as one who devises a definite recipe for making bread from flour.

Not satisfied with merely designing the mix, he has, in addition, devised means of checking his own "recipe" through the use of test cylinders. These cylinders, which are generally six inches in diameter and twelve inches high, are made by taking concrete as it is being poured into the forms and placing it in specially prepared molds. After being allowed to harden for a predetermined number of days, weeks or months these cylinders are taken to the laboratory where they are crushed in order to measure the strength of the sample concrete.

This phase of the Inspection and Testing Engineer's work is important enough to merit more description than is possible here—and interesting enough to read like a Jules Verne story. A discussion of steel awaits, however.

When we turn to steel our problem, while basically the same as that of cement, becomes more complicated. Steel has thousands of widely varying uses, is made to many specifications according to its intended purpose, and is a vastly differing material even as from a single mill. Steel, unlike cement, is generally used just as it comes. Since there are a great number of uses for steel, there must consequently be many different kinds of steel to meet each requirement efficiently. It would seem natural to suppose, therefore, that the tests which are designed to measure the qualities of steel would be equally numerous. Such, however, is not the case. Generally speaking, there are just two tests which are always used, and two additional tests which are used occasionally. One of the more important is the tensile-strength test, which consists of pulling apart a sample of the steel to ascertain its strength and elasticity; the other is a bending test—to measure its ductility—which consists simply of bending the test piece either until it breaks or to some predetermined angle. The two minor tests consist of (1) a "hardness" test—which is made by pressing a steel ball into the metal, and from the size of the impression and the pressure applied computing the relative hard-

(Moffett-Russell Photo)

JOHN J. O'BRIEN

Mr. O'Brien, president of the Standard Gas and Electric Company and H. M. Byllesby and Company, was born in Chicago, April 2, 1869. He received his education in public, parochial and business schools. His first employment was with the Pullman Company when he was eighteen years old. Two years later, in 1889, he became associated with the Chicago office of the United Edison Manufacturing Company, predecessor of the company which was merged with the General Electric Company in 1892. He continued in charge of accounting, for the Chicago office territory of the General Electric Company, until 1902, when he became associated with the late Colonel H. M. Byllesby in the formation of the Byllesby organization. He served as treasurer and general auditor until the death of Colonel Byllesby in 1924, at which time he was elected president.

Mr. O'Brien is also officer and director of the Standard Gas and Electric Company, H. M. Byllesby and Company, Byllesby Engineering and Management Corporation, Standard Power and Light Corporation, Northern States Power Company, Louisville Gas and Electric Company, Oklahoma Gas and Electric Company, Philadelphia Company, Market Street Railway Company, San Diego Consolidated Gas and Electric Company, Southern Colorado Power Company, The California Oregon Power Company, Mountain States Power Company, and Deep Rock Oil Corporation. These companies supply 1,662 communities in twenty states and in Mexico, and serve a population of approximately six million. He is also a director of the Pacific Gas and Electric Company and the Harris Trust and Savings Bank. Mr. O'Brien is a member of the Union League, Mid-Day, Electric, Butterfield Country, Chicago Golf, and Lake Shore Athletic clubs of Chicago; Lawyers, Recess, and Bankers of New York; Pendennis, of Louisville; and Duquesne, of Pittsburgh. During the summer of 1929 Mr. O'Brien qualified for membership in the "Hole-in-One" club. His other chief form of recreation is billiards.

In 1890 he was married to Miss Julia Hoy (died, 1895), of Chicago. Mr. O'Brien has one daughter, Katherine J. (Mrs. H. F. Carbaugh), with whom he makes his home.

ness; (2) the "impact" test—which measures the ability of the steel to with-stand sudden shocks. But, in addition to physical tests, chemical analyses and inspection are necessary.

Steel is really iron to which have been added exact quantities of other chemical elements to impart special qualities. Such elements as carbon, sul-phur, and phosphorous are always present. To these may also be added silicon, manganese, magnesium, copper, nickel, chromium, molybdenum, and a host of others; one may give greater strength, another may prevent cor-rosion, still another may increase its resistance to wear. To determine these special qualities, physical tests alone, such as pulling, bending, and twisting, are not enough—it is only by taking a sample of the steel apart chemically (analyzing) and measuring the quantity of each of its component elements that quality may be determined.

Even testing and analyzing is not enough. Steel is rolled, hammered, or poured into the shape in which it will be used. If through human error, these shapes become cracked, or bent, or contain any defects, it matters little how perfect the steel may be otherwise. A close visual inspection, there-fore, is necessary before the steel may be used in some skyscraper, or as a rail, a wheel, or for any of many other purposes.

Thus, it is seen how materials in general have been scientifically tested in order that they might be used efficiently and safely in the structures, pavements, and development of Chicago.

THE RACQUET CLUB.   Rebori & Wentworth, architects.

(DeHaven Photo)

LEIF E. OLSEN

Mr. Olsen is a partner of Olsen and Urbain, Inc., architects, and treasurer of the Mandell Manufacturing Company, manufacturers of cardboard advertising displays. He was born in Chicago, Illinois, on July 18, 1892, and is the son of Ole and Inga (Abrahamsen) Olsen. He studied architecture in the Society of Beaux Arts Architects, and in the office of Otis and Clark. During the World War, he served in the Navy and had charge of the Project Department at Newport, Rhode Island. Following the World War, Mr. Urbain and Mr. Olsen organized the firm which bears their names.

They have designed many hotels, cooperative apartments, homes, estates, and industrial plants in and near Chicago. Some of the recent important works are the Jefferson Electric Company Plant at Bellwood, Illinois, The Petrolagar Plant at Niles Center, Illinois, the William C. Grunow residence at River Forest, Illinois, Mr. Grunow's estate at Lake Geneva, the Philip K. Wrigley estate at Lake Geneva, Wisconsin, the Mandel Lowenstine residence at Valparaiso, Indiana and many others. In 1920 Albert E. Mandell, Jules Urbain, and Leif E. Olsen, organized the Toymakers Inc., which later was reorganized into the Mandell Manufacturing Company.

On March 4, 1916, Mr. Olsen married Goldie H. Andersen, of Chicago, They have two children, Leif E., Jr., and Donal Allan.

(*Chicago Architectural Photographing Company*)
JACKSON BOULEVARD, LOOKING EAST

(*Fernand de Gueldre Photo*)

WALTER P. PAEPCKE

Mr. Paepcke, president, Container Corporation of America and Chicago Mill and Lumber Corporation, was born in Chicago, June 29, 1896, son of Hermann and Paula (Wagner) Paepcke. He was a student at the University School, Chicago, from 1904 to 1912, graduated from the Chicago Latin School in 1913, and received his A. B. (Bachelor of Arts) degree at Yale in 1917. Mr. Paepcke began his business career in 1917 as assistant treasurer of Chicago Mill and Lumber Company (now Chicago Mill and Lumber Corporation) and has been president since 1921. This organization is one of the largest producers of hardwood lumber, wood boxes, crates, veneer, and plywood. The Container Corporation of America has become, under Mr. Paepcke's direction, the world's largest producers of corrugated and solid fibre shipping containers, folding cartons, and paperboard. Among its recent developments is a paperboard insulation material for home construction, as well as industrial usage.

Mr. Paepcke is chairman of the board of K. W. Battery Company, and Chicago Mill Paper Stock Company; director, McWilliams Dredging Company. He enlisted in the United States Naval Reserve Force in May, 1918, and was later commissioned as ensign, being honorably discharged in April, 1919. He is a member of Phi Beta Kappa and Alpha Delta Phi fraternities, and his clubs are Mid-Day, Racquet, Harvard-Yale-Princeton, Yale, Onwentsia, and Shoreacres. He enjoys golf, tennis, and squash racquets.

On April 16, 1922, Mr. Paepcke married Elizabeth H. Nitze of Chicago. The children are Walter P., Jr. (died October 4, 1926), Anina H., and Paula A.

DRAMATIZING THE HISTORY OF CHICAGO AND THE OLD NORTHWEST TERRITORY

The Chicago Historical Society and Its Important Work

BY CHARLES B. PIKE
President, Chicago Historical Society

YOUNG, as cities go, Chicago has already its legends and traditions. Its earliest visitors were men of fame and importance. Marquette, Joliet, La Salle and Tonti all tramped its sandy marshes and carried their canoes and supplies over the mud flats of the portage that separated the Chicago and the Des Plaines rivers. In 1679 La Salle entered the Illinois River and named it for the tribes of the surrounding region. The river named the territory when it was organized in February, 1809, and later the state when it came into existence in 1818. In 1833 Chicago was incorporated as a town, and in 1856 its historical society was organized.

Dedicated to the preservation and recording of Chicago's history the Chicago Historical Society has gradually broadened its province until it now dramatizes the history of the old Northwest, as well as of the entire United States. Progressive men leave their imprint on everything they touch and on every society with which they become actively associated. The Chicago Historical Society has been singularly fortunate in having always had as its trustees the foremost men of the city. Its founders were men whose names have gone down in history as the great statesmen, merchants, and bankers of their time. A list of the Society's presidents reads like the Dictionary of American Biography. It is therefore not surprising that each

(*Chicago Architectural Photographing Company*)
The Chicago Historical Society's building in Lincoln Park, near North Avenue.
Graham, Anderson, Probst & White, architects.

of the Society's buildings has been the most modern of its time, embodying the new and unusual features of museum construction, new methods for handling historical material, and new ways of attacking old historical problems.

Like its predecessors the new building of the Society will no doubt mark a step forward in historical museum technique. Standing amid the spreading lawns of Lincoln Park, near the Saint-Gaudens' statue of Lincoln, this red brick Georgian building with white limestone trim is one of Chicago's most beautiful examples of Colonial architecture. This Colonial

A SHRINE OF LINCOLN WORSHIPERS

The Lincoln Parlor, homelike and cheerful, is among the most popular of the Chicago Historical Society exhibits. Here is reproduced, with its original furniture, the front parlor of the Lincoln home in Springfield.

feeling is carried throughout the interior, with thirty-eight period rooms dramatizing the important epochs of American history from the days of Columbus to the present date. Beginning with the Spanish Exploration Room the visitor starts out on a tour of American history from the wreck of the Santa Maria off the coast of Santo Domingo on Christmas Eve, 1492, to the signing of the Armistice at the end of the World War. The visitor may walk through the important days of American history in an hour and a half. In that time he may pause to look in the mullioned windows of Paul Revere's North Square house in Boston, visit the Mount

Pleasant country seat of a wealthy Philadelphia gentleman, look into the west parlor of Mt. Vernon, trace the trend of the western migrations and the construction of the transcontinental railroads. He may gaze at Chicago as it looked before the great fire of 1871 and in the days of the World's Fair of 1893, pictures which are but two in a series of eight dioramas in the Chicago Diorama Gallery. Here the visitor-in-a-hurry can get a bird's-eye view of Chicago's history, a fifteen minute drama that he will not soon forget. It is not often that one lives to see a whole city going down to destruction in the grip of a great conflagration as he can in the diorama of the Chicago Fire, nor can he see an exciting horse race in old Washington Park every day merely by turning an electrical switch as he can do at the Chicago Historical Society. In a word, the Society has made history come to life—it has dramatized events that have stood as barren skeletons in our minds from the days of our childhood when dates in history were learned by rote.

With the opening of its new building the Chicago Historical Society embarks on a new period of usefulness to the teacher and student, as well as the man-in-the-street. Its library of 50,000 volumes includes many rare and out-of-print books and first editions, and an equal number of manu-

(*Howe and Arthur Photo*)

WHERE RELICS OF THE PIONEERS ARE GATHERED

The Early Pioneer Room, with its rugged beamed ceiling, was designed especially as a background for the Dr. Otto L. Schmidt collection of material associated with the early days of Illinois and the Old Northwest Territory.

President
CHICAGO
HISTORICAL
SOCIETY

(Du Bois Photo)

CHARLES B. PIKE

Mr. Pike, president of the Chicago Historical Society, was born in Chicago, Illinois, June 29, 1871, son of Eugene S. and Mary (Rockwell) Pike. He graduated from Harvard University in 1893 and from Harvard Law School in 1896. He was admitted to the Illinois Bar in 1898 and practiced law in Chicago for four years. In 1901-1902 he was vice-president of the Western State Bank and was president of the Hamilton National Bank and the Merchants Safe Deposit Company from 1903 to 1910. After retiring from banking, he assisted his father in the management of his real estate. On his father's death in 1916, he became the managing trustee of the Eugene S. Pike Estate Land Trust. During the War, Mr. Pike was Civilian Aide to the Adjutant General and Chairman of the Central and Western Departments of the Military Training Camps Association, the main Civilian Agency of the War Department for recruiting and inducting specialists into the various technical branches of the Army and the thirteen branches of the General Staff and for examining candidates for the Field and Coast Artillery Officers' Schools. Since 1922, he has been president of the Military Training Camps Association, with headquarters in Chicago, and Chief Civilian Aide to the Secretary of War—serving Secretaries John W. Weeks, Dwight F. Davis and Patrick J. Hurley in this capacity.

In 1927, Mr. Pike was elected president of the Chicago Historical Society. He was active in securing a site for the Society in Lincoln Park and in financing and supervising the building of its new Historical Museum and Library, with its up-to-date equipment, and planned to visualize the history not only of Chicago, but of the United States from the discovery of America to the immediate present. This educational, civic and patriotic project was opened to the general public on November 12, 1932. Mr. Pike sponsored the organizing of the Racquet Club of Chicago and was elected its first president in 1924, holding this office until his resignation in 1929. Mr. Pike is a member of the Chicago, University, Casino, Saddle and Cycle, Old Elm, Shoreacres, Onwentsia, Attic and Harvard clubs of Chicago, the Racquet and Tennis Club of New York and the Bar Harbor and Kebo Valley (president) clubs of Bar Harbor, Maine.

On May 18, 1898, in Washington, D. C., he married Frances Alger of Detroit, daughter of General Russell A. Alger, who was then Secretary of War.

scripts. Three thousand newspapers and thousands of maps and prints are at the disposal of all who care to visit the library. In the Chicago fire of 1871 and again in the fire of 1874 great destruction was wrought in the book collections and in the valuable group of manuscripts which included the original draft of Lincoln's Emancipation Proclamation. Many of these early books it has never been possible to replace. The Chicago Historical Society Library is particularly rich in material dealing with early frontier days of the old Northwest. It has a large George Rogers Clark collection, hundreds of early French manuscripts, diaries of early travelers, and account books of trappers and early storekeepers. In this great storehouse you will find letters of La Salle and Tonti, letters from Lincoln to Douglas, surveys made by George Washington, reports of pioneer Chicago firms, original copies of Indian treaties, and directories and newspapers of all kinds.

In its new building the Chicago Historical Society will enlarge its Educational Department. Not only have children's work rooms been provided for, but a large auditorium with motion picture and stereopticon equipment will be available for pageants and plays of all kinds. The Society expects, moreover to develop a series of lectures for adults on current topics, as well as historic events, at the same time continuing its valuable work among the school children of Chicago.

Some years ago the Chicago Historical Society, in conjunction with the Board of Education, worked out a series of lectures to be given to school children on Saturday mornings. These lectures supplement the work done in history in the public, private, and parochial schools of the city. Tests are given at the end of each lecture. The children fill in the test sheets and take them back to school. In this way, the student fixes in his own mind the information just gathered and returns to his class with an accurate synopsis of the lecture.

Another important educational activity of the Chicago Historical Society is the Junior Citizens Club which was formed four years ago for the purpose of spreading information about the functions of our city, state and national governments, as well as the responsibilities of citizenship. Its growth has been phenomenal. Begun as an educational project with headquarters in the building of the Chicago Historical Society, the Junior Citizens Club has grown into a loosely knit federation of individual Americanization clubs under the general supervision of a group of educators and business men.

The principal and teachers of each school in the city pick from the children in their charge fifteen to twenty pupils who have good scholarship averages and who have shown an interest in civic affairs. This group of students at their first meeting elect a president, vice-president, secretary and treasurer of the club, as well as special administrative, legislative, educational, publicity and social committees. The Junior Citizens Clubs study important events in American institutions of government from

(*Moffett-Russell Photo*)

ALBERT J. PIXLEY

Mr. Pixley, president of Pixley and Ehlers Restaurants, was born in Portage, Wisconsin, in 1879, son of Jacob and Augusta (Bachman) Pixley. He received his education in the public and high schools of that city. His first job in Chicago was in the restaurant of E. W. Rieck. With Mr. Pixley's help, Mr. Rieck built a second restaurant and put him in charge, so that at the age of nineteen he became a restaurant manager. A few months later, Mr. Rieck decided that the second restaurant was more than he cared to handle and urged Mr. Pixley to buy the place. He found he had saved only twenty-five dollars so he persuaded his good friend, Mr. W. J. Ehlers, to sell his barber shop and join him, which he did. A tailor advanced the remaining one hundred dollars, and they started in the restaurant business. Some time later Mr. Ehlers was forced to retire because of illness and Mr. Pixley became president of the company, which now owns fourteen restaurants in Chicago, and, in addition, a bakery on Madison street.

In the windows of many of the Pixley and Ehlers restaurants tantalizing pies and pastries of all sorts are prepared and baked before the bulging eyes of Chicagoans and visitors. In 1930, when business conditions became bad, Mr. Pixley said to his 500 employees: "We will not cut wages, nor lay anybody off (except for cause), nor reduce bonus payments." Mr. Pixley does business strictly on a cash basis, all bills being paid every week. He is a member of the Chicago Athletic Club, Oak Park Country Club, and the Swan Lake Shooting Club, and his favorite recreations are hunting and golf.

On April 25, 1900, he married Julia L. DeMoney, of Chicago.

the earliest days to the present. Pageants and plays are written and produced and an attempt is made to reach the parents through the children and interest them in the life of their communities. The unusual popularity of the Junior Citizens Club proves conclusively that it has a definite place in the life of the coming generations. The Chicago Historical Society plans, therefore, to extend its activities and to advance the welfare and usefulness of the Junior Citizens Club by every means in its power.

The Chicago Historical Society was organized by its founders to institute and encourage historical inquiry, to collect and preserve the materials of history and to spread historical information. It is not always easy to pick out historical events that will be of far-reaching influence in the future, when these take place in everyday life. The Chicago Historical Society does not attempt to do so except in a very broad way. It collects the materials of present-day civilization as they concern the life of the city, state and nation. Well aware that the cultural, as well as the industrial future of this country will be very unlike that of the past, the Chicago Historical Society feels, that by the accumulating of valuable materials of present-day history, its great collection can serve all who care to consult it, as a springboard from the past to the future.

A Victorian Parlor of the early 1850's. The rosewood furniture, from the Terrace Row home of Mrs. Tuthill King, is the gift of Mrs. George Henry High. The candelabra and the clock, gifts of Mrs. Eliphalet W. Cramer, were originally presented to James Spencer by the Prince of Wales, later Edward VII. The music box is from the John B. Drake home, and the fire-place from the Mahlon D. Ogden home.

(*Howe and Arthur Photo*)

(Moffett-Russell Photo)

CONRAD H. POPPENHUSEN

Mr. Poppenhusen, attorney, was born at College Point, Long Island, New York, on July 21, 1872, son of Herman C. and Caroline S. (Funke) Poppenhusen, and is a descendant of Conrad Poppenhusen, who came to the United States from Hamburg, Germany, in 1841, and became prominent in railroad activities in New York. Mr. Poppenhusen was sent to the Gymnasium at Kiel, Germany, for his early education, 1880-1889, returning to the United States to complete his studies. He took up the study of law and was admitted to practice in 1892. He continued his study of law, however, at the old Union College of Law (now Northwestern University Law School), graduating in 1894.

In 1899, after practicing alone for several years, he formed the firm of Gregory, Poppenhusen and McNab. In 1914 he entered the firm of Newman, Poppenhusen and Stern, and in 1928, following the death of Mr. Newman and Mr. Stern, organized the firm of Poppenhusen, Johnston, Thompson and Cole, with offices at 11 South La Salle street, of which he is the senior partner. He is a director of the Central Republic Trust Company, Fairbanks Morse & Company, Central-Illinois Securities Company, Chicago, and the State Bank and Trust Company, Evanston; is a member of the American, Illinois State and Chicago bar associations, the Association of the Bar of the City of New York, the Law Club, and Phi Delta Phi Fraternity, and is president of the board of trustees of the National College of Education, Evanston, Illinois. His clubs are the Chicago, Electric, Mid-Day, Old Elm, Glen View, Evanston, Midwick, Chicago Athletic, Union League, and Press. He takes an active interest in civic progress and public affairs and for diversion plays bridge and golf.

On June 25, 1895, he married Harriet G. Gunn, of Evanston, Illinois. Their children are Conrad H., Jr., and Nancy.

SEEING CHICAGO FROM THE BUS TOPS
"Open Air to Everywhere" Service Popular With Visitors and Townsfolk Alike

BY GARRETT T. SEELEY
Vice-President, Chicago Motor Coach Company

ADDING a metropolitan touch to Chicago within recent years, and im-parting a picturesque bit of color to the scene, are the motor coaches, plying the boulevards with their groups of sight-seers or their regular daily passengers.

With the coming of the motor coach, Chicago has taken on the aspect of New York or London, and there were reasons why this twentieth century transportation had to come.

Completion of the Michigan Boulevard link bridge, together with the lake front development of the last decade, has resulted in the development of a new retail business district, centering at Wacker drive and Michigan avenue. This district is now served by bus. Likewise, the bus lines furnish the only direct means of mass transportation to the Art Institute, Field Museum, Soldier Field, the Adler Planetarium, the Shedd Aquarium, and the Century of Progress exposition grounds.

The Chicago Motor Coach Company is the second oldest, and also one of the largest and most successful organizations of its kind in the United States. While it is a definite factor in meeting the transportation require-ments of Chicago's vast and growing population, the popularity of its serv-

BOATING IN LINCOLN PARK

(*Underwood and Underwood Photo*)

RUFUS W. PUTNAM

Major Putnam, president of the Maritime Engineering Corporation and secretary-treasurer of the Leathem Smith-Putnam Navigation Company, was born in La Crosse, Wisconsin, June 30, 1891, and is the son of William Rice and Jane (Willard) Putnam. He received his college education at the United States Military Academy, West Point, being an honor graduate of the class of 1913. He was commissioned to Corps of Engineers, United States Army, and served in all grades from second-lieutenant to that of lieutenant-colonel during his service with the army, which terminated upon his resignation in 1926. Major Putnam's military service included various engineering assignments in this country and with the American Expeditionary Forces in France.

From 1921 to 1926 he was United States District Engineer for the Chicago River and Harbor District. Since resigning from the service, he has been engaged in consulting engineering, specializing in marine operations. He was chief engineer for the Commercial Club of Chicago from 1926 to 1928 in connection with the preparation of a report on the "Harbor Plan of Chicago." His interests during the past few years have been along the lines of developing water transportation; his connection with the Leathem Smith-Putnam Navigation Company is evidence of this as this company is a pioneer in the field of barge transportation. This company has designed and is operating a special type of lake-going barge, carrying about 2,000 tons of sand or gravel, and so designed as to go under the Chicago River bridges without requiring them to open, which should be of special interest to Chicagoans who must cross one or more of our bridges every day. The development of this type of boat has been Major Putnam's hobby for the past few years. He is a member of the Chicago Engineers Club, Electric Club, Traffic Club, and Riverside Golf Club; director of Chicago Regional Planning Association and the Chicago Regional Port Commission; and a past president of the Western Society of Engineers.

On September 4, 1914, he married Caroline Frances Hough, of Rochester, New York. Their children are Persis, Rufus Willard, and Benjamin Olney.

ice is due largely to the fact that its routes are laid over the city's famed boulevard system and through its parks. Thus, to the visitor, a motor coach ride is the equivalent of a long sight-seeing tour. Most of Chicago's beauty spots and show places may be viewed from the top of a bus at the expense only of a dime or two.

Curiously enough, the idea for such a transportation system originated from John Hertz, father of the Yellow Cab service. With his genius for discerning opportunity, Mr. Hertz saw that adequate bus service would serve a definite need not only to the new and expanding business district, but as a civic asset in advertising Chicago's attractions to outsiders and in bringing residents in closer touch with the beauties of their city.

ONE OF CHICAGO'S MANY BATHING BEACHES

Mr. Hertz's first step was to purchase the old Chicago Motorbus Company, long a failing enterprise, which operated over a route of about ten miles on the North Side. This pioneer concern was taken over in 1922. At the same time Mr. Hertz obtained the services of the one man in the United States who was most likely to make a success of the new venture. This man, John A. Ritchie, president of the Fifth Avenue Coach Company of New York City, was regarded as the most able bus line operator in the country.

Mr. Ritchie had attracted wide attention because of the manner in which he had replaced red ink with black on the ledgers of the New York company, which had been anything but a gold mine. In connection with the civility campaigns which he inaugurated, he had published a series of pam-

(*Underwood and Underwood Photo*)

ROBERT ISHAM RANDOLPH

Col. Randolph, director of operations for A Century of Progress Exposition, Chicago's (1933) World's Fair, and president of the Chicago Association of Commerce, 1930 and 1931, was born in Chicago, April 14, 1883, the son of Isham and Mary Henry (Taylor) Randolph. He studied at Cornell University, and in 1904 was appointed assistant engineer of the Sanitary District of Chicago. From 1908 to 1911 he served as secretary of the Internal Improvement Commission of Illinois, and from 1911 to 1913 as secretary of the Rivers and Lakes Commission of Illinois. He was secretary of Isham Randolph and Company, consulting engineers, from 1913 to 1921, and is now vice-president of the Randolph-Perkins Company, consulting engineers.

As a private soldier, Col. Randolph served on the Mexican border with Battery C, 1st Illinois field artillery, in 1916. In 1918 he was a major in command of the 535th Engineers, American Expeditionary Forces, and later was breveted lieutenant-colonel, commanding the 381st Engineers, Officers' Reserve Corps. An enthusiastic advocate of inland waterways, Colonel Randolph has been equally active in the cause of crime prevention. As head of the Citizens' Committee for the Punishment and Prevention of Crime, the famous "Secret Six," he has won international recognition for his ruthless prosecution of Chicago's public enemies and for his fearless defense of Chicago's reputation. Col. Randolph is a director of the Citizens' Association and president (1932) of the Mississippi Valley Association. He is a member of the American Society of Civil Engineers, the Western Society of Engineers, the University, Engineers, Commercial, and Riverside Golf clubs, and the Psi Upsilon Fraternity.

He was married October 17, 1912, to Martha A. Maclean of Riverside, Illinois.

phlets on public relations. One of these, "A Harvest of Thoughts on Civility," so rang the bell that the first edition was snapped up overnight, and a number of subsequent printings were necessary. The slogan of the Chicago Motor Coach Company is "Service with a smile."

The company continued to operate at first only over the single North Side line. In a short time, however, permission was obtained from the Illinois Commerce Commission to extend the service to the boulevards of the South Side. Later a West Side service was established.

Under expert management and public understanding the new company enjoyed immediate prosperity and popularity. As Mr. Hertz had dreamed, it became a valuable advertisement for the city. Visitors went away from Chicago extolling its scenic and architectural beauties. Since the Chicago Motor Coach Company was established, it has multiplied its service approximately sixteen times. It maintains five garages, and two maintenance shops. More than 150 miles of routes are operated with 550 buses, and it is the preferred mode of transportation of about sixty million people annually.

The company has more than 1,200 employees on its payroll. The average daily mileage is 38,000.

The company has continually added to and improved its service. One of its most important money-saving policies, from the standpoint of the rider, was the inauguration, a few years ago, of a liberal free transfer system. This makes it possible to ride from one end of the city to another—a distance in excess of twenty-seven miles—for one fare.

Never, under the present management, have the buses failed in an emergency. Pageants and athletic events at Soldier Field have attracted hundreds of thousands of spectators, but the Motor Coach Company has handled the crowds competently and with dispatch.

(Gordon Studio Photo)

DAVID M. RAPPORT

Mr. Rapport, president of Rapid Roller Company, manufacturers of printing press rollers, was born in Chicago, March 10, 1885, son of Max and Hannah Rapport. Because of the death of his father he was reared in an orphans' home until fourteen years of age. He began his business career as a newsboy and later served an apprenticeship of four years with one of Chicago's reputable builders of printing machinery, studying drafting nights. Mr. Rapport got his technical education at Lewis Institute, Chicago. While working in his apprenticeship, he studied the operation of printers' rollers and developed ways of improving them. In 1913 he invented the first lithographic roller ever made which did away with the use of sheepskin and leather and since that time has evolved many other types of rollers. Because there was no machinery in existence to carry out his inventions, he designed and built new machines for this purpose.

In 1917 Mr. Rapport organized the Rapid Roller Company and he designed the machinery used in his plant. In the Rapid Roller Company plant is a complete chemical laboratory, as well as the manufacturing machinery constructed according to Mr. Rapport's ideas. Experiments are being conducted at all times to improve rollers. Mr. Rapport derived the first word in the name of his company from the first three letters of his own name and adopted "Mercury," the name of the winged Roman deity who was messenger of the gods, as his trade-mark. Mr. Rapport is a member of the Chicago Association of Commerce, Printing Trades Craftsmen, Executives, and Covenant clubs. His favorite recreations are handball and swimming.

He married Freda Savage, of Chicago, December 31, 1917. Their children are Maxine and Laurence.

CHICAGO AS A CENTER OF THE DANCE
An Art Form That Has Many Local Exponents and Admirers
BY MARK TURBYFILL

Author of "The Living Frieze," "A Marriage With Space." Dance critic, *The Chicagoan*

In 1850 Chicago heard its first performance of Grand Opera, which, as the program states, "concludes with a Pas de Deux." The small, two-story, wooden building which housed the theater, burned down the following evening. In 1928 Harriet Monroe wrote in *Poetry* of the dancer, "Adolph Bolm leaping to interpret the soaring skyscraper."

In Oriental countries similarities of form in architecture and dancing are evident. But in Chicago, has anyone seen a *port de bras* inspired by the opening and closing of the Michigan Avenue Link bridge; a *pirouette* set spinning by example of the Tribune tower's flying buttresses?

When civic enthusiasm presses the question, "What is Chicago's influence upon the dance?" it is the curious observation of a provocative philosopher and writer, Mr. G. Gurdjieff, who slyly called himself a "dancing teacher," which comes to mind. Visiting Chicago in 1924 with his phenomenal and indefatigable dancers, Mr. Gurdjieff found time to discuss various types of energy; and added knowledge to amazement by "revealing" the source of Chicago's proud strength: the population, he said, drew energy into the very fibers of their being from the sea of blood spilt from thousands of hogs and cattle slaughtered daily at the stockyards!

About the year 1865, in the wind-swept village of Fullersburg, then seventeen miles northwest of Chicago, was born Loie Fuller, the dancer. "They transformed the bar into a sleeping-room and there it was that I first saw light," she wrote in her *Fifteen Years of a Dancer's Life*. With the spirit of the Windy City blowing its will through agitated yards of her draperies, and with the projection of rainbow lights upon them ("It's a butterfly!" "It's an orchid!" thousands who saw her cried) she precipitated throughout the world a new idea of manipulating light, form, and movement upon the stage.

During three seasons in this age of incandescent light, the Chicago Allied Arts, Inc., raised, and finally lowered (December, 1926) its eloquent curtain upon which a suave ballerina came careening over a horizon of brilliantly illuminated (Chicago) skyscrapers. Newspapers agreed that the ballets presented by this organization were "cleverly arranged and admirably danced." But when they gave *La Farce du Pont Neuf,* there were differences of opinion. Needless to say, no sounds such as issued from Mme. Herscher-Clement's score were ever heard on Chicago bridges. "The music," declared one critic, "is the most futile, infantile conglomeration of sounds heard here in some time."

To have done with conglomerations, and to exclaim (in well modulated voices) "Welcome to our City!" to a creative synthesis of music, painting, and the dance, was precisely the hospitable and ambitious aim of those enthusiasts who organized the Chicago Allied Arts. Music, chosen principally from the works of modern composers, among whom were Chicago's own John Alden Carpenter and Leo Sowerby, was directed by Eric DeLamarter. Charm and wit enlivened the curtains, settings and costumes designed by Nicolas Remisoff. The ballets and dances, arranged by Adolph Bolm, became a vivid entity of the synthesis.

During these performances Chicago had its first opportunity to see the dancing of Tamara Karsavina of the Russian Ballet. Ruth Page, Caird Leslie, Amata Grassi, Berenice Holmes, Harriet Lundgren, Paul DuPont, Vera Mirova, Maria Montero, Edna McRae, Marcia Preble were among the many dancers who contributed to the variety and spirit of the productions. Organized in 1924, the Chicago Allied Arts, Inc., flowered but three brief seasons; yet it has been the only civic institution of significant proportions dedicated to the art of the dance of which the United States can boast.

The giant strides of trade which make Chicago the world's leader as a production center do not cover the globe merely with packing house products, common brick, varnish, telephone equipment, mail order merchandise. No. "Chicago leads the world in the manufacture and distribution of musical instruments and also radio and radio accessories," statistics say. The already versatile correspondence curriculum adds dance instruction from Chicago, and reaches a high point of ingenuity with lessons written by Chicagoans, signed with alluring Russian pseudonyms, and sold to the world by garrulous full page advertisements. "I can teach you to dance like this!" exclaim the captions, referring to accompanying illustrations of pretty girls doing "jazz toe," Spanish, and quasi-Oriental dances. Thus the city incubates and broadcasts over the nations its brood of mail-taught coryphées, and ministers to their Terpsichorean urge with music by radio, and with musical instruments manufactured in Chicago.

As for the jazz released from every corner of the globe by these instruments, everyone knows that it was once "an underground waif," "a low noise in a low dive"; but some forget to remember that it was Chicago (again!) that made jazz its protégé, gave it a vibrant send-off commanding prestige.

"There is considerable discussion," writes Paul Whiteman, "over exactly who did invent the term 'jazz band,' with many authorities giving the honor to Bert Kelly of Chicago, who described a group of musicians that he hired out to the Boosters' club at the Hotel Morrison as a 'jazz band.' The Boosters' club promptly raised its prices, alleging that the new-fangled jazz came high."

And so Chicago, moving on the shore of the great ocean of jazz, communicated convulsions to the whole world. Dancers, composers, painters, poets, producers, treading European shores, felt the tidal wave of jazz, and continued to work in its tempo and rhythm. In the fascinating works of Picasso, Picabia, Leger, Cocteau, Stravinsky, Milhaud, Honegger, Ravel, Kreutzberg, Massine, Balanchine, Diaghileff, it requires only eyes and ears to recognize the influence of jazz, a highly contagious and characteristic product of Chicago.

Probably the most notable of the ballets produced by the Chicago Opera Company were *The Birthday of the Infanta* and *Boudour*, both given during the season of 1919-20. Music for the *Infanta* was composed by John Alden Carpenter, settings by Robert Edmund Jones, choreography by Adolph Bolm, with Ruth Page dancing the role of the *Infanta*. Felix Borowski composed the music for *Boudour*, Norman Bel Geddes designed the décor, the late Andreas Pavley, and Serge Oukrainsky arranged the choreography, and Anna Ludmila danced the principal feminine role.

Opera in Chicago has always had the disposition to entrust the direction of the ballet to Europeans. Among these have been Luigi Albertieri, Messrs. Pavley and Oukrainsky, Adolph Bolm, Vecheslav Swoboda, Laurent Novikoff.

It remained for the Ravina Opera Company to entrust its ballet to an American, a Chicagoan. In 1926 when Ruth Page became ballet mistress of the Ravina Opera, the dancing was regarded as something of a gratifying surprise, perhaps even a sprightly interpolation. Then audiences and critics alike began to observe that with the entrance of the ballet there was established a higher degree of visual enjoyment; and that plastic harmonies, designs for the eye, were as essential as those aimed for the satisfaction of the ear.

Long before the birth of the "great American noise," before Chicago had made jazz its protégé, dance developments of another character were taking place here. These were the experiments of the greatest dance innovator of the age, Isadora Duncan. That her first productions were not, however, completely appreciated, has been vividly suggested by Harriet Monroe.

"The triumph of genius," she writes, "seems such an easy thing to the applauding world—a victory inevitable, writ in the stars from the beginning! But who would have foreseen it on that evening long ago when a lanky girl and her brother—ill-nourished, ill-dressed—tried out their dances in a Chicago drawing-room generously lent out of pity, and were advised by the kindly hostess and her satiric-smiling guests to give up their strange Terpsichorean antics."

As for schools of the dance in Chicago, they are too numerous to catalogue. Among the many capable teachers of Chicago are Hazel Sharp, Merriel Abbott, Edna McRae, Berenice Holmes, Serge Oukrainsky.

In the concert field and in Chicago's dance consciousness the name of Bertha Ochsner is rapidly becoming significant. Miss Ochsner explores the mental countries of religious fanatics; the regrets of a princess about to become a queen. She searches out strange meanings in the movements of animals, birds, and fish, and builds a dance of minutely accurate pictures or analogies. She dances her storms of feeling, but they are less savage than

(G. Dobkin Photo, Atlantic City, N. J.)

FREDERICK H. RAWSON

Mr. Rawson, chairman of the board of the First National Bank of Chicago and the First Union Trust and Savings Bank, was born in Chicago, May 30, 1872, the son of Stephen W. and Emily (Holbrook) Rawson. After his graduation from Yale University in 1895, he began his career as entry clerk for the Union Trust Company. He made rapid progress and in 1901 was elected a vice-president of the company. In 1925 he was chairman of the board, and when the Union Trust Company was merged with the First National Bank in 1929, Mr. Rawson was co-chairman of the board of the combined institution. He has held his present office of chairman since 1930.

His wide range of interests is indicated by his directorships in various organizations and by his club memberships. He is a director of the Mercantile Trust and Savings Bank, the Miehle Printing Press and Manufacturing Company, the Chicago, Burlington and Quincy and the Baltimore and Ohio railroad companies, and of Wilson and Company. He is a trustee of Field Museum of Natural History, and a member of the Bankers, Chicago, Saddle and Cycle, Mid-Day, Onwentsia, Old Elm, Racquet, and Shore Acres clubs, the New York Yacht Club, and the Cocoloba Cay Club of Miami.

Mr. Rawson was married January 10, 1907, to Edith Kennett of Chicago. The children are Frederick Holbrook and Kennett Longley.

those of Mary Wigman or Angna Enters, with whom she has something in common.

There are other younger dancers who have banded together to form The Chicago Little Theatre of the Dance. Their contributions, up to the present have been, however, too few or too slight to command more than mention of their endeavors and enthusiasms.

20 NORTH WACKER DRIVE BUILDING
Graham, Anderson, Probst & White, architects.

(*Melvin H. Sykes Photo*)

FRANK C. REED

Mr. Reed, vice-president of the Westinghouse Electric Elevator Company, was born in Mercer County, Pennsylvania, January 1, 1879, son of Alexander S. and Loretta (McEwen) Reed. He received his early education at a country school and Grove City College, Pennsylvania, graduating with the class of 1900. In 1903 he graduated from the Massachusetts Institute of Technology, Boston, Massachusetts, with the degree of B. S. (Bachelor of Science). After graduation he entered the employ of the Westinghouse Electric & Manufacturing Company, East Pittsburgh, Pennsylvania, as an apprentice, and has been in its employ continuously since that date. After serving as an apprentice for two years, he became identified with the industrial sales department, where he remained until January 1, 1921, when he was transferred to the Philadelphia office, as branch manager of the Huntington, West Virginia, territory. There he remained until June 1, 1927, when he was made sales manager of the Westinghouse Electric Elevator Company, in Chicago, and in March, 1931, he was made vice-president.

The Westinghouse Electric Elevator Company manufactures passenger and freight elevators. Its elevators are installed in such buildings as the Merchandise Mart, 20 North Wacker Drive, new Post-office, and Stevens Hotel buildings, in Chicago; Carew Tower in Cincinnati; the Gulf Oil Corporation building, Koppers building, and Cathedral of Learning, in Pittsburgh; the Fisher and First National Bank buildings in Detroit; the R. C. A., Daily News, Rockefeller Center, and Bankers' Trust buildings in New York; and in many larger government and other outstanding buildings in all sections of the country Mr. Reed is a director of the Westinghouse Electric Elevator Company, a veteran of the Spanish-American War and a member of the Sons of the American Revolution. He is a member of the University Club of Pittsburgh, the Medinah Athletic Club of Chicago, and the Hinsdale Golf Club, Hinsdale, Illinois.

Mr. Reed married Mary Boyd Firth of Mercer, Pennsylvania, on August 30, 1909.

HAWTHORNE—A CITY WITHIN A CITY
A Manufacturing Plant Which Has Its Own Police and Fire Departments, Power House, Gas Works, and Water Supply

BY C. L. RICE
Vice-President, Western Electric Company

FROM a stretch of prairie to the largest manufacturing plant in Illinois in the brief span of a quarter of a century! Such has been the growth of that city within a city, the Western Electric Company's great Hawthorne plant.

For more than sixty years Western Electric has been identified with Chicago. Its first workshop in Kinzie street employed only a handful of men, but the advent of the telephone brought about an era of swift and amazing expansion.

The Hawthorne plant, employing in normal times 30,000 Chicagoans, manufactures most of the telephone equipment for America. Its entire output is consumed by the Bell System. In addition to this huge industrial center on the southwest margin of Chicago, the company maintains two other large plants in the East, and a chain of distributing houses reaching from coast to coast.

For many of its 18,000 varieties of raw materials Hawthorne is dependent on the rest of the world. The gold miner of Alaska, the mica digger of India, men and women of every land and clime are producing goods which enter into the manufacture of telephone equipment.

Physically, Hawthorne is a modern industrial plant with 86 buildings containing over 3,000,000 square feet of available floor space. One never suspects in viewing the exterior that behind these buildings is an inner court, beautifully landscaped. There are winding streets and sidewalks, and seas of green lawns dotted with floral islands. Hawthorne is, in fact, a city in itself. It has its own police staff, a fire department, a completely equipped hospital, cooperative stores, a laundry, a railroad, a power house, a gas works, restaurants, and even its own water supply. Each month enough electricity is used to illuminate 450,000 average homes—enough to take care of a city the size of Memphis, Tennessee. In the same period gas enough to supply a city as large as Dallas, Texas, is generated and consumed.

Mechanically, Hawthorne is the wonder workshop of the world. Nowhere else is such complicated apparatus built in such large quantities. There are 13,000 different pieces of telephone apparatus and 125,000 different kinds of parts are required in their production. These are made at the rate of more than six billion parts in a normal year—and made to such accurate dimensions that any part will fit any similarly designed telephone anywhere.

From a human standpoint, Hawthorne typifies America in that it is truly a great melting pot of the nations. While 80 per cent of the em-

(*Chicago Architectural Photographing Company*)

A night time view of Randolph street, one of Chicago's many amusement centers.

ployees are native born, the other 20 per cent represent close to 60 different nationalities. An employees' club, the Hawthorne Club, carries on an extensive social, athletic, educational and mutual welfare program that gives this widely diversified family a common meeting ground.

Airplane view of Hawthorne plant of Western Electric Company, "the world's telephone workshop."

(Photo by Loubell Studios)

C. L. RICE

Mr. Rice, as vice-president of the Western Electric Company in charge of its Hawthorne Works, heads the largest single manufacturing unit in Illinois, an institution which has a normal working force of 30,000 and a weekly pay-roll of approximately $1,000,000. He was born in Pittsfield, Massachusetts, August 5, 1879, and is the son of Robert Addison and Corinthia (Dunham) Rice. Mr. Rice is president of the Chicago Safety Council, and since 1929 has led this organization in its extensive campaign to reduce accidents in the industries, homes, and on the streets of the city.

His position in Illinois' largest manufacturing industry has made him an active worker in the Illinois Manufacturers' Association. He is a member of the board of directors and the executive committee, and chairman of the civic affairs committee of the Chicago Association of Commerce. He is a member of the Public Affairs Committee of the Union League Club, a member of the Electric Club, a member of the Western Society of Engineers, the La Grange Country Club, and a number of fraternal organizations including Alpha Sigma Phi. He is vice-president of the First National Bank of La Grange, a director of the Cicero State Bank, and president of the La Grange Park District Commission. Mr. Rice holds degrees from Massachusetts Agricultural College and Boston University. Being one of the outstanding authorities on telephone manufacture, he has been in charge of telephone plants both here and in Europe during thirty years of association with the Western Electric Company.

He married Adelaide Crist, of New York City, June 10, 1903, and they have five children, Adelaide (Mrs. Vaughn L. Johannessen), Carolyn, Barbara, Winifred, and Charles L., Jr.

FROM HORSE CAR AND CABLE CAR TO MODERN STREET CAR AND TRACKLESS TROLLEY

Coming Decade to Witness Vast Expansion Program

BY GUY A. RICHARDSON

President, Chicago Surface Lines

IT was not until well into the twentieth century that the horse car faded from the Chicago scene. Its last survivor was an owl car which went tinkling along Wells street, carrying night workers home.

Nor does one have to look far back into Chicago's yesterdays to see the clanking cable car, oil lighted and stove heated, the "gripman" bundled in a fur coat against the icy blasts of winter, a few hardy passengers occupying the open wooden seats of the "grip" car, preferring the fresh if frosty air to the questionable comforts of the trailer.

Back in 1856, in the days of the omnibus, Chicago had a population of 86,000 scattered over eighteen square miles within the city limits, and a few thousand more living in the suburbs. The town was still only a few feet above the lake level, and the roads, with the exception of a few blocks of cobblestone or plank, were unpaved and often muddy. In that year a franchise was granted to Charles B. Philips and Roswel B. Mason for the construction and operation of a horse car line.

Financial depression delayed the project, and in 1858 another franchise was issued to Frank Parmelee, Liberty Bigelow, and Henry Fuller who were to operate a car line, provided that work were commenced by November 1 of that year, and tracks laid on the three projected lines by January 6, 1859. The first spadeful of earth was turned on the former date by Lieut. Gov. William Bross at State and Randolph streets.

The line, however, met with public opposition. In order to retain their franchise, the concessionaires laid tracks in State street between Randolph and Madison, imported two old cars from Troy, N. Y., and ran them back and forth over the two-block right of way.

The Chicago City Railway Company was incorporated in February, 1859, and the first unit of the system was built on the South Side. The "bob-tail" cars were mounted on a single truck. The crew consisted only of the driver. The passenger entered from the rear platform and deposited

THE BANKERS BUILDING
Burnham Brothers, Inc., architects.

(J. D. Toloff Photo, Evanston, Ill.)

GUY A. RICHARDSON

Mr. Richardson, president of the Chicago Surface Lines, was born in Boston, Massachusetts, May 28, 1882, son of Charles Edgar and Edwina Marston (Russell) Richardson. He attended elementary schools and Mechanic Arts High School at Boston. From 1901 to 1904 he was with the Boston Elevated Railway. In 1905 he became identified with Stone & Webster at Calumet, Michigan, and in Seattle, Washington, and for several years did expert work on railways in Chicago, Philadelphia, Rochester, New York, and Brooklyn. During the World War period he was drafted by the United States Shipping Board to assist in the laying out of a transportation system to serve the Hog Island ship yard near Philadelphia. From 1919 to 1923 Mr. Richardson was vice-president, director, and member of the executive committee of the Philadelphia Rapid Transit Company. From 1921 to 1923 he also was a director and member of the executive committee of the International Railway Company of Buffalo, New York.

Mr. Richardson came to Chicago in 1923 as vice-president, general manager, and member of the board of operations of the Chicago Surface Lines, of which he became president in February, 1932. He is a director of the First National Bank and First Union Trust and Savings Bank. He was president of the Union League Club during 1931, and is a member of the Mid-Day, Industrial, Chicago, and Economics clubs. He is president of the American Electric Railway Association; member and past president, Illinois Electric Railways Association; member, Western Society of Engineers, American Institute of Electrical Engineers, and Chicago Association of Commerce; executive committee, Civic Federation of Chicago; and chairman of the committee on surface transportation, A Century of Progress Exposition, Chicago's (1933) World's Fair.

On November 4, 1908, Mr. Richardson married Frances L. Putnam of Mount Sterling, Illinois, and they have two children, Martha and Robert Winsor.

his fare in an inclined slot, which conveyed the coin into a glass-covered box where, falling in, it rang a bell. For the sake of warmth, the floors were strewn with straw. The North Chicago City Railway Company was incorporated in the same year.

In 1861, another company, the Chicago West Division Railway, was chartered to serve the West Side. It began operating two years later, running cars in Madison and Randolph streets from State street to Union Park.

With the North, South, and West sides connected with the business district by rail, steam dummies were used to convey passengers from the south limits at 39th street to 55th street, and on the North Side, from Diversey to Graceland Cemetery along Evanston avenue (Broadway).

During the early '60's, the street railways, without intending to, developed into banks of issue. Small coins were scarce, and passengers began paying their fares in postage stamps. But as this medium of exchange proved unsatisfactory, the operating company issued commutation tickets for ten rides, to be punched by the conductor. Chicagoans eagerly siezed upon these to take the place of currency in other transactions. The tickets, punched or unpunched, found their way into the contribution box at church, or were tendered in liquidation of small debts. Such was their popularity that they were even counterfeited.

The cable car came in the '80's. It had been invented by a San Francisco engineer faced with the problem of getting horse cars up the steep inclines. The cable car speeded up transportation to a maximum of fourteen miles an hour, but it was not until the advent of the trolley that Chicago had anything like an adequate street railway system. Traction history of this period is closely identified with the colorful career of Charles T. Yerkes, Chicago's first real "traction magnate."

Today Chicago street cars transport about 79 per cent of the passengers carried by the three main local transportation systems. The Chicago Surface Lines, one of the largest and best equipped systems in America, comprises 1,107 miles of track and 56 miles of bus routes, and operates 3,864 cars and buses. It has the largest installation of trolley buses in the world.

While the lines are owned by four separate companies, they have been operated as a unit since the "unification" ordinance of 1914 went into effect. The lines carry more than 700,000,000 revenue passengers a year, representing, with transfers, nearly 1,300,000,000 rides. Some 16,000 employees are carried on a pay-roll amounting to $30,000,000 annually.

The average ride for each fare paid is in excess of four miles, and, owing to a liberal transfer system, it is possible to ride 37 miles for a single fare.

In 1930, taking advantage of legislation enacted by the General Assembly, the city council adopted an ordinance providing for the consolidation of the surface and rapid transit systems under one operating company.

The ordinance provides also for the construction of subways in the central business district by the city and their use by the new operating

Augustus Saint-Gaudens' statue of Abraham Lincoln, at the south entrance of Lincoln Park.

corporation. Provision is made further for extensions and improvements amounting within ten years to approximately $200,000,000.

Together with the $100,000,000 which will be spent by the city for subway construction, this will result in the investment of more money for transportation improvement in the coming decade than has been spent heretofore on all local transportation properties.

(*Trowbridge Photo*)
BURNHAM BUILDING
Burnham Brothers, Inc.

JOHN A. RITCHIE

Mr. Ritchie, president of the Chicago Motor Coach Company, president of the Omnibus Corporation, and chairman of the board of directors of the Fifth Avenue Coach Company of New York, was born in Freeport, Illinois, October 8, 1878, and received his education there. His first position was that of clerk in the office of the local freight agent of the Illinois Central. Later he became a clerk to the superintendent of this railroad at Fort Dodge, Iowa. After coming to Chicago, he became chief statistician of the Illinois Central Railroad. He attracted the attention of the late Theodore P. Shonts, who at that time was chairman of the board of directors of the Inter-borough Rapid Transit Company of New York and had holdings in a great many railroads. Mr. Shonts made him his personal statistician and in 1918, Mr. Ritchie, then forty years old, was elected president of the Fifth Avenue Coach Company. The company had been a failure from the first, but in four years under Mr. Ritchie's management, riding increased from 22,000,000 to 60,000,000 passengers a year. An important factor in his success was his public relations policy of unfailing "courtesy and service." A civility campaign inaugurated by him attracted wide attention throughout the nation.

Mr. Ritchie came to Chicago in 1922 at the invitation of John Hertz, then president of the Yellow Cab Company. Mr. Hertz had long dreamed of establishing a great motorbus system which should operate over the city's world-famous boulevards. "I'd have started it before," he exclaimed, "but in order to make it the success I dreamed I wanted to get the services of the best motorbus man in the country. He was John A. Ritchie, who had made such a success in New York."

The new forty-two-story FIELD BUILDING, Chicago's largest office structure. It is the first office structure in Chicago to be air-conditioned, the basements and the first four floors being so equipped. It also is the first local office building to have concealed radiation, and to be equipped with truscon aluminum windows. A modern drinking water system provides a fountain unit for each office, and for the first time in the Loop alternating electric current is provided.

Looking forward to the time of the subway, the Marshall Field Estate, owner of the building, has made provisions to permit an entrance from the subway trains to the basement on the Clark street side. Graham, Anderson, Probst & White, architects.

(Melvin H. Sykes Photo)

WALTER A. ROGERS

Mr. Rogers, president of Bates and Rogers Construction Company, Chicago, was born in Milwaukee, Wisconsin, January 19, 1868, son of Alexander H. and Martha (Ross) Rogers. He received his degree in Civil Engineering at the University of Wisconsin in 1888 with special honors in mathematics. Mr. Rogers entered railway service in the engineering department of the Wisconsin Central, where he remained from 1890 to 1891; until 1892 he was in the engineering department of the Northern Pacific, and until 1901, of the Chicago, Milwaukee & St. Paul (now Chicago, Milwaukee, St. Paul & Pacific Railroad Company). In 1901 he assisted in forming Bates and Rogers Construction Company, of which he has been president since 1904. Bates and Rogers Construction Company, civil engineers and contractors, is a nation-wide institution, serving railroads, public utilities, industrial concerns, governments, cities, et cetera.

Mr. Rogers is a member and past president of the American Railway Bridge & Building Association, member and past president of the Associated General Contractors of America (president, 1920), member of the American Society of Civil Engineers, Western Society of Engineers, and associate member of American Railway Engineering Association. His clubs are the Union League, University, Engineers, Glen Oak Country, Congregational of Chicago, Chicago Golf and University Club, of Madison, Wisconsin.

On July 1, 1891, he married Julia Cushing, of Wauwatosa, Wisconsin, and they have six children, Lester C., Margaret G., Ross W., Carl R., Walter C., and John W.

THE VAST MACHINERY OF SOCIAL SERVICE IN CHICAGO

Where the Neighborliness of Pioneer Days Still Survives

BY EDWARD L. RYERSON, JR.

IN 1832 an early resident wrote from Chicago to a relative in the East, "I already know the complexion of this country. It is a bilious country, with no trees to break the lightning, no hills to soften the thunder, and a wind to blow the hair off your head."

Chicago was built on a malarial swamp, by men and women who knew hardship and adversity. Social service, in those pioneer days, was as simple as it was sincere; a neighborly impulse of help to those in trouble. There was poverty, then as now, but there was no visiting nurse or country doctor to help the first Chicagoans through their many ailments, from the prairie itch to a cholera epidemic. There were no pre-natal clinics and Infant Welfare Societies, no children's homes or child-placing organizations. Orphans— and there were many—were taken in by friends or sent back to relatives in the East. Every neighbor was a visiting nurse, and every mother was a midwife.

It is a far cry from those pioneer days to the present complicated social service machinery of Chicago. Two qualities, however, that characterized the men and women of that young and struggling city have grown with the years and are the underlying motives of all that is being done in social work today: a warm-hearted answer to the cry of helplessness and need, and a tough-hearted defiance of adversity.

As the city grew, periods of growth alternated with periods of calamity. In good times we made great strides in education, building, and individual prosperity. In bad times, the old neighborly impulse of help to the unfortunate reasserted itself, and we perfected our social services. The friendly offices that were at first performed by neighbors for each other were gradually taken over by religious or non-sectarian groups. Relief societies, orphanages, homes for the aged, social settlements and family welfare societies came into existence.

Still the city grew and as the lives of its people became more complex, the cooperative trend in social service gained strength. Each new step was taken as an answer to some calamity. During the panic of 1857, a few scattered relief organizations banded together to form the old Chicago Relief and Aid Society. During the Civil War, that association combined with the Christian Union, the Citizens' Relief Society and the relief branch of the Young Men's Christian Association. The Chicago Fire of 1871 brought $5,000,000 into the city to be distributed by our swiftly growing social agencies. During the panic of 1883 the Charity Organization Society was formed. The black winter of 1895 gave birth to the Bureau of Associated Charities. With the hard times of 1907-8, all these forces joined hands to form the United Charities of Chicago.

(Moffett-Russell Photo)

GEORGE W. ROSSETTER

Mr. Rossetter, president of the Chicago Association of Commerce (1932) and senior member of the firm of George W. Rossetter and Company, certified public accountants, was born in Gilman, Illinois, January 31, 1879, the son of George W. and Mary A. (Flood) Rossetter. Mr. Rossetter represents the tenth generation of his family in America, the family having been established here by Edward Rossetter who came to America from England in 1630 and settled in Windsor, Connecticut. Mr. Rossetter's grandfather, Asher Rossetter, who came to Chicago in the early '40's, was the proprietor of the American House, one of the city's early hotels. Mr. Rossetter began his career as a public accountant here in 1902, and prior to establishing his own company was a partner in the firm of Haskins and Sells.

After attending the second officers' training camp at Fort Sheridan in 1918, he was commissioned as first lieutenant, and went overseas with the 326th machine gun battalion of the 84th division and later transferred to the 144th machine gun battalion of the 36th (Texas and Oklahoma National Guard) division. He is a director of the Chicago Crime Commission, chairman of the National Organization to Reduce Public Expenditures, a director of the Citizens' Association, trustee of Armour Institute of Technology, and a member of the National Economic League. He is also a member of the Sons of the American Revolution, the American Legion, the Forty and Eight, the Veterans' Corps of the 131st Infantry, 33d division, the American Institute of Accountants, the American, Illinois, and Minnesota societies of certified accountants, the Accountants Club of America, the Union League, Economic, Knollwood, Forty, and Exmoor Country clubs, India House, New York, and Beta Alpha Psi. He is an enthusiastic trout fisherman and horseman, and takes a lively interest in government and politics.

Mr. Rossetter was married October 16, 1913, to Marjorie Aylesworth Mihills. The children are George M., William A., and Thomas B.

All this time the cooperative idea had been growing. Catholic and Jewish charities developed centralized leadership. Day nurseries and settlements formed federations. Another idea, too, was taking root in the minds of thoughtful people. Our intricate modern life demanded that neighborliness be trained and informed to answer the needs of a complex age. The young profession of social service was crystalizing standards of education and technique. Schools of social work developed either separately or in connection with our leading universities, and our philosophy of philanthropy broadened to include recreational, educational, protective, preventive and a host of other activities, so that we came at length to think of social service as much more than charity. We began to realize it as embracing every effort that strives to give normal people a fair chance to develop their personalities, or works to improve the environment in which we all live.

While our private social agencies, supported by the gifts of benevolent citizens, were first multiplying and then centralizing their efforts, our public social work, supported by taxes, was compelled to enlarge its program to meet the needs of a swiftly growing city. Our Juvenile Court was born. In 1925 the Cook County Bureau of Public Welfare was created by an act of legislature. Its employees are under the civil service law and its procedure accords with the best social service practices. It is under the control of the County Board of Commissioners, and of an advisory board composed of representatives of our leading public and private social agencies and of our schools of social work. There has always been a fine spirit of team work between our County Bureau of Public Welfare and the voluntary social agencies of this city.

Chicago has grown from a few cabins huddled around a log fort, to the second largest city in the United States. Her social services have grown from the neighborly impulses of those first pioneers, to vast and intricate structure. There are now about 140 child-welfare organizations in Chicago, including homes for children, day nurseries, and societies that place children in family homes. There are at least 200 organizations in the health field, 50 homes for the aged, 45 summer camps, 30 family welfare agencies, 50 community centers and settlements, 25 civic reform associations and 250 parks and playgrounds. In normal times the money spent by our public and private social agencies in their work for the health and happiness of our people is considerably in excess of $30,000,000.

Any business of this size requires an engineering or planning department. In Chicago, this need is met by our Council of Social Agencies, a federation of 206 major social service organizations of the city. This council is controlled by a board of directors selected from its member agencies, representing both public and private social work as well as all creeds and races. It is not a financial federation. Each member agency has, in the past, raised and controlled its own funds.

(*Walinger Photo*)

EUGENE A. RUMMLER

Mr. Rummler, patent lawyer, was born in Kalamazoo, Michigan, April 20, 1872, son of Joseph J. and Jenny R. (Sittig) Rummler. He attended the public and high schools of Detroit and received his B. S. (Bachelor of Science) degree in mechanical engineering at the University of Michigan in 1898. He began as a draftsman in the engineering department of the Detroit Water Works, studying law nights, and was later with the Detroit Dry Dock Company and the Crescent Shipyards, Elizabeth, New York. He has been a member of the firm of Rummler, Rummler and Woodworth, patent attorneys, since 1901. He is one of the original patentees of the "postage meter," which is widely in use throughout America. He is a director of the Haynes Corporation, industrial engineers, and Hasbrouck Haynes, Inc.

Mr. Rummler was president of the Village of Winnetka, Illinois, from 1915 to 1917, chairman of the Winnetka Zoning Commission during 1920 and 1921, and is now chairman of the Winnetka Plan Commission. He is a member of the Patent Law Association, Western Society of Engineers, Society of Industrial Engineers (president, Chicago Chapter, 1923-24; national vice-president, 1925; national treasurer since 1927), also member of the Chicago Association of Commerce, Chicago Regional Planning Association, Art Institute of Chicago, and Field Museum of Natural History. He was chairman of the Court of Honor of the Boy Scouts of Winnetka and was chairman of the congregation of the Winnetka Congregational Church. His clubs are City, and Engineers, and his recreations are gardening, yachting, golf, and motoring.

In June, 1903, Mr. Rummler married Clara J. Wenborne of Buffalo, New York, and their children are Charles W., Rosalia, Frederick S. (died 1928), and Emma.

The economic crisis which began in 1929, however, taxed our social service machinery almost to the breaking point, and joint emergency relief campaigns for private funds were necessary to help finance our private social work, while our public agencies were obliged to ask help from the state legislature and the national Congress. The partial assumption of nation-wide responsibility for unemployment relief by the federal government marked a new step in social service. The policy of Chicago and its neighboring communities in asking and accepting such assistance was quite clearly defined. Public funds, raised by taxes will in the main be used for unemployment relief and disbursed through our public social agencies. Behind these stand our private social agencies, a solid second line of defense. Their chief responsibility will still be to perfect family service, encourage recreational, educational and preventive work, and sustain the morale of Chicago's men, women and children. And back of both public and private social service, inspiring and directing their efforts, is the same old impulse of neighborliness that stirred in the hearts of our earliest pioneers.

VIEW SHOWING THE GLEAMING BEAUTY OF DOWNTOWN CHICAGO
AT NIGHT

(Underwood and Underwood Photo)

EDWARD L. RYERSON, JR.

Mr. Ryerson, president of Joseph T. Ryerson & Son, Inc., was born in Chicago, December 3, 1886, son of Edward Larned and Mary Pringle (Mitchell) Ryerson. He received his preparatory school education at the Hill School, Pottstown, Pennsylvania; he obtained his Ph. D. (Doctor's) degree from the Sheffield Scientific School at Yale University in 1908; and attended the Massachusetts Institute of Technology in 1909. Mr. Ryerson has been identified with the Joseph T. Ryerson & Son, Inc., organization since September, 1909. He is a director of the Northern Trust Company and of the Quaker Oats Company. He is a commissioned captain R. M. A., Air Service of the United States.

In 1930 Mr. Ryerson was appointed vice-chairman of the Governor's Commission on Unemployment and Relief and chairman of the Budget and Relief Committee. In 1931 he became president of the Joint Emergency Relief Fund of Cook County; chairman of the Governor's Commission on Unemployment and Relief; a member of the President's National Advisory Committee on Unemployment and Relief; and chairman of the Illinois Emergency Relief Commission. He is a trustee of the University of Chicago, member of the Corporation of Yale University, president of the Council of Social Agencies of Chicago, secretary of the Sunday Evening Club, a member of the board of the Chicago Community Trust, and a member of the executive committee of the Chicago Plan Commission. Mr. Ryerson's club affiliations are Chicago, University, Commercial, Commonwealth, Saddle and Cycle, and Onwentsia.

Mr. Ryerson married Nora Butler, of Evanston, Illinois, October 6, 1914. Their children are Nora, Edward, and Morton.

CHICAGO—AN ART CENTER

BY C. J. BULLIET

Art Critic, The Chicago Daily News, Author of "*Robert Mantell's Romance*,"
"*Apples and Madonnas*," "*The Courtezan Olympia*," "*Firebrands of Art*."

A T the age of twenty-two, Chicago became "art conscious." It's an infantile age, as cities go, but then the still youthful and lusty squatter on the southern tip of Lake Michigan always was precocious.

It was in 1855 that an Irish carpenter by the name of O'Brien—Martin O'Brien—set aside a corner in his little shop on Lake street near State for the special accommodation of his customers who had been having him frame their pictures, such as they were.

This picture-framing branch of carpentry became so thriving, that, on the very day Fort Sumter fell (April 13, 1861), O'Brien opened on Lake street near his carpenter's shop a new shop devoted exclusively to the making of picture frames and the selling of chromos to be framed, and that was Chicago's first art gallery and the young city's first "art center."

Chicago grew, artists came to town along with the butchers and the bakers, among them G. P. A. Healy, painter of crowned heads of Europe, but also of uncrowned American heads, wherein whirred the brain wheels of industry. Healy was Chicago's first international painting celebrity. Martin O'Brien's shop was his Chicago hang-out.

There were Chicagoans who were getting rich. They began to patronize Healy and other painters, supplanting the chromos on their walls with "hand-painted pictures."

By 1866, "art interest" had so crystallized that there was formed an association of artists and art lovers under the name Chicago Academy of Design. It was primarily a club for the discussion of art topics, but thither came students to see pictures and to copy them. Martin O'Brien inserted in his advertisements a clause: "N. B. Paintings and Chromos rented for the purposes of copying in oil."

In 1871, the great fire destroyed the headquarters of the academy. The club was kept intact, but lay dormant until 1878, when it adopted the title "The Chicago Academy of Fine Arts," chartered the following year at Springfield. George Armour was elected president. In 1882, the name was amended to read "The Art Institute of Chicago," which persists to this day.

Charles L. Hutchinson was chosen presi-

Section of modern decoration by John Norton on the ceiling of the Daily News building concourse.

(*Moffett-Russell Photo*)

JOSEPH T. RYERSON

Mr. Ryerson, treasurer and member of the board of directors of Joseph T. Ryerson &
Son, Inc., was born in Chicago, November 21, 1880, the son of Edward Larned and Mary
Pringle (Mitchell) Ryerson. He was educated at Sheffield Scientific School, Yale University, where he received his Bachelor of Philosophy degree in 1901. After leaving
college he entered the employ of the American Sheet Steel Company (now the American
Sheet and Tin Plate Company of the United States Steel Corporation), Vandergrift, Pennsylvania, but a year later joined the firm of which he is now a director. He served as
vice-president and treasurer from 1916 to 1923, and as president and treasurer from
1923 to 1929. Since 1929 he has been treasurer and a member of the board of directors.

Mr. Ryerson's hobby is collecting "Chicagoana." He built the Chicago room on top
of his residence at 1406 Astor street to house his collection. As a boy he collected World's
Fair tickets at the Exposition of 1893. His Chicago collection contains, in addition to
rare prints, maps, lithographs, etchings, photographs, histories, and early directories, a
complete file of the World's Fair Puck, published from the Puck building on the Exposition grounds. On the shelves of Mr. Ryerson's "Chicago room" will be found also his
grandfather's published account of his arrival here in 1842, his experiences during the
great fire of 1871, and the rebuilding of the city. There are also many first edition and
"association" books by Chicago authors, including Finley Peter Dunn's "Mr. Dooley," and
novels dealing with the Chicago scene, among which are lurid murder mysteries and
"penny dreadfuls." Mr. Ryerson secured his treasures in Europe as well as America.
For the encouragement of Chicago photography he has at times offered a prize at the
Camera Club's international exhibition.

Mr. Ryerson is junior warden of St. James Episcopal church, and is treasurer of the
Girls Latin School of Chicago. He is chairman for 1932-1933 of the Trades and Industrial division of the Emergency Welfare Fund of Cook County; a director of the
Chicago Association of Commerce, the Illinois Chamber of Commerce, and the Personal
Loan and Savings Bank; a trustee of the Museum of Science and Industry, Chicago Historical Society, Art Institute of Chicago, and St. Luke's Hospital. Mr. Ryerson is repre-
Continued on page 549

dent, and held the office until his death in 1924. Associated with him were such men as Mr. Armour, Frank G. Logan, Samuel Nickerson, Edward E. Ayer, Clarence Buckingham, Edward B. Butler, Levi Z. Leiter and, a little later, Martin A. Ryerson.

The Art Institute of Chicago started in rented quarters at the corner of Monroe street and Michigan avenue. It then bought the southwest corner of Michigan avenue and Van Buren street, and, in 1885, erected a building with a brown stone front, four stories high, with class rooms and an exhibition gallery. There was little money left in the treasury after the building was completed. But the association, undismayed, bought $1,800 worth of plaster casts of antique sculpture, with a "sum met by subscriptions, membership dues and an issue of bonds secured on the property."

Dawned 1892 and the activities looking toward the World's Columbian Exposition. In apportionment of the money, President Hutchinson and his associates persuaded the fair officials to allot $200,000 for a permanent picture museum. It was too late to get the galleries ready for the paintings imported for the fair. But the present Art Institute of Chicago on the lake front came into being, and, in its uncompleted state, was used as headquarters for various women's activities in connection with the Fair. The Institute was dedicated as an art museum in December following the close of the exposition. It cost the $200,000 plus $425,000 paid for the corner the association was vacating—bought seven years before for $45,000.

The Art Institute, from its inception in 1866 as the "academy," was the center of all of Chicago's art activities until the Columbian Exposition. The rank-and-file of Chicagoans were not particularly interested, but there was growing up a slowly-widening group of art lovers and of persons interested in art for social reasons. Also, the school operated in connection with the institute began to grow and to become known in an ever-widening circle. But "art" was for the classes instead of the masses.

The Columbian Exposition changed all this. Chicago and the entire West suddenly was galvanized. The directors of the Fair, who were doing everything in a big way, including the Ferris wheel, brought over from Europe a tremendous picture show—the biggest that had ever crossed the Atlantic. "Fine Arts" began to mean something to the man in the street.

Rich people who saw the pictures at the fair were impelled to buy. Commercial establishments sprang up in rivalry with Martin O'Brien's. Native painters began to get commissions, private and public. Lorado Taft, sculptor, and Oliver Dennett Grover and Ralph Clarkson, painters, head the list of Chicagoans who profited almost to this day directly and handsomely from impulses born in the excitement of the Fair.

When time came to send the borrowed pictures back to Europe, the promoters of the new museum pooled their resources. In a gallery named for Mr. Hutchinson was installed a collection of old masters, purchased by President Hutchinson and Vice-president Ryerson with the assistance of

(*Matzene Photo*)

FRED W. SARGENT

Mr. Sargent, president of the Chicago and North Western and the Chicago, St. Paul, Minneapolis and Omaha railways, was born in Akron, Iowa, May 26, 1876, the son of Edgar Wesley and Abbie E. (Haskell) Sargent. He received his LL. B. (Bachelor of Laws) degree from the Iowa State University in 1901 and his LL. D. (Doctor of Laws) from Lawrence College, Appleton, Wisconsin, in 1929. Mr. Sargent began his practice of law at Sioux City, Iowa, in 1901. He was appointed general solicitor of the Chicago & North Western Railway, Chicago, in 1920. From 1923 to June, 1925, when he became president of both railways, he acted as vice-president and general counsel for the Chicago & North Western Railway and the Chicago, St. Paul, Minneapolis & Omaha Railway Company.

Mr. Sargent is a member of the American, Illinois State and Iowa State bar associations; a director of the Continental Illinois National Bank & Trust Company, the Merchandise Bank & Trust Company, the United States Chamber of Commerce, and the Illinois Bell Telephone Company. He is a trustee of Northwestern University, Lake Forest Academy, the Julius Rosenwald Museum of Science and Industry, Field Museum of Natural History, and the Northwestern Mutual Life Insurance Company. He is also general chairman of the Committee on Public Expenditures for the City of Chicago. His club affiliations are the Commercial Club of Chicago, Industrial Club of Chicago, Chicago Club, Union League Club, Old Elm, Glenview (Chicago); Minneapolis Club, Minneapolis, and Minnesota Club, St. Paul, Minnesota; Des Moines Club, Des Moines, Iowa.

Mr. Sargent married Mary Minier, of Flandreau, South Dakota, January 9, 1902. Their children are Minier, Haskell and Fredrica.

the first Marshall Field and Sidney A. Kent. Among these pictures is Rembrandt's "Girl at the Half Open Door," rated now one of the finest of all Rembrandts, and worth ten times the price paid for the whole collection.

Henry Field, Marshall's son, had been collecting the then fashionable Barbizons, and he loaned these pictures, forty-four of them, including Breton's "Song of the Lark," still the best-loved picture in the museum.

(*Frederick O. Bemm Photo*)
A vista through the galleries of the Chicago Galleries Association.

Mrs. Potter Palmer, "advanced" in her art tastes, had sat for the "daring" Zorn for a portrait during his visit to the fair. Mrs. Palmer had been collecting the French "Impressionists," too, partly out of friendship for Mary Cassatt.

These and others gladly hung their pictures on the museum's walls, and the impulse persists, Chicago collectors being known the world over for the generosity with which they share their treasures with the people.

The Art Institute continued on as the center of Chicago's art interest, its collections growing and its school increasing in size until it became the largest art school, in the number of students, in the world. There were numerous small activities outside the institute, but it was not until the advent of "Modernism" that any important rivalry grew up.

"Modernism" came in 1913 with the so-called "Armory Show," housed in New York in one of the city's numerous armories, soon to be the scene of sterner activities. The "Armory Show," with its rebel painting and sculpture, excited outcries here, as in New York and Paris, against "acade-

PAUL SCHULZE

Mr. Schulze, patron of the arts and president of Paul Schulze Biscuit Company, was born in Osterode, at the foot of Harz Mountains, Germany, June 13, 1864, son of Gustav and Henrietta (Roeper) Schulze. He attended the high school at Osterode and came to the United States in 1883, becoming a clerk in a store in Big Stone City, South Dakota. In 1887 he was with a wholesale hardware house in Minneapolis, and from that year until 1891, was a bookkeeper for a wholesale flour house in St. Paul. In 1891 he came to Chicago as a representative of the Washburn-Crosby Company of Minneapolis, which he represented until 1902. In 1893 Mr. Schulze organized, and became president of the Schulze Baking Company, and in the same year he became a naturalized citizen.

Under Mr. Schulze's leadership of twenty-eight years, the Schulze Baking Company became one of the largest in the United States, covering nine cities. In 1921 he sold out his interests in the baking company and acquired the business of F. Westerman and Company, operating under the name of Quaker Biscuit Works and the McMahon Biscuit Company, in the cracker biscuit business, which he incorporated in 1924 as the Paul Schulze Biscuit Company of which he is president. This company manufactures crackers, cookies, and biscuits, and has branches in Des Moines, Iowa; Hastings, Nebraska; Decatur and Rockford, Illinois; Milwaukee, Wisconsin; and South Bend, Indiana.

Mr. Schulze, who is interested in art, has been president of the Municipal Art League of Chicago since 1929. He is vice-president of the Association of Arts and Industries, treasurer of the Chicago Galleries Association, and governing member of the Art Institute of Chicago. In memory of their son, Walter, who died in the American Air Service in 1918, Mr. and Mrs. Paul Schulze founded, in 1924, the Walter H. Schulze Gallery of American Paintings in the Institute. He is a member of the Field Museum of Natural History, Chicago Historical Society, and Illinois Historical Society. He was vice-president, a member of the advisory board and is now treasurer of the Illinois Manufacturers' Association. For more than twenty-five years Mr. Schulze has been a trustee of the Concordia Normal School located at River Forest, Illinois. His clubs are Union League (chairman of the art committee), German, Cliff Dwellers, Arts (director), Palette and Chisel (vice-president), Skokie Country, Army Athletic Association (West Point, New York), and National Arts (New York).

On May 24, 1892, he married Ida Johl of Faribault, Minnesota; children, Walter (killed in World War), Paul, Jr., Helen Louise (Mrs. Edgar F. Burch), and Victor Hugo.

mic art"—and the Art Institute, which harbored the exhibition, became the center of attack from the rebels.

But the war intervened, and the mimic battles of the artists became hopelessly lost in the roar of iron canon in France. It was not until after the Armistice that the art war broke out again.

The first gun in the battle was fired by the Arts Club of Chicago, which had on its walls on Armistice Day itself its first exhibition of "Modernism." Around this exhibition soon were surging all the passions that had lain in abeyance since the "Armory Show."

The Arts Club, headed by a group of rebels in taste, with Mrs. John Alden Carpenter as president and Miss Alice Roulier as head of the exhibition committee, combed Europe for the best in "Modernism," and its shows soon were eclipsing in interest the shows of the Institute, and there was an added furore.

Then, the Chicago "rebels" got together and formed in 1922 the No-Jury Society of Artists. These artists exhibited in their annual shows whatever they chose, without having to submit their work to a jury.

The Art Institute, the Arts Club and the No-Jury Society are still the main focal points of Chicago's art activities.

Nothing else revolutionary developed for a decade, until the summer of 1932, when, for thirteen days in Grant Park, just south of the Art Institute, the artists of Chicago camped on park benches and on the grass and sold their pictures direct to passers-by. It was an innovation inspired by the depression, and was hugely successful financially.

As an art center, Chicago, a century young, is decidedly alive.

An inspiring modern design of forty-nine stories at One North La Salle Street.
K. M. Vitzthum Co., Inc., architects.

(*Moffett-Russell Photo*)

LEO J. SHERIDAN

Mr. Sheridan, president of L. J. Sheridan & Company, specialists in business property developing, renting, building management and financing, was born in Chicago, April 24, 1897, the son of John J. and Mary Ellen (Guhin) Sheridan. After his graduation from Lane Technical High School in 1915, he became associate editor of the Brick and Clay Record, a position which he held until 1918. After returning from the service he went with S. W. Straus & Company, first as assistant to the senior vice-president, then as chairman of the committee in charge of the construction and operation of the Straus Building. In 1927 he was made vice-president and director of S. W. Straus & Company and of the Straus Investment Corporation, in charge of the western real estate and finance division. He resigned in 1929 to organize the company he heads today, which, in addition to its general real estate activities, acts as exclusive agents for the forty-nine-story One La Salle Building, twenty-three-story Builders Building, and the McKinlock Building.

As a second lieutenant in the aviation corps Mr. Sheridan served as an instructor in flying at Fort Worth, Texas, in 1918 and 1919, and he is still actively interested in aviation. He is a member of the Chicago Association of Commerce, the Chicago Real Estate Board, the National Association of Building Owners and Managers, and the Building Managers' Association of Chicago. His clubs are the Union League, Tavern, Briergate Country, and Chicago Athletic Association.

Mr. Sheridan was married, June 26, 1921, to Irene S. Leader of Chicago. The children are Donald Tilden, Irene Mary, Mary Claire, and Catherine Patricia.

NORTHWESTERN UNIVERSITY—ITS IDEALS, TRADITIONS, AND RECORD OF PUBLIC SERVICE

A Pioneer Institution That Has Consistently Contributed to the Welfare of the Community

BY WALTER DILL SCOTT

President, Northwestern University

IT is not what a university has that counts, but what it does. Northwestern University has had no "angel"—no one outstanding benefactor. It has been built up by gifts from thousands of loyal citizens and loyal alumni. Realizing what it means to the community, more than 10,000 people a year make gifts to this institution, and their donations in the last ten years have amounted to $30,000,000.

The standards of admission to Northwestern University are high. Only about a third of those who apply are admitted, and these are recruited largely from the honor rolls of accredited high schools and preparatory schools.

While recognized as a Methodist institution, Northwestern University is by no means denominational. The only religious requirement is that one half the members of its board of 33 trustees be Methodists. Its 8,000 full

Entrance to the Milton H. Wilson campus of Northwestern University in Evanston, showing University Hall at the left and Harris Hall at the right.

President
NORTHWESTERN
UNIVERSITY

WALTER DILL SCOTT

Dr. Scott, president of Northwestern University, was born in Cooksville, Illinois, May 1, 1869, son of James Sterling and Henrietta (Sutton) Scott. He graduated from the Illinois State Normal University in 1891, received his A. B. (Bachelor of Arts) degree from Northwestern University in 1895, graduated from the McCormick Theological Seminary in 1898, and received his Ph. D. (Doctor of Philosophy), from the University of Leipzig in 1900. Dr. Scott has received the honorary degree of LL.D. (Doctor of Laws) from Cornell College, in 1921, and from the University of Southern California, in 1932. He was appointed instructor in psychology and education and director of the psychology laboratory, Northwestern University, in 1900; made professor of psychology and head of the psychology department in the College of Liberal Arts, 1905; became professor of advertising in the School of Commerce, in 1909; appointed professor of applied psychology in the School of Commerce, in 1912. He has also served as special lecturer at Columbia and Chicago universities, and as director of the Bureau of Salesmanship Research of the Carnegie Institute of Technology, 1916-1917.

During the war he served as chairman of the committee on classification of personnel in the United States army. He was awarded the Distinguished Service Medal "for specially meritorious and conspicuous service in originating and putting into operation the system of classification of enlisted personnel now used in the United States Army." He is now a colonel in the United States Reserves. Following the war he founded and was president (1919-1921) of the Scott Company, engineers and consultants in industrial personnel, with offices in Chicago, Philadelphia, and Dayton. He was president of the American Psychological Association in 1919-1920 and was elected president of Northwestern University in 1920. He is a trustee of the Wesley Memorial Hospital and the Presbyterian Theological Seminary of Chicago; vice-chairman of the board of the National Advisory Council on Radio in Education; and a member of the American Council on Education (chairman, 1927), American Psychological Association, Phi Beta Kappa, Delta Mu Delta, Sigma Xi, Phi Delta Kappa, and the American Legion. Some of his club affiliations are University (Chicago, Washington, Evanston), Commercial, Union League, City (Chicago), Glenview Golf, et cetera. He is the author of several volumes; his books dealing with the application of psychology to business are probably the best known. Dr. Scott married Anna Marcy Miller, July 21, 1898. Their children are John Marcy and Sumner Walter.

time students, drawn from nearly every State in the Union, and representing every important country in the world, include approximately 800 Jews and almost the same number of Catholics.

The College of Liberal Arts alone has an enrollment of 2,500. The Schools of Law, Medicine, Dentistry, Engineering, Commerce, Music, Speech, and Education, and the Graduate School account for the remainder of the students. The faculty includes many members who give no class-room instruction, but act as advisors to the undergraduates.

The University has many outside interests. It is concerned with socio-logical research, visiting nurses, infant welfare, heart disease, children's theaters, crime detection, church music, athletics. It maintains a university settlement in one of Chicago's "melting pot" districts.

The subjects taught and problems investigated are designed to relieve human suffering and increase human happiness. The courses are selected for their vocational as well as for their cultural value. They seek to train students for a life of service.

More than eighty years ago, on May 31, 1850, a group of nine Chi-cagoans met in the law office of Grant Goodrich over a harness shop in Lake street to discuss the founding of a university that would fill a definite need in the growing Northwest.

At that time, no academic degree had ever been conferred west of Chicago. Chicago was a city of only 28,000. No railroads had yet reached it from the populous East, and those seeking a higher education journeyed east to Yale or Harvard. But each son who selected an eastern university was costing his family in the neighborhood of $1,000 a year.

Why, these nine men asked, should not this new Northwest have a Yale or Harvard of its own for the education of its sons? Backed by Chicago families, and supported not only by Chicago, but by the entire territory, such an institution of higher learning, they believed, could per-form a service which would be expanded as the city grew.

That day, in the law office over the harness shop in Lake street, the foundation of Northwestern University was laid. The records show that on January 28, 1851, the original charter to "The Northwestern Univers-ity" was granted without debate by the Illinois Legislature, a mere incident in the day's routine. Later it was decided to omit the article and have the institution known merely as Northwestern University.

Dr. John Evans, a physician of striking personality, who had come to Chicago from Indiana, and who took a keen interest in education, acted as chief advisor to the sponsors. He was aided and inspired by the counsel of Orrington Lunt and other outstanding men.

Land was purchased at Jackson and La Salle streets, and it was intended to build a college there. But a more desirable site was found in a clump of woods a few miles north of the city on the lake front. The original down-town property, the present site of the Continental Illinois Bank, is still owned by the University.

(Covington Studio Photo)

SHERMAN J. SEXTON

Mr. Sexton, president of John Sexton and Company, was born in Chicago, September 12, 1892, son of John and Anna Louise (Bartelman) Sexton. He was educated at the De Paul University of Chicago, of which university he is now a member of the Executive Committee of the Board of Trustees. He has been associated since 1911 with the firm of John Sexton and Company, wholesale grocers of Chicago and Brooklyn, which was founded by his father. He has been president of the company since 1926. John Sexton and Company specializes in supplying foods for hotels, restaurants and institutions and through nationwide distribution of quality foods to this exacting clientele has become America's largest distributors of No. 10 canned foods. The number ten can serves twenty-five to thirty portions of food to the can. Mr. Sexton pioneered the sale of frozen foods to large hotels and restaurants, in which field his firm holds an outstanding leadership. The company manufactures a large assortment of foods in its own modernly equipped plant located at Illinois, Orleans and Kingsbury streets. All foods distributed by the company are packed especially for it and in each case are packed in large size containers to meet the needs of those who feed many people each day. The company has never sold retail grocery stores.

Mr. Sexton has also been vice-president of the Great Lakes Transit Corporation of Buffalo, New York, since 1919. This corporation operates a fleet of eighteen express package freighters and three palatial passenger ships, the Octorora, Tionesta and Juniata. Both the passenger and freight ships make all the principal ports of the Great Lakes during the navigation season. He is a member of the Chicago Athletic Association, Knollwood and Edgewater Golf clubs. His favorite recreation is golf. Mr. Sexton has for many years been a member of the Executive Committee of the Catholic Charities of Chicago.

On November 1, 1916, he married Alice Jordan Conners, and they have three children, William C., Alice C., and Shirley Ann.

McKinlock campus from the tower of the Furniture Mart showing Passavant hospital at the left, and from left to right the Montgomery Ward memorial building housing the schools of medicine and dentistry, Wieboldt hall, the school of commerce, Levy Mayer hall, the school of law, and the Elbert H. Gary library of law.

Dr. Evans helped to finance payment for an option on a tract of 379 acres. It was agreed to clear the land adjacent to Lake Michigan, erect a building on a suitable spot, lay out streets, and create a village. The village was given the name of Evanston in honor of Dr. Evans, who was the first president of the University's board of trustees. Similarly, the streets of the village were named from early faculty members and trustees. A tract of 70 acres was set aside for a campus. Some of the primeval oaks that stood there when the land was cleared were spared, and are still standing. Gradually the University's holdings were increased to 700 acres. This was subdivided and sold year by year to Chicagoans who wished to make Evanston their home. Space was arranged for parks and public school sites, and land was offered free to churches that would build there. The campus reservation was expanded to 140 acres.

It was not until five years after that first meeting over the harness shop that, on November 5, 1855, ten hardy students pushed their way over the muddy roads of the frontier city of Chicago and arrived in Evanston to enroll in the new university. They sought out a rather pretentious frame

(Laveccha Studio Photo)

WILLIAM JONES SMITH

Mr. Smith, member of the architectural firm of Childs and Smith, was born in Philadel-phia, Pennsylvania, May 26, 1881, son of Uselma Clarke Smith and Fannie (Mitcheson) Smith, of Scotch and English descent. He received his A. B. degree at Central High School of Philadelphia; B. S. (Bachelor of Science) in Architecture at the University of Pennsylvania in 1903; and A. D. G. (Architecte Diplomé par le Gouvérnement Français) at the École des Beaux Arts, Paris, 1907.

Mr. Smith started his architectural career with Cass Gilbert of New York in 1907. In 1909 he came to Chicago and joined Holabird and Roche where he remained until 1912, and since that year has been a member of the firm of Childs and Smith. He is in partnership with Frank A. Childs and O. H. Breidert. He was associate professor in charge of senior design at Armour Institute of Technology from 1924 to 1929. Childs and Smith are architects for many buildings in Chicago, as well as in other cities through-out the country. Some of them are: State Bank and Trust Company of Evanston; First National Bank & Trust Company, Hamilton, Ohio; First National Bank, Davenport, Iowa; Hardware Mutual Insurance Building, Stevens Point, Wisconsin; Central Manu-facturers Insurance Building, Van Wert, Ohio; American Bankers Insurance Building and 1448 Lake Shore Drive Apartment Building, Chicago; associate architects of Mc-Kinlock Campus Buildings, Northwestern University. Mr. Smith served as captain in the 319th Engineers, United States Army, and was instructor in engineering of infantry officers, and regimental instructor in French during 1917 and 1918. He is a member of the Plan Commission of Winnetka; member of the committee of the Burnham Library of Architecture; member of the American Institute of Architects (allied arts committee; vice-president, Chicago Chapter, 1932); member of the Art Institute of Chicago and the Architectural Guild of the Episcopal Diocese of Chicago. His clubs are Union League, Cliff Dwellers, and The Little Room (Chicago). His recreations are golf, crafts-manship, and reading.

On June 30, 1914, he married Mary Van Horne of Zanesville, Ohio. Their children are William Mitcheson, Van Horne, and Sidney Stockton.

building of three stories at Hinman avenue and Davis streets, and took up their studies without further ceremony.

That building, removed from its original site, but still cherished, is known today as "Old College," and houses the School of Education. It is here, annually in May, that the big purple candle is lighted and allowed to burn for fifteen minutes, while graduates in all parts of the world hold reunions, light smaller candles, intone the ritual for which Bishop Stewart wrote the inspiring words, and sing "Quaecumque sunt vera."

The institution which had such a modest beginning has grown until today it ranks as one of the outstanding educational centers of the country. Its financial resources are close to $50,000,000 and the enrollment has increased from that original ten to 16,000 full time or special students, with a faculty of more than 1,000.

Northwestern University was created to fill a very definite niche in the West and Northwest and there have been among its faculty and students men and women of renown. Northwestern has turned out men who have become presidents of other universities, who have become governors of various States and who have gone to both houses of Congress.

The University soon outgrew its single building. In 1868, University Hall was completed. It is a picturesque old building, ivy covered and ornamented with a high clock tower.

Other buildings followed rapidly. Today the Evanston campus extends for almost a mile along the shore of Lake Michigan. On this campus are the College of Liberal Arts, the Graduate School, the School of Speech, the School of Commerce, the School of Engineering, the School of Music, the School of Journalism and the School of Education. Over to the north is Dyche Stadium, inclosing one of the finest athletic fields in America.

Plans for the future development of this campus call for an expenditure of 100 million dollars in the next fifty years. These plans include a group of new science buildings, a new building for the School of Education, a Women's building, a new building and theater for the School of Speech, a Gothic chapel, a library and a new building for the School of Music.

Work on the first unit in this development project was started when ground was broken for the new $1,250,000 Deering Memorial Library, the gift of the family of the late Charles Deering, formerly chairman of the board of the International Harvester Company and a lifelong friend of the University.

The plans also call for the extension of the Evanston campus a quarter of a mile or a half mile out into Lake Michigan. East of the campus probably will be a lagoon and east of the lagoon a public park, a landing field for airplanes and a boulevard.

The Board of Trustees recently named the Evanston campus in honor of two of Northwestern's principal benefactors. The south part, extending as far north as Willard place, is now known as the Milton H. Wilson

HARRY W. SOLOMON

Harry W. Solomon is president of Transcontinental Hotels, Inc.; vice-president in charge of property service and hotel operations for S. W. Straus & Co.; member of Cook County Assessor's advisory committee on personal property taxes for Chicago hotels and apartment houses; vice-president of Milwaukee Terminal Co.; secretary of Manor Realty Co., and vice-president of Pere Marquette Building Corporation, New Orleans. He is an officer and member of numerous bondholder's committees. He was born in 1893. Mr. Solomon has been called "America's Greatest Host." Under his supervision stretches a vast domain of office building skyscrapers, hotels and apartment house properties extending all the way from the Great Lakes region to the Gulf of Mexico and westward up and down the Pacific coast. In Chicago some of these properties include the Straus Building, the Medical and Dental Arts and Old Dearborn Bank buildings, the Belmont, Lake Shore Drive, Sovereign, Allerton, Sherry, Plaisance, Southmoor, and many other hotels. Similar properties are located in Cincinnati, Dallas, Los Angeles, San Francisco, Detroit, Cleveland, and elsewhere throughout the United States.

Regarded as one of America's foremost authorities on building and hotel operations, Mr. Solomon is essentially an operator and not a banker. He devised the widely heralded system of centralized control by which nineteen hotels in the Chicago area alone under his command saved more than half a million dollars in operating expenses in less than two years' time, and this in the face of adverse conditions. An intense student of hotel operations and management, Mr. Solomon spent more than sixteen years learning the details of this business from actual construction work on up to management and reorganization of properties, effecting sensational economies and increasing revenues on the basis of efficiency alone. It is said of him that he is as equally at home among the footings of a new project as he is in the penthouse of a de luxe hotel or apartment dwelling of which he has built scores.

He is married and has two children, Lawrence and Shirley. His hobbies are golf, boxing and aviation.

Campus; and the section north of the Garrett Biblical Institute to Lincoln street, where are situated Patten Gymnasium, the Dearborn Observatory, and the men's dormitories, is designated as the James A. Patten Campus.

University hall on the Milton H. Wilson campus of Northwestern University in Evanston.

The Dearborn Observatory on the James A. Patten campus of Northwestern University.

On the Alexander McKinlock Memorial Campus in Chicago, at Lake Shore drive and East Chicago avenue, are the professional schools of the University: the Medical School, the Dental School, the School of Law, and the downtown divisions of the School of Commerce and the Medill School of Journalism.

As far back as 1913, plans were being discussed for the consolidation of all the professional schools of the University on a single downtown campus on the near north side. In 1915, a preliminary draft was drawn by the committee on endowment in which the purchase of the tract at Lake Shore drive and Chicago avenue was strongly advised. Two years later an option on the site was obtained.

William A. Dyche, business manager of the University, was doing valiant service persuading the trustees of the University that the site should be purchased, and interesting particularly the late Milton H. Wilson, without whose generosity the project never could have been carried out.

Finally, on June 15, 1920, the Trustees voted to purchase the nine-acre tract for $1,420,260. A year later, announcement was made of the receipt of a gift of $250,000 from Mr. and Mrs. George A. McKinlock in memory of their son who had lost his life in the World War, and by order of the Trustees the new Chicago campus was named in his honor.

ALBERT A. SPRAGUE

Col. Sprague, wholesale grocer and commissioner of public works, was born in Chicago, May 13, 1876, the son of Otho Sylvester Arnold and Lucia Elvira (Atwood) Sprague. After attending the Chicago public schools he entered St. Paul's School, Concord, New Hampshire, and from there went to Harvard University, where he received his Bachelor of Arts degree in 1898. Returning to Chicago, he entered the wholesale grocery firm of Sprague, Warner & Company, of which firm he is now a director, having served also as president and chairman of the board.

Col. Sprague was chairman of the Chicago chapter of the American Red Cross at the time of America's entry into the World War, but he resigned this position to attend the Officers' Training Camp at Fort Sheridan. He received his commission as major in the infantry, was assigned to the 341st regiment, 86th division, and detailed to headquarters. He was intelligence officer of the 86th division at Camp Grant, also commanding officer of the 2d batallion, 341st infantry at Camp Grant and in France. He sailed for France in July, 1918, and two days before the signing of the Armistice was advanced to the rank of lieutenant-colonel. He returned to the United States in March, 1919, was honorably discharged a few days later and is now a colonel in the Officers' Reserve Corps.

Col. Sprague entered public life in 1923, when he was appointed commissioner of public works by the late Mayor Dever. He was again appointed to this position in 1931 by Mayor Cermak. In 1924 he was the Democratic candidate for the United States Senate. His interest in Chicago's cultural and philanthropic enterprises is reflected in the many trusteeships he holds. He is a trustee of Field Museum of Natural History, the John Crerar Library, the Children's Memorial Hospital, Rush Medical College, the Chicago Symphony Orchestra, the Shedd Aquarium, the Museum of Science and Industry, and the Sprague Memorial Institute. He was recently elected a member of the board of overseers of Harvard University. He serves as vice-chairman of the Chicago Plan Commission. Col. Sprague is also a director of the Continental Illinois National Bank & Trust Company of Chicago, the Chicago & North Western Railway, the Calumet & Arizona Mining Company, and the B. F. Goodrich Company. He is a member of the University, City, Mid-Day, Commercial, Saddle and Cycle, Onwentsia, and Old Elm clubs.

He was married June 22, 1901, to Frances Fidelia Dibble of Rye Beach, New Hampshire. The children are Albert Arnold, Jr., Laura, and Otho S. A.

In 1923, Mrs. Elizabeth J. Ward gave the University $1,000,000 augmented by the sum of $3,000,000 in January, 1924, to be used for the erection of a building as a memorial to her husband, the late A. Montgomery Ward. The building was to house the laboratories and clinics of the Medical and Dental Schools. In March, 1926, Mrs. Ward added another $4,000,000 to her original gift, the income from which was to be used for scholarships, research and increased instructional facilities.

Mrs. Ward visioned a great medical center in the heart of Chicago on the McKinlock campus. In making her gift, she stressed the service the University is rendering.

Last year the Medical School in its clinics gave treatment to more than 100,000 persons and the Dental School performed more than 100,000 operations. This same ideal of service extends throughout the University, as is evidenced by the fact that the legal aid bureau of the School of Law last year gave legal aid to more than 8,000 persons, the speech clinic in the School of Speech treated 550 persons afflicted with defects in speech, and the psychological clinic extended its service to approximately 300.

Since the completion of the Montgomery Ward Memorial building, Passavant hospital has been built on the McKinlock campus and the Wesley Memorial hospital has drawn up plans for the construction of a $5,000,000 building there. Proposed plans for the campus also include a maternity hospital, a children's hospital and a general university hospital. When all of these buildings will have been completed, the McKinlock campus will be one of the world's greatest medical centers.

Other buildings on the McKinlock campus are the Levy Mayer Hall of Law, home of the School of Law, the gift of Mrs. Levy Mayer; the Elbert H. Gary Library of Law, the gift of the late Judge Elbert H. Gary; the Wieboldt Hall, home of the School of Commerce and the School of Journalism, made possible by a gift of $625,000 from the Wieboldt Foundation.

Mere size is not an evidence of success and size alone does not justify itself. Yet in the case of Northwestern University the material growth that has been witnessed has gone hand in hand with the spiritual growth. Increased facilities have led to increasing service, have justified increased vision and have focused recognition upon the real worth of our endeavors.

This growth in the intangible means for the accomplishment of magnificent purposes has been made possible by the donations of those who have been profoundly convinced that the spirit of service, the high ideals and the adequacy of administration were sufficient to the task imposed.

A metropolitan university such as Northwestern is not a cloistered institution. It takes itself seriously and tries to contribute to the welfare of the community. Northwestern University today is making distinct contributions to the welfare of this community, through its clinics, the research of distinguished scholars, and other agencies; and the Northwestern Uni-

(Moffett-Russell Photo)

DR. BENJAMIN M. SQUIRES

Dr. Squires, arbitrator, was born in Neptune, Richland county, Wisconsin, October 12, 1889, son of Mark Abraham and Mary Angeline (Page) Squires. He obtained his preparatory education in the public schools, then his B. A. (Bachelor of Arts) and M. A. (Master of Arts) degrees from the University of Wisconsin and his Ph.D. (Doctor of Philosophy) degree from Columbia University. He studied medicine in Germany. Dr. Squires was special agent, United States Bureau of Labor Statistics, 1914 to 1916; commissioner of conciliation, United States Department of Labor, 1916 to 1920; member, Alaskan Board of Mediation and Arbitration, 1916; administrative member and chairman, New York Harbor Wage Adjustment Board, 1917 to 1918; executive secretary, National Adjustment Commission, 1919 to 1920; and statistician and assistant, Employers' European Commission appointed by U. S. Department of Labor, 1919. He lectured on industrial relations, Columbia University, 1919; was investigator for the United States Coal Commission, 1923; lectured on political economy, University of Chicago, 1924 to 1929; and has been impartial chairman for the Cleaning and Dyeing Industry of Chicago, since 1930.

He is chairman of the Trade Board; chairman, Board of Arbitration, and chairman, Unemployment Insurance Fund, Chicago Men's Clothing Industry; professorial lecturer, Department of Economics, University of Chicago; chairman, General Advisory Board, Illinois Department of Labor; and executive secretary of Governor Emmerson's Unemployment Commission during 1930. Dr. Squires is a member of the Cosmos Club, Washington, D. C.; a director, Chicago City Club; member, Quadrangle Club; life member of the Press Club, and chairman, Committee on Industry and Trade, Social Science Research Council.

On March 26, 1924, he married Margaret J. Regan of Chicago, and they have four children, Benjamin Mark, Mark Page, Mary Page, and Barbara Joan.

versity of tomorrow will strive to make these contributions even greater and more significant through its faculty, its graduates, its progress in the methods of instruction, and its increased physical equipment.

(*Fairchild Aerial Surveys, Inc.*)

DYCHE STADIUM AS SEEN FROM THE AIR

(*Blank & Stoller, Inc., Photo*)

EUGENE M. STEVENS

Mr. Stevens, chairman of the Federal Reserve Bank of Chicago, was born in Preston, Minnesota, February 1, 1871, the son of Andrew J. and Clara Morgan (Bentley) Stevens. He received his education in the public schools. From 1887 to 1891 Mr. Stevens was with the Winona (Minn.) Wagon Company. He was in the employ of F. H. Peavey & Company, Minneapolis (grain merchants), 1891 to 1901, and organized Stevens, Chapman & Company (investment bankers), also of Minneapolis, which continued from 1901 to 1917. Mr. Stevens became vice-president of the Illinois Trust & Savings Bank of Chicago in 1917, which later merged with other banks under the name of the Illinois Merchants Trust Company, and became president of the latter institution in 1927. After the merger in 1929 with the Continental National Bank and Trust Company, he was president of the new organization, the Continental Illinois Bank and Trust Company, until November, 1930. He was appointed Class C director and chairman and Federal Reserve agent of the Federal Reserve Bank of Chicago, January 1, 1931. Mr. Stevens is also director of the Diamond Match Company since 1924; of the Texas Corporation since 1928; and of Wilson & Company, Inc., since 1926.

He is a trustee of the University of Chicago and is president of The John Crerar Library, Chicago. He was a member of the executive committee of Liberty Loan campaigns of the Chicago Federal Reserve District. His club affiliations are Chicago, Commercial, The Attic, Bankers, Glenview Country, and Old Elm.

In 1899 Mr. Stevens married Mary Frances Rolfe of Stacyville, Iowa. Their children are Eugene M. and Charles Rolfe.

CHICAGO'S LEADERSHIP IN OIL REFINING
Converting Millions of Barrels of Oil Into Commercially Important Products

BY KEITH FANSHIER
Petroleum Editor, Chicago Journal of Commerce

FEW think of Chicago as an "oil town." Applied to this city of millions of inhabitants, the words seem incongruous—reminiscent of gushers, mushroom oil camp communities, easy money, booming growth and as sudden decay. Yet the fact is, Chicago is an oil town. More, it is the biggest oil town in the world.

Chicago, unknown to most of its residents and most outsiders, is the world's greatest oil market—meaning the greatest market for refined petroleum products. More oil is sold in, from and through Chicago than any other point on earth.

The oil industry was built on the enterprise of the individual, the producer, seeking the oil. Today the important part played by Chicago reveals a reversal of trend. The oil is seeking the individual, the consumer. Around the southern tip of Lake Michigan has been built up an industrial entity that acts as a magnet, drawing millions of barrels of crude and refined petroleum annually by pipe line, by rail, by waterway, by highway, toward this great central market from the producing districts.

Not only is Chicago the strategically important market and sales center, but the Chicago region is the seat of one of the World's leading refining districts. Located as the hub of a great circle of oil producing fields, yet

Chicagoland's greatest refinery—an airplane view of the Standard Oil refinery at Whiting, Indiana, one of the largest complete refineries in the world, if not the largest. The process of cracking oil originated here.

(Blank & Stoller, Inc., Photo)

EDWARD G. SEUBERT

Mr. Seubert, president of the Standard Oil Company of Indiana, was born in Syracuse, New York, June 20, 1876, the son of Nicholas and Johanna (Neumeister) Seubert. He was educated in the Syracuse high school, and as a boy not yet sixteen, was given employ- ment as a mechanic's helper at the Whiting refinery of the Standard Oil Company of Indiana, which had been organized only two years previously. Mr. Seubert advanced steadily to positions of greater and greater responsibility, chiefly in the accounting division. He served as auditor from 1911 to 1919, as assistant secretary and assistant treasurer from March to November, 1919, and was elected to the directorate in that year, when he was advanced also to the position of secretary and treasurer.

From 1920 to 1927 he held office as vice-president, and in 1927 was elected president. On the elimination in 1929 of the position of chairman of the board, he became chief executive of the company. As an officer and director Mr. Seubert has played a major role in the development and growth of the Indiana company. Some of the most vital steps in its expansion have been made under his administration, with resulting increase in the strength of the company's position as one of the leading units in the oil industry.

Mr. Seubert is a member of the Union League, Old Elm, South Shore Country, and Flossmoor Country clubs.

crowded by none, Chicago is destined to become an oil refining center second to none. Already its refining capacity is measured in terms of hundreds of thousands of barrels daily. The dozen or more plants in the immediate vicinity of the city rank among the best, most efficient, and most complete refineries in the world. In these refineries in and around Chicago are manu-factured hundreds of separate products, ranging from high grade, volatile gasolines to the finest of table candles; from heavy, viscous fuel oils for industrial use to bland toilet, cosmetic and medicinal preparations.

The fields of petroleum utilization are enormous. The world demands petroleum derivatives. Deprived of them, our present-day civilization would totter. Probably no raw material is as essential to our well-being as petro-leum. On the farm, in industry, in the sick room, in the beauty parlor, in the home, on the high seas and below them, in the jungle, on the desert and in the air, this strange, mysterious substance plays its ever-increasing part. And forced to the utmost, the Chicago refining community could take care of a large share of the country's requirements.

Great, integrated corporations in and around Chicago and the central region generally have built upon petroleum far-flung industrial empires ex-tending throughout the nation and abroad. Thousands of independent dis-tributors keep in touch with developments here, in serving their trade. Hundreds of thousands of retail outlets make Chicago's petroleum products available to all.

The future may well be amazing, judged by our present knowledge and our standards. Packed away within a single one of all the billions of droplets of oil finding their way into the Chicago district are elements which may well go far toward shaping the destiny of the nation and the world. Man knows comparatively little about the make-up and the possi-bilities of petroleum, even now. But it is known that vast fields of un-touched utilization lie open, when man knows enough about this material to harness and develop it. Toward this end, large numbers of petroleum technologists are working today.

Petroleum will write its own history and carry along with it to logical destiny whatever is intimately associated with it, as is the Chicago region. As an industry it has well substantiated its ability to withstand adverse economic conditions. The little service station around the corner stands as a symbol of a force that will go far toward determining what is to come, just as it has influenced what has happened in the past. Chicago will have an important place in that picture.

(*Moffett-Russell Photo*)

AMOS ALONZO STAGG

Mr. Stagg, athletic director and football coach at the University of Chicago, was born in West Orange, New Jersey, August 16, 1862, the son of Amos Lindsley and Eunice (Pierson) Stagg. He attended Yale University where he was one of their greatest athletes; received his A.B. (Bachelor of Arts) degree in 1888. In 1891 he graduated from the International Y. M. C. A. College at Springfield, Massachusetts, which school conferred on him the honorary degree of Master of Physical Education, in 1912. He received the honorary degree of Master of Arts from Oberlin College, in 1923. Summers, during 1889, 1890 and 1891, he was director of athletics of the Northfield (Massachusetts) Students' Conference and the Lake Geneva (Wisconsin) Students' Conference. Mr. Stagg, as a member of the original faculty, became associate professor and director of the department of physical culture and athletics of the University of Chicago, 1892. He was made professor in 1900. Mr. Stagg holds an acknowledged position as one of the cleverest and most resourceful of coaches. He has made many contributions to the technique of football and as senior member of the Football Rules Committee he has had an important influence in shaping the development of the game. In 1931 his alma mater sent its football team west for the first time in history to play Mr. Stagg's fortieth Chicago team, in recognition of the fact that his "significant service to the best interests of college athletics is national rather than local in its influence."

Mr. Stagg represented the University of Chicago at the Inter-Collegiate Conference of Faculty Representatives, 1896 to 1911. He has been a member of the Football Rules Committee since 1904; member of the American Committee of the Olympic Games at Athens, 1906, London, 1908, Stockholm, 1912, Antwerp, 1920, Paris, 1924, and Amsterdam, 1928. He was coach of the middle distance runners of the American Olympic team, Paris, 1924. He was president of the Society of Directors of Physical Education in Colleges in 1911 and 1912 and of the Western Alumni Association of Phillips Exeter Academy, in 1924. He was presidential elector for the Progressive Party in 1912. Mr. Stagg is athletic adviser for the Order of De Molay. He is a fellow of the American Physical Education Society and a member of Sons of the American Revolution, National

Continued on page 549

CHICAGO COMPLETES GREAT CIVIC IMPROVEMENTS
Developments Which Have Added to the City's Commercial and Recreational Facilities

BY JAMES SIMPSON
Chairman, Chicago Plan Commission

FIFTY or seventy-five years ago no one, not even a prophet, could have foreseen Chicago's destiny. But in 1907, the city was growing so rapidly that it was apparent that some guidance was needed. City planning was a new idea in those days, but its value was so well understood in Chicago that the Commercial Club decided to draw up a comprehensive city-wide plan for future development.

Accordingly, in 1908, a Plan of Chicago was published and submitted to the city with the recommendation that a commission be appointed to study it and advise as to its execution. Thus the Chicago Plan Commission came into existence, but as a purely advisory branch of the city government. It was vested with no executive authority. The Chicago Plan was then, as now, merely an influence. It has been called "one of the city's most splendid conceptions since the World's Fair," of 1893.

To unimaginative people, the plan at first seemed visionary, Utopian. A "Chicago beautiful" was an excellent thing, they agreed, but hardly practical. It was a pretty picture, an artist's dream.

Yet the character of the Commission was such as to inspire public confidence. The men who composed its membership were practical citizens, the kind who have the ability to make dreams come true. If Chicago had to be taken apart and reassembled; if entire square miles of buildings must be razed to make room for new streets; if land had to be reclaimed from Lake Michigan; if the river had to be unkinked, well, why not? The difficulties were by no means insurmountable. Legal proceedings, pickaxes, steamshovels, and cement mixers could toss them aside.

The most urgent problem was the reclamation of the waterfronts, lake and river, and their conversion into esplanades and parkways. The next in importance was the acquisition, before land prices became prohibitive, of the forested areas on the city's outskirts. A third problem was one of street widening and extension; of providing adequate connections between the central business district and outlying sections, and of connecting these various sections. A fourth problem was that of unifying Chicago's railroad terminals.

Many of these colossal projects have been carried out and others are in more or less advanced stages of construction. A former Chicagoan who had not visited the city since 1910 would hardly recognize it. He would see the Loop no longer strangled by the elevated railroad structure, but extending from Canal street to the lake, and from Roosevelt road to Chicago avenue. He would see a new "front yard" east of the Illinois Central right of way, extending for miles along the lake. The Field Museum, the vast

Chairman
CHICAGO PLAN COMMISSION

(Blank & Stoller, Inc., Photo)

JAMES SIMPSON

Mr. Simpson, chairman of the Chicago Plan Commission and chairman of the Commonwealth Edison Company, The Peoples Gas Light and Coke Company, and the Public Service Company of Northern Illinois, was born in Glasgow, Scotland, January 26, 1874, the son of William and Isabella (Brechin) Simpson. He was brought to Chicago by his parents in 1880. After attending the public schools and a business college, he secured his first job—a clerkship in the cashier's office of Marshall Field & Company. This was in 1891. Within a year he had been picked by Mr. Field for his personal staff, and it was later, as confidential secretary to Mr. Field, that he received the training which was to carry him to the head of the great organization. On the death of Mr. Field in 1906 he was made second vice-president and assistant to the president, and in 1917 was elevated to the first vice-presidency. He became president of Marshall Field & Company in 1923, and was later chairman of the board, resigning in 1932 to head the public utility companies. It was during his regime as president of Marshall Field's that the store for men was built and the huge Merchandise Mart, the world's largest commercial building, was completed.

It is as chairman of the Chicago Plan Commission that Mr. Simpson has contributed most signally to the city's betterment. Under his leadership such projects as the Wacker Drive improvement, the Outer Drive extensions, and the straightening of the Chicago River have been carried out. During the World War he was a director of the Chicago chapter of the American Red Cross. In 1918 he went to France to assist in the Red Cross work overseas. He was also a member of the Capital Issues committee and civilian aide to the secretary of war for the 6th Corps Area. As his private responsibilities have increased, his civic and philanthropic cares have multiplied. He is a director of Rush Medical College, the Children's Memorial Hospital, and the Scottish Old People's Home; treasurer of the Chicago Fresh Air Hospital; and a trustee of Field Museum of Natural History, the Sunday Evening Club, and the Otho S. A. Sprague Institute. To Field Museum he gave the Simpson Theater, and Simpson Hall is named in his honor.

Continued on page 549

amphitheater of Soldier Field, the Shedd Aquarium, the Adler Planetarium, the Aladdin city of the Century of Progress Exposition stand where the waters used to roll. He would see a double-decked esplanade, Wacker drive, extending along the river front where the noisome and congested South Water street market once stood. He would see Michigan avenue, today one of the world's show streets, spanning the river and sweeping on northward through an entirely new commercial district. He would see the new Union Station and the new postoffice. A new "La Salle avenue." A new "South Parkway." A new Ogden avenue. A new outer drive, continuous from Jackson Park to Evanston, with the exception of the new bridge at the mouth of the river, which is now (1932) under construction but temporarily halted due to lack of funds. Visiting the outskirts of the city, he could drive through miles of woodland whose natural beauties have been assured to Chicago for all time because of the vision embodied in the great Plan of Chicago.

Today no inland city has a more beautiful waterfront than Chicago. The outer drive, now virtually twenty-five miles in length, will eventually be carried from the Indiana state line to Milwaukee. Burnham Park, connecting Grant and Jackson parks, provides a recreation ground six miles in

length, containing 1,139 acres and 343 acres of inclosed waters, bathing beaches and lagoons. Lincoln Park has been steadily advancing along the lake front, offering unrivaled facilities for tennis, golf, trap shooting, riding, swimming, and yachting; and new park lands equal in area to those along the southern shore of the lake.

The produce market, for many years an eyesore, cluttered up as it was with tumble-down buildings, and choked with trucks and wagons, has been removed to a new and more convenient site on the West Side, and replaced by a boulevard as splendid as any to be found in Paris. Wacker drive, already a mile and a quarter in length, named in honor of Charles H. Wacker, for seventeen years chairman of the Chicago Plan Commission, lined with impressive skyscrapers, and carrying traffic on two levels, is to be extended eastward to the lake and southward into the south side railway terminal area.

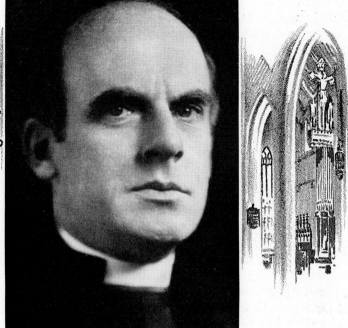

(*Moffett-Russell Photo*)

THE RT. REV. GEORGE CRAIG STEWART

Bishop Stewart, head of the Episcopal Diocese of Chicago, was born in Saginaw, Michigan, August 18, 1879, the son of George Forbes and Katharine (Craig) Stewart. He was graduated from the Evanston Academy in 1898, entered Northwestern University, and received his Bachelor of Arts degree in 1902. While still an undergraduate he was ordained to the Methodist ministry, and from 1897 to 1900 was pastor at the Calumet Heights Church. He was graduated from the Western Theological Seminary in 1903, and experiencing a change in faith, became a deacon and priest of the Protestant Episcopal Church. After serving for one year as rector of the Glencoe church, he came to St. Luke's, Evanston, at that time a comparatively small congregation, numbering only 200, and with property valued at $5,000. Twenty-six years later, when he left St. Luke's, it was a congregation of 2,000, and its property was valued at $1,000,000. In 1915 he received his Doctor of Literature degree (L.H.D.) from Kenyon College, Gambier, Ohio. In 1917 the Doctor of Divinity degree was conferred upon him by Northwestern University, and in 1930, he was given the Doctor of Sacred Theology degree by the Western Theological Seminary.

Bishop Stewart was secretary of the war commission of the Protestant Episcopal Church in 1918, and was chaplain of Evacuation Hospital No. 6, with the American Expeditionary Forces. He has been a delegate six times to the General Convention of the Protestant Episcopal Church. He is a member of the National Council and of the department of religious education of that church, a director of the Church Congress (Protestant Episcopal), of the Religious Education Society of America, and of the National Economic League. He is a trustee of Northwestern University and of the Western Theological Seminary; also a fellow of the Ecclesiological Society, vice-president of the Evanston Council of Boy Scouts, and a member of the Art commission of Evanston. He was elected bishop of the Diocese in 1930. Bishop Stewart is in demand as a preacher by universities from coast to coast, and has lectured on homiletics at the Western Seminary and at The College of Preachers. He is the author of The Colors of the Re-

Continued on page 549

The opening in May, 1920, of the Michigan avenue bridge, linking the North and the South Park systems, marked a new era for Chicago. Since then, all the old turnstyle bridges have been replaced by bridges of the bascule or cantilever type, the Wabash avenue, La Salle street, and Franklin-Orleans spans being the most recent. Not only has Wabash avenue been carried across the river for the first time, but a new and wider North La Salle street now extends from the City Hall to Lincoln Park. Bridge construction comes within the province of the city's Department of Public Works, of which Colonel Albert A. Sprague is commissioner. Colonel Sprague is also vice-chairman of the Chicago Plan Commission. The third official of the Plan Commission is vice-chairman Michael Zimmer, warden of Cook County Hospital.

Under the recommendations of the Plan Commission some twenty major street widening projects have been carried out. Roosevelt road, widened from 66 feet to 108 feet from Ashland avenue to Canal street, and carried by a new viaduct over the south branch of the river and the railroad tracks to Michigan avenue, has become one of the city's main arteries, and is to be continued to the lake front. With the completion of the Union Station in 1925, Canal street was elevated and widened. In preparation for the extension of Dearborn, La Salle, Wells, Franklin, and Market streets to the South Side, the river has been straightened at a cost of millions of dollars, the greater part of which cost was borne by the railroad companies. Dingy old South Park avenue has become a section of the new South Parkway. Ogden avenue has cut its way from Lincoln Park to the West Side. Ashland avenue and Western avenue have been widened in accordance with the Chicago Plan and Damen avenue has been opened on the north.

Electrification of the Illinois Central's suburban system at a cost of $25,000,000 has given Chicago the best suburban service in the world, a service superior to anything offered by New York's subway. Noiseless, smokeless trains running at the speed of sixty miles an hour whisk the passenger from the Loop to Hyde Park in about six minutes. Completion of a new and palatial terminal station for this line will see the materialization of another Chicago Plan Commission undertaking.

The depression of 1929-1932 delayed work on a comprehensive subway system which, had the era of prosperity continued, it was hoped would be completed in time for the opening of A Century of Progress Exposition. The subway, however, will come in time. Another major project, outlined by the Plan Commission, is a system of grade separation superhighways radiating from the heart of Chicago to all parts of the city.

The Chicago Plan also provides for aviation field sites, sites for filtration plants, and greater navigation facilities for the river and the harbor. It is a plan which, if adhered to and carried out as necessity requires and as financial resources permit, will assure the city's consistent progress.

President
PRESBYTERIAN
THEOLOGICAL
SEMINARY
CHICAGO

(Doose' Studio Photo)

REV. JOHN TIMOTHY STONE

Dr. Stone, president of the Presbyterian (formerly McCormick) Theological Seminary and pastor emeritus of the Fourth Presbyterian church, was born in a suburb of Boston, September 7, 1868, the son of Timothy Dwight Porter and Susan Margaret (Dickinson) Stone. The family moved to Albany, New York, in 1876, where Dr. Stone graduated from high school in 1887. Dr. Stone was graduated in 1891 from Amherst College, and was class orator. He was graduated from Auburn Theological Seminary in 1894, and was ordained in the Presbyterian ministry at Utica, New York, in June of the same year. He has received honorary degrees from nine universities and colleges: Doctor of Divinity (D.D.) from the University of Maryland and from Amherst College in 1919; Doctor of Laws (LL.D.) from Emporia College in 1913, Occidental College in 1914, Coe College in 1917, LaFayette College in 1923, and Northwestern University in 1926; Doctor of Sacred Theology (S. T. D.) from Columbia University in 1919; Doctor of Letters (Litt. D.) from the University of Vermont in 1923.

He was pastor of Olivet Church, Utica, from 1894 to 1896; Presbyterian Church, Cortland, New York, from 1896 to 1900, and of the Brown Memorial Church, Baltimore, from 1900 to 1909. Two years after he began his pastorate in Chicago, the new Fourth Presbyterian church, a model of Gothic architecture, was erected in North Michigan avenue near Delaware place, at a cost of $850,000. Dr. Stone served this church for over twenty years before becoming president of the Presbyterian Theological Seminary. He is a director of the Chicago Bible Society, the Presbyterian Ministers' Fund of Philadelphia, Presbyterian Hospital, and Presbyterian Home. In 1913 and 1914 he was Moderator of the General Assembly of the Presbyterian Church in the United States, and from 1920 to 1922 was chairman of the Committee which reorganized and consolidated the various boards of the Presbyterian Church.

He is also a trustee of the Half-Orphan Asylum, a past chaplain of the National Society of Sons of the American Revolution and of the Illinois chapter of the same society, and is now national chaplain of the Founders and Patriots of America. Dr. Stone is the author of Footsteps in a Parish, Recruiting for Christ, The Life of Whitfield, That Friday Night, Everyday Religion, Christianity in Action, and of numerous other books and monographs on educational and religious themes. He is a member of the University and Union League clubs, and of the Delta Kappa Epsilon Fraternity.

He was married, June 22, 1932, to Miss Marie Briggs of Chicago.

TRADITIONS OF THEODORE THOMAS PRESERVED IN THE CHICAGO SYMPHONY ORCHESTRA

A Famous Institution and Its Influence on the Life of the Community

BY HENRY E. VOEGELI

Manager, Chicago Symphony Orchestra

ORCHESTRA Hall, Chicago's superb temple of music, and the home of the Chicago Symphony Orchestra, is a monument to Theodore Thomas. But it is more than that. It is a symbol of the cultural aspirations of the city.

In its Symphony Orchestra Chicago has a priceless asset. It has added immeasurably to Chicago's prestige as a musical center. It has raised the musical standards of the community to a high level. It has been the inspiration of thousands of professional and amateur musicians. It has developed in Chicago's army of school children an appreciation of the best in the art form it interprets.

While the shadow of Theodore Thomas will remain ever in the background of this splendid organization, we must go even farther back than the first concerts given in Chicago by this pioneer for the beginnings of the Orchestra.

Let us turn back the pages of history to 1850. Chicago at that time was a crude and rapidly growing city, but among its residents were men of culture, men who were jealous of the monopoly in the finer things of life held by such eastern cities as New York, Philadelphia, and Boston.

The first serious attempts at implanting musical culture in Chicago were made by Hans Balatka, who, with the support of this group of public-spirited citizens, organized the Philharmonic Society, which for several years provided Chicago with high-class musical programs, and paved the way for Theodore Thomas. This organization, however, owing to the many discouragements it encountered, was forced to disband, and for a time Chicago had to do without orchestral music.

Then, in 1869, Mr. Thomas, who was touring the country with his New York orchestra, included Chicago in his itinerary. So favorable was his reception that a return engagement was arranged for, and the following year, the ensemble was heard here in a series of seven concerts, the programs including works altogether new to local music lovers.

In 1877, however, a more extended season was announced, and the delightful summer night concerts in the Exposition Building were inaugurated. The success of these led in 1890 to the founding of the Orchestral Association, which is today the governing body of the Chicago Symphony Orchestra.

During the thirteen years of these concerts, the popularity of Mr. Thomas grew, and more and more Chicago was beginning to adopt him and his musicians as her own. Thus, when the prospects for his orchestra in the East seemed hopeless; when New York failed to provide him with

(*Underwood & Underwood, Washington, D. C., Photo*)

FREDERICK A. STOCK

Dr. Stock, conductor of the Chicago Symphony Orchestra, was born in Julich, Germany, November 11, 1872, the son of Frederick Carl and Maria Stock. He became a naturalized citizen of the United States in 1919. His father, a bandmaster in the Prussian Army, began his musical education at the age of four, at which time he was given a small violin to play upon. At the age of fourteen Frederick Stock was admitted to the Cologne Conservatory where he spent four years in intensive study and practice of the violin under Japha, and theory and composition under Franz Wullner, Zöllner, Gustav Jensen and Humperdinck. He was graduated in 1887 and for the next eight years was a violinist with the Cologne Municipal Orchestra.

In 1895 he was requested by Theodore Thomas to join the Chicago Orchestra, which he did as viola player in the fall of that same year. Under the guidance of Thomas, who took a personal interest in his protégé's welfare, Stock was soon given more and more of the director's tasks. As a signal of recognition and respect for Stock's gifts as a composer, Thomas, in 1903, conducted Stock's "Symphonic Variations." At the death of its founder, Frederick A. Stock, as was the wish of Theodore Thomas, became permanent director of the Chicago Symphony Orchestra in 1905. Dr. Stock has conducted several performances of Wagnerian opera for the Civic Opera Company of Chicago (1923). He received the decoration of Chevalier, Legion of Honor (France) in 1925. The honorary degree of Doctor of Music has been bestowed upon Dr. Stock by Northwestern University, 1915, University of Michigan, 1924, University of Chicago, 1925, and Cornell College, Mount Vernon, Iowa, 1927. He has been appointed general music director of A Century of Progress, Chicago's (1933) World's Fair. Besides the one mentioned above he is the composer of a number of works for orchestra, string quartette and chorus.

Dr. Stock married Elsa Muskulus, of Fulda, Germany, May 22, 1896. There is one daughter, Vera F. (Mrs. Alfred M. Wolfe).

a hall, and no endowment fund was forthcoming, Mr. Thomas accepted the invitation of Chicago to make his permanent home here.

He brought with him sixty artists, and augmented his ensemble with musicians recruited from the local ranks. Some of these, indeed, had worshiped the music master from afar, mostly from gallery seats at the Exposition Building performances. The Orchestral Association accepted full financial responsibility, and Chicago had its "Thomas Orchestra."

The first concert under the new regime was given in the Auditorium in 1891, and the first season scheduled twenty Friday afternoon public rehearsals and the same number of Saturday night concerts.

Despite the acclaim with which the Orchestra was received, it cannot be denied that the early days of its existence were discouraging. For one thing, the Auditorium was far too large. It would have been much easier to play to a smaller house filled to capacity than to an audience which rattled around, as it were, like a dried pea in a pod. At that time there was no subscription list and the size of the audience was determined more or less by weather conditions or the popularity of counter attractions. Also it was difficult to obtain musicians of the desired virtuosity. There was no training school for ensemble players such as is provided for today by the Civic Orchestra, an offshoot of the Chicago Symphony, which was formed in 1919. It must be admitted, too, that Chicago, in the "Gay 90's" was interested more in things material than in things spiritual.

Nowadays it is different. Chicago has a passion for music. The dictates of fashion alone make attendance at the Symphony Concerts almost imperative. Subscription seats are handed down from father to son, from mother to daughter. They are treasured by Chicago's *haute monde* as a priceless asset. Seats for the popular concerts are snapped up far in advance. The conservatories of music are turning out highly accomplished artists in such numbers that the problem of their absorption is a grave one. The Chicago Symphony Orchestra, with long waiting lists both of subscribers and musicians, is virtually a closed corporation.

Never did the Chicago spirit come to the front more ebulliently than when the campaign was launched to erect in Michigan avenue a shrine of music worthy of the organization which was making musical history here. Millionaires and shop girls alike contributed to the building fund, the amounts given ranging from twenty-five cents to $25,000, and totaling $600,000. More than 7,500 Chicagoans, including hundreds of school children, subscribed.

In 1904, the dreams of Theodore Thomas were realized. The Chicago Symphony Orchestra at last had a home of its own, and a magnificent home, at that. On the night of the dedication, the music master received one of his greatest ovations. A few weeks later, Chicago and the rest of the nation were mourning his death. To Theodore Thomas Chicago owes a debt of gratitude that can never be repaid.

(*Rayhuff-Richter Photo*)

GUSTAVUS FRANKLIN SWIFT

Mr. Swift, third president of Swift & Company, is the second chief officer to bear that name, the company having been founded by his father, Gustavus Franklin Swift, Sr. The present chief executive was born in Chicago, March 1, 1881. He was educated in the Chicago public schools and business colleges. While still in school he spent much of his time after school hours in the Chicago Union Stock Yards with his father and older brothers. Here he learned the rudiments of livestock buying. After finishing school, Mr. Swift's first real job was in the buying end, where he became a weight taker in the hog buying department. After serving his apprenticeship here, he became a buyer and later was sent by his father to the packing house market, where he learned how meat is bought by the retail dealer.

Following an apprenticeship in selling to the retail trade, Mr. Swift worked in the general superintendent's office in order to attain a grasp of the operating end of the packing business, and it was as an operating executive that he first began to make himself felt in the business of the company. After some time spent also in the provision end of the packing business, he took charge of that branch of the work. While engaged in this he made several surveys of European markets and learned first hand the needs of the various nations to which Swift & Company was shipping its products. On January 6, 1916, G. F. Swift was elected a vice-president and director of the company. He was elected to the presidency of Swift & Company on January 8, 1931. Always careful and thorough in his ways, Mr. Swift's grasp of all angles of Swift & Company's business is most comprehensive. He also found time to take an active part in the organization of the Institute of American Meat Packers and has served for a number of years as head of its department of public relations. His clubs are Chicago, Industrial, Onwentsia, Casino, Saddle and Cycle, and Shoreacres.

He married Marie Fitzgerald, June 10, 1907, and they have four children, Geraldine, Marie, Gustavus F. III, and Jane Gertrude.

His successor, Frederick A. Stock, the present conductor, was brought by Mr. Thomas from Cologne. The son of a Prussian bandmaster, he was born and reared in the grim shadow of bastions and guns. Early in life, however, he showed a predilection for the musical rather than the military profession. Under the practical guidance of his father, he spent long hours at his violin. Graduated with honors from the Cologne Conservatory, he became a member of the Cologne Orchestra, where he was discovered by Mr. Thomas on one of his many trips abroad. In the Fall of 1895, the young musician came to Chicago. His ability and character at once won him the favor of his leader, who selected him for special work and development.

During those trying years when the future of the Orchestra was in the lap of the gods, Stock and Thomas worked side by side, often for the very existence of the organization, and when the latter laid down his baton, it was Frederick A. Stock who took it up. For a quarter of a century he has remained faithful to his trust, ever strengthening, ever building, until today the Chicago Symphony Orchestra stands as a living monument to the ideals, dreams, and aspirations of these two great figures in the world of music.

It was Mr. Stock who inaugurated the Children's Concerts. These, made up of forty-five minutes of music, interspersed with charming explanatory talks and slides, were from the start an unequivocal success. The children are encouraged to participate in the singing, and to answer questions put to them by the director. The concerts dovetail with the music courses of the public schools, courses which were introduced and organized through the influence of the Orchestral Association.

Each individual player of this great orchestra is a virtuoso on his chosen instrument, if not on several instruments. Some are American-born; some foreign-born, but each is a master. The roster of the orchestra is a roll of honor. Because of the loyalty of the members, vacancies are few, but the Civic Orchestra, governed jointly by the Orchestral Association and the Civic Music Association provides for younger players a convenient stepping stone. Many of its members have been graduated to symphony orchestras in other cities.

LAW
—
BUSINESS
—
BANKING
—
COMMERCE
—
CIVIC
AFFAIRS
—
FOREIGN
RELATIONS

(Harris & Ewing Photo, Washington. D. C.)

SILAS H. STRAWN

Mr. Strawn, senior member of Winston, Strawn & Shaw, was born in Ottawa, Illinois, December 15, 1866, the son of Abner and Eliza (Hardy) Strawn. He graduated from the high school in Ottawa in 1885, taught school for two years, and was admitted to the Illinois Bar in 1889. He has received the degree of Doctor of Laws from the University of Michigan, Northwestern University, Knox College, and Lake Forest College. Mr. Strawn practiced law in Ottawa from 1889 to 1891 and in Chicago since then. He has been senior member of the firm of Winston, Strawn & Shaw since 1918. He is chairman of the executive committee of Montgomery Ward & Company, director and member of the executive committee of the First National Bank and the First Union Trust and Savings Bank of Chicago, director and general solicitor of The Alton Railroad Company, director of the Electric Household Utilities Company, director of the Wahl Company, chairman of American Committee and vice-president of the International Chamber of Commerce, delegate of the International Chamber of Commerce at Rome, 1923, Stockholm, 1927, Amsterdam, 1929. He was honorary vice-president of the Chamber of Commerce of the United States in 1928 and president in 1931-1932. Mr. Strawn is also a member of the executive council of the American Society of International Law. He was a delegate from the United States Government to the Chinese Customs Tariff Conference at Peking, 1925-1926, and the United States Commissioner and chairman of the International Commission of Extra-territorial Jurisdiction in China, 1925-1926. He has served as president of the Chicago Council on Foreign Relations and was chairman of the Citizens' Committee for Tax Reform and Financial Relief of Chicago, 1929-1930.

Mr. Strawn was president of the Chicago Bar Association in 1913-1914, president of the Illinois State Bar Association, 1921-1922, and president of the American Bar Association in 1927-1928. He is a trustee of the Carnegie Endowment for International Peace, of the Field Museum, and of Northwestern University. His club affiliations are Chicago Law, Commercial (ex-president), Industrial (ex-president), Chicago, University, Chicago Athletic Association (honorary member), Mid-Day (ex-president), Casino,
Continued on page 549

THE CHICAGO STADIUM—THE WORLD'S GREATEST INDOOR ARENA
Where Presidential Candidates Have Been Nominated and Trained Elephants Have Performed

HAD it existed in the Ancient World, the Chicago Stadium, out on West Madison street, would have been included among the "Seven Wonders." It is the world's largest building of its kind.

Here Herbert Hoover and Franklin D. Roosevelt were nominated for the Presidency by the National Conventions of their respective parties. Here during the Rodeo, cowboys have ridden bucking broncos and have bull-dogged steers. Acrobats, equestrians, aerialists, and trained elephants have performed in its arena or under its steel girders. Here six-day bicycle racers have competed, boxing tournaments have been held . . . tennis tournaments . . . ice hockey matches . . . indoor track meets . . . flower shows . . . operas.

The Stadium, an immense pile of steel and stone, was erected in 1929. It is a monument to the enterprise of Paddy Harmon, west side politician and philanthropist, whose body lay in state there shortly after the completion of the building.

As a convention hall, as a temple of sport, as a setting for great public spectacles, the Chicago Stadium relegates New York's new Madison Square Garden to the background.

(*Chicago Architectural Photographing Company*)
CHICAGO STADIUM.   Eric E. Hall & Company, architects.

(*Loubell Studios, Photo*)

SIDNEY N. STROTZ

Mr. Strotz, president of The Chicago Stadium Corporation, was born in Chicago, April 26, 1898, son of Charles N. and Clara A. Strotz. He attended St. John's Military Academy, Delafield, Wisconsin, and received his college education in the school of law at Cornell University. Immediately after his withdrawal from college he began extensive activities in the administration of various business enterprises in Chicago and in the East. In 1928 Mr. Strotz and his brother, Harold, organized and financed the Chicago Stadium, the largest building of its kind in the world, with a seating capacity of 25,000 persons. Upon the completion of this project, Mr. Strotz became secretary and treasurer of this organization, which he remained until 1930 when he succeeded the late Paddy Harmon as president. The Chicago Stadium, the world's greatest indoor arena, is the scene of boxing matches, bicycle races, conventions (notably the 1932 Republican and Demo-cratic), rodeos, circuses, exhibits, hockey games, flower shows, and even operas. The original cost of the Stadium was $7,000,000.

During the World War Mr. Strotz was with the 326th Batallion, Tanks Corps, in France for eighteen months. He is a member of the Chicago Athletic Association, the Steuben Club, and the Rotary Club. For recreation he enjoys golf, boating, and horse-back riding. He has many fine saddle horses on his plantation at Swans Point, Virginia.

He married Frances Vyse. There are three children, Shirley, Charles N. II, and Sandra.

The Stadium has a seating capacity of 25,000, but on special occasions has accommodated 30,000 people without crowding. It occupies an entire city block, with parking spaces at either end. The seats are arranged in tiers around an oval 244 feet long and 145 feet wide.

It manufactures its own weather and has its own refrigerating plant. The ventilating and cooling systems, under thermostatic control, deliver 6,000 cubic feet of conditioned air every minute. The $368,000 ice-making equipment can manufacture 600 tons of ice within twenty-four hours, and for hockey matches or skating, the entire floor can be converted into a rink. The following week perhaps it may blossom into a huge garden.

In the building of the Stadium special attention was given to acoustics, with the result that acoustically it is superior even to the Mormon Temple at Salt Lake City which heretofore had been considered peerless in such matters.

(Kaufmann & Fabry Co. Photo)

A PROFESSIONAL HOCKEY GAME AT THE STADIUM

A "super" amplifying system makes it possible for a whisper to be heard in the most remote corner of the building. Powerful batteries of floodlights can be focused on any section of the amphitheater as required.

Unique in respect to being the world's largest is the Stadium organ, in volume of sound the equivalent of twenty-five bands of 100 instruments each, or 2,500 orchestral pieces. The great organ plays simultaneously 40 harmonizing snare drums, 16 violins, 12 saxophones, 4 bass drums, 12 flutes, 9 clarinets, 6 trumpets, 7 French horns. More than 240 feet of pipes and 5,000 feet of wire have gone into its making. The range of controlled sound runs all the way from a bird note to a thunder storm, but its full power never has been tested. On several experimental occasions, its vibrations have shattered electric light bulbs.

(From drawing by Burkart)

CLEMENT STUDEBAKER, JR.

Mr. Studebaker was born in South Bend, Indiana, August 11, 1871, son of Clement and Ann (Milburn) Studebaker. His father was one of the founders of Studebaker Brothers Manufacturing Company, now The Studebaker Corporation. He received his preliminary education in the public schools of South Bend, and later attended Northwestern University. He began his business career as a member of Studebaker Brothers Manufacturing Company, becoming cashier and treasurer. Upon the merger and incorporation of The Studebaker Corporation, he became treasurer and first vice-president, later being elected first vice-president and chairman of the committee of control.

Resigning from his offices with The Studebaker Corporation in April, 1914, Mr. Studebaker for a time devoted his attention to other interests, and on April 16, 1915, was elected president of the North American Light & Power Company, in which capacity he served until his death on December 3, 1932. He was an officer or director of various subsidiaries including Illinois Power and Light Corporation, Iowa Power and Light Company, Missouri Power & Light Company, Kansas Power and Light Company, and Des Moines Electric Light Company. He was also chairman of the board of Illinois Terminal Railroad System and president of the Illinois Traction Company and Illinois Traction, Inc. Following the example of his father, Mr. Studebaker was a trustee of Chautauqua Institution and of DePauw University. He was also trustee of Illinois Wesleyan University, of Bloomington, Illinois, and a past president of the Indiana Society of Chicago. He was a member of the following clubs: Chicago, Union League, Attic, Traffic, The Tavern, Glenview, of Golf, Illinois; Abenaqui of Rye Beach, New Hampshire; Tombigee, MacIntosh, Alabama; Grand Island Lodge, Bath, Illinois; Algonquin, of Boston; and the Lotos, of New York.

On April 27, 1893, Mr. Studebaker married Alice Rhawn, of Philadelphia, Pennsylvania. The children are Clement III, and Esther (Mrs. Peticolas).

Two restaurants, numerous conference rooms, public telephones, a private switchboard, telegraph and radio connections are among the Stadium's conveniences.

With main floor entrances on opposite sides of the building, balcony entrances at the four corners, and exits at either end, the Stadium can be emptied, even of a capacity crowd, within a few minutes.

The Stadium has its own staff of trained ushers, its own fire and police departments, the latter augumented by city police and firemen. President Sidney N. Strotz has tried to leave nothing undone that will make for the convenience, comfort and safety of the public.

There is something of interest going on almost all the time at the Stadium. Its conventions, expositions, entertainments, and sporting events have attracted nation-wide attention, thus adding to the fame of Chicago.

THE CHICAGO RIDING CLUB.   Rebori and Wentworth, architects.

(*Moffett-Russell Photo*)

WILLIAM J. SUTHERLAND

Mr. Sutherland, president of Mooney, Boland, Sutherland Corporation, international intelligence bureau, was born in Logansport, Indiana, November 3, 1863, son of George C. and Esther A. (Gerhart) Sutherland. He began as a clerk in a grocery store in Logansport in 1878. In 1880 he came to Chicago and was employed as a clerk in the Mooney & Boland Agency, the largest secret service organization in the country, which looks after the confidential matters of corporations and prominent individuals. Subsequently he became a partner, vice-president, and general manager of the western division, continuing in this capacity until 1918, when he became president of Mooney, Boland, Sutherland Corporation. This organization maintains offices in Chicago, New York, and Philadelphia, and has representatives all over the world. Mr. Sutherland is also president of Sutherland Incorporated and vice-president and general manager of the Employers' Protective & Bonding Association.

He is a member of the Chicago Association of Commerce, and his clubs are Chicago Athletic, Medinah Athletic, Hamilton, Press, Chicago Yacht, South Shore Country, and Business Men's Prosperity. He is the owner of Polo Farm at Wheaton, Illinois, and his favorite hobby is the raising of saddle horses. Many fine horse shows are held on his estate.

He married Ella M. Minnick, of Chicago, May 30, 1888.

CHICAGO'S ARCHITECTURE—IS IT BEAUTIFUL?
A Century of Progress Exposition Ushering in a New Architectural Era
BY THOMAS E. TALLMADGE, M.A., F.A.I.A.
Author of "The Story of Architecture in America"

WRITERS on the subject of Chicago's architecture have become very erudite in the last decade. In tracing our architectural history or in penning acid arguments on which was the first skyscraper we have often lost sight of the sheer beauty of some of our buildings. This little sketch, however, will be neither history nor controversy. It will merely be a humble attempt to appraise the beauty in its old-fashioned meaning of our architecture in both old and new fashioned guise.

Here we are brought face to face at once with age-old questions as to what constitutes beauty and whether we can condemn today what our fathers unanimously considered as beautiful yesterday or praise without qualifications what our descendents may regard as ugly, but we will pass

A RELIC OF OLDER CHICAGO

The Chicago Avenue Water Tower, the only structure of importance to survive the great fire of 1871. Once derided because of its mid-Victorian pompousness, the tower is regarded in a more favorable light today.

(Mayo's Studio Photo)

ARTHUR H. SWETT

Mr. Swett, president of the American Tag Company, was born in Worcester, Massachusetts, November 22, 1866, son of William O. and Charlotte M. (Heath) Swett, and is of American Revolutionary ancestry. He was educated at the Englewood High School and Cook County Normal School. He began his business career as secretary and treasurer of the American Playing Card Company, Kalamazoo, Michigan, in 1890. He was vice-president and manager of the Acme Flexible Clasp Company (now Acme Steel Company), of Chicago, from 1894 to 1898, and has been president and general manager of the American Tag Company since 1897.

This company designs and builds their own special machines for the economical production of tags, paper goods, etc., making it possible to start with a ball of string and a roll of paper stock and produce complete tags in one operation. These machines print tags on both sides in colors, die-cut, perforate, punch, number consecutively, gather, count in lots of one hundred or more, tie with string, and knot the end of same, all in one operation. The American Tag Company produces more than 2,000,000 tags a day; has more than $50,000 worth of stock dies of all sizes and shapes; and has its own electrotype foundry, as well as a department for making their own shipping cartons. This organization has offices in all the principal cities and has factories in Chicago and Newark. He is a member of the Chicago Association of Commerce and the Illinois Manufacturers' Association. His clubs are Chicago Athletic Association and the Ridge Country Club, and his favorite recreation is motoring.

In 1893 Mr. Swett married Emma Monroe of Chicago (deceased), and is the father of Arthur Hollister, Jr., Donald Monroe, William O. III, and Eleanor Emma. On January 11, 1911, he married Alice Beardsley of Chicago, and they have one son, Robert Wheeler.

these by. What are the buildings in Chicago today that most delight the eye?

Long before the war everyone laughed at and apologized for the mid-Victorian Water Tower sticking up like a huge nail through the long silver tape that is Michigan Avenue; but when in 1919 it was proposed to tear it down a howl of protest went up from esthete and Philistine alike. Why? Because it was useful? No. Because it was historical? Perhaps, in a degree; but I think the most potent reason was because we had come to consider it beautiful. Age itself can throw a veil of loveliness over a face or a piece of architecture which in its youth was harsh and unpleasing, especially if we have learned to love it. Sentimentality, however, cannot lead us into praise on the strength of loveliness of many buildings left to us of the seventies. Built in the gaunt and awkward fashion that our architects thought was the last word in the fashionable English Gothic or the stylish Mansard Roof Classic of Paris in the decade succeeding the fire, their bodies today seem to be all shrouded and waiting for the grave digger. One other familiar example of this ilk is the Potter Palmer palace. Beautiful or not as you are

A MONUMENT OF THE ROMANESQUE PERIOD

The Marshall Field Wholesale Building in North Wells Street, which was razed several years ago, was regarded in its time as a glorious monument to the Romanesque revival, of which its designer, H. H. Richardson, was a leading exponent.

(Moffett-Russell Photo)

NATHANIEL G. SYMONDS

Mr. Symonds, vice-president in charge of sales of the Westinghouse Electric and Manufacturing Company, was born in Ossining, New York, September 19, 1878, son of Henry Clay and Beatrice (Brandreth) Symonds. He received his early education at the Los Gatos (California) High School, and obtained his A. B. (Bachelor of Arts) degree in electric engineering at Leland Stanford University in 1901. His first position was with the Texas Consolidated Gold Mining Company as electrical engineer. In 1902 he joined the Westinghouse Church Kerr Company and the following year became district superintendent of stoker erection for the same firm. When the Westinghouse Machine Company became engaged in the manufacture of stokers, Mr. Symonds was assigned to East Pittsburgh. In May, 1905, he came to the Chicago sales office as stoker salesman, and in 1915, when the Westinghouse Machine Company was absorbed by the Westinghouse Electric and Manufacturing Company, he was appointed manager of the power division of the Chicago office. Three years later he became the industrial division manager; in 1921 was made Chicago district manager, in 1930 became commercial vice-president, and in October, 1932, was made vice-president in charge of sales.

The Westinghouse Electric and Manufacturing Company manufactures electrical equipment for central power stations, buildings, land and water transportation, etc.; in other words, equipment for the complete "electrification of industry," as well as electrical appliances for the home, such as Westinghouse electric refrigerators, ranges, washers, ironers, air conditioners, and many others. Mr. Symonds is a director of the Allcock Manufacturing Company, Ossining, New York, director of the Hinsdale (Illinois) State Bank, and served in the Illinois Reserve Militia during the World War. He is a member of the American Society of Mechanical Engineers, Kappa Sigma, and Rotary International. His clubs are Chicago, Union League, Electric, Hinsdale, Hinsdale Golf (Hinsdale, Illinois), and University at Pittsburgh. His principal interests, outside of his family and work, are golf and fishing.

He married Amy Irene Millberry, of San Francisco, California, December 25, 1901. Their children are: Henry Gardiner, Nathaniel Millberry, Amy Irene (deceased), and Cortlandt.

at liberty to consider it, it still sits like a Frederick Barbarossa clad in the ermine of other days; waiting, undoubtedly in vain, for the time when architecture shall call it back to rule again.

The Marshall Field Wholesale Building by H. H. Richardson and the Chicago Club by Burnham and Root were both glorious monuments of the Romanesque Revival, the style of architecture that overran the land in the eighties. These two buildings have been destroyed, the first, it would seem needlessly so. If one is interested in searching out other examples of this romantic and exotic style there is the Auditorium, the Congress hotel, the Newberry library, and the Rookery Building, not lovely perhaps, but vigorous and interesting members of one family.

Chicago's fame as a creator of the beautiful came with the World's Columbian Exposition of 1893. Here if ever was tested the dogma that beauty is its own excuse for being. Without logic or practicability the skin-deep loveliness of the Court of Honor brought a nation to her feet and launched if not a thousand ships, at least ten thousand architects on a new

THE "GOLDEN ENTRANCE" OF WORLD'S FAIR MEMORIES

One of the glories of the World's Columbian Exposition of 1903, this "Golden Entrance" to the Transportation Building, is a striking example of the Chicago school of architecture established by Louis Sullivan. It is somewhat reminiscent of the Moorish.

M. S. SZYMCZAK

Mr. Szymczak, comptroller of the City of Chicago, was born in Chicago on August 15, 1894, son of Stanley and Magdalena (Werner) Szymczak. He received his A. B. (Bachelor of Arts) degree at St. Mary's College, St. Mary, Kentucky, in 1914, his A. M. (Master of Arts) degree in 1918. He took graduate study at Mount St. Mary's Seminary, Cincinnati, Ohio, during 1914 and 1915 and received his A. B. (Bachelor of Arts) degree at De Paul University in 1917; A. M. (Master of Arts) degree in 1919; graduate study at New York University School of Commerce. He was an instructor in mathematics at St. Mary's College during 1913 and 1914; instructor in mathematics and history at De Paul University Preparatory School during 1916 and 1919; instructor in logic and public speaking at the College of Commerce, De Paul University, from 1919 to 1923; and professor of ethics, logic, and psychology in business, municipal government and business administration since 1923.

Mr. Szymczak is active in financial endeavors and organizations, and was director of several building and loan associations. He is a director of the First National Finance Corporation. In 1929 he became clerk of the Superior Court of Cook County and was appointed comptroller of the City of Chicago in 1931. He is an ex-commissioner of the Portage Park District and was general superintendent of the Cook County Forest Preserve District during 1927 and 1928. He is a member of the Izaak Walton League, Mercier Philosophical Society (organizer), Chicago Zoölogical Society (governing member), University Public Speakers Council (honorary president since 1921), Northwest Chamber of Commerce, Milwaukee Avenue Chamber of Commerce (president), State League of Building and Loan Associations (educational director), and Alpha Chi Fraternity. Mr. Szymczak is a lecturer on philosophy in business, and is a member of the Illinois Athletic, City and Iroquois clubs.

On January 15, 1916, he married Helen Marie Lappin of Chicago, and they have two children, Helen Josephine and Mary Elizabeth.

course. The recent transmutation of one of these buildings, the Palace of Fine Arts, from plaster and wood to stone and steel has proved that beauty is more than a fleeting smile and that architecture cast down to earth may rise again. This old World's Fair building reincarnated as the Rosenwald Museum is probably the most beautiful building in Chicago, surpassed in loveliness by but few in the whole world.

As a result of the World's Fair the twenty-five years from 1893 through the World War is known as the Eclectic period. Classic architecture predominated but Gothic in a new and more attractive garment returned. Of the first species there is the Art Institute, the Union Station and numerous houses in various phases of the Classic such as Georgian, French and Italian Renaissance; and of the Gothic, buildings of the University of Chicago such as the Harper Library; of Northwestern University in the McKinlock Campus, and the Fourth Presbyterian Church are typical.

Chicago as far back as 1888 had become known as the father of the skyscraper but the delusions of architectural grandeur given us by the Fair, caused such simple and logical, though perhaps not beautiful, solutions of an entirely new problem that existed in the Tacoma (destroyed), the Monadnock or the Reliance buildings to be discarded. The enormous number

(*Chicago Architectural Photographing Company*)
CHICAGO DAILY NEWS BUILDING AND PLAZA
Holabird & Root, architects.

(Jean Crunelle Photo)

LORADO TAFT

Mr. Taft, sculptor, author, teacher, and lecturer, was born in Elmwood, Illinois, April 29, 1860, the son of Professor Don Carlos and Mary Lucy (Foster) Taft. He is a graduate of the University of Illinois where his father was for many years professor of geology. He received his B. L. (Bachelor of Letters) degree in 1879 and his M. L. (Master of Laws) in 1880. From 1880 to 1883 he studied in Paris at the École des Beaux Arts, and independently. The honorary degrees that have been conferred on him are L. H. D. (Doctor of Literature), Northwestern University, in 1913; Litt. D. (Doctor of Letters), University of Colorado, in 1927; and LL. D. (Doctor of Laws), University of Illinois, 1929. Mr. Taft was an instructor in the Art Institute of Chicago from 1886 to 1907, a lecturer there from 1886 to 1929; a lecturer on art in the university extension department, University of Chicago, 1892 to 1902 and a professorial lecturer since 1909; and a non-resident professor of art at the University of Illinois since 1919. His principal works are Solitude of the Soul, in the Art Institute of Chicago; Black Hawk, in Oregon, Illinois; Columbus Memorial Fountain, in Washington, D. C.; Ferguson Fountain of the Great Lakes, in Grant Park, Chicago; Thatcher Memorial Fountain, in Denver, Colorado; The Fountain of Time, on the Midway Plaisance in Chicago; Lincoln, Urbana, Illinois; The Pioneers, Elmwood, Illinois; Alma Mater, University of Illinois; and The Crusader (Victor Lawson Memorial), Graceland Cemetery, Chicago.

Mr. Taft received the designer's medal at the Chicago Exposition, 1893; the silver medal at the Buffalo Exposition, 1901; and the gold medal at the St. Louis Exposition, 1904. He is a member of the American Academy of Arts and Letters, the National Academy of Design (A. N. A., 1909, N. A., 1911) and the National Sculpture Society; and honorary member of the American Institute of Architecture. He was appointed member of the Board of Art Advisers of Illinois, 1917 and 1929; member of the National Commission of Fine Arts, Washington, D. C., 1925 to 1928. He belongs to the Century (New York), Cliff Dwellers, City, and Quadrangle (Chicago) clubs. Mr. Taft is the author of The History of American Sculpture, 1903, and Recent Tendencies in Sculpture, 1921.

He married Carrie L. Scales, of Evanston, October 4, 1890 (died April, 1892). Mr. Taft was married a second time to Ada Bartlett, of Boston, February 11, 1896. They have three children, Mary, Emily, and Jessie Louise.

of huge office buildings erected in the loop in this Eclectic period, though painstakingly veneered by the architect with every ancient style and crowned, each one, with huge cornices, were not considered beautiful even by the man in the street. He called them "packing boxes." Typical examples are the Marquette Building, the Commonwealth Edison Building, the First National Bank Building. The most meritorious example of this old type, as we call it now, of skyscraper is the Peoples Gas Building. Here a skillful attempt was made to force beauty by texture and pattern. The Woolworth Tower in New York in the latter part of the period turned architects away from the box type, so unpopular with the laity, to the tower and the picturesque silhouette. Of these we have successful examples in the Wrigley Tower, the Straus Building and the Methodist Temple.

Throughout this era Louis Sullivan, Chicago architect and now acknowledged father of modernism in architecture, stormed and swore at his confreres for trying to put the new wine of skeleton steel construction into the old bottles of the ancient architectural styles. He even built such structures as the Schiller Theater (now Garrick), the Gage Building, and the Stock Exchange Building to show how "form should follow function," but in vain.

In 1922 came the famous Tribune competition. As a result, undoubtedly one of the most beautiful buildings in Chicago, the Tribune Tower by Raymond Hood, was erected. This building is Gothic and, as it proved, is the last of the Eclectics, for in this symposium of ideas for skyscrapers was an extraordinary design by a Finn, Eliel Saarinen. In Saarinen's drawings lay the solution of the skyscraper, a veritable philosopher's stone that would transmute the dross of eclecticism into the gold of the new architecture. Such corniceless and clean flanked buildings as 333 North Michigan, the Palmolive, the Daily News, the Marshall Field, one North La Salle, the Board of Trade, are all children of Saarinen's dream-mother.

The International Style as the new approach is being called, seems to be establishing itself as the architectural vehicle of the New Era now being born, as you have doubtless observed, with so much travail and with so much expense. Nor is it solely enveloping us in the cloudlike forms of the skyscraper. The Planetarium, the Chicago Motor Club, shops galore, residences in increasing numbers, and even a church or two proclaim the new dispensation. Even the 13th century architecture of the University of Chicago chapel owes its life to the new blood which is flowing in old veins. The Century of Progress Exposition is attempting to picture to you what the new architecture will be when the science of building has advanced so that its principles and forms can be applied to every sort of structure, and that brings us back to the problem that confronted us at the outset. What constitutes beauty? Will these strange shapes on the lake front, horrific to many of you, be acclaimed one day as were the colonnades on the Court of Honor? I feel that they may be. May I quote myself?

(*Walinger Photo*)

THOMAS E. TALLMADGE

Mr. Tallmadge, architect, lecturer and writer on architectural subjects, was born in Washington, D. C., April 24, 1876, the son of Louis Cass and Lida M. (Eddy) Tall-madge. He was graduated with the degree of Bachelor of Science from the Massachu-setts Institute of Technology in 1898, and was awarded the honorary degree of Master of Arts by Northwestern University in 1927. Since 1905 he has been a member of the firm of Tallmadge & Watson. Mr. Tallmadge has lectured on architectural history at the Art Institute and was professor of architecture at Armour Institute of Technology, and is serving as president of the Summer School of Painting at Saugatuck, Michigan. He was architect in chief of the Victory Loan decorations in Chicago in 1918.

He is president of the Art Commission of Evanston, a director of the Federated Council of Art Education, chairman of the board of art advisers of the State of Illinois, a member of the architectural commission for the restoration of Williamsburg, Virginia, a fellow of the American Institute of Architects, a governing member of the Art Insti-tute, vice-president of the Chicago Society of Etchers, and a director of the Chicago Regional Planning Association. Mr. Tallmadge is president of the Cliff Dwellers and a member of the Arts and Tavern clubs, the Lake Zurich Golf Club, Bear River Gun Club, Utah, the University Club of Evanston and of the Phi Beta Epsilon Fraternity. He was co-editor of The Significance of the Fine Arts, published in 1921, and is the author of The Story of Architecture in America, 1927, and of many brochures. With his partner, he is architect of many important buildings, chiefly ecclesiastical, such as First Methodist Church, Evanston, First Presbyterian Church, Chicago, Grace Lutheran Church, River Forest, Perkins Observatory, Delaware, Ohio, et cetera.

"A Century of Progress will be the luna moth of exhibitions, and only when the sun goes down behind the skyscrapers and darkness laps in from over the cool lake will the great buildings really open their myriad eyes and spread their damasked wings. Then, bathed and adorned with light—light innumerable of stains and splendid dyes that changes form and substance, that transforms, with the touch of Midas, earthborn structures into towers of ethereal gold, that now denudes, now covers with veils of changing mystery—the Exposition will be one of the most beautiful things that man has created."

THE WOMAN'S ATHLETIC CLUB
Philip B. Maher, architect.

(*Moffett-Russell Photo*)

ORVILLE J. TAYLOR

Mr. Taylor, attorney and partner in the law firm of Taylor, Miller, Busch and Boyden, was born in Sioux City, Iowa, September 8, 1885, son of Orville James and Eleanor Sarah (Harris) Taylor. After completing his elementary and high school education in the city of his birth, he matriculated at the University of Chicago and in 1909 received his LL.B. (Bachelor of Laws) degree at the Northwestern University Law School. In 1922 and 1923 he served as special assistant to the Attorney General of the United States, and together with the Hon. Jacob M. Dickinson, conducted the injunction proceedings against the shopmen's strike in the case of United States of America versus American Federation of Labor, et al. During the World War he attended the first Officers' Training Camp at Fort Sheridan and was there commissioned Captain of Cavalry and assigned for duty to the 86th Division at Camp Grant. In November, 1917, he was commissioned as Major, J. A., U. S. A., and served with his division overseas.

Mr. Taylor is a member of the Board of Education of Chicago; a member of the Chicago Plan Commission; a trustee of A Century of Progress, Chicago's (1933) World's Fair; member of the board of the Association Against the Prohibition Amendment, Illinois Division; member of the Chicago Real Estate Board; a director of the Chicago Stadium, and a director of L'Alliance Francaise. He is a member of the Chicago, Illinois and American bar associations; the Association of the Bar of New York; Chicago Law Institute; the Law Club; Legal Club; and American Branch of International Law Association; a member of the vestry of St. James Episcopal Church; is on the faculty, professor of law of private corporations, of Chicago Law School and is an American Legionnaire. His fraternities are Beta Theta Pi and Phi Delta Phi. His clubs are Chicago, Saddle and Cycle, Tavern, Attic, Chicago Riding, Exmoor Country, and Tippecanoe Lake Country.

On January 19, 1924, he married Catherine E. Apperson. His hobbies are golf and horseback riding.

THE CHICAGO MERCANTILE EXCHANGE AND ITS VAST OPERATIONS

Chicago, The World's Greatest Market for Butter, Eggs, Cheese, Poultry, Vegetables, and Fresh Fruits

WHEN Chicago speaks of its "Big Butter and Egg Men," it can do so without any exaggeration. "Big" is right. Since shortly after the Civil War, Chicago has been perhaps the most important dairy and poultry center in the world. This may be disputed by New York, but the fact remains that Chicago is without exception the world's greatest storage and distributing center for dairy products and poultry.

At first, when butter and eggs became of increasing importance to the farm industry, Elgin was the price-making center for the United States. The Elgin Board of Trade was formed in 1872, that city being considered the dairy capital of the Nation.

Before long, however, the men responsible for supplying Chicago with its daily quota of butter, eggs and poultry, and with shipping these commodities to the East, became discontented with the Elgin Board's restricted activities. The result was the formation of the Chicago Produce Exchange in 1874.

This Exchange at first handled not only, butter, eggs, cheese, and poultry, but fruits and vegetables as well. In 1898, the butter and egg divisions of the Produce Exchange divorced themselves from the organization and established the Chicago Butter and Egg Board. This Board functioned until 1919.

In that year, after prolonged discussion, it was decided that butter and eggs needed the facilities of a futures trading market, just as did grains, cotton and like commodities. This conviction had been growing steadily since shortly before the war.

The Butter and Egg Board was abolished and in its stead came into being the Chicago Mercantile Exchange. The Butter and Egg Board members formed themselves into an association operating not for profit, to handle "butter, eggs and other products" on a futures basis. Thus, from a beginning in 1874 there gradually evolved the greatest butter and egg market in the world and the formation of one of the most novel organizations in existence.

Just as the Chicago Board of Trade has provided facilities for trading in grains, so has the Chicago Mercantile Exchange provided a place where butter and eggs can be similarly handled. Hedging operations, speculative buying and selling and large scale merchandising operations are carried on daily on this Exchange.

Before many years after its organization, the Exchange found its quarters too cramped for its heavy business activity. As a result, the members decided to erect their own building. A site was purchased at the corner

(*Moffett-Russell Photo*)

LLOYD S. TENNY

Mr. Tenny, agricultural expert, and business manager of the Chicago Mercantile Exchange, was born in Hilton, New York, December 24, 1876, the son of Delos P. and Fannie Elizabeth (Lee) Tenny. On his graduation from the State Normal School at Brockport, New York, in 1896, he entered the University of Rochester, receiving his A.B. (Bachelor of Arts) degree in 1902. He was awarded a scholarship for research at the Marine Biological Laboratory, Woods Hole, Massachusetts, and in 1908 was engaged in post-graduate studies at Cornell. From 1911 to 1913 he was a member of the faculty at Cornell.

As first state leader of the county agricultural associations in New York, he assisted in establishing the first country farm bureaus. Entering the service of the Federal Government, he became in 1921 Assistant Chief of the Bureau of Agricultural Economics of the United States Department of Agriculture, in charge of the service and regulatory work of the Bureau, and in 1926, he was appointed chief of this Bureau, a position which he held for two years. Mr. Tenny was vice-president of the California Vineyardists Association from 1928 to 1929, and in the latter year, president of the Federal Fruit Stabilization Corporation of California. Since 1930 he has been business manager of the Chicago Mercantile Exchange, one of the great produce marts of the city. In 1921 Mr. Tenny served as a member of the Advisory Committee of the War Finance Corporation. He is a member of the Alpha Delta Phi Club of New York, the Cosmos Club of Washington, D. C., and the Midland Club of Chicago. He is the author of many magazine articles and published addresses.

Mr. Tenny was married June 1, 1907, to Abby Warn of Washington, D. C. They have three children, Fannybelle Lee, Stanley Warn and Lloyd Stanley.

of Franklin and Washington streets and a 17-story structure completed in 1928.

The Exchange occupies the second and third floors. Its trading floor ranks as one of the most spacious and most beautiful in the Nation, exceeded in size only by the new Chicago Board of Trade and the New York Curb floors.

The extent of the trading may be realized from the fact that a carlot of butter consists of 19,200 lbs. and a carlot of eggs 12,000 doz., and the Exchange handles between 50,000 and 70,000 carlots a year. In 1925, sales totalled 99,000 cars. The value of the products sold on the futures call in 1930 was $349,293,000 and in 1931 was $204,338,000. In both these years, prices were exceptionally low.

Huge dairy organizations, packing houses and brokerage concerns use the facilities of the Exchange extensively, the dairy concerns and packers largely for hedging operations, while the brokers supply their customers with information in order that the latter may speculate in butter and eggs. The turnover is rapid and the margins relatively small. Thus butter and eggs have become increasingly attractive in the past few years in the speculative market. In addition, hundreds and even thousands of smaller butter and eggs houses, storage houses, jobbers, and shippers have found hedging in butter and eggs their best means of insuring profit.

In 1931, the Exchange started branching into other lines. It placed potato futures on the board for trading. There were 5,000 cars sold in that year, a very poor year for the potato industry. In 1932, an even worse year, trading was much smaller, but the Exchange plans to increase this trading in the future while adding other commodities to its list.

As to Chicago and its Central Market fame, it has taken first rank in the dairy and poultry industries, due for the most part to its excellent facilities for handling these perishable products and its nearness to the heart of the great production area. While few persons realize this fact, it nevertheless is true that dairy and poultry products annually have a monetary value

(Kaufmann & Fabry Co. Photo)
MERCANTILE EXCHANGE BUILDING
Alfred S. Alschuler, architect.

(Harris & Ewing Photo)

SAMUEL E. THOMASON

Mr. Thomason, president and publisher of the Daily and Sunday Illustrated Times of Chicago, was born in Chicago, Illinois, January 24, 1883, son of Frank Davis and Diana M. (Bean) Thomason. He received his A. B. (Bachelor of Arts) degree at the University of Michigan in 1904 and his LL. B. (Bachelor of Laws) at Northwestern University in 1906. He was admitted to the Illinois Bar in 1906, practicing in the office of Stuart G. Shepard until 1909, when he became a member of the firm of Stuart G. Shepard & Robert R. McCormick. From 1911 to 1918 he was a member of the firm of Shepard, McCormick, Thomason, Kirkland & Patterson. He was vice-president and business manager of the Chicago Tribune from 1918 to 1927. The Illustrated Times, of which Mr. Thomason is president and publisher, shows news events graphically and is of convenient tabloid size. He is also publisher of the Tampa (Florida) Tribune.

Mr. Thomason was president of the American Newspaper Publishers' Association, 1924-1926. He is a member of the American, Illinois State, and Chicago bar associations and Theta Delta Chi Fraternity. His clubs are University, Chicago, Legal, Mid-Day, Tavern, South Shore, Glen View, and Swannanoa.

He married Alexina E. Young, of Chicago, September 10, 1907. They have one daughter, Elizabeth, and a foster-son, Ralph.

more than twice as great as all grains and cotton combined.

We may stress that fact all the more in emphasizing Chicago's importance in this field of agriculture. Some idea of Chicago's leadership can be
gained from the following:

Receipts of butter in Chicago in a year total more than 3,000,000 tubs,
in the neighborhood of 200,000,000 pounds. Egg receipts total 4,000,000
cases and over, more than 120,000,000 dozen. Surplus stocks stored in
Chicago during flush production for use in low production seasons, reach
a peak of between 25,000,000 and 30,000,000 lbs. of butter, and egg holdings average between 50,000,000 and 65,000,000 dozen. This means that
in the huge cold storage warehouses of Chicago around 25 per cent of the
surplus stocks of the entire nation are held.

The peak holdings of frozen poultry in Chicago reach to around 3,000,-
000 pounds while the surplus cheese stocks on hand in Chicago warehouses
during a year run well over 2,000,000 pounds. This does not take into
account the thousands and hundreds of thousands of pounds of cheese and
dressed and live poultry sold daily and which never enters a warehouse
except for a short stay.

Nor has mention been made of the enormous quantities of milk shipped
into Chicago for reshipping elsewhere for manufacturing purposes. More
millions of dollars of value are represented in this item.

(Koehne Photo)

JOHN R. THOMPSON, JR.

Mr. Thompson, Jr., president of John R. Thompson Company, owners and operators of about one hundred and twenty Thompson's Restaurants in forty-two cities, was born in Chicago, September 2, 1894, the son of John R. and Rose (Holloway) Thompson. After graduating from Taft School, Watertown, Connecticut, in 1913, he attended Yale University and received his B. A. (Bachelor of Arts) degree in 1917. While a student at Yale he spent his vacations working in Thompson's Restaurants, obtaining first-hand experience that was useful to him, when, at the age of thirty, he became president of the Thompson Restaurant interests. The slogan, "Thompson's Restaurants Must Be a Good Place to Eat!" is substantiated by the fact that all the new restaurants have been built from the profits of preceding ones. A completely equipped laboratory tests all the food products for Thompson's Restaurants, most of which are open twenty-four hours a day.

In addition to his responsibilities as head of this great corporation, Mr. Thompson is president of John R. Thompson Securities Corporation, investment bankers; a director of the Chicago, North Shore and Milwaukee Railroad Company, and Personal Loan and Savings Bank. He is a life member of the Chicago Historical Society and of the Field Museum of Natural History and member of the Beta Theta Pi Fraternity. His club affiliations are University, Chicago Athletic, Racquet, Knollwood, Bob o' Link Golf, and the Yale Club of New York. His hobbies are horses and baseball.

On June 22, 1916, Mr. Thompson married Lois Bell, of Chicago, and they have three children, Eleonore Rose, Lois, and Pauline.

Chicago is truly a world center as far as the dairy and poultry indus-tries are concerned. The price paid for butter, eggs, poultry, cheese, etc., in Chicago is of great importance to the farmer in Iowa and to the buyer in the East. The Chicago prices are quoted all over the nation and recorded in London and Copenhagen as well. The price of butter in Chicago is of greatest interest in Australia, New Zealand and wherever else butter is manufactured in large enough quantity to be exported.

Of equal importance to the outside world is Chicago as a potato market, an apple market and as a market for other produce of a like nature. In the East, it is true that Boston leads as a potato market, distributing the crops of Maine and the southern coast states. But Chicago is the largest market for the fine Idaho russets and for the great quantities of potatoes produced in the Midwest.

Chicago has the facilities of a great produce market where auctions are held daily and where prices are determined daily. Thousands of carloads of potatoes travel to Chicago from Idaho, Colorado, Nebraska, Texas, Mis-souri, Kansas, Oklahoma, Iowa, Minnesota and Wisconsin, to mention only the heaviest shipping states. Likewise, apples roll in almost by trainloads throughout the shipping season, and citrus fruits, as well as various other farm products, are governed as to price by the Chicago quotations.

(*Kaufmann & Fabry Co. Photo*)
SOUTH WATER MARKET—CHICAGO'S PRODUCE DISTRIBUTING CENTER
Thielbar & Fugard, architects. McLennan Construction Company, contractors.

(Gibson Photo)

REV. JOHN THOMPSON

Dr. Thompson, pastor of the First Methodist Episcopal Church (Chicago Temple), was born in Nenthead, England, the son of Jonathan and Hannah (Erwine) Thompson. He was educated at the London Polytechnic, the Wesleyan Methodist Theological School, Oxford University, and the Garrett Biblical Institute of Evanston, from which he received his Doctor of Divinity (D.D.) degree in 1921. Dr. Thompson was engaged for several years in city missionary work in London. He came to the United States on a visit in 1892 and was invited to remain permanently here. He was ordained to the ministry in 1897 and received his citizenship papers in the same year. Prior to coming to the Chicago Temple, he had held two pastorates in Chicago, the first at Grace Church, the second at the Hyde Park Church. He has been pastor of the Chicago Temple since 1920.

Dr. Thompson is a trustee of Garrett Biblical Institute and of Wesley Memorial Hospital, and since 1914 has been superintendent of the Chicago Home Missionary and Church Extension Society, which is doing missionary work among twenty-five nationalities in Chicago. He is editor of The City Foursquare, and as a contributor to the church press has for many years furnished weekly pages interpreting current events. He is the author of "The Soul of Chicago" (1920).

Dr. Thompson was married June 8, 1888, to Jane Cousin of England, the mother of his two children, Sarah Hannah (Mrs. W. A. Gamon) and Howard Newton. His second wife was Ruth Clegg of Chicago. They were married October 16, 1907.

CHICAGO'S EVERYDAY HEROES, THE BLUECOATS

The Distinguished Record of the City's Police Force

BY JOHN I. HOWE

Detective, Chicago Police Department

CHICAGO has an undeserved reputation for crimes involving violence, and many Europeans are persuaded, indeed, that life is unsafe on Chicago's streets.

It is true that many of Chicago's crimes, such as the operations of the "car barn bandits" and the more recent St. Valentine's day "massacre" have been spectacular. It is also true that modern inventions, especially the automobile and the machine gun, have made the criminal more resourceful than ever.

The newspapers, moreover, either because their editors have been graduated from the night police beat, or because of the theory that it is more wholesome to give widespread publicity to crime and bring it out into the open, have focused the spotlight on crime, and have overestimated its news value.

In the days when the open saloon and the gambling house provided the underworld with a safety valve, there was less crime in Chicago than today. It can no longer be denied that prohibition, bringing with it a golden opportunity for gain by traffic in illicit liquors, has produced a new especially audacious type of criminal, has increased the influence of the gangster, and developed an unholy alliance between politics and organized crime.

Chicago's police department has been faced with problems that were inconceivable at the beginning of the century, and in order to cope with the outlaw has had to resort to every aid offered by science. Members of Chicago's police force have studied ballistics under Col. Calvin Goddard at Northwestern University's classes in scientific crime detection. They have been enrolled in the courses in police administration conducted by the University of Chicago. The radio, of course, is the latest contribution of science to the prevention of crime. Bulletins sent out constantly on a short wave length from the radio station in the Police Building are picked up not only by other stations but by the cruising squads as they patrol the streets.

As for Chicago's crime record, statistics easily available will show that it is proportionately far below that of many other cities. In comparison especially with certain southern cities, where the slaying of a negro is not regarded as news, Chicago can be said almost to have an enviable record.

That Chicago's bluecoats are indeed the "finest" needs no further proof than that offered by the annual police games at Soldier Field. The exhibitions of horsemanship, marksmanship, boxing, wrestling, and field athletics have won the admiration of the thousands who have witnessed them.

Evidence of the individual heroism of Chicago's policemen is seen in the collection of stars in the office of the police commissioner. Each star in this galaxy represents the supreme sacrifice on the part of its former

(*Lewis-Smith Photo*)

ORVILL W. THOMPSON

Mr. Thompson, president and general manager of the Commercial Instrument Corporation of Chicago, was born in Vermillion, South Dakota, November 15, 1879, son of Myron D. and Anna Thompson. He attended the University of South Dakota. In 1913, he began with James P. Marsh and Company, manufacturers of steam specialties, in Chicago, and was president until 1929, when this organization became part of the Commercial Instrument Corporation, which also comprises the following: Connecticut Telephone and Electric Corporation, Meriden, Connecticut; Tiffany Manufacturing Company, operated as Tiffany Division of Connecticut Telephone and Electric Corporation; The American Paulin System, Inc., Los Angeles, California; Sargent Company, Chicago; and Carl Norgren Company, Denver, Colorado.

Mr. Thompson was a member of the South Dakota State Senate from 1906 to 1908 and was appointed colonel of the South Dakota National Guard in 1903. His clubs are University, Exmoor Country, The Tavern, Midland, Everglades (Palm Beach, Florida), and The Cloud (New York City). He is a member of the Phi Delta Theta Fraternity and one of three life members of its Scroll Endowment Trustees.

In 1913 Mr. Thompson was married to Blanche Gilson, of Knovxille, Iowa.

wearer. They tell the story of unsung, everyday heroes who have marched steadfastly and without thought of personal safety, to a rendezvous with death. They tell of gun duels in dark alleys, of fights against tremendous odds, of truly noble deeds done quietly and simply in the routine discharge of duty.

The great Chicago fire of 1871; the railroad strikes of 1877 and 1894; the Haymarket riot of 1886; the Iroquois fire, the teamsters', stockyards, and street car strikes, the race riots, the Eastland disaster—all have tested their mettle.

Need of adequate protection against the lawless element was felt as far back as the Fort Dearborn days. To the fast-growing community that was young Chicago flocked gamblers and adventurers, men who held the idea that the world owed them a living, and were bent on getting it without being overscrupulous. Prosperity, loose society, unrestricted immigration brought fortune seekers and individualists, some of whom needed careful watching.

Before Chicago's incorporation as a town, constables acted as peace guardians. In May, 1837, Chicago elected a "high constable." His election marked the beginning of the Chicago Police Department.

It was in 1854 that Chicago had its first experience with a mob. In a Fourth of July speech of that year Stephen A. Douglas had made a bitter attack on the Free Soilers and the Know Nothings. His political enemies in Chicago determined to give him a warm reception on his return home. Douglas arrived in Chicago on August 25 to find the town in arms against him. Despite warnings and threatening letters, he decided to speak at a meeting to be held in the old Market Hall. Mayor Milliken, a Democrat,

DES PLAINES RIVER, WITH FOREST PRESERVE ON BOTH SIDES

(Underwood and Underwood Photo)

CHARLES M. THOMSON

Mr. Thomson, lawyer, was born in Chicago, the son of James and Julia (Marsh) Thomson. He is a graduate of Washington and Jefferson College, receiving his Bachelor of Arts degree in 1899 and his Master's degree in 1902. He attended Northwestern University Law School, receiving his Bachelor of Laws degree in 1902. In that year he began his practice of law in Chicago.

In the spring of 1908 Mr. Thomson was elected to the Chicago City Council. He was reelected twice, in 1910 and 1912. In November of the latter year he was elected to Congress from the Tenth Illinois District, where he served from 1913 to 1915. In June, 1915, he was elected a Judge of the Circuit Court of Cook County. In 1917 the Supreme Court of Illinois appointed Judge Thomson a member of the Appellate Court for the First District where he continued to serve until 1927, when he returned to the practice of his profession, becoming associated with the firm of Chapman and Cutler, where he has continued since that time.

In October, 1905, he married Bessie Holbrook of Chicago. They have two children, Dorothy and John Holbrook. Their home is in Winnetka.

presided, and took every precaution to preserve the peace. A heckler in the audience supplied the spark that touched off the explosion. An exchange of repartee was followed by a hostile demonstration. Pandemonium broke loose. The "Little Giant" was surrounded by a maddened mob. A cordon of police, augmented by citizens, managed to break through the crowd and rescue him. This sudden outcropping of mass violence left Chicago wondering what would have happened if the city had not had a few well disciplined policemen.

Dr. Levi D. Boone, candidate of the American or Know Nothing party, was elected mayor in March, 1855. The entire city government fell under the control of this party. Race prejudice ran high, and every applicant for employment under the new administration was obliged to prove that he was born on American soil. The city council passed an ordinance providing for a police force of ninety men, every man to be a native American. This discriminatory measure was enforced despite the fact that half the population of Chicago was of foreign birth. Today, the flower of many nationalities is represented on the force.

When Mayor Boone raised the liquor license fee from $50 to $300, and tried to enforce a Sunday closing ordinance, he stirred up a hornets' nest. The rear and side doors of the whisky shops remained open to natives, but the German beer gardens were, by order, closed tight. The Germans resisted, and more than 200 arrests were made. One of the German saloon keepers was made defendant in a test case, whereupon a mob of 500 or more sympathizers marched solidly upon the court to demand a verdict in their favor. The mob was dispersed, but it reassembled later in the day, this time armed with deadly weapons. In Clark street, between Lake and Randolph, the rioters were confronted by a body of police. A battle followed, with casualties on both sides. The mob was defeated. The Chicago police, in their first significant test of strength, had proved equal to the occasion.

In 1871, the force numbered about 310 men. They showed of what stuff they were made during the tragic days of October 8, 9, and 10 of that year, when the entire city from De Koven street on the south to Lincoln Park on the north was swept by flames. Many of these bluecoats themselves had homes and families. Despite the fact that their homes had been wiped out and the fate of their loved ones was in doubt, they remained at their posts day and night, protecting property, aiding the firemen, and maintaining law and order to the best of their ability.

In July, 1877, transportation was paralyzed by a strike affecting the great transcontinental railroad lines. At a mass-meeting in Market street, soap-box orators harangued the crowd, denouncing capital and the police, but the meeting adjourned without violence. A few days later, a similar gathering became so menacing that the police intervened and dispersed the agitators by the use of blank cartridges. Everywhere, however, mobs were proceeding from shop to shop, demanding that the workers lay down their tools and join the strikers. Mayor Heath, sensing a crisis, called upon the

(Fernand de Gueldre Photo)

GEORGE PAULL TORRENCE

Mr. Torrence, president of the Link-Belt Company, of Chicago, was born in Bethel, Connecticut, February 24, 1887, son of George P. and Mary (Ferguson) Torrence. Graduated from Purdue University as Bachelor of Science in Mechanical Engineering, he began his business life with the Ayer & Lord Tie Company in Arkansas, followed by a two-year shop apprentice course in the Pittsburgh shops of Westinghouse Air Brake Company. In 1911, he entered the employ of Link-Belt Company in Indianapolis.

After successively holding various managerial positions with Link-Belt Company, including that of vice-president and general manager of Indianapolis operations, Mr. Torrence was elected director of the company in 1931, and president in March, 1932, with headquarters in Chicago. The company manufactures elevating, conveying, excavating and power transmitting machinery. Mr. Torrence is a director of Fletcher Trust Company in Indianapolis, and a member of the Indianapolis Board of Trade, the University Club of Chicago, the Evanston Country Club, the Alpha Tau Omega Fraternity, and the honorary fraternity of Tau Beta Pi.

On September 3, 1912, he was married to Florence Abbott at Wawasee, Indiana. There are three children, George Paull, Jr., Dorothy, and Haskell.

citizens and the police to crush the rioting at any cost. Several bloody skirmishes resulted. One mob assembled at the C. B. & Q. roundhouse in West 16th street, bent on wrecking the place. An advancing police squad was met with a barrage of stones and bullets. Revolvers in one hand, clubs in the other, the police charged the mob, and after an hour's fight, broke it up. Again Chicago's everyday heroes had made good. They were lauded on all sides for their pluck and courage.

They were to receive another baptism of fire on May 4, 1886, the day of the Haymarket riot. A group of anarchists had scheduled a meeting at the West Side market place. Incendiary speeches were in progress, and the mob was being worked up to a dangerous pitch when Inspector Bonfield drew up his forces, marched to the scene of trouble, and ordered the speakers from the platform. A sputtering noise was followed by a terrific explosion, and a volley of pistol shots was directed against the police. The police, recovering from the shock, returned the fire. Men on both sides fell dead or wounded. The police victims are still honored today at memorial services held by the survivors. A monument has been erected in their memory.

The Pullman strike of 1894 spread to Chicago. Rioting followed, but was put down by the police. At the Iroquois fire, the police fought their way into an inferno and carried to safety scores of maddened, panic-stricken people. The early years of the century brought the prolonged stockyards strike and the bitter strike of the teamsters, again taxing the resources of the police department. The south side race riots would have been much more serious had it not been for the effective work of the police. When the city was thrown into confusion by the street car strikes, the police likewise preserved order and prevented rioting. One of their most gruesome jobs was the rescue of hundreds of bodies from the capsized excursion steamer, the Eastland.

In their more peaceful duties they have acquitted themselves admirably. The handling of hundreds of thousands of people on such occasions as the Eucharistic Congress, the Dempsey-Tunney fight, and the Army-Navy football game at Soldier Field is all to their credit. In every Memorial Day parade, the blue ranks of the police, on foot or mounted, and the police band have made only the most favorable impression.

Chicago's police department has grown until the force now numbers 6,700 men, including a fine company of "Mounties." Owing to their watchfulness, citizens live here in less fear of their lives and property than the citizens of any other large community. New York, Philadelphia, and Los Angeles are grappling with the same problems that confront Chicago, for in these cities the underworld is well organized, well supplied with money, and resourceful. Chicago's crime rate is, of course, affected by its many nationalities and by its geographical location, but despite its emphasis by the newspapers, it is no greater than that of other cities in which the same problems obtain.

(Matzene Photo)

HOWARD VAN SINDEREN TRACY

Mr. Tracy, president of Rogers and Tracy, Inc., stocks and bonds, was born in Louisville, Kentucky, October 8, 1887, son of Howard and Bessie (Lindsley) Tracy. He was educated at private schools and under tutors, later at Northwestern Academy, and from 1906 to 1908 attended Harvard University. He served as a partner in the firm of A. E. Butler and Company, stocks and bonds, of Chicago, until 1914, was executive and director of John Burnham and Company from 1916 until 1924, and since that time has been president of Rogers and Tracy, Inc. He was also a director of Holland-St. Louis Sugar Company of Michigan and of Tracy & Avery Company of Ohio, and is regarded as an authority on sugar.

Mr. Tracy is an active member of the Chicago Association of Commerce. He was the organizer in 1919 and first president, now secretary, director, and member of the executive committee of the Investors Protective Bureau, Inc., which was established to cooperate in the effective administration of the Illinois "blue sky" law and to assist in the suppression of bucket shop and fraudulent securities evils. This Bureau has been highly successful and has been widely copied throughout the United States. He has been an Illinois delegate to various waterways congresses, a director of the Advertising Council of the Association of Commerce, an active member and director of the Chicago Crime Commission, and is one of the leaders in Chicago civic affairs. He was consulted in the drafting of the Illinois "blue sky" law, and originated the idea of "Class C" securities. He is a member of the Chicago Historical Society, life member of the Art Institute of Chicago, and has written tariff articles used in Republican presidential campaigns. He is interested in historical research and has one of the largest private collections of rare autographed letters in America. He is a member of the Harvard-Yale-Princeton, Mid-Day, The Tavern, Evanston Country, Indian Hill Winter, and Barrington Hills Country clubs. His principal recreations are music, hunting, horseback riding, and various other sports.

On April 19, 1916, Mr. Tracy married Ruth Wilbur Alexander of Nashville, Tennessee (divorced 1925), and they have one daughter, Anne Alexander.

CHICAGO'S VAST UNDERGROUND TRANSPORTATION SYSTEM

Tunnels That Relieve Traffic Congestion and Bring the Railroad to the Shipper's Door

FEW Chicagoans as they go about their business in the Loop are aware of the vast network of tunnels under their very feet or give much thought to the subterranean labyrinth along whose corridors electric trams weave in and out freighted with hundreds of thousands of tons of goods. A descent into these Stygian realms and a tour of the dark catacombs is an experience never to be forgotten, though the Tunnel System makes no pretenses of being a scenic railroad.

Should its operations suddenly be suspended, however, pedestrians and motorists on the surface would realize immediately that something extra-ordinary had occurred, for the resulting traffic jam would be almost un-believable.

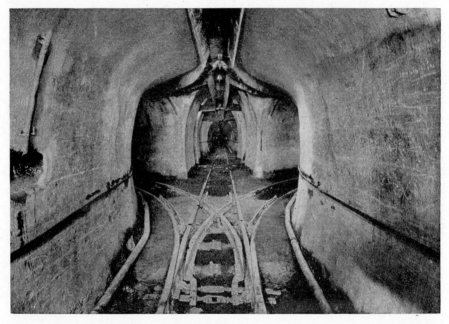

A four-way intersection and three-way switch.   The tunnels have 128 such intersections.

An airplane soaring over the Loop represents the uppermost level of transportation. The trams shuttling back and forth in the tunnels repre-sent the nethermost stratum. Between the two are the elevated structures, the city streets, and the river.

In the course of a year some 600,000 tons of package freight are moved through the Chicago freight tunnels. To this volume may be added 300,000 tons of coal, cinders and waste materials and, during normal times when

(*Underwood and Underwood Photo*)

SHERMAN W. TRACY

Mr. Tracy, president of Chicago Tunnel Company, which operates a railroad sixty-two miles long under the downtown district of Chicago, was born in Brevard, North Carolina, November 29, 1866, son of Samuel Joseph and Arminda Catherine (Hogsed) Tracy. He began his business career as a telegraph operator for the Hocking Valley Railway in 1883; then was with the I. I. & I. Railroad as agent in Indiana; and later was an accountant and auditor at Kankakee, Illinois. From 1907 to 1908 he was in Chicago as a statistician for the New York Central Railroad. From 1908 until 1912 he was superintendent of car service and auditor for the Indiana Harbor Belt Railroad at Hammond, Indiana.

Mr. Tracy joined the Chicago Tunnel Company and associated companies in 1912 as vice-president and has been president since 1916. He is also president of the Chicago Warehouse and Terminal Company and the Chicago Tunnel Transport Company and is vice-president of the Chicago Tunnel Terminal Corporation. Mr. Tracy is a member of Union League, Traffic, and Olympia Fields Country clubs.

He married Mary Alice Carr, February 14, 1889. Their children are Agnes Veronica (deceased) and Oswald Crawford.

there is considerable building going on, a vast amount of excavated clay.

Many of the great buildings in the central business district receive their coal through the tunnels, instead of on the surface, and dispose of cinders and ashes in the same way. Waste material is hauled by tunnel to a dis' posal station, loaded on scows and dumped far out in the lake.

The tunnels are connected by side lines, shafts, and elevators with many shipping concerns and warehouses, and with all railroad freight terminals. Their facilities are brought within reach of shippers, not located on tunnel lines, by four universal freight stations, strategically located outside the congested loop. The business concerns which use these stations find it economical to do so because the tunnels are a common carrier, subject to the same rules and regulations as other railroads. They issue through bills of lading over all lines. A shipper may deliver a single load, containing shipments to a dozen or more destinations, at one station where the sorting and routing will be done and the necessary shipping papers issued. Thus the shipper is relieved of the delay and expense incident to a dozen hauls through crowded streets to a dozen different railroad freight houses.

The tunnel system, which permits these extensive operations, is oper' ated by two affiliated corporations, the Chicago Tunnel Company, which, since the expiration of the original franchise, leases the bores from the city, and the Chicago Warehouse & Terminal Company, which owns the ap' proach tunnels, the shafts and elevators and the universal stations. The tunnels, in aggregate distance, extend 62.5 miles under the streets. There is a tunnel under nearly every street in the Loop. They extend south to Sixteenth street, west to Halsted street, north to Erie street and under Grant Park to Field Museum and the terminals and warehouses near the mouth of the river. They pass under the river eleven times. Most of the material for filling in the lake to make Grant Park was supplied by tunnels at no cost to the public. No other city in the world has such a system

Shipping room of a large commercial house. Showing how freight is loaded on to tunnel cars at commercial houses. Cars are moved to elevator by electric motor truck, in foreground.

(From Drawing by John Doctoroff)

MELVIN A. TRAYLOR

Mr. Traylor, president of the First National Bank of Chicago and the First Union Trust and Savings Bank, was born in Breeding, Kentucky, October 21, 1878, the son of James Milton and Kitty Frances (Harvey) Traylor. His home was a log cabin in the hills, remote from the railroad. He attended school in a log schoolhouse, his term ending at corn shucking time. Later he rode on horseback to the county seat to attend the High School in preparation for a teacher's examination. After four months of study he returned with his certificate, and for two years taught a small grade school near his birthplace. In 1898, at the age of twenty, in a suit of eight dollar "store clothes" and with sixty dollars in his pocket, he set out for Texas, traveling on horseback and by stage to Campbellsville, Kentucky, where he saw a railroad train for the first time. At Hillsboro, Texas, he clerked in a general store in the morning, earned his meals by working nights in a hotel, slept in the loft of the fire station, and studied law in his spare time. He was admitted to the Texas bar in 1901. In 1904 he was elected assistant county attorney of Hill County, Texas. The following year he abandoned law and went to work as cashier, janitor, and night watchman in the Bank of Malone, Texas, without pay. In 1907 he became cashier of the Citizens National Bank of Ballinger, Texas, was later vice-president, and when this bank consolidated with the First National, he was elected president of the combined institution. His wide knowledge of cattle loans, acquired during his stay in Texas, led to the vice-presidency of the Stock Yards National Bank of East St. Louis, Illinois, and in 1914 he came to Chicago as vice-president of the Live Stock Exchange National Bank, of which he became president in 1916.

During the World War he made a distinguished record as director of sales in Chicago for the Liberty Loan campaign, and in 1919 went to the First National Bank as vice-president. He has headed this institution since 1925. Mr. Traylor is a director of the U. S. Gypsum Company, the Standard Oil Company of Indiana, the Pan-American Petroleum & Transport Company, the General Electric Company, and the National Broadcasting Company. He is president of the Shedd Aquarium Society and a trustee

Continued on page 550

for the hauling of freight, or such connections between railroad freight
terminals. The tunnels, within the limits of their capacity, extend every
railroad to the shipper's door.

Strangely enough, the tunnels as a freight carrying system were an accident. The bores were originally intended to carry the wires and cables of
an independent telephone system and to lease space for similar purposes to
other concerns. This plan was several years in failing and it was during this
process that the tunnels as freight carriers were evolved. The costs of the

Nothing in the way of safety appliances is wanting, and, as a final protection the employees
have been carefully trained. There has never been a major accident in the tunnels.

(*Koehne Studios, Inc.*)

JULES URBAIN, JR.

Mr. Urbain is a partner of Olsen and Urbain, Inc., architects, and secretary of the Mandell Manufacturing Company, manufacturers of cardboard advertising displays. He was born in Chicago, Illinois, on January 24, 1894, son of Jules and Anna (Hommerding) Urbain. He studied architecture in the Society of Beaux Arts Architects, and in the office of Otis and Clark. During the World War, Mr. Urbain served in the Navy Department at Great Lakes, Illinois, as designing architect for Public Works in the 9th, 10th, and 11th Districts. Immediately after the World War, Mr. Olsen and Mr. Urbain organized the firm which bears their names.

Some of the recent important works of this firm are the Petrolagar Plant at Niles Center, Illinois, the Jefferson Electric Company Plant at Bellwood, Illinois, the William C. Grunow residence at River Forest, Illinois, and Mr. Grunow's estate at Lake Geneva, Wisconsin, and the Mandel Lowenstine residence at Valparaiso, Indiana. In 1920, Leif E. Olsen, Jules Urbain, and Albert E. Mandell, organized the Toymakers Inc., which later was reorganized into the Mandell Manufacturing Company.

On December 28, 1922, Mr. Urbain married Charlotte Selbman, at Chicago.

failure were heavy and the millions of dollars in losses were distributed among many venturesome investors. The tunnels have, however, won a place for themselves with the shippers. They have, in fact, made their facilities indispensable to Chicago. They are built into Chicago's scheme of freight distribution which covers a great territorial area and there is emphatic testimony that they not only save Chicago shippers time—by expediting freight movements at the initial point—and money—by eliminating or reducing costs of truckage—but they reduce the truck investment. Shippers who can avail themselves of tunnel service can make one truck do the work of several.

In the freight tunnels Chicago has one asset which cannot be measured in dollars and cents. The tunnels, running in silence 42 feet below the surface of the streets, divert from the street surface 5,000 to 6,000 heavy truck movements a day. In the business center of a great city, where a new traffic problem seems to follow the solution of every old one, the importance of such relief is hard to estimate and harder still to overestimate. Even if it seeks to build on reality, the imagination will fail to create an adequate picture. Such a number of trucks, normally spaced, would extend in a double line from Madison street north to Waukegan. The potentialities of jams, blockades, collisions and accidents are startling. But add this vast amount of heavy, cumbersome traffic to the already congested streets of the mile-square Loop and the districts immediately adjacent, and the potentialities are increased manyfold.

Street traffic problems, since the advent of the automobile, are far-reaching. The character of cities, the returns from taxes, the values of business property, the returns in rent, trade and commerce itself, have all been profoundly affected by this great increase in vehicular traffic.

Traffic engineers are unanimous in agreement that the freight tunnels have been the largest single contributor to the maintenance of the Loop as an efficient business district, to the maintenance of real estate values therein, and, therefore, to the maintenance of city income from taxes.

The tunnel system is, therefore, not only an asset to the merchants and shippers of Chicago and to the railroads but is as well a municipal and a civic asset.

The original franchise under which the Chicago Tunnel Company operated, expired February 20, 1929. By the terms of that ordinance, the tunnels became the property of the city on that date. After long negotiations they were leased to the Chicago Tunnel Company for a term of thirty years beginning in July 1932, and for a further term unless one of the parties to the agreement notifies the other of intention to terminate.

Shippers, railroads, city and company are, therefore, assured of the continuance of this unique and efficient freight service for a long time to come.

(Kaufmann and Fabry Photo)

MALCOLM D. VAIL

Mr. Vail, life insurance actuary, was born in Highland Park, Illinois, October 4, 1888, son of Henry Sherman and Jennie (McCulloch) Vail. In 1908 he graduated from Lake Forest (Illinois) Academy, and received his A. B. (Bachelor of Arts) degree at Cornell University in 1912. He has been in the life insurance business in Chicago since 1912 as member of the firm of H. S. Vail and Sons. He served in U. S. Navy Aviation Corps during 1918 and 1919, and received the commission of ensign.

He is a member of the Life Insurance Underwriters' Association, American Legion, U. S. Veterans of the World War, and is a Beta Theta Pi. His clubs are University, Adventurers, Chicago Yacht, (vice-commodore, 1932) Officers of World War. His principal recreations are sailing, hunting, and riding, and he may often be seen sailing his well-known "Gossoon II" in Chicago's front yard.

On April 4, 1916, Mr. Vail married Margaret Nye, of Cleveland, Ohio, and they have three children, Katherine Lewis, Malcolm Dennison, Jr., and Henry Sherman II.

(Shigeta-Wright Photo)

Ceres, goddess of grain and harvest, overlooking the trading floor of the Board of Trade.
Mural by John Norton.   Holabird & Root, architects.

LOUIS L. VALENTINE

Mr. Valentine, patron of the arts and philanthropist, was born in Lexington, Illinois, May 10, 1865, son of William and Eva (Joerger) Valentine. In 1927 he retired from the furniture manufacturing business, which he had entered as a youth, learning cabinet making from his father. He founded the Valentine-Seaver Company, manufacturers of upholstered furniture, in 1889. Relieved of business details, Mr. Valentine devotes much of his time to aiding the cause of the underprivileged boy. During 1930 and 1931 he was president of the Chicago Boys' Club, Inc. He is now a trustee of the Union League Foundation for Boys' Clubs, a director of Off-the-Street Club, and a director of the Boys' Clubs of America, the national organization. Mr. Valentine believes an investment in boyhood pays big dividends and advocates building more clubs, in order to keep boys busy and out of trouble during their unoccupied time. He is a director of the Illinois Academy of Fine Arts and of the Municipal Art League of Chicago, and president of the Chicago Galleries Association, which provides a permanent gallery for the display and sale of the best work of Chicago and western artists and interests the general public in art and in acquiring beautiful pictures for their homes. During the past six years the Chicago Galleries Association has been instrumental in the sale of more than one-half million dollars worth of fine paintings. One may become a member of the Chicago Galleries Association Circulating Department for twelve dollars a year and this fee entitles one to take one of the smaller sized pictures home and then exchange it for another picture every thirty days. This naturally increases the interest in art and brings about the sale of many of the paintings. The Galleries have a splendid central location at 220 North Michigan avenue, comprising five large exhibition galleries with the latest modern lighting equipment, which is ideal for effectively displaying the works of leading artists.

Mr. Valentine is a collector of fine paintings, sculpture and ivory carvings. His favorite pastimes are fishing, hunting and golf. He is a member of the Union League, Illinois Athletic, Lake Shore Athletic, Chicago Yacht, Cliff Dwellers, and Westmoreland Country clubs.

On November 24, 1898, he married Anna Louise Paul of Wisconsin Rapids, Wisconsin.

CHICAGO, ITS BAZAAR STREETS AND DEPARTMENT STORES

Merchants Who Have Added To The City's Fame

CITIES of the ancient and the medieval world rose to high position largely through the enterprises of their merchants. Chicago, too, has had and has its outstanding merchants, and to them owes much of its prestige.

State street, with its great department stores, each a "World's Fair" in itself, and Michigan avenue, with its specialty shops, are among the world's most famous bazaar streets. State street's show windows set the styles for merchandise display.

From Chicago's department stores an army of buyers goes out to the fashion centers of Europe to bring back the latest creations of the cou-tourier. From every country in the world come articles of use or beauty, to delight the shopper.

Chicago is said to be the birthplace of the department store in this country. It was H. G. Selfridge, a Chicago merchant, who introduced American methods in department stores of London.

The history of department stores in Chicago is the history of the city itself. It is the story of pioneer merchants who, losing everything but the goodwill of their customers in the great fire of '71, started to build their fortunes anew.

Identified with the growth and development of the department store in Chicago were Potter Palmer who, foreseeing the trend of business, led the exodus of retail merchants from Lake street to State, and Marshall Field, who insured the Illinois Central terminals for the downtown district.

Among Chicago's other merchants were Levi Z. Leiter, Marshall Field's first partner, and John G. Shedd; Charles Netcher and Edward and Charles W. Pardridge, founders of the Boston Store; E. J. Lehman, founder of The Fair; Samuel Carson, John T. Pirie, and Andrew MacLeish who entered into a partnership in 1864 under the name of Carson Pirie Company; the Mandel brothers, Simon, Leon, and Emanuel.

Others have brought the department store to the outlying districts, creating new shopping centers there.

The department store of today is an outgrowth of the general store of fifty or seventy-five years ago. Although the kind of merchandise sold remains essentially the same, the variety has been tremendously increased and the quality improved. The service too is highly specialized. Every convenience that can be thought of—rest rooms, tea rooms, writing rooms, expert shopping service—is at the disposal of customers. The local delivery service, requiring fleets of motor vehicles, extends far out into the suburbs.

Selling has become specialized. In the days when Chicago was younger, each salesman had his own following, and he sold throughout the store.

(Moffett-Russell Photo)

WILLIAM P. VARNEY

Mr. Varney, manager of the Chicago branch of the Hydraulic Press Brick Company, was born in Weston, West Virginia, February 19, 1872, son of John W. and Mary E. (Urbach) Varney. After attending the public schools of Loudon County, Virginia, he was a student at the Oak Dale Academy at Lincoln, Virginia. He began his business career with the Hydraulic Press Brick Company at Washington, D. C., in 1893, was sales manager of the company from 1905 to 1909, and has since been manager of the Chicago branch. Many office and industrial buildings in Chicago, as well as thousands of homes, are constructed with "hydraulic brick" furnished by the Hydraulic Press Brick Company. A few of them are the Wrigley Building, Carbide and Carbon Building, Builders' Building, Blackstone Hotel, the new Jefferson Electric Company Building at Bellwood, and many others.

Mr. Varney is a member of the American Ceramic Society, American Face Brick Association, Illinois Manufacturers' Association, and Chicago Association of Commerce. His clubs are: Chicago Athletic, Architects, Builders, Executives, Lake Shore Athletic, and Chicago Motor. His recreations are golf and automobiling.

On December 9, 1900, he married Mamie E. Cockrell, of Alexandria, Virginia, and their children are Charles William, Francis Carleton, Margaret Virginia, Vivian (Mrs. Malcolm M. Swift), William P., Jr., Edna, Ralph, and Alice May.

There were German-speaking salesmen with German followings, Swedish salesmen with their Swedish trade.

Rules for employees of that day would seem curious now. Employees were required to attend church regularly, and were forbidden to smoke while waiting upon customers. The stores were open six nights of the week.

John Wood, of Carson, Pirie & Scott's retail store, recalls the time when as a "light watcher" his duties consisted of turning on the lights when the sky was clouded and turning them off when the sun shone. "In the Spring," says Mr. Wood, "when April showers would alternate with sunshine, I was often kept so busy at this job that I felt like a one-man track team."

There were of course no telephones, typewriters, cash registers, or adding machines in the early days. Horse-drawn street cars and "handsome equipages" brought customers to the store. Often the proprietor himself, who met the shoppers at the door, would be called on to prevent a runaway.

Most of Chicago's dry-goods stores remained dry-goods stores until the World's Columbian Exposition, when they added such departments as groceries, furniture, shoes, and musical instruments.

Early advertising was based almost wholly on price-appeal, with no attempt to emphasize either quality or style. Thus, an advertisement in the Chicago Daily News of July 2, 1877, featured the following bargains for the "Fourth," men's linen suits, $2.25; ladies' fine gloves, 10 to 50 cents; white skirts, 59 cents to $1.00; sunbonnets, 15 cents; ladies' shoes, $1.00.

It was not until the gay '90's that style began to creep in. Plush capes with tight waists, leg-of-mutton sleeves, and Columbian collars were presented as the latest mode. High-heeled shoes, the subject of heated discussion by physicians, were recommended as "the thing for evening wear."

Today, to the appeal of price, style, and quality, is added color appeal. Linoleums of brilliant hues, tile cretonnes to match, and clocks to harmonize, kitchenware of red, green, yellow or blue—color in the kitchen, color in the bedroom, color in the living room—are making the home cheerful. Fashion experts, interior decorators and other specialists have been added to the sales staff—a far cry from the German speaking salesman and his German speaking trade.

As the line of demarcation between the dry-goods store and the department store is somewhat vague, the exact number of department stores in Chicago is not accurately known. The study of department store sales in 1926, the federal census year, embraces only 39 stores, but is extremely interesting. Sales by these establishments total $361,000,000, 18.2 per cent of Chicago's aggregate retail business—first among merchandising concerns.

These figures, however, do not begin to tell the story. They fail to take into account the many new department stores which have sprung up in the outlying and suburban districts. They indicate in a general way, however, that the department store in its development has kept pace with the swift, forward strides of the city.

(*Moffett-Russell Photo*)

HENRY B. VOORHEES

Mr. Voorhees, vice-president and executive representative in Chicago of the Baltimore & Ohio Railroad Company, vice-president, in charge of all departments, of the Alton Railroad Company, and president of the Baltimore & Ohio Chicago Terminal Railroad Company, was born at Saratoga Springs, New York, January 22, 1876, son of Theodore and Mary E. (Chittenden) Voorhees. He was a student at the College of the City of New York, 1891-1892, and in 1896 received the degree of Civil Engineer from the Rensselaer Polytechnic Institute. He began his railway career in 1897 as assistant supervisor of the Philadelphia & Reading Railway, and filled various positions with that company before going to the Baltimore & Ohio as assistant division engineer in 1901. He was promoted to assistant to general superintendent of transportation of that line in 1903, and then became superintendent of the Philadelphia division in 1905, serving in the latter capacity until 1910. From 1910 to 1911 he was assistant to president, and the following year served as general superintendent of transportation. From 1912 to 1917 he was general superintendent of the southwest district of the Baltimore & Ohio at Cincinnati.

In 1917 he returned to Baltimore and was general superintendent of transportation of the Baltimore & Ohio and affiliated lines until 1919, this being the period of Federal control during the World War. From 1919 to 1924 he was general manager of the New York terminal lines of the Baltimore & Ohio, at the same time being vice-president and general manager of the Staten Island Rapid Transit Company. He became general manager of the Western Lines of the Baltimore & Ohio in 1925 with headquarters at Cincinnati. Serving four years at Cincinnati, Mr. Voorhees became vice-president and executive representative in Chicago of the Baltimore & Ohio on June 15, 1929. He also has been president of the Baltimore & Ohio Chicago Terminal Railroad Company since June 15, 1929. Mr. Voorhees has been vice-president of the Alton Railroad Company since July 18, 1931. He is a member of Sigma Xi and Delta Kappa Epsilon fraternities. His clubs are the Chicago, Union League, Saddle and Cycle, and Olympia Fields of Chicago, the Queen City of Cincinnati, and the Maryland of Baltimore.

On October 20, 1903, Mr. Voorhees married Ethel Roland of Reading, Pennsylvania; died, February 27, 1924. There are two sons, Roland and Harlow C. On August 8, 1925, Mr. Voorhees married Grace Ferguson Anderson of Cincinnati.

Spire of Chicago's First Skyscraper Church, the Chicago Temple Building.
Holabird and Root, architects.

(*Blank and Stoller, Inc., Photo*)

RUSSELL S. WALCOTT

Mr. Walcott, as an architect, has designed many of the fine residences along Chicago's North Shore as well as in other parts of the country. He was born in Chicago, May 28, 1889, son of Chester P. and Martha Cook (Howe) Walcott. After graduating from Princeton University in 1912, he studied and traveled in Europe and served his years of apprenticeship as a draftsman in the office of Howard Shaw and other prominent architects.

During the war he was in the American Expeditionary Forces as sergeant in Company A, 335th Battalion, Tank Corps, and upon his discharge, in 1919, formed a partnership with his brother, Chester H. Walcott, for the practice of architecture. He was a member of the firm of Clark and Walcott from 1920 until 1922, after which he practiced for six years alone. In 1928 the present partnership of Russell Walcott and Robert Work was organized.

On October 12, 1917, he married Eugenia M. Buffington of Chicago.

TREATMENT AND PRESERVATION OF WOOD
CONSERVING AMERICA'S GREAT TIMBER RESOURCES

Despite Vanishing Forests, Chicago Holds Her Own as a Lumber Port

CONDITIONS in the lumber trade have changed significantly within recent years. Time was when the Chicago river front bristled with masts of lumber schooners bringing their cargoes of pine from the boundless forests of Wisconsin and Michigan, and later from Minnesota.

Chicago, because of its favorable location as a Great Lakes port, and its unrivaled rail connections, became the largest lumber port in the world, and lumber did much to establish Chicago's commercial supremacy over other Mississippi Valley cities.

Chicago lumbermen would bid for lumber at the cargo market at the foot of Franklin street; the ships would be towed to the yards of the purchasers, where the lumber was unloaded, piled, and seasoned. Not a few Chicago lumber merchants owned and operated their own fleets.

In those days, the lumber arriving by boats, was shipped to New York, Philadelphia, and other eastern markets; to the prairie States, and to the South and the Southwest. Wood was cheap and plentiful, and furnished about the only building material.

The forests at that time seemed inexhaustible. America was rich in natural resources; no immediate scarcity threatened, and the conservation movement was unheard of. But, despite their vast extent, the northern forests were gradually denuded. Wasteful methods of cutting and disastrous forest fires hastened the time when the supplies would run precariously low. Gradually the lumber camps moved back into the interior. No means of treating wood to prolong its life had been discovered.

By 1890 the timber resources of Wisconsin, Michigan, and Minnesota were greatly diminished. As the lumber camps receded, mills were built nearer the source of supply. Chicago as a lumber port was slipping.

Then the southern forests came to the rescue. For a while, more pine from the South reached Chicago than from the North. But eventually these forests, too, began to fail.

Today, though the picturesque lake schooners have disappeared, Chicago is again coming to the front as a lumber distributing center, but most of the lumber reaching the city is cut on the Pacific coast.

Late in the day, but perhaps not too late, scientific forestry combined with the scientific treatment of the finished product, is coming to the rescue of the forests. Waste is being eliminated at each end, and the prodigal use of lumber has been checked.

An entire industry, based on the preservative treatment of wood, has sprung up to avert the threatened scarcity of timber without restricting its use for the many purposes for which it is adapted.

(Puffer Photo)

WILLIAM T. WATKINS

Mr. Watkins, chairman of the board of Joyce-Watkins Company, was born in Chautauqua County, New York, January 30, 1860, and is the son of Sherman Sheldon and Julia Jane (McGlashen) Watkins. He was educated at the public schools of Red Wing, Minnesota, and began his business career as a purchasing agent of the "Soo Line" (Milwaukee, St. Paul and Sault Ste. Marie Railway) in 1886, continuing with this railroad until 1895. In 1897 he became vice-president of Bradley-Watkins Company, later president of Pillsbury-Watkins Company, both of which are now liquidated. He was vice-president of Joyce-Watkins Company from 1906 to 1909, president from 1909 until 1932, and is now chairman of the board. He is president of Watkins Creosoting Company, Arrow Transportation Company, and director of Wyoming Tie & Timber Company.

Mr. Watkins is a member of the Art Institute of Chicago, and his clubs are: Union League, Mid-Day, Chicago Athletic, Chicago Yacht, Evanston Club, Evanston Golf, and Gulf Hills (Mississippi). His favorite recreations are horseback riding, yachting, and golf.

He married Louise Genevieve, daughter of G. D. Williston of Lake View, Illinois, September 3, 1884. Their children are: Louise Genevieve (Mrs. Ricker Van Metre), Carrie Armine (Mrs. A. R. Joyce), William Wynne (who is president of Joyce-Watkins Company) and Sherman Sheldon.

Certain chemicals, it was found, would double or treble its life by pre-venting decay and guarding it from attack by insect pests—the two great enemies of wood.

Chemically treated, it becomes a highly satisfactory and economical construction material, and since less lumber is thus required for replace-ment, the drain on the forests is materially lessened.

Chicago is the center of this wood-preserving industry, which is guar-anteeing to future generations an abundant timber supply. Among the pioneers of the new industry is William T. Watkins, who, from his execu-tive offices in Chicago, directs the activities of his plant outside the city, where wood is treated with coal-tar creosote and zinc chloride to prolong its life.

From a modest beginning back in the '70's, when a few thousand rail-road ties were treated in a small cylinder, the industry has progressed until at the present time, 134 pressure treating plants, with cylinders ranging from six to eight feet in diameter and from 100 to 175 feet in length, turn out billions of feet of processed timber annually. The treated products include railroad ties, mine ties and timbers, cross-arms, poles, wood blocks, railway and highway bridge timbers, and piling.

While this industry had its beginning in an effort by consumers to effect economy by prolonging the life of timber, the success of that effort and the rapid growth of the wood processing business have been hailed nationally as the most efficient and practical means yet found to prevent waste of forest products.

For, as President Coolidge said in 1924, addressing the National Con-ference on Utilization of Forest Products, "a tree saved is a tree grown. . . . We hold the resources of our country as a trust. They ought to be used for the benefit of the present generation, but they ought neither to be wasted nor destroyed. The generations to come also have a vested interest in them."

(*Chicago Architectural Photographing Company*)
CHICAGO'S "FRONT YARD," A VIEW TAKEN FROM GRANT PARK

(Blank & Stoller, Inc., Photo)

CHARLES R. WALGREEN

Mr. Walgreen, president of the Walgreen Company which operates drug stores in 129 cities scattered through thirty states, was born in Knox County, Illinois, October 9, 1873, the son of Charles and Ellen (Olson) Walgreen, and was educated in the public schools and the Dixon Business College, Dixon, Illinois. He began as an apprentice in a drug store at Dixon, and became a registered pharmacist. Mr. Walgreen entered the retail drug business in Chicago in 1902, and in 1909 the business was incorporated, with two drug stores in operation. The Walgreen Company has enjoyed a steady growth. In 1920 there were nineteen units, doing an annual business of $1,500,000. Fifty more stores were added in the next five years, bringing the net sales to more than $9,000,000 annually. In 1932 the company was operating 471 stores in such important cities as Chicago, New York, St. Louis, Detroit, Indianapolis, Kansas City, Dallas, Milwaukee, Minneapolis, Nashville, Philadelphia, Pittsburgh, Rochester, N. Y., Salt Lake City, and Sacramento, and serving 144,000,000 customers. In addition, the company has two stores at A Century of Progress Exposition, one of them housed in its own building. It is the second largest chain drug store enterprise in the United State. The company has its own laboratories for the manufacture of drugs and toilet articles and for research work. It maintains creameries in Ohio and Illinois and large ice cream plants in Chicago and other cities. The Walgreen candy plant has an annual capacity of 5,000,000 pounds.

Mr. Walgreen served in the Spanish-American War as a private in Company L, 1st Illinois Volunteers. He is a member of the commission on the Fort Dixon Memorial to Abraham Lincoln, and of the Gorgas Institute, and donor of the Walgreen essay prize in 1930 and 1931. He is a director of the First National Bank of Chicago and First Union Trust and Savings Bank, and of the Dixon National Bank; of the National Chain Store Association, the Associated Chain Drug Stores, and the Northwestern University Associates; also a founder member of A Century of Progress Exposition, Chicago's (1933) World's Fair. He is a member of the Rotary, Beverly Hills and South Shore Country clubs, and of the Chicago Athletic Association.

Mr. Walgreen was married, August 18, 1902, to Myrtle R. Norton of Normal, Illinois. Their children are Charles R., Jr. and Ruth (Mrs. Justin W. Dart).

HARDWARE — A STUDY IN EVOLUTION
A Business That Reflects Chicago's Changing Tastes and Needs

PERHAPS no more striking commentary on the changes brought by modern science and invention into the everyday lives of all of us is to be seen than in the evolution of the wholesale hardware store. Hardware has an interesting story to tell of human progress, of advances in our mode of living from the days of the blacksmith shop and the kerosene lamp to the day of the garage and electricity.

In the attractive displays of golf clubs, radio sets, fishing tackle, and mechanical toys which now line the shelves and counters of the whole-sale hardware establishment we can see reflected the changes brought about by twentieth century manners.

One hardware house alone, Hibbard, Spencer, Bartlett & Co., which has been identified with Chicago for more than seventy-five years, will serve to illustrate this evolution.

Despite the fact that the automobile, electric light, the gas range, the washing machine, the central heating system, and other improvements and inventions have rendered obsolescent if not obsolete many of the items formerly carried by this pioneer firm, the number of items on its catalog has increased from 20,000 to 60,000 within recent years.

Only twenty-five years ago, at least one out of every four items sold had to do with a horse, a wagon, or a buggy. Today, the very names of these articles have all but passed out of the English language. Collars, straps, buckles, halters and chains, flynets, clevises, and wagon body rods are in small demand. Horseshoes, horseshoe nails, blacksmiths' anvils and bellows, which once formed the foundation of the hardware merchant's stock in trade, are left to gather rust today like Boy Blue's little tin soldiers. The felloe oiler, which prevented a hot-box in a buggy, has likewise faded from the picture.

Almost coincident with the exit of the horse and buggy came the fare-well to the kerosene lamp and all that went with it. As recently as thirty years ago, half an entire floor in the Hibbard, Spencer, Bartlett plant was given over to lamp goods and lanterns. There were stable lanterns, bicycle lanterns, dark lanterns, kitchen lamps, student lamps, raised or lowered on a rod, overhead parlor lamps, cleverly contrived with chains for their adjustment. The wick and chimney business alone was considerable. Today the company still carries a few lamps and lanterns, but the volume of such business is a mere trifle. Electric lighted homes and pocket flashlights for out-of-doors have brought about the change.

Combine harvesters have cut into the sale of steel forks and other farm tools. Concrete and steel have greatly reduced the consumption of nails. Because of the vast amount of preparation of building material at the mill, even to the boring of holes, fewer carpenter's tools are needed now than formerly.

GREEN DUCK
COMPANY

(Koehne Photo)

WILLIAM U. WATSON

Mr. Watson, president of Green Duck Company, manufacturers of adver-tising novelties, was born in Girard, Illinois, April 5, 1883, and is a son of Larken Burwell and Martha Susan (Keysear) Watson. He attended the public and high schools of Girard, Illinois, North Manchester (Indiana) College, Brown's Business College at Jacksonville, Illinois, and later studied at the Armour Institute of Technology, Chicago.

Mr. Watson began his business career in the Pitner Gasoline Lighting Company at Springfield, Illinois, where he was branch manager from 1909 until 1910, when he moved to Chicago to become general manager of the Sunderland Manufacturing Company. In 1921 he resigned from this company to become president and owner of the Green Duck Company, world's fore-most manufacturers of badges, advertising buttons, metal advertising novel-ties, name plates, emblems, etc. He is also president and owner of the Green-duck Metal Stamping Company of Chicago. He is a member of the Beach View Club and his favorite recreation is fishing.

On April 25, 1906, Mr. Watson married Madeleine de Sprangh Mason of Jacksonville, Illinois, and they have one son, John Robert.

The vogue of ready-made clothing has reduced to a great extent the amount of home sewing. Hibbard dealers used to sell thousands of dozens of pairs of scissors and shears each year, but today the sales are a mere fraction of what they were.

The tin shop is all but extinct. Before the days of better public laundries and stationary wash-tubs or washing machines in the home, the tinsmith manufactured wash boilers for family use, purchasing his tin as well as copper for the bottoms from the hardware companies. Today this business is all but gone.

Along with the wash boilers has gone part of the tinware that once went into the dairy industry. Tank cars for carrying milk have supplanted millions of cans.

Central heating has reduced to a negligible minimum the demand for stoves and stovepipes.

The biggest sales outlet for shotguns had always been the boys growing up on farms. Today, with families on farms fewer and smaller, even though city folk have more leisure for hunting and trapshooting, shotgun sales in the last twenty years have barely held their own.

Pocket knives have been hit by the automatic pencil which requires no sharpening. The metal cuspidor, once handled in carload lots, has almost disappeared.

But new times have created new demands. Just now we are in an era of color. More paint is used than at any previous time in the world's history. Kitchen ware now comes in cheerful colors. Garden tools have color schemes.

Toys, which were practically unheard of in hardware stores a generation ago, have now become an item of tremendous importance. As people have come into greater wealth, they have begun to think more about luxuries. Thousands of families spend more money annually on toys alone than would once have bought a horse and buggy.

The householder may no longer require an ax or a cross saw, for his winter fuel is supplied largely by the

1325 ASTOR STREET APARTMENTS
Rebori & Wentworth, architects.

(Fernand de Gueldre Photo)

JOHN WENTWORTH

Mr. Wentworth, a great-nephew of "Long John" Wentworth, who was one of the most famous of Chicago's pioneers and who was twice mayor of Chicago, was born in Chicago, September 24, 1892. He is the son of Moses Jones Wentworth and Lizzie Shaw (Hunt) Wentworth. He graduated from Harvard University, A. B. (Bachelor of Arts) degree, 1914; was a captain in the Aviation Service during the World War, serving with the 94th and 49th Squadron, A. E. F. In 1924 he became vice-president of Rebori, Wentworth, Dewey & McCormick, Inc., a firm engaged in general architectural practice. Among their work are the Racquet Club, 1325 Astor Street, The Cudahy Memorial Library, the Riding Club, and Curtis Airport.

He is chairman of the Architectural Committee of the Chicago Plan Commission. He is a member of the Chicago, Saddle and Cycle, Racquet, and Tavern clubs.

Mr. Wentworth was married in 1924 to Harriet Brown, of Baltimore.

gas and oil companies. But he spends more money for golf clubs than he ever did on tools for more productive forms of manual labor.

The man who would have been content once with a bamboo fishing rod requires a steel rod and the very latest artificial lures. Paved roads and the automobile have made it possible for the fisherman to go far beyond the limits of his own locality. If there are no fishing waters near home, he can reach the Minnesota or Wisconsin lakes and streams almost over-night.

Improved agricultural methods call for millions of yards of paper mulch. . . . Profits once made by the hardware dealer on bicycles are now made on radios. . . . Electrical devices of all kinds have become house-hold necessities.

(Kaufmann & Fabry Co. Photo)

Warehouses and industrial plants just north of the downtown district. The Hibbard, Spencer, Bartlett & Company building is in the left foreground.

Few Chicago firms have had as interesting a history or have been longer in business than Hibbard, Spencer, Bartlett & Co. The house was estab-lished in 1855 by William Gold Hibbard, who came to Chicago in 1849 from Cortland, N. Y. The first store occupied a four-story building in South Water street, equipped with a windlass for hoisting heavy goods, and a chute for lowering boxes to the basement. In 1857, the house of Tuttle, Hibbard & Co., as it was then known, was wiped out by fire, but more commodious quarters were opened in Lake street. Franklin F. Spencer, who entered the firm about that time, was its first traveling salesman, his territory being confined largely to Iowa. Today the firm has sales repre-sentatives in every State in the Union and in several foreign countries. The great fire of 1871 again reduced the stock to molten metal and left the Lake

CHARLES J. WHIPPLE

Mr. Whipple, president of Hibbard, Spencer, Bartlett and Company, was born in Chicago, July 10, 1885, son of Charles Backus and Almira (Hayward) Whipple. He received his preparatory education at the Chicago Manual Training School and obtained his B. S. degree in Electrical Engineering at the University of Michigan in 1907. He became an apprentice at the Western Electric Company in June, 1907. In February, 1908, he started with Hibbard, Spencer, Bartlett and Company, wholesale hardware, as a stock clerk, later becoming a salesman, and then a sales correspondent. Mr. Whipple became superintendent of Hibbard, Spencer, Bartlett and Company in 1913; was made general manager in 1916; and in 1920 was elected vice-president and in 1926, president.

During the World War he was associated with the Committee on Personnel of the Adjutant General's Department, and installed the first personnel system at Camp Dodge during the summer and fall of 1917. For the duration of the War, he served as Personnel Supervisor of the Military Camps in the Central West. Mr. Whipple is a director of the Chicago Railways Company. He is vice-president of the Employers' Association of Chicago, member of the Northwestern University Vocational Council, president of the Chicago Home for the Friendless, and a member of Alpha Delta Phi Fraternity and Tau Beta Pi Honorary Society. His clubs are Chicago, University, Industrial, South Shore Country, and Barrington Hills Country. He has contributed many articles to hardware trade journals and has spoken on trade problems to association gatherings. His principal recreation is golf.

Mr. Whipple married Elsa Kempf, of Ann Arbor, Michigan, April 2, 1910. Their children are Pauline Elizabeth and Charles John, Jr.

street building in ruins. Business was carried on temporarily in Mr. Hibbard's Prairie avenue home. Customers responded generously to an appeal to pay their outstanding obligations promptly. Orders were filled from New York, and new supplies were rushed to Chicago from New York and Milwaukee. The Hibbard stable was jammed with hardware, and a big shed was erected in the garden. The drawing room space not filled with desks was stored with cutlery. The clerks slept on the floor and ate in the kitchen.

Business was resumed finally in Lake street, but in 1903, the firm erected a tenstory building near the State street bridge, which was occupied until the Wacker drive improvement forced the company out. The present fourteenstory plant at 211 East North Water street was uncompleted, but the wreckers had arrived, and it was necessary to remove a $3,000,000 stock without delay. A temporary storehouse was found, and the gigantic moving job was managed.

Today, the firm occupies one of the most modern commercial homes in America, a plant in which more than 1,000,000 square feet is devoted to the display of hardware. Steamships, freight trains, and cars of the Illinois Tunnel Company load and unload goods at the back door.

(*Courtesy, Curtis Lighting, Inc.*)

McJunkin Building at Wilson Avenue and Broadway—an interesting example of the way various Chicago buildings are floodlighted to concentrate attention on the location.

(*Moffet-Russell Photo*)

HAROLD F. WHITE

Mr. White, member of the law firm of White and Hawxhurst, was born in Chicago, December 8, 1877, son of Captain Lyman A. and Annie Hungerford (Ferris) White. After receiving his LL.B. (Bachelor of Laws) degree from Lake Forest University in 1901, he was admitted to the Illinois Bar and became associated with the late Albert N. Eastman in practice in Chicago the same year. He has been a member of the firm of White and Hawxhurst and its predecessors continuously since that time.

Mr. White is a director of several industrial and financial organizations in Chicago and other cities. He is a director of the United Charities of Chicago, former chairman of the Legal Aid Committee, member of the American and Illinois State Bar associations, member of the Chicago Bar Association, life member of the American Law Institute, and member of the Association of the Bar, City of New York. He is a life member of the Art Institute of Chicago, member of the Field Museum of Natural History, member and ex-president of the Municipal Voters League; and member of the Chicago Historical Society, Chicago Geographical Society, and Delta Chi Fraternity. His clubs are Union League (member Public Affairs Committee), City, Law (ex-president), Commercial (secretary, 1930-1932), Quadrangle, Arts, South Shore Country, and the Chikaming Country of Lakeside, Michigan, (president). His favorite diversions are golf and the drama. His home is frequently the gathering place of a group interested in the writing of scenarios and producing of plays for their own amusement.

On June 21, 1904, he married Catharine Eddy Cleaver of Chicago. Their children are Roger Quincy, who is practicing law with his father, Harold Ferris, and Philip Cleaver.

GREAT LAKES, WHERE CORN-FED BOYS ARE TRANSFORMED INTO SAILORS

U. S. Naval Training Station and Fort Sheridan Giving a Martial Aspect to the North Shore

CHICAGO, though nearly a thousand miles removed from the eastern seaboard, has in the United States Naval Training Station at Great Lakes one of the four stations maintained by the Navy Department for giving the apprentice seaman his preliminary training.

Also on the North Shore, at Highland Park, is located Fort Sheridan, an important U. S. Army post, permanently garrisoned by troops. Here, during the World War, an Officers' Training Camp was maintained, and hundreds of fine young officers were turned out. Fort Sheridan serves also as the summer training camp of the Citizens Army, and is well equipped for the purpose. The camp is open to young men within the prescribed age limits who can meet the physical requirements, and offers them an opportunity to perfect themselves in military maneuvers, rifle, and artillery practice. The "regulars" stationed at Fort Sheridan are always in demand to lend a martial tone to Chicago's Memorial Day and Armistice Day celebrations, and always make a splendid showing.

One of the thrills of Chicago life is the annual Army Show at Soldier Field, where aircraft roar overhead or fly in close formation, sham battles are fought, and exhibitions of high jumping and polo are staged by cavalrymen and officers.

Fort Sheridan, with a commanding site on the lake front, is about twenty-five miles north of Chicago, and can be reached by automobile from the city, via Sheridan road or other routes, in about three-quarters of an hour. Great Lakes is only a short distance farther north. Both institutions are well worth a visit.

The growth of Great Lakes has been almost miraculous, though why the station came to be the most productive in the world, and why such an astonishing development should have taken place so far inland is still a puzzle to the seaboard sections of the country.

If Great Lakes has proved anything in the twenty-one years of its existence, it has proved that the corn-fed boy of the western prairies and the Mississippi Valley can make as good a sailor as the lad from Maine or Massachusetts.

Great Lakes draws its material—and good material it is—from the farms, the small towns, and the cities of the Middle West. It occupies a tract of land 182 acres in extent, on a high plateau, overlooking Lake Michigan. The buildings and equipment of the station represent an investment of $3,500,000. The magnificent plant, together with its ideal location and picturesque surroundings, make it an excellent school for the young naval apprentice.

(*Blank & Stoller, Inc., Photo*)

JOHN E. WILDER

Mr. Wilder was born in Lancaster, Massachusetts, April 16, 1861, son of Charles Lewis and Harriet Ellen (Harris) Wilder. He was president of Wilder and Company, tanners and leather merchants of Chicago, and chairman of the board of J. W. and A. P. Howard Company, tanners of Corrychrome at Corry, Pennsylvania, until his death on July 26, 1932. He received his B. S. (Bachelor of Science) degree at the Massachusetts Agricultural College in 1882 and began his business career as a clerk with Wilder and Hale in November of that year. He became a salesman in 1883 and a partner in 1886. The firm changed the name in 1887 to Wilder and Company of which he was vice-president from 1906 to 1919, and from that year until his death he was president.

Mr. Wilder was president of the Illinois Manufacturers' Association during 1905 and a member of the board of directors from 1906 through 1914. He was one of the original organizers, and from 1909 to 1915 was president, of the Tanners Association of America (now called the Tanners Council of America). For more than thirty years he was an active trustee of Beloit College and was an honorary trustee until his death. From 1900 to 1916 he was president of the Illinois Y. M. C. A. and for twenty-five years was an active director of the Evanston Y. M. C. A. He was chairman of the finance committee which made a drive to raise funds to construct their new building. He was president of the Evanston Y. M. C. A. for five years and for ten years before his death had been an honorary director. Mr. Wilder was president of the board of trustees of Chicago Memorial Hospital and a director of the Central Republic Bank and Trust Company. His clubs included Union League and Glenview Golf.

Mr. Wilder married Laura Hurlbut of Oak Park, Illinois, (died January 23, 1915) on April 14, 1886. The children are Laurence, Emery H., Lois (Mrs. Robert M. Landreth), and Antoinette (Mrs. Charles A. Ball). On September 8, 1917, he married Fanny Morse Barnhart.

During the World War the station became the main source of man-power for the navy. From April 6, 1917, to November 2, 1918, Great Lakes received for training no less than 125,000 men. During this period, 96,779 men were transferred to sea duty, while the special schools organized to provide intensive training for such recruits as could qualify, graduated 17,356 men.

This was an achievement on which the West could pride itself—an answer to the scoffers who, when the idea of establishing a naval training station on the shores of a fresh-water lake was first broached, either tried to laugh it down, or classed it as a glaring example of congressional "pork."

Established by Act of Congress April 27, 1904, on a site donated by the Commercial Club of Chicago, it was still being ridiculed when it was opened October 28, 1911, and dedicated by President Taft.

Recruits for the station are selected with meticulous care, and only those who conform to the Navy's high mental, moral, and physical stand-ards are accepted. The "rooky's" instruction starts soon after his arrival. He is first taught how to care for the outfit of clothing issued to him, and is impressed with the fact that personal neatness is a prime requisite in the Navy. Then he learns some of the more simple squad evolutions and com-pany drills, and receives rudimentary instruction in seamanship, signaling, ordnance, in swimming, and in the Swedish system of calisthenics.

The more advanced instruction in seamanship involves learning how to knot and splice rope, how to sew canvas, as well as practical work in the handling of hawsers and heaving lines, and the handling of boats with oars and under sail. The use of the log and the lead line is explained and the recruit is shown how to make soundings. He learns how to box the com-

PATTEN GYMNASIUM, NORTHWESTERN UNIVERSITY, EVANSTON
George Maher, architect.

KENNETH L. WILSON

Mr. Wilson, director of athletics at Northwestern University, was born in Atwood, Illinois, March 27, 1896, the son of Charles and Nelda (Gross) Wilson. In 1920 he received his B.S. (Bachelor of Science) degree from the University of Illinois. He was a member of the football, basketball, and track teams during his years there and captain of the basketball team his senior year. Mr. Wilson was a member of the United States Olympic track team of 1920, Antwerp, Belgium, competing in the javelin event. Following graduation, he spent a year as an assistant on the athletic staff at Illinois. From 1921 to 1925 he was director of athletics at Drake University, Des Moines, Iowa, where he was instrumental in building up the Drake Relays into a meet of national proportions.

Since 1925 "Tug" Wilson has directed athletic activities at Northwestern. Dyche Stadium was erected during his second year as director. His judgment in the selection of his coaching staff has been confirmed by the growing list of championships won by the university teams in all lines of intercollegiate sports. Mr. Wilson is an ardent golfer, and president of the Kildeer golf club, 1931 and 1932.

In 1924 he married Dorothy Shade of Lexington, Illinois. They have one daughter, Nancy Ann.

pass, how to steer a ship, and how to determine a ship's speed. He is in-structed also in anchor drill, collision drill, and signal drill.

Instruction in ordnance work is given principally by means of an indoor target range. Advance work is given in an outdoor range.

The young men are at all times surrounded by the best influences. Re-ligious services are held at stated intervals; the chaplain mingles freely with the boys and generally acts as their big brother. Athletic sports such as boxing, baseball and football are encouraged. The station's reservation is ample for field sports, and a well-equipped gymnasium furnishes splendid facilities for physical development. A well-stocked library is at the disposal of the recruit, while billiard and pool rooms and bowling alleys give him a wide range of selection as to the matter of utilizing his spare time.

Amateur theatricals, minstrel performances, movies, band concerts, and weekly "liberty" break the monotony of the training.

On Armistice Day, 1918, Great Lakes had spread itself over 1,200 acres of land, had 775 buildings, including nine great drill halls, and was training nearly 50,000 men.

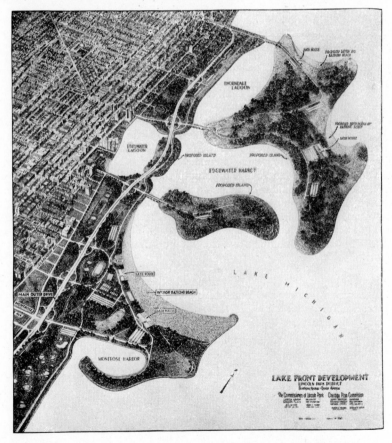

LAKE FRONT DEVELOPMENT, LINCOLN PARK DISTRICT

(Blank & Stoller, Inc., Photo)

THOMAS E. WILSON

Mr. Wilson, president of Wilson & Co., meat packers was born in London, Ontario, July 22, 1868. He came to Chicago in 1877. After graduating from high school, he became a clerk with the Chicago, Burlington & Quincy Railroad in 1886. In 1890 he went to work for Morris & Company. He rose rapidly and in 1905 became vice-president, then, upon the death of Edward Morris in 1913, president. He resigned in March, 1916, to become president of Sulzberger & Sons Co., which became Wilson & Co. in July of that year.

Under Mr. Wilson's direction, Wilson & Co. has become one of the world's largest meat packing concerns, with plants in important cities of North and South America and branches in Europe. Mr. Wilson was the organizer and is chairman of the National Committee on Boys' and Girls' Club Work and has founded scholarships and special awards to encourage farm boys' and girls' work. He was first president of the Institute of American Meat Packers, which organization he was instrumental in forming. Mr. Wilson is a director of the International Live Stock Exposition; a director of the Wabash railroad, and president of the Oklahoma City Stock Yards Co. and vice-chairman of the National Live Stock Meat Board, Chicago. He is a director of the First National Bank; the First Trust & Savings Bank; the Stockyards National Bank. He is a member of the Senior Council of the Chicago Association of Commerce; past president of the Industrial Club and a member of the Commercial Club of Chicago, and a life member of the Field Museum of Natural History. He is a member of the Chicago Athletic Association, Old Elm, Chicago Club, Commercial, Onwentsia Country, Saddle & Sirloin, Post and Paddock, Forty, Knollwood, Shoreacres (founder member), Union League, Mid-Pines Country Club, Pinehurst, North Carolina; Congressional Country Club (life member), Rockville, Maryland; and the American Club of London, England. Breeding of pure blooded cattle, hogs, horses and poultry is his hobby. His Edellyn Farms are known the world over, and his entries have won premuims at live stock shows for years.

Mr. Wilson was married to Elizabeth L. Foss, of Chicago, November 1, 1899, and has two children, Mrs. Harry J. (Helen) Williams and Edward Foss.

BANKS WHERE MERCHANDISE, INSTEAD OF MONEY, IS DEPOSITED

Chicago's Public Warehouses and Their Functions

A BANK in which goods, instead of money, are deposited; a bank on which you can write a check for merchandise, or from which you can receive a negotiable receipt for goods deposited.

Such is the public merchandise warehouse, of which there are many in Chicago, contributing to the city's prestige as the great distributing center of the Middle West.

Chicago's public warehouses are located strategically along the sidings of the railroads. They are busy places. Freight is being loaded and unloaded constantly. Fleets of motor trucks deliver merchandise to their doors or remove it to its destination.

The activity of the public warehouses is a good index of business conditions throughout the country. Here the commercial and industrial pulse of the nation can be felt.

The public warehouses serve not only the Chicago manufacturer, but act as the Chicago representative for thousands of out-of-town manufacturers eager to reach the Great Central Market of which Chicago is the hub.

Because their customers want what they want when they want it, the manufacturers find it essential to carry "spot stock" in Chicago. Here their products are on hand to fill the demand created for them by advertising and other sales effort. No actual selling is done at these warehouses, but outside of that, they function as branch offices for the manufacturer.

From the latter's standpoint, the routine of the warehouse is simplicity itself. The manufacturer ships a consignment of his goods to the warehouse, sending a manifest in advance and indicating of what the shipment consists. On its arrival, the warehouseman will check the shipment and report any shortage or damage, and furnishing claim papers if necessary. The goods are stored. Proper receipts are issued, and accurate books, like those of a bank, are kept for each type of goods in storage.

As sales are made, the manufacturer or his Chicago sales representative issues an order like a bank check, instructing the warehouseman to deliver to the customer from the stock thus deposited what the order calls for. The jobber cashes his order at the warehouse and gets the merchandise, or the warehouse will deliver it to his door. In the case of rail shipments, the special package car service operated by the carriers out of Chicago is available, consisting of the daily departure of package cars destined to 3,000 specific cities and gateways. Arrangements are made for routing shipments via water and motor carriers when required.

Because of Chicago's excellent warehousing facilities, many merchants find it unnecessary to employ Chicago sales representatives. Depending on advertising to create a demand for their products, they furnish the warehouseman with a list of their customers, and authorize him to accept orders

(*Walinger Photo*)

PERCY WILSON

Mr. Wilson, president of Percy Wilson and Company, real estate, was born in Chicago, October 31, 1890, son of Charles W. and Myra (Schuermann) Wilson. At the age of sixteen, he entered the employ of the real estate firm of Frederick H. Bartlett with a salary of $6.00 a week. In the evenings and on Saturday afternoons he was an usher in old McVicker's Theatre for an additional $3.50 a week. From 1907 to 1909 he attended evening classes at the Chicago College of Law (since merged with Kent College of Law). In 1908 he became advertising manager of the real estate firm of Frederick H. Bartlett; from 1911 to 1914 he was in charge of the colonization of 20,000 acres in Arkansas, and the liquidation of the firm's holdings in southern Illinois, Indiana, Ohio, and Colorado; in 1916 he was made an assistant general sales manager; in 1923 he became general sales manager and member of the firm; and in 1924 he was elected a director and appointed treasurer. In 1926 he organized Percy Wilson & Company, of which he is president, and in 1927 he became president of Wilson Finance Company. Mr. Wilson has personally sold or directed the sale of more than one hundred distinct projects; has sold thousands of individual homes in Chicago; and has colonized thousands of acres of land in various parts of North America. It is estimated that these transactions have totaled over $100,000,000 worth of real estate to no less than 100,000 purchasers.

During the late war he was a member of the American Protective League and a four minute speaker. He is a well-known lecturer, and has spoken before many organizations, schools, and universities. He is the author of several articles on salesmanship and character attributes of successful men, and has also written a booklet on Chicago real estate. He is a director of the Chicago Better Business Bureau; a vice-president and director, and chairman of the subdivision division publicity committee of the Chicago Real Estate Board; member of the Real Estate Securities Exchange Committee, realty division of the Association of Commerce, Cook County Real Estate Board, Chicago Board of Underwriters, and Chicago Mortgage Bankers Association. He is a member of the Chicago Galleries Association, the Art Institute and the clubs of which Mr. Wilson is a member include: Mid-Day, Barrington Hills Country, Knollwood, and Chicago Athletic. His favorite recreations are golf and horseback riding.

On January 1, 1918, he married Barbara Frances Heggie, of Chicago, and the children are Patricia, Theodore, and Robert.

from them in accordance with their credit standing. The use of the credit list saves time in handling orders, reduces sales expense, and eliminates consignment selling.

Besides using Chicago public warehouses for carrying "spot" stocks to maintain and increase their sales volume, some manufacturers find that having a stock of their goods here is a protection in case of fire or shut-downs due to labor troubles. Because of their fire resistant construction, the warehouses enjoy a low insurance rate on all goods carried.

The out-of-town manufacturer also can save money by the "storage in transit" privileges offered to them by the railroads. Their goods, sent to Chicago under this privilege, are held here pending sale. When finally sold, the freight rate is the same as if they had been shipped directly from the factory to their destination.

No statement of the many-sided activities of Chicago public warehouses would be complete if it failed to mention the financial services rendered to the manufacturers. Chief of these is the issuance of warehouse receipts which may be used as collateral for loans. A manufacturer may turn over to a public warehouse the whole or part of his stock of readily marketable goods, and receive therefore a negotiable receipt issued in his name, or a non-negotiable receipt issued in the name of his bank. Banks frequently lend as much as 70 per cent of the value of the commodity stored when warehouse receipts are offered as collateral. Warehoused goods, by becoming segregated assets, are available for loans in a manner not possible when they are merged with the owner's general assets. Thus, a growing business in need of additional capital is easily accommodated.

Chicago manufacturers find it to their advantage to make use of public warehouse facilities especially in storing raw materials and containers. In order to take advantage of a favorable market, they often purchase these in large amounts, depositing them in the warehouse until needed in production. On these, too, negotiable receipts are issued, thus releasing much of the capital the materials represent, and leaving it free for continued production or expansion.

Warehousemen call themselves "bankers of merchandise" and consider that their responsibility with respect to goods in their custody is as sacred as a bank's responsibility would be with respect to the equivalent in money. The granting of a license by the state is contingent upon the warehouseman's ability to file with the state a bond issued by a recognized surety company to assure the faithful performance of his obligations under the law. Long-established public warehouses in Chicago have earned an enviable reputation among manufacturers for their responsibility as merchandise bankers and for the wide diversity and excellence of their service.

(*Blank & Stoller, Inc., Photo*)

JOHN HEATH WOOD

Mr. Wood, president of Standard Varnish Works, manufacturers of varnishes, paints, and allied specialties, was born in Chicago, June 24, 1883. He is the son of John H. Wood, a director of Carson Pirie Scott and Company, and Myrtle (Heath) Wood, and is a grandson of Monroe Heath, mayor of Chicago from 1876 to 1879. He received his preparatory education at the Manual Training School of Chicago and from 1902 to 1904 attended the University of Wisconsin. He began his business career in the factory of Heath and Milligan Manufacturing Company, manufacturers of paints, in 1906, and served as works manager of this company from 1916 to 1918, when he became connected with the Standard Varnish Company of Chicago as general sales manager, later becoming president. When this Chicago firm merged with the Standard Varnish Works of New York, Mr. Wood became vice-president of the combined organizations and in 1931 was elected president of the Standard Varnish Works, which has factories in Chicago, New York, Linden, New Jersey, and Detroit. He divides his time between the Chicago and New York offices.

Mr. Wood is a member of the Chicago Athletic Association, South Shore Country Club, Flossmoor Country Club, Beverly Country Club of Chicago, Commonwealth Club of Chicago, and New York Athletic Club of New York.

On June 6, 1906, he married Pauline Verdin of St. Louis, Missouri, and they have two children, Bernice and Elizabeth Heath.

CHICAGO AS THE NATION'S ICE BOX

If all the transportation systems entering Chicago should be tied up by strikes or blizzards, the city would still have enough food supplies in its "family refrigerator" to last for many days.

The central distributing point for meats and other perishable farm products, Chicago is the nation's ice box.

Refrigerated space operated by Chicago's cold storage warehouses increased from 3,000,000 cubic feet in 1900 to 23,000,000 cubic feet just prior to the World War. The war, requiring as it did, the storage of immense supplies for the overseas troops, resulted in a sudden expansion of cold storage facilities here, but the emergency was adequately met. Normal requirements today call for approximately 55,000,000 cubic feet of space.

The public cold storage warehouse is not a depository for hoarding foodstuffs. On the contrary, it acts as a stabilizer in the prices of perishable foodstuffs both to the producer and to the consumer. It assists in the orderly marketing of food products and in their more even distribution.

In these refrigerated warehouses are carried a wide range of perishables which are kept at proper temperature and under proper humidity conditions from the season of plenty to the time of scarcity. Cold storage warehousing provides the consumer at all times with an ample and wholesome food supply, and offers a year-round instead of a seasonal market to the producer. Of perishable food commodities thus stored, only those of the highest quality are held against future needs.

Thus the "Cold Storage" label on foods is actually a guarantee of their wholesomeness. The art of mechanical refrigeration has attained such perfection that meats, fruits, vegetables, eggs, and dairy products may be kept fresh and without deterioration over long periods of time. Their preservation not only insures a steady supply to the American table and awards productive efforts, but forestalls profiteering in times of scarcity. So far as any element of speculation is concerned, cold storage merely evens up prices, preventing disastrous extremes.

In fact, the cold storage warehouse is to the city and the nation only what the household refrigerator is to the American family. Ever taking thought of the morrow, it provides against seasons of low production and precludes the possibility of shortage and unreasonable prices.

Mechanical refrigeration was introduced in Chicago during the '80's. Prior to that time natural ice was used, but early methods permitted of no system of temperature or humidity regulation such as obtains today.

(Blank & Stoller, Inc., Photo)

HENRY C. WOODS

Mr. Woods, executive vice-president and director of the O'Gara Coal Company, director of the Addressograph Company, the Associated Telephone & Telegraph Company, and Frank H. Woods, Inc., was born October 24, 1895, son of Frank H. and Nelle (Cochrane) Woods. His business interests branch out from Chicago to practically every country on the globe.

In 1916 he left Yale to join the French Ambulance Corps, later recalled to finish his college course. When war was declared, he joined the army and, as an officer of light artillery, was in the front line of battle until he was gassed at Chateau Thierry. Invalided home in May, 1918, he entered the course of the Harvard Graduate School of Business. He is a member of the Harvard-Yale-Princeton, University, Yacht, and Indian Hill Country clubs. He is a member of the American Legion and the Boy Scouts, in both of which organizations he is actively interested. He enjoys yachting, horseback riding and tennis.

In 1920 he married Elouise Bixby and they have one son, Henry C., Jr.

LINCOLN PARK, CHICAGO'S MOST POPULAR PLAYGROUND

A People's Country Club Enjoyed by Millions

NAMED in honor of Abraham Lincoln, Lincoln Park, Chicago's great north side playground, has a colorful history which dates back to the days of the martyred President, whose statue by Saint Gaudens at the south end of the park, is a shrine for thousands of pilgrims yearly.

It was in 1865, at the close of the Civil War, that Lincoln Park came into being, supplanting an old burial ground, where a single tomb remains, a link between the present and the past.

Incredible changes have come since this strip of land on the lake front was reclaimed from a graveyard and dedicated to the health and happiness of the living.

Where once Victorias and broughams rolled over the graveled drive-ways, limousines and motor buses speed along over sweeping boulevards. Golf, which was unknown in America when Lincoln Park was young, now attracts armies of its devotees to the two courses available to the public there today.

An area of 300 acres, half a mile wide and a mile and a half long, has developed into a "People's Country Club" of 800 acres stretching three and a half miles along the shores of Lake Michigan, and creeping north-ward day by day as millions of cubic feet of sand, sucked from the shallow lake bottom off the Indiana shore are being added to the "made land" of the Park.

The cost of filling in this land comes to $53,000 an acre, but the land thus formed is valued at $1,000,000 an acre. When plans now under way have been completed, some 1,050 acres will have been added to the present area, bringing the total area up to 1,850 acres with a shore line approxi-mately eight miles in length.

Under the efficient administration of Warren Wright, president of the Lincoln Park Commissioners, and his associates, the program of expansion

African leopard.

Barbary lion.

(*Walinger Photo*)

PHILIP B. WOODWORTH

Mr. Woodworth, engineer and patent lawyer, was born in Auburn, New York, October 19, 1865, son of Thomas Bell and Mary Gertrude (Smith) Woodworth. He received his B. S. (Bachelor of Science) degree at Michigan State College in 1886, his degrees in mechanical and electrical engineering at Cornell University in 1890, and attended the University of Berlin during 1891 and 1892. He was assistant professor of physics and engineering at Michigan State College from 1892 to 1899, and from 1899 to 1917 was professor of engineering, later dean of engineering, at Lewis Institute in Chicago. He served in the war plans division of General Staff, United States Army, from 1917 to 1921. He was president of the Rose Polytechnic Institute at Terre Haute, Indiana, from 1921 to 1923, and has been a member of Rummler, Rummler and Woodworth, patent attorneys, since 1907.

Mr. Woodworth is a member of the bar of the Supreme Court of Indiana, American Institute of Electrical Engineers, Western Society of Engineers, American and Chicago Bar Associations, Chicago Patent Law Association, Tau Beta Pi, Phi Delta Theta, and Founders and Patriots of America. He received the honorary degree of Doctor of Science from Michigan State College in 1920. His clubs are University, Cornell, and Michigan State College of Chicago. Mr. Woodworth is interested in genealogy and has written several articles on this subject.

In 1893 he married Lucy M., daughter of the late President Clute of Michigan State College and the University of Florida. They have four children, Paul Merrylees, Robert Clute, and Gertrude Elizabeth and Marion Merrylees, who are twins.

and beautification has been further accelerated by recent court decisions permitting condemnation of private property for park purposes. After years of litigation, a precedent has been established providing for confiscation of riparian rights and restoring to the people the shore line of Lake Michigan.

One of the most recent improvements is the new Waveland golf course, one of the sportiest in the Chicago metropolitan area. A new 33-acre yacht harbor is being built north of the picturesque Belmont harbor.

One of the Park's major attractions, of course, is the zoo, with its collection of nearly 500 animals and 2,500 birds. The zoo has grown enormously within recent years with the addition of a new lion house, a new house for aquatic birds, an ultra-modern new monkey house, and the aquarium and fish hatchery. From the hatchery, 4,000,000 lake trout, silver salmon, and rainbow trout are transferred to Lake Michigan every year, and 14,-000,000 wall-eyed pike go to the restocking of near-by inland lakes and streams.

The Sunday crowds during the summer average from 750,000 to 1,-000,000. As many as 1,000 family picnics have been held in Lincoln Park in a single day. Not less than 500 larger groups hold their outings in the park in a single summer. It is nothing unusual for the crews to gather up sixty tons of rubbish—two carloads—on a Monday morning during the picnic season. Oak street beach on a Monday morning after a hot day will yield as much as fifteen tons of trash, and perhaps 1,200 empty milk bottles.

LINCOLN PARK GARDENS, WITH CONSERVATORY IN BACKGROUND,
FAMOUS THE WORLD 'ROUND

(Blank & Stoller, Inc., Photo)

WARREN WRIGHT

Mr. Wright, president of the Lincoln Park Board of Commissioners and of Calumet Baking Powder Company, was born in Springfield, Ohio, on September 25, 1875, the son of William Monroe and Clare Lee (Morrison) Wright. He obtained his education in the public grammar school, high school, and in business college; then, in 1890, entered the employ of the Calumet Baking Powder Company as an office boy. Within nine years, or in 1899, he became president. He is also a director of the General Foods Corporation and Paramount-Publix Corporation, both of New York; chairman of the National Realty and Investment Company; president, Warren Wright, Inc.; and director of John R. Thompson Company, the First National Bank of Chicago and First Union Trust and Savings Bank, and the Upper Avenue Bank, of Chicago.

He was appointed commissioner of the Lincoln Park Board by Governor L. L. Emerson and was elected president by his fellow commissioners. Mr. Wright is a member of the Chicago Athletic Association, the South Shore Country, Exmoor Country, Glenview Country, Bob O' Link Country, Chicago Yacht, and Post and Paddock clubs. His recreations are golf, fishing, and hunting.

March 25, 1919, he married Lucille Parker of Maysville, Kentucky, and they have one son, Warren, Jr.

The Sunday throngs will include visitors from nearly every State in the Union.

For its daily water supply, the Park's private pumping station draws 15,000,000 gallons of water from the lake.

In addition to the zoo and aquarium buildings, the Park's permanent buildings include the new colonial home of the Chicago Historical Society, the Laflin Memorial, housing the Chicago Academy of Sciences, the refectory, with its breezy pavilion, and the conservatory, where a marvelous collection of plant life is always on display. Among the exhibits under the glass dome is the $50,000 collection of orchids founded by the former Chicago merchant, H. G. Selfridge. The annual fall chrysanthemum shows are veritable carnivals of bloom, introducing scores of rare varieties of this gorgeous flower. The approach to the conservatory is through formal gardens, seen to best advantage perhaps, in early Spring, in tulip time, when they are a riot of color. Fountains and statuary enhance their beauty. Near-

The elephant "Deed-a-day"

Sika deer from Formosa.

by is an old-fashioned "grandma's" garden, where one may wander among the pinks, candy-tuft, and forget-me-nots. There is also a dreamy lily pool. A five-acre bird sanctuary, vocal with the flutings of its feathered inhabitants, is planted thick with berry bushes and carpeted with wild strawberry plants.

One may enjoy almost any kind of sport in Lincoln Park. In addition to the two golf courses there are seventy grass and clay tennis courts, thirty-three baseball diamonds, seven football gridirons, and twelve horseshoe courts. There are roquet courts for followers of that gentle sport. The equestrian will find the five and a half miles of bridle path greatly to his liking. In one of the sequestered lagoons the fly-caster may prove his skill. Ample lawns provide space for archery ranges. The Lincoln Park Trap Shooting Club has its headquarters on one of the new extensions on the lake front, and the traps are open to the public. The two main lagoons are merry with boating parties in the summer and with skaters in the winter. The sailing of toy yachts is a sport which has become increasingly popular among the younger set of late. The Lincoln Park Boat Club is provided

JAMES GLENDENNING WRAY

Mr. Wray, senior partner of J. G. Wray & Company, consulting engineers of Chicago, was born in Janesville, Wisconsin, May 19, 1872, son of James Glendenning and Helen (Edgar) Wray. He graduated from the University of Wisconsin in 1893, receiving his degree in Electrical Engineering. From 1902 to 1916 he was chief engineer for the Chicago Telephone Company. From 1911 to 1916 he was chief engineer for the following telephone companies: Wisconsin, Michigan State, Cleveland, and Central Union. He was vice-president of the Standard Telephone Company from 1927 to 1928; president, United Telephone Company, 1927-1929; and president, Southeastern Telephone Company, 1929-1931. Mr. Wray is now senior partner of J. G. Wray & Company, Chicago, and of Wray-Parsons and Company, real estate subdividers and builders of Waukegan, Illinois. He is president of Pa Wray Pickle Company and of St. Louis Blue Print and Supply Company.

Mr. Wray was a member of the Society for the Promotion of Engineering Education, 1910 to 1920; Illuminating Engineering Society, 1910 to 1918; University Club, Madison, Wisconsin, 1910 to 1915; and Electric Club, 1910 to 1915. He is president of the Wisconsin Society of Chicago and a member of various business and social organizations including the Chicago Association of Commerce; University, City, Midland, and Skokie Country clubs; and University of Wisconsin Club of Chicago (former president, secretary, and treasurer). Mr. Wray is a Fellow in the American Institute of Electrical Engineers (chairman of Chicago section for three years); member, Western Society of Engineers; Fellow, American Association for the Advancement of Science; and member, Illinois Academy of Sciences. He is a member of the Glencoe, Illinois, Park Board and has been a member of its Plan Commission. He was formerly a member of the Wilmette, Illinois, Board of Education (president, 1917 to 1919), member of Board of Visitors, University of Wisconsin, 1909 to 1912, and director, Chicago Missionary Society.

He married Clara May Williams of Chicago, Illinois, September 25, 1895; children, Florence Vivian (Mrs. Allen H. Ward), Ernest Lee (deceased), Alice May (Mrs. J. A. Bailey), Ethel Lois (Mrs. Stanley D. Grace), Helen Norma (Mrs. J. D. Emrich, Jr.), James Glendenning, Jr., and Clara Grace.

with a fine course for its racing shells. There are public beaches at Oak street and Diversey boulevard, and these are augmented by a children's bathing beach. Belmont Harbor shelters a large fleet of yachts and motor boats. Hundreds of motor craft find additional anchorage in the slip at the south end of the Park.

But all this is only the beginning. On the north, the proposed exten-sion will reach from Montrose avenue to Devon avenue, a distance of two and a half miles. It will consist first of a mainland peninsula of 396 acres, lying between Montrose and Foster avenues, which will contain the new Montrose yacht harbor, and a 39-acre bathing beach in line with Wilson avenue.

The next section will be a mainland strip 171 acres in extent, lying between Foster and Devon avenues, bordered by three islands with areas of 31, 37, and 467 acres respectively. On the latter, at Devon avenue, will be a 9-acre bathing beach. Between the second and third islands will be another yacht shelter of 238 acres, to be known as Edgewater Harbor.

A portion of the new park will be landscaped in a formal manner, while the larger part of the island areas will be devoted to picnic grounds and playfields, all easy of access yet removed from the main traffic ways. On the mainland peninsula will be built two large bath houses, two children's play-grounds with shelters, fields for football and baseball, courts for basketball, handball, and quoits, a running track, and a ski jump.

"When the present expansion is completed," says Mr. Wright, "the people of Chicago will have a playground which will rival anything of its kind in the world. It will give Chicago an uninterrupted highway bordering on the lake shore and extending almost the entire length of the city, and will be the realization of a civic hope and dream of many years.

"When asked for funds to carry out this stupendous program, the voters responded generously and without hesitation, knowing that the money de-rived from the bond issues would be expended honestly and efficiently and in their interests. The Lincoln Park Commissioners are doing all in their power to merit such confidence."

The new Outer Drive link, to be carried over the main channel of the Chicago river at its mouth by a two-leaf trunnion bascule bridge, will con-nect the Lincoln Park and the South Park systems.

(*Moffett-Russell Photo*)

CLARK CHITTENDEN WRIGHT

Col. Wright, of the architectural firm of Nimmons, Carr & Wright, was born in Liberty-ville, Illinois, July 3, 1880, son of Caleb Frank and Emma Jane (Price) Wright. He received his preparatory education at Beloit College Academy and during his vacations worked as a carpenter on building construction. He later became a student at the Chicago School of Architecture, and after two years of training started his architectural career as a draughtsman and building construction superintendent. He has been actively engaged in architectural and building construction in Chicago since 1900, and has been a member of the firm of George C. Nimmons & Co., later Nimmons, Carr & Wright, since 1915. This firm has enjoyed a nation-wide practice and has erected buildings in more than one hundred cities and twenty-seven states of the United States. Some of the Chicago projects are the Sears, Roebuck and Co. stores, Olympia Fields, Ravisloe and Flossmoor Country Clubs, Cracker Jack plant at Clearing, Central Service Station of the Commonwealth Edison Company, and American Furniture Mart, associated with N. Max Dunning.

Col. Wright was commissioned major of the Quartermaster Corps in January, 1918, lieutenant colonel in 1918 and finally colonel U. S. A. assigned to duty with the Construction Division of the Army, where he had charge of the construction of Army Hospitals and all construction work in Army Cantonments and Embarkation Camps. He is a member of the American Institute of Architects, the American Society of Civil Engineers, the Society of American Military Engineers and the Illinois Society of Architects. He is a member of the Exmoor Country Club, the Tavern and the Chicago Yacht Club, of which he is now commodore (1932). His principal recreation is yacht racing and for twenty-five years he has taken an active part in major yacht racing events on Lake Michigan. His present schooner yacht, "Privateer," is an active contender in all long distance races, including the famous Mackinac race.

Col. Wright married Lillian Griggs, of Streator, Illinois, April 29, 1920.

(*Chicago Architectural Photographing Company*)

ON THE LEFT ARE THE WRIGLEY BUILDINGS, BUILT BY
WILLIAM WRIGLEY, JR.

(*Kaufmann & Fabry Co. Photo*)

THE CHICAGO NATIONAL LEAGUE BASEBALL PARK—HOME OF THE CUBS

(*Fernand de Gueldre Photo*)

FRANK LLOYD WRIGHT

Mr. Wright, architect, was born in Richland Center, Wisconsin, June 8, 1869, the son of William Russell Cary and Anna Lloyd (Jones) Wright. He studied civil engineering at the University of Wisconsin, entering with the class of 1888, and began his practice as an architect in Chicago in 1893. Mr. Wright has spent many years in Japan, and the modern architecture of Japan to no small extent reflects his influence. He was the architect of the Imperial Hotel of Tokio, Japan, a building which, because of the unique engineering principles employed, successfully withstood the great Japanese earthquake which destroyed the city. Mr. Wright's work has been characterized in America as "The New School of the Middle West," and in Europe as "The American Expression in Architecture." He was one of the first Americans to appreciate and understand the beauty of Oriental art, of which he has been an outstanding collector. A priceless collection of these works was destroyed several years ago by a fire which swept his summer home, Taliesin, at Spring Green, Wisconsin. He is an honorary member of the Académie Royale des Beaux Arts d'Anvers, to which he was elected in 1927; an "extraordinary honorary member" of the Akademie der Kunst (Royal Academy) of Berlin, and an honorary member of the Instituto Central de Architectos of Brazil. He is a member of the Fine Arts and Phi Delta Theta fraternities and of the Players club of New York.

Mr. Wright is the author of many books on architecture published in America and Europe, and of an interesting autobiography which made its appearance in 1932. His publications include An Interpretation of Japanese Prints, 1912; In the Cause of Architecture (essays), 1909-1923; Ausgefuhrte Bauten und Entwurfe, Sonderheit, and Wendingen, published in Europe in 1909, 1910, and 1925 respectively; Modern Architecture, 1931; The Nature of Materials, 1932; and The Disappearing City, 1932. He maintains offices in Chicago, Los Angeles, and Tokio, Japan. During the past year he has founded and built the Taliesen Fellowship on his farm near Spring Green, Wisconsin, where seventy-seven apprentices are studying architecture as the essential structure of all art and life.

Mr. Wright has been married three times, first to Catherine Lee, who was the mother of Lloyd, John, Catherine, David, Frances, and Llewellyn. His second wife was Miriam Noel, and his third, Olga Lazovich of Montenegro, the mother of his youngest daughter, Iovanna.

CHICAGO NEEDS SUPERHIGHWAYS

Elevated Express Thoroughfares are Vital to Traffic Movement

BY HUGH E. YOUNG

Chief Engineer, Chicago Plan Commission

YEAR in and year out, for the past ten years at least, there have been nearly one thousand more automobiles added to Chicago's total number of vehicles each and every week. Every day in the year almost a quarter of a million automobiles from outside the city enter Chicago and traverse its streets, most of them finding their way into the heart of the community.

No doubt the late depression has reduced the number of new automobiles added to Chicago's total each week, but there is no letting up in the number of outside cars which find their way into the city. As a matter of fact, this number is constantly increasing with the improvement of state and county highways leading to and from Chicago. And with a return to normal conditions there is no reason to expect anything else than that the sale of new automobiles will likewise return to normal.

So we have a condition where more vehicles are continually being placed in service upon the streets of Chicago and where an ever larger number of vehicles are coming into the city every day. With this, in contrast, is the small amount of highway improvement within the municipal limits which is going forward. As a result of its years of study of the traffic problems, the Chicago Plan Commission has reached the conclusion that the next necessary step toward providing relief from traffic over-congestion lies in the provision of a complete system of elevated, grade-separation highways within Chicago, radiating out fan-shaped from the central business district and extending to the municipal limits on all sides, there making contact with the county, state and national improved highway systems.

So far only one route in this general system has been definitely recommended by the Chicago Plan Commission. That is the one known as Avondale Superhighway, which parallels the Chicago & Northwestern Railroad right-of-way for ten miles from Jefferson to the loop. At Jefferson it ends in the focal point of some ten or twelve major state and county highways, and in the loop it provides half a dozen connections with important north-and-south and east-and-west city streets. For nine miles of its ten mile length, the superhighway is planned to be 210 feet wide, consisting of an elevated express highway 160 feet wide, mainly built on solid fill like the adjacent railroad embankment, and in addition a local street, adjacent to the private property at the normal street level. Inclined roadways or ramps will connect the elevated express highway with Chicago's normal street system at strategic intervals. The remaining mile does not provide this local, low-level roadway, because the express highway is to be built above the railroad tracks, which in this section are not elevated but lie on the normal surface of the ground.

The first question which naturally arises in thinking of superhighways

(Fernand de Gueldre Photo)

WILLIAM WRIGLEY, JR.

Mr. Wrigley, manufacturer and sportsman, was born in Philadelphia, September 30, 1861, the son of William and Mary A. (Ladley) Wrigley, and died in Phoenix, Arizona, January 26, 1932. At the age of thirteen he began work in his father's soap factory, and after mastering the details of production, was for seventeen years a traveling salesman for the firm. In 1891 he came to Chicago as a distributor for the factory's products, and as a sales promotion device, introduced the premium system. He became the largest distributor of premiums in the world. Among the articles offered as inducements to customers was chewing gum, and noting the popularity of this article, he decided to concentrate on its manufacture. As the business grew, he increased his advertising appropriations until the firm, William Wrigley, Jr. Company, the largest manufacturing concern of its kind in the world, ranked also among America's leading advertisers. Today the company operates a fifteen-acre plant in Chicago, as well as factories in Toronto, Canada, London, England, Frankfort, Germany, and Sydney, Australia. The Wrigley Building in North Michigan avenue is one of the architectural landmarks of the city.

Mr. Wrigley retired from the presidency of his company in 1925, being succeeded by his son, Philip K. Wrigley, but remained active in the firm as chairman of the board. He was a liberal contributor to hospitals, local charities, and organizations for the education and welfare of children. The decorations on the north pylons of the Michigan avenue bridge were his gift to the city.

In the field of sports Mr. Wrigley was principal owner of the Chicago National League baseball club, the Cubs, and of the Angel City baseball club of Los Angeles; also as the promotor of the Catalina Channel swimming race of 1926, which attracted international interest and was won by George Young, a Canadian.

In 1919 he purchased Catalina Island, off the coast of California, built a home there and a baseball park which served as winter training grounds for the Cubs, and transformed the island into a pleasure resort visited annually by hundreds of thousands of tourists. Mr. Wrigley acquired the Arizona Biltmore properties at Phoenix and was developing a winter resort there at the time of his death. He was a director of

Continued on page 550

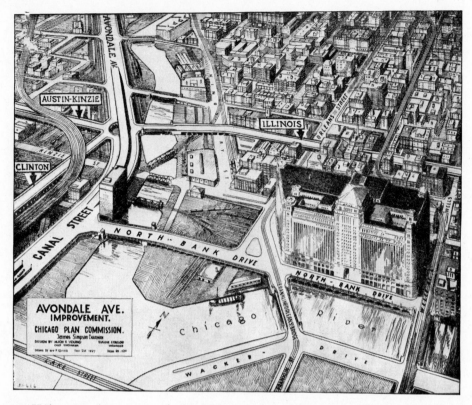

is: What conditions justify building an elevated street? The principal condition necessary, in my opinion, is an amount of traffic of such volume and character that the saving in time by eliminating delays due to cross traffic and turning traffic will justify the cost involved in the construction of the elevated thoroughfare. The average value of traffic has been estimated to be 2.2c per car minute. Having determined the approximate number of vehicles which can reasonably be expected to use an elevated highway daily, and having estimated the amount of time each vehicle will save by using the superhighway, multiplying the number of vehicles by the time saved and multiplying this again by 2.2c will give a fairly accurate idea of what amount can justifiably be spent for such an improvement.

Not only the volume but also the character of the traffic is important. It is obvious that in order to justify elevated grade-separation highway construction a large percentage of the traffic must be that which is ordinarily classed as "through-bound," that is, that each vehicular trip will be of sufficient extent to justify the provision of a continuous and uninterrupted elevated right-of-way. Consequently, my opinion is that the main economic factor which justifies the construction of an elevated street is a large enough volume of long distance traffic to justify spending the amount of money the structure will cost in order to produce the benefits that will result. In other words, when the saving in time and distance—expressed

(*Fernand de Gueldre Photo*)

WILLIAM A. YAGER

Mr. Yager, president of Arms-Yager Railway Car Company, was born in Piqua, Miami County, Ohio, January 14, 1864, and is the son of George and Mary Frances (Statler) Yager. He attended the public and high schools at Piqua, and later, Cincinnati Commercial College. Mr. Yager was one of the incorporators of the Arms Car Company in 1885, and continued with the company as secretary and treasurer, then vice-president and president, later president of the reincorporated company that is now called The Arms-Yager Railway Car Company, which specializes in the leasing of baggage car type of passenger equipment, and special freight cars. In 1904 Mr. Yager patented a convertible passenger equipped car. This equipment is adapted for the transportation of storage mail, baggage, express-commodities, fruits, vegetables and live stock in passenger train service. The cars are universally used by all railroads and express companies in the United States and Canada.

Mr. Yager is a member of the Art Institute of Chicago and Ohio Society of Chicago. His clubs are Transportation, Veteran, Chicago Athletic Association, Mid-Day, Lake Shore Athletic, Exmoor Country, Saddle and Sirloin, Knollwood, and Chicago Yacht. His principal recreations are fishing, horseback riding, and traveling.

On August 17, 1910, he married Ella H. Nimocks of Minneapolis, Minnesota.

in dollars—fully warrants the improvement from an economic viewpoint. Of course, the humanitarian factor is of great importance too, because grade-separation highways will not only naturally reduce automobile accidents by eliminating points of cross traffic movement but of even greater importance, the provision of separate routes for high speed traffic will eliminate all causes of accidents to pedestrians and children because pedestrians will not be permitted on the superhighways.

The second question which invariably arises is: What does an elevated superhighway cost per mile? This, of course, depends upon what kind of a superhighway it is, where it is located, how wide it is and other factors of construction involved. For example, the structure could consist of steel

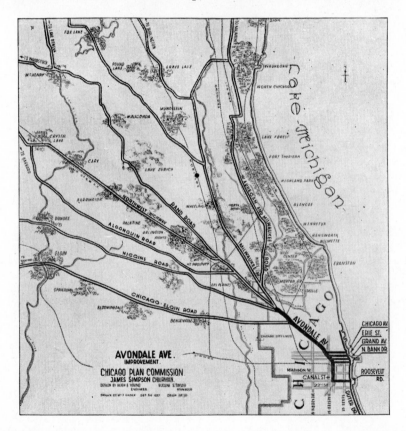

or concrete construction resting upon pile foundations, or it could consist of solid fill of the customary type of construction, which costs only about one-third as much as steel encased in concrete. Therefore, placing these superhighways along elevated steam railroad lines, and continuing the railroad embankment across the width of the elevated street to a concrete retaining wall will affect the cost both because of this type of construction and the proportion of solid fill there may be in each superhighway. In

(Root Photo)

HUGH E. YOUNG

Mr. Young, chief engineer of the Chicago Plan Commission, was born in Anamosa, Iowa, and is the son of Joseph C. and Sarah J. (Charity) Young. He graduated from the Anamosa High School and the University of Iowa, receiving his degree in Civil Engineering in 1905. He came to Chicago during the same year and for the next nine years was employed in the engineering departments of the Illinois Steel Company, American Bridge Company, Chicago, Milwaukee and St. Paul Railroad Company and Union Pacific Railway. In 1914 he was appointed by the Civil Service Commission of Chicago to the position of engineer in charge of the design of Chicago's bridges. He designed the Wells Street, Michigan Avenue, and Franklin-Orleans Street movable bridges, and many other similar structures. He also developed plans for many improvements, including Wacker Drive, the straightening of the Chicago River, many street widenings, as well as various bridges and improvements for other cities, such as movable bridges for Detroit, Michigan, and the new lighting system for the City of Evanston, Illinois.

Mr. Young is now chief engineer of the Chicago Plan Commission and consulting engineer for the Commissioners of Lincoln Park and South Park Commissioners in charge of the design and construction of the Outer Drive improvement and the Lincoln Park extension work, two outstanding accomplishments. An illustration of the Lincoln Park extension work between Montrose avenue and Foster avenue, as well as Mr. Young's article relating some of his ideas about superhighways are included in this book. He is a member of the American Society of Engineers, Western Society of Engineers, American Institute of Electrical Engineers, Illuminating Engineering Society, the Sigma Alpha Epsilon Fraternity, and the "I" Fraternity at the State University of Iowa. His clubs are the Illinois Athletic Club and Rolling Green Country Club.

In 1911, he married Gabrielle Bock, and they have two children, Burton Hugh and Robert Elleson.

both types the steel and concrete construction is used wherever cross streets pass beneath the superhighway.

Upon two separate occasions the City of Chicago has endeavored to begin the construction of a superhighway. The first effort was in connection with the Avondale Superhighway for a start upon which a bond issue of $5,000,000 was placed upon the city ballot a few years ago.

Subsequently the West Chicago Park Commissioners were desirous of creating an elevated boulevard extending through the west side. This route was known as the Austin-Kinzie route and a $20,000,000 bond issue was submitted in referendum to the voters of the West Park District.

Each of these attempts was defeated, but the fact remains that Chicago cannot forever continue to compel all its traffic to use the same narrow, inadequate, over-congested thoroughfares that were laid out in the days of our grandparents, when the city was only one-tenth of its present size, and when faithful old Dobbin was the only known motive power for street vehicles, long before modern automotive transportation methods were even dreamed of. The grade-separation superhighway really originated in Chicago, and despite the fact that New York and other cities have appreciated the value of this idea and have actually put it into use by building elevated streets while Chicago has yet to make a start upon actual superhighway construction, yet I have every confidence that when Chicago fully awakes to the pressing need for separating local and through-bound vehicular traffic, it will carry out a comprehensive superhighway system with a speed that will amaze the rest of the country.

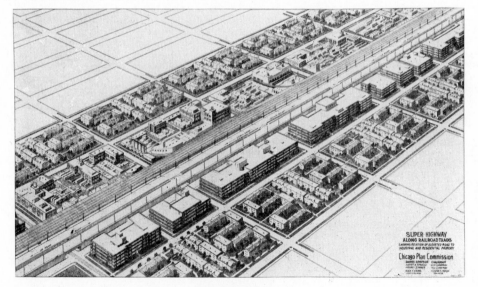

Superhighway along railroad tracks, showing relation of elevated road to industrial and residential property.

President
CHICAGO
REAL ESTATE
BOARD
1924
•
NATIONAL
ASSOCIATION
of REAL ESTATE
BOARDS
1928
•
CIVIC
FEDERATION
of CHICAGO
1922 - 1923
•

(Photo by Atlantic Foto Service)

HENRY G. ZANDER

Mr. Zander, pioneer real estate man and vice-chairman of the Federal Home Loan Bank of Evanston, was born in Rendsburg, Schleswig-Holstein, Germany, October 4, 1869, the son of Claudius C. and Margot (Van Staeding) Zander. He attended the Gymnasium at Rendsburg, and after coming to Chicago entered the North Division high school, from which he was graduated in 1886. His first business connection was made in the same year when he became associated with Martin Van Allen, whose real estate firm, established in 1854, was then the oldest in the city. Continuing his education, he was graduated as a civil engineer from Grant's School, Chicago, and later received his Bachelor of Laws degree from John Marshall Law School. In 1889 he became Mr. Van Allen's junior partner, and in December, 1891, he organized the firm of Henry G. Zander & Co. In May, 1892, he formed a partnership with George F. Koester under the firm name of Koester & Zander. This firm, which became in time one of the oldest and most successful in Chicago, remained in business for thirty-three years, when it was dissolved by the death of Mr. Koester. In 1927 Mr. Zander, with whom were associated his two sons, Henry G., Jr. and Karl M., organized the firm of Henry G. Zander & Company, specializing in real estate investments and mortgage loans.

Mr. Zander was a pioneer in zoning and city planning and was a leader in the fight for adopting the brokers' license law in Illinois. He was elected president in 1924 of the Chicago Real Estate Board, which organization he had served as director, and in 1928 was president of the National Association of Real Estate Boards. As chairman of the National Association's committee on federal legislation and taxation he secured the repeal of the stamp tax on deeds and of other provisions, which were costing the profession millions of dollars annually. Mr. Zander is a director of the Civic Federation, of which he was president in 1922 and 1923; a director of the Illinois State Realtors' Association, and a member of the Union League, Mid-Day, Iroquois, City, German, Ridgemoor Country, Barrington Hills Country, Minocqua (Wisconsin) Country, and Michigan North Woods clubs. He was president of the German Club for two years. His recreations are golf and fishing.

Mr. Zander was married in 1895 to Charlotte M. Keitel of Chicago. Residence, "The Oaks," Cuba Township, Barrington, Illinois. His two sons are still associated with him in business.

CHICAGO'S ACCOMPLISHMENTS, CHICAGO'S LEADERS, CHICAGO'S REAL ESTATE— A TRINITY INSEPARABLE

BY C. L. PERKINS
Editor of the Magazine, REAL ESTATE

CHICAGO'S acres, as soil, are worth no more than many other equal por-tions of the earth's surface. Chicago's acres, however, cannot be valued as soil. Chicago was predestined to greatness. Its very location made it the inevitable home and workshop of millions, produced its leaders, and gave incentive to their accomplishments.

Chicago's real estate, in the heart of the world's richest agricultural region, the Mississippi Valley, at the meeting place of coal and iron, at the hub of rail, water, and air transportation, has always had, and will continue to have a guarantee of increasing value underwritten by Nature.

As real estate prices have mounted, Chicago has found means of putting its land to a higher and higher use. It was in Chicago that the first steel-skeletoned skyscraper was built—an edifice which was to revolutionize com-mercial architecture. Chicago was the first city to double deck a business thoroughfare, and was the first city to pass a zoning ordinance.

Rising land values have been reflected, especially in the last two decades, in building construction. Ornamental façades, grand rotundas, and inside light wells are disappearing. Efficiency is written into every line of the modern skyscraper which, with its graceful towers and setbacks is replacing the structure of the packing box type.

(*Chicago Architectural Photographing Company*)
ILLINOIS LIFE INSURANCE COMPANY
Holabird & Roche, architects.   Avery Brundage Company, general contractor.

Chicago's real estate history is replete with fascinating tales, some of them almost unbelievable. Pages could be devoted to them.

It is told of John Kinzie, the first white settler, that when exercising his right to a quarter section of land, he accepted only 102 acres, rejecting the additional 58 acres on the ground that they were not worth the trouble of developing. Today the Kinzie farm is the site of the Wrigley Buildings and its neighboring skyscrapers. Would anyone turn down a gift of 58 acres in this section of the city if it should be offered to him now?

Then there is the story about W. B. Ogden, Chicago's first mayor, and perhaps its first real estate dealer. Ogden wished to sell a tract of land, about five acres in extent, to a friend of his named Prindeville. He offered it on what was known as "Canal time" —one fourth down, and the balance in one, two, and three years. Prindeville had no money which he wanted to invest, and refused to buy the land.

"Well," said Ogden, "I will take back the land at the end of a year if you're not satisfied."

Still Prindeville would not buy.

"I'll give you a year's time on the first payment."

"No."

"Look here, Prindeville," said Ogden, "that's not the way to get along. When you deal in Chicago real estate, the proper way is to go in for all you can get, and then go on with your business and forget about the land. It will take care of itself."

But Prindeville remained obdurate. Ogden finally sold the tract to another man, and within six months this purchaser made $4,000 by reselling only a small part.

TRUSTEES SYSTEM BUILDING
Thielbar & Fugard, architects.
McLennan Construction Company, builders.

There's a thrill in realizing that in the brief span of a hundred years the unit of sale for downtown property has shrunk from five-acre tracts to a square foot.

Robert Cavalier Sieur de La Salle saw the possibilities of the site of Chicago more than 250 years ago. In honor of the French explorer, J. Thompson, when recording the first plat of Chicago, named one of the streets La Salle. Almost as interesting as the story of La Salle himself is that of the thoroughfare which bears his name.

The plot of land extending from Madison street to what is now Roosevelt road, and from State to Halsted streets, intersected by La Salle street, was originally set aside as public school property. In 1833, that school section was put up at auction. Its 144 blocks were disposed of at an average price of $6.72 an acre. The sum realized—$38,865—was said at the time to have been "beyond expectations."

SEARS, ROEBUCK & COMPANY, CHICAGO
Nimmons, Carr & Wright, architects.

Not far from where the new Board of Trade building now stands brooding over this busy canyon, a young couple walking to church became mired, and were rapidly sinking, when their cries brought help. This was 90 years ago. Had their grandchildren been so fortunate as to own a single lot near the scene of this mishap, they would have been financially independent for life.

Chicago has made many serious mistakes in the past, but of recent years has done much to offset them. One mistake was in allowing temporary frame buildings to be erected after the great fire of 1871. Prior to 1883, there were no zoning laws of any kind, but an ordinance passed by the city council in that year prohibited the erection of "livery stables, blacksmiths' shops, and foundries in residence districts" without the consent of the property owners affected. Today Chicago is developing, under the influence of a well-balanced building code, a zoning system and, above all, a city plan which looks far into the future.

Increasing real estate values both within the city limits and in the nearby suburbs are reflected not only in the towering skyscrapers but in residential buildings. The mansion of the Victorian era, together with the single family residence has given way in the city to the modern apartment building and the apartment hotel, while in the suburbs, the small home, rather than the family mansion, is predominant. Many of the most pretentious private estates have been subdivided into 40- and 60-foot lots.

As improved transportation facilities, the extension of "L" lines and suburban lines, the automobile, and the motor bus, have expanded the city, Chicago has outgrown the Loop, and many thriving business centers, with their banks, theaters, and department stores, have been developed in the outlying districts and in the suburban towns.

The Loop itself has been constantly expanding. With the completion of the Michigan avenue bridge, business crossed the river, and with the extension southward of Dearborn, Wells, and other streets, an entirely new retail district will be opened up south of the loop.

Chicago at present may be slightly overbuilt, but the population is increasing steadily, and within a few years, as has happened over and over in the past, there will again be a shortage of homes and office space, and real

(*Chicago Architectural Photographing Co.*)
1540 LAKE SHORE DRIVE
Huszagh & Hill, architects.
Avery Brundage Company, general contractor.

estate values, city and suburban, will be due for another jump. The coming of air transportation will considerably hasten this day.

A replica of Fort Dearborn on the shore of Lake Michigan at Twenty-sixth street. Once inside the stockade of this historic Fort, time turns back more than a century, and one can sense the courage of those who founded the village that has become America's second city.

VINCENT BENDIX
Continued from page 49
York; Bendix-Stromberg Carburetor Company, South Bend, Indiana; Scintilla Magneto Company, Sidney, New York; Delco Aviation Corporation, Dayton, Ohio; Pioneer Instrument Company, Brooklyn, New York; Bendix-Cowdrey Brake Tester, Inc., South Bend, Indiana; Julien P. Friez & Sons, Inc., Baltimore, Maryland; Charles Cory Corporation, New York City; Bendix Products Sales Company, South Bend, Indiana; Bendix Research Corporation, East Orange, New Jersey; Eclipse Machine Company, Ltd., Walkerville, Ontario; and the Eclipse Textile Devices, Inc., Elmira, New York. Affiliated companies are Bendix-Westinghouse, Automotive Air Brake Company, Pittsburgh, Pennsylvania, and the Lubrication Corporation, South Bend, Indiana.

King Gustav of Sweden conferred upon him the insignia of the Order of the North Star. He has been awarded the Linné medal by Sweden. He recently bought the famous Potter Palmer home in Chicago and also maintains a home in South Bend, Indiana. Mr. Bendix is the sole donor of the Golden Pavilion of Jehol to Chicago's (1933) World's Fair and is also donor of the collection of East Asiatic ecclesiastic art exhibited in the Liljevalch Hall of Art in Stockholm.

Mr. Bendix is a member and past president of the Society of Automotive Engineers, trustee of the Armour Institute of Technology, and member of the Field Museum of Natural History, the Art Institute of Chicago, Union League Club, Bob O'Link, Midlothian Country, Forty, Riding, and Lake Shore Athletic clubs (all of Chicago). He is also a member of the Detroit Athletic Club, South Bend Country Club, the Indiana Country Club, the Toledo Club, the Elmira Club, and the Woodmont Rod and Gun Club of Michigan.

JAMES HENRY BREASTED
Continued from page 63
American Council of Learned Societies, 1931-1934; was chairman of the United States delegation to the 18th International Congress of Orientalists at Leyden, in 1931; is a member of the Academic Commission of the Berlin Egyptian Dictionary; is a trustee of the American Schools of Oriental Research, 1930-1933. Dr. Breasted is a corresponding member of the Royal Academy of Sciences at Berlin and the American Geographic Society; foreign member of Academie des Inscriptions et Belles Lettres, Historical-Philosophical Class of the Bavarian Academy, and Archaeologisches Institut des Deutschen Reiches; president of the American Oriental Society, in 1918; member of the American Philosophical Society (vice-president 1927-1932); honorary member of the Society of Antiquaries, London, and the Royal Asiatic Society; and member of the National Academy of Sciences and the American Historical Association (president, 1928). Dr. Breasted is the author of numerous books and articles on Oriental civilization and history. He was awarded the Rosenberger medal for his contribution to the history of civilization, in 1929; the gold medal of the Geographic Society of Chicago, in 1929; and the gold medal of the Holland Society of New York, in 1930.

Unusual combination of distinguished scholar and able administrator, Dr. Breasted has established the Oriental Institute of The University of Chicago as the world center for the study of the rise of civilization. Dr. Breasted, foremost Orientalist of the world, in December of 1931 realized the hopes of forty years when he dedicated the new building of the Oriental Institute, a laboratory for the investigation of man, his origins and his civilization. Today (1932), he is directing an army of thirteen field expeditions on a 3,500-mile front extending from the Upper Nile Valley to Persia, the largest archaeological organization in the world.

Dr. Breasted married Frances Hart, in Berlin, Germany, October 22, 1894. Their children are Charles, James Henry, and Astrid.

ARTHUR HOLLY COMPTON
Continued from page 125
author of (monograph) Secondary Radiotrons Produced by X-rays, 1922, X-rays and Electrons, 1926, and numerous articles on scientific subjects.

Dr. Compton is the leading representative of the new era in the science, as his noted predecessor, Albert A. Michelson was the foremost figure of the "classical regime" of exact measurement, and is recognized as one of the great scientists of the world. Thirty-five years old when he was awarded the Nobel Prize by the Swedish Academy of Sciences, in 1927, Dr. Compton has made a long series of significant contributions to the new concepts of physics. He also was awarded the Rumford Gold Medal by the American

Continued on page 546

COMPTON—Continued

Academy of Arts and Sciences in 1927 and the Gold Medal of the Radiological Society of North America, in 1928. His particular field is that of analysis of the fine structure of matter and of the production of radiant energy from matter. In the discovery of the "Compton effect" he demonstrated that X-rays, and presumably light waves and all other forms of radiant energy, seemingly act like corpuscles, or projectiles, as well as like waves. Other of his achievements in the analysis of X-rays have been his determination of the index of refraction of the rays; the absolute measurement of wave-lengths with ruled gratings, and the measurement of the intensity of rays reflected from crystals, all preliminary to the discovery of the "Compton effect." He has recently used the "Compton effect" in extraordinarily delicate measurements of atoms. During the past year he has traveled 50,000 miles as the leader of a world survey to measure the intensity of cosmic rays.

CHARLES G. DAWES
Continued from page 147

Service Medal by the United States, Companion of the Bath (British), Commander of Saints Maurice and Lazarus (Italian), Order of Leopold (Belgian) in 1919, and Commander Légion d'Honneur (French) in 1919.

He was appointed first director of the United States Bureau of the Budget, 1921, by President Harding and established the existing budgetary system of the United States. In 1923 the Reparations Commission appointed him as president of the committee to investigate the possibilities of the German budget—the resulting "Dawes Plan" was put into effect September 1, 1924. He was nominated by the Republican National Convention for vice-president of the United States and elected November, 1924, for the term of 1925-1929. He was awarded the Nobel Peace Prize for 1925, jointly with Sir Austen Chamberlain, British foreign secretary, and turned over his share of the prize to the endowment of the Walter Hines Page School of International Relations. Mr. Dawes was American Ambassador to the Court of St. James from 1929 to 1932. He was chairman of the Economic Commission of American Experts that visited Santo Domingo in 1929 and reorganized their financial system; first president of the Reconstruction Finance Corporation (1932); chairman of the finance committee of A Century of Progress, Chicago's (1933) World's Fair since 1929. He is a member of the Chicago, Commercial, Union League, University, Onwentsia, Glenview, Evanston, and Evanston Country clubs. He is the author of The Banking System of the United States, 1892; Essays and Speeches, 1915; A Journal of the Great War, 1921; and The First Year of the Budget of the United States, 1923.

General Dawes married Caro D. Blymyer, of Cincinnati, Ohio, January 24, 1889, and their children are Rufus Fearing (deceased), Mrs. Carolyn Ericson, Dana McCutcheon, and Virginia.

J. FRANK GRIMES
Continued from page 229

of the Marketing Specialists, Inc., and vice-president of Chicago Offset Printing Company. He is a life member of the Art Institute of Chicago, and his clubs are Illinois Athletic, Medinah Athletic, Medinah Country, Briargate Golf, and Shawnee Country. His favorite recreation is golf.

Mr. Grimes married Barbara C. Adam, of Chicago, January 28, 1903. Their children are John Franklin, Donald Robert, Douglas Adam, and Helen Margaret.

OTTO F. HUNZIKER
Continued from page 265

industry. In 1930 he was selected as one of the ten "Master Minds of Dairying." In 1932, Purdue University conferred on him the honorary degree of Doctor of Science in appreciation of his skillful and unselfish service as professor and chief of the dairy department of this institution, work which has contributed to the permanent advancement of agriculture in this and other countries.

In 1905 Mr. Hunziker married Florence Belle Burne of Ellicottville, New York, and their children are Thelma Belle (Mrs. Raymond A. Tipple), Florence Louise, Karl Otto (deceased), Walter Burne, Isabelle Mary, and Otto Frederick.

EDWARD N. HURLEY
Continued from page 267

national Chamber of Commerce, and the Chamber of Commerce of the United States, for which he is Director of Foreign Commerce. He is a member of the Northwestern University Associates, the Academy of Political Science, Field Museum of Natural History, the Chicago Zoölogical Society, and the Chicago Council on Foreign Relations; a trustee of the University of Notre Dame and of A Century of Progress Exposition, Chicago's (1933) World's Fair.

He has been decorated with the Cross of the French Legion of Honor, the Order of Ta Cho Cha Ho of China, the Laetare Medal of Notre Dame, is a Grand Officer of the Crown of Italy, and a Knight of St. John of Malta. Mr. Hurley is a member of the Metropolitan Club (Washington, D. C.); the Recess and India House clubs (New York); the Union League, Mid-Day, Chicago Golf, Post and Paddock, Racquet, Chicago, and Attic clubs, and of the Chicago Athletic Association (Chicago), and the Jefferson Islands Club (Maryland). He is the author of The Awakening of Business, 1916, The New Merchant Marine, 1920, and The Bridge to France, 1927.

Mr. Hurley was married September 20, 1891, to Julia Keeley of Chicago (died 1900). On July 24, 1905, he was married to Florence Agnes Amberg of Chicago (died September, 1932). The children are Helen Mary (Mrs. William A. Ryan) and John R. The children of his first marriage are Edward N. Jr., and Raymond J.

FRANK KNOX
Continued from page 287

Hoarding, was largely responsible for putting millions of dollars of hoarded money into circulation. He is an active member of the Newspaper Publishers' Association, and was organizer of the New England Newspaper Alliance. Col. Knox believes in "giving the public the facts and letting the readers draw their own conclusions."

He is a member of the Chicago, Commercial, Wayfarers, Cliff Dwellers, Glen View, and Sky-Line of Chicago, the Derryfield, Calumet, Country, and Army and Navy clubs of Washington, D. C., the University and City clubs of Boston, and the Lotus and Advertising clubs of New York City. He was married December 28, 1898, to Annie Reid, of Alma, Michigan.

WALLACE R. LANE
Continued from page 295

New York City, and Illinois State bar associations. His clubs are the University, Mid-Day, Yale, Brown (president, 1923), Glenview, Shawnee (Chicago), University (Washington), Rhode Island Country (Providence), and Fall River (Mass.) Yacht. And he is a member of Beta Theta Pi, Phi Alpha Delta, Pi Gamma Mu, and Book and Gavel fraternities. He is a contributor of many articles on legal subjects to law journals and other publications.

On July 2, 1901, he married Gertrude Gardner, of Swansea, Massachusetts, and their children are Esther (Mrs. George T. Moore), Josephine (Mrs. George D. Busher), and John W.

SALMON O. LEVINSON
Continued from page 303

In 1929 he founded and endowed the William Edgar Borah Outlawry of War Foundation at the University of Idaho. He is the subject of an article by John Dewey on "Apostles of World Peace," appearing in the World Unity Magazine in 1929, and his work has been favorably commented on by the late Dr. Eliot of Harvard, William Hard, and others. He is the author of the Levinson Plan for the readjustment of German reparations, allied and interallied debts, European appeasement and world peace, issued in 1927, and of a supplementary plan for compromising the war debt situation, which appeared in the New York Times and other newspapers, April 7, 1932, and was later incorporated in the Congressional Record by request of Senator Borah. He contributed the article on "Agression, International," in the Encyclopedia of Social Sciences (1926), and has written a score of pamphlets and magazine articles on the outlawry of war. Mr. Levinson is a member of the American, Illinois, State and Chicago bar associations, and is a member of the Association of the Bar of the City of New York. Is chairman for outlawry of war. He is a member of the Hamilton, City, Standard, and Ravisloe Country clubs of Chicago and the Webhannet Golf Club of Kennebunk Beach, Maine.

Mr. Levinson was married in 1884 to Helen Bartlett Haire of Chicago, who died in 1904 survived by three children, Horace Clifford, Ronald Bartlett, and Helen Winthrop. In 1914 he was married to Ruth Langworthy of Pittsburgh, Pennsylvania, the mother of his youngest son, John Oliver.

FRANK G. LOGAN
Continued from page 309

Paliolithic specimens. For this research work in France and North Africa through the Logan Museum, the French government conferred upon Mr. Logan the distinguished insignia of the "Palms." The honorary degree of LL.D. (Doctor of Laws) was conferred upon him by Beloit College in 1922. Mr. and Mrs. Logan also established a Medical Research Fund at the University of Chicago, endowing three annual fellowships, and enriched the Chicago Historical Society by a gift of his famous collection of Abraham Lincoln and John Brown relics, including the famous shawl and coat and the last bit of President Lincoln's writing.

Mr. Logan finds his keenest pleasure, outside of his family life, in the varied activities in the field of art, education and science. His clubs are the Union League, City, Onwentsia, Shore Acres, Cliff Dwellers, South Shore Country, Congressional Country Club, Washington, D. C., and the Riviera Country Club, Los Angeles, California.

He married Josephine Hancock, daughter of Colonel John Lane Hancock of Chicago, June 15, 1882. Their family comprises one daughter, Mrs. Charles A. Munroe, and four sons, Stuart, Howard H., Spencer H., and Waldo H.

Mrs. Logan has been greatly interested in painters', sculptors', and musicians' work to such an extent that she has established winter quarters for the exhibition and sale of their productions at 9 West Washington street. Among her own accomplishments is her book of verse, published by Kroch, called "Lights and Shadows," and there have been many encomiums bestowed on it as philosophy in verse. She has also been invited and has become a member of the "Midland Authors," the National Pen Woman's League, and the Bookfellows' Society.

NATHAN WILLIAM MacCHESNEY
Continued from page 311

of the White Elephant of the Kingdom of Siam. Some of MacChesney's activities in public and civic life are as follows: member of the Illinois Commission on Uniform State Laws (president, 1913-1917); member of the National Conference of Commissioners on Uniform State Laws (president, 1922-1925); member of executive committee of the Chicago Plan Commission; member of the Chicago City Council Crime Commission; member of Air Board of Chicago; chairman of the Uniform Judicial Procedure Committee of the American Bar Association (vice-president, 1925-1926); president, 1915-1916, Illinois State Bar Association; chairman of the committee on public relations of the Chicago Bar Association; charter member of the American Law Institute; member, American Institute of Criminal Law and Criminology (president 1910-1911); president, Northwestern University Press; director, United Charities; trustee, Northwestern University; director of the Illinois Children's Home and Aid Society; member of the Association of Commerce; member of the committee of the Chicago World's Fair Centennial Celebration for 1933; and a director of the Boulevard Bridge Bank and the Central Life Insurance Company. Mr. MacChesney is a member of the Sons of the American Revolution, Society of the War of 1812, Sons of Veterans, Grand Army of the Republic, and the American Legion. He is a member of Phi Kappa Psi, Phi Beta Kappa, Phi Delta Phi, and the Order of the Coif, the honorary legal scholarship fraternity. His clubs are University, Chicago, Racquet, Union League, City (vice-president 1927-1931), Knollwood, Chicago Law, Chicago Literary, Chicago Yacht, and Tavern, all of Chicago; Metropolitan, of Washington, D. C.; Army and Navy of New York; and Lawyers Club of Ann Arbor, Michigan. He is author of Abraham Lincoln, The Tribute of a Century; Challenge to American Ideals; Principles of Military Law; and Principles of Real Estate Law.

Mr. MacChesney has lectured on constitutional, military, and international law at various universities, including Northwestern University, University of Illinois, and the University of Wisconsin, and has represented this country abroad and various foreign countries here from time to time, particularly Siam.

General MacChesney married Lena Frost of Riverside and Chicago, Illinois, December 1, 1904. They have two sons, Alfred Brunson III, and Gordon.

ALONZO C. MATHER
Continued from page 321

was passed in the United States Congress stating that no structure or bridge could be built in international waters without a special act of Congress. This bill ended Mr. Mather's dream of a memorial bridge. The result of Mr. Mather's plans, although carried out by others, is the great Peace Bridge, commemorating the one hundred years

Continued on page 549

MATHER—Continued

of peace between the two neighboring countries, which was dedicated in 1927 and which affords a de luxe highway connecting the United States and Canada at Buffalo. The river frontage Mr. Mather had acquired at Fort Erie, Ontario, which he had intended to be used in connection with the construction of the bridge, he donated to the Queen Victoria Park Commission, and it is now called Mather Park.

In 1927 Mr. Mather built the "Mather Tower" on Wacker Drive, one of the tallest and most beautiful office buildings in Chicago. He has always been interested in the Art Institute of Chicago, of which he is a life governing member, and a few years ago presented to the Institute the "Mather Addition." He is a member of the Chicago Association of Commerce, and Illinois Manufacturers' Association, the Union League Club, and was one of the first active members in the organization of the First Regiment. He is prominent in both business and social circles.

JOSEPH T. RYERSON
Continued from page 411

sented on the board of governors of the Casino, Racquet, and Tavern clubs, and is a member of the Chicago, Commercial, Attic, Shoreacres, Onwentsia, and Saddle and Cycle clubs; and of the Racquet and Tennis, Squadron A, Coffee House, and Yale clubs of New York; also the Valley Club, Santa Barbara, California.

He was married December 29, 1909, to Annie Lawrie McBirney of Lake Forest, Illinois. The children are Joseph T., Mary McBirney, Annie Lawrie, and Ellen Larned.

AMOS ALONZO STAGG
Continued from page 435

College Athletic Association (chairman of the track and field committee since 1921); Psi Upsilon and Skull and Bones fraternities (Yale); Quadrangle, University and Olympia Fields Country (president, 1916-1919) clubs. He is the author of Treatise on Football (Stagg and Williams), 1893, and Touchdown, 1927. The athletic field of the University of Chicago was named "Stagg Field" in his honor, 1914.

Mr. Stagg married Stella Robertson, of Albion, New York, September 10, 1894. Their children are Amos Alonzo, Ruth, and Paul.

JAMES SIMPSON
Continued from page 437

He financed the famous Roosevelt expedition into the Pamirs which enriched the Museum with hundreds of rare specimens. Mr. Simpson's hobby is mountain climbing and he is one of the few who have scaled the almost inaccessible peak that dominates Harrison Pass in the Sierras. He is director and deputy chairman of the Federal Reserve Bank and a director of the New York Central Railroad. His clubs are the Chicago, Mid-Day, Commercial, Saddle and Cycle, Old Elm, Racquet, Casino, Onwentsia, Shore Acres, Post and Paddock, Sheridan Yacht, and Sanganois, and the Links and River clubs of New York.

He was married December 1, 1903, to Jessie McLaren of Chicago. The children are James, Jr., John McLaren, and William.

THE RT. REV. GEORGE CRAIG STEWART
Continued from page 439

public, 1915; Evolution: a Witness to God, 1921; What Is My Life Work?, 1925; Spanish Summer, 1928; and Six Altars, 1929; The Call of Christ, 1931; The Face of Christ, 1932; and is homiletic editor of the Anglican Theological Review. He is a member of the Delta Upsilon and Delta Rho fraternities, the University, Glenview, Skokie, and Westmoreland clubs.

Bishop Stewart was married, March 31, 1902, to Mary Gertrude Clyde of Chester, Pennsylvania. The Stewarts have two sons, John Clyde and George Craig, Jr. A daughter, Katharine, was taken by death.

SILAS H. STRAWN
Continued from page 447

Saddle and Cycle, Old Elm (Chicago) Chevy Chase (Maryland), Burning Tree, Metropolitan (Washington, D. C.), Century Association (New York), and National Golf Links of America. Mr. Strawn has also served as president of the United States Golf Association.

Mr. Strawn married Margaret Stewart, of Binghamton, New York, in 1897. There are two daughters, Margaret (Mrs. James A. Cathcart) and Katherine (Mrs. Wesley M. Dixon).

MELVIN A. TRAYLOR
Continued from page 485

of Northwestern University, the Newberry Library, and Berea (Kentucky) College. He was vice-president in 1925 and 1926 of the American Bankers' Association, and president in 1926 and 1927. He was president of the Illinois Bankers Association in 1923 and 1924. He is a member of the Art Institute, the American Economic Association and the Southern Society of Chicago, past president of the U. S. Golf Association, and a member of many clubs. These include the Chicago, Bankers, Mid-Day, University, Press, Iroquois, Commercial, Saddle and Cycle, Saddle and Sirloin, Glenview, Old Elm, and Racquet, and the Recess Club of New York. At the National Democratic Convention of 1932, Mr. Traylor was placed in nomination for the Presidency of the United States.

He was married, June 8, 1906, to Dorothy Arnold Yerby of Hillsboro, Texas. Their children are Nancy Frances, and Melvin A., Jr.

WILLIAM WRIGLEY, JR.
Continued from page 533

the Erie Railroad and of the First National, and First Union Trust & Savings, and the Boulevard Bridge banks. He was a trustee of Field Museum, a member of the executive committee of the Chicago chapter, American Red Cross, and a member of the Loyal Legion. He attended several National Republican conventions as a delegate from Illinois. He maintained residences in Chicago, Lake Geneva, Phoenix, and Pasadena, as well as on Catalina Island.

Mr. Wrigley was married, September 17, 1885, to Ada E. Foote. Their daughter, Dorothy W., is the wife of James R. Offield; their son, Philip K., a veteran of the World War, and the present head of the Wrigley interests, married Helen Atwater of New York, and has two daughters, Ada Blanche and Dorothy.

THIS BOOK
Compiled and Published by

GLENN A. BISHOP

in collaboration with

PAUL T. GILBERT